Long-Term Care
Managing Across the Continuum

Fourth Edition

John R. Pratt, MHA, FACHCA, LFACHE

Retired Professor of Health Administration
Saint Joseph's College
Standish, Maine

JONES & BARTLETT
LEARNING

World Headquarters
Jones & Bartlett Learning
5 Wall Street
Burlington, MA 01803
978-443-5000
info@jblearning.com
www.jblearning.com

Jones & Bartlett Learning books and products are available through most bookstores and online booksellers. To contact Jones & Bartlett Learning directly, call 800-832-0034, fax 978-443-8000, or visit our website, www.jblearning.com.

Substantial discounts on bulk quantities of Jones & Bartlett Learning publications are available to corporations, professional associations, and other qualified organizations. For details and specific discount information, contact the special sales department at Jones & Bartlett Learning via the above contact information or send an email to specialsales@jblearning.com.

08656-0

Production Credits

VP, Executive Publisher: David D. Cella
Publisher: Michael Brown
Associate Editor: Lindsey Mawhiney
Editorial Assistant: Nicholas Alakel
Production Manager: Tracey McCrea
Senior Marketing Manager: Sophie Fleck Teague
Manufacturing and Inventory Control Supervisor:
   Amy Bacus

Composition: Cenveo Publisher Services
Cover Design: Scott Moden
Manager of Photo Research, Rights & Permissions:
   Amy Rathburn
Cover Image: © Taewoon Lee/ShutterStock, Inc.
Printing and Binding: Edwards Brothers Malloy
Cover Printing: Edwards Brothers Malloy

Library of Congress Cataloging-in-Publication Data
Pratt, John R., author.
   Long-term care : managing across the continuum / John R. Pratt. — 4.
      p. ; cm.
   Includes bibliographical references and index.
   ISBN 978-1-284-05459-0 (pbk.)
   I. Title.
   [DNLM: 1. Long-Term Care—organization & administration. 2. Delivery of Health Care, Integrated—organization & administration. 3. Health Facility Administration. 4. Long-Term Care—trends. WX 162]
   RA997
   362.16068—dc23
                    2014039674

6048

Printed in the United States of America
19 18 17 16 15   10 9 8 7 6 5 4 3 2 1

Dedication

Prior editions of his book were dedicated to long-term caregivers. This edition is dedicated to those who matter most, the consumers who rely on the long-term care system for their quality of life.

Contents

CHAPTER 3 ■ Toward an Ideal System 55

PART II ■ Long-Term Care Service Providers 87

CHAPTER 4 ■ Nursing Facilities 89

CHAPTER 6 ■ Assisted Living — 151

CHAPTER 7 ■ Senior Housing — 177

CHAPTER 8 ■ Community-Based Services   193

PART III ■ Interaction Within the Continuum   229

CHAPTER 9 ■ Competition, Cooperation, and Integration   231

New to This Edition

The following changes/additions are new to this edition:

- Addition of a chapter dealing with the Affordable Care Act (Obamacare), recognizing that it will still be developing for years to come, but providing a sound foundation for understanding it and any future developments. The chapter will not attempt to cover all of the many aspects of ACA, but will focus only on its impact on long-term care.
- References to ACA in other chapters as appropriate.
- Updates in all chapters to cover changes in care delivery, regulations, etc.
- Updates to references.
- Separation of the chapter titled, "Leadership and Culture Change in Long-Term Care" into two chapters: "Leadership in Long-Term Care" and "Culture Change in Long-Term Care," as both have developed enough to warrant chapters of their own.

Foreword

The profession of long-term care administration is one that provides many wonderful opportunities, some considerable challenges, and very significant responsibilities. In the past 25 plus years of my professional experience in this field, the one constant has been that of change. It is absolutely critical to remain connected and current at all times to provide effective, relevant leadership. John Pratt has again updated his comprehensive text with this fourth edition dedicated to long-term care knowledge and practical insight. This provides an excellent read for both those new to the profession and those with experience looking to gain a new perspective to assist in improving their leadership and management skills.

Leaders in this profession need to be prepared to collaborate across a growing continuum of care and services to meet the demands of a new generation of seniors who are more informed, focused on preventive approaches, and desire active engagement. This text provides a broad picture describing how the long-term care system developed as well as how it continues to evolve. It clearly describes the primary types of long-term services provided across the continuum so the reader comprehends the landscape. In this edition, Mr. Pratt continues his commitment to keeping this trusted text—which is utilized both as a college text and as a reference to professionals—pertinent by making significant changes to include the impacts of changes in the care delivery system, regulations, and legislation affecting long-term care. This includes an additional chapter dedicated to setting a foundational understanding of the Affordable Care Act's influence on long-term care that will continue to shape the future. He has also focused chapters specifically on leadership and culture change in long-term care, which is noteworthy. This text continues to be listed as a reference for the national licensing examination prepared by the National Association of Long-Term Care Administrator Boards, which indicates the value of the material.

I have had the privilege of seeing Mr. Pratt's passion in assisting new leaders succeed in their roles through his dedication both through his teaching in the classroom and through this effort expanding his encouragement and guidance through his writing. Long-term care is very complex, and this text provides logical and concise attention needed to get to the heart of matters that are critical to excellent leadership. It is written in a manner that is intended to engage the reader well beyond what is written on the page.

The focus of your leadership is critical to be successful in managing during these turbulent times, targeting the most important priorities from the multiple daily demands for your time and attention. Mr. Pratt does an excellent job of pointing out the importance of quality improvement and a customer-driven culture, while at the same time providing cost-efficient, yet effective care and services that will help your organization to be competitive in the market. My hope is that this text will challenge your thinking and cause you to even more fully engage your mind and soul in this very important work that impacts the lives of so many. This is a rewarding career that is critical with the tsunami of seniors in the upcoming years that will need care and services as the baby boomers age. I am one of those baby boomers who will be counting on engaged and dedicated leaders such as you to carry on the mission of leadership as this profession continues to grow and evolve to meet the constantly changing consumer needs and demands. Thank you in advance for all that you will do to ensure that future is strong and bright!

Tom Syverson, CNHA
Executive Vice President/Chief Operating Officer,
The Evangelical Lutheran Good Samaritan Society

Preface

In a time when change is the rule in most businesses, the field of long-term care is changing faster and more dramatically than most. There are seemingly constant changes in regulations and in reimbursement methodology. The field is undergoing a great deal of redefinition of the roles of institutional and community-based providers. Those in public policy positions affecting the delivery of long-term care are trying to balance a much-needed increase in emphasis on home health care and other alternatives to institutional care with the realization that there is still a valid place in the system for a variety of institutional service providers. New levels of care, or at least new names and rules for existing types of care (assisted living, subacute care), are being created constantly. Long-term care providers must focus on integration with other players in the healthcare system while, at the same time, experiencing competition from those same players. These changes, whether considered individually or collectively, place huge demands on those who manage the organizations providing long-term care.

As change takes place and the field becomes more sophisticated and diverse, successful long-term care administrators will face tougher challenges than any they have seen before and will have to bring new skills to their jobs. They will have to possess the ability to change with the times and to manage their organizations while under considerable pressure. They will need to be flexible enough to adapt to different management settings or to provide services that are different from those with which they may have been familiar. It is no longer enough to be expert in home health care, skilled nursing care, or residential care. Tomorrow's long-term care managers will be expected to possess those skills essential to managing larger, more complex organizations, which will probably include multiple segments of the continuum of care.

At a very minimum, they must understand:

- The differences and similarities among the many long-term care service providers
- How the various segments of long-term care fit together to form an overall system
- The issues affecting them all, individually or collectively
- The skills they will need to succeed in that system

This text supplies that information and gives those managers a solid foundation on which to build their expertise. It is aimed at providing a comprehensive view of the field as it exists today, of the changes taking place in that continuum now and in the near future, and of the skills managers need to survive and prosper. It is a practical management reference for all long-term care administrators, long-term care being defined as including all institutional and noninstitutional providers of chronic or long-term care services (nursing facilities, assisted living, subacute care, senior housing, adult day care, home health care, and hospice).

It should be noted here, before some critic (rightfully) points it out, that long-term care does not represent the entire continuum of care. That is acknowledged. The full continuum, as explained early in the text, is a lengthier and more comprehensive list of services, including acute care (hospitals and physician services) and preventive health care at one end and social services, such as housing and transportation, at the other.

Long-term care, however, is such an integral part of the overall continuum and interacts so intimately with the rest that it deserves special examination. Thus, the focus here is on the organization portion of the continuum of care, showing what it is, where it fits, and the nature of its relationships with other segments.

This book has been written for two separate but closely related segments of a common audience: long-term care administrators who are currently practicing and future administrators being trained in long-term care administration in college and university programs. It is academic enough to meet the latter need, but it is practical and not overly theoretical, allowing it to serve both groups.

In the first group are many of today's long-term care managers who have extensive experience providing one type of service (e.g., nursing facility care, home health care) but who have limited knowledge of or contact with other segments of the field. They can no longer be content to be expert in a single specialty area. They must learn about the entire continuum of care and be prepared to manage anywhere within it.

The second group of long-term care managers for whom this book is written consists of those who are being educated through college degree programs to fill the many positions being created as the field expands. With the expected increasing need for long-term care, and consequently for long-term care managers, caused by the aging of our society, those college programs must be supported. It is intended as a comprehensive text for students in these programs, giving them a good understanding of the field they plan to enter. The first, second, and third editions have been used as a required text in dozens of college and university programs. Their feedback has been of great assistance in updating the text material.

This book should also be of interest to others interested in the topic, including policy makers, regulators, and consumer advocates. Because it presents a comprehensive view of the continuum of long-term care, it provides readers with both an overview and a moderately detailed view of various aspects of the continuum.

There are several excellent textbooks dealing with the specific types of day-to-day activities involved in managing each of the different segments of the long-term care field, such as nursing facilities, subacute care, home health care, and assisted living. They cover knowledge of applicable regulations and the detailed procedures and practices involved in hands-on administration (e.g., admission, resident/client classification, grievance procedures) of particular types of long-term care organizations. None addresses the entire long-term care continuum. On the other hand, there are several good texts dealing with the continuum of care from a broad, policy-oriented, macro/sociological viewpoint.

The approach here is different from these others in that the focus is on management in different segments of the continuum, not just definition of the continuum itself. It deals with management within the continuum as such and goes beyond definition to compare and contrast the different service providers and the impact of change on them.

The text is divided into five sections. Part I, "Introduction: The Changing Long-Term Care Scene," presents an overview of the long-term care continuum as it exists today. It includes an explanation of how long-term care reached its current state and looks at where the system is—or should be—going. Chapter 1 defines long-term care, including its various segments, and examines the dynamics particular to the overall field. Chapter 2 addresses the Affordable Care Act of 2010 (ACA) and its impact on long-term care. That impact is also reflected in other chapters as appropriate. Chapter 3 discusses the goals toward which we should aim in seeking an ideal long-term care system, based largely on the *Criteria for Designing or Evaluating a Long-Term Care System*, a copy of which is included as Appendix A. The *Criteria* were developed by me, your author, with assistance from a group of long-term care experts. They present benchmarks for measuring a long-term care system, as well as the steps needed to attain those benchmarks.

Part II, "Long-Term Care Service Providers," includes chapters devoted to each of the major long-term care service providers, with a goal of providing readers with a good understanding of each of those individual provider types. Chapters 4 through 8 include descriptions and overviews of each service, the types and numbers of consumers served, financial aspects, staffing and human resource issues, legal and ethical issues, particular management challenges and opportunities, and other pertinent information, such as any significant trends affecting the service. All chapters in this section have been written in a similar format, for the purpose of making comparison of the various providers easier.

Part III, "Interaction Within the Continuum," turns to investigating the broader aspects of long-term care, showing how the individual players interact to produce the system as it now exists. It also relates to the ideal long-term care system described in Part I and discusses implications for providers, regulators, payers, and consumers. Covered in this section are chapters addressing issues relevant to all long-term care providers, including the movement toward more competition, cooperation, and integration; external forces controlling long-term care, such as regulation, licensure, and accreditation; reimbursement; quality; and ethical issues.

Part IV, "Managing in the Long-Term Care System," recognizes that managers in long-term care organizations need certain skills if they and their organizations are to survive and succeed. The chapters in this section (covering governance and administration, leadership, culture change, technology and marketing/community relations) identify these skills and present helpful information about obtaining and maintaining them.

The final section, Part V, "The Future: Continuing Change," discusses the future of long-term care. Chapter 19 examines trends that are likely to affect the field; Chapter 20 offers suggestions for managing in this millennium.

In preparing this book, I decided that it should go beyond a mere description of long-term care and the pieces that make it a whole. I also wanted to tie those pieces together and delve more deeply into why they exist and how they interact with each other and with the rest of the continuum of care. Thus, you will find many opinions expressed herein. These opinions are based on my extensive experience and view of the field as it exists now and into the coming decades and are intended as a source of enrichment for the text.

Readers will notice an inevitable overlap from chapter to chapter because I covered many topics/issues from a variety of different perspectives. For example, the topic of consumer choice is referenced in numerous sections as it impacts so much of the long-term care system and those who manage within it. Similarly, while there are separate chapter segments dealing with financing, regulation, and ethical issues, those topics are also covered in the chapters dealing with individual provider types (e.g., nursing facilities), showing how they are affected. This gives readers an opportunity to see such topics from different perspectives, and is intended as a means of providing a comprehensive, multidimensional view of the long-term care system. I hope you will find this book informative and perhaps even enjoyable reading.

John Pratt

About the Author

John Pratt is a retired Professor of Health Administration at Saint Joseph's College in Standish, Maine. Prior to entering retirement in 2013, he had been Director of the Health Administration programs that are designed for working adult healthcare professionals and are taught online. He was also Director of the Long-Term Care Management Institute at the college. Prior to moving to academia, he served as a health care administrator for 25 years. He is a Fellow of the American College of Health Care Administrators (ACHCA) and a Life Fellow of the American College of Healthcare Executives (ACHE). He has served on the board of directors of ACHCA and chaired that organization's education committee. He has also been active in the National Association of Long-Term Care Administrator Boards (NAB). He has been a regular presenter at professional conferences and an active contributor to professional journals.

Introduction: The Changing Long-Term Care Scene

Long-Term Care Today: Turbulent Times

■ Introduction

More than 3 decades ago, management guru Peter Drucker (1980) wrote about the need for managers to manage for change during turbulent times. He was talking about business in general, which was experiencing and continues to experience changes at the very core of its operating styles. It may have taken a while for the field of long-term care to catch up with other businesses in that respect, but the 1990s and early 2000s saw it reach full status as an industry that is also deeply engrossed in turbulent times. While acute care—primarily meaning hospitals—achieved that somewhat dubious distinction a number of years earlier, not far behind other industries, long-term care has taken a bit longer. Yet, today, the symptoms of that organizational turbulence are seen in all aspects of long-term care.

Competition among long-term care providers has become much more common than has been experienced in the past, not only from similar types of providers (nursing homes, community-based home care agencies, government-run mental health institutions), but also from new entries in the field (assisted living, new housing options). There was a time when any form of advertising was considered bad form throughout the healthcare system. Now, healthcare providers, including all types of long-term care providers, are engaging in regular, often highly sophisticated (and correspondingly expensive) advertising, utilizing all of the tools available to them through the commercial media. It is somewhat ironic in a system with more than enough demand to go around (a topic we discuss in more detail later) that long-term care organizations are competing for consumers. The explanation for that seemingly odd fact is that they are competing for those consumers with certain types of reimbursement, particularly those who are able to pay for their own care.

Long-term care providers have increasingly experienced the need to operate in a highly efficient, cost-effective manner, as third-party payers have become much more restrictive in defining the types and amounts of costs for which they will pay. That has led to the previously unthinkable—downsizing, including layoffs. It has also motivated many providers of long-term care to engage in various forms of reengineering, attempting to maintain or expand their particular portion of the market through reorganization. The forces the long-term care system is now feeling are forces that have been acting on other segments of the healthcare industry for several decades. Those forces have seen some hospitals close because they were unable to demonstrate their need or were unable to compete with others with whom they shared a service area. Other hospitals have formed healthcare networks, resulting in mergers, formal affiliations, and contract management agreements as a means of survival. Long-term care providers had not, until about a decade ago, been involved in those networks, nor had they been pressured to become so.

That all changed, with a rapidity that caught many long-term care providers unprepared. No longer could those previously isolated providers in the long-term care system remain aloof from the rest of the system. No longer could they stay within their own limited spheres of activity and service as they had in the past. The players in long-term care in the beginning of this millennium had to be aware of, and be prepared to deal with, unprecedented changes. They came to expect and anticipate competition and intrusion not only from other segments of that system, but also from hospitals and from entrepreneurial newcomers from outside of the conventional system.

The strategic position of traditional long-term care facilities, primarily nursing homes, was not unlike the position of the United States prior to World War I, finding it difficult to recognize that other players were entering the arena in which they had long played. Like the United States during that time, traditional long-term care organizations now realize that they can no longer survive in an isolationist mode. They came to realize—some willingly, some reluctantly—that they represent only small portions of an ever-expanding industry. Your author teaches a class called "Leadership in Health Administration" to adult healthcare professionals enrolled as part of their coursework for college degrees in health care or long-term care administration. The course is both wholly online and a hybrid, taught through a combination of 5 weeks of online classes and 1 week on campus. Students come from all over the United States and from numerous other countries, and they represent the full gamut of training and experience in various segments of the healthcare industry. Most are healthcare managers, ranging from first-line supervisors (charge nurses, department heads) to chief executive officers (CEOs) of hospitals, nursing homes, or other healthcare organizations. They come to the class with a great deal of experience in all phases of the healthcare system. In fact, during one class, one of the students conducted a survey and determined that the students in that one class represented a total of 370 years of healthcare experience and represented a cross-section of healthcare and long-term care professionals.

Class sessions in recent years have demonstrated two significant trends not seen in earlier groups. First, the number of students engaged in some aspect of long-term care has grown significantly compared with those working in acute care. Second—and more dramatic by far—is the proportion of students who are undergoing, or have undergone, some type of downsizing, reengineering, or reorganization. The end result, the result most critical to the individual managers involved, is that they have had to adjust their career goals and have had to find new ways in which to participate in this, their chosen field. While organizational change is common throughout the healthcare industry, there seems to be some correlation between the number of individuals affected and the number involved in long-term care.

There appear to be two converging trends at work here. First, there are those already engaged in some form of long-term care who are experiencing the trauma of organizational turnover and who are seeking to find more secure positions within that system. Second, and probably of more importance to the future of the long-term care industry, are those whose entire experience has been in acute care but who are now seeing long-term care as a better opportunity for career advancement. Together, these two groups are a very real, sometimes poignant, reminder of the turbulence taking place in the long-term care system today.

The degree to which long-term care organizations have evolved and continue to evolve, the disruption of established routines, the unsettled future of the industry, the threats to organizational stability, and the rapid pace with which the environment is changing are all symptoms of the times. They describe not so much the status of the long-term care system today, but rather the dynamic forces acting on that system and the way in which it has reacted to those forces.

Before we investigate how those forces affected the evolution of long-term care, we need to define the system as it exists today and why it exists in the first place.

■ Defining the Long-Term Care System

Let us begin with definitions of a couple of terms, and then put them aside, for they serve only to set the stage for a more detailed discussion. First, the long-term care system is often defined according to what sets it apart from other forms of health care. In doing so, the terms chronic care and long-term care are generally used interchangeably. Both are used in the context of an extended type of care that is required over long periods of time, with temporary, short-term breaks, but which goes on in most cases for the remainder of the individual recipient's life. In fact, the term extended care was commonly used for a time to describe what we now define as long-term care. Long-term care is also thought of, not always accurately, as any care after acute care.

While both terms, *chronic care* and *long-term care*, are used at one time or other in this text, the term *long-term care* will predominate. That is not because there is anything wrong with the term *chronic care* but because it is less commonly found in general usage.

Second, when defining the long-term care system in terms of those who provide its services, *long-term care* has been used most often in reference to nursing homes exclusively. Although that is an inaccurate application of the term, it has evolved over time because, as discussed later in this chapter, nursing homes have traditionally been the predominant providers of long-term care services. As other providers and other types of long-term care services have developed and will undoubtedly continue to develop, it is only right that the more all-encompassing use of the term be used, and it will be herein.

In reviewing this material, your author ran across a new term (at least to him). The term *long-term services and supports (LTSS)* refers to the broad range of services and infrastructures to help frail older people and younger people with disabilities remain independent; this term has gained wider use and appears to be more descriptive of services people with disabilities need in their daily lives. The term is used in P.L. 111-148, the Patient Protection and Affordable Care Act of 2010 (ACA), to refer to a range of supportive services for these populations (O'Shaughnessy, 2011b, p.1). While *long-term care* will be used more frequently in this text, *long-term services and supports* will be used when appropriate. Do not be confused by these terms as they are essentially interchangeable.

Perhaps the long-term care system is best defined in terms of the people who require and use it. A person who uses long-term care is described in one instance as "a person who requires someone else to help him with his physical or emotional needs over an extended period of time" (Day, 2013). Another, more detailed description of long-term care consumers is "those persons requiring healthcare, personal care, social, and supportive services over a sustained period of time" (Continuing Care Council, 1992, p.1). The type of consumers who use long-term care is discussed at length later in this chapter. It has been reported that "about 11 million adults age 18 and older, almost 5 percent of the total U.S. adult population, receive LTSS. Of those 18 and older, the majority of adults receiving LTSS are 65 years and older (57 percent), but a substantial proportion are adults between the ages of 18 and 64 (43 percent)" (O'Shaughnessy, 2011b, p. 2).

■ How the Long-Term Care System Came About

Long-term care, as we know it today, has taken a long time to develop. Unlike the acute care (hospital) system, which became highly institutionalized in the mid-19th century, a formal system of long-term care took much longer to evolve. In fact, during most of the 20th century it was what one writer described as "a comparatively drab backwater in the overall scene of U.S. health care" (Goldsmith, 1994, p. 5). The public knew little about long-term care and cared not much more. There was not the clearly identifiable population of seriously ill or injured, difficult for the community to ignore. Nor, with notable exceptions such as tuberculosis, did those needing long-term care pose as great a threat to the community as did patients involved in active epidemics.

Instead, until quite recently, most long-term care was provided by informal care-givers, such as families and friends (a topic discussed in more detail later), religious organizations, and community groups formed specifically to help those less fortunate than themselves. During the 19th century, and well into the 20th, families took care of their own members when possible. Several generations lived together, with the young caring for the old and the old caring for the young. It was a widely accepted way of life. While it can generously be assumed that such care was usually motivated by a sincere desire to help, or an inherent sense of obligation, there were other motivations as well. There was a stigma attached to admitting need for assistance from others. It was believed that responsible members of society avoided accepting charity whenever possible, often to the point of causing considerable hardship for themselves and their families. In addition, people were often ashamed to admit that a family member was physically or mentally handicapped, apparently based on a feeling that they were somehow at fault for the family member's affliction.

Whatever the reasons, most long-term care was provided at home. What few institutional resources were in place consisted of homes for those with no family able or willing to provide for them. Mostly, those resources took the form of almshouses or poor farms, perpetuating the negative societal image of those needing help simply to survive. Those homes usually cared for people with a variety of needs, with little distinction made between serving those requiring mere shelter and food and those needing supervision and functional assistance closer to what is now known as long-term care. The elderly, homeless, unemployed or unemployable, and people unable to care for themselves (including those with moderate levels of mental illness or retardation) were housed together and received much the same care. Whether sponsored by church groups, fraternal or ethnic organizations, or community-based charities, it was essentially a voluntary form of welfare. People qualified more often because of poverty than because of illness. This was the primary method of providing services for the needy up to the 1920s (Goldsmith, 1994). There are numerous reasons for the way the long-term care system developed, including the growing role of government in long-term care financing; the impact of regulations; past successes; and efforts to reduce healthcare costs.

The Growing Role of Government in Long-Term Care Financing

Through the first 2 decades of the 20th century, there was very little government involvement in long-term care, happening only when private resources could not be found. Even when public agencies stepped in to help out, it was usually at a level close to the community. Long-term care institutions, usually in the form of asylums, were sponsored by local, county, and occasionally state agencies. Those institutions were created as much to protect society from the necessity of having to see those unfortunates as it was to protect those receiving the care. Thus, long-term care institutions were often built on large tracts of land far away from community centers. Many public facilities still exist on those large, remote sites, although a community may have grown up around them.

That situation was to change irrevocably in the 1930s. The Great Depression caused the numbers of people unable to care for themselves to multiply many times, seemingly overnight, far outreaching the resources available through family and voluntary sponsorship. With passage of the Social Security Act of 1935 and other, related welfare programs, the federal government became deeply involved in care of society's needy, particularly the aged, blind, and families with dependent children. This has been identified as the indirect beginning of the nursing home industry (Goldsmith, 1994) from which the many other forms of long-term care have grown.

Over the next several decades, the federal government expanded its role in financing care of the needy and of those requiring certain specific levels of health care. It did so by passing numerous amendments to the original Social Security Act. This was especially true during the 1960s, with passage of the landmark Medicare and Medicaid amendments (Title XVIII and Title XIX). With the advent of Medicare and Medicaid came funding for hospital and medical care for the elderly and for those who could not afford such care. That funding produced a variety of results for different people and organizations. For most individuals, it meant relief from the increasing cost of getting care or being able to get needed care for the first time. For hospitals and doctors, it meant a new source of revenue, a reduced need to provide free care, a greatly increased demand for their services, and far more regulations and paperwork. For both state and federal government, it meant a new commitment to providing services for their constituents and an ongoing problem in finding the funds to do so.

Unfortunately, those planning the Medicare and Medicaid programs greatly underestimated the impact of those programs. They based their projections of need largely on the number of people being served at the time, with a modest increase expected. In fact, there was a large, unanticipated reservoir of need that was not being met, specifically because of the lack of funding for it. Many people had gone without all but the most critical medical care when they had to pay for it themselves or when they had no way of paying for it. When reimbursement became available through these government programs, they soon flooded healthcare providers, seeking help.

While Medicare and Medicaid—with their new availability of payment for care and the resulting larger-than-expected demand for services—had the greatest impact on hospitals and physicians, they also provided both direct and indirect stimulus for the slowly developing nursing home industry. Medicare included coverage for certain limited types of long-term care, in the form of skilled nursing facilities (SNFs) providing high-end nursing home care. Medicaid provided an even broader range of nursing home coverage.

Although often confused by the public, even to this day, the two programs contain significant differences. Medicare was designed to serve the elderly, the blind, and certain categories of the permanently disabled, without regard to ability to pay, while Medicaid serves the medically indigent—those unable to pay for their own health care.

There are other differences in the two programs beyond the varying eligibility requirements. Medicare coverage is intentionally limited, both in what health care it covers and in the duration of the coverage. Medicaid provides more extensive coverage, in effect for as long as the person needs it and as long as that person can meet the financial means test required to qualify, but still does not cover all long-term care services.

Those differences have had a significant effect on long-term care as it has developed. Medicare, with its limitations on coverage, often stops paying for long-term care when much more care is needed. At that point, individuals and families are forced to spend down (i.e., use up their own financial resources) in order to become eligible for Medicaid. In addition, while Medicare is a federally funded program, Medicaid is funded by a combination of federal and state taxes. As demand for long-term care services has grown over the decades, many states have found themselves struggling to pay for their shares of the funding for those services. The Medicaid Act provides certain levels of coverage below which states cannot go, but gives the individual states considerable leeway in determining what and how much they can cover. Some states provide much more than others, resulting in (1) inequities in coverage, (2) movement by recipients from one state to another where benefits are more liberal, and (3) attendant difficulty for some states in funding the programs.

Today, Medicaid is the dominant source of payment for long-term services and supports (LTSS), followed by out-of-pocket payments by individuals and families. Of all U.S. spending on LTSS, the Medicaid program is the principal payer. One report showed that:

> in 2011, Medicaid paid for 62.3 percent ($131.4 billion) of all LTSS spending. Out-of pocket spending by individuals and families accounted for about 21.6 percent ($45.5 billion) of spending. Other sources, including Medicare, private insurance and other private and public sources paid the balance. (O'Shaughnessy, 2011b, p. 4)

Another law that has impacted financing of health care (including long-term care) is the Older Americans Act. It was intended to help people age 60 and older maintain maximum independence in their homes and communities, with appropriate supportive services, and to promote a continuum of care for the vulnerable elderly. The 1965 Act "represented a turning point in financing and delivering community services to the elderly. Before then, federal and state governments played a limited role in providing social services and LTSS to older people" (O'Shaughnessy, 2011a, p. 4).

The Impact of Regulations on Development of the Long-Term Care System

The effect of Medicare and Medicaid on the long-term care system has not been limited to that caused by the nature and amount of reimbursement provided. With any government program that provides funding comes regulation. The government, at whatever level, simply wants to protect its investment and issues regulations to do so. In the case of Medicare and Medicaid, the regulations have been extensive—both in the scope of their coverage and in the length of the written regulations themselves. As with most other healthcare regulations, they are intended to ensure accomplishment of two objectives: that care paid for by the government is of sufficiently high quality and that it is purchased at the lowest possible price. The impact of the regulations relating to these two laws, and other related regulations, on the providers of long-term care has been great. That impact has ultimately been felt by the consumers of care. Just as available services are determined in large part by the amount of reimbursement for them, so are they influenced by the regulations governing them. When providers of care have seen that the cost of meeting regulations has been too high in relation to the revenue available for providing that care, those services have ceased to exist. On the other hand, when regulations have made it easier for providers to balance cost, revenue, and quality, services have generally been more available.

Federal and state healthcare regulations have often been used to accomplish a third objective: limiting or expanding the availability of services in specific segments of the industry or in defined geographic locations. This is done to improve access in underserved areas or to reduce costs attributed to oversupply in other areas. Some such regulations are specifically designed to do just that—to affect the availability of services. Perhaps the two most notable regulations in that category are the Hill-Burton Act (the Medical Facilities Survey and Construction Act of 1946) and the Certificate of Need provisions in the National Health Planning and Resources Development Act of 1974.

The Hill-Burton Act built hospitals in underserved areas from the late 1940s until well into the 1960s. The act provided funding for those hospitals but used regulations related to that funding to influence where new hospitals were built. At first, there was little, if any, direct impact on long-term care, but increasing the availability of hospitals in rural areas eventually had a positive impact on other services, including long-term care. Also, a 1954 amendment to the act made some nonprofit long-term care facilities eligible for construction funding, but only in severely restricted instances.

Several decades later, in a direct reversal of the intent of Hill-Burton, certificate of need (CON) programs were enacted, designed to reduce the amount of expansion of healthcare facilities. The federal law mandated that each state develop a CON program requiring approval before any new construction or expansion could take place. Those regulations had a much more direct impact on long-term care than did previous laws, because nursing homes were covered by their provisions. Although largely dismantled during the 1980s, CON laws are still in effect in some states, with widely varying degrees of enforcement.

Other notable federal laws include the Omnibus Budget Reconciliation Act (OBRA) of 1987 and the Affordable Care Act of 2010. OBRA was designed to improve the quality of care in nursing facilities and imposed strict new regulations and monitoring. The ACA's impact on long-term care is yet to be fully realized and understood.

The Results of Past Successes

Much of the development of the long-term care system has resulted from the many improvements in medical care over the past century. The healthcare system's ability to prevent many previously fatal illnesses and to treat others has kept people alive longer, producing an ever-increasing population needing extensive long-term care of one sort or another. Not only are more people living to use long-term care services, but they are living long enough to need long-term care over a period of many more years.

This progress has been extremely beneficial to the elderly, but it has also caused certain problems for long-term care providers and policy makers. These successes in extending longevity created an additional demand for services and an increased level of expectation of further clinical advances. While those problems should have been anticipated, little attention was given to them or to their solutions. One early long-term care administration text did predict that these breakthroughs would "magnify the difficulties and ambiguities in defining the role of the elderly and in setting priorities for long-term care programs" (Levy & Loomba, 1977, p. 572) and called for "drastic changes in long-term care and healthcare programs to meet the needs of a more vigorous aged population" (Levy & Loomba, 1977, p. 571).

However, it should not be assumed that nothing was done in response to that and similar warnings. Many groups and individuals worked hard to change attitudes and practices concerning the elderly, some with considerable success. However, those programmatic efforts have been hard pressed to move with the rapidity of clinical advances or with the speed at which the elderly population was growing and changing.

Such dramatic medical procedures as organ transplants, replacement of knees and hips with artificial joints, and nonsurgical correction of cataracts became commonplace. They and a multitude of similar procedures unheard of in earlier generations have come to be thought of as almost routine and we are now experiencing much more sophisticated tools and procedures. Any one of them has the potential to extend an individual's life or functional independence for decades, and it is not uncommon for some people to benefit from several of them over a period of years. Yet, while these medical advances extend life—and allow individuals to overcome or postpone specific functional disabilities—their health may be worsening in other areas, compounding the need for long-term care. For example, an artificial joint replacement will allow a person to be more independent physically, but other concurrent complications such as loss of sight or hearing may create other long-term care needs.

Efforts to Reduce Healthcare Costs and Their Impact on Long-Term Care

Government programs, such as Medicare and Medicaid, have not been alone in trying to reduce their costs for health care. Private insurance companies, employers who are the largest purchasers of insurance, and individuals paying their own bills have all become increasingly concerned about rapidly escalating costs. As a result, several new forms of healthcare financing and delivery developed, most notably managed care. That emphasis on cost-effectiveness affected the long-term care system quite significantly, especially through the practice of reducing institutionalization to the barest minimum.

Because of rising costs, particularly in acute care settings, third-party payers have increasingly pressured providers to reduce lengths of stay, even when that meant discharging patients to other levels of care. Some payers, particularly managed care organizations (MCOs), have placed preset limits on how long patients may stay in a hospital for treatment of a given illness. The result is that many such patients have been transferred to long-term care organizations requiring much more care than would have been the case in the past, a practice that came to be known as "quicker and sicker" discharges.

These pressures on providers to discharge patients at predetermined times was not new. From its earliest inception, Medicare denied reimbursement for care beyond certain points. The law included a section requiring providers to conduct a process known as utilization review, intended to ensure that the Medicare system did not pay for care beyond that which was determined to be necessary. New trends were the increased involvement of other payers and the compressing of allowable lengths of stay.

This trend affected the long-term care system in several ways. First is the increased level of care required in the various segments of long-term care. People who would have remained in hospitals in the past are now cared for in nursing homes. Many of those who used to receive care in nursing homes are now getting their care in assisted living or residential care facilities or at home. That, in turn, has produced other changes in the system. It has increased the acuity of patients at each level, has changed staffing requirements accordingly, and has forced facilities and agencies to add new services to meet the increased needs of their clients. It also led to development of several new types of care delivery, such as assisted living and subacute care.

The trend toward quicker and sicker discharges has also been a factor in the development of integrated care systems or networks. As providers have attempted to respond to pressures to move patients to the lowest acceptable level of care, some have found that they needed to obtain services to which they can refer those patients. Others are on the receiving end of referrals and have discovered the advantages of allying themselves with referral sources as a means of maintaining a high occupancy level.

Long-term care providers have become much more market conscious and competitive as a result of these pressures. While some have sought to protect their niche in the market by affiliating with integrated networks, others have actually begun providing the services themselves. Hospitals have increasingly converted portions of their facilities to long-term care programs as a means of filling empty beds and securing a place to which they can discharge their patients. Both hospitals and nursing homes have begun to add home healthcare services as a continuation of that trend.

The Components of the Long-Term Care System

Long-term care evolved slowly at first, but stimulated by the many competing pressures discussed herein, it has developed into an extremely complex system that consumers and providers alike have difficulty understanding. There are many players involved, including consumers, providers, payers, and regulators. The payers and regulators have had, and will continue to have, major influence on how the long-term care system develops and functions.

At this point, and as a means of setting the stage for later discussions, let us identify the consumers and providers of long-term care.

The Consumers of Long-Term Care

One indication of the complexity of the long-term care system is the fact that those individuals using the system do not even carry a commonly agreed-upon label, a descriptive name. When they are in acute or subacute care settings, they are called patients. In most other long-term care institutions, they become residents. Yet, community-based care providers usually refer to them as clients. A couple of decades ago, one author even referred to them as constituents, pointing out the reciprocal relationship inherent in the interface between those seeking care and those providing it (Kissick, 1994). It is an intriguing idea, but what those users of long-term care have in common is that they are consumers, which is what they will be called herein.

Unlike in the acute healthcare system, long-term care consumers are not usually defined by a single disease or condition. Instead, they require services because of functional disabilities—limiting their ability to function independently (Evashwick, 2005). While those functional disabilities may be caused by one or more specific diseases, it is the disability itself that is addressed by long-term care, rather than the disease. In fact, long-term care consumers typically suffer from more than one underlying ailment, resulting in the functional deficits. An individual might have functional limitations caused by a combination of such diseases as hypertension, diabetes, arthritis, and heart disease, any one of which could be disabling by itself. In addition, it is not uncommon for the chronically ill, particularly the elderly, to also suffer some loss of cognitive ability. They also suffer from some form of dementia or some loss of cognitive ability. The Alzheimer's Association estimated that 5.2 million Americans of all ages had Alzheimer's disease in 2013. This includes an estimated 5 million people age 65 and older and approximately 200,000 individuals younger than age 65 who have younger onset Alzheimer's (Alzheimer's Association, 2013). Any inability to understand the nature of their disability and to follow their care plan makes it that much more difficult to care for them or to assist them in caring for themselves. Chronic disease and combinations of chronic diseases affect individuals to varying degrees and may impact an individual's life in different ways. The increasing prevalence of multiple chronic diseases "presents a complex challenge to the U.S. health care system, both in terms of quality of life and expenditures for an aging population" (Freid, Bernstein, & Bush, 2012, p. 6).

Elderly Users of Long-Term Care

Consumers of long-term care represent a broad spectrum of people who rely on the system for assistance. They are largely, though not exclusively, elderly. While a growing number of nonelderly need long-term care for a variety of reasons, it is still the aged members of our society who use the lion's share of long-term care services. The most elderly among them (those over 75 and even over 85 years of age) use the long-term care system at a disproportionate rate.

Their numbers are growing rapidly, and are projected to continue to grow. The Federal Interagency Forum on Aging-Related Statistics (2013) reported that in 2010, 40 million people age 65 and over lived in the United States, accounting for 13% of the total population. The agency also reported that the older population grew from 3 million in 1900 to 40 million in 2010, while the oldest-old population (those age 85 and over) grew from just over 100,000 in 1900 to 5.5 million in 2010. That dramatic growth is not over, but it can be expected to grow even more in the future. The older population in 2030 is projected to be twice as large as in 2000, growing from 35 million to 72 million and representing nearly 20% of the total U.S. population (Federal Interagency Forum on Aging-Related Statistics, 2013).

Yet, even those consumers who fall into the broad category of "elderly" or "aged" can no longer be lumped together as a homogenous, easily defined entity. As their numbers have grown, and as the medical and care delivery innovations described earlier make it possible for an increasing variety of individuals to join that select group, they have become more diverse. That diversity has produced a broad range of interests, differing personal values, and considerable disagreement about what constitutes an optimum quality of life. No longer can long-term care consumers be cared for in a one-size-fits-all delivery system. Their needs are as diverse as they are. Providers, payers, regulators, and long-term care policy makers have all had to learn to differentiate among these dissimilar consumers to find new ways to accommodate them and their needs. While many innovative solutions have been found, the effort has been of only limited success to date.

No longer can we predict what elderly individuals would prefer when it comes to making decisions about such critical topics as medically prolonging life, self-determined death, and using biomedical technologies to postpone aging. They (the elderly) have forced society in general, and the providers of long-term care in particular, to recognize them as individuals with individual desires and needs, not as an easily defined cluster of people with common, easily solved problems.

They have learned to exert their rights. They have the right to have a say in their care. They no longer are willing to simply do what the professionals determine to be best for them. Instead, they are learning to be more assertive in selecting the care they receive. Increasingly, they are demanding the right to choose quality of life over treatment. That has forced providers to include elderly consumers more in developing care plans. Elderly consumers have the right to live and receive care in their own homes when possible or in a homelike atmosphere if institutionalization is required. As a result, nursing facilities and other institutional providers have paid more attention to facility design and furnishings.

In addition to the aging of the population, major economic and social changes are occurring, including possible changes in Medicare and Medicaid and changes in how the elderly are served. This function may well affect the nature of key social relationships and institutions that define the environment for older persons (Waite & Plewes, 2014).

The Elderly as a Political Force

One result of the growth of the elderly, both in numbers and in their need for long-term care services—not a minor result by any definition—has been their growing economic and political power. Three and a half decades ago, the elderly were described as "not well organized for exerting political influence" (Levy & Loomba, 1977, p. 571). Yet, since the 1990s, the elderly have become a potent, well-organized, much-listened-to constituency. They are better informed than previous generations and have become increasingly assertive in voicing their concerns. Formal organizations of the aged, such as AARP, the Council of Senior Citizens, and the Gray Panthers, have learned how to exert their influence effectively in Congress and in state legislatures. The extent of that influence and the ability of those advocacy organizations to mobilize constituent support produced a major surprise for many of the nation's elected officials when they succeeded in defeating a well-intended catastrophic insurance law. That law would have required a larger than previously experienced contribution by the elderly. In defeating the measure, they sent a clear message that they not only did not want it, but would not abide having such decisions made about them without their input.

More recently, older Americans, led and supported by those well-organized advocacy organizations, have demonstrated their strength in debates over virtually all major policy issues affecting them, including the Affordable Care Act, Medicare restructuring, and how state and federal Medicaid funds are allocated among different types of long-term care providers. They have become a force to be reckoned with, demanding a major role in determining their futures and accepting the responsibility that goes with that role.

Nonelderly Long-Term Care Users

While the elderly are by far the most visible group of users of long-term care services, there are younger consumer populations to be considered. In fact, the elderly (defined here as age 65 or older) make up only about 63% of the total long-term care population. The remainder are 64 and younger. In 2007, a total of 404,400 children and 1.3 million adults under age 65 used long-term services and supports (Kaiser Family Foundation, 2011). This can include children, people of any age who are suffering from injuries, people with AIDS, and those who have some type of mental disease. Just like elderly patients, these patients rely on long-term care services to help them live more regular lives. People in these categories are somewhat more likely to be suffering from a single, albeit disabling, disease or condition than are the elderly. Like the elderly, they rely on long-term care services to assist them in carrying on their everyday lives as closely to normal as is possible, given their functional constraints.

The Physically Handicapped

Those who need long-term care due to one of the many different types of physical disability are a very special group of consumers. Their care needs are complex and intensive. Their functional limitations are frequently extreme yet are often combined with a near total absence of mental or emotional disability. They have high expectations for themselves, are generally quite knowledgeable about their afflictions, and are often demanding—thus providing major challenges for the long-term care system.

Some of the physically handicapped are in need of long-term care from the time of their birth, if they are handicapped as the result of congenital defects or birth accidents. Although largely unrecognized by the public as users of long-term care services, these handicapped children may, as the result of the good care they receive, live to be adults. They include patients with such debilitating diseases as spina bifida, muscular dystrophy, and cerebral palsy. As administrator of a facility devoted to caring for patients such as these for more than a decade, your author witnessed innumerable cases in which families of these patients would have been effectively destroyed had it not been for the long-term care services available to them.

They (those suffering from congenital illness) are joined by an unfortunately growing number of young adults needing long-term care because of physical (e.g., traumatic head injury) and/or chemical (e.g., drug overdose) accidents. Taken together, these younger-than-usual long-term care consumers represent only a small percentage of the overall long-term care consumer population. However, as individuals, they are some of the most fragile members of society, and they and their families are among those most reliant on the long-term care system for sustenance and support. They are among the heaviest individual users of the full range of long-term care services, and use those services for many years—much longer than typical elderly long-term care consumers—thus creating a disproportionate burden on the long-term care system.

Like the elderly, these younger chronically ill persons, particularly those with spinal cord injuries and those suffering from AIDS, have become politically active. Advocacy organizations, representing mostly young adult paraplegics and quadriplegics, were largely responsible for passage of the Americans with Disabilities Act (ADA), which forced businesses and organizations to make significant changes in physical accessibility to their buildings and in their employment and customer service policies. AIDS advocates have been nearly as effective.

The Mentally Ill/Mentally Retarded

Another, even less visible, segment of the long-term care consumer population includes those suffering some type or degree of mental illness or mental retardation. They, often being afflicted from birth or at a relatively early age, also use highly intensive long-term care services for many years. As a group, they have long received less attention than their elderly or physically handicapped counterparts. Several factors have contributed to that, including the relative difficulty involved in diagnosing and categorizing their illnesses, and most of all, the societal stigma traditionally attached to the mentally ill or retarded, or to anyone who acts differently from what is considered normal. Attempts to remove some of that stigma have included use of the term *intellectual disability*. Intellectual disability is a term used when a person has certain limitations in mental functioning and in skills such as communicating, taking care of him- or herself, and social skills. These limitations may cause a person to learn and develop more slowly than others. They may also take longer to learn to speak, walk, and take care of their personal needs such as dressing or eating. They can learn many but not all of these skills (NICHCY, 2011).

The Baby Boomers: Current and Future Long-Term Care Consumers

The past few years have seen a new population of consumers who have impacted the system more than any single group to come before them. They are known as baby boomers, the name given to the large number of people born in the period following World War II, between 1946 and 1964. When the first of them began to retire, around the year 2011, approximately 40 million Americans were 65 and over. According to the Federal Interagency Forum on Aging-Related Statistics (2013), "The older population in 2030 is projected to be twice as large as their counterparts in 2000, growing from 35 million to 72 million and representing nearly 20 percent of the total U.S. population" (p. 2). That growth in the number of elderly will translate to corresponding growth in the number of chronically ill or disabled requiring long-term care services. One source notes that 12 million Americans are expected to need long-term care in 2020 (O'Shaughnessy, 2011b). Their impact on the long-term care system will go far beyond mere numbers, however. They will be better educated and will demand much more from the system.

Providers of Long-Term Care

Long-term care is primarily health care and is usually thought of in that sense. However, because it is more geared to the consumer's level of independent functioning than to medical condition alone, other societal forces play a significant role in the success of that care. Social and economic factors such as availability and affordability of housing, homemaking assistance, and transportation, while not always thought of as part of long-term care, often determine how well the long-term care system works for an individual consumer. Long-term health care is usually so closely intertwined with those nonhealth services that the two systems (health and social) should not be treated as separate. Yet, in reality, they usually are. To attempt to fully discuss all of the other social service systems that affect long-term care would be somewhat prohibitive—and probably confusing. Thus, this book's primary focus is on the long-term healthcare system and includes the providers most directly related to that system. While there is not a distinct section dealing with other societal forces, they and their impact are referenced throughout with inclusion of the term *long-term services and supports*. The exception to that is housing, which has become so important to long-term care, with its many new options.

The current system of long-term care providers has developed in a seemingly hit-or-miss fashion. That is largely because it has grown in response to three factors that are not necessarily orderly themselves: (1) need, (2) demand, and (3) availability of reimbursement. Each is influenced to some degree by the others. To begin with, need and demand are not synonymous, particularly where consumers are not primarily responsible for payment, as is the case in long-term care. As demonstrated, there is considerable unmet need in the long-term care system, often because there is no reimbursement available. On the other hand, consumers sometimes want services that they really may not need—especially if they know that third-party reimbursement for those services is available.

The types and numbers of long-term care service providers available today are directly the result of those three factors (need, demand, and financing). When one, two, or all three of them are present to a sufficient degree, providers of specific services appear. As a result, the mix of provider organizations and the respective roles of each in the system are constantly changing. Even the names associated with specific provider types tend to change with alarming regularity. More often than not, those name changes come about as the result of some new regulation and its definition of the provider. For example, what were formerly called "nursing homes" are now referred to as "nursing facilities" because of the Omnibus Budget Reconciliation Act (OBRA) of 1987. "Boarding homes" are now "residential care facilities." Some terms such as *extended care* were created by earlier regulations, but they have long since been replaced in common usage by others, again created by later legislative action.

All of this makes for a very confusing situation. Providers must keep up with pertinent regulations affecting the classification of their services. Regulators, on the other hand, must strive to keep up with changes initiated by the providers. Ultimately, it is consumers who are caught in the middle. Even when, as is usually the case, changes take place in the best interests of the consumers, it becomes very difficult for anyone to understand the makeup of this ever-changing system. As the old saying goes, "You can't tell the players without a program."

Nursing Facilities

Formerly called nursing homes, nursing facilities are healthcare facilities licensed by the states offering room, board, nursing care, and some therapies. They include facilities certified by Medicare as skilled nursing facilities (SNFs) and others that used to be called intermediate care facilities (ICFs), the primary difference being the amount of nursing care and the number of therapies provided. Skilled nursing facilities provide 24-hour nursing care plus such other services as intravenous therapy, oxygen therapy, wound care, physical therapy, occupational therapy, speech pathology, and nutritional teaching. Nonskilled facilities provide less intensive nursing care and may offer some of the other services, but do not do so on a regular basis.

Skilled nursing care centers serve individuals who have increasingly complex medical conditions and extensive needs for care and support, as demonstrated by measures of both physical and cognitive function. An analysis by the American Health Care Association (2013) concentrating on five activities of daily living (bathing, bed mobility, transfer, toilet use, and eating) found that

> nearly all (95.2 percent) of those individuals who enter a center for a Medicare-covered, post-acute stay required assistance with four or five of these activities. Among long-stay residents (for at least one year), 85.6 percent needed that same level of assistance. In addition, almost two-thirds (61.1 percent) of long-stay residents have dementia, while only 37.7 percent of Medicare admissions have dementia. (p. 4)

Subacute Care

One of the newer terms in long-term care, *subacute care* has grown as a cost-effective alternative for those individuals needing more than nursing facility care and less than hospital care. Subacute care facilities or units provide highly skilled nursing care, therapies, and more medical supervision than nursing facilities. It is highly focused care designed to bridge between acute and long-term care, with a relatively short length of stay (although longer than is typical of acute care hospitals). In subacute care, multidisciplinary teams work toward a goal of moving the patient to home or a lower level of care.

Both government payment sources (primarily Medicare) and managed care organizations favor subacute care as a means of providing intensive, high-quality care at a lower cost. Hospitals and nursing facilities see it as a means of filling empty beds and gaining a growing portion of the healthcare market.

Assisted Living/Residential Care

Assisted living/residential care provides relatively independent seniors with assistance and limited healthcare services in a homelike atmosphere. The Assisted Living Federation of America defines assisted living as "a long-term care option that combines housing, support services and health care, as needed. Assisted living is designed for individuals who require assistance with everyday activities such as meals, medication management or assistance, bathing, dressing and transportation" (Assisted Living Federation of America, 2013, p. 1).

Elderly Housing Options

Elder housing includes simple housing (owned and rental), age-restricted retirement communities, senior apartments, cohousing, independent living, congregate housing, and continuing care retirement communities (CCRCs). This is a growing area of long-term care, both in size and importance.

Community-Based Services

Increasingly, both to satisfy the desire of long-term care consumers and to save costs, care is being delivered in the community, not in institutions. The most prominent types of such community-based care services are home health care, adult day care, and hospice care.

Home healthcare services are provided in the consumer's home. Those services might include any combination of the following: care management, nursing care, therapies, dietary consultation, wound care, or homemaker services. They are not provided on a round-the-clock basis, but for a few hours daily as needed. Home health care is seen as a major means of avoiding institutionalization.

Hospice care provides emotional and physical support for persons with terminal illness. It is usually provided in the home, often by volunteers.

Adult day care provides daily (not overnight) services for chronically ill individuals who are not able to function on their own but are able to live at home with the assistance of informal caregivers. It provides meals, social and educational activities, assistance with personal care, and supervision for the care recipient. At the same time, it provides a few hours of relief for the caregivers, often allowing them to maintain employment.

■ The Argument Over Institutional Versus Noninstitutional Care

Long-term care providers are often categorized as either institutional or noninstitutional. Nursing care, assisted living care, subacute care, and housing services are usually considered to be institutional care because most of their care is provided in facilities developed for that purpose. Home care, adult day care, and hospice care are usually provided in the consumer's home; thus they are thought of as noninstitutional (community-based) care.

The distinction, however, is not as clear as it seems. Hospice care regularly has both an institutional and noninstitutional component. So does assisted living in some situations. Adult day care is often provided in nursing facilities, but it is essentially community based. Also, provider organizations are increasingly offering not only multiple levels of institutional care, but also noninstitutional services such as home care. For that reason, in the following discussion, the distinction will be between institutional and noninstitutional services, not among providers.

One of the primary ways in which payers have tried to reduce healthcare costs in recent years has been an increased emphasis on community-based, noninstitutional services (such as home care) and an ongoing effort to reduce the number of nursing home beds. Shifting of funding from institutional to noninstitutional services, combined with changing eligibility rules designed to accomplish the same end, has been quite successful in the past several decades. These efforts have been strengthened by a decision by the U.S. Supreme Court, known as the Olmstead decision, that unnecessary segregation of individuals with disabilities in institutions may constitute discrimination based on disability, that the Americans with Disabilities Act may require states to provide community-based services rather than institutional placements for individuals with disabilities, and that states have an obligation to move individuals with disabilities from institutional settings into more integrated settings in the community. While home care services have grown significantly during that time, the number of nursing homes has declined. For example, the number of nursing homes in the United States dropped by 6% between 2001 and 2011 (Centers for Disease Control & Prevention, 2013).

The reasoning behind such efforts has been twofold:

1. Long-term care consumers, particularly the elderly who make up such a large portion of that population, prefer to receive care in their own homes.
2. Home care is less expensive than institutional (nursing home) care.

Both of those arguments are valid in their broadest sense. Yet, both have shortcomings when put into practice.

First, the idea that most people would prefer to be cared for at home is a no-brainer. Of course they would! While some individuals recognize and want the security and socialization that comes with institutional care, most are more comfortable in their own homes, surrounded by familiar objects. It is only natural that people feel more secure and less threatened in the homes that they have built for themselves and, of major importance, homes in which they are in command. When they are uprooted, frequently after having spent as much as a half-century in the same environment, and are forced to live in a communal setting over which they have little control, they are understandably unsettled, uncomfortable, and distressed.

Yet, advocates of community-based care continue to conduct study after study showing that people prefer to be cared for at home. They would do well to refocus their efforts toward identifying those long-term care consumers who would be better served by care in their homes.

As for the idea that home-based care is less expensive—it is, when used in moderation. When taken as a whole, institutional care (from the most expensive subacute or skilled nursing care to the less expensive assisted living care) is more costly than home care. Yet, when compared on an hour-by-hour basis, it is less expensive to care for institutional residents with a staffing of one staff person for multiple residents than it is for one-on-one home care. Numerous studies have shown that home-based care, contrary to popular belief, is not necessarily less expensive. Much of the reason for that is that nursing facilities and home care agencies tend to serve different populations, with those requiring more intensive, continuous care going into institutions and those who are less frail being cared for at home.

To a degree, the argument over home-based versus institutional care is somewhat specious and irrelevant. It generates more emotional response than factual, for a couple of reasons. To begin with, it is not an either/or situation. There is enough demand for long-term care services to go around. The rapidly growing population of elderly (and others) needing long-term care will ensure that the supply of services—in whatever form—is not likely to overtake the demand for such services in the foreseeable future.

Also, some individuals are better cared for at home, while others would be better served in nursing homes or other long-term care institutions. Consumers who can generally care for themselves with the support of certain types of assistance—such as help with activities of daily living (ADLs), including feeding, bathing, dressing, toileting, and transferring—are capable of home-based care, which is less expensive and which poses less of an intrusion on their independence. Such care, usually available on an à la carte basis, permits them to maintain their all-important sense of self-reliance, providing only that level and extent of care that is needed. It has the added advantage of being flexible enough to easily expand or contract as the consumer's needs change.

Conversely, institutional care provides the security, supervision, medical/nursing oversight, and functional assistance needed by those long-term care consumers who are generally unable to function safely and adequately with minimal support. It is constant, as opposed to periodic care.

The difficulty of determining accurately how many residents currently in nursing facilities could be appropriately cared for in community-based care is illustrated by one report that placed that number somewhere between 5% and 11%. That wide range in identifying how many could be moved from nursing homes to home care or community-based personal care homes is the result of inconsistency in how they are defined, either narrowly or broadly. The point worth noting here is not which of these definitions is most accurate, if any, but that there is little agreement on how to determine the appropriateness of different types of care. It is a question not easily answered, because those trying to make the determination of what is appropriate are alternately influenced by issues of cost, quality, and choice.

■ Long-Term Care as Part of a Continuum

One approach to defining the interrelationship among long-term care providers is to consider them collectively as a continuum of care. Dr. Connie Evashwick was one of the earliest (and still one of the leading) advocates for considering our health and social system as a comprehensive, integrated continuum of care. In her book *The Continuum of Long-Term Care*, she defines a continuum of care as "an integrated, client-oriented system of care composed of both services and integrating mechanisms that guides and tracks clients over time through a comprehensive array of health, mental health, and social services spanning all levels of intensity of care" (Evashwick, 2005, p. 4).

Also, the term *continuum of care* may be used to refer to the overall system as we are doing here, or it may refer to a specific subsystem serving a defined geographic area or a particular service population, such as an integrated care network. The elements of a continuum remain the same. It is client oriented, comprehensive, and integrated.

The Continuum Is Client Oriented

Long-term care and other health and social services should revolve around the consumers (clients), rather than forcing the consumers to revolve around the services. An ideal long-term care system is often defined as client-oriented, meaning that it is not provider-oriented or payer-oriented. We use the somewhat stronger term *consumer-driven* herein. That term was chosen after lengthy debate as a way to denote that the consumers should have some control in how and when they use the long-term care system. Whichever term is chosen, the point is that the client (consumer) is the focus of the system and all of its components.

The Continuum Is Comprehensive

A long-term care system, be it localized or the overall U.S. long-term care system, must provide all of the services needed by its consumers if it is to be a true continuum. A list of services should include at least health promotion/illness prevention, ambulatory care, inpatient acute care, residential long-term care, community-based long-term care, and housing. It should be noted that services are being added all of the time. The consumers involved may require any or all of those services at one time or another. The key is being able to match the services to their needs (Evashwick, 2005). A continuum also covers more than the services usually associated with long-term care. It includes services such as acute care and housing services if it is to be considered comprehensive. If any of the services are missing, or if they are not appropriate for a particular consumer's needs, gaps in coverage are created.

The Continuum Is Integrated

Evashwick (2005) emphasizes that a continuum of care is an integrated system of care—it is "more than just a collection of fragmented services, but one that includes mechanisms for organizing those services and operating them as an integrated system" (p. 4).

Dr. Bruce Vladeck, former head of the U.S. Health Care Financing Administration (HCFA)—now known as the Centers for Medicare & Medicaid Services (CMS), the agency that oversees Medicare and Medicaid—presented an entirely different and enlightening way of looking at the continuum (Vladeck, 1987). Although his descriptions of the continuum were written 2½ decades ago, they have stood the test of time. In that text, he described the continuum of care in common, easy-to-understand terms. Perhaps his most valuable contribution is in identifying what the continuum is not.

First, "it is not a ladder, which has been the accepted model for much of health care but simply does not fit the users of long-term care services" (Vladeck, 1987, p. 4). The ladder concept suggests that everyone progresses (or regresses) from acute care through the various levels to the other extreme of the continuum. An often unrecognized fact about long-term care is that it is not static. Most individuals using long-term care move from one level of need to another on a random, unpredictable basis. It was long assumed that long-term care was a one-way street, moving from relative independence to complete dependence. As more discrete types of care have become available, it has been shown that most long-term care recipients move relatively often from one level of care need to another. They may regress from one level of functional independence to a lower level for a time, only to regain their ability to care for themselves (usually as the result of good therapy services). Periodic episodes of acute illness are not infrequent, particularly with the frail elderly. Experience has shown that long-term care is a dynamic process. Any individual may well move from one level of care to another, from one type of care delivery modality to another, and back again, perhaps several times over a period of years.

For the same reasons, the continuum of care is not "a set of concentric circles" (Vladeck, 1987, p. 5). A set of concentric circles is another frequently used means of visualizing the continuum of care, with acute services at the hub and less intensive services in the outer circles. All this model really does is change the direction of perceived movement from up/down (in the ladder model) to inside/out. It has many of the same flaws as the ladder concept, in that long-term care consumers do not move smoothly from one ring to another. They often utilize portions of services from several levels of care.

One of the most popular organizational tools of the 1990s was the matrix. A three-dimensional matrix model is another way of describing the continuum of care, but as Vladeck explains, it still falls short. As he says, "It fails to take into consideration the many human dimensions involved" (Vladeck, 1987, p. 7).

He goes on to develop a couple of his own metaphors, a user-friendly computer and a root system, to describe the continuum. Actually, they are not much better. In trying to understand the concept of a continuum of care, we should try to avoid getting too tangled up in visual images. Rather, we should work at understanding that it is a comprehensive, integrated system designed to meet the very complex needs of a highly vulnerable population. Its shape is not important, but the results are.

■ Strengths and Weaknesses in the Long-Term Care System

The long-term care system, being very much in the middle of a turbulent time, has both strengths and weaknesses. Let us look at the more prominent of them.

Strengths

The long-term care system, while less than perfect, has provided essential care to a very large, very diverse population for a long time. While it is human nature to dwell on the weaknesses of the system (a prerequisite to overcoming those weaknesses), the system also has its strengths, which should not be overlooked.

Response to Changing Needs

Even as it has been evolving, the long-term care system has responded to the changing needs of its consumers. In fact, that responsiveness has been a cornerstone of its evolution. As new needs have arisen, new modes of delivery have developed to meet them. For example, as new or newly identified diseases such as Alzheimer's disease have come along and have produced an entirely new set of consumer needs, new treatment methods have been found to better care for those particular populations.

The Long-Term Care System's Uniquely American Nature

The long-term care system in the United States has evolved in ways that fit the attitudes of our particular society. The system has resisted efforts to impose on it those elements that appear to work in other societies. That may not appear to all readers as a strength, but it represents certain values that are somewhat unique to this culture, including strong reliance on personal responsibility, resistance to heavy government involvement, and fierce defense of individuals' right to choice. Whether we agree with each of those, they represent ideas that are deeply ingrained in American society. The seemingly haphazard way in which the long-term care system has developed is a form of recognition that there are vast geographic, ethnic, economic, and social differences in this large country and that it will be difficult to find any monolithic system that meets all of those needs equally.

The Dedication of Caregivers

There are many criticisms of the current long-term care system, as we shall see. However, the vast majority of people working in long-term care are highly dedicated to the welfare of those for whom they care. It is that dedication that has allowed the long-term care system to survive its turbulent history and to serve its consumers as well as it has. There are far too many situations where the quality of long-term care and the quality of life of those dependent on such care are sacrificed because of incompetent or greedy providers. However, emphasis on those situations overlooks the many providers and their staff members whose primary allegiance is to their consumers. (Note that later herein, the poor image of long-term care providers is identified as part of what is wrong with the current system.)

Increasing Focus on Customer Service

In recent years, the long-term care system has become increasingly concerned with what has been known in other industries as customer service. As long-term care consumers have become more aware of their options, and have been more willing to demand amenities that will improve the quality of their lives, they have in effect become better consumers. It is to the credit of the providers in the long-term care system that they have sought ways of providing those amenities. They have often turned to successful companies such as Walt Disney Enterprises and some of the large hotel chains to learn how to make the long-term care they provide more satisfactory and more responsive to the needs and wants of their customers.

Critics will say that they have done so only because of the increasingly competitive nature of the field. That may sometimes be the case, but the motivation for this focus on customer service is of less importance than the end result, which has been a major benefit for both those using the services and the system itself.

Development of Innovative Types of Care

For a variety of reasons—including the desire to provide better service, the need to secure a larger portion of a competitive market, and simple creativity—the long-term care system has shown considerable capability to create new and innovative ways of meeting the needs of their consumers.

Aging in Place—One such innovation is known as "aging in place." It is based on acknowledgment of the need to tailor services to the particular requirements of individuals. Aging in place recognizes that consumers' long-term care needs vary from time to time and is designed to bring services to them rather than moving them to where the services are available. The idea is that long-term care recipients should live in a stable, homelike setting that is familiar and comfortable, in which services can be provided. The difficulty in implementing the concept lies in the logistics required to have all necessary services available at a reasonable cost. There have been, and continue to be, numerous highly successful projects aimed at solving that problem.

Multilevel Facilities—Multilevel facilities are a variation of aging in place—long-term care facilities that provide several different levels of care in the same location. While not allowing residents to stay in the same specific setting as aging in place would, multilevel facilities do allow them to stay in the same facility. Such facilities provide some or all of the services of the long-term care system. Most common are the more traditional institutional services, nursing facilities (skilled and nonskilled), assisted living/residential care, and various types of supported independent living arrangements.

When individuals need a different level or type of care, either temporarily or permanently, they move from one floor to another or one unit to another, staying within the overall organizational campus. In doing so, they remain in a familiar environment, with familiar staff, subject to familiar rules and regulations. A particularly valuable aspect of such an arrangement is that it minimizes separation of elderly couples. Even if one of them needs to move to another unit, the spouse is not all that far away and can visit regularly.

Adult Day Care—These programs were designed to provide relief for family members who provide long-term care for relatives in their homes. In such programs, the consumer spends a few hours a day in a supervised setting outside the home, often within a nursing facility. The concept recognizes the need of such caregivers for some free time to hold jobs or to attend to their own matters. In many cases, adult day care availability is the difference between keeping the care recipient at home with his or her family or having to institutionalize him or her. In addition, day care provides valuable social interaction, including structured activity programs.

Long-term care providers have also found an especially innovative and highly successful variation of adult day care—inclusion of pediatric day care in long-term care programs designed primarily for the elderly. Pediatric day care has been around for a long time, providing safe, supervised babysitting activities for preschool children while their parents work. In time, various long-term care organizations, particularly nursing facilities, began offering on-site child day care for their employees as a recruitment and retention benefit. They discovered the value of allowing the children and the elderly residents to interact, benefiting both groups. Many long-term care organizations now schedule joint activities for the children and the residents, creating a simulated grandparent–grandchild relationship.

Integration Efforts

Perhaps the most significant and promising innovation in the long-term care system has been the move toward more integration of services. Development of integrated health systems (IHSs) has progressed rapidly in recent years. They represent an important development in the evolution of the long-term care system toward a true continuum of care. Some integrated systems are still in relatively early stages of their development, with developers learning what works and what does not. Others have worked through that phase. While some such experiments failed, those that have succeeded are sound, tested organizational forms able to better serve the needs of their customers.

Weaknesses

It would be an understatement to say that the current long-term care system has its flaws. Its weaknesses and the need to overcome them in such a dynamic environment pose major challenges for all involved with the system: providers, payers, regulators, and policy makers. The rapid growth in the number of people needing long-term care now and projected to need it in the near future compounds the need to find some solutions fast. Let us look briefly at some of the weaknesses in the long-term care system as a prelude to seeking ways to address them.

A Reimbursement-Driven System

All of the above has created one of the greatest problems with the long-term care system as it exists today: it is reimbursement-driven! Providers have come forward to meet needs for which there is reimbursement, but have been understandably reluctant to create services for which they will not be paid, or for which reimbursement is extremely limited.

The long-term care system, like the rest of the American healthcare system, is reimbursement-driven rather than consumer-driven. The type and amount of service available to individual consumers is more often than not dependent on the type and amount of financial coverage they have. Whether they are covered by private insurance or government programs such as Medicare or Medicaid, their services are restricted to those included under that program. Eligibility requirements, co-pay responsibility, duration of coverage, and selection of providers all affect the availability and accessibility of services, and all vary depending on the reimbursement source.

Instead of focusing primarily on the needs of individual consumers, the system focuses on payment availability, resulting in gaps in services for many consumers. For example, people whose insurance provides coverage for home care services may be able to stay at home, while others with the same functional disabilities might have to be admitted to a nursing facility because their coverage is limited to institutional care. The length of time spent in a specific type or level of facility is also dependent on the source of third-party reimbursement. These problems have been exacerbated somewhat by the advent of managed care which, while being more efficient, has tended to impose more restrictions on the types and amounts of care received, based on cost. It is unclear at this time whether the Affordable Care Act will change this for better or for worse.

The financing and payment system is dysfunctional for all parties to it—providers, payers, consumers, all of whom feel it either (1) costs too much or (2) brings too little revenue. How we pay health care providers does little to provide incentives to improve quality, value, and efficiency (Kovner, Knickman, & Jonas, 2011).

Inequitably Distributed Services

Long-term care services are not equally available to all who need them. This is partly, but not entirely, due to the nature of long-term care reimbursement. Other factors contributing to that inequality include limitations caused by geographic and political boundaries and uneven availability of certain types of professional staff. Availability of care can depend on whether those needing it have reimbursement coverage or on the source of that coverage. Where they live can also make them eligible or ineligible, as can other demographic factors such as age or socioeconomic status. Even when they are eligible, services are often not available to them.

Any or all of those factors can contribute to long-term care being available to some and not to others. One of the biggest challenges for the long-term care system is making services available and accessible to all who need them. Without such equity, the system is not seamless nor can it be considered a true continuum.

A Fragmented and Uncoordinated System

The long-term care system is fragmented, consisting of numerous parts that should be interrelated and integrated but are not. That fragmentation comes from several sources, including the many different payers and types of reimbursement, the independent nature of providers, and not least of all by the fragmented regulations governing the system.

To begin with, the lack of coordination in the system affects providers of care. It has become popular in recent years to talk of creating a level playing field, meaning that all players in the game have equal opportunities, face similar obstacles, and play by the same rules. In long-term care, there is no level playing field—nor any semblance of one. Different segments of the industry (e.g., providers, payers, regulators) each have their own set of forces determining how they proceed. Those forces usually involve financing or regulations. As noted earlier, uneven availability of reimbursement is a major reason for the fragmentation of the system. Uncoordinated regulations also contribute to that problem. Nursing facilities are subject to different rules and regulations than are home care agencies or even more closely related services such as assisted living. Some types of care, such as subacute care, are caught in the middle, with regulations from both acute care and nursing care applying to them. Multilevel long-term care organizations often have to meet several differing, often competing regulations.

Even within one provider type, there are also differences from one geographic area to another. For example, by federal law all states must license nursing home (nursing facility) administrators. Yet, there are no overall standards governing how they do so, and there is great variation from one state to another. One organization, the National Association of Long-Term Care Administrator Boards, continues to work toward some degree of uniformity in that area, but it still has work to do.

While this fragmentation makes it difficult for providers of long-term care services to do their jobs, the real impact is on the consumers. The providers deliver different services in different situations, to different consumer groups, and in response to different regulations. Consumers end up working with numerous providers at the same time, with little if any coordination. Each provider works within its own arbitrarily defined boundaries, presenting consumers with a confusing mishmash of rules to understand and follow.

The effect of all of this goes beyond mere confusion and inconvenience. It can also result in inferior care. A nursing home may send a resident to a hospital for treatment of an acute episode of illness, without filling the hospital staff in on all of that person's other care requirements. The hospital, in turn, may make discharge plans for a patient without knowing all of his or her social needs. Some of that is caused by poor planning and communication among providers of different levels of service, but much of it is caused by the fragmentation of the overall system.

A Mix of Health and Social Services

The long-term care system includes or relies on a mix of health-related elements and others that are more social or economic, such as housing and transportation. Remember that the need for long-term care is generally triggered by a functional limitation resulting from a disease or condition, not by the disease or condition itself. Assistance in overcoming that functional limitation often includes services traditionally thought of as social services. Providing appropriate housing, meals, transportation as needed, and financial or legal assistance may have a significant impact on the success of the more health-related long-term care services. Indeed, the availability or unavailability of those other services often becomes a determinant in whether long-term care is needed at all.

While health and social services can never be totally separated, they frequently involve different providers, reimbursement sources, and/or regulations. Arbitrary boundaries between long-term care and social services abound. That separation makes it very difficult to achieve any type of coordination.

Multiple Entry Points Into the System

The fragmentation, inequity, and lack of coordination that are seemingly inherent in the long-term care system produce a result that makes it very difficult for consumers to access services: the many different points at which they enter the system and the different steps required to reach services from those multiple entry points. An individual consumer's need for long-term care may be identified while in the acute (hospital) system, may come from interaction with the social services system, or may come directly from home—without any prior contact with those other systems. Depending on which of these routes is followed, there may be significant differences in eligibility requirements, reimbursement, and duration of care. Even worse, should the consumer leave the long-term care system and reenter at a later time, he or she may have to start all over.

Overshadowed by the Acute System

The long-term care system has long taken a backseat to the acute care system. Hospitals, with their ever-increasing ability to save lives and cure illness, have been far more dramatically imprinted in the minds of the public than the less glamorous, ongoing long-term care, with several unfortunate results for long-term care. First, healthcare professionals, particularly doctors and nurses, have not been as likely to see long-term care as a desirable career option. Thus, there is a shortage of medical professionals trained in long-term-care-related areas such as geriatrics. Despite efforts to convince the medical profession of their worth, the numbers of practicing geriatricians are falling seriously behind needed levels. Doctors, physician assistants, psychiatrists, nurses, psychologists, pharmacists, social workers, and other healthcare professionals specially trained in the care of older adults will be in short supply. The American Geriatrics Society (2013) notes that "With the supply of geriatricians in jeopardy; older adults will not receive the care they need." It has been difficult to get those who do move from an acute care setting to long-term care to realign their thinking from a medical model to a more holistic model—to go from a cure mentality to a care mentality.

Second, both reimbursement policies and regulations affecting the long-term care system tend to be adapted from the acute care system rather than being created specifically for long-term care. An example of that is the Medicare requirement of an acute hospital stay as a prerequisite for certain types of long-term care. The original purpose of that requirement was to avoid inappropriate and unnecessary use of long-term care services, particularly in nursing homes. It was based on the concept that only a physician could determine the need for long-term care, and then only after hospitalization. The irony is that it sometimes served to create inappropriate and unnecessary hospital stays as a means of justifying entry into the long-term care system. There is great need to move away from that philosophy toward one more suitable for long-term care.

Acute care tends to focus on and treat a person's medical condition, while long-term care looks at the total picture, the entire individual.

Poor Public Image

The long-term care system has long suffered from an unfavorable image among the public. Because nursing homes have been the predominant type of provider in years past, they have been the focus of much of that bad publicity.

Anecdotal evidence of poor care is not hard to come by. For example, one study by the Henry J. Kaiser Family Foundation (2013) of public attitudes about nursing homes found that:

> the public's attitudes about nursing homes are mixed. Around a third say nursing homes are doing a good job serving health care consumers, around a third say they are doing a bad job, and the rest say they do a mixed job or that they don't know. (p. 1)

That same study revealed that many Americans believe that at least some nursing home residents suffer abuse from staff (Kaiser Family Foundation, 2013). While there has undoubtedly been organizational and personal abuse in the long-term care system, it is not nearly as rampant or as serious as such articles suggest.

Also, nursing homes are fighting a societal perception. They have been seen by an entire generation as places where someone goes to die or places where family members can get rid of a burdensome relative. These negative images often translate into tougher regulations and/or opposition to funding of long-term care. The system will be hard put to implement significant change without addressing its image problem.

Inadequate Support for Informal Caregivers

The long-term care system relies heavily on an informal group of caregivers who supplement its formal services. About 65.7 million people are informal caregivers, defined as "an unpaid individual (a spouse, partner, family member, friend, or neighbor) involved in assisting others with activities of daily living and/or medical tasks" (National Alliance for Caregiving, 2012). A typical caregiver in the United States is a 46-year-old female, who has some college education, works, and spends more than 20 hours a week providing care to her mother (National Alliance for Caregiving, 2012). They are usually not recognized as an integral part of the formal long-term care system, nor do they receive adequate support, although there have been encouraging steps in that direction. Hospice care programs assist families in caring for relatives with terminal conditions by providing both physical and emotional support. Respite programs provide periods of relief from caregiving chores, benefiting both patient and caregiver.

Yet, little has been done systemwide to recognize the degree to which these informal caregivers augment the formal long-term care system or to provide financial or other support and incentives for them. By failing to do that, the long-term care system is also failing to take full advantage of a potentially significant resource.

A Confusing and User-Unfriendly System

All of these weaknesses in the current long-term care system, when taken together, result in a system that is extremely difficult for consumers and potential consumers to access and use effectively. The fragmentation and the lack of coordination of services, financing, and regulations only serve to make the system confusing and unfriendly to anyone who must rely on it. Many an experienced expert in some aspect of long-term care has discovered, when confronted with dealing with the system on a personal basis, that it is very difficult to understand and use. If the experts find it difficult, imagine what the nonexperts encounter when attempting to access long-term care.

■ Summary

Today's long-term care system is, indeed, in a state of turbulence. It is a system that is growing at a rate far in excess of its apparent ability to accommodate to the changing needs. A host of external and internal forces is at work pushing the system to change. Yet, it is a system that has grown and developed in a random, reactive, and sometimes haphazard manner. Its history has been one of meeting needs as they become apparent, rather than anticipating those needs in a proactive approach. It is fragmented, difficult to access, and overly dependent on the vagaries of a reimbursement system that is changeable at best, fickle at worst.

On the other hand, it is a system that does respond (eventually) to demonstrated needs, one that somehow manages to provide services to those who need them the most. It is a system that depends on the dedication and ingenuity of those directly providing services to meet the changing needs of the system's consumers even when faced with confusing, sometimes incomprehensible, rules and regulations.

It is a system struggling to respond to a rapidly changing environment with creative and innovative methods of delivering services to a population that is discovering its ability to influence its own future. The worst characteristic of the current long-term care system is its lack of coordination and uniformity. Paradoxically, its best characteristic is its flexibility and ability to accommodate the different needs and wants of its many consumers.

■ Vocabulary Terms

The following terms are included in this chapter. They are important to the topics and issues discussed herein and should become familiar to readers. Some of the terms are also found in other chapters but may be used in different contexts. They may not be fully defined herein. Thus, readers may wish to seek other, supplementary definitions of them.

AARP
activities of daily living (ADLs)
adult day care
Affordable Care Act (ACA)
aging in place
Americans with Disabilities Act
assisted living/residential care
baby boomers
Centers for Medicare & Medicaid
   Services (CMS)
certificate of need (CON)
chronic care
clients
community-based care
continuum of care
functional disabilities
home health care
hospice care

informal caregivers
institutional care
integrated health systems (IHSs)
integration
long-term care
long-term services and supports
managed care
Medicaid
Medicare
multilevel facilities
multiple entry points
noninstitutional care
nursing facilities
quicker and sicker discharges
residents
Social Security Act of 1935
subacute care

■ Discussion Questions

The following questions are presented to assist you in understanding the material covered in this chapter. They tend to be general but lend themselves to detailed answers, which can be found in the chapter.

1. What factors have led to the development of the long-term care system as it currently exists?
2. What are some of the strengths and weaknesses of the current long-term care system?
3. Who uses long-term care services, and why do they use them?
4. Who are baby boomers, and what is their impact on the long-term care system?
5. What is and has been the role of informal caregivers in the long-term care system?
6. What is a continuum of care, and where do long-term care services fit in that continuum?
7. What types of services make up institutional and noninstitutional care?
8. What effect have government regulations had on the financing of long-term care?

■ References

Alzheimer's Association. (2013, October 30). *2013 Alzheimer's disease facts and figures*. Chicago, IL: Alzheimer's Association. National Institutes of Health Press Releases. Retrieved from http://www.alz.org/downloads/facts_figures_2013.pdf.

American Geriatrics Society. (2013). *Demand for Geriatric Care and the Evident Shortage of Shortage of geriatrics healthcare providers*. Retrieved from http://www.americangeriatrics.org/files/documents/Adv_Resources/demand_for_geriatric_care.pdf.

American Health Care Association. (2013). *2013 Quality report*. Washington, DC: American Health Care Association.

Assisted Living Federation of America. (2013). *Consumer options: What is assisted living?* Retrieved from http://www.alfa.org/alfa/Assisted_Living_Information.asp.

Centers for Disease Control & Prevention. (2013). *Nursing homes, beds, residents, and occupancy rates, by state: United States, selected years 1995–2011*. Retrieved from http://www.cdc.gov/nchs/data/hus/2012/109.pdf.

Day, T. (2013). *What is long term care?* Retrieved from http://www.longtermcarelink.net/eldercare/long_term_care.htm.

Drucker, P. (1980). *Managing in turbulent times*. New York, NY: Harper & Row.

Evashwick, C. (2005). *The continuum of care* (3rd ed.). Clifton Park, NY: Thomson Delmar Learning.

Federal Interagency Forum on Aging-Related Statistics. (2013, July 31). *Older Americans 2012*. Hyattsville, MD: Federal Interagency Forum on Aging-Related Statistics. Retrieved from http://www.agingstats.gov/agingstatsdotnet/Main_Site/Data/2012_Documents/docs/EntireChartbook.pdf.

Freid, V., Bernstein, A., & Bush, M. (2012). *Multiple chronic conditions among adults aged 45 and over: Trends over the past 10 years*. NCHS data brief, No. 100. Hyattsville, MD: National Center for Health Statistics.

Goldsmith, S. (1994). *Essentials of long-term care administration.* Gaithersburg, MD: Aspen Publishers.

Kaiser Family Foundation. (2011, October 11). *Medicaid's long-term care users: Spending patterns across institutional and community-based settings.* Retrieved from http://kaiserfamilyfoundation.files.wordpress.com/2013/01/7576-02.pdf.

Kaiser Family Foundation. (2013). *National survey on nursing homes.* Retrieved from http://kaiserfamilyfoundation.files.wordpress.com/2013/01/kaiser-newshour-national-survey-on-nursing-homes-highlights-and-chartpack.pdf.

Kissick, W. (1994). *Medicine's needs versus finite resources.* New Haven, CT: Yale University Press.

Kovner, A., Knickman, J., & Jonas, S. (2011). *Jonas and Kovner's health care delivery in the United States* (10th ed.). New York, NY: Springer.

Levy, S., & Loomba, P. (1977). *Long-term care administration: A managerial perspective* (Vol. II). New York, NY: Spectrum Publications.

National Alliance for Caregiving. (2012). *Caregiving in the U.S.* Washington, DC: National Alliance for Caregiving.

NICHCY. (2011, January). *Intellectual disability.* Retrieved from http://www.parentcenterhub.org/repository/intellectual.

O'Shaughnessy, C. (2011a, December 13). *The Aging Services Network: Serving a vulnerable and growing elderly population in tough economic times.* Retrieved from http://www.nhpf.org/library/details.cfm/2880.

O'Shaughnessy, C. (2011b, February 1). *National spending for long-term services and supports (LTSS), 2011.* Retrieved from http://www.nhpf.org/library/details.cfm/2783.

Saint Joseph's College of Maine (1992). Criteria for designing or evaluating a long-term care system. Standish, ME: Saint Joseph's College. (p. 1).

Vladeck, B. (1987). The continuum of care: Principles and metaphors. In C. Evashwick & L. Weiss (Eds.), *Managing the continuum of care* (pp. 3–10). Rockville, MD: Aspen Publishers.

Waite, L., & Plewes, T. (2014). *New directions in the sociology of aging (2013).* Washington, DC: The National Academies Press.

The Affordable Care Act

Author's Note: The Affordable Care Act of 2010 (or "Obamacare" if you prefer) is very much a work in progress. Even as of this publication 5 years after its passage, many segments of it are still to be implemented, some have been delayed, changes are being made, and there has been an ongoing effort by its critics to repeal it in whole or in part. As a result, it is nearly impossible for this text to be completely up to date concerning the act. From the time I finish writing to actual publication, changes are inevitable. However, I have made a sincere attempt herein to give you a sound foundation on which to build a basic understanding of the act and its implications for long-term care and to guide you in seeking more information.

—John Pratt

Learning Objectives

After completing this chapter, readers will be able to:

1. Discuss how the Affordable Care Act came to be and the factors leading to its passage.
2. Discuss the content of the Affordable Care Act of 2010.
3. Identify and discuss the impact of the Affordable Care Act on long-term care providers and consumers.
4. Identify and discuss the issues still remaining in the Affordable Care Act.

■ Introduction

When Barack Obama was elected president of the United States in 2008, he made health care reform the signature domestic goal of his presidency. *Time Magazine* commented as follows: "Having staked the success of his presidency on the longstanding Democratic dream of universal health care, President Obama finally achieved victory, bringing an end to a yearlong partisan struggle" (Tumulty, 2010). While the Affordable Care Act was a substantial victory for the president, it was, and remains, highly controversial and certainly did not bring an end to the partisan struggle. While the relationship between the two major parties had been somewhat less than cordial before introduction of the bill, the interaction after it has regularly been described as "rancorous."

The stated aim of the ACA was

> to increase the quality, affordability, and rate of health insurance coverage for Americans, and reduce the costs of health care for individuals and the government. It provides a number of mechanisms, including mandates, subsidies, and insurance exchanges, to increase coverage and affordability. (Genesis Financial, 2013)

The mandates require individuals to have insurance coverage and businesses to provide coverage or pay fines. Health insurance exchanges will be set up in each state to provide a marketplace where individuals and small businesses can buy insurance (with a government subsidy if eligible). The law also requires insurance companies to cover all applicants within new minimum standards and offer the same rates regardless of preexisting conditions or sex.

Even the name fosters discussion, often heated. The act was originally titled "The Patient Protection and Affordable Care Act." Earlier on, the "Patient Protection and" portion was dropped to make it easier to say and identify as the Affordable Care Act (ACA). Because it was so completely identified with President Obama and his agenda, critics began calling it "Obamacare." However, the president turned that around on them, accepting the term and even using it himself. His administration even created a website named Obamacare Facts, explaining (spinning?) it positively. Both sides continue to use the term. In our discussion, we will refer to the law as "The Affordable Care Act" at times, "Obamacare" at others, and mostly (for convenience) as "the ACA."

■ History/Passage of the Law

The bill passed without a single Republican vote, and 34 Democrats also voted against it. Republican attempts to filibuster the bill were defeated by Senate President Harry Reid (D-NV) who used a budgetary process called "reconciliation" to pass the bill with only 51 votes. That allowed House Democrats to approve the Senate version; although many of them disliked it, they were promised fixes through reconciliation (NBCNews.com, 2013).

Passage in that form only increased the differences between the bill's supporters and its detractors. Critics complained that the reconciliation process bypassed normal legislative channels and that the 2,000-plus page bill had not been adequately discussed. House Speaker Nancy Pelosi (D-CA) famously said "we have to pass the bill so that you can find out what is in it" (Christopher, 2013). Various public polls at the time (and since) showed that more than 60% of Americans did not approve of the law.

Constitutionality of the Law

The constitutionality of the act was challenged, specifically targeting one provision of the act known as the "individual mandate." That provision requires most individuals to purchase health insurance or pay a penalty (Pitts, 2013). The petitioners argued that the government did not have the authority to force individuals to purchase a product or service. On June 28, 2012, the United States Supreme Court upheld the constitutionality of the Affordable Care Act based on the argument that Congress has authority to impose the mandate under its power to tax and spend and that the individual mandate was, in fact, a tax.

Implementation

The act was designed to be implemented over several years. The administration chose to begin with some of the more popular portions (requiring policies to be issued regardless of any medical condition, allowing people under age 26 to be covered by their parents' insurance, etc.). Those sections were implemented first. Other more controversial regulations (increased taxes, expansion of Medicaid, etc.) were designed to be spread out over later years. Implementation of some sections has already been postponed by the Obama administration.

Regulations

Any new law results in a plethora of regulations to implement it. The ACA is no exception. Various estimates are that it has spawned anywhere from 10,000 to 30,000 pages of new regulations, and 5 years after the law's passage, more regulations are sure to come. Again, we need to remember that only a portion of those regulations apply to long-term care. Throughout this discussion, keep in mind that each section and provision of the law we cover has associated regulations. We may or may not discuss those regulations specifically, but they are always there.

Funding of the ACA

The ACA is funded by a combination of taxes and cost offsets (reductions). Major taxes include a much-broadened Medicare tax on incomes over $200,000 for individuals and $250,000 for joint filers, an annual fee on insurance providers, and a 40% excise tax on "Cadillac" insurance policies. There are also taxes on pharmaceuticals, high-cost diagnostic equipment, and a 10% federal sales tax on indoor tanning services. Cost offsets are from intended cost savings such as changes in the Medicare Advantage program relative to traditional Medicare (Genesis Financial, 2013).

Even the Obama administration says "ObamaCare's cost is estimated at up to net cost of $1.36 trillion dollars by 2023" but goes on to say, "Although ObamaCare's net costs are in the trillions, the law actually reduces the growth in health care spending by tens of billions each year, reduces health care costs for many Americans, helps to insure tens of millions and is estimated to result in an overall net decrease of the deficit" (ObamaCare Facts, 2014). The Congressional Budget Office (2014) projects a net cost of $36 billion for 2014 and $1,383 billion for the 2015–2024 period.

Cuts in Medicare

To finance part of the new spending, spending and coverage cuts are made to Medicare. A 2012 Congressional Budget Office (CBO) report updated the amount of money Obamacare cuts out of Medicare from $500 billion to a whopping $716 billion between 2013 and 2022 (Senger, 2012). Among those Medicare cuts would be:

- Reduction in funding for Medicare Advantage policies: $132 billion
- Reduction in Medicare home healthcare payments: $40 billion
- Reduction in certain Medicare hospital payments: $22 billion (Genesis Financial, 2013)

Note that these were projected cuts as of September 2013 and may change as time goes on.

■ Impact on Long-Term Care

Our focus here is on long-term care. Therefore, our discussion will be about how Obamacare affects that segment of the healthcare spectrum. Although the act itself runs to more than 2,400 pages, the majority of provisions in the act, including many of the more controversial, are tangential to long-term care and will not be covered herein.

During formulation of the ACA, it was thought that long-term care would be a potential cost saver because this type of coverage would not be needed immediately and the government could build up its reserves and help lower the cost of the ACA (Loureghy, 2013). That, of course, would not lower the cost but—if true—would simply delay it.

Many people are still unaware that long-term care is not included several years after passage of the ACA. Nationwide Financial Retirement Institute's 2014 survey revealed that:

> more than seven in 10 affluent baby boomers mistakenly think the Affordable Care Act will cover their long-term care (LTC) costs in retirement. According to the poll conducted by Harris Interactive of 801 Americans over 50 with at least $150,000 in household income, only 28 percent know that the Affordable Care Act does not cover LTC costs. (Nationwide Financial, 2014)

Health Insurance Exchanges

As of October 1, 2013, the ACA included health insurance exchanges—online marketplaces for health insurance. Under this provision, people can use their state's insurance exchange (marketplace) to obtain coverage from competing private healthcare providers. They can use a calculator to see if they qualify for Medicaid and CHIP subsidies (ObamaCare Facts, 2013). These exchanges are significant to our discussion here because they *are not* designed to include long-term care.

■ Shifting Focus Away From Institutional Care

Much of the focus of the ACA is on redirecting long-term care consumers and services away from institutions such as nursing facilities and assisted living and toward less intensive home and community-based services, such as home health care, hospice, etc. While this strategy has been in place by both state and federal governments for years, the ACA gives it new impetus. Following are some of the ACA options relating to that focus.

CLASS Act

Considered by many to be the most important of these is the Community Living Assistance Services and Supports (CLASS) Act, described by the Urban Institute as "a voluntary employment-based public long term care insurance program intended to provide a private financial base for disability-related services and supports during working years and in old age" (Urban Institute, 2010). The CLASS Act was the primary way of addressing long-term care needs through the ACA. It would establish a national long-term care insurance program. The concept was that an individual would contribute to the CLASS program for 5 years before benefits would become available. That would allow the program to build up a fund before drawing on it.

However, the CLASS program was not to be. Its long-run sustainability came under scrutiny and it was suspended indefinitely on October 14, 2011. The Department of Health and Human Services (HHS) stated that it was unable to implement a long-term financially stable CLASS program. Thus, the most important segment of the ACA dealing with long-term care never came into existence. If a newer version, modified to be more financially viable, should emerge in the future, the impact of the ACA on long-term care will be greatly increased.

Community First Choice Option

The ACA Community First Choice Option provides a 6% increase in federal Medicaid matching funds to states for providing community-based attendant services and supports within their Medicaid program. It is intended to allow people to more easily receive services in the community rather than being in a hospital or nursing home (HHS.gov, 2012).

Balancing Incentive Payments Program

The Balancing Incentive Payments Program is another of the ACA provisions designed to keep long-term care consumers out of costly institutions. It is aimed at removing barriers to providing long-term care in people's homes and communities. The Pew Charitable Trust reports that:

> States participating in the $3 billion program receive a higher federal match for all of their spending on home and community care through September 2015, provided they reduce the red tape and confusion that caretakers, elders and those with disabilities typically encounter when they attempt to find alternatives to nursing homes. (Vestal, 2014)

Money Follows the Person Program

Another of the ACA provisions designed to keep long-term care consumers out of costly institutions is the "Money Follows the Person" program. In an attempt to address Medicaid's continuing institutional bias, the ACA includes a number of Medicaid home and community-based services options. To reinforce those options, the ACA extends the Money Follows the Person program originally created as part of the Deficit Reduction Act of 2005 through September 30, 2016. It also shortens the nursing home residency requirement from 180 to 90 days (Miller, 2012).

Spousal Impoverishment Protections

The ACA extends mandatory spousal impoverishment protections to spouses of people receiving home and community-based services. The National Association of State Units on Aging describes the change as follows:

> Current federal law protects the financial interests of spouses of certain Medicaid beneficiaries by allowing the spouse of a nursing facility resident to keep a minimum share of the couple's combined income and assets. The ACA addresses the institutional bias that applies these spousal protections only to nursing home residents by extending the protections to spouses of Medicaid beneficiaries who receive home and community-based services. (NASUA, 2014, p. 1)

No Wrong Door System—Aging and Disability Resource Centers

The "No Wrong Door" system supports state efforts to streamline access to long-term services and supports and simplify access to long-term care services for the elderly and individuals with disabilities. No Wrong Door systems as described by the Center for Disability and Aging Policy "are designed to serve as highly visible and trusted places available in every community across the country where people of all ages, incomes and disabilities go to get information and one-on-one person-centered counseling on the full range of options" (Administration for Community Living, 2014). They provide information and assistance to both consumers and professionals and serve as the entry point to publicly administered long-term services, including those funded under Medicaid.

The No Wrong Door program is delivered through aging and disability resource centers, one-stop locations designed to provide comprehensive information and assistance to people of all income levels and all types of disability. The ACA is providing $10 million per year in grants to states to improve and expand their aging and disability resource centers. Medicaid was recently approved for $400,000 in additional Money Follows the Person funding to support the aging and disability resource centers (Vestal, 2014).

Health Homes

Health homes were created by the ACA, effective January 1, 2011. Health homes "are designed to be person-centered systems of care that facilitate access to and coordination of the full array of primary and acute physical health services, behavioral health care, and long-term community-based services and supports" (Kaiser Family Foundation, 2011). Through that coordination and integration, the health home model of service seeks to better meet the needs of people with multiple chronic illnesses and to improve healthcare quality, clinical outcomes, and the patient care experience, while also reducing costs.

Dual-Eligible Initiative

The ACA created a new Medicare–Medicaid Coordination Office within the Centers for Medicare & Medicaid Services to coordinate care for individuals who are eligible for both Medicaid and Medicare. The office is charged with making the two programs work together more effectively to improve care and lower costs (Nicolella, 2012). It will seek to improve quality and access to care, simplify processes, and eliminate regulatory conflicts and cost-shifting that occur between the Medicare and Medicaid programs, states, and the federal government.

■ Other Provisions Impacting Long-Term Care

While the law's provisions listed previously are focused on redirecting long-term care consumers and services away from institutions and toward less intensive home and community-based services, there are other sections of the law that also impact long-term care and long-term care providers. They are discussed in the following sections.

Improving Nursing Home Quality

A stated goal of the ACA is to increase transparency in nursing homes. The act requires increased disclosure of detailed information concerning ownership, staffing, expenditures, and compliance. This obviously involves new and/or changed regulations and rules for providers to follow. Other provisions relate to culture change and the use of information technology, improving quality, and preventing elder abuse and neglect (Miller, 2012).

Pay-for-Performance

Pay-for-performance (P4P) is "an umbrella term for initiatives aimed at improving the quality, efficiency, and overall value of health care. These arrangements provide financial incentives to hospitals, physicians, and other healthcare providers to carry out such improvements and achieve optimal outcomes for patients. Pay-for-performance has become popular among policy makers and private and public payers, including Medicare and Medicaid. The Affordable Care Act expands the use of pay-for-performance and encourages experimentation to identify designs and programs that are most effective" (James, 2012). Studies have shown that financial incentive plans such as P4P can improve quality in management of chronic diseases, such as diabetes and heart disease.

Bundling

The Bundled Payments for Care Improvement initiative is a new payment model created by the Affordable Care Act (ACA). Payment arrangements include financial and performance accountability for episodes of care. It is hoped that these models will lead to higher quality and more coordinated care at a lower cost to Medicare (CMS, 2013). Under these arrangements, payment is paid to a single entity for a defined episode of care rather than individual payments to individual service providers. In that episode of care, services might include inpatient hospital, physician, outpatient therapy, and postacute care services. The episode of care must be initiated with a hospitalization and continue for 30 days after discharge. The Medicare program already has considerable experience with bundled payments for sets of services: inpatient hospital services are bundled into stays, skilled nursing facility (SNF) services are bundled into days, and home-health-agency (HHA) services are bundled into episodes (Feder, 2013).

The goal of the bundled payment approach is to improve care coordination and to control the cost of an episode of care. Providers are rewarded for delivering more services. The entity receiving the payment becomes responsible for all services required. It arranges for acute and postacute care services to be available and for the other acute and long-term care providers who are involved.

The entity receiving the payment keeps any difference between the payment and episode costs, but is responsible for any costs above the payment amount. It could reduce costs

by eliminating unnecessary services delivered during the episode, avoiding hospital readmissions, coordinating services across all providers and facilities to avoid duplication and waste, and delivering the most efficient mix of services for the patient. Alternatively, the entity could reduce costs by stinting on care or avoiding high cost patients. (Dummit, 2011, p. 3)

The Centers for Medicare & Medicaid Services (CMS) is testing four models of bundling differentiated primarily by how an episode of care is defined. The models are:

- *Model 1*—Bases the episode of care on the acute care inpatient stay.
- *Model 2*—Bases the episode of care on the acute care inpatient stay and a post-acute care period.
- *Model 3*—Bases the episode of care on the postacute care following a hospital stay.
- *Model 4*—Bases the episode of care on the acute care inpatient stay, but pays the hospital one bulk payment for all services rendered (Tabar, 2013).

Accountable Care Organizations

Accountable care organizations (ACOs) are CMS's new model of coordinated care by physicians, hospitals, and long-term care providers. They have a goal of reducing hospital readmissions, reducing quality variations, and managing risk. The ACOs function under a bundled payment methodology as described previously. The ACOs will contract with long-term care providers for postacute care, and the ACOs will be held accountable for the quality outcomes associated with that care. An ACO may be made up of a group of physicians, hospitals, and other suppliers of services. However, ACOs that impact long-term care providers are almost exclusively hospital-based organizations. Although the ACO model is touted as a cost saver in the long run, the investments needed for the initial changeover to an ACO are not cheap, meaning that large, urban hospitals and integrated delivery networks are more likely to participate in an ACO than small, rural, or stand-alone hospitals.

In an appearance at the Second Annual ACO Summit in Washington, DC, in June 2014, Mark Parkinson, the president and CEO of the American Health Care Association, stated:

It is obvious that nursing facilities play a vital role in the care continuum within the ACO frame work, noting the large chunk of Medicare expenditures going to skilled nursing facilities (SNFs). SNFs can help ACOs be successful in providing lower cost care settings with high quality care. (Parkinson, 2013)

Many long-term care providers have concerns about being so reliant on hospitals or hospital systems for their reimbursement. They understand that the ACOs controlled by those organizations may not give them due respect and input. These fears are based on a long history of relationships between the two segments of the continuum of care but are not always founded on facts. For the ACO system to work, all parties involved have to learn to work together.

Medicaid Expansion

Another key provision of the Affordable Care Act is expansion of Medicaid. Medicaid provides health coverage to millions of Americans, including children, pregnant women, parents, seniors, and individuals with disabilities. It consists of both federal and state funding. Federal law requires participating states to cover certain population groups (mandatory eligibility groups) and gives those states the flexibility to cover other population groups (optional eligibility groups). States set individual eligibility criteria within federal minimum standards. In the past, Medicaid had not covered all low-income adults because eligibility was restricted to specific categories of low-income individuals, such as children, their parents, pregnant women, the elderly, or individuals with disabilities. In most states, adults without dependent children were ineligible regardless of their income, and income limits for parents were very low. The ACA aimed to fill in gaps in coverage by extending Medicaid eligibility (Kaiser Family Foundation, 2014).

The ACA expands Medicaid eligibility to include all individuals and families with incomes up to 133% of the poverty level. In *National Federation of Independent Business v. Sebelius*, the Supreme Court allowed states to opt out of the Medicaid expansion, and some states have done so. As of May 22, 2014, 26 states and the District of Columbia were implementing the Medicaid expansion, 20 states were not moving forward, and 4 states were considering it (The Advisory Board Company, 2014). Those states not participating can set their own eligibility thresholds, which may be below the ACA mandated level. Many states do not make Medicaid available to childless adults at any income level. Because subsidies on insurance plans purchased through exchanges are not available to those below the poverty level, this may create a coverage gap in those states (Genesis Financial, 2013).

The expansion of Medicaid is controversial in many states because those states will bear increased costs ranging into the millions of dollars. The ACA provides payment for most of those costs for the first few years, but states opting to expand their Medicaid programs will have to maintain that extended coverage and the associated costs.

Asset Recovery

Medicaid has generally allowed states to recover Medicaid long-term care payments against a recipient's estate. However, Medicaid does permit the spouse of a long-term care recipient to keep some of the recipient's assets to protect that spouse against impoverishment. The Affordable Care Act creates a new category of Medicaid recipients—adults with incomes under 133% of the poverty level—and changes income and asset eligibility rules for others who were already eligible. This raises questions about how existing rules regarding asset transfers, liens, estate recoveries, and posteligibility income apply to persons eligible for Medicaid based on the new ACA rules (Jost, 2014).

Readmissions Reduction

The Medicare hospital readmissions reduction program (HRRP) was created as part of the Affordable Care Act. HRRP assesses penalties on hospitals with high readmission rates for patients with certain medical conditions. Approximately $280 million in penalties was assessed in fiscal year 2013 for readmissions between 2009 and 2011 (Coberly & Scanlon, 2013). The program has been criticized for failing to consider socioeconomic and other factors on readmissions. In support of those criticisms, recent research, published in the *Journal of General Internal Medicine*, notes that a patient's age, income, race, employment status, and other social factors can play a role in outcomes and readmissions (Hoban, 2012).

The readmissions program resulted from various studies showing that elderly patients experienced a high level of readmission to hospitals following discharge. A study by the Robert Wood Johnson Foundation found that one in eight Medicare patients was readmitted to the hospital within 30 days of being released after surgery in 2010, while one in six patients returned to the hospital within a month of leaving after receiving medical care (Robert Wood Johnson Foundation, 2013). Another study by the Department of Health and Human Services showed that readmissions of seniors to a hospital within a month of discharge declined in 2013. The all-cause 30-day hospital readmission rate for Medicare beneficiaries was 17.5% last year. That's a drop from 18.5% in 2012 and the higher rates than that for several years prior (Newman, 2014).

It should be noted here that those studies do not indicate where the elderly patients were discharged to—home, a rehab facility, or another destination. However, this program impacts long-term care providers to whom the patients are discharged.

Medicare Advantage Plans

A Medicare Advantage Plan is defined by Medicare (Medicare.gov, 2014) as

> a type of Medicare health plan offered by a private company that contracts with Medicare to provide all your Part A and Part B benefits. Medicare Advantage Plans include Health Maintenance Organizations, Preferred Provider Organizations, Private Fee-for-Service Plans, Special Needs Plans, and Medicare Medical Savings Account Plans.

Thus, they are actually managed care organizations.

With passage of the Affordable Care Act, there was widespread concern that the plans would be eliminated or made more expensive as a way of funding the ACA. However, on Monday, April 7, 2014, the Centers for Medicare & Medicaid Services (CMS) announced a group of changes that it says:

> sets a stable path for Medicare Advantage and implements a number of policies that ensure beneficiaries will continue to have access to a wide array of high

quality, high value, and low cost options while making certain that plans are providing value to Medicare and taxpayers. (CMS.gov, 2014, p. 1)

Should that happen, it would go a long way toward reassuring Medicaid Advantage plan holders.

In that announcement, CMS further reports that:

Medicare Advantage premiums have fallen by 10 percent and enrollment has increased by 38 percent to an all-time high of more than 15 million beneficiaries. Today, nearly 30 percent of Medicare beneficiaries are enrolled in a Medicare Advantage plan. Furthermore, enrollees are benefiting from greater quality as over half of enrollees are now in plans with 4 or more stars, a significant increase from 37 percent of enrollees in such plans in 2013. (CMS.gov, 2014, p. 1)

Medical Device Tax

The 2.3% medical device tax imposed by the Affordable Care Act was one of a number of revenue-raising provisions to finance the act. According to the Congressional Research Service, this tax, which took effect in January 2013, is projected to collect approximately $38 billion of excise tax revenues over the next 10 years, resulting in $29 billion of net revenues, after accounting for offsets from other taxes. Most medical devices become subject to a 2.3% excise tax collected at the time of purchase as long as they are being sold to medical providers, including such items as examination gloves and catheters that are used in long-term care (Gravelle & Lowry, 2013). This is one of the most controversial taxes imposed by the ACA, and there have been numerous attempts to block it.

Employer Mandate

The ACA employer mandate is a requirement that all businesses with over 50 full-time equivalent employees provide health insurance for their full-time employees or pay a penalty. The mandate, which was set to begin in 2014, was delayed until 2015/2016. Businesses with 50–99 full-time equivalent employees will have to start insuring workers by 2016, while those with 100 or more will need to start providing health benefits in 2015 (Cordero, 2014). A February 2014 report by the Congressional Budget Office projects that the full-time workforce will lose roughly 2 million people overall by 2024 as a result of the Affordable Care Act (Mullaney, 2014). The ACA defines full-time work as 30 hours or more a week, and some employers may cut workers' hours below that level to avoid the mandate, but there has been discussion in Congress to change the definition of full-time work to 40 hours a week. This is intended to protect workers in companies with 50 full-time employees from having their hours cut by companies seeking to stay under the threshold.

Because many long-term care providers have relatively small staffs, the impact of this mandate will not affect them. However, larger facilities/systems will be impacted, and it would be wise for all to keep abreast of changes in the mandate.

Projected Staff Shortages

The Affordable Care Act promises to create millions of newly insured consumers. They threaten to overwhelm a delivery system that was already strained. Workforce shortages have existed for decades and are likely to get much worse under the ACA. The Heritage Foundation warns that:

> A system overload is inevitable. Pent-up demand from those waiting for a plastic card and attracted by the promise of "free" or heavily subsidized services is expected. Training new health professionals takes years. Without more graduates from nursing and medical schools, individuals and families will face longer wait times, greater difficulty accessing providers, shortened time with providers, increased costs, and new frustrations with care delivery. (Anderson, 2014)

When one combines the expanded care requirements with the shortage of personnel and limited resources, the prognosis is grim. The changes built into the law will mean increased workloads, heavier regulation and new penalties, and lower payments—not what the law's creators intended.

■ Summary

Few would disagree that the Affordable Care Act (ACA) of 2010 is the most significant health-related piece of legislation since passage of the Medicare and Medicaid amendments of 1965. Whether you support it or disagree with it, it is significant. Many of its provisions, such as requiring policies to be issued regardless of any medical condition, allowing people under age 26 to be covered by their parents' insurance, etc., are beneficial to consumers. Other more controversial provisions such as increased regulations, increased taxes, etc., cause problems for providers.

Not all of the provisions of the ACA directly impact long-term care providers or consumers. In fact, with the suspension of the CLASS program, there is little in the act that provides coverage for long-term care. Yet, some do affect long-term care indirectly. It is those provisions that are the focus of our discussion herein.

As has been pointed out repeatedly, the ACA and its implementation are not finished products. Changes are still occurring several years after the law's passage for several reasons. First, the implementation was planned to take place over a period of several years. Second, critics of the law, both in Congress and elsewhere, continue to challenge it. Third, the Obama administration has changed or deleted sections that were not working (such as suspending the CLASS program). Further changes should be expected.

There has been an effort herein to discuss the important aspects of the ACA and to lay a foundation for further study. By the time readers get to this point, it is more than likely that some changes will have happened. Therefore, you are urged to seek additional information. There is a great deal of it available on the Internet and in publications. Just be careful as you read it, as much of what you will find is opinion, not fact.

■ Vocabulary Terms

The following terms are included in this chapter. They are important to the topics and issues discussed herein and should become familiar to readers. Some of the terms are also found in other chapters but may be used in different contexts. They may not be fully defined herein. Thus, readers may wish to seek other, supplementary definitions of them.

accountable care organizations (ACOs)
Affordable Care Act (ACA)
asset recovery
aging and disability resource centers
Balancing Incentive Payments Program
bundling
Centers for Medicare & Medicaid Services (CMS)
CLASS program
community-based services
Community First Choice Option
Congressional Budget Office
cost offsets
Dual-Eligible Initiative
employer mandate

health homes
health insurance exchanges
hospital readmissions reduction program (HRRP)
individual mandate
institutional care
Medicaid
medical device tax
Medicare
Medicare Advantage plans
Money Follows the Person program
No Wrong Door system
Obamacare
pay-for-performance (P4P)
reconciliation
spousal impoverishment protections

■ Discussion Questions

The following questions are presented to assist you in understanding the material covered in this chapter. They tend to be general, but lend themselves to detailed answers, which can be found in the chapter.

1. What factors led to passage of the Affordable Care Act?
2. What are the provisions of the Affordable Care Act that benefit consumers?

3. What are the provisions of the Affordable Care Act that directly impact long-term care providers?
4. What is meant by bundling?
5. What is an Accountable Care Organization (ACO), and how does it work?
6. What is the CLASS Act, and why was it suspended?
7. What is pay-for-performance (P4P), and how does it improve quality?
8. What is the hospital readmissions reduction program (HRRP), and how does it affect long-term care organizations?

■ References

Administration for Community Living. (2014, April 16). *Aging & Disability Resource Centers Program/ No Wrong Door system*. Retrieved from http://www.acl.gov/Programs/CDAP/OIP/ADRC/index .aspx#.

The Advisory Board Company. (2014, May 28). *Where the states stand on Medicaid expansion*. Retrieved from http://www.advisory.com/daily-briefing/resources/primers/medicaidmap.

Anderson, A. (2014, March 18). *The impact of the Affordable Care Act on the health care workforce*. Retrieved from http://www.heritage.org/research/reports/2014/03/the-impact-of-the -affordable-care-act-on-the-health-care-workforce.

Centers for Medicare and Medicaid Services (CMS). (2013). *Bundled Payments for Care Improvement (BPCI) Initiative: General information*. Retrieved from http://innovation.cms.gov/initiatives /Bundled-Payments/index.html.

Christopher, T. (2013, November 17). *The Context Behind Nancy Pelosi's Famous 'We Have to Pass the Bill' Quote*. Retrieved from Mediaite, LLC: http://www.mediaite.com/tv /the-context-behind-nancy-pelosis-famous-we-have-to-pass-the-bill-quote.

CMS.gov. (2014, April 7). *CMS ensures higher value and quality for Medicare health and drug plans*. Retrieved from http://www.cms.gov/Newsroom/MediaReleaseDatabase/Press-releases/2014-Press -releases-items/2014-04-07.html.

Coberly, S., & Scanlon, J. (2013, June 21). *The Medicare Hospital Readmissions Reduction Program: Time for an update?* Retrieved from http://www.nhpf.org/library/details.cfm/2930.

Congressional Budget Office. (2014, April 14). *Updated estimates of the effects of the insurance coverage provisions of the Affordable Care Act, April 2014*. Retrieved from http://www.cbo.gov /publication/45231.

Cordero Certified Public Accountants. (2014). *The Obamacare employer mandate delayed*. Retrieved from http://www.corderocpa.com/obama-news/the-obamacare-employer-mandate-delayed.php.

Dummit, L. (2011, March 28). *Medicare's bundling pilot: Including post-acute care services*. Retrieved from http://www.nhpf.org/library/issue-briefs/IB841_BundlingPostAcuteCare_03-28-11.pdf.

Feder, J. (2013, August 1). Bundle with care—rethinking Medicare incentives for post–acute care services. *New England Journal of Medicine, 369*, 400–401. Retrieved http://www.nejm.org/doi/full/10.1056 /NEJMp1302730.

Genesis Financial. (2013, September). *Health care reform—What you need to know*. Retrieved from http://genesisfinancial.biz/genesis/health-care-reform/.

Gravelle, J., & Lowry, S. (2013, December 13). *The medical device excise tax: Economic analysis*. Retrieved from http://www.fas.org/sgp/crs/misc/R43342.pdf.

HHS.gov. (2012, April 26). *HHS announces new Affordable Care Act options for community-based care.* Retrieved from http://www.hhs.gov/news/press/2012pres/04/20120426a.html.

Hoban, S. (2012, October 22). *Study suggests social factors play a role in hospital readmissions.* Retrieved from http://www.environmentsforaging.com/news-item/study-suggests-social-factors-play-role-hospital-readmissions.

James, J. (2012, October 11). *Pay-for-performance.* Retrieved from http://www.healthaffairs.org/healthpolicybriefs/brief.php?brief_id=78.

Jost, T. (2014, February 14). *Implementing health reform: Medicaid asset rules and the Affordable Care Act.* Retrieved from http://healthaffairs.org/blog/2014/02/24/implementing-health-reform-medicaid-asset-rules-and-the-affordable-care-act.

Kaiser Family Foundation. (2011, January). *Medicaid's new "health home" option.* Retrieved from http://kaiserfamilyfoundation.files.wordpress.com/2013/01/8136.pdf.

Kaiser Family Foundation. (2014, August 7). *How will the uninsured fare under the Affordable Care Act?* Retrieved from http://kff.org/health-reform/fact-sheet/how-will-the-uninsured-fare-under-the-affordable-care-act.

Loureghy, E. (2013, October 9). *Long-term care insurance and the Affordable Care Act.* http://www.blufftontoday.com/bluffton-sun-city/2013-10-09/long-term-care-insurance-and-affordable-care-act#.VBcni7l0xHy.

Medicare.gov. (2014). *Medicare advantage plans.* Retrieved from http://www.medicare.gov/sign-up-change-plans/medicare-health-plans/medicare-advantage-plans/medicare-advantage-plans.html.

Miller, E. (2012). The Affordable Care Act and long-term care comprehensive reform or just tinkering around the edges? *Journal of Aging & Social Policy, 24*(2), 101–117.

Mullaney, T. (2014, February 25). *CBO: Affordable Care Act will reduce full-time workforce by more than 2 million in the next decade.* Retrieved from http://www.mcknights.com/cbo-affordable-care-act-will-reduce-full-time-workforce-by-more-than-2-million-in-the-next-decade/article/332700/.

NASUA. (2014). *Long-term care in brief: Explaining the HCBs spousal impoverishment protections.* Retrieved from http://www.nasuad.org/documentation/aca/NASUAD_materials/ltcb_protectionforHCBSrecipients.pdf.

Nationwide Financial. (2014, February 21). *Most boomers mistakenly think Affordable Care Act covers long-term care costs.* Retrieved from http://finance.yahoo.com/news/most-boomers-mistakenly-think-affordable-153000372.html.

NBCNews.com. (2013). *Health care: A timeline of the overhaul bill's passage.* Retrieved from http://www.nbcnews.com/id/35986022/ns/politics-capitol_hill/t/health-care-timeline-overhaul-bills-passage.

Newman, E. (2014, June 1). *Readmission numbers drop.* Retrieved from http://www.mcknights.com/readmission-numbers-drop/article/351330.

Nicolella, E. (2012, January 12). *The Affordable Care Act's impact on long-term services and supports.* Retrieved from http://www.healthcare.ri.gov/documents/01_09_12%20Exec%20Comm%20Presentation.pdf.

ObamaCare Facts. (2013). *What is the Obamacare health insurance exchange marketplace?* Retrieved from http://obamacarefacts.com/obamacare-health-insurance-exchange.php.

ObamaCare Facts. (2014). *What does Obamacare cost?* Retrieved from http://obamacarefacts.com/costof-obamacare.php.

Parkinson, M. (2013, June 14). Presentation "Long-Term Care Providers in ACOs" at the second annual ACO summit, Washington, DC.

Pitts, C. (2013, August 1). *How to make sense of the individual mandate.* Retrieved from http://www .sbnonline.com/2013/08/how-to-make-sense-of-the-individual-mandate.

Robert Wood Johnson Foundation. (2013, February). *The revolving door: A report on U.S. hospital readmissions.* Retrieved from http://rwjf.org/en/research-publications/find-rwjf-research/2013/02 /the-revolving-door--a-report-on-u-s--hospital-readmissions.html.

Senger, A. (2012, August 1). Obamacare robs Medicare of $716 billion to fund itself. *The Daily Signal.* http://dailysignal.com/2012/08/01/obamacare-robs-medicare-of-716-billion-to-fund-itself/.

Tabar, P. (2013, January 31). *CMS announces test sites for bundled payment program.* Retrieved from http://www.ltlmagazine.com/news-item/cms-announces-test-sites-bundled-payment-program.

Tumulty, K. (2010, March 23). *Making history: House passes health care reform.* Retrieved from http:// www.time.com/time/politics/article/0,8599,1973989,00.html.

Urban Institute. (2010). *Disability and long term care.* Retrieved from http://www.urban.org/health_policy /long-term_care.

Vestal, C. (2014, January 17). *ACA spurs state shift in long-term care.* Retrieved from http://www.pewtrusts .org/en/research-and-analysis/blogs/stateline/2014/01/17/aca-spurs-state-shift-in-longterm-care.

Toward an Ideal System

After completing this chapter, readers will be able to:

1. Identify the characteristics of an ideal long-term care system, with particular attention to accessibility, quality, and cost.

2. Describe what it means for the long-term care system to be consumer driven, including an understanding of consumers' rights and the responsibilities that go along with those rights.

3. Identify the roles of formal and informal caregivers and ways for those resources to be coordinated.

4. Define the components of a full and uniform assessment of a consumer's service needs.

5. Discuss the need for incentives for providers and consumers to improve the quality and effectiveness of care and to use the long-term care system wisely.

■ Introduction

Having seen earlier in this text what the current long-term care system looks like, let us now look at how an ideal system might appear. A truly ideal long-term care system does not, and probably never will, exist. The needs of the consumers are too great and change too regularly for that to occur. In addition, other forces acting on the long-term care system are so dynamic it is unlikely that any system can react to them in an optimum way. Forces such as managed care, limits on funding availability, piecemeal regulations, and competition from within and without the system will keep the system off balance for years to come. In addition, we can safely say that the future will bring new pressures on the system that we cannot even imagine today.

However, there are certain characteristics that would be present in an ideal system—elements that would be essential for the system to be successful. In this chapter, we examine those characteristics.

The basis for our discussion is a document entitled *Criteria for Designing or Evaluating a Long-Term Care System* (Saint Joseph's College of Maine, 1993) (termed simply *Criteria* hereafter). The *Criteria* were developed by the Continuing Care Council and the Long-Term Care Management Institute of Saint Joseph's College for use in designing a new long-term care system or for evaluating any current or proposed long-term care system. The *Criteria* were created during the early days of the health-care reform debates in the 1990s. During those debates, which actually focused on healthcare financing more than on healthcare delivery, long-term care was barely discussed. When it was, it was pretty much an afterthought. When questioned at the time about their failure to consider long-term care in the administration's reform plans, one official stated that it would simply be too expensive to include it.

Given that mindset at the national level, many groups around the country got involved in attempting to positively influence the future of health care in general and long-term care in particular. The *Criteria* came about as the result of one such effort, a symposium, held in Rockport, Maine, in September 1991. The symposium, Vision 2000: Defining New Models for Long-Term Care, was cosponsored by the Maine Health Care Association, the Home Care Alliance of Maine, the Maine Chapter of the National Council of Senior Citizens, and the Area Agencies on Aging. Over a period of 3 days, your author, serving as "symposiarch," engaged more than 200 participants in an effort to define an ideal long-term care system. Those participants came from more than 20 organizations representing long-term care consumers, providers, regulators, and payers.

The tone of the symposium was set by Bruce Jennings, then assistant director of the prestigious Hastings Center, who defined a moral vision for long-term care, and Dr. Warren Davidson, a geriatrician from Monckton, New Brunswick (Canada), who described his experiences with long-term care consumers. The symposium participants then proceeded to work together to identify the essential elements of an ideal long-term care system. It was a valuable exercise of constructive interaction among representatives of the various segments of the system, in which they gained an understanding of each other's seemingly irreconcilable points of view and developed a remarkable degree of consensus on the issues.

From the notes taken during that symposium, the *Criteria* evolved, primarily through the efforts of the Long-Term Care Management Institute. They were reviewed, critiqued, and refined by the Continuing Care Council, a long-term care advisory organization made up of representatives from all segments of the long-term care system, an organization that also developed as a result of the 1991 symposium.

Let us use the *Criteria* as a foundation for construction of a long-term care system as it should be. While each criterion is important in its own right, it is only when taken as a whole that they represent an optimum system. It is recognized that there is some duplication and overlapping of criteria, but that serves to emphasize the importance of certain aspects of long-term care. The criteria are stated as general precepts against which a long-term care system should be measured. Each of them is accompanied by several statements identifying the benchmarks a system must accomplish to meet that particular criterion. In our discussion, we examine why those benchmarks are important and how they might be achieved. Although developed more than 2 decades ago, the *Criteria* have stood the test of time amazingly well and are as relevant today as they were then.

■ Criterion I. The long-term care system should be based on recognition of the needs, rights, and responsibilities of individuals.

The system should be for and about those who use long-term care. Its consumers are individuals, and they deserve to be treated as such, with dignity and respect. Long-term care involves the most intimate aspects of their lives, and the system's ultimate goal should be no less than to enable them to function at their highest achievable level. It should do everything possible to assist them to live as valuable members of society. They do have value. The system's job is to recognize and maximize that value.

A. The long-term care system should be consumer driven.

Availability and utilization of long-term care services should be based on the needs of the consumers of those services, rather than on the needs of providers, reimbursement agencies, or politicians. The current long-term care system is largely reimbursement driven, with the availability or lack of availability of services being dependent on the availability of funding for those services. The system should do more to make those services available when and where they are needed by consumers without concern for financing or eligibility.

To achieve that end, the system will have to overcome many logistical difficulties. It will have to find ways to provide the right mix of services for all consumers, recognizing them as individuals, even though their needs vary greatly. There are many factors causing those differences. First, there is their uneven distribution throughout rural, urban, and suburban areas, with all of the variations of need caused by that distribution. The need for services will also vary according to other demographic factors, including age, education level, and availability of family or other informal caregivers.

Even if providers try to provide a broad enough range of services to meet the needs of all, and even if adequate funding exists, those providers can be expected to encounter other problems, including regulatory prohibitions and finding the right types and number of properly trained staff.

Not only should consumers be the primary focus of services, they should also play a major role in determining which services to access, and when. While the terms *client-centered*, *consumer-oriented*, and *consumer-focused* are used frequently, the preferred term here is *consumer-driven*. It was chosen carefully, and only after considerable debate, because it more accurately defines the consumers' role in an ideal long-term care system. They should be positioned to take charge of their own care as much as possible, and the system and all of the players in it have an obligation to do all possible to assist them.

That is not to say that consumers must always get all of the services they might want. One of the problems with the current system is the attitude by many that they are entitled to services because somebody else is paying for them. That attitude must change for the system to have any chance of success, but it will not be easily done. Here we get into the difficult area of balancing consumer wishes with actual needs. Should the long-term care system guarantee that consumers may use any services they wish, whenever they wish, or should there be some requirement to justify actual need? How are their real needs measured, and by whom?

These are not questions that are easily answered, but there is hope that a satisfactory balance between wants and needs can be achieved by careful definition of eligibility criteria. Those criteria should be developed with input from both consumers and providers. One solution may be that overall parameters will be set, within which the consumers are allowed to choose the services they receive. Another is that the system might be built on the basis of a cafeteria plan with built-in incentives for consumers to use it appropriately. Such incentives could include co-pay provisions or other financial motivators. Consumers have shown that they can and will use the system wisely if given incentives to do so.

B. The long-term care system should meet all consumer needs.

An ideal system should address the full range of consumer needs, rather than meeting only some of them. It must be a comprehensive, full-service system, providing all needed long-term care services, including both in-home care and a full range of institution-based services. Unavailability in that system of any single service can have major consequences both for the consumer and for the rest of the system. For the consumer, it can mean a less desirable outcome or a lengthened care process. For the system, it could mean having to compensate for the unavailable service by providing care in an inefficient, costly, perhaps ineffective manner.

In addition to meeting those consumer needs inherent in long-term health care, if the system is to be comprehensive, it must also arrange for or have connections to other social needs, such as housing and transportation. Otherwise, the continuum will be neither complete nor effective. Long-term care consumers should not have to be concerned with which system they are in or with having to know how to move from one system to another.

C. The long-term care system should focus on the individual, recognizing that individuals have unique needs.

Consumers of long-term care services vary greatly, and their needs vary accordingly. To begin with, their particular functional disabilities have the most direct impact on determining what services are necessary. Their ability or inability to perform any of the activities of daily living (feeding, bathing, transferring, toileting, and dressing) defines their level of independence, which in turn creates the need for services. For example, someone who needs assistance in bathing and dressing can probably get by with one or two visits each day by a home care provider, while another person who needs assistance with feeding and toileting would probably be better served in a long-term care facility where assistance is available at all times.

Long-term care needs relate to the functional disability a person has, not to the underlying illness or condition causing the disability. However, the nature of that illness or condition also has a bearing on the extent of services needed. This is particularly true if cognitive ability is affected in any way. If he or she is unable to make care-related decisions on his or her own, it adds an entirely new dimension to determining what is best for him or her. People suffering from brain damage, Alzheimer's disease, or simply old age require different types and intensities of service than those with cardiac problems or those with degenerative bone disease. The long-term care system should be flexible enough to recognize those needs and to adapt the services provided accordingly.

However, the system needs to go beyond matching services to the functional limitations impacting those using it. Personal characteristics such as age, gender, and ethnic background also play an important role in defining consumers as individuals. Those limitations may also be related to, or caused by, other factors (psychological, social, and financial) that must be considered.

The long-term care system should recognize all of these differences and have the capacity to match services to them. It will not be easy, but it is essential.

D. The long-term care system should respect different cultures and cultural values.

The United States is a mix of many cultures and ethnic groups, each of which has its own set of values and practices resulting from those values—practices that are central to their lifestyles. The long-term care system should be capable of recognizing those differences and at least attempting to accommodate them. For example, people from Asian cultures appear to place more importance on caring for elderly family members at home than do members of some Western societies. A flexible long-term care system would take that into account in deciding which services to make available.

One of the more visible differences among cultures is the type of food preferred. Being able to eat the foods we like plays an important part in how we define the quality of our lives. Yet, until recently, most nursing facilities paid little attention to satisfying the seemingly exotic culinary wishes of their residents, ignoring their importance. More and more of them are now finding ways to meet those wishes. An ideal system would go much further in doing so.

The long-term care system should recognize and adapt to these and other, equally important, cultural differences, taking into account matters such as religious observances and personal choice of dress. These are important elements of what defines people as individuals and as members of particular cultures. What they do may not be as different as how they choose to do it. How they go about their daily activities is usually a result of a lifetime of cultural and environmental influences. The long-term care system owes them the respect shown by accommodating them as much as possible.

In addition to cultural traits, each consumer has personal habits and lifestyle peculiarities that also have developed over many years. An ideal system would go to great lengths to address each individual's personal and cultural preferences in an attempt to raise the quality of life for that person. While attempting to do that raises the issue of conflict between individual desires and the wishes of the larger community, it is an issue that must be faced.

E. The long-term care system should promote quality, dignity, and self-improvement for consumers.

A primary goal of long-term care is assisting people with disabilities (including those functional disabilities brought on by advancing age) to live a more satisfying and productive life; thus, the system should be built on a foundation of respect for those individuals. There should be an underlying philosophy that all of us, not only those of sound body, are valuable members of society.

The system should demonstrate that it values older adults and those with chronic disabling conditions. It can do that in many ways. To begin with, respect for consumers can be shown in the way providers interact with individual consumers. They should deal with the person, not with the disability. The system can also do so in a more global manner. It can promote a positive approach to living with chronic illness and dependency. There should be no stigma attached to being old or disabled, yet today there is. All of the participants in the long-term care system can help to remove that stigma by showing that consumers are valued for who they are, not for the disability they have or for what they cannot do. This is an area wherein the long-term care system can, and should, lead.

The long-term care system, and society in general, should allow long-term care recipients to continue to contribute to life and to the community. Each of them has something to offer, be it nothing more than their years of experience. The system should place emphasis on allowing people to make whatever contribution they can. We all have a need to be needed, perhaps our greatest need. Our self-worth is diminished if we feel that we are not contributing something useful to those around us. One of the ways in which the system can, and does, allow its consumers to contribute is by promoting their highest achievable level of functioning and by showing society in general, and people as individuals, that they do have value. However, even that is not always enough. Once that has been accomplished, the system needs to be creative in matching each person's skills and functional abilities to productive tasks and finding ways for them to contribute, sometimes in ways that they would not have imagined.

We are not saying here that the current system is doing nothing in this area. To the contrary, it has done much. Long-term care providers already do much to make it possible for elderly and handicapped people to be useful members of society and should be applauded for what they do. However, such efforts are usually localized, not systemic. The system must do much more to ensure that all consumers benefit.

F. The long-term care system should balance consumer rights and responsibilities.

A truly consumer-driven long-term care system would expand the rights of those relying on the system. They would be much more influential in terms of their roles in it, as they should be. However, those rights should carry with them corresponding responsibilities. Both long-term care consumers and their families should be allowed and encouraged to participate in designing and implementing plans of care, including making care-related decisions. After all, who has more at stake in the outcome than they? That does not mean that they should ignore the advice of long-term care professionals, but that they should be actively involved in the process. As members of the care team, they should accept their share of accountability for the success of the team's efforts. In doing so, they would find incentives to do their utmost to cooperate with—and support—the care plan, thus greatly improving the likelihood of success of that plan.

In addition to their involvement in the actual plan of care, consumers must also take greater responsibility for their own lifestyle choices, choices that affect the success or failure of the care plan. If the long-term care system, or the overall healthcare system, is to meet their needs in an optimum fashion, they should be expected to do whatever they can to support that plan and to improve their level of independence. They should refrain from practices that are harmful or actions that jeopardize their ability to function. That may mean giving up long-held practices such as smoking or eating foods that are not good for them.

At this point, we begin to get into some difficult areas of philosophy and ethics. In asking people to make such lifestyle changes, we are in effect limiting something we strongly advocate: their right to choose. However, that right is not all-inclusive. Long-term care consumers, particularly those living in nursing facilities or other group settings, must accept their responsibility as members of the larger care community. That often means subordinating their personal needs and desires to the interests of the larger group. To a degree, the success of any type of long-term care can be measured by how well those interests are balanced and by the relative satisfaction (happiness) of all involved.

Lastly, consumers in the long-term care system should share some responsibility for financing their care when it is appropriate for them to do so. Whether it involves co-payment, purchase of long-term care insurance, or some other form of financial participation, they should make some contribution if they are able to. That would relieve some of the pressure on the system to pay for the services they receive. Accepting some degree of financial responsibility, no matter how small, also gives consumers an incentive to use the system wisely and appropriately. There should, of course, be exemptions for those who cannot afford to pay anything. There must be a safety net to ensure that no one is denied services on the basis of finances, but the extent to which those who can contribute do so impacts the success of the overall system.

G. The long-term care system should offer consumers a choice of service providers and service delivery modalities.

As we have noted repeatedly, the consumer's right to choose should be respected and encouraged whenever possible. Without multiple options, however, there is little opportunity for choice. The long-term care system should provide consumers with numerous types of choices. First, they should have choices among kinds and levels of care. They should have a choice between home care or care in a nursing facility, providing those types of care that are appropriate for them. However, in making those choices, they should understand that there may be trade-offs involved. For example, a nursing facility usually means some loss of independence but, in return, provides more security and a higher level of care and assistance. Home-based care, on the other hand, swaps a lower level of service for a higher level of independence. The consumer should be provided with enough information to understand those differences and to make an intelligent decision.

To the degree possible, consumers should also have multiple providers to choose from within each type of care. Ideally, those providers would each deliver the same quality of care, but would offer differences in amenities, style, and/or ambiance, factors important to an individual's lifestyle. Consumers should have the option of choosing between facility A and facility B.

■ Criterion II. The long-term care system should be easily accessible.

Accessibility to services depends on several components, including availability of those services, financial coverage, physical logistics (location, style, etc.), and the degree of complexity of the consumer's needs. The long-term care system should address all of those factors individually and collectively in the interest of providing maximum accessibility with a minimum of hassle for those using it.

A. The long-term care system should be universally accessible.

Ideally, services should be available to all who need them, not limited to certain groups. Availability should be based primarily on functional, not financial or political, criteria.

People should be deemed eligible for services on the basis of their need for assistance in overcoming or living with functional disabilities. For example, a person's ability to accomplish activities of daily living (ADLs) should play a significant part in the eligibility decision.

Many portions of the current system already utilize ADLs as a criterion for eligibility, but they usually also include other criteria, such as financial status, enrollment in group insurance plans, or the nature of the consumer's underlying illness or condition. In the ideal system, those other factors would not be included in determining access to services. In reality, the current system is far from that ideal, but it can move closer to it, perhaps in incremental steps, placing increasing emphasis on functional needs as opposed to other qualifying factors.

Functional criteria should be uniform, both in content and in application. All consumers and potential consumers of long-term care services should be treated equally and should be measured against the same standards. The process of applying those criteria must be equitable. It is not easy to maintain that equality and fairness when dealing with so many different consumers.

B. The long-term care system should be user friendly.

The system should be uncomplicated for the consumer to access and use. However, that is easier said than done. The system should be based on a sound, demonstrated philosophy of customer service. While there has recently been considerable well-intended attention given to customer service in the current system, it is still very difficult for anyone to understand or use. That lack of understanding leads to inefficient and often inappropriate use of the system. Even those who are involved in one aspect or another of long-term care—the experts in the field—experience that difficulty when confronted with using the system for themselves or for family members. It often comes as somewhat of a shock for them to realize what it is like to be on the other side, to experience the fragmentation, duplication, confusion, and impersonality of the system. If they find it so puzzling and overwhelming, imagine how intimidating it is for a consumer who has had little or no contact with long-term care, particularly an elderly person. In an ideal long-term care system, or one even approaching the ideal, that would not be the case. Entry into the system and advancement from one segment of the system to another would be easy and user friendly.

Paperwork required by the long-term care system should be minimal and should be understandable to the vast majority of consumers. It should avoid jargon, acronyms, and technical terms. Nevertheless, the system should recognize that many consumers will still need assistance, no matter how simplified it becomes. Assistance in completing necessary paperwork should be readily available.

Financing and approval processes should be simplified as much as possible. The long-term care system should be coordinated to the point where consumers do not have to submit to repeated documentation of their eligibility. Once accepted into the system, they should not need reapproval until some significant aspect of their situation changes. The numerous, repetitive approval processes inherent in the current system are annoying and time consuming. They are also very unsettling for people who worry about whether they will still maintain critical eligibility. It is important to them to know that their status in the system is secure.

In a system that is truly user friendly, there should be no excessive delays in service. Again, this is not just a matter of customer convenience, although that is a very important consideration. Delays in meeting the needs of long-term care consumers may actually reduce their functional independence and may eventually increase the amount of care required.

C. The long-term care system should provide care in the least restrictive environment.

The system should facilitate the provision of care in the setting and service modality that will provide the best combination of appropriate care, quality of life, and cost-effectiveness for each individual. The caregiving environment should provide each consumer with an optimum level of freedom and independence. In doing that, it will be important for all of the participants in the long-term care system—including providers, payers, regulators, and consumer advocates—to understand that the least restrictive environment will be different for each person. While a person's home is most commonly the least restrictive environment, it is not always the case. The amount of assistance needed by an individual may actually be more easily accomplished in a more formal, institutional setting that then results in more real independence. The location wherein long-term care is provided is an important determinant in making the system accessible.

D. The long-term care system should encourage single-site care availability.

The system should be designed to provide, to the degree possible, all necessary services to consumers without requiring them to deal with multiple sites and/or providers. Availability of several needed services in one setting makes it much more convenient for the consumer, and this convenience is an element central to accessibility. Current aging in place programs and the growing number of organizations providing multiple types and levels of care in single locations are recognition of the value consumers place on having those services easily available. Single-site availability is often more than a matter of simple convenience. Such programs also allow spouses to remain together, or at least nearby, even when their individual care needs vary. They make it possible for people to receive care in familiar surroundings, with familiar caregiving staff, should their conditions change. Because those changes are frequently of relatively short duration, not having to move from setting to setting avoids a great deal of disruption in their lives.

In the ideal long-term care system, payment mechanisms and associated regulations would be designed to encourage and facilitate more provision of single-site availability

5RATT, JOHN R.

LONG-TERM CARE: MANAGING ACROSS THE CONTINUUM.

4TH ED.   Paper   576 P.
SUDBURY: JONES & BARTLETT LEARNING, 2015

TEXTBOOK--ADV. UNDERGRAD. W/ ONLINE ACCESS.

ISBN 1284054594   **Library PO#** FIRM ORDERS

		List	83.95	USD
8395 NATIONAL UNIVERSITY LIBRAR		**Disc**	5.0%	
App. Date 4/13/16 SHHS	8214-08	**Net**	79.75	USD

SUBJ: LONG-TERM CARE FACILITIES--U.S.--
ADMINISTRATION.

CLASS RA997   DEWEY# 362.160973   LEVEL ADV-AC

YBP Library Services

5RATT, JOHN R.

LONG-TERM CARE: MANAGING ACROSS THE CONTINUUM.

4TH ED.   Paper   576 P.
SUDBURY: JONES & BARTLETT LEARNING, 2015

TEXTBOOK--ADV. UNDERGRAD. W/ ONLINE ACCESS.

ISBN 1284054594   **Library PO#** FIRM ORDERS

		List	83.95	USD
8395 NATIONAL UNIVERSITY LIBRAR		**Disc**	5.0%	
App. Date 4/13/16 SHHS	8214-08	**Net**	79.75	USD

SUBJ: LONG-TERM CARE FACILITIES--U.S.--
ADMINISTRATION.

CLASS RA997   DEWEY# 362.160973   LEVEL ADV-AC

of services, not discourage it as is often the case today. Currently, facilities attempting to offer multiple levels and modalities of care must comply with different, sometimes conflicting, regulations. They also find that some of the services they offer are reimbursable by third-party sources and others are not. To be easily accessible, the system must move to reduce or eliminate that fragmentation.

■ Criterion III. The long-term care system should coordinate professional, consumer, family, and other informal caregiver resources.

There are many resources potentially available to long-term care consumers, including professional (provider) resources and informal resources provided by family members, other volunteer caregivers, and sometimes the consumers themselves. Currently, these resources are not well coordinated, if they are coordinated at all. Chronic conditions are different from acute conditions and require a different kind of care. There needs to be more of an integrated network of professional expertise combined with a far greater reliance on informal (nonprofessional) caregivers.

A. The long-term care system should integrate professional, community, family, and other informal caregiver efforts.

The various sources of available support must be integrated if consumers are to take fullest advantage of the system. Without such integration, they will encounter frequent, disruptive gaps in availability of services. Equally troublesome is costly duplication of effort. A well-designed long-term care system would avoid those two extremes. It would meld those professional and nonprofessional resources into a partnership wherein each segment assists the other, ultimately benefiting the consumers they serve.

B. The long-term care system should evolve from the current medical model to a holistic model of service delivery.

The overall healthcare system in this country is based primarily on acute and episodic care. It should encourage more involvement of nonmedical personnel in caregiving and in problem solving. The field of long-term care is much broader than just its clinical components. The system needs to strengthen its focus on care as opposed to cure. There are many nonclinical professionals who currently provide valuable services, but they still operate largely under a medical model. The system should focus its efforts more on the whole individual and less on specific clinical or functional characteristics. Many nontraditional care delivery methods, such as wellness programs, have found a place in the long-term care system. The system needs to do much more to encourage them and to stimulate new, innovative programs.

C. The long-term care system should involve families in case management and care delivery.

The system should make better use of informal caregivers as an integral part of formal care plans. Family members already play a valuable role in many cases, particularly in home-based care but also in institutional settings. Experts have described family caregivers as the "backbone" or the "bedrock" of the LTSS workforce (Levine, Halper, Peist, & Gould, 2010). As one early long-term care text put it, "The family invented long-term care of the elderly well before that phrase was articulated, making the shift from episodic short-term care sooner and more flexibly, more willingly, and more effectively than have professionals and the bureaucracy" (Eisdorfer, 1989, p. 259). Their efforts should be better coordinated with the efforts of professional caregivers to allow them to perform at their best. In fact, they would usually benefit from being given an opportunity to work under the supervision of those professionals.

The system should also facilitate informal caregiving by providing more assistance, even financial resources, to family caregivers. Studies have shown that approximately 87% of Americans who need long-term care receive it from informal, or unpaid, caregivers (NAC and AARP, 2009). Yet, there usually comes a time when those informal caregivers can no longer provide all of the care needed. In many cases, only a relatively small amount of assistance would be required for them to continue providing the care at home.

The past several decades have seen considerable change in the structure of the typical American family. The need for both husband and wife to work, growing distances separating family members as they move for employment-related reasons, and an increasing incidence of single heads of household have all contributed to making it more difficult for families to care for their own. They are the foundation of our nation's LTSS system, but they need help. They need somewhere to turn for information, support, and respite. As the nation ages and future generations have fewer children on whom to rely for support, a more adequate system of LTSS will be critical to ensure that older adults and people with disabilities have the support services they need (Reinhard, Kassner, Houser, & Mollica, 2011).

As the large population of baby boomers and subsequent generations continue to age, these societal trends will continue and expand. They will make it less easy to find informal caregivers. The ultimate impact on the system will be a need for more readily accessible formal services.

Until relatively recently, there was not a lot of empirical research into the degree to which family caregivers prevent institutionalization, but the Agency for Healthcare Research and Quality (AHRQ), the health services research arm of the U.S. Department of Health and Human Services (HHS), is conducting studies in that area. AHRQ works to improve delivery and coordination of primary care services to meet the need for high-quality, safe, effective, and efficient clinical prevention and chronic disease care (AHRQ, 2013). Several other agencies have also come forward with newer research. That type of research is sorely needed to support the anecdotal evidence so observable among caregivers. The pressure on informal caregivers, be they family, friends, or others, is of considerable consequence. They are subject to physical, emotional, and financial strain. One study showed that more than one in three caregivers (37%) say no one else provided unpaid help to the person they cared for during the past year. Among caregivers who say someone else did provide assistance during the past year, one in three (34%) say they provide most of the unpaid care, and 10% say they split the care 50/50 (National Alliance for Caregiving, 2009). They must balance their caregiving duties with their jobs and/or their responsibilities to other family members. Programs providing assistance to them would be beneficial almost beyond imagination.

There are many excellent programs already in existence, but they are not uniformly available. One such type of assistance is adult day care. Adult day care provides daytime relief for caregivers and a supervised, stimulating setting for the person receiving the care. It regularly allows family members to remain employed without necessitating placement of the long-term care consumer in an institutional setting. Other similar programs, such as hospice and respite care, also provide assistance to the informal caregivers in the form of actual services. Hospice care helps those with terminal illnesses by assisting with caregiving chores and lending moral and spiritual support. Respite care is designed to relieve the primary caregivers from their duties for short periods of time, while maintaining the level of care given.

There is very little, if any, availability of direct financial assistance for informal caregivers. Yet, it would often be much less expensive to provide a small amount of reimbursement to them than to utilize the more formal types of services. There are several barriers to doing that. One is the question of quality assurance. There are many existing processes for checking the competency of professionals, but it is much more difficult to do so with informal caregivers. Government agencies and insurance companies are reluctant to provide financing for care unless they have assurances of its quality. They are concerned not only about the welfare of the recipients of that care, but also about possible liability should someone be injured.

There is also the usually unspoken, but very real, issue of competition with the formal system. Organizations representing healthcare professionals tend to resist attempts to allow what they see as potential replacement by untrained civilians.

■ Criterion IV. The long-term care system should be an integral part of the health and social system to promote integration, efficiency, and cost-effectiveness.

Long-term care cannot exist in a vacuum, nor can it meet all of the needs of its consumers. It is only one segment of the overall societal system, one of several subsystems. Like the other subsystems—acute health care and various social services—long-term care meets some of the needs of those who depend on it but must rely on its complementary counterparts to meet the rest. In an ideal system, those disparate elements would be integrated, interactive parts that make up the whole.

There has been much movement toward integration within the healthcare system in recent years, but much more is needed. Ties, both formal and informal, between acute care and long-term care organizations should be increased and enhanced. Doing so will expand the capabilities and expertise of each of them.

A. The long-term care system should include a full continuum of services.

Consumers in that larger system should experience no break in services from one sub-system to another. They should not have to worry about differences in accessibility, financing, or quality. The system should be virtually seamless, a term that has become popular in describing a system without gaps.

While the system needs to be comprehensive in the breadth of services it provides, it also needs depth in terms of its ability to provide similar services to vastly differing groups of consumers. The services provided in the system should be designed such that they will meet the needs of all with chronic illness, not just the elderly. Because the elderly are such a large part of the population using long-term care services, we tend to think only in terms of them. However, there are many others who need long-term care and whose needs may be somewhat different. Younger long-term care consumers (such as handicapped children, young adults handicapped by traumatic injury or AIDS, and those suffering from mental disease or intellectual disabilities) each have their own specific needs.

Meeting those needs adequately often means special care units, additional training of long-term care personnel, and, most importantly, an understanding of long-term care consumers of all types and their varying requirements. Units or facilities designed to specialize in caring for a particular segment of the long-term care consumer population have become more popular, but they still face several barriers inherent in the current system.

Providing a full continuum of services also requires changes in the way professional personnel are trained and distributed. Physicians, for example, have traditionally been drawn to the more visibly attractive types of care, primarily acute care. The number of fully trained geriatricians is still small relative to other specialists, but that is changing slowly as medical schools have begun to put more emphasis on primary care (including chronic care), spurred in part by federal funding incentives. The system has to do much more to provide an adequate number of physicians and other clinical specialists if it is to meet the growing numbers of persons needing long-term care in the near future. There appears to be consensus that the United States faces a crisis in adequately staffing its long-term care sector. The aging of the baby boomer generation is beginning to stretch an already overburdened long-term care sector, which suffers from workforce shortages due to a variety of factors (Holzer, 2008).

Nurses have also tended toward acute care in the past, in most cases a reflection of the nature of their training as well as the excitement involved in faster-paced care settings, not to mention the higher salaries. There has been some positive change in that area also. New types of long-term care, such as assisted living and subacute care, with their more visible success, seem to be attracting more nurses away from the acute sector. Also, the organizational turbulence described earlier in this text has hit the acute care sector particularly hard and somewhat earlier than long-term care, resulting in layoffs and downsizing, which has left many nurses looking for other career opportunities, most for the first time. They have found long-term care to be different and more attractive than they had previously thought it to be.

Physicians and nurses are not the only professionals that the long-term care system has had trouble recruiting. It has experienced similar difficulties with other employee groups. Long-term care relies much more heavily than acute care on certified nurse assistants and others with less formal training. Because of their lack of specialization, they have more employment opportunities outside of the long-term care system, often at a higher rate of pay. The work they do is not glamorous; it is often unpleasant and physically demanding. While most long-term care employees find intrinsic rewards in caring for the functionally disabled (fortunately), their tangible rewards are not all that great.

Improvements to date in the training and recruitment of staff are only the beginning of what will be required in the long-term care system of the future. Creative approaches to using existing and potential future categories of personnel more efficiently and effectively are needed.

How well the long-term care system is able to find innovative ways to utilize personnel and care settings depends in large part on the extent to which it is able to identify and differentiate among the several types of consumers. It must be built on an acceptance of their differences and an understanding that creative care methods are needed.

B. The long-term care system should include a full and uniform assessment (initial and ongoing) of the consumer's needs.

All involved with the long-term care system need to have a better awareness of the extent to which people needing care differ and of the alternative system components that are required to service them. The first step in meeting all of their needs is identifying and quantifying those needs. We have made progress, but the long-term care system cannot function optimally unless we continue to improve on that understanding.

Improved understanding requires an assessment that is comprehensive and detailed. It requires an assessment that addresses all of the individual's needs, including medical, social, and financial. There should be one review process that takes these factors into account, rather than several different, uncoordinated processes. It must focus on the whole person, rather than the parts that make up that whole. To accomplish such a comprehensive appraisal, the several parts of the system have to work together more closely and have to share information about those they serve. They have to break down barriers to coordination, barriers that may be caused by any number of factors, including professional parochialism, financial competition, and technological naiveté. Any system that intends (or wishes) to be integrated must make both clinical and financial information about all clients available at all service sites almost instantaneously.

We noted earlier in this discussion that services should be available on the basis of the functional needs of each person, not on the needs of, or for the benefit of, those who pay for care. That is not to say, however, that there can be no financial involvement in assessing the need for care. Those who can contribute financially to meeting their needs should do so. The costs of providing long-term care are great; the system should take advantage of any and all opportunities to reduce the impact of those costs, including participation by those consumers who are able to do so. What the system must avoid is using the financial portion of the initial assessment to determine if care is to be provided, rather than how it will be reimbursed.

If the long-term care system is to provide good care—to say nothing of promoting integration, efficiency, and cost-effectiveness—it must be built on an understanding of chronicity. The assessment that determines which services a person gets must reflect that understanding. Historically, there has been so much focus on the acute care system and those it serves that there has been little attention paid to the specific needs of the chronically ill and the differences between the two groups. Yet, chronic illness can cause changes in health status and quality of life. There has been a great deal of conspicuous progress made in curing illnesses, but somewhat less in caring for those with chronic maladies. That shortcoming has not been intentional, nor was it based on any conscious discrimination against long-term care or those who need it. It has been simply a case of the most demonstrably devastating (i.e., life-threatening, painful, or disfiguring) diseases and conditions receiving the most attention, getting the lion's share of available resources, and benefiting from the most sensational clinical advances.

Clinical innovations such as organ transplants, reversal of birth defects, and life-extending surgical procedures fully deserve the attention they have received, but so are new long-term care delivery methods. They may not be as interesting to the public, but are every bit as important to the consumers involved.

C. The long-term care system should provide emphasis on, and reimbursement for, illness prevention efforts as an integral part of the overall system.

While preventive services are not usually seen as part of the long-term care system, their impact on the system must be considered, because that impact can be significant and long-lasting. For example, strokes and heart attacks are among the largest reasons people become functionally disabled and require long-term care. Yet, experience has shown that the number of strokes and heart attacks can be reduced greatly with early prevention efforts, including smoking prevention or cessation, proper diet, and exercise. Similarly, other debilitating diseases such as osteoporosis can be avoided, or at least delayed with early treatment. AIDS, which could potentially become one of the leading causes of long-term care disability, can be prevented.

While these and many other disabling diseases can be avoided with adequate prevention efforts, others are not yet avoidable. We have not found ways to prevent diseases such as multiple sclerosis, muscular dystrophy, and Parkinson's disease, but research continues toward that end. Prevention or cure of any of those diseases would significantly reduce the need for long-term care. Look at the impact of the Salk and Sabin polio vaccines or the virtual elimination of tuberculosis by modern antibiotics. With the sophistication of current medical research, similar discoveries are very possible.

However, remember that it is not the disease that leads to long-term care. It is the disability resulting from that disease. Even without the ability to prevent the disease, early and effective treatment can delay that disability in many cases. That treatment is a form of prevention.

Illness prevention efforts and the degree to which they are successful will play a role in shaping the future of the long-term care system. Their impact on the system may not be felt to any significant extent in the near future, but current emphasis on prevention will pay off in the long run and must be an integral part of the overall system. What one author (Kodner, 1993) has termed "preventive gerontology" should become an integral and accepted part of the long-term care system. There has been one small step in that direction. The 1997 Balanced Budget Act expanded Medicare coverage of cancer screening, bone-density tests, and services for diabetes patients. The changes provided Medicare beneficiaries with preventive testing that has been effective with other populations. Title IV of the Affordable Care Act is titled, "Prevention of Chronic Disease and Improving Public Health," but it is still unclear how much effort will go toward chronic disease.

D. The long-term care system should be planned and coordinated to reduce fragmentation and inefficiencies.

As we have noted here repeatedly, long-term care must be integrated with the other subsystems into an overall system if it is to be effective and efficient. However, there is another dimension to such integration. It should also integrate systemwide coordination with local and regional autonomy.

Earlier, we referenced Dr. Connie Evashwick's description of a continuum of care (Evashwick, 2005). Her definition applies to both an overall system and a variety of local or regional systems. A major challenge facing policy makers now and in the future is finding ways to integrate many independent continuums into a coordinated whole without impinging unnecessarily on their individual independence and autonomy.

The difficulty of finding that balance is reflective of the healthcare reform debates of the early 1990s. One reason for the failure of those debates to produce a national healthcare system (in reality, they were looking at a national healthcare financing system) was the participants' inability to agree on the respective roles of the federal and state governments. That disagreement is shown by the current resistance of state governments to the controversial expansion of Medicaid proposed in the Affordable Care Act (ACA). A 2012 decision of the U.S. Supreme Court found the mandate unconstitutional, giving states the freedom to choose whether to expand the welfare program. Melding local or regional continuums of care into an overall long-term care system will be every bit as difficult. Yet, it must be done if that overall system is to be at all successful.

E. The long-term care system should be based on outcome-oriented accountability.

If the system is to achieve any significant level of integration and coordination, it must include ways to hold each of its elements accountable. Providers of long-term care services should have a high degree of accountability both to those using their services and to those paying for the services. To attain that accountability, the system should focus on outcomes, not on process as is largely the case with the current system.

To begin with, the system should be designed to gauge results, particularly as they affect quality of life, instead of looking at how those results are obtained. There are three basic ways of measuring quality: structure, process, and outcome (Donabedian, 1988). To date, long-term care quality has been measured largely according to process and structure. Process-based measurement focuses on how the services are provided and whether they follow accepted procedures. A somewhat simplified example of a process measure is the Omnibus Budget Reconciliation Act (OBRA) requirement governing the frequency of meals and bedtime snacks in nursing facilities. While its intent is presumably to ensure that residents of those facilities receive adequate nutrition, the regulation, like so many others, holds the provider accountable for what it does and how it does it, not for achieving the desired result.

Structure-based measurement also looks at how things are done but addresses the organizational configuration of providers as a means of evaluating their ability to perform. Again using OBRA as an example, providers must maintain prescribed staffing levels. It is assumed that those staffing requirements, when met, will ensure a base level of care quality.

Outcome measures evaluate quality based on the success of the end result. In a system in which outcome measures are the rule, providers would be held accountable for producing the desired effect for the consumer, not for how they went about doing it.

As we might imagine, process and structure measures require a great deal of documentation and paperwork, both of which are frustrating for providers. In any system, even one that bases accountability on outcomes, there must be documentation, but there should be an attempt at elimination of unnecessary paperwork. Time spent by providers doing paperwork is time not spent providing care.

However, providers are not the only ones burdened by paperwork in the current system. Consumers, their families, and their advocates must also wade through mounds of paper, first to determine eligibility, then to secure and maintain reimbursement. For them, the forms they must complete are not only onerous, but very confusing. An ideal system would find ways to simplify the process for them.

A long-term care system that was truly outcome-oriented would contain incentives to improve the quality of care delivered rather than inspecting for lack of quality. The emphasis should be on rewarding providers for giving care that is above average. Currently, providers are reviewed by state surveyors to determine if they meet a minimum level of quality and are cited if they fall below that minimum in any area. That aspect of the system must be maintained to the extent that providers must not be allowed to give substandard care, but the emphasis should be on exceeding the minimum whenever possible.

Most long-term care providers will tell you that they could do a better job than they are doing at present but that there are disincentives in the system that make it very difficult for them to do so. Many of those disincentives are built into the current method of reimbursement. It pays on the basis of process and structure. There is little, if any, financial reward for exceeding the minimum levels of quality on which reimbursement is based or for producing better outcomes.

The long-term care system should be flexible enough to promote innovation and positive change. Not only is innovation not encouraged in the current system, it is actually discouraged. There is so much emphasis on strict adherence to process and structure it is very difficult to innovate. The system should seek new and better ways of meeting the needs of long-term care consumers and reward providers who advance those new methods. Successful business organizations recognize the need to set aside funds for research and development into better operating methods. The long-term care system can afford to do no less.

In addition to being outcome based, the standards against which quality is measured should be consistent, both in their development and application. Presently, standards of care vary considerably, depending on several factors. They differ according to the source of payment for services. Public and private reimbursement sources often have different requirements, as do individual payers even within those categories.

Managed care programs have introduced an entirely new element into the equation by placing more emphasis on cost-effectiveness than do traditional insurance plans. While cost-effectiveness and operational efficiency do not always affect quality of care directly, the degree to which they are required cannot help but have some impact on it. That impact is not always negative, by any means, nor is there any intent here to imply that managed care programs are any less concerned about providing high-quality care. What it does mean is that the standards against which providers are measured may be made up of a different balance of those elements.

Within Medicaid—the primary funding source for many long-term care providers, particularly nursing facilities—standards vary from state to state. OBRA went a long way toward reducing that variation by setting much more rigid national standards to which state Medicaid programs and the providers they oversee must adhere. However, there is still considerable leeway for individual states to impose standards that are different. That inconsistency is particularly problematic for the increasing number of long-term care organizations doing business in multiple state jurisdictions.

Reimbursement is not the only source of inconsistency in the development and application of standards of care. Those standards also vary based on regulations, which may or may not be linked to reimbursement. Standards often differ from one type of provider to another. While the method and location of care delivery are different depending on whether the provider is a nursing facility, an assisted living provider, or a home healthcare agency, the quality of care given should be the same. Thus, the standards against which that quality is measured should be the same. Again, that is not easy to accomplish using process or structure standards. Outcome-based standards would lend themselves much more readily to consistent application.

■ Criterion V. The long-term care system should be adequately and fairly financed.

Even a long-term care system that is consumer driven, not reimbursement driven, is heavily influenced by the amount of financing available and by the method by which that financing is applied. The emphasis should be on ensuring that it is adequate and applied fairly. In such a system, providers will not always have all of the reimbursement they desire, nor will payers always be able to reduce that reimbursement as much as they may wish. Adequate financing means enough to provide the desired level of quality, while fairness requires a balance between cost-effectiveness and meeting the wishes of consumers. Quality of care must always be the common denominator.

A. The long-term care system should utilize public and consumer resources to ensure universal access to services.

All available resources, public and private, should be considered in providing services for current and future consumers. A feature of the current long-term care system that promises to become even more prominent in any future system is that demand for services will always place a great strain on available financing. For that reason, the system must do a better job utilizing all potential funding resources, including both public and private.

Public funding of long-term care—usually Medicare and Medicaid—will be especially hard hit unless alternative methods are found. That means that new, innovative means of factoring in private financing must be found. It means greater emphasis on public/private partnerships, a concept beginning to receive attention. There have already been a number of attempts to develop such partnerships. During the early part of the last decade, the Robert Wood Johnson Foundation funded a number of demonstration projects. They were designed to provide incentives to increase private participation in long-term care financing, with an ultimate objective of reducing the demand on public funding, freeing it for use as a financial safety net for those who need it.

Much of the focus of those and other public/private partnership efforts is on getting consumers to purchase private long-term care insurance. To date, while such insurance is generally available, with many coverage and payment options, there has not been a rush by consumers to purchase it. There are several reasons for that. First, if long-term care insurance is to be cost effective, with premiums set at an affordable level, it should be purchased while the consumers are relatively young. As with most insurances, the premium rates escalate greatly if people wait until they are likely to need it before making their initial purchase. For example, at age 75, the premium is estimated at two and a half times greater than if purchased at age 65 and six times higher than if bought at age 55 (Alexander, 2013).

Today's young adult and middle-aged populations are beset by many other financial demands that they see as more pressing than securing protection against something that might happen in the distant future or might not happen at all. Various studies have shown that they are not preparing adequately for old age or retirement. Faced with more immediate concerns such as getting by on a daily basis, putting the kids through college, and taking care of their own parents, they tend to not show much concern with something as far off as long-term care.

Second, many of them have little awareness of long-term care, what it entails, or what it costs, although as more baby boomers reach middle age, they are beginning to gain that awareness. They have been called the "sandwich generation" because so many of them are caring for both their children and their parents. As they find it necessary to gain entry for their parents into the long-term care system, they encounter their own problems dealing with that system. Many of those problems revolve around financial coverage or the lack of it. An increasingly common response from them is "I want to find a way to prevent the necessity of my children having to go through this when I get old and need long-term care." One solution for them is to purchase private long-term care insurance.

Lastly, there is the belief by many consumers that public funding sources (the government) will take care of them. Their taxes support those sources, so why should they pay again? The long-term care system of the future will need to do much more than the current system to educate consumers about the system, its requirements and shortcomings, and their role in it (see criterion VI).

B. The long-term care system should provide incentives for consumers to use services in an appropriate and cost-effective manner.

The overall cost of the system can be controlled by avoiding excessive and unnecessary use. There will always be the potential for wasteful, inappropriate use of long-term care by consumers, but much can be done to reduce it. The current system's disincentives for providers were discussed earlier. There are also inherent disincentives for consumers. It is not uncommon for payers to require an acute care stay or a visit to a physician's office as a prerequisite for some types of long-term care. They do so to ensure that the care is justified. Unfortunately, when those rules are rigidly cast, they result in unnecessary use of the most expensive types of care. As an example, people using home-based care on an extended basis often must see a physician periodically to maintain their eligibility. That office call is often pro forma, serving no other purpose than to meet the rules.

While consumers of long-term care need to be better informed about how to use the system, they are much more aware of its problems than we give them credit for. Just about any discussion with a long-term care consumer produces anecdotes about receiving unneeded care or unused medical supplies because Medicare paid for them. In general, they do not wish to abuse the system or use it excessively. It is up to the system to assist them in using services wisely and appropriately.

C. The long-term care system should provide incentives for consumers to self-finance their care.

Long-term care consumers and their families should be encouraged to pay for their own care when possible. The fundamental purpose of public funding should be to provide for those who cannot provide for themselves. There has been discussion of late about requiring some form of means test to qualify for Medicare—either limiting it solely to the medically indigent elderly or requiring some degree of financial participation by consumers based on their ability to pay. That concept has been advanced as a way of preserving the Medicare system, which is in danger of dissolution as demands on it exceed its funding capability. It is a concept vigorously resisted by the elderly and their advocacy groups, groups that have shown their political muscle in the past. They argue that they have paid into the Medicare trust fund for years and now deserve to benefit from it, regardless of their own financial status. Proponents of the idea counter with the argument that other taxpayers should not be subsidizing the very wealthy.

Medicaid, unlike Medicare, was designed from the first as a welfare-like payment mechanism to help those without other sources of payment for care. Those who need long-term care, be they elderly or not, may qualify for Medicaid, but are required to spend down their assets before it takes effect. That perception has created a great deal of concern. It has also caused considerable controversy as consumers and their lawyers seek ways to protect property or savings that they intended to pass on to their children and grandchildren, creating an unplanned entitlement program at the expense of Medicaid. Government, on the other hand, is working hard to prevent them from getting a free ride. In 1996, federal legislation made divesting of assets for the purpose of qualifying for Medicaid illegal.

If consumers are to be expected to pay for some or all of their care in lieu of having Medicare or Medicaid do it, they are going to expect something in return. The system will need to provide incentives as well if such drastic changes are ever to be accepted. One type of incentive that is a cornerstone of the public/private partnerships described earlier would allow people to shelter and pass on more of their assets in return for providing portions of their own long-term care coverage through purchase of insurance. Although there are many ways to do that, the goal is to reduce the amount of public funding required by encouraging consumers to provide private coverage. Any plan that does that successfully will have a significant, positive impact on both Medicare and Medicaid.

Another type of incentive that seems to receive favorable review is the tax break. Whether it rewards them for paying for their long-term care directly or for purchasing insurance, a tax deduction or credit provides a tangible incentive for those who support the public system with their taxes. Again, there has been some progress along those lines, but only a beginning. The Health Insurance Portability and Accountability Act of 1996 allowed taxpayers, for the first time, to treat long-term care insurance premiums as deductions similar to other health insurance premiums. An increasing number of states are offering various tax incentives, including deductions, credits, or both, for the purchase of private long-term care insurance.

Even the financial support for family caregivers mentioned when we discussed criterion III would be a form of incentive. They would, in effect, be making in-kind contributions through their time and effort. The cost of the care they provide, even with some added subsidy, is still much less than the cost of similar care provided in a formal setting.

If the long-term care system is to survive financially, it must find other, creative ways to reduce the burden on the public financing portion of that system. The innovative efforts that have been tried to date are heartening, but they must be expanded greatly.

D. The long-term care system should avoid causing impoverishment of consumers and families.

While consumers and their families should be encouraged to contribute to the cost of their care, that contribution should be limited to prevent undue hardship. There is little to be gained in the long run by depleting all of the assets of long-term care consumers and their families. It only speeds up the process by which they come to rely more heavily on public funding sources. Yet, failure of the system to provide adequate financing, and overly zealous attempts to hold families accountable, often combine to cause exactly that type of hardship. A system that is fairly financed would do all possible to avoid causing harm in the name of doing good.

Many long-term care consumers and their families today find themselves caught in a dilemma. They do not have adequate resources to pay for long-term care out of their own pockets but are not poor enough to be eligible for government programs such as Medicaid. The only way they can qualify for assistance is to become medically indigent.

E. The long-term care system should provide incentives for providers to develop cost-effective measures.

Just as providers of long-term care services could improve the quality of care if given incentives to do that, so could they also improve the cost-effectiveness of the system. Holding them to one-size-fits-all process and structure standards that determine how they provide care leaves little opportunity for innovation. Nor are there many financial rewards for operating in an efficient, cost-effective manner. The long-term care system should allow more flexibility to innovate, realizing that quality must never be jeopardized by cutting costs. Incentives to function more efficiently could include allowing the providers to actually share in the cost savings but might be nothing more than increased freedom to be creative without being penalized for doing so. Many successful organizations have long known that those people closest to the work—on the front lines, so to speak—are the ones most likely to conceive and implement better ways of working. That fact was rediscovered with much fanfare a few years ago by Dr. W. Edwards Deming and his total quality management (TQM) processes. TQM utilizes front-line workers to improve both product quality and cost-effectiveness. While many providers in the long-term care system have embraced TQM and successors such as continuous quality improvement, the system as a whole could do much better in providing incentives for providers to be cost effective.

F. The long-term care system should develop payment mechanisms that allow efficient providers to adequately compensate staff and that allow for appropriate operating surplus and/or return on investment.

One way of getting providers to operate more efficiently is to reimburse them in a manner that encourages them to employ well-qualified, properly trained staff. That does not necessarily require that they be reimbursed more, although one of the major complaints by providers is that they cannot hire adequate staff because of their reimbursement levels. If some providers are efficient enough to provide high-quality care by hiring superior staff, the system should include some flexibility in its payment scheme that would allow them to apply some of their cost savings to paying those staff at adequate rates. In the long run, the system would benefit.

Another incentive for providers would be an allowance for an appropriate operating surplus or return on investment. The operative word here is appropriate, meaning neither too much nor too little. The stories we hear of long-term care providers making exorbitant profits are all too common and all too true. However, they do not represent the majority of providers. Yet, the current system, in an effort to avoid those extremes, makes it difficult for others to even make the type of return on investment deemed acceptable in other industries. It has been said that most regulations are designed to deal with the worst 2 percent of those they cover. The other 98 percent are penalized because of them.

The long-term care system is made up of an unusual mix of for-profit and not-for-profit providers. Both sectors should continue to have significant roles in the future, and the rules and regulations that govern the system should be adaptable enough to accommodate both. There was a time when some segments of health care, most notably hospitals, were primarily not for profit and were expected to operate at a loss as a community service. That is no longer true, even for hospitals. Providers of care, regardless of the nature of their ownership, must now operate efficiently and above the break-even line if they are to survive. The long-term care system should recognize that it is in its long-term best interests to allow providers to get an appropriate return on investment and to encourage them to reinvest in their organizations.

G. The long-term care system should operate within the limits of a well-conceived budget.

It might appear to be stating the obvious to say that the system needs to have a well-conceived budget. However, the current system does not, nor has it ever. It is fragmented, with numerous discrete parts, and it is sadly lacking in coordination. It should function within the same budgetary constraints as the organizations of which it is composed. Those constraints often result in limiting available funds. Of perhaps as much importance, a well-conceived budget spells out how those funds may be used. It also includes clear benchmarks by which progress can be measured. More than anything else, a sound budget lets all of those governed by it know exactly what they have available in the way of resources and the parameters within which they must stay.

Developing such a budget for the long-term care system is an ideal that may be extremely tough to accomplish. A budget is not something that is easily developed or implemented in pieces or in incremental steps, but rather tends to become viable only when all pieces come together. Thus, we are not likely to see any major progress on this goal in the near future.

Integrating the separate payers, public and private, into a unit that would be cohesive enough to function within a single budget is a daunting task. Getting the many discrete, dissimilar providers under such an umbrella promises to be even more so.

H. The long-term care system should provide significant flexibility to enable consumers to meet long-term care needs as each consumer defines those needs.

The financing of the system should reflect the needs of individuals (as identified in criterion I). There is no way the system can be truly consumer driven if the financing mechanism(s) cannot accommodate different types of care and needs. Long-term care consumers want simplified access to a wide range of services and a predictable payment mechanism (Evashwick, 2005).

Meeting this goal will require an intriguing blend of flexibility and coordination. In the long-term care system, services should determine financing rather than financing determining services. As we have pointed out before, the services received by any individual consumer should be based on that individual's needs. Ideally, financing would not be part of that calculation of service need, but would only come into play afterward.

I. The long-term care system should be based on uniform financial eligibility criteria.

When financial criteria are applied, they should be uniform. Remember, financial criteria should be used only to determine the type and amount of payment received from a consumer, not to decide whether services are provided. Those criteria should not eliminate anyone from eligibility for coverage, nor should they make a difference in whether they receive services. They must only be applied in the interests of determining how much the individual will pay. The standards used in that determination should be comprehensive enough to apply to all consumers fairly. They should be fair and equitable in their design and in the way they are practiced.

■ Criterion VI. The long-term care system should include an education component to create informed consumers, providers, reimbursers, and regulators.

The gaps between the current long-term care system and an ideal system are great. Bridging those gaps will not be easy. Perhaps the best weapon for doing so is education. Only when all involved understand the nature of long-term care—how it works and how it could work—will there be significant progress.

A. The long-term care system should include community education.

The public must be informed about long-term care, including available service options, limitations, and access methods. One of the most striking characteristics of the current system is the general lack of understanding about what the long-term care system offers, how it is accessed, who is eligible, and what is covered. While those who manage the system—the providers, payers, regulators, and policy makers—have done a pretty poor job of educating the public, they are not the sole cause of the problem.

There are numerous other factors at work here. To begin with, as we explained earlier, the system is so complicated it tends to defy easy understanding. Second, the public has not been particularly interested in becoming better educated concerning long-term care, nor have they really had to be. It, like other forms of health care, has historically been provided for them, with little emphasis on whether they understood it or wanted it. They had little say in the matter, or at least thought so. One of the reasons they have not been interested in learning more about long-term care is that they have been given the impression that it would be provided for them. So, why worry? Neither Medicare nor Medicaid was meant to meet all of the healthcare needs of the elderly or the medically indigent, but the political hoopla with which they were introduced led many to believe that they would.

Times have changed and with them, the need for public education. No matter how good the system is, people cannot use it effectively unless we turn them into informed consumers. Our ability to do that will be critical to the success of any future system of care. None of these *Criteria* can be realized without an effective education component. To date, that component has been mostly ineffective.

There is an interesting, and paradoxical, aspect of this problem. If we were to search out and catalog the consumer information that now exists concerning long-term care, the amount of such information available would probably be surprising. So would the quality and accuracy of that information. So, why is it not getting to consumers? Why is it not effective in making them better informed? The problem is not always lack of information, but often involves ineffective delivery of that information. While much information is currently available, it is not meeting the need. Barriers to achieving the ideal include consumer apathy; fragmented, conflicting, and/or overlapping sources of information; and inadequate, inconsistent methods of delivering the information.

In part, for the reasons just mentioned, consumers are not really looking for it, nor do they yet see the need for it. When they do seek information about long-term care, it is usually when they need to access the system immediately, which is too late in most cases. At that point, they are too emotionally involved and under too much pressure to fully comprehend all of the necessary information. To be effective, consumer education must take place long before the onset of need for services. It should preferably take place over a period of years so that consumers and their families are prepared to make the necessary choices.

Another reason long-term care information does not get to consumers adequately is that it is fragmented, comes from many uncoordinated sources, is not comprehensive, and is not uniformly available. Elderly advocacy organizations such as AARP (formerly known as the American Association of Retired Persons) and the National Council of Senior Citizens provide a great deal of information. Yet, by their very nature, those organizations cover very broad areas of interest to the elderly, such as retirement planning, leisure activities, and investments. Their focus on long-term care tends to be more related to protecting the rights of their constituents, but with limited information about how to actually access and use the long-term care system effectively.

On a more local level, area agencies on aging (triple *A*s) usually provide a great deal of information about local long-term care services and how to find them. They also cover a much broader scope than just long-term care. However, because it is so critical to those they serve, long-term care issues are prominent with them. The draw-back with the triple *A*s is that they serve a defined constituency of the elderly and do not cover the full spectrum of long-term care consumers.

Providers often supply information for consumers. Some, motivated by both a sincere desire to serve and a wish to increase their market share, have been quite inno-vative. Toll-free information telephone lines, media advertisements, and public lectures are becoming common. Some have even opened their own "storefront" information centers, providing access and referral materials. They, of course, focus on their own services, not those of competitors. Retirement planning seminars, available to orga-nizations or other groups, include information about long-term care.

Consumers seeking an overall education about long-term care must examine all of these sources and attempt to assimilate the information on their own. That assumes that they know where to look in the first place—not a simple task in and of itself.

The system must find better methods of coordinating available information, supple-menting it when necessary, and bringing it to the attention of the public. Technological advances will assist somewhat. As more people have gained access to the Internet, they have found a great deal of information about long-term care readily available. Infor-mation is already available on computer disks and CD-ROMs and through interactive computer education programs for those who are computer proficient. While many of the elderly are not computer literate, an increasing number are. For some, other, more traditional information delivery modes work best, while others rely heavily on web-based information. The answer to what works best for the general public is all of the above. A variety of consumer education methods is required. As with the long-term care system itself, coordination is critical to the success of these efforts.

B. The long-term care system should include education for providers.

The system should provide for more geriatric education for physicians and others dealing with the elderly. Far too often, healthcare professionals fail to understand the differences between the elderly and younger patients. As we age, we encounter changes in our physiology that play a large part in determining our care needs. Changes such as increasingly fragile bones must be taken into account when treatment plans are developed. While those changes occur more slowly for some than for others, they can be expected by most. In addition to those physical changes, there may also be some decrease in memory or other cognitive ability.

Healthcare providers cannot serve the elderly adequately without a good under-standing of the aging process. They must be trained to recognize the stages of that process and to treat their patients appropriately. Today, many are not. One of the most common results of that lack of training is the tendency to treat all older people as physical and mental invalids. They are individuals, with individual abilities, desires, and needs.

As the locus of care shifts more and more from hospitals to long-term care facilities or agencies, the need to educate healthcare professionals about the needs of the chronically ill will grow. While most long-term care providers understand those needs and respond well to them, other providers, including those in acute care, need to be educated more than they are at the present time.

C. The long-term care system should educate young, healthy persons to better prepare them to cope with chronic illness.

The time to deal with chronic illness and its accompanying disability is long before the onset of that illness. The long-term care system should place more emphasis on preventive education of future consumers. A better understanding of chronicity will lead to better acceptance of chronic illness in individuals and family members, and more effective, efficient use of available resources. Both they and the overall system will benefit.

When long-term care consumers do not know how to use the system, inappropriate use of services by those consumers is unavoidable. That inappropriate use of services means less-than-optimum results for the consumers. It is also inefficient. Young and middle-aged people are accustomed to using acute care services and are comfortable accessing them. They usually have little experience dealing with long-term care, do not understand what is available, and simply avoid it. They can learn to use the full continuum, but not without a consistent, concentrated consumer education effort.

■ Summary

Through the *Criteria for Designing or Evaluating a Long-Term Care System*, we have attempted to define the long-term care system as it should look. It is an intriguing and challenging exercise. However, it must be more than just a mere exercise. The gaps between the current system and the ideal are wide. Bridging those gaps requires a concentrated, coordinated effort by all segments of the long-term care field.

It may be too optimistic to think that the ideal can be achieved. However, we can come closer to it than we are today—and must do so if the system is to survive and prosper. The growth in the elderly population projected over the next several decades as the baby boomers age will test the system's ability to respond as it has not been tested before. The combination of increasing need and diminishing, or at least static, resources will require that new, more efficient delivery methods be found. Yet, the quest for efficiency and cost-effectiveness must not, in any way, compromise quality of care. Long-term care consumers will be better informed and will demand more and better services as a result. The system, its providers, and those who pay the bills must be ready to respond to those demands.

In describing what an ideal long-term care system would look like, it has been necessary to point out the shortcomings of the current system. In doing that, the impression may have been created that the situation is hopeless, that there is little good happening now. That was not the intent. There is much in the current long-term care system that is exemplary. There are many innovative providers who are finding ways to better serve the chronically ill. And they are not alone. Regulators, payers, and policy makers are working to find new solutions to the problems of the system.

■ Vocabulary Terms

The following terms are included in this chapter. They are important to the topics and issues discussed herein and should become familiar to readers. Some of the terms are also found in other chapters but may be used in different contexts. They may not be fully defined herein. Thus, readers may wish to seek other, supplementary definitions of them.

AARP (American Association of Retired Persons)	geriatrician
	informal caregivers
AIDS	long-term care insurance
Alzheimer's disease	Omnibus Budget Reconciliation Act
Area Agencies on Aging	of 1987 (OBRA)
baby boomers	public funding sources
chronicity	respite care
co-payment	sandwich generation
consumer-driven	single-site care availability
consumer responsibilities	uniform assessment
consumer rights	uniform financial eligibility criteria
functional disability	universally accessible

■ Discussion Questions

The following questions are presented to assist you in understanding the material covered in this chapter. They tend to be general, but lend themselves to detailed answers, which can be found in the chapter.

1. What is meant by a consumer-driven long-term care system?
2. What are some of the rights and responsibilities of long-term care consumers?
3. What are the components of accessibility to long-term care services?
4. What is meant by a uniform assessment?
5. What is the role of illness prevention in long-term care?
6. What are some incentives that might be provided to encourage providers to operate more effectively and efficiently?

7. What are some incentives that might encourage consumers to use the long-term care system more effectively and efficiently?
8. What is the role of education in creating a long-term care system that closely approximates the ideal?

■ References

Agency for Healthcare Research and Quality (AHRQ). (2013). *Prevention and chronic care resources.* Retrieved from http://www.ahrq.gov/index.html.

Alexander, R. (2013). *Avoiding fraud when buying long-term care insurance: A guide for consumers and their families.* Retrieved from http://www.alexanderinjury.com/library-fraud-1.

Donabedian, A. (1988). Quality and cost: Choices and responsibilities. *Inquiry, 25,* 90–99.

Eisdorfer, C. (1989). *Caring for the elderly.* Baltimore, MD: Johns Hopkins University Press.

Evashwick, C. (2005). *The continuum of care* (3rd ed.). Clifton Park, NY: Thomson Delmar Learning.

Holzer, J. A. (2008, October). *Long-term care worker shortage.* Retrieved from http://www.hpm.org /de/Surveys/JHSPH_-_USA/12/Long-Term_Care_Worker_Shortage.html.

Kodner, D. (1993). Long-term care 2010: Speculations and implications. *Journal of Long-Term Care Administration, 21*(3) (1993), 82–86.

Levine, C., Halper, D., Peist, A., & Gould, D. (2010). Bridging troubled waters: Family caregivers, transitions, and long-term care. *Health Affairs, 29*(1), 116–124.

NAC and AARP. (2009, November). *Caregiving in the U.S. 2009.* Retrieved from http://www.caregiving .org/data/Caregiving_in_the_US_2009_full_report.pdf.

National Alliance for Caregiving. (2009). *Caregiving in the United States.* Bethesda, MD: The National Alliance for Caregiving. Retrieved from http://www.caregiving.org/pdf/research/Caregiving_in_the _US_2009_full_report.pdf.

Reinhard, S., Kassner, E., Houser, A., & Mollica, R. (2011). *State scorecard on long-term services and supports for older adults, people with physical disabilities, and family caregivers.* Washington, DC: AARP.

Saint Joseph's College of Maine. (1993). *Criteria for designing or evaluating a long-term care system.* Standish: Saint Joseph's College of Maine.

Long-Term Care Service Providers

Nursing Facilities

After completing this chapter, readers will be able to:

1. Define and describe nursing facilities and how they developed, where they fit in the continuum of care, the services they offer, and who uses them.

2. Identify sources of financing for nursing facilities.

3. Identify and describe regulations affecting nursing facilities.

4. Identify and discuss ethical issues affecting nursing facilities.

5. Identify trends affecting nursing facilities in the near future and describe the possible impact of those trends.

■ Introduction

Herein we present a description of nursing care facilities, including a discussion of where they fit into the current long-term care system, how they developed, and where they are likely to be going in the near future. It includes a description of consumers, services offered, staffing, and financing issues. There is also a discussion of ethical issues and management challenges facing this particular type of provider and identification of some of the trends to watch in coming years.

If we were to ask a random sample of people, "What is a nursing facility?" it is likely that most of them would not know what you mean. The term *nursing facility* is a relatively new one and primarily a regulatory term. Yet, if you asked those same people, "What is a nursing home?" they would all know what you were talking about. Although their perceptions might vary a bit, they would all have an understanding of the essence of what constitutes a nursing home. In fact, many of them would probably have some fairly strong opinions about nursing homes, including what is right and what is wrong with them.

Those old ideas about nursing homes are as outdated as the name. A nursing home is a facility that provides residents with a room, meals, personal care, nursing care, and medical services. Nursing homes provide care to residents with chronic conditions requiring long-term care or for those needing a shorter term acute recovery period after hospitalization. Their residents need assistance with activities of daily living (ADLs), which include bathing, dressing, eating, toileting, transferring in and out of chairs or beds, and continence. They may also have cognitive limitations due to Alzheimer's disease or another form of dementia (Metlife Mature Market Institute, 2012).

For many years, the nursing home has been synonymous with long-term care. In fact, the term *long-term care* has been used most often to refer to nursing homes exclusively. Although that exclusive use of the terminology is no longer accurate, it continues and will not change easily. Newer terms, such as *nursing facility*, will help clarify the role of these specific long-term care organizations and differentiate them from others in the overall continuum of care. It is also hoped that others will adopt the stand taken by this book in referring to long-term care as a system, not as a single type of provider.

According to the American Health Care Association (AHCA), there are currently more than 15,000 nursing facilities in the United States, with a total of nearly 1.7 million beds (AHCA, 2014). The term *nursing facility* comes from federal legislation, specifically the Omnibus Budget Reconciliation Act of 1987 (OBRA). It includes facilities licensed by the states offering room, board, nursing care, and some therapies. They include those certified by Medicare as skilled nursing facilities (SNFs) and what used to be called intermediate care facilities, the primary difference being the amount of nursing care provided.

■ How Nursing Facilities Developed

Nursing homes grew out of early charity-based forms of care for people without family or others to care for them (Kaffenberger, 2000). They really came into their own, however, when the federal government became involved with assisting the needy, beginning with passage of the Social Security Act in 1935. The Medicare and Medicaid amendments in the 1960s provided funding of sorts and stimulated growth of the nursing home industry.

For nearly a quarter of a century, nursing homes were the dominant form of long-term care. They provided an institutional alternative to extended hospitalization. As hospital costs began to rise significantly and pressure grew to find less expensive forms of care, nursing homes became more attractive, at least to those paying for the care. Nursing homes also served (and continue to serve) as homes away from home for the elderly and others needing assistance with daily activities and some level of medical care merely to survive.

As important as nursing homes have been in the U.S. healthcare system, their history has been turbulent. The image of the nursing home industry has been tarnished repeatedly, in a number of ways. To begin with, they became known to many elderly as the place you go to die, a reputation transferred from hospitals of earlier years. That reputation reflected not on the quality of care, but on the reality that nursing homes were where people went when there was little chance of improvement. As institutions, they were properly seen as the choice of last resort. Unfortunately, that reputation did not endear them to potential residents who felt they were being put away.

Add to the reluctance of the elderly to go to nursing homes the guilt often felt by families who can no longer provide adequate care at home, and nursing homes found themselves faced with a market population who saw admission to their facilities as a failure. Yet, because there were few, if any, alternatives available to those individuals and their families, nursing homes had little trouble maintaining satisfactory occupancy rates. As a result, they did little to overcome the negative image.

The poor reputation of the nursing home industry cannot be blamed completely on the reluctance of the elderly to accept institutionalization. Throughout much of their history, there have been far too many instances of inadequate care, incompetent management, and even fraud and resident abuse. It is not your author's intent here to condemn all nursing facilities past or present. Today, the field is characterized by high-quality care, competent management, and caring staff. Even during the darker years, the majority of facilities did an excellent job.

It was others who hurt the industry so much, to say nothing of the damage done to individual residents and their families. Numerous investigations exposed instances in which the care provided was so bad as to be abusive. High-profile cases showed residents being exploited both physically and financially. Some nursing home administrators were unscrupulous, others incompetent. The result was that an important segment of the continuum of care, one on which so many vulnerable elderly relied, produced far too many instances of inexcusably bad care. The entire industry suffered.

Why did these situations occur so frequently in nursing homes, particularly when it was not the case with other types of healthcare providers? There are many possible reasons. Some blame the predominantly for-profit nature of nursing homes. They identify the profit motive as a factor in the problems in nursing home quality, citing cases wherein owners and administrators were more interested in making money than in the welfare of the residents in their facilities. Interestingly, we are now hearing that same argument applied to managed care organizations. There can be no doubt that it is an accurate assessment in individual cases (both when applied to nursing facilities and to managed care organizations), but it is an inappropriate and unfair categorization of either industry as a whole. There are many examples of for-profit nursing facilities providing excellent care, and making a profit, but only after meeting the needs of residents.

Part of the blame for examples of both poor care and inadequate management in nursing homes over the past few decades must be borne by the industry itself. Even those owners and administrators who provided good care in their own facilities did relatively little to police the industry in which they operated. Unlike hospitals, an industry with a long history of community oversight, nursing homes operated pretty much on their own. They seldom had representative governing boards to ensure their adherence to missions of community service, as did most hospitals. There was little incentive to provide free care when needed nor to accept admissions regardless of insurance coverage.

That is not necessarily because hospitals had higher standards or were more concerned with the welfare of the needy in the community than were nursing homes, although their record in that area was better. They simply had more built-in oversight mechanisms. First, the nature of their constituents allowed less freedom to choose whom to serve. Hospital patients were (and still are) suffering from acute, often life-threatening, conditions requiring immediate treatment. Nursing homes dealt with people needing long-term, postacute care, which could be delayed. Such delays might cause considerable inconvenience, even suffering, but it was not of the urgent nature of hospital care.

As a result, hospitals have for years been under much more intense public scrutiny than nursing homes. Any failure on their part to provide prompt, high-quality care usually became the subject of damaging public disclosure. That was not so with nursing homes, except in the most extreme situations. Instead of dealing with acute, even emergency, care for generally young, socially active members of society, nursing homes' constituents were elderly, somewhat invisible members of society. Their care needs, while important, were of the more routine, not-so-dramatic variety and generated little public interest.

The higher level of scrutiny of hospitals also included government and private sources of reimbursement. To begin with, hospitals were reimbursed by numerous large payers, including Medicare, Medicaid, Blue Cross, and a variety of private insurances. As early as the 1950s, and particularly from the 1960s on, those reimbursement sources exerted a considerable amount of influence on hospitals, requiring that they be responsive to the needs of their patients, to the community, and to the payers themselves. That influence was not nearly as strong when it came to nursing homes, because most of those reimbursement sources provided little, if any, coverage for long-term care.

Finally, in the early 1970s, public exposés of the nursing home industry caused federal and state governments to get involved. Regulations governing the operation and administration of such facilities were enacted, imposing increasingly strict standards for care and putting in place complex mechanisms for checking on compliance with those regulations. Following a period of relatively less government involvement (an assessment that will be hotly challenged by any nursing facility administrators practicing during that time), the federal government again stepped in with the far-reaching OBRA. That act imposed detailed, highly restrictive regulations on nursing facilities, covering everything from levels of nursing coverage to the type and amount of training required for certified nurse assistants (CNAs).

For these reasons, and probably others not covered here, the nursing home industry has long been plagued by a negative image. Again, it must be stressed here that the industry's overall image problems should not be applied indiscriminately to all nursing facilities, nor should the outstanding, unselfish efforts of the majority of facilities and their staffs be overlooked. Nevertheless, the industry has had much to overcome.

To a large degree, it has done so. A number of professional, regulatory, and other industry associations have worked hard to improve the quality of care provided in nursing homes (now called nursing facilities), the administration and governance of those facilities, and in turn the reputation of the overall field. Professional associations like the American College of Health Care Administrators have done much to improve the level of education and training of those who run nursing facilities, as have trade groups such as the AHCA and its state affiliates. Regulatory organizations in each state license both nursing facilities and their administrators. Quasiregulatory organizations, including the National Association of Long-Term Care Administrator Boards, oversee the training and licensure of nursing facility administrators, working to ensure that those facilities are operated by competent, qualified managers. In response to the work of such organizations, there has been rapid growth in the number of college and university degree and certificate programs providing management education specific to the long-term care field.

It is hard to envision any other industry that has undergone more examination of its actions than nursing facilities. That scrutiny has been deserved for the most part and has produced positive results. It continues today, with both consumer advocacy groups and government agencies questioning the degree to which the elderly are institutionalized and arguing for more home- and community-based types of care.

■ Philosophy of Care

One of the more difficult questions facing the healthcare system today is where to draw the line (if a line is really needed) between acute care and long-term care. Nursing facilities find themselves sitting solidly astride that line. For many years, they have been providing a variety of health and nonhealth services. Their residents have many combinations of needs, some of which are health care related (receiving medications, dressing of wounds, monitoring of medical conditions such as diabetes) and others that are not (supervision, room and board). For them, the ideal is not having to worry about categorizing the care they give, but instead doing what is needed by the residents. Yet, they are licensed categorically and reimbursed according to those categories.

Medical Versus Social Model

The debate over care given in nursing facilities tends to focus on whether it should be based on a medical model or a social model. Much of our healthcare system is based on what has come to be known as the medical model of care. That means simply that the care given is determined by physicians and is aimed at repairing clinical conditions or diseases or overcoming the results of accidents or other medical misadventures. The emphasis is on the clinical condition, not on the person suffering from that condition. There is nothing wrong with that. It is their rightful role.

Long-term care organizations, on the other hand, deal with people who have a variety of conditions—some medical, some social, some financial. Their focus is on care not cure. Those organizations, including nursing facilities, are there to meet the everyday needs of the elderly and other vulnerable individuals. When the needs of their consumers include medical needs beyond their ability to handle, care is transferred to the acute (hospital) healthcare system. Short of those acute episodes, and often when the acute episodes have been resolved, nursing facilities provide the rest of the care needed by those who rely on them.

The varied care requirements of the people served by nursing facilities and other long-term care organizations were well described by the Continuing Care Council, an organization affiliated with the Long-Term Care Management Institute at Saint Joseph's College of Maine. The council, whose mission was "to bring together a diverse group of individuals for the purpose of advancing a consumer-driven system of long-term care" (Continuing Care Council, 1992), has defined consumers of long-term care as "those persons requiring healthcare, personal care, social services, and other supportive services over a sustained period of time" (Continuing Care Council, 1992, p. 2). The Continuing Care Council no longer exists, but these definitions have stood the test of time. Meeting such an extensive spectrum of needs requires that long-term care providers operate on the basis of a holistic philosophy of care. It means that they must approach their constituents as individuals defined by distinctive personalities, strengths, weaknesses, and varying degrees of functional disability or limitation. In caring for them, long-term care providers cannot (at least should not) focus on the clinical causes of disabilities, but rather must attempt to develop an overall care plan that overcomes or minimizes the disabilities.

Nursing facilities often find themselves caring for people who do not fit into other niches within the continuum of care. Their consumers cannot be cared for safely or adequately at home, but do not need the more intensive (and expensive) care provided in hospitals, or even in subacute care facilities. As discussed earlier, nursing facilities are not always the location of first choice.

A Multidisciplinary Approach

As a result, they have to be prepared to provide a wide range of services, with less ability to be selective in what they offer. To do that, most rely on a multidisciplinary approach to care. They utilize a combination of medical, social, residential, and other allied professionals to provide needed services, blending those disciplinary specialties to develop and implement care plans for individual consumers. A distinguishing characteristic of nursing facilities is the extent to which the various professional disciplines intermingle. While some may be more influential than others, it is considerably different from the physician-dominated acute care system.

Family Involvement

Another distinguishing characteristic of long-term care in general, and nursing facilities in particular, is the degree to which family members are involved in the care of the primary consumer. In many cases, the family becomes somewhat of an extension of the resident, making decisions when that person is incapable of doing so and assisting in providing some aspects of care. Nursing facilities and their staffs find it beneficial to utilize those family members, if for no other reason than to maintain a vital link to the consumer's past.

■ Ownership of Nursing Facilities

Traditionally, nursing facilities have been owned mostly by for-profit organizations. That has changed but slightly in recent years. In 2013, according to the American Health Care Association (2013a), 68% were for-profit, 25% were nonprofit, and a small number (6%) were government owned. Fifty-five percent were owned by national multifacility chains. A 2012 survey of long-term care costs by the Metlife Mature Market Institute (2012) found that 86% of all nursing facilities surveyed were freestanding facilities. The rest were physically connected to or on the same grounds as an assisted living community (9%), hospital (5%), or both (<1%). Eleven percent of those surveyed had an associated assisted living unit or wing, and 8% were part of a continuing care retirement community. Under the bundled payment program of the Affordable Care Act, where a single entity receives a sum of money to cover the costs of an episode of care spanning two or more providers, the number of affiliation agreements between hospital systems and long-term care facilities has grown and will continue to grow.

■ Occupancy

The overall occupancy rate for nursing facilities shows a declining trend from a high of 89% in 2007 to 86% in 2013 in spite of a growing elderly population. This suggests a decrease in nursing facility use that is likely a result of the expansion of home/community-based services (AHCA, 2013a).

■ Services Provided

Nursing facilities, in part because of their history as being the lone providers of long-term care in many cases and in part because of their role as the provider of last resort, have traditionally been at the heart of the continuum of care. It is not uncommon for them to cover multiple portions of the continuum, providing a range of services in one institution. Yet, nursing care is still generally the primary care type—and the foundation on which other services are built.

Services in a typical nursing facility include nursing, physical therapy, occupational therapy, speech therapy, medical and dental services, medications, and laboratory and X-ray services as needed. Some of these services may be obtained through agreements with other healthcare organizations, such as hospitals. A small percentage of nursing homes provide adult day care services, often open to residents of the nursing home as well as the community. Some offer adult day services to the community only while others offer them to residents of the nursing home only (Metlife Mature Market Institute, 2012).

■ Special Care Units

As nursing facilities tried to meet the needs of a wider variety of residents, many facilities created special care units (SCUs). Those units enabled them to more effectively provide care that may be different from the care that is provided for the majority of residents. In 2013, 6% of total nursing facility beds in the United States were in special care units (AHCA, 2013a). There are several prevalent types of special care units and reasons for their creation.

Special Care Units Based on a Specific Diagnosis or Disability

One of the most common reasons for developing a special care unit is to meet the unique needs of residents who have special care requirements because of a specific disease or condition. In some cases, the uniqueness reflects special treatments called for by the condition. In others, it is because a group of residents with certain conditions or disabilities do not mix well with the general population of residents. Often, it is a combination of the two.

Alzheimer's Disease Units

One of the most common reasons for creation of special care units is for the care of residents suffering from Alzheimer's disease. According to the Alzheimer's Association (2013a), nearly 60% of all nursing home residents suffer from Alzheimer's disease or a related disorder. Their disability is cognitive impairment. It makes it difficult for them to remember simple everyday tasks and to take care of themselves. Yet, most are not physically disabled. Some special care units are designed to meet the specific needs of individuals with Alzheimer's disease and other dementias. In 2013, 72% of special care units in nursing facilities were dedicated to Alzheimer's disease (AHCA, 2013a). SCUs can take many forms and exist within various types of residential care. In such units, persons with dementia are most often grouped together on a unit within a larger residential care facility (Alzheimer's Association, 2013b). Successful

Alzheimer's disease units have also found that residents respond to certain activities and to additional types of stimulation not needed by others. In many multilevel nursing facilities, Alzheimer's disease residents are separated for most of their care but do mingle with other residents in some group activities.

Mental Health and Units Devoted to Individuals With Intellectual Disabilities

Another group of residents who are institutionalized primarily because of some degree of cognitive impairment, or at least an inability to care for themselves, are those suffering from mental illness or intellectual disabilities (formerly called mental retardation). Like residents with Alzheimer's disease, they need an environment that protects them from their own actions. The closing of many of the large state mental hospitals of the past and the heavy emphasis over the past several decades on deinstitutionalization of the mentally ill and intellectually disabled have resulted in nursing facilities having more residents with cognitive difficulties. More than 50 percent of residents in assisted living and nursing homes have some form of dementia or cognitive impairment, and that number is increasing every day (Tilley & Reed, 2009).

However, that percentage is much higher in some states. For example, a 2013 report, *Dementia in Maine: Characteristics, Care and Cost Across Settings,* showed the numbers to be much higher in Maine. That is in part because Maine has the highest percentage of elderly of every state in the union. The report showed that across all long-term care settings in the state combined, almost half of the people served have some form of Alzheimer's disease or dementia. The percentage of people with dementia increases with each higher level of care. Two thirds of the people in nursing homes have a diagnosis of dementia. If those with impaired decision-making skills are also included, "8 out of 10 people in nursing homes in Maine either have dementia or impaired decision-making" (Fralich, 2013, p. 7).

While many such residents have traditionally been mixed in with others in nursing facilities, the increasing volume of them and the greater-than-before severity of their behavioral problems have encouraged many facilities to create special care units for them.

Brain Injury Units

Another group of residents needing special care for a unique combination of physical and behavioral disabilities is the growing population of people with traumatic brain injury. They tend to be young adults who have suffered massive head trauma in motor vehicle accidents or other similar mishaps, although they may be of any age. Also, there is an unfortunately increasing incidence of young people suffering brain injury as the result of drug overdoses. Regardless of the etiology of the injury, they require supervision to protect themselves and others from sometimes violent actions. In addition, they often have accompanying medical conditions needing attention and treatment. While many brain-injured residents are cared for in acute or subacute care units because of the severity of their injuries, an increasing number are finding their way to nursing facilities. When the number of such residents becomes high enough to warrant it, special care units seem to be the most effective way of caring for them.

Residents With AIDS

A last type of special care unit based on the cause of the disability is one designed for care of people with acquired immune deficiency syndrome (AIDS). Residents with AIDS have distinctive needs from many other types of residents. To begin with, their condition is usually considered to be terminal, though there is ever-increasing hope for improved care. While a large percentage of the residents in a nursing facility will end their lives there eventually, those with AIDS can expect to die in a shorter time. During their time as nursing facility residents, they are likely to suffer from a number of severe side effects and secondary diseases or conditions (sometimes called opportunistic conditions), causing them to require a higher degree of emotional and medical support.

Like those with brain injuries, they tend to be young adults, whose problems may need to be addressed differently from those of the elderly. And, unlike others with Alzheimer's disease, mental illness, intellectual disability, or brain injury, residents with AIDS must be in an environment that protects them from transient infections and protects other residents and staff from contracting AIDS.

Special Care Units Based on Age

Special care units in nursing facilities are not always designed to separate residents because of medical condition or disability. Sometimes they are created because a group of residents is of a significantly different age range than the more typical resident population.

Pediatric Nursing Care Units

Some units have been built specifically for children. Those units are designed to meet the special physical and emotional needs of children with chronic illness. While not many in number, they are extremely important to those children and their families. Experience has shown that they do better in separate units, with other children, and with staff experienced in pediatric care.

Young Adults

Some nursing facilities have found success creating special care units for young adults, including those in their late teens. In addition to those who are institutionalized because of traumatic injury, there may be others with disabilities caused by such diseases as muscular dystrophy, cerebral palsy, or multiple sclerosis. Even though their underlying disabilities and/or conditions may vary, they have a valuable commonality of interests. They can be very supportive of each other.

Your author was formerly the administrator of a long-term care hospital with a mix of handicapped patients of all ages. A lesson learned early on was that handicapped teenagers were teenagers first and handicapped second. They actively sought the same lifestyle as normal teenagers, including their music, dress, and other interests. They did not mix well with elderly residents any more than they would in any other living situation. Once a special unit was created for them, the quality of their lives—and of the lives of other residents—improved significantly.

SCUs in nursing facilities offer numerous advantages, including the efficiency of grouping residents with common care needs; the ability of staff to focus on, and become expert in, that type of care; and creating support groups of and for the residents. The growth of SCUs is not without controversy. Critics cite segregation from the rest of the facility, the lack of interaction with other residents, the stress on staff of caring for such severely impaired residents, and other similar issues. However, if the residents are evaluated properly, they can be placed either in the SCU or with the general population. It appears that the popularity of special care units will continue, although perhaps within more carefully defined parameters.

■ Consumers Served

Skilled nursing facilities serve people who have increasingly complex medical conditions and extensive needs for care and support, as demonstrated by measures of both physical and cognitive function. In an analysis concentrating on five activities of daily living (bathing, bed mobility, transfer, toilet use, and eating), it was found that more than 95% of those individuals who enter a facility for a Medicare-covered, postacute stay require assistance with four or five of these activities. Of those staying for at least 1 year, 85% need that same level of assistance (AHCA, 2013b).

For many Americans, the move to a nursing facility is a permanent one. The nursing facility resident may have a chronic condition, a need for assistance with multiple ADLs, or a cognitive impairment requiring a level of care that prevents him or her from living independently or at lower levels of care. Nursing facilities strive to provide a secure environment and an array of services to meet their needs (Metlife Mature Market Institute, 2012).

Average Length of Stay

Increasingly, skilled nursing facilities take care of two distinct groups of individuals: those who need rehabilitation after an acute illness or hospital stay and those who need long-term care because they are unable to live independently at home or in an assisted living facility (AHCA, 2013a). The average length of stay for short-term care in a skilled nursing facility is approximately 27 days (MedPAC, 2013), while the average long-term care stay is greater than 365 days (Jones, 2012). This much shorter length of stay will allow the facility to serve many more people coming from hospitals for short-stay, postacute care (AHCA, 2014). In spite of the frequency with which nursing facilities provide other services, they tend to serve a relatively homogeneous population, one that can be defined quite well in terms of age and care needs. Let us examine them briefly.

Age

Most nursing facility residents are elderly, meaning over age 65. It has been estimated that the average age upon admittance to a nursing facility is 79 and that 40% of individuals who reach age 65 who will enter a nursing home during their lifetimes (Benz, 2012). As they live longer, more and more of them are reaching ages of 75 and even 85. The impact on the facilities is that those older residents require heavier levels of care as they age. Also, they require that care for longer periods of time.

Care Needs

Individual consumers are admitted to nursing facilities because of functional disabilities, resulting from a number of medical or physical conditions. The care they receive varies, depending on the nature and intensity of those disabilities, and is based on the need for assistance with ADLs. Those ADLs include dressing, bathing, eating, toileting, and transferring. The percentage of residents with severe ADL impairment has been increasing. In 2005, 42% of residents required assistance with four or more ADLs. In 2009, more than half required that level of assistance (CMS, 2010). Nursing facilities are required by OBRA to conduct a "comprehensive, accurate, standardized, reproducible assessment of each resident's functional capacity" (Brown, 2001, p. 3) on all residents at the time of admission. While care plans including therapies can improve a person's functioning in those areas, those functions can be expected to deteriorate over time. Just maintaining current levels is a challenge for staff in nursing facilities.

Many nursing facility residents have both physical and mental disabilities. While not mentally ill as such, many have limitations in their cognitive ability, meaning they may have trouble remembering how to care for themselves or are unable to make decisions for themselves (Stein, 2008).

Gender Mix

Women have historically made up the majority of residents in nursing facilities. According to the U.S. Census Bureau, in 2011, 66% of nursing home residents were women, and 34% were men (Metlife Mature Market Institute, 2012). That reflects their longer average life span and perhaps a lifelong reliance on their husbands to handle many daily chores. Whatever the reason, they dominate institutional long-term care.

In summary, the typical resident is a woman about 87 years old who is mobile but needs assistance with approximately two to three activities of daily living (ADLs). She would have two to three of the Top 10 chronic conditions (NCAL, 2011).

■ Market Forces Affecting Nursing Facilities

There are several factors that can be instrumental in determining admission of consumers to nursing facilities. Those factors are important in understanding the position of these facilities in the long-term care system. They also influence where (to which specific facility) residents are admitted.

Need-Driven Versus Choice-Driven Admissions

As has been discussed earlier, admissions to nursing facilities have traditionally not been because the individual involved wanted to be institutionalized, but rather because there was a need that could not be met otherwise. That is still true with today's nursing facilities, although there have been some changes. Elderly and other functionally disabled people generally prefer to remain in their homes and often resist admission to nursing facilities. The administrators and staffs of those facilities have to keep that in mind in helping new admissions to adapt to an institutional environment.

Nursing facilities have, however, made significant progress in changing that attitude. They have begun by changing the environment to make it much less institutional and more homelike. Using a combination of architectural innovations, programming initiatives, and staff education, many nursing facilities have created living environments that are very attractive and pleasant. Living in those facilities is as much like living at home as is possible, given the individual's disabilities and care needs. The desire for a more homelike environment in nursing homes has gained momentum in the increasingly popular culture change movement.

Those facilities have also begun to aggressively market their organizations, focusing on such factors as quality of life and personal independence. By making more of the public aware that their facilities do not conform to the old stereotypes and by letting people know what is available, they are helping educate several generations about the changes taking place. As potential residents and their families learn more about the choices available to them, they are more likely to make those choices based on what the resident might want, rather than relying only on the care needed.

Family- and Physician-Initiated Admissions

A second factor affecting how admissions to nursing facilities are determined centers on who actually makes the choice. Much of the time that choice is not made by the primary consumer, the resident. Instead, because the decision is delayed until the latest possible moment, the person most involved is no longer capable of making such an important decision because of physical or mental limitations. When that happens, the decision to admit, and where to admit, becomes the responsibility of family members. That decision is heavily influenced by other healthcare professionals, including the family physician. If the consumer has been involved in a hospital admission, other professionals (such as discharge planners, social workers, or utilization review staff) play a large part in the decision. Again, that situation is changing, although slowly, as the result of the consumer education efforts described earlier. The more information future generations of consumers have about the entire continuum, the better equipped they will be to make sound choices and the more willing they will be to make those choices before the situation becomes an emergency.

Hospital Readmissions

Under the Affordable Care Act's Hospital Readmissions Reduction Program, hospitals that readmit excessive numbers of Medicare patients within 30 days of discharge now face significant penalties. The maximum penalty is 1% of a hospital's Medicare reimbursement, but that will increase to 3% in 2015 (CMS, 2013a). One in five patients discharged from the hospital returns within 30 days, and hospital readmissions cost Medicare $17.4 billion in 2010. Since almost one fourth of these beneficiaries are readmitted to SNFs (AHCA/NCAL, 2014), this has placed a considerable amount of pressure on the long-term care facilities. In 2013, the Department of Health and Human Services included recommendations from the Medicare Payment Advisory Commission to have SNFs join hospitals in accountability for avoidable 30-day hospital readmissions. As part of the 2014 budget proposal, SNFs with high rates of Medicare rehospitalizations would have payments reduced by 3% beginning in 2017 (Hoban, 2013).

Location Relative to the Resident's Family

When a person has to make the change from living at home or with relatives to living in a nursing facility, the potential trauma of that change is lessened if the nursing facility is close to the consumer's former home. Visits by family and friends are very important in maintaining an emotional link with the past. Depending on the extent and nature of the person's disabilities, there are other links that are almost as valuable. Being treated by the same physician or dentist or taking trips into the community can help. Even reading a familiar newspaper or watching television news about familiar people and places can be important to people who have lived in a community for many years.

As valuable as those links are, it is not always possible to be admitted to a facility close to home. There may not be enough facilities with services needed by the consumer in the area, or the consumer may have special care requirements that cannot be satisfied in those facilities that are available. The type of financial reimbursement available may also limit the choices.

Alternative Types of Care (or Lack Of)

A last factor affecting if, when, and where people are admitted to nursing facilities is the availability of other types of care that might serve just as well or even better.

Home healthcare services come to mind as the most likely alternatives to nursing facility admission. Frequently, the availability of such alternatives is the deciding factor concerning nursing facility admission. When home care services are available, they may negate the need for institutionalization or at least delay it. Other long-term care services—such as assisted living, subacute care, home care, adult day care, and hospice—can have the same type of impact. They may make admission to a nursing facility less desirable or even unnecessary.

When these services are not available, the likelihood of admission to a nursing facility grows. That is not necessarily bad, in and of itself, but it is obviously in every consumer's best interests to have a number of alternatives from which to choose.

■ Regulations

Nursing facilities operate under the oversight of a large number of regulations, as do all healthcare organizations. In fact, Bruce Yarwood, former president and CEO of the American Health Care Association and the National Center for Assisted Living (AHCA/NCAL) described long-term care as "one of the most highly regulated industries in the country" (Yarwood, 2007, p. 39). A report by the Working Group on Long-Term Care of the U.S. Department of Labor (2000) was even more critical of long-term care regulation, saying:

> The regulatory and inspection process has become so adversarial that it is counterproductive and demoralizing to the actual caregivers. Many of these regulatory processes, inspections and surveys appear to be outdated and do not improve the quality of care offered. Rather they increase costs and reduce the quality of care that is able to be provided.

Caregivers and provider facilities certainly agree with that sentiment. They have long complained that they have to spend so much time and effort to responding to regulations, inspections, and surveys that they cannot provide the quality of care they desire to. The working group went on to say:

> These excessive regulations have affected the LTC provider facilities financially. Many are unable to pay their skilled nursing and assistant staff competitive wages. As a result, caregivers are becoming more and more discouraged with the regulations and leaving the field altogether, seeking higher paying employment in traditional medical facilities. (U.S. Department of Labor, 2000)

Those regulations originate at the national, state, and even local government levels. Their purposes are generally to ensure that (1) care received by consumers is safe and of high quality, (2) care is not unnecessarily expensive for consumers or government agencies, (3) services are as uniformly accessible as possible, and (4) the rights of workers are protected. Let us look briefly at those regulations, the agencies that develop and implement them, and their impact on nursing facilities.

Most such regulations stem, either directly or indirectly, from federal legislation, particularly the Social Security Act of 1935 and the many amendments that have been attached to it over the past several decades. Most notable of those amendments are Titles XVIII and XIX, which created the Medicare and Medicaid programs, respectively. Because those programs represented the federal government's first major incursion into healthcare financing, they came with extensive regulations to ensure that those funds are spent effectively. The other federal legislation with the most impact on nursing facilities is OBRA. Also known as the Nursing Home Reform Act, it changed federal law by instituting higher standards for patient care. The law increased staffing requirements and established a number of resident rights, including the right to be free from abuse, mistreatment, and neglect.

Not all regulations come about as the result of legislation. For instance, in 1999, the U.S. Supreme Court handed down a decision known as the Olmstead decision, *Olmstead v. L.C.* [527 U.S. 581 (1999)]. The court ruled that:

> the unnecessary segregation of individuals with disabilities in institutions may constitute discrimination based on disability and that the Americans with Disabilities Act (ADA) may require states to provide community-based services rather than institutional placements for individuals with disabilities, and that states have an obligation to move individuals with disabilities from institutional settings into more integrated settings in the community. (U.S. Department of Justice, 2011)

A decade and a half later, the impact of *Olmstead* is still being determined, but it is safe to say that some consumers have benefited and some providers have suffered financially trying to meet the requirements. Some state agencies have used it as authentication of their efforts to shift funding away from institutional providers to community-based services.

Regulations Affecting Residents

The regulations with the most direct impact on nursing facilities are those directly affecting the care given to residents in those facilities. They are multitudinous, very detailed, and sometimes in conflict with other applicable regulations.

OBRA, Medicare, Medicaid, and state licensing regulations prescribe the level and types of care given, the types and numbers of professional staff needed, the layout and condition of the facility, and many other specific details of how care is provided. Other regulations directly affecting residents in nursing facilities include the Older Americans Act and the ADA.

Regulations Affecting Employees

Employees of nursing facilities are also affected by numerous regulations designed to protect them. Those regulations are associated with a number of laws and regulatory organizations, including the Occupational Safety and Health Administration, the Department of Labor Wage and Hour Division, the Equal Employment Opportunity Commission, state worker's compensation acts, the ADA, the Fair Labor Standards Act, the Family Medical Leave Act, and too many others to list here.

Regulations Affecting Building Construction and Safety

Regulations pertaining to environmental safety also apply. Nursing facilities must conform to the Life Safety Code, the Occupational Safety and Health Administration, and local building codes to ensure that residents live in an environment that is safe and comfortable.

■ Financing Nursing Facilities

Nursing facilities receive financing from several sources. Government funding (mostly Medicare and Medicaid) commands a large portion of the long-term care reimbursement picture. At any point in time, Medicaid is the payer for services for nearly two thirds of persons being served in nursing facilities. The payer mix for for-profit, not-for-profit, and government-owned facilities varies. Government-run facilities average 67% coverage by Medicaid followed by for-profit centers at 66%, and not-for-profit facilities at 55% (AHCA, 2013b). As more nursing facilities have ventured into subacute care and/or skilled nursing, the Medicare portion has risen. Also, as coverage by private long-term care insurance grows, albeit slowly, it will have more of an impact on the reimbursement mix of nursing facilities.

Although rates vary, the average cost of a semiprivate nursing home room in 2013 was $84,000 per year, while the average cost of a private room averaged more than $94,000 (Carman, 2013). Routine daily rates usually include room, board, nursing care, therapeutic activities, and social services, with other services such as physical therapy and speech therapy usually being charged separately. There are several variables that affect the actual amount paid by a nursing facility resident. The first is, of course, the type and amount of coverage. While the facilities may have a standard charge, some sources such as Medicare and Medicaid pay less than the full charge.

Medicare places some hard and fast restrictions on coverage in nursing facilities:

- It covers only skilled nursing care.
- It must follow a three-day qualifying hospital stay.
- It is limited to 100 days per benefit period.
- It requires a co-payment of $148.00 a day for the 21st through the 100th day of skilled nursing care (Piper, 2012).

Medicaid generally provides full coverage for residents who meet financial qualifications, although the rate is set by the state Medicaid agency and is usually less than full cost. In 2012, state Medicaid programs, on average, reimbursed nursing facilities less than 90% of their allowable costs incurred for Medicaid patients. This represented the lowest percentage since 1999 (Eljay, LLC, 2012). Other variables affecting the rates paid by various reimbursement sources include the specific services used, the number of ADLs with which assistance is needed, and factors such as private versus two-bed rooms.

■ Staffing and Human Resource Issues

Nursing facilities are faced with a number of issues surrounding staffing. As is true of all long-term care and other healthcare organizations, it is an industry that is worker intensive. That means that there is more emphasis on staffing than on use of machinery or technology. Payroll is typically the largest component of the facility's overall expenses. Maintaining the required number of staff members is almost as difficult as maintaining their training and the quality of the work they provide.

Nature of the Workforce

Nursing facilities utilize a staffing mix that combines both highly trained and relatively untrained staff, working side-by-side. The American Health Care Association says that skilled nursing care centers "employ registered nurses (RNs), licensed practical nurses (LPNs), nurses with administrative duties (ARNs), nurse practitioners, certified nursing assistants (CNAs), therapists, housekeeping staff, dietary staff, social services staff, and administrative staff to take care of individuals and meet their needs and preferences" (AHCA, 2012). They must provide both clinical care (including giving medications, changing dressings, and monitoring medical conditions) and nonclinical care (such as assisting with the ADLs that healthy, nondisabled people take for granted). In addition to these nursing and custodial services, nursing facilities are increasingly providing rehabilitation services such as physical therapy, occupational therapy, and speech pathology. Balancing those services in a fashion to best satisfy the care needs of their residents, individually and collectively, requires effort and vigilance.

Nursing

As the name *nursing facility* implies, the primary care of the residents is provided by nursing staff. In the context of nursing facilities, nursing staff consists of registered nurses, practical nurses, and nurse aides. Government regulations, particularly OBRA and Medicare, specify the numbers of staff on duty on each work shift and the mix of personnel categories making up that staff. One requirement that separates nursing facilities from certain other types of long-term care organizations is that there must be licensed nurse coverage on all shifts. For skilled nursing facilities, as defined under

Medicare, the staffing ratio must be higher. Several states have also implemented regulations requiring nurse coverage even beyond that required by the federal government.

Certified Nurse Aides

The largest category of staff in most nursing facilities is that of CNA. CNAs are nonlicensed paraprofessionals who provide most of the hands-on care (Singh, 2010). While nurse assistants have been the primary component of staffing in nursing facilities for years, OBRA imposed strict new regulations concerning their training and qualifications, developing a new definition of certified nurse assistants. Those CNAs must receive a minimum amount of training and must be certified by a state agency as having received such training or otherwise being judged competent.

Medical Coverage

Unlike hospitals, which need large medical staffs to provide their physician-centered care, nursing facilities require only medical supervision and the availability of medical coverage. That coverage is not less important but is needed less often and is usually not as intensive. As the continuum of care continues to shift downward, with each segment caring for people with higher care needs than in the past, both the frequency and intensity of medical coverage in nursing facilities will also continue to increase.

OBRA regulations mandate that each facility have a medical director responsible for oversight of the clinical care provided in the facility. The medical director does not have to be and seldom is, except in some very large facilities, full-time. He or she must coordinate medical coverage, develop and implement clinical policies and procedures, and provide direct care as appropriate. In fact, because of the difficulty in finding physicians willing to attend nursing facility residents for the reimbursement available, the medical director is often the physician of record for many residents.

Other medical coverage is usually provided by physicians employed on a consultant or contract basis. They make regular visits to the facility and are available for emergencies. The facilities also maintain transfer arrangements with area hospitals for those emergency situations and acute episodes requiring more care than can be provided by them.

Other Specialists

In addition to physicians, nurses, and nurse assistants, nursing facilities must have a number of other disciplines represented to adequately provide services, including pharmacists, dietitians, social workers, and therapists. There are several ways of securing those services. First, of course, is to hire them on a full- or part-time basis. That is not always possible because of shortages in some areas of certain professionals. It may also not be feasible for either of a couple of other reasons: (1) an individual facility may not need the full-time services of some professional specialties, and (2) they may not be able to afford such services. The result is that some groups of professionals are made available on a contract basis. It is acceptable, even to financing and regulatory bodies, to provide those services on a consultant basis, as long as the services are adequate in scope and quality.

Recruitment and Turnover Issues

Nursing facilities, like most other healthcare providers, are experiencing staffing shortages, and those shortages are expected to become worse in coming years. The aging of American society will affect long-term care in several ways. First, the number of people who will need long-term care is growing. At the same time, the number of people available to care for them is declining, in part because of the number of them who are retiring. According to the AHCA, in 2011, the overall turnover rate for all nursing facility employees was 45% and was highest among nursing care staff (50%) (AHCA, 2012).

Nursing facilities often experience difficulty in recruiting staff. They have problems with competition on several fronts. To begin with, they must obviously compete with similar nursing facilities and other long-term care organizations for all categories of staff. However, much of their strongest competition for their most highly trained staff—including nurses, therapists, and medical coverage—comes from hospitals. In most areas, hospitals pay higher salaries for similar specialists. Also, many healthcare professionals prefer the more acute, more exciting world of hospitals to the more routine care given in nursing facilities. There has been an historic lack of respect for long-term care by many acute care professionals.

Nursing facilities must also compete for the less highly trained, lower paid members of their staffs, particularly certified nurse assistants and employees in their dietary and housekeeping departments. In addition to other healthcare facilities, there is strong competition for their employees from other businesses. It has been widely reported that fast-food restaurants and retail stores pay higher wages than many nursing facilities. Because nursing facilities are highly regulated, including their expenditures, their ability to raise wages may be severely limited. Wages are not the only reason for competition from those other businesses. Their training requirements are minimal, choices of work shifts may be better, and their workers do not have to clean up after residents who may be incontinent or deal with them when they are disagreeable. Because of these issues, nursing facilities may have difficulty maintaining staff morale. It is critical that facility administrators strive continually to do so, because staff discontent will undoubtedly be reflected in the care they give and in the morale of residents.

■ Legal and Ethical Issues

Nursing facilities share the same ethical issues as other long-term care organizations. They also share the same legal responsibility to protect their constituents' rights and to act ethically, even in some difficult situations. Nursing facilities, however, need to be particularly sensitive to a variety of such issues. The clinical care they provide is closer to hospital care than that of other long-term care organizations that provide primarily residential care. On the other hand, they must provide that care over much longer periods of time than hospitals. Although home healthcare agencies often provide much of the same types of care as nursing facilities, they do not have 24-hour responsibility. As a result, the likelihood of legal and ethical questions arising is higher in nursing facilities.

Let us look briefly at how ethical issues in long-term care affect nursing facilities in particular.

Day-to-Day Quality-of-Life Issues

There is probably no more important issue for residents in nursing facilities than personal autonomy. Even though they must live in an institution, they seek, and deserve, as much control over their own lives as is possible. Autonomy has many aspects and means different things to different residents. For some, it means being able to decide what to eat and when to eat it. For others, it is being able to accept or refuse treatments. For the staff of the nursing facilities, it means trying to accede to the individual resident's wishes without compromising the quality and effectiveness of the care given to that resident. It is not an easy process, given the range of physical and mental disabilities suffered by the residents of the typical facility. Many residents are not totally competent to make important decisions by themselves. Facility staff must find ways to ensure that such decisions are made with the best interests of the resident in mind. In doing that, they must give great credence to what they believe to be the wishes of the resident, protecting that person's autonomy whenever possible.

Another autonomy-related issue that arises in nursing facilities—probably more often than in other long-term care organizations—is the issue of individual choice versus group choice. In any group living situation, individuals are not always able to have all of their desires granted if those desires have a negative effect on others in the group. In nursing facilities, that issue may revolve around whether a resident can have a private room. Such rooms might not be available. More and more facilities are providing them, but even then, the resident's reimbursement coverage may not allow it. Other variations of this issue tend to center on day-to-day activities such as meals, bedtime, entertainment (television, radio), and visitors. It is not unlike other group living arrangements such as college dormitories, military barracks, or summer camp, except that residency in a nursing facility is much more permanent and the residents have fewer options to get away or to create their own alternatives.

Nursing facilities have made great strides in making the living environment more pleasant and homelike. Part of that has been creating more opportunities for residents to do their own thing, to have as much choice in how they live as possible.

End-of-Life Issues

Nursing facilities have always had to deal with death of their residents. The fact is many of their residents will live there for the rest of their lives. However, the legal and ethical issues related to end of life have taken on new prominence. As the acuity levels rise in those facilities and more focus is placed on quality of life versus the extension of life, opportunities for critical decision making increase. Administrators and staff of nursing facilities must be prepared to address the desires of their residents to forgo life-sustaining treatment or to otherwise dictate how they spend the last few months of their lives. As has happened in other segments of health care, they have become more sensitive to those desires and recognize the need for open discussion of end-of-life issues.

That discussion has stimulated, and been further stimulated by, federal legislation concerning the rights of patients/residents to make decisions about their care and to make their desires known. The Patient Self-Determination Act of 1990 required that everyone admitted to a healthcare facility be informed of their rights to create advance directives, spelling out their wishes in the event of future inability to express those wishes themselves. Those advance directives usually take the form of a living will or power of attorney. The act also requires healthcare providers to abide by the desires of the consumer in such cases to the best of their ability, even when they disagree with those desires.

■ Management of Nursing Facilities

Managing any long-term care organization is challenging. It is not meant to be easy. Managing facilities that have such a long, not always positive, history as do nursing facilities is especially challenging. Today's nursing facility administrators—and there are approximately 16,000 of them (AHCA, 2014)—must not only meet the challenges of change, but also must overcome the public image associated with the past. An administrator of any long-term care organization must be knowledgeable about the organization and the industry in which it functions, must be willing to make difficult decisions that affect the lives of others, and must provide leadership for the staff of the organization. It is not a job for everyone, but the rewards are commensurate with the challenges. The highest of those rewards is the satisfaction of having played an important role in protecting and helping some very vulnerable people.

Management Qualifications

Administrators of nursing facilities must be licensed by the states in which they practice, meeting minimum education and experience requirements. The idea is to ensure that they possess the essential qualifications for the job. That requirement was imposed by the federal government in 1967 as the result of numerous studies highlighting the shortcomings in the management of nursing homes at that time. However, while the federal government charged the states with licensure, it gave them little guidance concerning how they were to do it, and it did not set standards to be met.

The result has been great variance in pre-licensure requirements, particularly the type and amount of education required. Those requirements range from a high school diploma to a specialized college degree, and everything in between. The amount of hands-on experience required prior to licensure also varies from none in some states to as much as 2 years in others.

The National Association of Long-Term Care Administrator Boards coordinates the process of testing administrators of nursing facilities and administers a national licensure examination. In most states, administrators must also attend continuing education programs to maintain their licensure and to keep abreast of developments in the field. They are also represented by professional associations such as the American College of Health Care Administrators, which has developed both a code of ethics and a set of standards of practice for long-term care administrators.

Management Challenges and Opportunities

Management of any healthcare organization contains many challenges but also provides an equal number of opportunities. Managers of nursing facilities have more than their share. The industry was once described as "one of the most regulated, underpaid, poorly regarded, and least understood industries in the United States" (Gelfanc, 1993, p. 54). That definition is as true today as it was in 1993. Let us look briefly at some of the most common of those challenges.

Balancing Cost and Quality

Because nursing facilities are subject to such a broad range of regulations, most of which attempt to minimize cost and maximize quality of care, nursing facility administrators must constantly work at balancing those two forces. It is not as easy as many would believe. Nor do most administrators disagree with the desirability of achieving those goals. They care about the residents who depend on them. They also recognize the need to operate as efficiently as possible.

One of the benefits of the increasing competition in long-term care is that it separates those organizations that are successful from those that are not. It provides a very powerful incentive for administrators. The better they can provide high-quality care at low costs, the better accepted their facilities will be by the buyers of their services.

Integration of Differing Levels of Service

As we have noted repeatedly, the old model of a nursing facility that can limit its services to those narrowly defined by regulation is a creature of the past. Today, the most popular model is one of a multilevel facility providing several types of care, possibly including assisted living, home health care, and/or subacute care in addition to skilled care and nursing care. The challenge to the administrator is understanding which of those services are most appropriate for his or her organization and which are not. That means knowing the potential capabilities of the facility's staff and physical plant. It also means being foresighted and willing to look beyond traditional boundaries.

Coordination With Other Facilities and Organizations

No matter how much they are able to expand their service mix, few nursing facilities can afford to go it alone in this dynamic, complex field. They cannot be all things to all consumers. Successful nursing facility managers develop relationships with other organizations as a means of expanding the services they have available to their residents. It requires that those managers be well informed about the alternatives available to them, the needs of their consumers, and the strengths and weaknesses of their competitors.

■ Significant Trends and Their Impact on Nursing Facilities

There are many changes taking place in the entire field of long-term care, many of them likely to continue in the near future. Some are having more impact on nursing facilities than others. Although most have been touched on in the discussions in this chapter, their future significance is worth noting here.

Rising Acuity Levels

As healthcare costs rise, and pressure to find the most efficient, cost-effective forms of care rises with them, providers are seeing people who need more care than ever before. Nursing facilities find themselves right in the middle of that shift. They are being required to care for people with conditions that would have required them to be kept in hospitals in past years. At the same time, other types of long-term care, such as home health care, are being used to care for more of those who historically would have been residents in their facilities.

If nursing facilities are to successfully ride out this trend, they must each identify their particular niche in the continuum and make the most of it. If they fail to do that, they are likely to be pushed aside by others who are more farsighted and flexible.

Managed Care

While managed care affected only a relatively small number of residents in nursing facilities a few years ago, that is no longer true today. States are shifting Medicare and Medicaid clients into managed care systems, and health maintenance organizations are increasingly developing networks with nursing facilities. There is little doubt that the influence of managed care organizations on nursing facilities will continue to grow, given the number of people cared for in those facilities and the money spent on them. Nursing facility administrators must understand how managed care works and be proactive in preparing for it.

Other Reimbursement Trends

About the only thing certain about the current method of reimbursing nursing facilities is that it will continue to change. Several trends currently under way will have significant impact on those facilities, including those discussed here.

Prospective Payment

Several years ago, Congress mandated a prospective payment system (PPS) for long-term care facilities similar to that in place for hospitals for a number of years. SNFs are no longer paid on a reasonable cost basis or through low-volume prospectively determined rates, but rather on the basis of a prospective payment system whose payment rates are adjusted for case mix and geographic variation in wages and cover costs of furnishing Medicare-covered SNF services (CMS, 2013b). As with most new legislation, the reaction of industry experts was mixed.

Private Long-Term Care Insurance

The concept of privately purchasing long-term care insurance is still in its infancy, but it is destined to grow. It has been estimated that 7 to 9 million people had private long-term care insurance in 2010. They did so to protect their assets from the Medicaid spend-down requirement without resorting to legal gimmicks. That is borne out by the fact that 79% of long-term care insurance purchasers had more than $100,000 in liquid assets (Benz, 2012). To date, it is largely limited to individuals. As it becomes more attractive for employers to offer it as an option for their workers, preferably with some significant contribution by the employers, it will gain both attractiveness and volume. As that happens, nursing facilities will have another group of customers with whom to deal. That body of consumers—employers and individual premium payers—is not totally new but will certainly gain new prominence.

Payment Bundling

The Affordable Care Act created a system of payment bundling. As described by the American Health Care Association (2010):

> bundling is designed to align payment incentives and encourage efficiencies between acute and post-acute providers. Currently, the Medicare fee-for-service system has unique payment rules and amounts for each provider type. Under a bundled payment, a single entity would receive a sum of money to cover the costs of an episode of care spanning two or more providers. (p. 13)

This will be accomplished, in most cases, through accountable care organizations (ACOs)—networks of providers who work together to cover a defined patient population.

Rising Liability Insurance Costs

In recent years, a large number of high payout liability suits against all healthcare providers has caused liability insurance premiums to rise dramatically. Those rising costs have contributed to bankruptcies of nursing facility providers in several instances. In others, corporate provider organizations have withdrawn from certain states in which the situation is worst. There has been an effort in Congress to pass some form of tort reform to remedy this problem, but to date that effort has not been successful. If the situation persists, both access to care and the quality of care delivered may suffer.

Consumer Choice

Not all change of significance to nursing facilities is related to financing. Nearly 2 decades ago, your author said in an interview published as, "Taking Turns at the Crystal Ball: Long-Term Care Leaders Foretell the Future," that the single most important trend today, and into coming decades, will be the demand by consumers for more choice in their care (Pratt, 1996, p. 12). That demand has already been felt by many nursing facilities, and they have generally reacted positively and creatively. Those who have not will find themselves at a distinctive disadvantage unless they change.

■ Summary

Nursing facilities have a long history in providing long-term care. In fact, to many people, they are long-term care facilities. However, that perception is changing, just as these facilities are changing. The external pressures on them, discussed in this chapter, threaten their identity, individually and collectively.

Today's nursing facilities find themselves no longer dominating the continuum of care as they have in the past. Other providers have stepped forward to claim some of their consumers, as well as some of their funding. Tomorrow, they just may find their role in the continuum further diminished—in visibility, if not in importance. To avoid that, they need to be proactive. They must adapt to new forms of payment and organization and find their most advantageous place in the system. To their credit, most have already begun to do that—some very effectively.

As the continuum becomes more seamless, and as both providers and integrated organizations become involved in multiple segments of the continuum, the role of each is less distinct. While that is a positive step toward a system that is better coordinated and less fragmented, it poses a considerable challenge for individual facilities and their administrators.

Nursing Facilities Case: Mary

Mary is a resident in a nursing facility—and has been for the past 5 of her 87 years. Most of the time, she is withdrawn into her own little world, although she shows occasional signs of being alert to her surroundings, sometimes appearing to be confused by them. Her physical appearance is generally good. She is neat and clean, more due to the care and effort of the facility staff than to her own efforts. Her hair is brushed neatly, and her clothes are freshly laundered and pressed. She spends her time in a wheelchair because an arthritic condition makes it difficult for her to walk.

Mary does not participate in many of the organized activities of the facility, in spite of valiant efforts by the staff to get her to do so. She seems content most of the time to keep to herself, although her favorite spot is near the nurses' station where she is surrounded by activity. How much of it she actually absorbs is unknown, but she prefers to be at the hub of things. This lack of cognitive ability has come on gradually over a number of years, and her doctors have not felt the need to apply a specific diagnosis. Of more concern to them is her history of at least one heart attack, late-onset diabetes, and arthritis that has virtually destroyed her hips.

This is not the Mary we would have seen a few years earlier. Let us look at her background to better understand her and how she came to be a resident of the nursing facility. She has led what some would consider a difficult life. Married to a construction worker who often had to travel considerable distances to work sites and came home only on weekends, Mary bore most of the responsibility for raising four children. She was a very strong-willed, self-reliant person. That is important in understanding the extent of lifestyle change she had to overcome in her later years.

After being widowed before she turned 60, she continued to live alone in the family home for a number of years. Eventually, however, it became clear that she could not care for herself safely, largely because of the advancing arthritis in her hips. She agreed to move in with her daughter and son-in-law, a first step toward losing her independence. The situation was amicable. She had a room of her own but was fully included in the family's affairs, and she assisted in some chores, particularly cooking. Given the security of the living arrangements, she was able to continue knitting, sewing, and crocheting, something at which she was very talented. It allowed her to feel that she was contributing and useful.

However, the time came when Mary became forgetful and occasionally used poor judgment, making it unsafe for her to use the cookstove. She also posed a threat to herself should she fall or wander, and she could not be relied on to remember to take her medicine. She needed nearly constant supervision for her own protection. Because the daughter and son-in-law operated a business on the premises of their home, they were able to provide that supervision longer than most, but eventually even they had to face the reality of placing Mary in a more protective setting, probably a nursing home.

They were fortunate to find an excellent facility only a few miles from their home. It provided multiple levels of care and was affiliated with a nearby hospital. It offered the further benefit of being close to her former neighbors and friends, a fact made even more important because her remaining three children all live out of state and are unable to visit regularly.

Thus, in spite of the feelings of guilt that are experienced by most families when faced with placing a loved one in institutional care, Mary was admitted to the Mountainview Health Care Facility.

Because of her age and lack of personal finances, Mary's care in the facility is covered by a combination of Medicare and Medicaid. Her essential needs are met, and although there are few extras, her needs are modest. Family members provide new clothes and personal items as needed. Some items, such as eyeglasses and dentures, are covered by Medicare or Medicaid, although the process of approving the expenditures can sometimes be lengthy and cumbersome. The time that approval takes is a nuisance for Mary—especially since she has a habit of misplacing or losing her glasses and dentures. For the staff at Mountainview, however, it is more of a feeling of frustration. They want the best for all of their residents and would rather be spending their time caring for them than doing paperwork. However, they also realize that Mary brings some of on it by her own actions, and they sympathize with the staff processing the paperwork on the other end.

Mary, as her cognitive ability and sense of reality have progressively decreased, has slipped ever more into her own imaginary world. That has both advantages and disadvantages for the facility staff. On the plus side, she usually requires little actual care, other than seeing to it that she takes her medication and that her heart condition and diabetes are monitored and treated as necessary. On the other hand, her lack of reality makes her difficult to live with. She resents roommates, thinking of her room as the home she remembers. For a long time, she refused to attend any of the many group activities arranged by the facility staff. After much questioning, they eventually found that she thought that all of those events were funerals, and she dislikes funerals.

Mary's retreat into her imaginary world has been harder on her children. She no longer recognizes them and has no concept of how often they visit. They have increasingly felt a mix of gratitude for the excellent and humane care provided by the facility staff and a sense of loss because of their decreased involvement in her life.

However, that situation has recently taken a significant turn, placing them in a position of making a difficult, but important, decision on Mary's behalf. The arthritis has caused her hips to deteriorate to the point where she not only is unable to walk, but is uncomfortable even sitting in a chair or wheelchair. They decided to approve the surgery for hip replacements to make her more comfortable.

■ Vocabulary Terms

The following terms are included in this chapter. They are important to the topics and issues discussed herein and should become familiar to readers. Some of the terms are also found in other chapters but may be used in different contexts. They may not be fully defined herein. Thus, readers may wish to seek other, supplementary definitions of them.

activities of daily living (ADLs)
acuity levels
advance directives
Affordable Care Act
American College of Health Care
    Administrators
American Health Care Association
    (AHCA)
Americans With Disabilities Act
AIDS
Alzheimer's disease
autonomy
brain injury units

certified nurse assistants (CNAs)
deinstitutionalization
end-of-life issues
Equal Employment Opportunity
    Commission
Fair Labor Standards Act
Family Medical Leave Act
holistic philosophy of care
intermediate care facility
Life Safety Code
living wills
managed care organizations
Medicaid
medical versus social model

Medicare
multidisciplinary approach to care
National Association of Long-Term
    Care Administrator Boards
nursing facility
nursing home
Occupational Safety and Health
    Administration
Older Americans Act

Omnibus Budget Reconciliation Act
    of 1987 (OBRA)
Patient Self-Determination Act of
    1990
power of attorney
prospective payment system (PPS)
skilled nursing facility (SNF)
Social Security Act of 1935
special care units (SCUs)

■ Discussion Questions

The following questions are presented to assist you in understanding the material covered in this chapter. They tend to be general but lend themselves to detailed answers, which can be found in the chapter.

1. What is a nursing facility? How does the name *nursing home* relate to it?
2. How did nursing facilities develop?
3. What types of services are provided by nursing facilities? Who uses them?
4. How are nursing facilities financed?
5. What regulations govern the operation of nursing facilities? Who does the regulating?
6. What types of professional and paraprofessional staff work in nursing facilities?
7. What are special care units (SCUs) in nursing facilities? Why do they exist?
8. What are some of the ethical issues faced in nursing facilities?
9. What trends are most likely to affect the operation of nursing facilities in the future?
10. In reference to the case at the end of this chapter, consider the following:
    a. Should Mary's family members authorize double hip replacement?
    b. What factors should be considered?
    c. Who else, if anyone, should be consulted?
    d. What are the implications of that decision on the parties involved: Mary, her children, the facility staff?
    NOTE: As is so often true, both in case analysis and in real life, there is no single right answer here. The purpose of the question is to get you thinking about the many aspects of making such a decision for someone else.

■ References

Alzheimer's Association. (2013a). *Choosing care providers*. Retrieved from http://www.alz.org/living_with_alzheimers_choosing_care_providers.asp.

Alzheimer's Association. (2013b). *Special care units.* Retrieved from http://www.alz.org/join_the_cause
_special_care_units.asp.

American Health Care Association (AHCA). (2010, November). *Maximizing the value of post-acute care.*
Retrieved from http://www.aha.org/research/reports/tw/10nov-tw-postacute.pdf.

American Health Care Association (AHCA). (2012). *2011 AHCA staffing survey report.* Washington,
DC: American Health Care Association. Retrieved from http://www.ahcancal.org/research_data
/staffing/Documents/2011%20Staffing%20Survey%20Report.pdf.

American Health Care Association (AHCA). (2013a). *LTC stats: Nursing facility operational characteristics report.* Retrieved from AHCA Research: http://www.ahcancal.org/research_data
/oscar_data/Nursing%20Facility%20Operational%20Characteristics/LTC%20STATS_PVNF
_OPERATIONS_2013Q2_FINAL.pdf.

American Health Care Association (AHCA). (2013b). *2013 quality report.* Washington, DC: American
Health Care Association.

American Health Care Association (AHCA). (2014, March). *Trends in nursing facility characteristics.*
Retrieved from http://www.ahcancal.org/research_data/trends_statistics/Documents/Trend_PVNF
_FINALRPT_June2013.pdf.

American Health Care Association/National Center for Assisted Living (AHCA/NCAL). (2014). *Issue
brief: Hospital readmissions.* Retrieved from http://www.ahcancal.org/advocacy/issue_briefs
/Issue%20Briefs/Readmissions_IB.pdf.

Benz, C. (2012, August 9). *40 must-know statistics about long-term care.* Retrieved from http://news
.morningstar.com/articlenet/article.aspx?id=564139.

Brown, J. (2001). *Nursing home resident assessment quality of care.* Retrieved from Office of the Inspec-
tor General: https://oig.hhs.gov/oei/reports/oei-02-99-00040.pdf.

Carman, A. (2013, September 1). *Room charges now top $94K.* Retrieved from http://www.mcknights
.com/room-charges-now-top-94k/article/310032.

Centers for Medicare and Medicaid Services (CMS). (2010). *Nursing home data compendium, 2010.*
Washington, DC: Centers for Medicare & Medicaid Services. Retrieved from http://www.cms.gov
/Research-Statistics-Data-and-Systems/Statistics-Trends-and-Reports/DataCompendium/2011
_Data_Compendium.html.

Centers for Medicare and Medicaid Services (CMS). (2013a, August 2). *Readmissions reduction program.* Retrieved from http://www.cms.gov/Medicare/Medicare-Fee-for-Service-Payment/Acute
InpatientPPS/Readmissions-Reduction-Program.html.

Centers for Medicare and Medicaid Services (CMS). (2013b, July 31). *Skilled nursing facility PPS.*
Retrieved from http://www.cms.gov/Medicare/Medicare-Fee-for-Service-Payment/SNFPPS/index
.html?redirect=/snfpps.

Continuing Care Council. (1992). *Continuing Care Council operating protocol.* Standish: Saint Joseph's
College of Maine.

Eljay, LLC. (2012). *A report on shortfalls in Medicaid funding for nursing center care.* Washington, DC:
American Health Care Association.

Fralich, E. A. (2013). *Dementia in Maine: Characteristics, care and cost across settings.* Portland: Muskie
School of Public Service, University of Southern Maine.

Gelfand, Lawrence (1993). Frustrations of a nursing home administrator in the 1990s. In *Long-term care:
Management scope and practical issues* (p. 54) Philadelphia, PA: The Charles Press.

Hoban, S. (2013, August 16). *SNFs soon may face penalties for avoidable readmissions.* Retrieved from
http://www.ltlmagazine.com/news-item/snfs-soon-may-face-penalties-avoidable-readmissions.

Jones, C. (2012, April 8). *Characteristics and use of home health care by men and women aged 65 and over*. National Health Statistics Reports number 52. Retrieved from http://www.cdc.gov/nchs/data/nhsr/nhsr052.pdf.

Kaffenberger, K. (2000). Nursing home ownership: An historical analysis. *Journal of Aging & Social Policy*, 2(1), 35–48.

MedPAC. (2013). *Health care spending and the Medicare program*. Washington, DC: Medicare Payment Advisory Commission.

Metlife Mature Market Institute. (2012). *Market survey of long-term care costs*. New York, NY: MetLife.

NCAL. (2011). *Resident profile*. Retrieved from National Center for Assisted Living: http://www.ahcancal.org/ncal/resources/Pages/ResidentProfile.aspx.

Piper, K. (2012, December 31). *Medicare premiums, co-payments, and deductibles for 2013*. Retrieved from http://www.piperreport.com/blog/2012/12/31/medicare-premiums-co-payments-deductibles-2013/.

Pratt, J. (1996). Taking turns at the crystal ball: Long-term care leaders foretell the future. (R. Peck, Interviewer), *Nursing Homes*, 45(20), 11–19.

Singh, D. (2010). *Effective management of long-term care facilities* (2nd ed.). Sudbury, MA: Jones and Bartlett Learning.

Stein, R. (2008, March 18). *One in seven Americans age 71 and older has some type of dementia*. Retrieved September 23, 2008, from Washington Post: http://www.washingtonpost.com/wp-dyn/content/article/2008/03/17/AR2008031701881.html?sub=new.

Tilley, J., & Reed, P. (2009). *Dementia care practice recommendations for assisted living residences and nursing homes – Phases 1 and 2*. Retrieved from http://www.alz.org/national/documents/brochure_dcprphases1n2.pdf.

U.S. Department of Justice. (2011, June 22). *Statement of the Department of Justice on enforcement of the integration mandate of Title II of the Americans With Disabilities Act and* Olmstead v. L.C. Retrieved from http://www.ada.gov/olmstead/q&a_olmstead.htm.

U.S. Department of Labor. (2000, November 14). *Report of the Working Group on Long-Term Care*. Retrieved from http://www.dol.gov/ebsa/publications/report2.htm.

Yarwood, B. (2007). *The future of facility-based long term care in america: Nursing homes and assisted living facilities*. Richmond, VA: Genworth Financial.

Subacute and Postacute Care

After completing this chapter, readers will be able to:

1. Define and describe subacute and postacute care for the purpose of clarifying these confusing terms.

2. Identify where subacute care fits in the continuum of care, the services it offers, and the consumers who use it.

3. Identify sources of financing for subacute care.

4. Identify and describe regulations affecting subacute care.

5. Identify and discuss ethical issues affecting subacute care.

6. Identify trends affecting subacute care for the near future, and describe the impact of those trends.

■ Introduction

This chapter describes subacute (and postacute) care—an often-misunderstood segment of the continuum of care—discussing its development, reasons for that development, and where it currently fits in the continuum, as well as the nature of the consumers who use subacute care and what they seek from it. It is misunderstood because it contains several elements that frequently overlap and are referenced by different names. The terms *subacute care* and *postacute care* cover some, but not all, of the same services. In fact, discussing both subacute care and postacute care in the same chapter could be called arbitrary. However, we do so in an attempt to bring some clarity to the issue.

We discuss postacute care primarily in the context of explaining the terminology. The chapter explores issues related to financing, staffing, and regulation as they impact subacute care, and it identifies several trends promising such impact in the future.

■ What Is Postacute Care?

Postacute care (PAC)

is designed to improve the transition from hospital to the community. Post-acute care includes the recuperation, rehabilitation, and nursing services following a hospitalization that are provided in skilled nursing facilities (SNFs), inpatient rehabilitation facilities (IRFs), and long-term care hospitals (LTCHs), and by home health agencies (HHAs) and outpatient rehabilitation providers. (Dummit, 2011, p. 3)

■ What Is Subacute Care?

While we get to a more detailed definition of subacute care later, for now let us use a simple, straightforward definition. It is "a level of care needed by a patient who does not require hospital acute care, but who requires more intensive skilled nursing care than is provided to the majority of patients in a skilled nursing facility" (CA Subacute Care Unit, 2012). One author suggests we think of subacute care as:

a passageway through which increasing numbers of patients travel. What happens during that experience can range from a set of basic rehabilitation services to a much richer array of therapy, teaching, and medical progress. Medical, and often psychosocial, complexity characterizes subacute care. (Buxbaum, 2009)

■ What Is the Difference Between Postacute Care and Subacute Care?

Both subacute and postacute care are substitutes for acute care, resulting in less cost to the system and to third-party payers and in more convenience for the patient. However, there are differences as shown by the following:

Subacute Care	Postacute Care
May be either after or in place of acute care	Happens after acute care
Provides inpatient services	Provides outpatient services
Provides medical and nursing care	Provides nursing and/or nonmedical care

Postacute care may even be provided following subacute care as an outpatient follow-up to inpatient subacute care.

■ Postacute Care

We begin this discussion with a look at who provides postacute care. Postacute care may be provided in or by several different types of providers, including the following:

- Inpatient rehabilitation hospitals and units
- LTCHs
- Skilled nursing facilities
- Home health agencies (CMS, 2012)

Each of the multiple PAC settings specializes in certain types of care and therapies, allowing patients to receive a diverse array of services ranging from intensive medical, rehabilitation, and respiratory care to in-home follow-up, such as changing dressings or administering medication. Patients receive a unique set of services in each PAC setting, though some services may be available in more than one setting. Selecting the most appropriate setting for a given patient may involve multiple factors. Some patients may benefit from care at multiple PAC settings during a single episode of illness (AHA, 2010). Because both skilled nursing facilities and home health agencies are discussed in detail elsewhere, we discuss them here only as they relate to the others in postacute care or subacute care. Let us examine the other two categories (inpatient rehabilitation facilities and long-term care hospitals) here. It is also worth noting that postacute care may also be provided in outpatient settings and adult day care. However, these services are not covered by Medicare and are not significant in terms of the number of patients utilizing them as postacute care.

Inpatient Rehabilitation Facilities

In a broad sense, rehabilitation services are measures taken to promote optimum attainable levels of physical, cognitive, emotional, psychological, social, and economic usefulness and thereafter to maintain the individual at the maximal functional level. The term is used to denote services "provided in inpatient and outpatient settings, ranging from comprehensive, coordinated, medically based programs in specialized hospital settings to therapies offered in units of hospitals, nursing facilities, or ambulatory centers" (AHA, 2013). Subacute rehabilitation care provides continuity of care for patients who no longer require hospitalization but still need skilled medical care in a rehabilitation facility. Subacute rehabilitation is recommended when a patient is not functionally able to return home. Instead, during recuperation, patients receive rehabilitation in a skilled nursing facility. Medicare requires that skilled nursing facilities provide an intensive rehabilitation program, and patients who are admitted must be able to tolerate 3 hours of intense rehabilitation services per day. For classification as an IRF, a percentage of the IRF's total patient population during the IRF's cost reporting period must match 1 or more of 13 specific medical conditions (CMS, 2012).

In 2001, the Centers for Medicare & Medicaid Services (CMS) published a prospective payment system (PPS) for Medicare IRFs as required by the Balanced Budget Act of 1997. The payment system, which became effective January 1, 2002, significantly changed how inpatient medical rehabilitation hospitals and units are paid under Medicare.

The number of inpatient rehabilitation facilities declined slightly in 2009 after remaining stable for several years before that (MedPac, 2013).

Long-Term Care Hospitals

LTCHs "typically provide extended medical and rehabilitative care for patients who are clinically complex and may suffer from multiple acute or chronic conditions. Services may include comprehensive rehabilitation, respiratory therapy, cancer treatment, head trauma treatment, and pain management" (CMS, 2012, p. 7).

LTCHs are certified as hospitals, meeting the same minimum staffing requirements, range of services, and life-safety standards. In addition, LTCHs are required to have an average Medicare length of stay of more than 25 days, which is intended to ensure that their patients are medically complex. LTCHs that are located within an acute care hospital—the fastest growing segment of these providers—are subject to additional requirements that limit the share of their patients admitted from the host hospital. The number of LTCHs rose from 278 in 2001 to 432 in 2009. In spite of a moratorium on new LTCHs beginning in October 2007, the number of these facilities continued to grow through 2010, then remained constant from 2011 to 2012 (MedPac, 2013). In some areas of the country where they are not available, acute care hospitals and SNFs substitute (Dummit, 2011). IRFs are either freestanding facilities, sometimes called rehabilitation hospitals, or rehabilitation units located within acute care hospitals (Singh, 2010).

While Medicare covers LTCHs, there has been concern that they are not an efficient use of resources. Although each of the other types of postacute care (IRFs, skilled nursing facilities, and home health) has standardized data collection and systems, no assessment instrument is mandated for LTCHs (CMS, 2012).

Use of Postacute Care

About one-third of hospital patients go on to use postacute care. The most common, single, postacute care destination for beneficiaries discharged from acute inpatient care hospitals is a skilled nursing facility. Although some episodes involve multiple settings, they generally include only one postacute setting (MedPac, 2013).

Medicare Conditions of Participation

Postacute providers must also meet different conditions of participation. For example, physicians must be integrally involved in care provided in rehabilitation facilities and long-term care hospitals, but are required to visit an SNF patient only once every 30 days for the first 90 days and every 60 days thereafter. Requirements for physician involvement in home health care are even less stringent.

Rehabilitation facilities are required to have 75% of their admissions in 1 of 10 specific diagnoses related to conditions requiring rehabilitation services. LTCHs' only condition of participation in addition to those required of all hospitals is to have an average Medicare length of stay greater than 25 days (MedPac, 2013).

As one can see, Medicare is a major factor influencing postacute care services due to its reimbursement of those services and the rules that go with that reimbursement. Postacute care currently makes up about 11% of Medicare's total spending (MedPac, 2013). The CMS has been concerned that the system for reimbursing and monitoring postacute care is poorly defined and contains some inconsistencies, and it has implemented a postacute care reform plan. That plan calls for a demonstration project to assess the system and develop reforms (MedPac, 2013).

Bundled Payments

Like other Medicare-certified providers, postacute care providers will be impacted by the CMS's Bundled Payments for Care Improvement initiative. Under the Bundled Payments initiative, organizations known as accountable care organizations will enter into payment arrangements that include financial and performance accountability for episodes of care. The hospital-based accountable care organizations will receive the Medicare payments for all other services and will contract with long-term care providers for postacute care. Medicare will pay the accountable care organizations for covered services delivered during an episode of care that is initiated with a hospitalization and continues for 30 days after discharge (Dummit, 2011). The accountable care organizations will then pay the contracted providers and will be held accountable by the CMS for the quality outcomes associated with this postacute care.

Readmissions

The Affordable Care Act of 2010 reduces payments to hospitals for greater-than-expected readmissions, decreasing payments for all Medicare discharges in the prior year. Acute care hospitals and PAC providers will work to reduce rehospitalizations (AHA, 2010).

■ Subacute Care

Having hopefully clarified the terms *subacute care* and *postacute care*, we focus the remainder of this chapter on subacute care, referencing postacute care as needed.

How Did Subacute Care Come to Be?

Subacute care is probably one of the newest entries into the continuum of care. (*Probably* is used here because of the rapidity with which new types of care and mutations of established types of care are emerging.) It is also one of the fastest growing segments of the healthcare delivery system. Over the past several decades, it has grown and developed, slowly at first, then more rapidly. It has also become somewhat better defined. At first, it was best defined by what it was not. It was not really acute care, nor was it long-term care. It was pretty much anything that fell in between the two. As the healthcare field reacted to the forces at work on it during the 1980s and 1990s (forces such as pressures to be cost effective, increased demand for consumer choice, and competition between providers), subacute care found its niche. It became a defined service instead of a somewhat nebulous gap filler.

Defining Subacute Care

Subacute care

> includes post-acute services for people who require convalescence from acute illnesses or surgical episodes. These patients may be recovering but are still subject to complications while in recovery. They require more nursing intervention than what is typically included in skilled nursing care. (Singh, 2010, p. 15)

It is a level of care needed by a patient who does not require hospital acute care but who requires more intensive skilled nursing care than is provided to the majority of patients in a skilled nursing facility. Subacute patients are medically fragile and require special services, such as inhalation therapy, tracheotomy care, intravenous tube feeding, and complex wound management care. Pediatric subacute care is a level of care needed by a person less than 21 years of age. These patients generally use medical technology to compensate for the loss of a vital bodily function (CA Subacute Care Unit, 2012).

Philosophy of Care

Subacute care is specific care rendered for very specific reasons. Conditions that may be appropriate for inpatient subacute care include but are not limited to:

- Cardiac recovery
- Oncology recovery—receiving chemotherapy and radiation
- Pulmonary conditions
- Orthopedic rehabilitation
- Neurological disorders/cerebrovascular accident
- Complex wound management
- Intravenous therapy (Anthem, 2013)

Initially, subacute care was seen as a form of postacute care, or treatment rendered immediately after acute hospitalization. Over time, it also began to be used in place of acute hospitalization, both as a cost-saving measure and in the interests of providing treatment in the least restrictive location and manner.

It is generally thought of as a transitional phase of care, moving the patient to home or to a long-term care facility in a short time. However, there are other variations. There seem to be four generally agreed-upon categories of subacute care, best defined by Kathleen Griffin in her *Handbook of Subacute Care,* which has become the authority on the subject (Griffin, 1995). The first category she identifies is transitional subacute care, which is usually quite short term, serving as a means of transitioning from highly intensive hospital units while maintaining the availability of acute care if needed. As such, transitional units are usually located at or near hospitals and operated by those hospitals.

A second type of subacute care is referred to as general subacute care. Lengths of stay are somewhat longer for those receiving general subacute care than those in transitional units. Patients needing ongoing therapy or monitoring fall into this group. General subacute care units are apt to be owned and operated by either hospitals or nursing facilities (Griffin, 1995).

The third category is chronic subacute care. These units care for patients with serious chronic conditions requiring services such as ventilator or intravenous therapy. Their average stay is longer than the transitional or general subacute care units, but most patients stay only about 60 to 90 days before they are transferred to a lower level of care or before they die (Griffin, 1995).

The last category described by Griffin is long-term transitional subacute care. It is usually hospital-based care for patients with more complex medical problems who need more intensive (but still not acute) care over a longer time before transitioning to home or another level of care (Griffin, 1995).

Thus, subacute care, as a portion of the continuum, is best defined in terms of the type, amount, and duration of care given. There is emphasis on staff with skills in assessment of patients' conditions and the ability to adjust treatment plans as needed. They must also be skillful at managing specific conditions such as strokes or post–cardiac surgery and in performing specific procedures such as ventilator therapy or pain management. Although Griffin's book is 2 decades old, these categories and definitions are still valid and one of the best ways to differentiate the various forms of subacute care.

Ownership of Subacute Care Units

As noted earlier, subacute care is identified by the services offered, not necessarily by who the providers are. Often, subacute care is provided by existing hospitals or freestanding nursing facilities. Increasingly, both groups are becoming part of integrated healthcare networks. Subacute care units, when affiliated with hospitals or nursing facilities, are usually classified as SNFs by Medicare for reasons of reimbursement and are often the result of reclassifying beds in a designated unit.

Freestanding SNFs are the most prevalent form of subacute care, followed by hospital-based units. The hospital-based units generally function as swing-bed units, allowing the patient to change classification without actually moving.

An important trend in ownership of subacute care units, a trend supported by all available studies, is the large proportion owned and operated by chains, either regional or national. They have the financial resources and staff expertise to develop and operate such services where many independent owners do not.

Services Provided

Services provided in subacute care units vary depending on the nature of the population served, but might include the following:

- Rehabilitation
- Physical and occupational therapy
- Respiratory therapy
- Cardiac rehabilitation
- Speech therapy
- Postsurgical care
- Chemotherapy
- Total parenteral nutrition
- Dialysis
- Pain management
- Complex medical care
- Wound management
- Ventilation care
- Other specialty care

Planning how care will be delivered to consumers is important in all forms of health care, but the terms *care planning* and *case management* have taken on more importance in subacute care than in some of those others, largely due to the influence of reimbursement sources. Care planning is discussed next; case management will be discussed later in this chapter.

Care Planning

A key to successfully providing subacute care is good care planning. It involves assessing each individual patient's needs, developing a care plan to meet those needs, and constantly reviewing the care plan and adjusting it as needed. If not done carefully, by qualified staff, care planning may produce negative results, including longer-than-necessary lengths of stay or inadequate treatment. The former results in excessive costs to the organization. The latter leads to dissatisfied patients, which, in turn, may lead to dissatisfied reimbursement organizations.

The care plan begins with a detailed assessment of each patient. Members of the interdisciplinary team must have assessment skills in addition to knowing how to provide specific treatments. The entire team is involved in the assessment process, and each member has something specific to offer. It is their collective evaluation that results in a good care plan. Together, they develop care goals for the patient—goals that might focus on returning the patient to home, improving or maintaining the level of functional independence, stabilizing a medical condition, or any of a variety of similar end results. Those goals must be accurately defined and clearly understood by all involved, including the patient.

There must be clearly established admission criteria to determine the parameters within which the team may work. Those criteria should be explicit and include definitions of the types of patients and patient conditions for which the facility is qualified to care.

Care planning by the interdisciplinary team is not a one-time occurrence. It goes on throughout the course of treatment. It is generally recognized that the team will hold care-planning conferences to review the plan and the patient's progress at least weekly, more often if the patient's medical or functional status changes. It must be a dynamic process, capable of quickly identifying and assessing changes and responding to them in a timely and appropriate manner, which requires that the team members be skilled in assessment techniques.

These interdisciplinary team meetings should include all who are involved in the patient's care, as well as the patient, family members, and other caregivers. It is an information-sharing session as well as an opportunity to evaluate progress against the original care plan.

The care plan, including the assessment on which it is based and the periodic evaluation and adjustments of that plan, does not represent the end of the process by a long shot. To be successful, subacute care must include an outcomes-based measure of how well the program met its goals. There must be a process for determining the effectiveness of the treatment plan. That effectiveness is measured by changes in the patient's medical or functional status from the beginning of the program to the end. It also includes periodic measurement against predetermined benchmarks during the treatment process.

Measuring Quality of Care

There are numerous excellent tools available for measuring outcomes-based effectiveness. For example the CARF International (formerly the Commission on Accreditation of Rehabilitation Facilities) program evaluation system contains excellent processes for measuring functional outcomes. Providers have also dealt with a couple of other programs: quality assurance and continuous program improvement—also known as program improvement—that have been replaced by quality assurance and performance improvement (QAPI).

QAPI

QAPI is the merger of two complementary approaches to quality: quality assurance and performance improvement. Both involve seeking and using information, but they differ in key ways:

- Quality assurance is a reactive, retrospective process of meeting regulatory quality standards.
- QAPI is a proactive and continuous study of processes with the intent to prevent or decrease the likelihood of problems by identifying areas of opportunity and testing new approaches to fix underlying causes of persistent/systemic problems.

QAPI is a data-driven, proactive approach to improving the quality of life, care, and services in nursing homes. According to the CMS, the activities of QAPI "involve members at all levels of the organization to: identify opportunities for improvement; address gaps in systems or processes; develop and implement an improvement or corrective plan; and continuously monitor effectiveness of interventions" (CMS, 2013).

Whatever process, or combination of processes, a subacute care program chooses to utilize, there must be a method of measuring what the program accomplished on behalf of its patients. Patients will seek that information, as will agencies providing reimbursement, and any licensing or accreditation organizations involved. Even if they did not, the provider needs to know how well it is performing. Anecdotal evidence of patient satisfaction is valuable but should be supported by some type of tangible, quantifiable confirmation that the program is producing the results it expects and promises.

Outcomes measurement should not stop at discharge. Most subacute care services are aimed at producing results that will improve the patient's medical or functional status. If effective, those results will last, at least for a reasonable period. Yet, the very nature of the conditions being treated causes those results to diminish over time. An effective outcomes measurement program will extend beyond discharge far enough to document how well the treatment results lasted, usually at least 90 days. It provides the program with information about how well the patient was prepared for discharge, indicating the efficacy of follow-up arrangements and the preparation of the patient to continue treatments or to maintain the functional or medical status achieved while receiving subacute care.

Both quality and cost outcomes should be measured. It is obviously important that the quality and efficacy of care be proven. However, payment sources, particularly managed care organizations (MCOs), expect subacute care providers to document their efficiency as well.

Postdischarge measurement also provides a mechanism for detecting problems with the discharge planning process and sometimes with the plans themselves. It identifies potential slippage in the patient's status, indicating the need for further, more intense intervention. As such, it is an integral part of the entire treatment process. Just as there must be clear criteria for admission to the subacute care organization, so must there be criteria for discharge. The unit must have transfer agreements with appropriate facilities so that the care-planning team is able to discharge appropriately and in a timely fashion, without unnecessary delays or gaps in coverage.

Case Management

There is another element in managing the process of providing subacute care. It is case management, not to be confused with care management. While care management is concerned with the type and quality of care received, case management's primary goal is the cost-effectiveness of the care given.

The actual process of case management parallels the care-planning process, with many similarities. In fact, the case manager is an integral part of the interdisciplinary team and is involved each step of the way. The difference is that the case manager's focus is more on the degree of efficiency with which care is given. He or she manages the utilization of resources expended in providing care.

Case managers are often employed by payers, particularly MCOs, to protect their interests. Those external case managers often have powers to approve or disapprove treatment, including specific procedures. They seek to control high-cost procedures, limiting or eliminating expenses deemed unnecessary.

There may not always be an external case manager in subacute care, depending on the payer, but there will usually be an internal case manager employed by the unit. That person's job involves both patient outcomes and cost. The internal case manager is more closely involved with the patient care team than the external case manager is likely to be. In fact, one major role of the unit's case manager is to act as a liaison with the case manager employed by the payer and to negotiate with the payer's representative to secure authorization and payment for needed supplies, equipment, and procedures. He or she also functions as a liaison with other entities, including the clinical team, the patient, and the patient's family. Lastly, do not get the impression that the subacute care organization's case manager is only concerned with minimizing costs. That person is also the patient's advocate. A clinical background is very useful.

The role requires a combination of coordination, monitoring, and control. The internal case manager must be knowledgeable of the rules governing payment for services and must keep up with any changes in eligibility or coverage provisions that would affect reimbursement to the provider.

The use of case managers by the providers and payers has become standard practice in subacute care and some other types of health care. It is based on a sound philosophy of managing the process of providing care to ensure that it is efficient, cost effective, and not unnecessarily expensive. However, it raises certain questions and has led to some disagreement and controversy, particularly among healthcare policy makers. The case manager functions as a gatekeeper—the person who controls access to care. Who should be the gatekeeper? Can anyone objectively serve the three principal participants (the patient, the provider, and the payer)? When the gatekeeper works for the provider, the payer worries that unneeded services will be provided to generate revenue.

At the same time, the patient worries that the provider will skimp on services to save expenses. If the payer employs the gatekeeper, the provider and patient both worry that cost will take precedence over quality or even over required care. Lastly, if the patient or a surrogate (an ombudsman, legal representative, or other advocate) serves as gatekeeper, the provider and payers fear excessive use of services at their expense.

Who should be the gatekeeper? There is no easy answer. Perhaps the most effective, but certainly not the neatest or most efficient, solution lies in having three gatekeepers who each represent one of the parties. Through a system of checks and counterchecks, they keep each other in balance. The one who is most likely to be at a disadvantage is the patient, who has to rely to some degree on the good faith and honorable intentions of the others to act in his or her best interests. It is an interesting dilemma and one for which subacute care may be leading the way toward a system that comes closest to a solution. The relative newness of subacute care leaves more room for experimentation and innovation than some of the more traditional segments of health care. The major role played by MCOs in subacute care, when compared with nursing facilities, home care, and other forms of long-term care, is also increasing the popularity of case management. It is a concept that is here to stay, although its shape may change many times over the next few years.

Consumers Served

Subacute care serves a variety of types of patients, but it tends to treat more of some types than others. They are patients needing a high level of skilled care, generally with a defined treatment plan and timetable for discharge or transfer to another type of care. They need rehabilitation, monitoring, or other specialized treatment. People of all ages require and receive subacute care, but as with most long-term care, the majority are elderly.

■ Market Forces Affecting Subacute Care

Subacute care has grown in response to several factors in the healthcare environment.

Cost-Saving Efforts

The primary force has been financial. With the replacement of the historical, retrospective, cost-based method of reimbursing hospitals by a PPS, hospitals came under considerable pressure to keep lengths of stay in acute care as short as possible. At the heart of PPS was a system of diagnosis-related groups. Under the system of diagnosis-related groups, hospitals were being reimbursed for the episode of illness, not by the day. They sought ways to discharge patients earlier or to find less expensive settings for them. This set up a general movement within the healthcare system of patients to a lower level of care intensity. It, in turn, raised the acuity level of patients/residents at each level. Subacute patients did not need the high-end acute services offered by hospitals but needed more than traditional nursing facilities were equipped to provide.

Providers and reimbursement agencies alike quickly realized that a care/payment category in the middle made sense. Reimbursers—primarily Medicare—were able to pay a lower rate for subacute services than they would for acute care. Hospitals received a rate lower than their acute rate but more than a nursing care rate.

Diagnosis-related groups created another market force that also led to creation of more subacute care units. Hospitals found themselves, many for the first time, with low occupancy rates and entire units of empty beds. Creation of a new, in-between, level of care enabled them to fill some of those beds. It also allowed them to legitimately keep patients longer. By converting acute patient units to subacute care, they were able to make more efficient and effective use of their expensive buildings, equipment, and staff. The bundled payments program of the Affordable Care Act places more emphasis on coordination of effort between acute and subacute providers in reducing costs.

Managed Care

The most important market force driving the growth of subacute care, however, has been the emergence and rapid expansion of managed care. MCOs have found subacute care to be an excellent resource for them in their quest to find lower cost alternatives to acute hospitals.

Nursing care facilities have also found reasons to enter the subacute care arena, including making themselves attractive to MCOs. Their administrators are faced with both an opportunity and a challenge to meet higher demands for managed care (Singh, 2010).

Medicare and MCOs were not the only reimbursers seeking ways to reduce their costs. Others, such as private insurance companies, spurred on by their corporate customers, were also reacting to major increases in the cost of providing and insuring health care. They sought mechanisms for controlling those costs, including mandatory second opinions and preadmission authorization. Subacute care gave them an opportunity to cover needed care for their policyholders at a lower cost.

Many nursing facilities also foresaw the competition coming from hospitals and decided to get into subacute care as a means of expanding, or at least maintaining, their market share. Others were not as proactive, but many of them have come to realize that subacute care is an area that they can share with hospitals or be left out.

Choice

Another, nonfinancial force affecting the growth of subacute care was the rising demand by healthcare consumers for more choice in their care. They made it very clear that they want as much care as is necessary but do not want to be in what they see as more restrictive acute hospitals if it is not needed. Again, subacute care units provide them with a middle-ground alternative.

Regulations

Subacute care was created in part because of regulations (primarily those associated with the prospective payment system); thus, has it been further shaped and defined by regulations. Subacute care is similar to other parts of the continuum of care in that it is governed by a plethora of regulations. It is, however, somewhat different from the more established entities such as hospitals and nursing facilities because of its relative newness. It is still somewhat immature as a regulated industry segment, but it is rapidly catching up with the other provider groups.

Just as subacute care is neither hospital care nor nursing facility care as such, it has been treated as a kind of hybrid by regulators. Hospital regulations do not fit it well. Although applied to subacute care, they have not adequately met the needs of either providers or regulators in that area. Nor have nursing facility regulations. Those regulations were designed for other types and levels of care, with different patient populations, care goals, and staffing. Healthcare regulations dealing with quality of care, reimbursement, and management of one type of provider cannot readily be applied to another in a one-size-fits-all manner. That is particularly true when there are already several different sets of regulation applying to older types of service providers.

For example, federal law requires that all nursing facility administrators be licensed in their respective states, but there is no such regulation applicable to hospital administrators. If subacute care fits somewhere in between, should their administrators be licensed or not?

There is need for regulations tailored to subacute care. It is an established form of healthcare service. Although newer than most others, it has enough of a track record for regulators to use to create appropriate regulations that protect consumers from poor quality and the government from excessive costs. Current regulations do neither adequately. Yet, because they are being applied, they often serve as obstacles to providers who are trying to further refine this growing field.

Other regulations to which subacute care providers are subject come from several different sources, as do those covering other types of health care. However, the lack of subacute-specific regulations muddies the waters even more.

Medicare certification regulations cover areas such as staffing, length of stay, organizational form, patients' rights, and required services. Subacute care providers find it difficult to comply with them because there are discrepancies from one type of provider to another in some of those regulations.

Other regulations applying to subacute care are those associated with the Omnibus Budget Reconciliation Act of 1987 (OBRA). Also referred to as the Nursing Home Reform Act, OBRA made major changes in the long-term care industry. Its rules, which are very prescriptive concerning such things as facility design, staffing patterns, care plans, and services provided, are much more rigid than those to which hospitals are accustomed. However, they have been determined to apply to all SNFs certified by Medicare, including hospital-based units. Hospitals have found themselves hard pressed to conform to those more definitive regulations.

Medicaid regulations also affect subacute care providers, although they vary from state to state. There are often crossover regulations affecting both Medicare and Medicaid, particularly in terms of eligibility.

Subacute care providers are also subject to certificate of need (CON) regulations where CON laws still are in effect. Certificate of need laws were first passed to control new capital expenditures and services. The purpose of such laws was to limit overall healthcare spending by limiting expansion of services or the building of healthcare facilities. They have been scrapped in many states, but in those states still enforcing CON regulations, subacute care providers must go through a lengthy, and often expensive, review process in order to get approval to create a new subacute care service. Some states have created a virtual moratorium on certain types of new construction. Providers wishing to open a new unit then have to buy a CON approval from another provider, purchase an existing facility's licensed bed complement, or gain that approval through a joint venture with an organization that has already received such approval. It is not uncommon for potential subacute providers to avoid states with restrictive CON laws still in effect.

While inapplicable, fragmented regulations are the bane of any provider's existence, and the situation in subacute care is particularly bad, do not think that those providers are not capable of taking advantage of that confusion. They, like providers in any highly regulated industry, know where to find the loopholes and are surprisingly adept at leveraging the system to their advantage, which may lead to some unfortunate gamesmanship between regulators and the regulated, such as the purchase of CONs as just described. Also, some providers have taken advantage of the inability of regulations in those programs to prevent abuses. In response, the CMS—formerly the Health Care Financing Administration—implemented an all-out effort to make changes needed to stop them (Hyatt & Cornish, 1997). It was a laudable effort, but one that might have been avoided, at least in part, if a similar level of effort had been devoted to developing clear, applicable regulations to this new segment of the industry.

Some states have looked at separate regulations for subacute care but have not addressed subacute care directly. This only added to the already high level of uncertainty pervading the field of subacute care. Reform efforts have, however, often resulted in an increase in managed care, including coverage of public constituencies such as Medicaid patients. Those efforts, based in large part on a desire to save money, have indirectly benefited subacute care.

Before leaving this brief look at regulations, it should be noted that subacute care providers are also subject to other types of regulations just as are other healthcare providers and, in most cases, other industries. They are subject to regulations affecting employment and treatment of their staff that come from sources such as the Occupational Safety and Health Administration, the Wage and Hour Division of the U.S. Department of Labor, the Equal Employment Opportunity Commission, worker's compensation acts, the Americans With Disabilities Act, the Fair Labor Standards Act, the Family Medical Leave Act, and others.

They must also comply with regulations affecting building construction/safety such as the Life Safety Code and local building codes. The Occupational Safety and Health Administration and Americans With Disabilities Act also contain regulations concerning building construction and safety.

■ Accreditation

Voluntary accreditation and certification is much further ahead than regulation in attempting to ensure quality in subacute care. The Joint Commission (formerly the Joint Commission on Accreditation of Healthcare Organizations) and CARF International both took the early lead in implementing subacute care quality standards.

The Joint Commission, instead of developing an entirely new set of standards for subacute care, took portions of its existing hospital and long-term care standards and adapted them to fit this in-between level of care. Actually, the standards are changed little if at all, but the interpretation of those standards, on which the survey is based, was tailored to reflect differences in staffing, care plans, and physical facility requirements. It has worked surprisingly well, although it is not as refined as subacute-specific standards would probably be.

CARF International took a somewhat different approach. It was, after all, focused on rehabilitation and had considerable experience in accrediting agencies and organizations providing a variety of rehabilitation services, as compared with the Joint Commission's broader healthcare focus. Thus, CARF International included medical rehabilitation, including subacute care, under the overall umbrella of comprehensive rehabilitation programs. Three subcategories were developed, taking into account the different levels and types of rehabilitation care (acute or subacute), the provider location (hospital-based or freestanding skilled nursing facilities), and patient outcome goals. CARF International standards and survey processes have long been more outcome oriented than those of the Joint Commission, but the latter organization has made significant changes over the past few years to the point where it is also focused on outcomes. It should be noted here that CARF International merged with the Continuing Care Accreditation Commission in 2003, but that did not have any significant impact on subacute care accreditation.

The National Committee for Quality Assurance (NCQA) is directed primarily at MCOs. However, as subacute care providers or the parent organizations under which they operate wish to contract with MCOs, they must be aware of the NCQA standards, what they are, what they require, and how best to meet them.

Subacute care provider organizations that are part of MCOs will have to meet these standards. However, they are not alone. Other subacute care providers will also have to adopt strategies designed to comply with NCQA standards if they wish to compete successfully for managed care contracts.

Subacute care providers are seeking voluntary accreditation at a much faster pace than are traditional nursing facilities, perhaps reflecting the influence of hospitals, for whom accreditation is a long-standing norm. Accreditation is also a valuable credential for any organization trying to survive in a competitive marketplace to have. Many subacute care units are accredited by the Joint Commission, another group is accredited by CARF International, and a smaller group by state or other accrediting bodies.

In a business without clear regulations to govern it and document excellence or the lack of it, accreditation becomes an even more useful credential to have.

■ Financing Subacute Care

The problems stemming from attempting to use regulations designed for hospitals and/or nursing facilities with subacute care also affect the financing of those services. Because subacute care reimbursement has been in such a state of change, with new rules and formats occurring regularly and numerous demonstration projects under scrutiny, we do not get into a lot of detail about it in this chapter. If we did so, it would probably be out of date before the reader gets to it. Instead, we present a broad overview—enough to provide a basic understanding of how subacute care is financed.

There is no single payer for subacute services, nor is there any standardized payment mechanism. Medicare and private insurance are the primary source for subacute nursing home care funding. Medicare pays 68% while private insurance and individual self-pay account for 22%, with the remainder coming from other sources such as the patient or his or her family (ParentGiving, 2013).

Medicare

Just as Medicare had moved from a retrospective, cost-based payment system to a PPS for acute care hospitals some years earlier, subacute care made a similar move as the result of the Balanced Budget Act of 1997. Under the PPS, providers receive payment based on preestablished rates for specific services instead of receiving direct reimbursement for their costs.

Managed Care

One trend that does seem to be holding true is the increased influence of managed care in financing of subacute care. Recent information suggests that the managed care portion of subacute care is growing very rapidly. Not only are private MCOs growing, both in number and in size, but government programs are also moving in that direction. A majority of states have been experimenting with managed care for Medicaid patients as a cost-cutting measure. Several of the federal initiatives that have been proposed would also encourage managed care for both Medicare and Medicaid.

■ Staffing and Human Resource Issues

Like most other aspects of subacute care, staffing requirements fall somewhere between acute care staffing and nursing facility staffing. There are some basic elements, however, that must be included. Subacute care requires the coordinated services of an interdisciplinary team including physicians, nurses, and other relevant professional disciplines sufficiently trained and knowledgeable to assess and manage these specific conditions and perform the necessary procedures (Anthem, 2013).

An Interdisciplinary Team

First, the subacute care provider must adopt a philosophy of care based on an interdisciplinary team. There must also be an organizational structure that recognizes that approach and supports the philosophy, which is not enough in itself. The actual makeup of the team will vary somewhat but would include a program administrator, a medical director, case managers, and any or all of the following clinical disciplines: other physicians, nursing, social services, psychology, physical therapy, occupational therapy, speech-language pathology, respiratory therapy, recreation therapy, and dietary.

Program Administrator

There must be someone in charge administratively. That person might be called program manager, program director, administrator, or some variation of those titles. What is more important than the title is the clear responsibility and authority the person has for operation of the subacute care unit or facility. The program administrator, as we shall call the position for sake of simplicity, may have a related clinical background or may be trained in health care administration. Regardless of background, the person responsible for running the unit or facility must have good management skills.

Physicians

Physician coverage and direction is critical to the success of the subacute care program. There should be a medical director with designated responsibility for clinical oversight of the program, ensuring its integrity. The medical director may have other duties, including direct care of some patients, as long as those duties do not interfere with his or her primary duties. Ideally, the medical director will be trained in care of the types of patients to be treated. A medical rehabilitation unit would do well to appoint a specialist in internal medicine or a geriatrician. If the focus is more on physical reha-bilitation, a physiatrist would be preferable; for cardiac rehabilitation, a cardiologist; and so on. That may not be possible. The unit is very unlikely to treat only one type of patient; it may be hard to find a medical director with training appropriate to all of them, and such specialists are not always easy to find.

Gaps in medical specialty coverage can be filled with other physicians with the needed specialty training and experience. They may be hired on a full- or part-time basis, engaged as consultants, or allowed to admit and treat patients as independent contractors. The choice of method or methods for providing medical coverage depends on factors such as size of the program, number and type of services offered, and avail-ability of physicians with the desired specialties.

Physicians need to visit more often than in the traditional nursing facility, although generally not as often as in an acute hospital. The types of services offered and the acuity of the patients dictate the frequency of physician visits.

Nursing

Nursing coverage is also of critical importance. There must be 24-hour coverage by registered nurses. The actual amount of nursing care per patient per day depends on the type of treatment. Patients in transitional medical programs usually require more than some other rehabilitation patients. Some highly specialized subacute care, such as that in pulmonary rehabilitation or neurobehavioral programs, may require con-siderably more, even approaching acute staffing levels.

Staffing levels are subject to influence by the source of reimbursement. Government agencies such as Medicare and Medicaid have set minimum staffing requirements and maximum reimbursable expense levels, defining a pretty narrow range within which the provider must work. MCOs, with their focus on cost-effectiveness, have their own ideas about staffing. The provider must be aware of these stipulations, preferably before getting involved.

Other Professional Staff

Subacute care requires a mix of professional staff, including therapists, psycholo-gists, social workers, dietitians, and occasionally others. These disciplines, like the physicians, can be obtained through several different methods, including direct hire, consulting, and contracting through an independent company supplying such ser-vices. The volume of patient needs for a particular service component may not justify employment of full-time staff in some of these areas—and they may not be available. In such cases, the program may need to contract with an individual professional or with a contract firm. There are many excellent contract providers supplying specialty professionals to hospitals and nursing facilities. However, there may be disadvantages in using outside sources. For example, it is always easier to generate consistency of interest and effort with in-house staff.

Nonlicensed Staff

The subacute unit will also need a committed, well-trained cadre of nonlicensed workers, including nurse assistants and staff in housekeeping, maintenance, the business office, and medical records. They must also be in tune with the overall philosophy of the subacute program if they are to contribute to it.

Recruitment

Recruitment of staff is important to the success of the program. The proper number and mix of staff are needed for efficient operation. Staff also need to have training in the types of services provided. Those services may include some highly specialized treatments, such as dialysis, intravenous therapy, or wound management. There may be current staff with some of these capabilities if the subacute care program is being carved out of an existing facility or organization. If not, or if the subacute program is an entirely new venture, recruitment becomes particularly critical and must be given an appropriate level of attention and support. People with some of these specialized talents are often difficult to find. In fact, proceeding with development of a new program without ascertaining the availability of required staff ahead of time would be foolhardy at the least and could be disastrous at worst.

The degree to which the organization is able to acquire staff who already have education and experience will determine how much additional training is needed. There will always be some level of training necessary to make sure all staff are equally and adequately qualified. It must also be an ongoing process to keep staff sharp and up to date.

■ Legal and Ethical Issues

Subacute care providers entering the field of subacute care face a number of legal issues. Those issues fall into two general categories: (1) meeting licensure and reimbursement regulations and (2) professional liability.

Licensure and reimbursement issues revolve around getting approval to open and operate a subacute care unit and securing reimbursement for the services provided. These areas involving licensure and reimbursement are closely related. Regulations concerning licensure of the unit are, in many ways, the legal foundation on which reimbursement agreements are based. This is particularly true when the reimbursement, or even a portion of it, is derived from public sources, such as Medicare and Medicaid. Organizations seeking to open subacute care units should study these complex issues carefully, with the assistance of well-qualified legal counsel, preferably with experience in subacute care–related legal matters. Operators of nursing care facilities who are thinking of getting into subacute care should look carefully at several professional liability issues that may be new to them, including malpractice, incident reporting mechanisms, claims management, and credentialing of its professional staff.

■ Management of Subacute Care Units

The program administrator, while responsible for administration of the subacute care function, may fit into a variety of places within the overall organization. If the subacute care unit is a freestanding unit, functioning on its own, the administrator probably reports to a governing board. If it is part of a hospital or nursing facility organization, the subacute program administrator probably reports to an administrator at a higher level in the organizational hierarchy. The same holds true in a multiorganizational integrated healthcare network.

It is important that the administrator have access to needed staff and other resources to do the job effectively and successfully. If subacute care is a new venture for the organization, the administrator should be in place at the very beginning. He or she should have responsibility for staffing and recruitment of staff. The administrator (in any organizational setting) should have confidence in his or her staff. The best way to do that is to hire them. If a new facility is being built or if it requires major renovation of an existing space, the administrator should also be directly involved in that phase of development.

On an ongoing basis, the program administrator has overall responsibility for ensuring the quality of care given; for the effectiveness, efficiency, and productivity of staff; and for planning future activities. Those responsibilities, particularly ensuring the quality of care, may be met through the work of others, but the administrator remains accountable for their success. That requires a well-trained, skillful manager.

Management Qualifications

Subacute care administrators need the same skills as administrators of other healthcare organizations. Administrators of nursing facilities must be licensed by the states, but hospital administrators are not. With subacute care being so new and being delivered in both types of facilities, what assurance is there that the administrators are qualified? The American College of Health Care Administrators developed a program to certify subacute care administrators. That program, with its study materials, provided both training of subacute care administrators and documentation of their skills. It was a voluntary certification, but it was eventually dropped because of lack of interest by the professionals and lack of requirement for it.

Management Challenges and Opportunities

There are many reasons for creating a subacute care unit or facility. It provides an organization with many opportunities for expanded services. It is a means of gaining or protecting a market niche. Even if it only means finding new uses for currently underutilized beds or facilities, subacute care has much to recommend it. However, converting to subacute care also presents some formidable challenges. Let us look briefly at some of them.

Changing the Culture of the Organization

Any time an organization moves from one type of care to another, there are likely to be some changes in its culture. Each organization has its own culture based on a set of principles and/or beliefs that determine acceptable behaviors. Subacute care is just developing its own distinct culture, borrowing from both hospitals and nursing facilities and their established organizational cultures. Yet, either of those entities wishing to move into the subacute care arena must make some fundamental changes as well.

The dichotomy between nursing facilities and hospitals has been described as care versus cure. Acute care hospitals are accustomed to short lengths of stay, intensive medical and nursing care, and high-technology equipment. They, of necessity, place emphasis on curing the patient's particular malady.

Nursing care facilities, on the other hand, are used to caring for their residents for long periods of time. They focus on the overall person and that person's quality of life. Even the names given to these consumers of care reflect the differences. When in a hospital, they are called patients. When in a nursing facility, they are seen as residents.

Subacute care is more closely aligned with acute care. It requires relatively high-technology equipment. Services are aimed at treating a medical condition or functional limitation. Lengths of stay are shorter than in nursing facilities but longer than typical hospital lengths of stay. Required staffing patterns are higher than in nursing facilities but lower than in hospitals, both in terms of the staffing mix and the number of hours per day allocated to each patient.

The culture change involved in moving into subacute care is greater for nursing facilities than for hospitals. They must act more like acute care, turning their energies and resources to achieving short-term goals that center on improving a specific condition, instead of focusing on longer term goals related to the resident's quality of life. They must change their staffing to more closely reflect a medical model of care.

Hospitals moving to subacute care have to change their culture as well. Lengths of stay are longer than those to which they have been accustomed. They must adapt to lower staffing levels. Patients in subacute care expect more amenities related to their personal comfort. They are there longer, are usually not as ill as when in an acute care setting, and expect their living quarters to be more homelike.

These changes in organizational culture are not impossible to achieve. Indeed, many subacute care units have successfully been created out of both hospitals and nursing facilities. The biggest obstacle to doing that is an organization's inability or unwillingness to recognize that there are differences. It is not enough to simply change the name of a unit, transferring current attitudes and activities, and hoping it will work. Getting all staff, especially highly skilled physicians and nurses, to change their fundamental way of functioning is a challenge for any subacute care administrator.

Balancing Cost and Quality

It is a challenge for any healthcare organization to successfully balance quality of services with cost-effectiveness. Subacute care units are more focused on that than some other healthcare entities. There are several reasons for that, not the least of which is that subacute care came about largely as a means of providing care at a lower cost than in acute hospitals. Had that incentive not been present, it is doubtful that subacute care would have developed as rapidly as it has, if at all.

As was noted earlier, managed care is a major influence on subacute care. MCOs see subacute care as a viable alternative to higher cost treatment in acute care hospitals. As their influence on subacute care providers continues to grow, there is related pressure on those facilities to slash their operating expenses. With that cost-cutting effort comes a responsibility to ensure the continued quality of care. MCOs will not continue to contract with a subacute care provider, no matter how cost effective, if that provider cannot assure a certain level of quality. MCOs have more providers from which to choose; as competition increases in the subacute care industry, so does the need to develop meaningful measurements of facility quality. Achieving success in both cost-effectiveness and quality is not easy and presents an ongoing challenge for subacute care providers.

Coordination and Competition With Other Facilities and Organizations

Subacute care units have experienced, and can expect to continue to experience, a considerable amount of competition as others see the opportunities it presents. At the same time, subacute care units must interact with other organizations if they are to succeed. One of the challenges for any subacute care organization is maintaining a balance between the two forces of competition and cooperation. It must carefully analyze its operating environment, watching for potential collaboration opportunities as well as threats from competitors.

Subacute care is not an organizational entity that can stand on its own well. It must have sources of patients. Few subacute care patients are admitted without some prior admission to an acute hospital or some contact with an MCO and its affiliated hospital or medical staff. To succeed, the unit needs referral agreements with other levels of care. It also needs discharge opportunities for its patients.

Choosing those organizations with whom to associate and those with whom to compete requires a sound analysis and evaluation of the subacute care unit's own capabilities, its strengths, and its weaknesses, as well as the strengths and weaknesses of potential competitors or collaborators. The subacute care organization may not always have the option of choosing. Those other organizations will be going through the same analysis and evaluation process. The one that does so most effectively will be in the best position to determine its own partnerships.

Subacute care units, even those that are physically freestanding, tend to be affiliated with or owned and operated by hospitals or nursing facilities. Within those parent organizations, there is need to integrate the subacute services with others offered, while maintaining the separateness that is required for reimbursement and accreditation purposes. The physical plant, staffing, administrative oversight, and policies and procedures are all areas that should be addressed if that balance is to be sustained.

Physical Facility Considerations

As we have noted, subacute care units are often carved out of hospitals or nursing facilities. Neither of those facilities is ideal for subacute care, although for hospitals, it primarily means designating a section or a wing of the facility for subacute care. It must be a dedicated unit, either a separate facility, standing on its own, or, if part of a larger facility, physically separated from other patient units.

The unit may already have the necessary technology available. For nursing facilities, the magnitude of change is much greater. They must usually do more and spend more to convert to this different level of care. They should anticipate a significant investment in unit renovation and capital equipment, as well as in upgrading a variety of systems. They will probably have to upgrade the unit, including such improvements as adding piped-in oxygen, electric beds, and other equipment necessary for providing a higher level of care. If rehabilitation services are offered, there will likely be need for additional space for physical and occupational therapies. If the services are primarily medical, other clinical modifications will be needed.

A major change for many nursing facilities entering the subacute care business is the need for a sophisticated information system. Contracting with MCOs, documenting treatments and costs, and maintaining a successful outcomes measurement system require more data-handling capacity than many nursing facilities have traditionally had. NCQA standards require MCOs to practice utilization management. The MCOs, in turn, pass those utilization management requirements on to the providers with whom they contract. Nursing care facilities with strong information systems are more likely to be competitive for MCO contracts.

■ Significant Trends and Their Impact on Subacute Care

Change is a given in any specialty care area as new and relatively undefined as subacute care. Some change comes from trends in overall health care, some from trends more specific to long-term care, and some from trends within subacute care itself. All have the potential for causing significant, and sometimes dramatic, change within the subacute care field. We have discussed some of those trends in our earlier discussions, but let us summarize them briefly.

Managed Care

Clearly, the most important trend affecting subacute care is the increased influence of managed care. It has been a primary factor in the growth of subacute care to date and will continue into the future. Pressures to provide quality care at low cost will not diminish, further fueling the growth of managed care plans. As public entities become more experienced at applying managed care theories and practices to reducing their costs, the demand for niche providers such as subacute care will continue to expand.

That demand will encourage more and more organizations to try their hand in the area of subacute care. Not all will succeed. Some will fail because of poor planning, others because they did not provide adequate resources. A few will fail in spite of good planning and administration, simply because they are outdone by a competitor. Eventually, the field will mature and settle down some, but in the meantime there will be continued turmoil caused by new entries into the field and the resultant casualties.

Changes in Acuity Levels

As managed care and other cost-effectiveness measures continue to seek the least expensive form of care, the acuity level of patients in each type of provider will continue to rise, as it has recently. That trend is supported by consumers' desires to receive care in the most homelike setting possible. The impact on subacute care will be that patient treatments that, today, are provided in hospitals will be handled in subacute care units. That means that those units will require even more high-technology capabilities. At the other end, nursing facilities will be prepared for more of the treatments that are now commonly performed in subacute care.

Emphasis on Outcomes

Payment sources for subacute care, particularly private MCOs, will continue to emphasize outcomes as a basis for measuring organizational performance. Those outcome measures will contain both quality and cost-effectiveness components and will require that the two be balanced. As Medicare and Medicaid experiment more with managed care, it is likely that they will adopt some of the outcomes measurement systems developed in the private sector. Because they are also the primary regulators of subacute care, that may lead them away from some of the more intrusive forms of regulation, such as current survey formats, toward more outcome-oriented regulations. This may be simply wishful thinking, but there is some logic in seeing that as a trend.

■ Summary

Subacute care is the fast-growing child of the healthcare industry. Its clothes do not seem to fit. It is developing faster than it can learn the rules by which it should play, and it keeps experimenting with new and different ideas and approaches. New playmates keep appearing on the scene. Its parents—payers, regulators, and policy makers—are trying to keep up with it and, like any parent, are trying to keep it from injuring itself. However, they are finding it difficult to stay ahead of this exciting, but sometimes unruly, child they have created.

Like most children, subacute care will develop into a useful, productive adult of which its parents can be proud. The growth years may be difficult, but the very fact that it is a new industry segment and is ill defined and poorly regulated leaves room for innovation and creativity. The competition from different provider groups and from within those groups is already resulting in some outstanding examples of good care and good management.

Accrediting agencies such as the Joint Commission, CARF International, and NCQA have moved with relative speed to create standards for subacute care and are using measures based primarily on outcomes, as opposed to structure and process measures. Government regulators have not followed suit, at least at this time. They will have to if subacute care is to survive as a distinct and viable segment of the healthcare continuum.

The past several years have been exciting and challenging for all involved with subacute care. The next few years, as we move toward and into the next millennium, promise no less.

Subacute Care Case

This case involves two people. Both have been admitted to subacute care units following stays in an acute hospital. However, they are different in many ways, as is the type of care they receive. They are used here to demonstrate some of the differences in the segment of the continuum known as subacute care.

David is 17 years old. He was injured in an automobile accident several months ago. Suffering multiple fractures and some internal injuries, he has been in a hospital for several weeks. While his initial injuries have largely healed, with the help of several operations, he still faces a long, difficult period of rehabilitation. It is for that rehabilitation, as well as monitoring of his overall condition, that he has been transferred to a subacute care unit.

Joyce is 67. She has a long history of heart trouble and was admitted to the hospital following her last massive heart attack. That attack, coming on top of her already weakened heart condition, has left her in a semicomatose state. Her breathing is assisted by a mechanical ventilator, and she must be fed and medicated intravenously.

The subacute unit to which David was sent is known as a general subacute unit. It is operated by, and in conjunction with, a multilevel nursing facility. Joyce, on the other hand, was admitted to a chronic subacute care unit, operated by the hospital from which she was transferred. The difference between the two units is primarily the conditions they mostly treat and the kinds of staff and equipment needed to do what they each do best.

Both of them began their journey through subacute care with an assessment by multidisciplinary teams from the subacute units to which they were being transferred. Those assessments identified physical, medical, and mental conditions and developed individual care plans designed to best achieve the outcome goals identified for them. Because David appeared to be in need of physical rehabilitation, his assessment team was heavily weighted with therapists of one type or another, while Joyce's assessment team was much more nursing oriented.

David's outcome goal is to be able to return to his home and eventually back to school. The assessment team estimates that he will regain nearly all if not all of his previous functional independence. To achieve that, he requires intensive rehabilitation, including physical and occupational therapy. His care team is headed by a physiatrist and will focus on those therapies, although his medical condition will be watched.

Joyce's prognosis is not nearly as bright. The team assessing her agreed that she is unlikely to ever improve and sets a goal of maintaining her condition as well as possible until her death, something that is not likely to be that far distant. She does not need rehabilitation, although staff in the unit do some maintenance range-of-motion exercises with her to keep her physical condition from deteriorating. She does, however, require much more intensive nursing care and monitoring than does David and will be cared for under the watchful eye of a cardiologist.

Another difference, based on expected outcomes, is that David will receive close follow-up care after he is discharged to his home. He will probably continue some of his therapy on an outpatient basis and will be tested periodically to make sure he has not regressed in his quest for functional independence. Joyce, unfortunately, will not have that option.

While the probable results of their subacute care are expected to be so different, Joyce and David have a common reason for being transferred to those units. Their care needs are too high for them to be treated at lower levels, such as nursing facilities or at home. Yet, they do not need acute hospital care. A secondary, but very important, factor contributing to those transfers is the cost of care. David is covered by a managed care plan to which his parents belong. Joyce is eligible for Medicare. Both reimbursement sources want to give them the best care they can, but at the lowest possible cost.

Thus, these two people in such different situations both find themselves in subacute units, between hospital and nursing facility care levels. It is a kind of care that suits them both well. Until only a few years ago, David would have stayed in the hospital for many months, at an unnecessarily high cost. Joyce might have remained in the hospital also, but because she was unconscious and was going to die anyway, it is more than likely that she would have ended up in a nursing facility unprepared to provide her with the care she should have had.

■ Vocabulary Terms

The following terms are included in this chapter. They are important to the topics and issues discussed herein and should become familiar to readers. Some of the terms are also found in other chapters but may be used in different contexts. They may not be fully defined herein. Thus, readers may wish to seek other, supplementary definitions of them.

care management
care planning
CARF International
case management
case manager
certificate of need (CON)
chronic subacute care
continuous quality improvement
diagnosis-related groups
gatekeeper
general subacute care

interdisciplinary team
long-term transitional subacute care
managed care organizations (MCOs)
National Committee for Quality Assurance (NCQA)
quality assurance and performance improvement (QAPI)
skilled nursing facilities (SNFs)
subacute care
transitional subacute care

■ Discussion Questions

The following questions are presented to assist you in understanding the material covered in this chapter. They tend to be general but lend themselves to detailed answers. The answers to these questions can be found in the chapter.

1. What are postacute and subacute care?
2. Where is subacute care provided, and by whom?
3. What types of services are included in subacute care?
4. How and why did subacute care develop?
5. How is subacute care financed?
6. What regulations apply to subacute care?
7. What is the difference between care management and case management?
8. In reference to the case at the end of this chapter, consider the following:
   a. How can subacute care meet the needs of such different patients as David and Joyce?
   b. Should both be included in a single care category, or should different levels of care be created for them?
   c. Is subacute care really a response to patient needs, or is it a way of increasing financing for providers?

   NOTE: This question applies to the overall system, but applying it to the case will assist you in seeing the implications for those using the system.

■ References

AHA. (2014). *Rehabilitation*. Retrieved from American Hospital Association: http://www.aha.org/advocacy-issues/postacute/rehab/index.shtml.

American Hospital Association (AHA). (2010, June). *Maximizing the value of post-acute care*. Retrieved from http://www.aha.org/research/reports/tw/10nov-tw-postacute.pdf.

Anthem. (2013, May 9). *Inpatient subacute care*. Retrieved from http://www.anthem.com/medicalpolicies/guidelines/gl_pw_a050124.htm.

Buxbaum, R. (2009, March). *Subacute care: The road ahead*. Retrieved from http://www.annalsoflongtermcare.com/content/subacute-care-the-road-ahead.

CA Subacute Care Unit. (2012). *Subacute care*. Retrieved from http://www.dhcs.ca.gov/provgovpart/Pages/SubacuteCare.aspx.

Centers for Medicare & Medicaid Services (CMS). (2012). *Post acute care reform plan*. Washington, DC: Centers for Medicare & Medicaid Services. Retrieved from http://www.cms.gov/Medicare/Medicare-Fee-for-Service-Payment/SNFPPS/Downloads/pac_reform_plan_2006.pdf.

Centers for Medicare and Medicaid Services (CMS). (2013, June 5). *QAPI description and background*. Retrieved from http://cms.gov/Medicare/Provider-Enrollment-and-Certification/QAPI/qapidefinition.html.

Dummit, L. (2011, March 28). *Medicare's bundling pilot: Including post-acute care services*. Retrieved from http://www.nhpf.org/library/issue-briefs/IB841_BundlingPostAcuteCare_03-28-11.pdf.

Griffin, K. (1995). *Handbook of Subacute Health Care.* Gaithersburg, MD: Aspen Publishers.

Hyatt, L., & Cornish, K. (1997). Regulations to watch for in 1997. *Journal of Long-Term Care Administration*, pp. 21–23.

MedPac. (2013). *A data book: Healthcare spending and the Medicare program, June 2005.* Washington, DC: Centers for Medicare & Medicaid Services.

ParentGiving. (2013). *What is subacute nursing home care?* Retrieved from http://www.parentgiving .com/elder-care/skilled-nursing-facility-sub-acute/.

Singh, D. (2010). *Effective management of long-term care facilities* (2nd ed.). Sudbury, MA: Jones and Bartlett Learning.

Assisted Living

After completing this chapter, readers will be able to:

1. Define and describe assisted living facilities, where they fit in the continuum of care, the consumers who use them, and the services they offer.

2. Identify sources of financing for assisted living facilities.

3. Identify and describe regulations affecting assisted living facilities.

4. Identify and discuss ethical issues affecting assisted living facilities.

5. Identify trends affecting assisted living facilities in the foreseeable future, and describe the impact of those trends.

▪ Introduction

The Assisted Living Federation of America (2013) defines assisted living as "a long-term care option that combines housing, support services and health care, as needed. Assisted living is designed for individuals who require assistance with everyday activities such as meals, medication management or assistance, bathing, dressing and transportation." Many assisted living communities provide specialized services for people with Alzheimer's disease and other dementias (Polzer, 2013). In the continuum of care, assisted living bridges the gap between home care and nursing homes. It provides services for those who are unable to live independently but require less care than is provided by a nursing home (MetLife Market Institute, 2012). Assisted living is preferred by many individuals and their families because of its emphasis on resident choice, dignity, and privacy.

Throughout the remainder of this discussion, we use the term *assisted living* in the context of the preceding definitions. When other terms (e.g., *residential care*) are specifically indicated, such as in reference to a particular state's regulations, those terms are used.

There are a few other terms used in reference to senior housing that are sometimes confused with assisted living. To clarify them, definitions from the Assisted Living Federation of America (ALFA, 2013) are discussed in the following sections.

Independent Living

Independent living refers to:

> a residential living setting for elderly or senior adults that may or may not provide hospitality or supportive services. Under this living arrangement, the senior adult leads an independent lifestyle that requires minimal or no extra assistance. Independent living may also include rental-assisted or market-rate apartments or cottages. (ALFA, 2013)

Congregate Housing

Congregate housing "is similar to independent living, except that it usually provides convenience or supportive services like meals, housekeeping, and transportation in addition to rental housing" (ALFA, 2013).

Continuing Care Retirement Community

A continuing care retirement community is:

> a community that offers several levels of assistance, including independent living, assisted living, and nursing home care. It is different from other housing and care facilities for seniors because it usually provides a written agreement or long-term contract between the resident (frequently lasting the term of the resident's lifetime) and the community that offers a continuum of housing, services, and healthcare system—often all on one campus or site. (ALFA, 2013)

■ Assisted Living Workgroup

Perhaps because of the confusion surrounding assisted living, the U.S. Senate got involved. In August 2001, the Senate Special Committee on Aging convened a meeting of assisted living stakeholders to request that they work together and make recommendations to ensure high-quality care and services for all assisted living residents. Thus was formed the Assisted Living Workgroup, a group composed of more than 50 organizations representing various interests, including providers, consumers, and regulators as well as various aging, healthcare, and psychosocial interests. The Assisted

Living Workgroup made over 100 recommendations based on their discussions (CEAL, 2013). We refer to those recommendations and other Assisted Living Workgroup findings throughout this chapter.

■ How Assisted Living Developed

The concept of assisted living has actually been around for several decades, although not with that name. It has taken a couple of largely parallel tracks to get where it is today. On one track were residential care facilities. Known more commonly as boarding homes or boarding care facilities, their services were traditionally provided in small homes caring for one or several seniors. They were mostly providing nonmedical care and supervision and were often in the private homes of the service providers. As these facilities found themselves caring for larger numbers of people, the size of the facilities also grew, often moving away from small, "mom and pop" operations. Facilities owned and operated by state and local governments housed many residential care consumers with a heavy focus on the indigent.

On another track, a level of care much more like what we now know as assisted living developed in the form of independent living. In a way, the name was misleading. Independent living was not for people who could live independently. It was for people who, with a bit of assistance, could live more independently. Thus, the term *assisted living* is more accurate and gradually began to replace *independent living* in general usage.

In both cases, the primary goal has been to provide a setting in which individuals can attain those services needed to allow them to live with as much independence and dignity as possible, given their needs for support.

■ Philosophy of Care

Assisted living represents a philosophy to provide residential long-term care in a home-like environment that maximizes autonomy and independence for its residents. Assisted living brings the best of an independent home environment together with high-quality services unavailable at home. That philosophy is captured by the National Center for Assisted Living (NCAL) as doing the following:

- Maximizing residents' personal dignity, autonomy, independence, privacy, and choice
- Providing a homelike environment
- Providing personal care services, 24-hour supervision and assistance, activities, and health-related services
- Accommodating residents' changing care needs and preferences

- Minimizing the need to move when a resident's care needs increase
- Involving family and the community (Mollica & Houser, 2012)

Let us look at each in more detail.

Maximizing Dignity, Autonomy, Independence, Privacy, and Choice

Assisted living is based on the idea of providing only the amount of assistance needed to live in a manner as close as possible to the way the individual lived before, which requires that the person be allowed to do as much for him- or herself as possible. Being cared for in the most intimate activities surrounding one's life can mean loss of both independence and dignity. Assisted living facilities (ALFs) strive to prevent that loss. Residents are not only permitted to make many decisions for themselves, they are encouraged to do so. They have opportunities to choose their living arrangements (private room, shared suite, etc.), what they eat and where they eat it, and which activities they join. Being able to make such choices allows them to maintain a lifestyle surprisingly like that to which they have been accustomed. It also gives them the sense of autonomy and dignity they need. Living arrangements permit a high degree of privacy not possible in long-term care facilities providing a higher level of medical care, such as nursing facilities and hospitals.

Providing a Homelike Environment

Efforts are made to enhance this autonomy and independence by seeking to provide care in a homelike environment. Many ALFs offer residents a choice of either furnished or unfurnished units, generally consisting of single rooms or small apartments, including studios, one-bedroom units, or even two-bedroom units. The two-bedroom apartments usually involve a shared common space for two residents, each with his or her own bedroom. Such arrangements make it possible for the residents to create a living environment of their own choosing. Because they have space that is their own, they can decorate and furnish it with pictures, mementos, and even furniture from earlier in their lives. Some apartments include a full kitchen, while others have a kitchenette.

Providing Personal Care Services, 24-Hour Supervision and Assistance, Activities, and Health-Related Services

Assisted living communities provide a variety of personal care services including three meals a day plus snacks in a group dining room and a range of services that promote resident quality of life and independence.

One of the most important services provided is 24-hour supervision and assistance. This is accomplished with a minimum of intrusion on personal space and freedom but is there as needed.

Accommodating Residents' Changing Care Needs and Preferences

Residents in assisted living are often at a point in their lives where their functional status is far from constant. After all, they are there in the first place because they need some level of assistance, and they are usually elderly. Their status can change frequently, and, as a result, their need for care changes. Facilities strive to provide enough flexibility in their services to accommodate those changes easily and with as little disruption as possible. For example, a resident who is able to do all of her own cooking in her own kitchen may become unable to continue doing so because of either physical or mental capacity. When that happens, she can very easily switch to taking her meals in the facility's dining room. Such changes can also be made based simply on the resident's desire for change.

Minimizing the Need to Move When a Resident's Care Needs Increase

That ability to respond to changing care needs also allows residents to stay where they are in many instances when they would otherwise have to move to different facilities offering more intense levels of care, such as nursing facilities. They do sometimes have to move to such higher levels of care, but the philosophy of assisted living is to minimize such moves. To the degree feasible, services are brought to the resident in what has become her or his own home.

Involving Families and the Community

An important element of the philosophy of assisted living is to preserve the residents' ties to their families and to the community. When choosing a facility, proximity to children and other family members is important. Some of the services provided by most assisted living facilities (to be discussed in more detail later) are aimed at facilitating such ties. Family members are encouraged to be involved in facility activities, to join the residents at mealtime, and to take the residents out of the facility regularly. To the extent they are able, residents are helped to do the things they like in the community. Transportation is provided for shopping, church, and other community activities.

All in all, the philosophy of assisted living is to do just what it says—assist residents to live, with a high quality of life. A nationwide survey of seniors currently living in assisted living communities found that fully 93% feel satisfied with their community, including 68% who say they are very satisfied. The survey also found residents almost unanimously feel safe in their communities, with 99% of respondents reporting they feel safe (Allmon, 2013).

■ Ownership of Assisted Living Facilities

The majority of assisted living facilities are owned and operated by for-profit organizations. In fact, a 2011 study found that approximately 82% were for profit and the remainder were not for profit or were owned by government entities. Small facilities were more likely to be for profit (91%) than larger ones. Approximately one half were small facilities with 4–10 beds. The rest were medium facilities with 11–25 beds (16%), large facilities with 26–100 beds (28%), and extra-large facilities with more than 100 beds (7%) (Park-Lee et al., 2011, p. 1). That is a significant change from 2001, when 88% were for profit and only 12% were not for profit (ALFA, 2001, p. 5). A couple of reasons have been given for the dominance of for-profit ownership of assisted living facilities. They include the fact that most assisted living residents pay from their own funds or family funds. Because of the high degree of self-pay, for-profit investors are able to charge market rates unencumbered by government reimbursement restrictions. Second, the relative lack of government funding has meant a similar paucity of government regulation, making it easier and more attractive to invest in assisted living than in other types of long-term care; as can be seen from the shifting characteristics of ownership.

■ Services Provided

Assisted living residences typically provide or coordinate

- 24-hour supervision
- Three meals a day plus snacks in a group dining room
- A range of services that promote resident quality of life and independence, including:
  - Personal care services (help with eating, bathing, dressing, toileting, etc.)
  - Various healthcare services
  - Medication management
  - Social services
  - Supervision of persons with cognitive disabilities
  - Social and religious activities
  - Arrangements for transportation
  - Laundry and linen service
  - Housekeeping and maintenance (NCAL, 2013a)

While most assisted living facilities offer all of these services, it is not necessary for every resident to utilize all of them. In fact, beyond the basic housing and supervision, many of the services are provided on an à la carte basis, with the residents paying for only what they use. Residents are evaluated prior to, or at, time of admission to determine the services they need or desire. A service plan, not unlike a care plan in a healthcare facility, is developed and used as the basis for delivery of services. The service plan can be revised as needed and is reviewed on a periodic basis.

Personal Care Services

Most assisted living residents need some help with activities of daily living (ADLs). ADLs include dressing, bathing, eating, toileting, and transferring. A recent study showed that bathing is the most common activity with which residents need help (72%), followed by dressing (52%), toileting (36%), transferring (25%), and eating (22%). Thirty-eight percent received assistance with three or more of these ADLs, an additional 36% received assistance with one or two of the ADLs, and 26% did not receive assistance with any ADL (Caffrey et al., 2012, p. 3). In some cases, they need a large amount of assistance, in others only a small amount.

Healthcare Services

Healthcare services for residents in assisted living may include nursing care, assistance with taking medication, and therapy services. The types and intensity of services provided in most assisted living facilities are very similar to those services provided by home healthcare agencies in consumers' homes. In effect, that is what occurs, because the facility is their home. Some of those healthcare services are provided by facility staff, some by contract with outside agencies.

Medication Management

While most assisted living residents take their own medications, the community assists with managing those medications to assure that the individual takes them correctly.

Social Services

Assisted living facilities provide help with social service issues such as getting access to funding, contracting with outside services, and handling legal matters, much as do nursing facilities.

Supervision of Persons With Cognitive Disabilities

Many residents in assisted living suffer from some type of cognitive disability, although the extent of such disabilities may vary considerably. Cognitive disability means that an individual may have a level of dementia or may simply be unable to understand and follow directions. Alzheimer's disease is the most common form of cognitive disability in the elderly. Obviously, when the disability is too severe, they will need care in a setting other than assisted living. However, it can be progressive, starting with mild symptoms. A person may become forgetful, with potentially harmful results if not supervised. For example, a resident may fail to remember to take medications or even forget to eat. Of even more concern is the person doing his or her own cooking who fails to watch the stove after turning it on, or the person who might get lost in an unfamiliar setting. About half of the assisted living communities surveyed in 2012 provided Alzheimer's and dementia care for residents, 61% of which charge an additional fee for this service (MetLife Market Institute, 2012, p.9). The facility provides supervision to protect the residents. Interestingly, these may be the very problems that led the resident to assisted living in the first place.

Social and Religious Activities

Because it is so important that residents be able to continue a lifestyle as similar to what they are accustomed to as possible, facilities provide lively activity programs. They design the activities to best meet the interests and abilities of the residents in their particular facilities. However, some facility staff members become very creative.

Assisted living facilities usually provide religious services for their residents, facilitate visits by clergy, and provide transportation to religious services outside the facility for those residents able to attend them.

Exercise and Educational Activities

Maintaining a high level of functional independence requires staying active physically and mentally. Facilities provide activities that are more than just social. Their activities generally include age-appropriate exercises such as aerobics, gardening, and individual exercise equipment and mental stimulation through lectures, discussion groups, films, and library holdings. Technology is also used and understood by senior residents. A 2013 survey found that a large majority of seniors understand the importance of technology in helping them stay connected to family, friends, and the wider world. When asked which technologies they use frequently, 75% of seniors said cell phones, 68% said computers, 65% said the Internet, and 62% said email. Almost all seniors say that technology is important in helping them stay in touch with family and friends (87%), keep up with the world (84%), learn new things (80%), and stay mentally sharp (79%) (National Council on Aging, 2013). Successful assisted living communities have learned to adapt to those desires/needs.

Arrangements for Transportation

As noted earlier, some of the activities that are important to the residents require them to venture outside the facility. Transportation is provided by the facility or, when available, by community senior transportation services.

Laundry and Linen Service

Because the residents wear clothes of their own choice and furnish their living quarters to their own tastes, they need laundry and linen services beyond those expected in other healthcare settings such as nursing facilities and hospitals. Those services are provided by the facility.

Housekeeping and Maintenance

Similarly, keeping their living quarters clean and maintained can be difficult for some residents, although others are able to perform some housekeeping and maintenance functions themselves. The facilities provide the help needed.

While such services are provided in most assisted living facilities, the extent and nature of them may be determined by a combination of the rates charged, the ability of residents to take advantage of them, and state and local regulations.

■ Consumers Served

Consumers of assisted living are likely to be females in their 80s, although not exclusively. The National Center for Assisted Living reports that the average age is 87, with a population that is 74% female (NCAL, 2013b). That has changed somewhat from a 1998 survey that found the average to be 83, with a female/male distribution of 78% to 22% (Wright, 2001, p. 1). The high percentage of women in assisted living reflects the fact that they tend to live longer than men and need services longer. Individuals of either gender regularly reach a time when they can no longer function totally independently. When that happens, they become candidates for some level of long-term care. Those who require the most care are admitted to nursing care facilities, while others needing a lesser amount of care and/or supervision are excellent candidates for assisted living.

These consumers are highly likely to choose a facility that is within a few miles from their family members. That could be, in part, because the family members often play a large role in choice of facility. They want to be close to the resident, both for convenience and to maintain the ongoing relationship they have had.

Where They Come From
Residents come to assisted living facilities from a variety of settings, as indicated next:

Seventy percent moved from a private home or apartment.
Nine percent came from a nursing facility.
Nine percent moved from a retirement or independent living community.
Seven percent moved from a family residence (such as living with adult children).
Five percent came from another assisted living residence or group home (NCAL, 2013b).

Let us look at some of the reasons.
First, nearly three quarters go to an ALF directly from home. They probably have been living quite independently but can no longer keep up with the physical and mental demands of doing that. Perhaps they have been living alone with a family member visiting daily, and those support caregivers can no longer do it. On the other hand, many new ALF residents have been living with family members (spouses, children) who have provided supervision and care as needed. Perhaps the needs have simply become too much for that family member. Often, the final deciding factor is that the individual cannot be left alone for even a few hours because of the potential for accidents or injury.

The residents who move to an ALF from a nursing home are likely doing so because they have gained functional capacity. They may have received enough rehabilitation in the nursing facility to no longer need skilled nursing services. A defining factor in such cases is often the reimbursement available. Skilled nursing care is reimbursable under Medicare. Should a resident no longer qualify for that level of care, she/he would have to rely on other insurance or personal savings. Because the cost of residing in an ALF is much lower than in a nursing facility, the obvious choice would be to move. Besides, if the individual has regained that much functional capacity, the ALF offers much more choice and independence. Residents stay in assisted living facilities for varying lengths of time, but various research studies put the average at around 2.5 to 3 years.

If they come from a retirement or independent living community, it is probably because of decreased independence and functional ability.

Those who came from another ALF may be moving because of dissatisfaction with the services provided or the personnel providing them. More often, it is because of external factors, such as the family moving and the resident wanting to be close to them or the opening of a new facility closer to family. Some may move because their needs have changed and another facility can better meet those needs. Lastly, they might be forced to move because of inability to continue paying the rate at the facility where they have been. We discuss financing of assisted living a bit later, but the rates charged do vary considerably.

Where They Go

When it comes to leaving the assisted living facility, the most common destination is to a nursing facility (59%), generally because of loss of functional capacity. The second most common (33%) reason for leaving is the death of the resident. The remainder will move home or to another location (NCAL, 2013b). Many assisted living facilities do everything they can, within the bounds of resident safety, to continue caring for their residents even when death is imminent. Most will arrange for hospice or palliative care services from outside contractors if needed. Their intent is to allow the resident to die in what has come to be a familiar setting, surrounded by recognizable people.

■ Market Forces

There are several market forces at work that have affected the way assisted living has developed and how it is likely to develop in the future. Among these forces are seeking care alternatives, the impact on the residents' children, and cost-cutting efforts.

Seeking Care Alternatives

As long-term care consumers become better informed, they tend to seek alternatives to the usual forms of care such as nursing facilities. That means that they are less likely to accept the decisions of physicians and other healthcare professionals without questioning their options. They have many more choices available to them and will be increasingly willing to ask questions about their options. An older generation of long-term care consumers who felt that they had little choice but institutionalization is passing. Their children, the long-term care consumers of tomorrow, will seek other alternatives when such alternatives are available. Many of them will eventually require skilled nursing care, for which nursing facilities are most appropriate, but they will look for ways to delay that decision as long as possible. Assisted living is one such option because it provides a combination of a residential setting and relative independence.

Impact on Children

The children of a potential assisted living resident are often deeply involved in the decision to admit the parent to a residential facility. That has changed from previous generations for several reasons. First, the changing nature of the nuclear family unit in our society over the past several decades means that the grown children of elderly consumers are less able to care for them when the need arises. Two-wage-earner families have become more the rule than the exception, removing the possibility of a child (usually a daughter) being available as a full-time caregiver. When elderly people can no longer function totally alone, families do what they can, often taking the elder into their homes, much as was done by earlier generations. However, when the parent reaches the point where it is unsafe to be left alone for hours while the family members work, other alternatives become imperative.

The children (generally) want only what is best for the parent(s), but frequently feel a sense of guilt at no longer being able to take care of the parent(s). Placement in an assisted living facility where the parent has access to a range of services while maintaining as much autonomy as possible satisfies both needs.

It is also more common for parents and children to live far from each other, sometimes several states away. That makes it difficult if not impossible for the children to care for their parents adequately. ALFs offer a solution to their problem. Sometimes the facility chosen is close to a family member for frequent family interaction. In other cases, the father or mother selects a facility close to her or his home, facilitating interaction with familiar people and activities. Although the children may not live close to the facility, they experience the relief and peace of mind of knowing that the parent is safe and well cared for in a setting designed to provide a high quality of life in the parent's late years.

Cost-Cutting Efforts

As healthcare costs continue to escalate, including those relating to long-term care, those who must pay the bills look for less costly alternatives. Whether the payer is the consumer, the consumer's family, or some third-party reimbursement source such as private long-term care insurance or a government program, no one wishes to pay more than is necessary for the services needed and provided. When nursing facility care is the most appropriate solution, the higher cost is justified and accepted. However, when lower cost assisted living will suffice, it provides considerable savings. There are several possible beneficial results of those savings. If the payments come from the consumer, it may mean extending the length of time when care can be purchased out of limited family funds. If the family is contributing, it may mean less negative impact on their savings, which could then be used for other purposes. If the payment source is an insurance company or state Medicaid agency (remember that there are some situations in which Medicaid can be used to cover assisted living), the savings mean that more individuals can be covered.

These factors all contribute to the growing popularity of assisted living as a provider of long-term care. Their impact is likely to continue growing.

■ Regulations

Regulation of assisted living has been hit-or-miss at best. It has grown sporadically, much as has the field being regulated. While nursing facilities have been highly regulated for decades, it is only in the past few years that assisted living facilities have been regulated to any significant degree. However, state licensing agencies have been working diligently to make up for lost time. There is no national licensing of these services, but they are increasingly licensed by state governments. Even there, the lack of uniformity in terms of what the services are called and how they are defined leads to great misunderstanding. Eighteen states reported making regulatory, statutory, or policy changes impacting assisted living/residential care communities from January 2012 through January 2013. More than two thirds of state licensing agencies use the term *assisted living*, with *residential care* being second most prevalent (Polzer, 2013). However, there is still little commonality in the specifics of their regulations.

The Assisted Living Workgroup referenced earlier issued a report to Congress in April 2003. In that report the workgroup made several recommendations concerning regulation of assisted living facilities. Among them was a recommendation that a national center for excellence in assisted living (CEAL) be formed and funded to continue the work of the Assisted Living Workgroup and serve as an ongoing source of information and guidance to states regulating assisted living That CEAL was formed in 2004 with the following mission:

To foster access to high-quality assisted living by:

- Creating resources and acting as an objective resource center to facilitate quality improvement in assisted living
- Increasing the availability of research on quality practices in assisted living
- Establishing and maintaining a national clearinghouse of information on assisted living

- Building upon the work of the Assisted Living Workgroup
- Providing resources and technical expertise to facilitate the development and operations of high-quality, affordable assisted living programs to serve low- and moderate-income individuals (CEAL, 2013)

Its board of directors represents 11 assisted living organizations including:

- AARP
- Alzheimer's Association
- American Assisted Living Nurses Association
- American Association of Homes and Services for the Aging
- ALFA
- Consumer Consortium on Assisted Living
- LeadingAge
- NCAL
- NCB Capital Impact
- Paralyzed Veterans of America
- Pioneer Network

The CEAL also has an advisory council with representatives of 27 additional private and government agencies and organizations (CEAL, 2013).

Regulations Affecting Residents

There are federal laws that affect assisted living, but oversight occurs primarily at the state level (Polzer, 2013). There is considerable controversy about the nature of the regulations. Several assisted living organizations, such as the NCAL and ALFA, have advocated that regulation of assisted living should not follow the pattern of nursing facility regulation. Their concern is that nursing facilities follow more of a medical model than do assisted living facilities and the regulations thus need to be different. They argue that facilities should be judged (regulated) more on the basis of customer satisfaction and quality of life because those are the attributes that most assisted living residents prize most highly. Supporters of regulations focusing more on customer satisfaction and quality of life point to what they see as the failure of nursing facility regulations.

Other Regulations

Assisted living facilities must also comply with the same regulations relating to resident and employee safety (e.g., those of the Occupational Safety and Health Administration and the Life Safety Code) and employee rights (e.g., those of the Equal Employment Opportunity Commission and the Family Medical Leave Act) that other provider organizations do.

■ Accreditation

Assisted living facilities have a couple of options for accreditation. First, the Joint Commission began accrediting assisted living in 2000 under its former name, the Joint Commission on Accreditation of Healthcare Organizations. In 2003, CARF International (formerly the Commission on Accreditation of Rehabilitation Facilities) and the Continuing Care Accreditation Commission merged, combining their accreditation programs, enabling them to serve a wider variety of provider organizations.

■ Financing Assisted Living

As a segment of long-term care that is still evolving, assisted living is financed in a number of ways—ways that are changing as time goes on. That includes both the ways in which consumers are charged and the sources of reimbursement.

Costs/Charges

Because assisted living facilities vary so in the extent of services provided and in just how fancy those services and the living quarters are, costs also vary widely. Most ALFs charge a basic fee for core services, which are defined as room and board. Nationally, these basic rates averaged $3,550 monthly or $42,600 annually in 2012 (MetLife Market Institute, 2012, p. 4) with added charges for other services used. For example, the basic fee might cover one or two meals per day in a communal living room. Additional meals are prepared by many residents in their kitchens or kitchenettes. If they are unable to do so, or do not want to, they can arrange for the additional meals in the dining room at an added cost.

Services that are added, and bear additional costs, may be healthcare-related services. Nursing care and/or monitoring are typically extras. Nursing services may be provided by in-house staff if the ALF is large enough or is affiliated with a nearby healthcare organization. If, not, those services are contracted with a home care agency or other similar source. Nonhealth services may include a barber or beauty shop.

Another, increasingly popular type of pricing is the tiered approach, whereby several different bundles of services from which consumers can choose are offered. A 2010 study of assisted living facilities found that about half of them use a tiered-pricing model for bundled services, 24% use an all-inclusive rate model, and 17% use a fee-for-service model (NCAL, 2013a). Charges vary considerably due to type of facility, size and type of unit, and location.

Reimbursement

Private pay—use of an individual's own funds—remains the largest source of reimbursement for assisted living. Medicare does not cover it, although in some cases, there is some coverage under Social Security's Supplemental Security Income.

Medicaid is a small, but growing source of reimbursement. In 2010, about 4 in 10 served residents were receiving long-term care services paid by Medicaid. Overall, 43% of residential care/assisted living facilities had at least one resident who had some or all of his or her long-term care services paid by Medicaid (Park-Lee et al., 2011, p. 3). The primary reason for that is the need for states to find cost-effective alternatives to more expensive nursing facility care. Assisted living (often referred to as "residential care" by state Medicaid agencies) costs considerably less than does nursing facility care because of the lower requirement for expensive nursing care and therapies. State Medicaid agencies have several ways of paying for assisted living/residential care services, primarily through the use of authorized Home and Community Based Services (HCBS) waivers. Under this provision, states may apply to the U.S. Department of Health and Human Services for a waiver of certain federal requirements, allowing them to pay for home and community services for individuals who would otherwise require services in a skilled nursing care facility (CMS, 2013).

Other reimbursement for assisted living comes from private long-term care insurance and managed care organizations.

■ Staffing/Human Resource Issues

Assisted living facilities, like nursing facilities, are highly staff intensive, although there are some differences in the particular jobs.

Nature of the Workforce

While some assisted living facilities employ nurses and other clinical staff, they do not need to for provision of basic services. Most of the staff in ALFs is there to provide customer services such as preparing meals, housekeeping, and maintenance. Direct care is provided mostly by personal care attendants and certified nursing assistants. Nursing care is provided as needed. ALFs with a high proportion of residents with Alzheimer's disease or dementia must, of course, have a higher number of nursing staff for their protection. Other employees include activity directors, health and wellness staff, and those performing special services such as beauticians and nutritionists.

Customer Service Focus

The focus of staffing is on making the residents comfortable, happy, and safe. The customer service concept found in assisted living is not that different from what is found in hotels and resorts. That is not to say that nursing facilities are unconcerned with customer service—because they are, and most do it very well. However, their residents require such a high level of nursing care that they are not able to focus as much on nonclinical services. Besides, many of their residents are unable to take full advantage of services such as those offered in assisted living.

Assisted living residents are able to make many more decisions about what they do, as well as when and how they do it. Their privacy is important to them and is highly respected. Thus, the amount and type of direct interaction with staff may be less. Assisted living facilities also employ numerous specialty staff, either directly or as contract consultants, depending on the needs of their residents. For example, ALFs actively market their services, requiring that they staff marketing experts.

Staffing Regulations

Staffing levels in assisted living are much less controlled by regulation than in other levels of long-term care, although that is changing in many instances. Where state governments do regulate assisted living, some minimum staffing levels are not uncommon. This is particularly true for facilities caring for consumers with dementia. One problem many ALFs have with such regulations is that they tend to be based on a nursing facility model. After all, that is where most such regulating agencies have the most experience. In spite of the regulators' good intentions, the nursing care model of staffing is not a good fit in ALFs.

Training

The type and amount of required staff training and orientation for assisted living facility staff varies, but for the most part, relatively little training is required (Mollica & Houser, 2012). It generally consists largely of orienting staff to the philosophy of assisted living. Training in this area is particularly important to assisted living facilities, because employees coming from outside of health care or from other healthcare facilities may not be familiar with the services provided in ALFs. Those coming from outside have to understand the needs of the residents who, although the emphasis is on independence and as normal a lifestyle as possible, still do require assistance. The balance between serving and caring can be delicate, but it must be maintained. Even though residents may want to be very independent, they may not always be capable of the level of autonomy they desire. Staff members have to be trained to help as much as needed without doing something that would endanger the residents.

In assisted living facilities with substantial populations of Alzheimer's disease or dementia residents, it is much more common for additional training in this area to occur.

■ Legal and Ethical Issues

Assisted living facilities face legal and ethical issues similar to other long-term care providers. However, their focus on resident independence can create some difficult situations for them.

Autonomy and Decision Making

Most legal and/or ethical issues affecting assisted living facilities and their residents deal with the issue of how much autonomy is safe for each resident. They need to balance the residents' desire to be independent with the facility's responsibility to protect them from harm. That includes protecting residents from making bad decisions about the care they need. Many factors enter into the balance, including cognitive, physical, and functional ability; availability of assistance from family or friends; and the wishes of residents. Each of these can change—and eventually will. The capability of the facility to meet specific needs also plays a part.

A resident may become increasingly forgetful, yet insist on doing nearly everything for herself, including cooking, taking medications, and taking walks around the facility's grounds. Yet, facility staff do not think she can do all of these things safely. They want her to maintain her dignity, of which autonomy is such a significant part, but must take away some of that autonomy for her safety. Facility staff goes to great length to do that with sympathy and understanding. They enlist family members to help convince the resident that it is for her own good.

Assisted living facilities are faced with this dilemma all the time. A good example is the taking of medications. Unlike other levels of health care, where medications are administered by nursing staff, residents in assisted living usually take their own medicines. It is an important aspect of helping them have as much autonomy as possible, to feel as though they are living at home. Yet, most are not fully capable of remembering to take their medications appropriately and at the right times. It is common for the elderly, whether living in their own residence or in an assisted living facility, to take as many as five or six different medicines, each on its own schedule. Keeping track of those medications is no easy matter.

The role of the ALF staff is to supervise the taking of medications, to manage them. This is one area wherein many states do have some regulations. They usually consist of guidelines, rather than highly specific procedural requirements. Within those guidelines, ALFs develop their own policies and procedures. Those policies and procedures dictate how they manage residents' medications. In some cases, they have the medications administered directly by trained staff. In others, and more frequently, they provide the medicines to the residents and allow the residents to take them. There can be several variations of that. The staff may trust the residents to remove the pills from bottles or packages when they are supposed to take them. Or, they may count out the pills and put them in containers that separate them according to when they are to be taken. In either case, the staff keep records of each resident's medications and when they are consumed.

Medications, such as insulin, that are administered by injection or in some manner other than by mouth, require even more care. Many individuals have been self-administering such medications for years. If they are still able to self-administer their medicine, they are allowed to do so, but with some level of supervision. When they are no longer capable of doing it safely, staff will administer the medicine for them. What makes it more difficult is the issue of the residents' legal and ethical rights to remain in place.

Aging in Place

But, what happens when a resident's condition deteriorates to the point where the facility can no longer provide appropriate care? The seemingly easy answer is that the resident must be transferred to another facility that can provide the care, but that can be distressing for the resident. The wish of residents to stay in familiar surroundings with familiar friends, and the desire of providers to honor this wish, has led to a concept of aging in place. Aging in place, in its simplest form, means bringing the necessary services to the individual rather than making the individual move to where services are available. It is an admirable idea, and many facilities have made it available by expanding the levels of care they offer, becoming multilevel providers. They have a range of services available, often including independent living, assisted living, skilled nursing care, and even their own home care services.

However, the idea of aging in place has produced some problems for both providers and residents because of different interpretations of what it really means. In some cases, lawsuits have been filed, claiming that the facility has a legal obligation to provide whatever services a resident needs, no matter the cost or difficulty of doing so. Some state regulatory agencies have developed regulations based on a similar interpretation. In at least one state, authorities have ruled that a resident could not be moved from an assisted living unit in a multilevel facility to a skilled nursing unit a few feet away. They said that the resident could not be moved involuntarily, but that needed services had to be delivered on the assisted living unit. The ruling was appealed unsuccessfully.

Because of these problems, the NCAL, in its *Guiding Principles of Assisted Living*, recommends that the term *aging in place* not be used unless accompanied by an explanation that includes any health-related restrictions mandated by the residence and/or state regulation (NCAL, 2014).

In spite of these difficulties, which will be resolved in time, the idea of aging in place is a good one. Its basis is an attempt to do what is best for residents, a wish shared by all, even though there is disagreement about how to accomplish that end.

■ Management of Assisted Living

As with nursing facilities, administrators of ALFs find their work to be challenging, but rewarding. They have to deal with issues of regulations and reimbursement, but also get the satisfaction of serving their consumers.

Where ALF Administrators Come From

Assisted living managers come from several sources. First, many ALF administrators are licensed nursing facility administrators who have moved from that other kind of long-term care provider. They bring with them experience in providing services to the elderly and other long-term care consumers. They generally have a good understanding of the complex regulations and reimbursement mechanisms that characterize nursing facility operations. They also understand the difference between the cure philosophy of acute care and the care philosophy of long-term care.

However, they must adapt to a philosophy of care that is different from their experience in nursing facilities. They must also learn to deal with a resident population that is less severely ill and is capable of much more autonomy. Nursing facility residents require a higher level of nursing care by definition than do residents in assisted living facilities. Those nursing facility residents generally require assistance in more ADLs. In other words, more must be done for them. Assisted living residents can, and want to, do more for themselves. It takes some adapting for former nursing facility administrators to learn the different levels and types of staffing required in assisted living. That adaptation takes place very quickly in most cases, and they make excellent assisted living administrators.

Some administrators come from outside of the field of long-term care. Because such a high proportion of ALFs are owned and operated by for-profit organizations, successful business people from other disciplines see it as an attractive investment. They also must learn the types of customers (residents) they will be serving and the particular philosophy of care. While they may not be as familiar with long-term care as former nursing facility administrators, they often come with more extensive training and experience in marketing and customer service, both very important in a competitive assisted living environment.

A last group of assisted living administrators comes from within the field. They are assistant administrators and department heads who are familiar with the setting and the residents, and desire to become top-level administrators. They come with the advantage of knowing assisted living but usually require additional training in management skills.

Management Qualifications

As noted earlier, regulation of assisted living is still very much a work in progress. So is regulation of assisted living administrators. Nursing facility administrators must be licensed in all states. Not so with assisted living administrators. An increasing number of licensing jurisdictions are requiring their licensure, but there is little uniformity in those requirements. One factor adding to the confusion is that some states place responsibility for licensing nursing facility administrators and assisted living administrators in a single agency, while others utilize totally separate departments.

In most states that do license ALF administrators, the requirements are often significantly less rigorous than for nursing facility administrators. That is understandable, not because managing an ALF requires any less skill than managing a nursing facility, but because ALF administrator regulations are in the process of catching up. Nursing facility administrators have been licensed in all states for several decades—but even now have not achieved uniformity. Although the National Association of Long-Term Care Administrator Boards (NAB) has identified a baccalaureate degree as the desired minimum standard for nursing facility administrators, not all states have adapted their regulations to meeting that standard. Also, the licensing agencies have realistically recognized that they cannot expect to move from no regulation of ALF administrators to highly demanding and restrictive regulations in a single move. When they do begin regulating them, they usually have a large group of administrators who have not had to obtain the higher level of education and experience. Some states have set higher licensing requirements, but have grandfathered current administrators, at least temporarily. Others have set initial requirements somewhat lower, with the intent of raising them over time. In both cases, reaching the higher level of licensing requirements will take time.

A number of states have moved directly to more stringent regulation of ALF administrators, working with NAB. As with nursing facility (nursing home) administrators, NAB oversees a licensing examination designed to guarantee that licensed administrators have a solid command of the skills and knowledge deemed essential to their success and to the well-being of the residents they serve. NAB has set completion of a 40-hour, state-approved residential care/assisted living licensure course covering the NAB residential care/assisted living domains of practice, and one of the following combinations of education and experience as minimum qualifications to take the residential care/assisted living exam:

1. A high school diploma (or equivalent) plus 2 years' experience working in assisted living, which includes 1 year in a leadership or management position
2. An AA degree plus 1 year's experience working in assisted living, including 6 months in a leadership or management position
3. A bachelor's degree plus 6 months' leadership and management experience in assisted living (NAB, 2013)

While only some licensing jurisdictions require the NAB assisted living exam for licensure, that number is growing. Also, some states that do not require it for licensure recognize its value and accept it as one way of meeting their requirements. One can safely predict that state licensing of assisted living administrators will grow and that use of the NAB examination will become more commonplace.

As with nursing facility administrators, the American College of Health Care Administrators (ACHCA) has moved ahead of government licensing jurisdictions in setting standards for assisted living administrators. To be fair to the states, it is much easier for a private association to develop and implement new rules and standards than it is for government agencies that have to go through difficult and time-consuming legislative hoops to make significant changes. ACHCA has developed a professional certification program for nursing home (nursing facility) administrators and assisted living administrators.

While state licensure of assisted living (and other) administrators is designed to identify a minimally acceptable level of qualifications, the ACHCA professional certification program sets optimal standards for them. It "identifies and honors administrators and managers who are performing at an advanced level of knowledge and skill" (ACHCA, 2013).

■ Management Challenges and Opportunities

Challenges and opportunities for ALF managers are both similar to and quite different from those of nursing facility managers. They share the challenges of balancing cost and quality and integrating with other long-term care organizations. However, there are several challenges/opportunities that are either unique to ALFs or play a larger part in their management.

Developing an Organizational Identity

As indicated earlier, assisted living has only somewhat recently become a reasonably well-known, long-term care alternative. As a field, it is not all that well defined, at least not yet. A strength of assisted living is the freedom of providers to tailor their services to a particular resident population. However, that can also create confusion and lack of organizational identity. The challenge for the administrator is to develop an identity for his or her facility that is clear to both staff and residents. Without such an identity, it is difficult to market the facility's services. A critical part of marketing any product or service is making it stand out from the competition. That becomes very difficult if the organization's management is unclear what that is. An understandable vision of what the facility should offer is also essential to creating a strategic plan.

Interacting With Residents

It is not the intent of this section to suggest that interaction with residents is necessarily a challenge. It can be at times, but it is usually a pleasant and rewarding experience. Why it is listed here as a management challenge (and opportunity) is that ALF administrators have to adjust to the fact that they are much more personally involved with the residents than they would be in other types of long-term care. Typically, an ALF manager may spend half to three quarters of his or her time managing residents' care issues and communicating with families. Assisted living managers coming from outside of the healthcare field entirely are apt to find it even more difficult learning that it is all right to spend significant amounts of time visiting with residents, when they have been taught to delegate such matters. While it may take a bit of time to balance resident interaction with more traditional acts of management, the rewards of doing so are high.

■ Significant Trends and Their Impact on Assisted Living

Earlier, we discussed the factors that have led to the growth of assisted living as a viable provider of long-term care services. While those factors will continue to exert their influence for years to come, there are a couple of other trends to watch in the near future.

Movement Toward Agreement

As the result of efforts such as the work of the Center for Excellence in Assisted Living (CEAL), the *Guiding Principles for Assisted Living* developed by the NCAL, and numerous other agencies and organizations, the field of assisted living has begun to take on more coherence and stability. That trend should continue.

Increased Regulation

As a segment of long-term care that is growing both in size and in importance, assisted living cannot continue to be so largely unregulated—or so nonuniformly regulated. Both the state and national governments have an interest in, and responsibility for, protecting the residents in assisted living facilities. To accomplish that, they will have to continue to develop regulations to control how and where assisted living is provided. It can be hoped that they will listen to some of the discussion that occurred in the Assisted Living Workgroup and other forums in recent years and will avoid some of the mistakes of the past, developing regulations focused on the needs of assisted living consumers, rather than simply attempting to adapt regulations from other sectors of health care.

Growth in Coverage by Managed Care and Government

We have already seen increased interest in assisted living as a cost-effective alternative by both managed care organizations and state Medicaid programs. As those reimbursement entities experience continued cost inflation in all of health care, including long-term care, they will pay even more attention to assisted living as a way of saving money. It is possible that even Medicare, which does not now cover institutional care below the level of skilled nursing care, will come to see the value of covering assisted living and other less costly forms of long-term care. A major challenge will be providing that coverage without diminishing the extent or quality of services provided. The customer services provided in most ALFs make the difference between basic existence and a truly good quality of life for the residents. If, in the pursuit of cost-effectiveness, these new reimbursement sources attempt to delete or limit availability to those services, the objective will be lost.

Integration With Other Providers

Assisted living is one level of long-term care. While many assisted living facilities will succeed on their own, many will find that they can provide better services and prosper financially by joining with other types and levels of long-term care providers in integrated systems.

■ Summary

Assisted living is one of the most dynamic players in the very dynamic field of long-term care. While its development has been at times haphazard, it is here to stay and is approaching maturity. As it matures, we should see more consensus on what it is and how it is regulated, eliminating some of the current confusion for consumers, providers, and policy makers alike.

Assisted Living Case

Daniella had been an active person all of her life, having raised several children, caring for her family, and occasionally working outside of the home. Now, however, she is in her early 80s and widowed from her loving husband, Carlos. She has lived for the past several years with her daughter, Sophia, and son-in-law, Antonio, since suffering a heart attack and minor stroke that left her unable to live alone without some assistance and support. The arrangement has worked well, and she has been well cared for.

Now, however, Antonio has reached retirement age, and he and Sophia want to move to Florida. Daniella does not want to leave the community in which she has lived all of her life and move that far away. Her other children live in the area but have neither the room nor the resources to include her in their homes. What is she to do?

A home health nurse who comes in periodically to monitor her heart condition told her about a newly opened assisted living/residential care facility in their town. After much consideration, as well as some discussion among the family members, Daniella was admitted to that facility. It was private pay; the retirement income Carlos had left her made her ineligible for Medicaid, and the type of care was not covered by Medicare. Her supportive family also contributed to make this move possible, as it seemed to be just what she needed.

Initially, Daniella needed little help with ADLs, but she was somewhat forgetful and needed someone to make sure she took her medication when needed. In the assisted living facility, she had a very attractive efficiency apartment. The facility provided her with supervision, housekeeping and laundry services, and a communal dining room where she could get her meals (she could fix snacks in her apartment). It also provided social interaction with others, including a variety of activities to keep her mentally sharp and designed to help her maintain as much of her independence as possible.

Daniella thrived in the assisted living setting. She had her own place to live but was neither isolated nor without assistance when needed. Her children and grandchildren could visit her as frequently as she wanted (although Sophia and Antonio could not come from Florida quite as often as she would have liked), and even some of her friends from the community could visit her.

Over time, her health deteriorated slowly but persistently. She began having more difficulty accomplishing ADLs such as bathing and dressing herself. As that happened, the assisted living facility provided her with the additional services without her having to leave her familiar apartment. Eventually, she may need to move to a nursing facility, but for now, she is doing just fine as is.

■ Vocabulary Terms

The following terms are included in this chapter. They are important to the topics and issues discussed herein and should become familiar to readers. Some of the terms are also found in other chapters but may be used in different contexts. They may not be fully defined herein. Thus, readers may wish to seek other, supplementary definitions of them.

AARP
activities of daily living (ADLs)
aging in place
autonomy
caregiver
Center for Excellence in Assisted
 Living (CEAL)
cognitive disability

congregate housing
continuing care retirement
 communities
Joint Commission
medication management
residential care facilities
Senate Special Committee on Aging

■ Discussion Questions

The following questions are presented to assist you in understanding the material covered in this chapter. They tend to be general but lend themselves to detailed answers. The answers to these questions can be found in the chapter.

1. What is assisted living, and how does it differ from nursing facility care?
2. Who provides assisted living?
3. What services are usually included in assisted living?
4. How is assisted living financed?
5. What regulations apply to assisted living?
6. What are some of the ethical and legal issues affecting assisted living?
7. What trends are likely to affect assisted living in the future?

8. In reference to the case at the end of this chapter, consider the following:
   a. How have Daniella's needs changed since moving into the assisted living facility?
   b. How are those changing needs being met by the assisted living facility?
   c. If the assisted living services were not available, what would Daniella's options likely be?

NOTE: As is so often true, both in case analysis and in real life, there is no single right answer here. The purpose of the question is to get you thinking about the many possible scenarios and their implications.

■ References

Allmon, K. (2013, July 24). *Poll finds seniors in assisted living feel overwhelmingly satisfied and safe in their community*. Retrieved from http://www.businesswire.com/news/home/20130724006009/en.

American College of Health Care Administrators (ACHCA). (2013). *Certification*. Retrieved from http://achca.org/joomla/index.php/development/certification.

Assisted Living Federation of America (ALFA). (2001). *ALFA's overview of the assisted living industry, executive summary (2001)*. Fairfax, VA: Assisted Living Federation of America.

Assisted Living Federation of America (ALFA). (2013). *Definitions*. Retrieved from http://www.alfa.org/alfa/Senior_Living_Options.asp.

Caffrey, C., Sengupta, M., Park-Lee, E., Moss, A., Rosenoff, E., & Harris-Kojetin, L. (2012, April). *Residents living in residential care facilities: United States, 2010*. NCHS Data Brief No. 91. Retrieved from http://www.cdc.gov/nchs/data/databriefs/db91.pdf.

Center for Excellence in Assisted Living (CEAL). (2013). *Assisted Living Workgroup report*. Retrieved from http://www.theceal.org/component/content/article/2-uncategorised/15-assisted-living-workgroup-report.

Centers for Medicare and Medicaid Services (CMS). (2013). *Waivers*. Retrieved from http://www.medicaid.gov/Medicaid-CHIP-Program-Information/By-Topics/Waivers/Waivers.html.

MetLife Market Institute. (2012). *Market survey of long-term care costs*. New York, NY: Metropolitan Life Insurance Company.

Mollica, R., & Houser, A. (2012). *Assisted living and residential care in the states in 2010*. Washington, DC: AARP Public Policy Institute.

National Association of Long-Term Care Administrator Boards (NAB). (2013, July). *PB-02: RC/AL Study Guide for the Residential Care/Assisted Living Administrators Examination*, 2nd Ed. Retrieved from http://www.nabweb.org/pb-02-rc-al-study-guide-for-the-residential-care-assisted-living-administrators-examination-2nd-ed-updated-in-2010?page_id=857.

National Center for Assisted Living (NCAL). (2013a). *Assisted living community profile*. Retrieved from http://www.ahcancal.org/ncal/resources/Pages/ALFacilityProfile.aspx.

National Center for Assisted Living (NCAL). (2013b). *Assisted living resident profile*. Retrieved from http://www.ahcancal.org/ncal/resources/Pages/ResidentProfile.aspx.

NCAL. (2014). Guiding Principles for Assisted Living. Retrieved from National Center for Assisted Living: http://www.ahcancal.org/ncal/about/Documents/GPAssistedLiving.pdf.

National Council on Aging. (2013). *The United States of aging*. Washington, DC: National Council on Aging.

Park-Lee, E., Caffrey, C., Sengupta, M., Moss, A. J., Rosenoff, E., & Harris-Kojetin, L. D. (2011, December). *Residential care facilities: A key sector in the spectrum of long-term care providers in the United States*. NCHS Data Brief No. 78. Retrieved from http://www.cdc.gov/nchs/data/databriefs/db78.pdf.

Polzer, K. (2013). *Assisted living regulatory review*. Retrieved from http://www.ahcancal.org/ncal/resources/Documents/2013_reg_review.pdf.

Wright, Bernadette (2001). *Assisted living in the United States*. Washington, DC: AARP Public Policy Institute.

Senior Housing

After completing this chapter, readers will be able to:

1. Understand how senior housing developed and where it fits in the continuum of care.

2. Identify and define the components of senior housing.

3. Identify and describe regulations affecting senior housing providers.

4. Understand the financial, ethical, and managerial issues facing senior housing providers.

5. Identify and discuss trends in senior housing and its management.

■ Introduction

The number of elderly is growing rapidly, largely due to the aging of the baby boomers. Along with that growth is a correlate increase in the need of these seniors for living accommodations that meet their functional and personal needs. Many seniors do not require institutional care but still are not able to live in their traditional homes. Thus has developed the area of senior housing.

Even the U.S. Internal Revenue Service acknowledged that the relief of the distress of old age was not based on financial considerations alone and issued a ruling granting some exceptions for homes for the aged. That ruling recognized that the elderly face forms of distress other than financial, such as need for suitable housing; physical and mental health care; civic, cultural, and recreational activities; and an overall environment conducive to dignity and independence (Kastenberg & Chasin, 2004).

■ What Is Senior Housing?

Senior housing is not homogeneous, but rather there are several different types or versions. There are also numerous terms used in reference to senior housing that are similar and even overlapping and—unfortunately—used interchangeably much too often, which leads to much confusion. To clarify these terms, here are some definitions that are composites from several sources (ALFA, 2013; Cohousing, 2013; HelpGuide. org, 2013; Senior Housing Net, 2013; Senior Outlook.Com, 2013; SeniorResource. Com, 2013). It is important to distinguish them from assisted living. We repeat them here to clarify what we mean by senior housing and its options. We start with the options that are mostly housing arrangements and move toward the more complex options that offer a variety of nonhousing services.

Age-Restricted Housing

Age-restricted housing options offer home ownership or rental opportunities for adults 55 years of age and older, or sometimes 62 years and older.

Reverse Mortgage

One of the newest ways for seniors to meet their needs is the reverse mortgage. For seniors who are homeowners, a reverse mortgage, or home-equity conversion, is one way to pay for housing with services. They continue to live in their homes and receive monthly mortgage payments from a lending institution. It is a means of borrowing money from the amount the home is worth beyond any mortgage debt. There are a variety of lending institutions that provide this, regulated by the federal government. To qualify for this type of financing, the borrower must be age 62 or older, and there must be adequate equity built up. Sometimes the requirement is that they own their homes free and clear. There may also be restrictions on how they can use the funds, but the reverse mortgage may pay for:

- Eliminating an existing mortgage
- Long-term care insurance
- Hired caregivers to help with housekeeping or provide custodial care services
- Nursing home care for a spouse while a partner remains in the home

   The conditions of a reverse mortgage require the seniors to repay the loan if they cease to live in the home or, after their death, their heirs must pay back the loan, either through the sale of the house or with other funds. Because this way of paying for housing has an effect on their heirs, it can be a complex decision requiring much thought and discussion. It is an attractive option for only a small segment of the senior housing population, but it is still an option.

Age-Restricted Retirement Communities

An age-restricted retirement community can be like any other neighborhood or community except it is restricted to people usually 55 or over or 62 and over. It often involves purchase of property or condominiums. Differences in minimum age are usually established when the community entitlement is established. Those with a 55+ restriction require that at least one resident is 55 or older. Other residents must be over 18 but are permitted to be younger than 55. In a 62+ community, all residents must usually meet the age requirement. To be competitive and attractive to a retirement lifestyle, age-restricted communities usually offer amenities, activities, and services that cater to residents. Retirement communities are oriented toward an active lifestyle, or "younger-thinking" seniors. They might offer golf, tennis, swimming pool and spa, exercise rooms, and a variety of clubs and interest groups.

Senior Apartments

Another form of age-restricted housing is multiunit rental housing, or senior apartments, for older adults who are able to care for themselves. Most commonly, no additional services such as meals or transportation are provided. There are numerous reasons some seniors sell their homes and move to an apartment. It frees up equity that can then supplement income through interest or dividends earned through investment of the capital. The move also frees them from home maintenance and grounds keeping chores. Another reason is that living in a large complex of all seniors also affords a greater sense of security than living in a private home.

Cohousing

Cohousing is a variation of the housing options just described. It is a type of collaborative housing in which residents participate in the design and operation of their own neighborhoods. While not necessarily age restricted, it has become popular with seniors, and many cohousing communities are age restricted. Cohousing residents are consciously committed to living as a community. The physical design encourages both social contact and individual space. Private homes contain all the features of conventional homes, but residents also have access to extensive common facilities such as open space, courtyards, and a common house. Cohousing communities are usually designed as attached or single-family homes along one or more pedestrian streets or clustered around a courtyard. They range in size, the majority of them housing 20 to 40 households. Cohousing offers many opportunities for casual meetings between neighbors, as well as for deliberate gatherings such as celebrations, clubs, and business meetings. The common house is the social center of a community, usually with a large dining room and kitchen, lounge, and recreational facilities and frequently has a guest room, workshop, and laundry room. Communities typically serve optional group meals in the common house at least two or three times a week.

Independent Living

Independent living is another residential living setting for elderly or senior adults. It differs from the real estate options defined earlier in that it may or may not provide hospitality or supportive services. In this living arrangement, the senior requires minimal or no extra assistance and leads an independent lifestyle filled with recreational, educational, and social activities among other seniors. Residents usually have complete choice in whether to participate in a facility's services or programs. Sometimes referred to as elderly housing in the government-subsidized environment (see comments under "Financing"), independent living may also include rental-assisted or market-rate apartments or cottages.

Congregate Housing

Congregate housing is a form of independent living that differs in that it usually provides convenience or supportive services like meals, housekeeping, and transportation in addition to rental housing.

Continuing Care Retirement Community

A continuing care retirement community (CCRC) is a community that provides a continuum of care, offering several levels of assistance, usually including independent living, assisted living, and nursing home care—often all on one campus or site. It is also different from other housing and care facilities for seniors because it usually provides a written agreement or long-term contract between the resident (frequently lasting the term of the resident's lifetime) and the community.

Life Care Community

A life care community is:

> a form of CCRC that offers an insurance-type contract and provides all levels of care. It often includes payment for acute care and physician's visits. Little or no change is made in the monthly fee, regardless of the level of medical care required by the resident, except for cost of living increases. (Episcopal Homes, 2013)

We examine each of these options in more detail, including how they differ, as we proceed with our discussion.

■ Philosophy of Care

As shown by the somewhat lengthy definitions provided in the previous section, the various forms of senior housing are designed to give seniors the services and assistance they need while seeking to optimize their independence. While the options vary somewhat in the extent of support they provide, the philosophy is the same: helping seniors live as freely and self-sufficiently as possible. The variety of options they make available allows just about any individual to live to the maximum extent of his or her abilities.

■ Services Provided

Age-Restricted Communities

Age-restricted communities, whether they involve ownership or rental, provide the least amount of services of the various options. In effect, their services differ little from comparable communities with no age restriction. Some places may also provide different kinds of services to the people who live there, including meals, transportation, social activities, and other programs. They do, however, differ in that the focus of those activities and amenities is likely to be those most often utilized by the elderly and often designed with seniors in mind.

In some cases, the program does not provide services directly to seniors living in their apartments, but acts as a broker for those services.

Independent Living

Independent living units are for relatively healthy, active seniors.

Housing varies widely, from apartment-style living to freestanding homes, but in general, it is friendlier to the elderly, such as being more compact, with easier navigation and no maintenance to worry about. Most independent living communities offer amenities, activities, and services (HelpGuide.org, 2013).

While services may vary, independent living communities offer an independent lifestyle and the benefits of a full service community, such as meals in a restaurant setting, housekeeping, transportation, and various social activities. They may include wellness programs but typically do not include other care options (Senior Outlook.Com, 2013). Often, recreational centers or clubhouses are available on site to give seniors the opportunity to connect with peers and participate in community activities, such as arts and crafts, holiday gatherings, continuing education classes, or movie nights. Independent living facilities may also offer facilities such as a swimming pool, fitness center, tennis courts, a golf course, or other clubs and interest groups. Other services offered in independent living may include on-site spas, beauty and barber salons, daily meals, and basic housekeeping and laundry services (HelpGuide.org, 2013). Since independent living facilities are aimed at older adults who need little or no assistance with activities of daily living, most do not offer medical care or nursing staff. As with regular housing, though, residents can hire in-home help separately as required.

Many seniors choose this setting for the flexibility and freedom offered, the active lifestyle promoted, and the convenience of maintenance-free living. For some, being surrounded by a community of healthy, engaged seniors makes independent living a desirable option, too. Clearly a flexible option, independent living can accommodate a number of different lifestyle preferences. Some residents prefer privacy and self-sufficiency, while others will want to engage in more social activities (Seitzer, 2011).

Congregate Housing

Congregate housing usually provides the same basic services as most senior retirement apartment complexes, such as:

- Shared meals
- Full-time staff on duty 24 hours a day to assist residents
- Housekeeping
- Areas within the building for socializing with other residents
- Secure building
- Planned recreational and social activities

Beyond these basic services, congregate housing may have the following options, often for an extra fee:

- Laundry service
- Transportation for shopping and doctors' appointments
- Health monitoring
- Help with taking medications
- Assisted daily living (HelpGuide.org, 2013)

Typically, independent living units (including congregate housing) are not licensed for health care. Residents of independent living units may receive healthcare services from a contract agency.

Continuing Care Retirement Communities

CCRCs offer a broad range of service and housing packages that allow access to independent living, assisted living, and skilled nursing facilities. Some CCRCs are in a high-rise building; others are on extensive campuses. Seniors who are independent may live in a single-family home, apartment, or condominium within the continuing care retirement complex.

One of the major advantages of a CCRC is the option to move between the available housing environments as one's needs change. The range of services is based on the concept of aging in place and may include housing, health care, social services, and health and wellness programs (Singh, 2010). There is no moving required (except possibly to another building within the same community). The senior is still able to maintain relationships with spouse, friends, and other family members. If the person no longer requires nursing care, the care ceases, and he or she resumes an independent lifestyle within the same community (HelpGuide.org, 2013).

Life Care Community

One form of CCRC is a life care community, which offers an insurance type of contract and provides all levels of care for a monthly fee, sometimes even including acute care and physician's visits. The fee generally stays the same, except for possible cost-of-living increases (Episcopal Homes, 2013). A senior in such a community contracts in advance for a lifetime commitment from the community to care for them, regardless of their future needs.

Some continuing care retirement communities can accommodate residents with Alzheimer's disease or other forms of dementia.

Many have large campuses that include separate housing for those who live very independently, assisted living facilities that offer more support, and nursing homes for those needing skilled nursing care. With all on the same grounds, people who are relatively active, as well as those who have serious physical and mental disabilities, all live nearby. Residents then move from one housing choice to another as their needs change.

■ Ownership

The different forms of senior housing vary a bit in terms of who owns them.

Age-Restricted Communities

Age-restricted communities fall into two distinct categories: for-profit ownership and publicly owned. Many are built and owned by for-profit investors, catering to the desire of many seniors to live in these communities; they tend to be high-end, with many added (and often expensive) amenities. Other age-restricted communities are senior housing complexes built and subsidized by municipalities to serve the needs of their elderly—particularly those of limited financial means.

Independent Living

Market-rate, for-profit independent living communities compose the vast majority of the independent living sector, although there are a significant number of not-for-profit senior housing providers.

Continuing Care Retirement Communities

While many CCRCs are for profit, nonprofit organizations also sponsor some. Sponsors include religious, fraternal, and community organizations; universities; and hospitals. Some are companies specifically dedicated to development and operation of senior living communities (Seitzer, 2011).

The American Senior Housing Association represents senior housing operators, and their membership shows the many different forms of ownership. While most members are for-profit operators or financiers, the American Seniors Housing Association's membership also includes a significant number of executives from leading not-for-profit seniors housing providers. The American Seniors Housing Association's membership consists of both for-profit and not-for-profit operators, lenders and investors, and other prominent professionals. The association's membership owns and/or manages an estimated 600,000 units of seniors housing in the United States, with properties located in virtually all 50 states, Canada, and Europe (ASHA, 2010).

■ Consumers Served

There are more similarities than differences among the seniors who live in the separate types of housing.

Age-Restricted Retirement Communities

Those who choose these communities are apt to be younger than those choosing some of the other options, in part because 55+ communities define *senior* a bit younger than others. Many of their residents have retired early and seek the companionship of others of similar age and interests.

Senior Apartments

Although residents of senior apartments may be affluent, they are more likely to have moved to those units to preserve their assets by selling their homes that they may no longer need and cannot care for. Being widowed from a long-time spouse is often a catalyst for them to make the move. In addition, the availability of subsidized housing may be very attractive to them.

Independent Living

Senior independent living communities tend to cater to seniors who are very independent with few medical problems, living in fully equipped private apartments (A Place for Mom, 2013). Widowed, white females in their mid-80s make up the largest percentage of residents in independent living communities. Most of them have annual household incomes ranging from $25,000 to $75,000 and a total net worth ranging from $100,000 to $500,000. These communities are mostly private pay.

Continuing Care Retirement Communities

Many seniors enter into a CCRC contract while they are healthy and active, knowing they will be able to stay in the same community and receive nursing care should this become necessary.

In a 2009 study, the average age of recent movers into entrance-fee CCRCs was 81, and into rental CCRCs, 80.2 years. Two thirds of the survey respondents were women, but the proportion of male respondents increased as the age of the respondents increased: 29% of the male respondents age 77 or younger and 42% of those aged 88 or older were men. The majority of survey respondents (54%) were widowed, 35% were married, 6% were divorced, 4% were never married, and 1% were separated (Zarem, 2010).

■ Accreditation

Most senior housing is not accredited as are some other forms of long-term care. The exception is CCRCs. They are accredited by the Continuing Care Accreditation Commission.

■ Financing

The ways in which senior housing is financed differs both from one type to another and within the individual housing formats.

Age-Restricted Housing

As noted earlier, this housing varies from expensive high-end communities to government-subsidized senior villages. The latter may be financed by local communities or nonprofit organizations.

There is also some limited federal subsidization of senior housing through the Supportive Housing for the Elderly (Section 202) Program. HUD provides:

> capital advances to finance the construction, rehabilitation or acquisition with or without rehabilitation of structures that will serve as supportive housing for very low-income elderly persons, including the frail elderly, and provides rent subsidies for the projects to help make them affordable. (HUD.gov, 2013)

In general, eligibility is restricted to persons who are at least 62 years of age and have incomes below 50% of their area's median income.

Independent Living

Rents vary greatly depending on the region of the country, size of the living unit, services included as part of the base monthly fee, and the range of service amenities available within the community. Many communities offer a variety of unit types to choose from, including studios and one- and two-bedroom designs. The range of fees runs the gamut, but fees generally range from $1,500 to $3,500 per month (A Place for Mom, 2013).

Congregate Housing

The cost for this type of senior housing ranges from $500 per month to more than $4,000 per month. For $500 per month, a senior may get a small one-room apartment with its own bath, and a roommate; but such low rates are not available in all communities. In some instances, subsidized housing provides more amenities, including a private room. Three meals a day are usually included, plus activities and maid service. Many facilities accept seniors who are on SSI (Supplemental Security Income) and may require that they share an apartment with another senior. Private, nonsubsidized apartments begin at around $1,500 per month.

Residents of a congregate housing facility must pay for:

- Either the purchase price or monthly rent for their apartment.
- Security and cleaning deposits.
- A buy-in or entry fee into the facility (in some cases).
- Monthly fees for any optional services that they enroll in.

While most facilities have a rental agreement, many do not require a long-term financial commitment. Seniors may stay so long as they do not require more assistance than the facility can provide. If they do not like the facility, they can leave without penalty (HelpGuide.org, 2013).

Continuing Care Retirement Communities

CCRCs are the most expensive long-term-care solution available to seniors and may be unaffordable to those with low or moderate incomes and assets. CCRCs require a hefty entrance fee as well as monthly charges. Entrance fees can range from $100,000 to $1 million—an up-front sum to prepay for care as well as to provide the facility money to operate. Monthly charges can range from $3,000 to $5,000, but may increase as needs change (AARP, 2013).

Fees vary according to:

- Whether the resident owns or rents the living space.
- The size and location of the residence.
- The amenities chosen.
- Whether the living space is for one or two individuals.
- The type of service contract chosen.
- The current risk for needing intensive, long-term care (seniors who are in good health at the time they sign the contract can expect to pay less).

CCRC residents sign a binding, life-long contract at the beginning of their residency. If they break the contract later, they may forfeit the entrance fee. The three types of residential contracts, or fee schedules, are:

- *Life Care/Extensive Contract*—Provides unlimited long-term nursing care at little or no additional cost for as long as the nursing services are necessary.
- *Modified/Continuing Care Contract*—Provides long-term health care or nursing services for a specified period of time. After the specified care period, the resident is responsible for the additional cost.
- *Fee-for-Service Contract*—Requires that residents pay separately for all health and medical services and for long-term care (AARP, 2013).

■ Staffing

Because most senior housing options (with the exception of nursing facility and assisted living components of CCRCs) do not provide a great deal of health-related services, they are staffed somewhat similar to non–senior housing options. In that sense, they are much like the hospitality industry (hotels, apartment complexes, etc.), which means that staffing tends to include housekeepers, maintenance workers, groundskeepers, and office help.

To the extent that some health-related services are provided, they may be contracted out.

■ Management

Managers of senior housing range from for-profit owner/operators to hired administrators. There is no requirement that they be licensed or otherwise credentialed (again with the exception of the nursing facility and assisted living components of CCRCs). That does not mean that they are not competent or professional managers, just that there are no regulatory requirements pertaining to them.

■ Significant Trends and Their Impact on Senior Housing

There are several trends currently affecting senior housing. They are not all that different from the trends affecting other segments of the long-term care system.

Desire for More Options

Today's seniors seek (and demand) housing options that meet their needs and also are attractive, desirable places to live. This has led to them having access to a wide range of senior housing options, from moderately priced rental communities with basic services to more upscale rental and entrance fee communities with high-end services and amenities. Not surprisingly, seniors want access to a wide range of service amenities.

Most importantly, the industry has responded to seniors' desire to have access to a continuum of services in familiar homelike surroundings. Residents in need of minimal to moderate assistance have the option to pay privately for home healthcare services within the privacy of their apartment. For those requiring more extensive assistance, the vast majority of communities offer residents on-site access to licensed assisted living. Some communities also offer special care for residents with memory impairment.

Quality of Life

Seniors do not want their quality of life to decline when they move into senior housing; furthermore, they want it to actually improve. Many communities have responded by expanding their menu choices and hours of dining service and offering such service amenities as a wet bar, massage therapy, indoor swimming, a business center, banking services, concierge services, a fitness center, and movie theater. The physical designs have been adapted to accommodate seniors' demands for more spaciously designed apartments, greater choice of floor plans, and enhanced common areas that promote a more intimate dining and social experience.

High Occupancy Rates

As a result, demand for senior housing is at a record high with occupancy levels running at more than 90% throughout most of the country. At the end of 2012, occupancy stood at 89.0% for independent living properties, up 0.3 percentage points over the prior quarter (Magan, 2013).

■ Summary

Senior housing is not all that well known as a segment of long-term care, but it has long existed and is becoming much better recognized as a vital part of that system. It has developed largely in response to the desire of today's seniors for additional options concerning where (and how) they live. It is also a good example of how the long-term care system overlaps and interacts with other social systems in the overall continuum.

Senior Housing Case

Don and Rose have been married for more than half a century, and during that time, have never been apart for more than a few days. Now, they are faced with the possibility of having to live apart for the remainder of their lives. But to intelligently discuss the current situation, we must look at how it came to be.

Don, now 80, and Rose, now 71, have both been retired from active professional lives and, until 5 years ago when Don suffered a stroke, their personal lives were active as well. Upon giving up work, they moved to a CCRC in a southern state where they could take full advantage of the outdoors that they both loved so much. The CCRC provided them with the social support they sought, living among other seniors like themselves. They also traveled a lot and fully enjoyed their hard-earned retirement. However, after the stroke, Don was unable to do most of the things he had previously enjoyed. Rose, in part because she needed to care for Don and in part because she didn't want to do the things alone that they used to do together, also stopped most activities. She spent virtually all of her time and energy being Don's caregiver.

However, it eventually became too much for her. Don, who once played football, is nearly twice as large as Rose, making it very hard for her to help him with the activities of daily living such as bathing and dressing. To make matters worse, Rose does not really like to drive the family car, because Don generally did all of the driving when he was able to do so. Thus, she went out alone only when absolutely necessary.

As the caregiver burden became more and more difficult, Rose was able to get some assistance from the CCRC. It began providing staff for an hour or 2 daily to bathe and dress Don, delivered one meal each day, and a woman to come in and clean the house on a weekly basis. Those services sufficed for a time, but it soon became obvious that they were not enough. During the remainder of the day (and night) Rose had to do it all by herself. Don was becoming increasingly distraught over his inability to help Rose or even to take care of himself. Rose, on the other hand, was also becoming depressed and even found herself beginning to resent having to spend all of her time caring for Don.

She began thinking, reluctantly, about placing Don in the nursing facility located on the CCRC campus, but his medical requirements did not really require that level of care. However, the CCRC also had an assisted living facility, which was just what Don needed—at least at that point in time, and he was admitted. In addition to helping Don with the activities of daily living that he could not manage for himself (such as dressing, bathing, and making sure he took his medication when needed), the facility provided Don with supervision and with activities to keep him occupied that were designed to help him gain back some of his independence.

Rose visited regularly, but her depression continued. She simply missed Don too much. Her own health began to deteriorate as she neglected to eat properly and became more and more withdrawn from outside activities.

One day a neighbor of Rose's in the CCRC told her she should investigate the independent living apartments on the campus. After getting all of the necessary information, these apartments seemed to be designed just for her, so Rose moved in. It meant that she could more easily be close to Don and be part of his life. His need for supervision and assistance was still too great for him to live with her in her apartment, but they were only a short distance apart.

She could visit Don and he could visit her. They even play bingo together, with Rose helping Don to play. Rose no longer has to drive to see Don, and the facility provides transportation for shopping and other short trips.

This setting is just perfect for Rose and Don. His physical condition is not going to improve markedly, but he is learning to be more independent. In addition, being near him without the burden of being primary caregiver has lifted a load from Rose's shoulders. Perhaps most importantly, the assisted living facility is part of a larger, multilevel complex. That means that as Don's condition changes for the better or worse, he can be moved to the appropriate unit without having to be transferred to another facility. Rose will still be close to him, and should her own health worsen, will be able to get the services she needs as well.

■ Vocabulary Terms

The following terms are included in this chapter. They are important to the topics and issues discussed herein and should become familiar to readers. Some of the terms are also found in other chapters but may be used in different contexts. They may not be fully defined herein. Thus, readers may wish to seek other, supplementary definitions of them.

age-restricted communities
aging in place
cohousing
congregate housing
Continuing Care Accreditation
    Commission
continuing care retirement commu-
    nity (CCRC)
fee-for-service contract
independent lifestyle

independent living
life care community
life care/extensive contract
modified/continuing care contract
Section 202
senior apartments
senior housing
service amenities
Supportive Housing for the Elderly
    Program

■ Discussion Questions

The following questions are presented to assist you in understanding the material covered in this chapter. They tend to be general but lend themselves to detailed answers. The answers to these questions can be found in the chapter.

1. What is senior housing, and how does it differ from other types of long-term care?
2. Who provides the various types of senior housing?
3. What services are usually included in the various types of senior housing?
4. How is senior housing financed?
5. In reference to the case at the end of this chapter, consider the following:
   a. What different needs do Rose and Don have that are being met by the CCRC?
   b. If the multiple levels of service were not available, what would Rose and Don's situation likely be at this time? In the near future?
   NOTE: As is so often true, both in case analysis and in real life, there is no single right answer here. The purpose of the question is to get you thinking about the many possible scenarios and their implications.

■ References

AARP. (2013). *About continuing care retirement communities*. Retrieved from http://www.aarp.org /relationships/caregiving-resource-center/info-09-2010/ho_continuing_care_retirement_communities .html.

American Seniors Housing Association (ASHA). (2010). *About ASHA*. Retrieved from https://www .seniorshousing.org/about-asha.php.

Assisted Living Foundation of America (ALFA). (2013). *Definitions*. Retrieved from http://www.alfa .org/alfa/default.asp.

Cohousing. (2013). *What is cohousing?* Retrieved from http://www.cohousing.org/.

Episcopal Homes. (2013). *Common senior housing terms and definitions*. Retrieved from http://ehomesmn .org/terms-and-definitions/.

HelpGuide.org. (2013). *Independent Living for Seniors*. Retrieved from http://www.helpguide.org/elder /independent_living_seniors_retirement.htm.

HUD.gov. (2013, November 14). *Section 202 Supportive Housing for the Elderly Program*. Retrieved from http://portal.hud.gov/hudportal/HUD?src=/program_offices/housing/mfh/progdesc/eld202.

Kastenberg, E., & Chasin, J. (2004). *Elderly Housing*. Washington, DC: U.S. Internal Revenue Service.

Magan, G. (2013, January 26). *Senior housing: Occupancy is up, inventory is down*. Retrieved from http://www.leadingage.org/Seniors_Housing_Occupancy_is_Up_Inventory_is_Down.aspx?sz=585.

A Place for Mom. (2013, July 20). *Guide to senior housing options*. Retrieved from http://www .aplaceformom.com/senior-care-resources/articles/senior-housing-options.

Seitzer, M. (2011, July 27). *Why choose independent living?* Retrieved from http://www.seniorsforliving .com/blog/2011/07/27/why-choose-independent-living-2/.

Senior Housing Net. (2013). *Types of senior housing*. Retrieved from http://www.seniorhousingnet .com/?source=web.

Senior Outlook.com. (2013). *Glossary of senior housing terms*. Retrieved from http://www .senioroutlook.com.

SeniorResource.com. (2013). *Housing choices*. Retrieved from http://www.seniorresource.com.

Singh, D. (2010). *Effective management of long-term care facilities* (2nd ed.). Sudbury, MA: Jones & Bartlett.

Zarem, J. (2010). *Today's continuing care community*. Washington, DC: CCRC Task Force.

Community-Based Services

After completing this chapter, readers will be able to:

1. Understand how community-based long-term care services developed and where they fit in the continuum of care.

2. Identify and define the components of community-based long-term care services.

3. Identify and describe regulations affecting community-based service providers.

4. Understand the financial, ethical, and managerial issues facing community-based long-term care services providers.

5. Identify and discuss trends in community-based long-term care services and management.

■ Introduction

The long-term care services we have reviewed thus far (nursing facilities, assisted living facilities, subacute care, and senior housing) are known as institutional services because they are provided on site in an institution. (Reverse mortgages do not fit that description.) Herein, we look at services that are described as noninstitutional, but we employ the more definitive term *community-based* because that is where they are delivered. In this case, the term *community* is used in a broad sense that includes the consumer's home and other locations within the community. The services covered herein include home health care, hospice care, and adult day care.

Let us begin by looking at what each is and how it is defined.

What Is Home Health Care?

Home health care helps people maintain themselves in the least restrictive environment possible. Without home health care, some people would have to be in hospitals or nursing homes to receive the same services at a much higher expense (Singh, 2010).

Home health care includes both health and social services. They are delivered to recovering, disabled, chronically or terminally ill persons to enhance their ability to live in their homes (LTPACHIT, 2012). Here, it is important to clarify some similar terms that are sometimes used interchangeably: *home health care* and *home care*. Although they sound the same (and home health care may include some home care services), home health care is more medically oriented. Home care typically includes chore and housecleaning services, while home health care involves helping seniors recover from an illness or injury (Administration on Aging, 2013). For the purposes of this discussion, most of our focus is on home health care, and that term will be used to include both health and supportive services unless otherwise specified.

Home health care is "a formal, regulated program of care, providing a range of medical, therapeutic, and nonmedical services; delivered by a variety of health care professionals in the patient's home" (Jones, 2012). Home health care is delivered in the patient's home, even if that home is a long-term care facility (e.g., nursing or assisted living facility). The reason for providing home healthcare services in a long-term care facility would be that the facility does not offer some specific services needed by a resident.

Home health care may be provided when a person needs only intermittent care rather than full-time care such as would be given in a nursing facility. It usually involves visits to the home for only a few hours per day and a few days per week. When the patient needs more than a few hours of service or needs it every day, home health care is no longer as cost effective. Home health services are often provided following a hospitalization to assist in making the transition from hospital to home or to allow earlier discharge.

What Is Hospice Care?

Hospice care is end-of-life care. It focuses on helping a person with a terminal illness die with dignity and helping the family of that person or other informal caregivers deal with the loss of a loved one. Terminal illness is usually defined, at least in terms of eligibility for hospice services, as a medical condition with a prognosis of 6 months or less of remaining life, with little or no hope of improvement through therapeutic interventions or treatments.

What Is Adult Day Care?

Adult day care is defined by the National Institutes of Health (2013) as:

a form of long-term care that provides interim (less than 24-hour) supervision for individuals who cannot be without supervision or assistance. They do not need the more complete services of a nursing care facility or an assisted living facility. Adult day service programs provide health, social, and other services in a safe place, generally on weekdays. They are designed for adults with mental or physical impairments. They are also for adults who need time to socialize and a place to go when their family caregivers are at work.

◼ Origins and Development

These community-based long-term care services developed to meet different—but related—needs. What they have in common is that they are substitutes for institutional forms of care. That generally means that they are less costly and are more convenient for the consumers who use them. Their ability to provide care in a noninstitutional setting—often in the consumer's home—may mean a better quality of life. Let us look at how they came to be.

Home Health Care

Home health care began in the later part of the 1800s as a service of city health departments called visiting nurse services. They often supplemented the work of physicians at a time when doctors regularly made house calls. In time, these visiting nurse associations sometimes separated from the municipal government and became freestanding. They still relied heavily on funds contributed by the cities and private sources of philanthropy. As third-party reimbursement became more available, home healthcare agencies became even more independent.

In the 1980s and 1990s, as reimbursement sources, particularly Medicare and Medicaid, looked for ways to reduce their ever-increasing costs, there was a concerted move to divert long-term care residents from institutional care to home-based care.

Hospice Care

The word *hospice* stems from the Latin word *hospitium*, meaning guesthouse. It was originally used to describe a place of shelter for weary and sick travelers returning from religious pilgrimages. During the 1960s, Dr. Cicely Saunders, a British physician, began the modern hospice movement by establishing St. Christopher's Hospice near London. St. Christopher's organized a team approach to professional caregiving and was the first program to use modern pain management techniques to compassionately care for the dying. The first hospice in the United States was established in New Haven, Connecticut, in 1974 (Hospice Foundation of America, 2014). Over the past 4 decades, hospice care has grown rapidly, to the point where there are currently several thousand hospice care programs in the United States.

Adult Day Care

Adult day care developed from the concept of respite: providing a short reprieve from the responsibilities of caregiving for those who have a family member living with them who needs constant care and supervision. As society has moved from a more inclusive nuclear family, with several generations living together and caring for each other, to families that are separated by distance and/or where both spouses must work, some families were left with a situation in which both adults wanted to engage in full-time employment, but one of them needed to remain at home to care for an elderly mother or father.

At first, the respite came in the form of friends who came into the home for a few hours to relieve the caregivers. This led to hiring someone to do the same thing periodically. Eventually, centers were opened where several people could receive care at the same time, developing into today's adult day care.

■ Philosophy of Care

These community-based long-term care services are similar, but each has a core philosophy of care that identifies it.

Home Health Care

The philosophy of home health care is quite simple: to take health services to the consumer rather than requiring the consumer to go to where the services are delivered. There are several qualifiers defining who receives home health care. They are included in the Medicare eligibility requirements and are a good guide for defining home health care in general.

Physician-Ordered Care

Home health care must be ordered by a physician. Nonhealth services such as homemaking and other supportive services may be provided without a physician's order, but without that order they are usually not provided by a home healthcare agency. There are organizations that provide only such services. The physician ordering home healthcare services also participates in developing a plan of care for the patient.

Intermittent Care

If full-time care is not needed, the care provided can be intermittent care or care that is given fewer than 7 days per week or fewer than 8 hours per day. In most cases, home health care is provided for a few (3 to 4) hours at a time, several times a week. Different healthcare professionals (e.g., nurses, therapists, social workers) may visit on different days.

Homebound Consumers

The recipient of home health care must be essentially homebound, meaning unable to leave home without a major effort. The only exceptions are infrequent, short trips to get medical care or attend religious services.

Home health care may be short term or long term. Short-term care usually provides a transition from an acute episode of care to self-reliance. Patients can be released from a hospital or rehabilitation facility sooner if they can get the care they need at home. Follow-up nursing care and therapies are commonly used in this way. Long-term home health care is for people who need ongoing care because of an illness or a diminution of functional capability. They need the services over a period of time but only on an intermittent basis.

Hospice Care

Hospice is based on a concept of providing comfort and support to patients and their families when a life-limiting illness no longer responds to cure-oriented treatments. It neither prolongs life nor hastens death. The goal of hospice care is to improve the quality of a patient's last days by offering comfort and dignity (Hospice Foundation of America, 2014). A central concept of hospice is provision of palliative care, also called comfort care, which concentrates on providing pain and symptom relief. Hospice helps the terminally ill live out their last days with as little disruption as possible and with as much dignity as possible. At the same time, there is considerable focus on the family members. The physical needs of the patient are met, along with the psychological, emotional, and spiritual needs of both patient and family members. While most hospice care is provided in the home, in some cases it is necessary for the consumer to be admitted to a hospital or skilled nursing facility for care levels that cannot be provided at home. However, hospice agency staff and volunteers are usually still very involved.

By definition of hospice, consumers of hospice services are at or near the end of their lives. That fact by itself changes the focus of the services provided and the relationship between consumer and provider. Because the goals of hospice are so directly aimed at maintaining the comfort of the dying person, there is no rehabilitation component. In most other types of long-term care, there is some attempt to rehabilitate the person receiving the services, but this is not the case in hospice. Everyone—including the patient, his or her family, and the staff of the hospice—knows that the patient is going to die shortly. This greatly increases the emotional strain on all concerned.

Hospice care is not for everyone. Some patients and/or their families want all possible steps taken to prolong life. They do not fit the philosophy of hospice, nor does it fit their needs. Similarly, hospice care does not involve any acts that may speed up the dying process, such as assisted suicide.

Adult Day Care

Adult day care operates on a philosophy of providing needed services for both the person receiving the care and those responsible for that care. In this sense, it is somewhat different from other forms of long-term care. True, in all of long-term care, from nursing facilities to home care, family members are involved with care and are considered extended consumers. The difference with adult day care is a matter of degree. As service beneficiaries, the caregivers are nearly as important as the care recipients themselves.

Adult day care centers approach their care of consumers in a holistic manner, seeking to maintain and improve their quality of life while protecting them from injuries or neglect that might result from their inability to look after themselves. Independence is promoted, and self-confidence is improved. Social interaction with other consumers and the staff of the day care center helps them achieve a way of life that is as close to normal as is possible given their physical or cognitive impairments. It has been shown over and over that the improvements in functional independence carry over to their lives at home, making it better for them and their caregivers.

Generally, a care recipient can benefit from adult day care because:

- It allows him or her to stay in his or her community while the caregiver goes to work.
- It gives him or her a break from the caregiver.
- It provides needed social interaction.
- It provides greater structure to his or her daily activities. (FamilyCare America, 2013)

■ Ownership

Community-based long-term care services providers represent several different forms of ownership, including nonprofit, for profit, and government owned. Nonprofit, community-based, long-term care services may be owned and operated by religious organizations, community organizations set up for that purpose, or nonprofit hospital or healthcare systems.

Providers that are owned and operated on a for-profit basis may be independent or affiliated with a healthcare organization. Some are freestanding, with no ownership ties to others, while others are either part of a larger chain of similar agencies or a multilevel chain that includes several types of healthcare services.

Some community-based long-term care services are owned and operated by government, including local health departments and state agencies. Usually they are set up to provide services to indigent patients. With the increasing availability of reimbursement from Medicare and Medicaid, these agencies are not needed as much, and some have been disbanded or have become independent, privately run provider organizations.

The number affiliated with other healthcare providers has grown considerably in recent years as hospitals and even nursing care facilities have developed their own home health, hospice, or adult day care services to more effectively meet the needs of their patients/residents. Many long-term care facilities (e.g., nursing facilities, assisted living facilities) that do not have their own community-based care service programs contract with outside organizations to provide those services to their residents.

Home care services are usually provided by home care organizations but may also be obtained from registries and independent providers. Home care organizations include home health agencies; hospices; homemaker and home care aide agencies; staffing and private-duty agencies; and companies specializing in medical equipment and supplies, pharmaceuticals, and drug infusion therapy. Several types of home care organizations may merge to provide a wide variety of services through an integrated system.

As of 2012, more than 62% of agencies were freestanding proprietary agencies while 12% were hospital based (NAHCH, 2012).

Most hospice organizations are not for profit, but some are part of for-profit healthcare corporations. When hospice was first developing, most were organized on a model that relied primarily on volunteers. As reimbursement has become more available, there was a decided shift away from that model toward one that is a mix of professional staff and volunteers. Although not all hospice programs are certified by Medicare, most are.

From 1984 to January 2010, the total number of hospices participating in Medicare rose from 31 to 3,407, a nearly 110-fold increase. Of these hospices, 2,278 are freestanding, 578 are home health agency based, 531 are hospital-based, and 20 are skilled nursing facility based. There are also an estimated 200 additional volunteer agencies that are not Medicare certified (NAHCH, 2010b, p. 1).

The National Adult Day Services Association estimates that there are nearly 5,000 adult day centers in the United States serving over 270,000 participants and family caregivers (Harris-Kojetin, Sengupta, Park-Lee, & Valverde, 2013, p. 11). While some are freestanding centers, others are affiliated with a nursing home, assisted living community, senior center, or rehabilitation facility. Nearly three quarters of them are not physically connected to or on the same grounds as another type of facility (MetLife Mature Market Institute, 2012, p. 6). The high proportion of nonprofit and public ownership reflects the beginnings of adult day care as a service provided to those who needed it rather than as an investment. As adult day care has become more health oriented, there has been an increase in ownership by, or in affiliation with, healthcare facilities.

■ Services Provided

Community-based long-term care organizations provide many of the same services although in different amounts and formats and with different degrees of emphasis on certain services.

Home Health Care

Home care providers deliver a wide variety of healthcare and supportive services, including skilled care services and ongoing home care. One survey found that the services commonly used by home healthcare patients aged 65 years and over included the following proportions: "skilled nursing services (84%), physical therapy (40%), assistance with activities of daily living (ADLs) (37%), homemaker services (17%), occupational therapy (14%), wound care (14%), and dietary counseling (14%)" (MetLife Mature Market Institute, 2012, p. 70).

Nursing

Nursing is the primary skilled service provided and is at the heart of home health care. Nursing care includes assessment, monitoring, dressing changes, administration of medications, and education of the patient and the family caregivers. It is provided by both registered nurses (RNs) and licensed practical nurses.

Therapy

Several types of therapy are provided to home care consumers in their own residences, including physical therapy, occupational therapy, and therapy for speech/language pathologies. Physical therapy involves restoring or maintaining the mobility and strength of patients who are limited by physical injuries, using techniques such as exercise and massage. Occupational therapists assist them in overcoming limitations with the use of assistive devices and techniques. Speech-language pathologists are therapists who work with patients to improve or restore their ability to communicate.

Other Services

Some minor dental procedures, such as cleaning, checkups, and small fillings, can be done in the patient's home by dentists and/or dental assistants. Nutritional assessment and counseling assist the patient and his or her family or caregiver to provide the proper nutrition and learn how to plan diets appropriate to the patient's illness. Also, routine and special lab tests can be performed, with the specimens (blood, urine, etc.) being collected in the patient's home.

In the area of care management, social workers coordinate much of the care and arrange other services as needed. For personal care, home care staff helps patients who may have limitations in their ADLs, particularly with personal care (e.g., bathing, grooming, and dressing). Homemakers perform light housekeeping and other chores, which include some meal preparation when the family or other caregiver is unable to do so. Agency staff may also transport the patient to medical appointments and shop for the patient if needed.

Another very important service provided by home health agencies is education of the patient and family. Patients are taught how to do as much for themselves as possible and how to change their way of doing things, if necessary, to achieve more independence and less reliance on formal caregivers.

As with other forms of long-term care, home health care begins with an assessment of the needs of the patient. Although home health providers have long used such an assessment to better provide services, a standardized form of assessment has been developed by Medicare and home health providers. It is known as OASIS, which stands for Outcome and Assessment Information Set. OASIS is a method of collecting and monitoring data to improve outcome measures in home health care. The data cover the sociodemographic, environmental, support system, health status, and functional status attributes of the patient. They allow the Medicare program to measure patient outcomes on a large scale and provide information on which Medicare case-mix payments are based. Individual home health providers can also use the data for assessment and care planning for their patients.

In recent years, technology has played an increasing role in home health care. Diagnostic tests and treatments that previously could be done only in a healthcare facility or a doctor's office can now be administered safely and effectively at home. Monitoring devices, including telemonitoring, have become commonplace. Telemonitoring involves telecommunications devices in the home that record and send information to the patient's doctor or other healthcare professional. They are capable of recording and transmitting information such as blood pressure, heartbeat, and other vital signs. Other technologies enable the use of infusion pumps and other medication administration techniques.

Home health and hospice care agencies have increasingly adopted electronic health records and/or mobile technology. The most commonly used functionalities for agencies with electronic health records were patient demographics and clinical notes. For agencies with mobile technology, email and appointment scheduling were the most commonly used (Bercovitz, Park-Lee, & Jamoom, 2013).

Hospice Care

Hospice care agencies provide supportive and palliative care to people at the end of life. Hospice agencies focus on comfort and quality of life, rather than curative treatments (NAHCH, 2010b). The services provided in a hospice program are aimed at easing the pain of the patients and assisting them and their families in getting through this very difficult time.

The services usually provided are a mix of physical care and emotional support and include:

- *Physician Services*: Overall supervision of the care plan. The physician may be employed by the hospice or may be the patient's own primary care physician.
- *Nursing Services*: A full range of skilled nursing services, including monitoring, dressing changes, and comfort care.
- *Social Services*: Assistance with emotional and financial matters, making contact with outside agencies.
- *Counseling*: Psychological, spiritual, and nutritional counseling.
- *Medical Appliances and Supplies*: Providing needed items such as bandages, hospital room equipment, etc.
- *Pain Management*: Medication and other symptom relief.

- *Homemaker and Home Health Aide Services*: Personal care and assistance with housework.
- *Therapies*: Physical, occupational, and speech therapy to maintain optimum functional capacity for as long as possible.

These services are routinely provided by the hospice team in the patient's home, even if that home is actually a nursing facility or other long-term care setting. In addition, there are usually arrangements for temporary continuous home care or inpatient care for short periods if needed for pain control or other crises. Some hospices also offer respite services, placing the patient in a hospital or nursing facility for a brief time to give the caregivers a needed break from their physically and emotionally draining duties.

Prior to admission to a hospice program, the patient and family members meet with the hospice team to assess the specific needs of the patient. The assessment addresses the patient's illness and possible methods of pain and symptom management, functional disabilities requiring assistance, and any special nursing or therapy needs. It also involves a meeting with a social worker to evaluate any social service needs.

The team-oriented care requires a high level of communication and enables the team members to always know all of the aspects of the patient's care. This is particularly important in hospice care because terminally ill patients have needs and wishes that change as their disease progresses.

Adult Day Care

As with most long-term care providers, the specific services provided vary depending on the nature of the consumers served and the interests of the providers. Adult day care centers are generally grouped into two categories: social day care and health day care. There is a third group, dementia day care, but it is usually included in one of the other categories.

Social Model

The social model of adult day care is the original form and has been around since the 1970s. Its primary purpose is providing a safe and secure environment for people without significant healthcare needs but who may have some minor limitation in the ADLs. The social model provides consumers with relief from boredom and loneliness, conditions that can lead to feelings of isolation and depression. It allows seniors and others with some mild cognitive impairment to interact with others in a sheltered setting. Individuals with Alzheimer's disease are often candidates for social adult day care. They cannot be left alone because of memory loss or a tendency to wander, but in an adult day care center they can be supervised appropriately.

Services focus on socialization and recreation and may range from group singing and bingo to more challenging activities, depending on the cognitive levels of those participating. Communal meals and other group activities such as field trips add to the social interaction and sense of belonging.

■ Informal Caregivers

The family members of the consumers of community-based long-term care services must also be included as beneficiaries of community-based long-term care services. Often, the caregivers of long-term care consumers are spouses, children, friends, and volunteers. As one set of authors put it:

> recognizing the reality of family life today, we should define informal caregivers broadly, to include not only relatives but also partners, friends, neighbors, and others who provide or manage the care of a person with a serious illness or disability. (Levine, Halper, Peist, & Gould, 2010)

To distinguish them from those who give care as part of their jobs, they will be referred to here as informal caregivers. Formal caregivers are the staff members of healthcare organizations: nursing and assisted living facilities, hospitals, subacute care units, home care agencies, and hospice and adult day care programs. They are employed to work with consumers of long-term care. By contrast, informal caregivers do so as a matter of personal or familial obligation, friendship, or simply a desire to help someone less fortunate.

Informal caregivers play a huge role in providing care to long-term care consumers. They have been defined as the backbone or the bedrock of the Long Term Care Services & Supports (LTSS) workforce (Levine et al., 2010). This is particularly true for those consumers using hospice and adult day care, and those services provide much-needed relief for those caregivers. In addition to giving them a break from the physical and mental tasks associated with caregiving and providing specialized services beyond the capabilities of the informal caregivers, it may also make it possible for them to go shopping or hold a part-time or even full-time job, bringing in needed income for the family.

The sheer volume of care given by these informal caregivers is staggering. The Family Caregiver Alliance (2014) reports that:

> about 44 million Americans provide 37 billion hours of unpaid, "informal" care each year for adult family members and friends with chronic illnesses or conditions that prevent them from handling daily activities such as bathing, managing medications or preparing meals on their own. Family caregivers, particularly women, provide over 75% of caregiving support in the United States.

An estimated 78% of the elderly in need of long-term care receive that care from family members and friends, and 34 million caregivers provide care to someone age 50 or over (Benz, 2012). Women are slightly more likely than men to be caring for a loved one, as are adults ages 50–64, compared with other age groups (Fox & Brenner, 2012).

Anyone working directly with these consumers and their informal caregivers can tell numerous true stories of the burden of being a full-time caregiver. First, there is the added cost. Long-term caregiving has significant financial consequences for caregivers, particularly for women. Informal caregivers personally lose about $659,139 over a lifetime: $25,494 in Social Security benefits; $67,202 in pension benefits; and $566,443 in forgone wages (Family Caregiver Alliance, 2014).

Then, there are the nonmonetary costs. Caregiving responsibilities often lead to physical, emotional, and financial strain for caregivers, some of whom are in poor health themselves (Levine et al., 2010). Many times, especially when the caregiver is a spouse, his or her health may not be much better than the one for whom they care. They sacrifice much to care for their loved ones, often placing their own health in jeopardy. One such example involved an 84-year-old man who was in relatively good health for his age, providing around-the-clock care for his 89-year-old wife who had suffered several strokes. Although his family and others tried to assist, neither he nor his wife would accept any such help. It was not until he needed a total hip replacement himself that they finally agreed to get assistance.

This situation is very typical of family caregivers. They feel an obligation to do as much as they can and resist asking for outside assistance. There is also some amount of guilt at no longer being able to tend to a loved one as well as in the past. Services such as those provided in adult day care centers can give these family members valuable assistance and do it without taking away independence or breaking any of the bonds that exist. This helps them avoid the feelings of guilt. It stops short of taking a family member away to a nursing facility or other institutional setting, and that means a great deal to them.

■ Market Forces Affecting Community-Based Services

Community-based long-term care has grown as a result of a combination of factors.

Consumer Choice

Consumers of health care have always had a desire to stay at home. Admission to a hospital or long-term care facility puts them in a foreign set of surroundings when they are ill or hurting. The food is not what they are accustomed to, their schedule is disrupted, and they are subjected to tests and treatments that may be unpleasant. Although community-based long-term care services may not be able to eliminate the tests and treatments, receiving them in one's own familiar home or in a less institutional setting can greatly improve the situation.

The popularity of community-based services with consumers is largely due to its ability to prevent, delay, or at least minimize the need for those admissions. It has enabled many patients to remain in familiar surroundings for long periods of time—in some cases avoiding admission to a facility completely. Community-based services often make it possible for a family to stay together, even though the caregiver (spouse, child, or parent) may not be able to provide all of the care that is needed.

This movement toward consumers wanting to receive care in a manner that is as close to their normal lives as possible has affected all of health care and long-term care. Consumers want to have a larger say in their care and in decision making concerning that care. They are becoming better informed and are willing to demand services that meet their needs and wishes.

Cost-Effectiveness

Community-based care has also grown in popularity with those organizations that pay for health care because it is a cost-effective alternative to other, more intensive, forms of health care. A note of caution here: home health care, home-based hospice care, and adult day care are more cost-effective than other delivery methods if used appropriately—for a few hours per week. It is tempting to think of noninstitutional care as always being more cost-effective. However, if the needs of an individual consumer are such that intermittent care is not enough, home-based health care becomes more expensive. It is, after all, one-on-one care, whereas in institutional care, each staff member cares for several consumers. When the consumer needs care that is more than intermittent or needs nearly full-time supervision by trained staff, community-based care is no longer appropriate.

The agencies and organizations that pay for health care learned early on that community-based long-term care costs them less than full-time institutional care. Medicare began covering home health care when the program was enacted in 1965 and added hospice care later. In many states, Medicaid covers all three types of community-based long-term care services. The extent of such coverage continues to grow as Medicaid agencies seek less expensive forms of care. The national percentage of Medicaid spending on home and community-based services more than doubled from 20% in 1995 to 45% in 2010 (Kaiser Commission on Medicaid and the Uninsured, 2012). Managed care organizations (MCOs) and other insurance companies increasingly cover them as well.

Social and Demographic Changes

The dramatic growth in the number of elderly in this country has increased the need for all long-term care services and will continue to do so for the foreseeable future. More people need more care for a longer time. This has prompted development of new services such as community-based long-term care services.

In addition to the growth in demand for services caused by increased numbers of elderly, other societal changes have boosted that demand. The breakup of the close-knit family structure and increased employment of both spouses make it difficult for relatives to provide full-time care without assistance. Community-based long-term care services have helped to meet that need.

Competition Among Other Providers

Other providers of healthcare services, such as hospitals, nursing facilities, and assisted living facilities, are looking for new product lines and are getting involved in the business of adult day care. As competition among them increases, each such provider looks for ways to improve its position in the overall market, and adding a valuable new service before a competitor does gives them a considerable advantage.

■ Regulations

Regulations affecting community-based services fall into three general categories: (1) Medicare certification, (2) licensure of provider organizations, and (3) licensure of professional staff.

Medicare Certification

Home health and hospice care are covered by Medicare (adult day care is not). Any healthcare provider wishing to receive Medicare reimbursement must be certified by them and must comply with certain conditions of participation. These conditions cover the types of services provided, staffing, financial restrictions, and reporting requirements. For home health providers, the conditions also cover the OASIS assessment data reporting and the rules for calculating case-mix information used in determining the rate of payment. Although the Medicare hospice regulations cover many of the same requirements as those for other long-term care services, they are a bit different. For example, Medicare does not require that patients be essentially homebound as is the case with home care.

Licensure of Provider Organizations

Licensure of community-based service providers is handled at the state level. Medicare requires that agencies comply with state and local laws where such laws are in effect, but it does not specify that states must require licensure. Most, but not all, states do license home healthcare agencies, and nearly all states now license hospice providers. Most that do so do it in conjunction with Medicaid coverage of hospice services.

Not surprisingly, most of the states that do require licensure either base their regulations on or have regulations that closely reflect those of Medicare, although they may also add their own specific regulations. Some require that all licensed agencies abide by those regulations, but a few apply them only to Medicare-certified home health agencies.

Current codes, laws, and regulations governing adult day services are not uniform among the states. Although many states regulate adult day services to some degree, they are not federally regulated (MetLife Mature Market Institute, 2012). Typically, in those states that provide Medicaid reimbursement through various waiver programs, there are more regulations in place to protect that state's investment. Where licensing does exist, regulations usually cover space, safety, and staffing as with other forms of long-term care. As the number of centers grows, and particularly as more of them focus on health care, there will clearly be more regulations at both the state and national levels.

Licensure of Staff

Professional staff, such as physicians, nurses, and social workers, must be licensed by their state licensing boards regardless of what type of healthcare organization they work for. The state regulations are generally quite similar and allow movement from state to state.

■ Accreditation and Certification

Accreditation and certification are voluntary programs. Accreditation applies to provider organizations, and certification applies to individuals. Both attest to the fact that the organization or individual meets certain qualifications.

Accreditation

Home healthcare and hospice agencies may be accredited by any of three separate organizations: the Joint Commission, the Community Health Accreditation Program (CHAP), or the Accreditation Commission for Health Care.

The Joint Commission accredits most forms of healthcare providers, including hospitals, doctor's offices, nursing homes, office-based surgery centers, behavioral health treatment facilities, and providers of home care services (The Joint Commission, 2014). Home health and hospice care are accredited, but adult day care is not.

CHAP began as a joint venture between the American Public Health Association and the National League for Nursing in 1965. In 2001, it became an independent nonprofit corporation. CHAP accredits some community-based services, including home care and hospice. CHAP is "an independent, nonprofit, accrediting body for community-based health care organizations, which accredits nine programs and services" (CHAP, 2014).

The Accreditation Commission for Health Care accredits home health, home infusion, home medical equipment, hospice, aides, specialty pharmacy, mail order medical, and rehabilitation technology services as well as respiratory nebulizer medication pharmacy services and women's healthcare products and services.

Certification of Professionals

Individual health professionals also have the option of acquiring voluntary verification of their qualifications, called "certification." Such certification is usually provided through the appropriate national professional associations, such as the American Nurses Credentialing Center or the American Occupational Therapy Association. Because professional certification applies to individuals, they can carry it with them from job to job.

■ Financing of Community-Based Services

As is true of institutional care, financing of community-based long-term care services comes from a combination of government programs (Medicare and Medicaid), private insurance and managed care, and private out-of-pocket sources.

Medicare

Medicare is the largest single payer of home healthcare services.

Medicare spending accounts for about four tenths of home health expenditures. Other public funding sources for home health include Medicaid, the Older Americans Act, Title XX Social Services Block Grants, the Department of Veterans Affairs, and the Civilian Health and Medical Program of the Uniformed Services.

Medicare funding for home health care has been very volatile since its inception. As new groups of beneficiaries have been added, payment methods have changed, and as Medicare rates have fluctuated up and down, the impact on home health care has been considerable. The amount and availability of Medicare funding has affected the number of organizations providing services.

For example, from the time Medicare first began covering home health care in 1965, through the mid-1980s, the number of home healthcare agencies grew steadily, but leveled off in the mid-1980s, largely because of increasing Medicare paperwork and unreliable payment policies. Following a 1987 lawsuit and changes in payment policies, the number of home health agencies grew again. In 1997, however, portions of the Balanced Budget Act again reduced Medicare reimbursement, and the number of providers declined (NAHCH, 2010a). Since the full prospective payment system was implemented, the decline in the number of home health providers seems to have stopped.

With the prospective payment system, Medicare pays home health (and hospice) providers for each 60-day episode of care. The amount paid for that 60-day period is a set amount based on a standard rate and adjusted for the type and intensity of care provided, in what is known as a case-mix formula. The home health prospective payment system relies on a 153-category case-mix adjuster to set payment rates based on patient characteristics including clinical severity, functional status, and the need for rehabilitative therapy services. Medicare does not cover all home health care. It does not cover 24-hour care, prescription drugs, meals delivered to the home (e.g., Meals on Wheels), homemaker services, and personal care if that is the only care needed.

In its early years, hospice care relied on a combination of private pay from consumers and their families and contributions from philanthropies and social agencies such as the United Way. However, that changed substantially in 1982 with passage of the Tax Equity Fiscal Responsibility Act when hospice care became a Medicare entitlement. As a result, hospice care was suddenly available to millions of Americans.

Today, Medicare stands as the single largest source of hospice reimbursement. Hospice care is covered under the Medicare Part A benefit. Part A is the hospital insurance portion of Medicare, while Part B is the medical (nonhospital) portion. Medicare does not cover everything related to hospice care, although its coverage is quite broad. Services covered include physician and nursing services; medical equipment, such as wheelchairs or walkers; medical supplies, such as bandages and catheters; drugs for symptom control and pain relief; short-term hospital care, including respite care; home health aide and homemaker services; physical and occupational therapy; speech therapy; social worker services; nutritional counseling; and grief counseling for both the patient and the family.

Hospice services not covered by Medicare include treatments designed to cure the terminal illness, treatment or services not related to comfort care, care from another hospice that was not set up through the patient's own hospice, care from another provider that could be provided by the patient's own hospice, and room and board other than during periods of temporary respite care.

Medicare hospice coverage includes two 90-day benefit periods, followed by an unlimited number of 60-day benefit periods. Although Medicare hospice coverage depends on the physician certifying that the prognosis is for no more than 6 months of life, coverage can extend beyond that period given that the 6-month prognosis is only the doctor's best estimate.

There is also provision for patients to move out of and back into hospice care. In some cases, particularly those pertaining to patients with some forms of cancer, there are periods of remission when their health improves temporarily. When that happens, they leave hospice care and are covered by their regular Medicare or other insurance. If or when they need hospice care again, their Medicare hospice coverage resumes.

Medicare pays the hospice provider on a per diem basis. The per diem payment is expected to cover all services provided by the hospice. There are several different rates, varying according to the type and level of care provided. The different rates cover routine home care, continuous home care (24 hours/day), inpatient respite care, and general inpatient care. Costs often vary by the type of service, particularly the extent of health care services the participant requires. Medicare does not pay for adult day care, but expenses can be covered through a variety of other sources. Under the home and community-based services waiver program, Medicaid is the leading source of payment for adult day care (Singh, 2010). National average daily rates remain unchanged since 2011 at $70 per day. The average daily rate for adult day services programs operating using a medical/health model is $79, significantly higher than programs operating using a combined medical/health and social model ($71) or a social model alone ($63) (MetLife Mature Market Institute, 2012).

Medicaid

Medicaid is a program designed to cover health care for people who are medically indigent, meaning that their incomes are too low for them to afford to pay for care, and for those who have no health insurance. It is operated by the states under national guidelines, and the cost is split between the states and the national government. States must provide certain services but have the option of choosing whether to provide others. They must provide nursing services, home care aide services, and medical equipment and supplies, but they are not required to provide other services, including some that would be provided under Medicare. Therapies and social services are among those that the states may or may not provide. Hospice care is also optional.

Medicaid coverage of community-based services has grown, largely because state governments are seeking ways to reduce their costs, and these services are one way to do that. However, the rates paid by some state Medicaid programs are lower than those for other programs, and some agencies do not accept patients with Medicaid coverage only.

Although not universal, most states offer a hospice benefit as part of their Medicaid coverage. Their payment methods and rates are similar to those of Medicare, with some minor differences from state to state.

Some state Medicaid programs pay for adult day care. Most of these do so through federal waivers that allow them to waive some Medicaid rules in order to use less costly services. Other Medicaid funds come through Title III of the Older Americans Act.

One community-based government program that has proven particularly successful is the Program of All-Inclusive Care for the Elderly (PACE). PACE features a comprehensive service delivery system and integrated Medicare and Medicaid financing. The PACE model is a Medicare program that enables states to provide PACE services to Medicaid beneficiaries as an optional Medicaid benefit, allowing most participants to continue living at home.

Although PACE services can be provided at home or in other facilities, most are provided at adult day care centers. PACE programs provide social and medical services primarily in an adult day health center, supplemented by in-home and referral services in accordance with the participant's needs. The PACE service package must include all Medicare- and Medicaid-covered services and other services determined necessary by the interdisciplinary team for the care of the PACE participant (LTPACHIT, 2012).

The PACE program is capitated, meaning that providers are paid a set rate for each person covered rather than on a fee-for-service basis. Such capitation allows providers more flexibility than they would otherwise have. The number of PACE programs continues to grow.

Private Health Insurance and Managed Care

Private (or commercial) insurance companies, including MCOs, are also increasingly providing coverage of community-based care. Traditional insurance was slow to add such coverage, but insurance policies specifically designed for long-term care often do include it. Also, as more and more types of MCOs have developed—including health maintenance organizations and preferred provider organizations—that coverage has expanded. Again, the primary impetus for this growth has been efforts to improve cost-effectiveness.

While MCOs have been slower to cover adult day care than they have to cover home health and hospice care, they are becoming increasingly interested in it and are including it among their covered benefits. Other private insurance coverage of adult day care has also been minimal, but as long-term care insurance programs gain popularity, that coverage will increase. However, it still represents a very small portion of the financing of adult day care and will for some time to come.

Also, most (80% or more) employees in company-sponsored health insurance plans have access to hospice coverage. This remains true whether they are covered by traditional insurance or a managed care contract.

Private, Out-of-Pocket Financing

A substantial amount of community-based care is paid by the patients themselves or their families. It may be because they have no other coverage or because they fail to meet the qualification requirements of other programs. Sometimes self-pay serves to provide limited services until patients qualify, or after they cease to qualify, for other programs. For example, most adult day care has traditionally been financed by the consumers themselves or their families. This is still the case, although other sources of financing are becoming available. Because these sources of funding are so fragmented and limited, the families or other caregivers usually have to come up with some funds of their own.

■ Staffing and Human Resource Issues

Community-based care services are personnel intensive; that is, payroll for staff is the largest portion of the budget. They rely on a mix of professional and nonprofessional staff working as a care team. The team includes nurses (both RNs and licensed practical nurses), aides, therapists (physical, occupational, speech), social workers, and numerous other specialists.

Nurses are generally the care coordinators, regularly evaluating the nursing care needs of each patient, adjusting the care plan accordingly and keeping the supervising physician and other members of the care team informed about the condition of the patient, any changes in that condition, and the progress of the patient. The nurse is also instrumental in providing the patient and family with the education they need to optimize their contribution to the care plan.

Licensed practical nurses assist the RNs, providing many of the nursing services needed. They are allowed to perform many treatments and nursing procedures under the supervision of an RN.

Aides are seen by many as the backbone of community-based care because they provide such a large number of the routine services to patients. They work under the supervision of the professional nurses and therapists and provide most of the personal care. That care includes assistance with ADLs and assisting them with self-administered medications and therapist-ordered exercises. Aides in Medicare-certified home health agencies must complete a training program covering specified competency areas. They must also undergo a periodic competency evaluation and in-service training as needed.

Physical and occupational therapy may be provided either by registered therapists or by certified therapy assistants under the supervision of the therapists. Therapists evaluate the patient's therapy needs, develop the plan of care, and oversee the work of therapy assistants when they are involved. Therapy assistants have less training and essentially carry out the treatments ordered by the therapists. The actual extent of the duties they can perform is regulated by state licensing agencies and varies somewhat from state to state. Speech therapy is provided by registered speech pathologists.

Medical social workers assist the team with assessing social and emotional factors affecting the patient's treatment plan. They also assist the patient and family in accessing community resources, resolving financial issues, and interacting with other providers. Because of the bewildering array of information needed by providers and payers, to say nothing of the many rules and regulations governing health care, patients and their families welcome the assistance given by the social worker. As a result, they often feel very close to these workers. Some social service tasks can be performed by social service aides.

While all forms of community-based care involve an interdisciplinary team that includes healthcare professionals, in the case of hospice the team is more likely to include clergy and/or other bereavement counselors and to place more emphasis on inclusion of the patient and a family member or primary caregiver. In keeping with the concept of hospice as a means of giving terminally ill patients more control over their lives, the hospice team involves them regularly and directly in decision making. Volunteers also help in many ways. Some help with household chores such as cleaning and cooking. Others provide transportation for the patient to and from appointments or take a family member shopping or to other engagements. They may stay with patients for a short time to give caregivers an hour or two off to attend to their personal needs (not to be confused with respite care, which usually involves several days at a time). Sometimes the greatest contribution made by a volunteer is simply being available to talk to the patient or caregiver.

Medical care and supervision of patients in community-based care are usually provided by the patient's own personal physician, although the service provider—particularly in hospice care—may also have a medical director involved.

As noted earlier, most hospices began with a largely volunteer staff. Although that has changed in favor of the highly specialized professionals listed earlier, volunteers still play a large role in most hospice care. The volunteers are often friends or relatives of the hospice patient who want to help in any way they can. Other volunteers give their time and services simply because they want to assist anyone who needs them. In either case, the volunteers are screened and trained by the hospice staff to ensure that they are appropriately integrated into the individual's care plan.

Adult day care centers are staffed by a combination of professional and nonprofessional employees, with the proportion of each determined by the nature of the center (social or health model) and the particular services offered. Both social model and health model day care centers have staff trained in personal care, activities and/or recreation, and nutrition. They may also have positions such as activity coordinator, recreation assistant, drivers, and cooks. Adult day healthcare centers have more healthcare professionals available, either part time or full time, including physicians; nurses; physical, occupational, speech, and recreation therapists; nutritionists; and social workers. There is also usually a category comparable to the certified nursing assistants found in nursing facilities or the home health aides found in home health agencies. They are often called program aides or health aides.

■ Legal and Ethical Issues

Most legal and ethical issues in home health and hospice care center on the fact that the care is delivered in the patient's home, not in a more structured setting such as a long-term care facility. This means that the providers have less control of the care setting and how well the patient complies with the care plan. The legal and ethical issues affecting adult day care centers are similar to those found in other forms of long-term care, centering on the rights of the consumers. The following are some of the issues providers of community-based services face.

Patient Noncompliance

The providers strive to give the patient as much autonomy and participation in making care-related decisions as possible. However, when professional opinion differs with patient choice, it can be difficult for all involved. Patients are expected to conform to the treatment plan even when staff members are not present, but that does not always happen. The plan may require that the patient adhere to a restrictive diet because some foods are contraindicated and might even be harmful. Getting patients to avoid those foods when they desire them may be difficult. Patients with late onset diabetes may

cheat on their diet by sneaking candy bars when no one is looking, which undermines the treatment plan. How does agency staff deal with this issue? In reality, it usually comes down to a combination of education, a bit of scolding, and realization that such cheating is likely and the treatment plan will need to be adjusted accordingly. This is not as great a problem for adult day care because of the on-site supervision, but it still happens.

Patient Safety

A much more serious issue arises when staff suspects that the patient is in an unsafe situation in the home or is perhaps subject to neglect or abuse by a family member or other person. They must look out for the welfare of the patient but cannot afford to make unfounded accusations. If their suspicions have merit, they are legally and ethically obligated to report those suspicions to the appropriate authorities. In such instances, the agency will gather its entire staff, including administrators and perhaps even legal counsel, to review the facts and reach a decision.

Patients' Rights

As with other forms of long-term care, the issue of patient's rights is of great concern, and community-based providers have to be continuously cognizant of these and other legal and ethical issues and must attempt to anticipate them and deal with them in a careful, deliberative manner. This requires that they be well informed about such issues, even though laws and regulations change with regularity.

The Decision to Accept Hospice Care

One issue that is common to hospice care is denial. Acknowledging the fact that you are terminally ill is difficult at best, traumatic at worst. We all know, at least philosophically, that we are going to die eventually. However, most believe it to be far into the future. For the patient who is eligible for hospice care, there is the need to accept that death will occur sooner rather than later. This is not easy for the patient or for family and friends, and it becomes an ethical issue as it relates to the way in which they address the impending death and the decision to accept hospice care.

Sometimes it is more difficult for loved ones to accept the inevitable death of a loved one than it is for the patient. There can also be feelings of guilt or feelings that more could have been done to prolong life or even to accomplish a cure. These emotions are normal but can often lead to unintended, but still harmful, attempts to influence the patient and professional care providers. A spouse or child who is in denial may convince the patient that hospice is not needed, or at least not yet.

Healthcare professionals may also contribute to the difficulty by refusing to believe that there is nothing more they can do for the patient. The great advances made in recent years in prolonging life, and even in defeating some formerly certain death-causing conditions, have led to the belief that there is always something else to be tried. It is important that neither family members nor health professionals be allowed to inappropriately deny someone the benefits of hospice care. Late hospice intervention can limit those benefits. The best way to avoid delayed hospice care is education of all involved. Some hospice patients fool the professional prognosticators by living longer than the anticipated 6 months. What should be done then? The answer is simple: extend hospice care. However, acceptance of that answer by patients, family, and healthcare workers is not always that simple or easy. Although all involved are happy that death has been delayed, there is also a feeling of confusion and even guilt. They may ask themselves "Did we jump the gun, enrolling in hospice too soon?" These concerns are usually unfounded. However, they should be addressed early on to help avoid the emotional problems they cause.

Inequitable Access

There is great variation in access to hospice services from state to state, from urban to rural areas, and even within geographic regions. To the extent that access to appropriate care, including community-based services, is a right, this is an ethical issue.

■ Management

Administrators of community-based service providers are not regularly licensed as are nursing facility administrators and, in some states, administrators of assisted living facilities. However, Medicare conditions of participation spell out several qualifications for an administrator of a Medicare-certified home health agency. The administrator must be a licensed physician, an RN, or have training and experience in health service administration and at least 1 year of supervisory or administrative experience in home healthcare or related health programs. As already noted, there are several organizations accrediting home health agencies. Those organizations do have standards for administrative performance and leadership.

Medicare requirements for management of hospice care are quite general, essentially requiring that the agency has a governing body responsible for overall operation and a qualified individual to manage it (NHPCO, 2014). Medicare also allows a hospice to contract with another entity to furnish services to its patients, but the hospice retains professional management responsibility.

There is little in the way of commonality in terms of qualifications for administrators of adult day care centers. Those states that license adult day care centers usually require a combination of education and/or experience but are quite liberal in allowing substitutions of one for the other. When the center is part of a larger, long-term care organization, such as a nursing care facility or home care agency, the requirements for that entity usually apply.

■ Management Challenges and Opportunities

As is the case with other types of long-term care, managers of community-based services must deal with issues of balancing cost and quality, complying with numerous regulations, staffing shortages, and maintaining ties to the community and referral organizations. There are, however, several challenges that are unique to them.

Supervision of Staff—Home Health and Hospice Care

Unlike most other types of long-term care, hospice and home health agencies send staff members out to provide services in patients' homes. Although more than a single staff member may visit the patient concurrently on occasion, this is not the norm. Most of the time they visit separately, meaning that staff members work most of the time without direct supervision. This does not apply to staff of adult day care because they work within a more formal setting.

Supervisors must rely on use of standardized procedures, reporting methods, and documentation to evaluate the quality and productivity of their staff. Each patient is different, with a different care plan, and staff providing services must know and follow that particular care plan. The manager of the agency has to be well organized and must have an ability to judge the work of subordinates without always being able to observe them directly. Technology has provided some added tools in recent years, including electronic note taking and telemetry, both of which allow the on-site staff to record what they are doing and allow the supervisor to follow along or review the records at a later time.

Hospice—Coordinating Professional and Volunteer Staff

All healthcare organizations rely to some extent on volunteers to supplement their paid employee staff. However, in the case of hospice, the volunteers are a much more integral part of the overall staffing, both in numbers and in what they do. They are, in most instances, fully participating members of the interdisciplinary team. This means that they must receive a special amount of training and supervision not found in most other volunteer situations. They are directly involved with the patient and family and may even be family members or close friends. This places an emotional burden on them, and they carry a significant responsibility, which means that the manager of the hospice also carries a special responsibility to ensure that they fulfill their roles appropriately. It is not always easy and demands more time and effort on the part of the manager than is the case with many other long-term care organizations.

Hospice—The Emotional Element

Whether paid professionals or volunteers, hospice staff have to deal with helping people prepare to die. No matter how well trained and conditioned the staff may be, there is still a toll taken. They work very closely with the patients and families for months, only to have those patients die. It is important that the management of the hospice prepare them for the emotional aspects of their duties. They need to be taught and reassured that their job is to improve the quality of life of the patient and family and even to improve the quality of dying. They are not there to prevent death and must not see it as a defeat. Most hospices provide counseling and support for their staff as well as for the patients and families. It is the job of the manager to see that such support is in place.

Cultural, Religious, and Ethnic Differences

Few aspects of our lives depend as much on our cultural, religious, and ethnic backgrounds as our approach to dying. Each individual is exposed to these influences from birth and even inherits certain traits based on them. By the time we become elderly, as are most hospice patients, these influences have pretty well determined who we are and what we think. When it comes to thinking about impending death, there are many different approaches. A hospice has to be cognizant of those differences and adapt the organization's services to respect and accommodate them. Ethnic and cultural differences can mean that what one patient might appreciate is insulting to another.

Some hospices serve a relatively well-defined patient population with few cultural, religious, or ethnic differences, but these are not the rule. When the patients are more diversified, it presents the management of the hospice with a considerable challenge. Understanding how each patient and his or her family feel about death is crucial. When there is a clergy member already involved, the hospice works with that person. If not, they must decide whether the patient wants such involvement and, if so, arrange it.

Community and Philanthropic Groups

Although reimbursement for hospice services has become much more common and available, most hospices still rely to some extent on community agencies such as the United Way and other philanthropies for financial support. This situation requires a portion of the manager's time and effort and requires that he or she be a bit of a fund raiser and community ambassador, all while managing the operations of the organization.

■ Significant Trends and Their Impact on Community-Based Services

Community-based care is, at the same time, a well-established form of health care and a still-developing field. The basic services provided have long been, and continue to be, nursing, therapies, and personal care. However, new services are added periodically, and old services are refined and improved. In addition to trends relating to services, there are significant trends in service delivery, financing, and organization.

Consumer Choice/Quality of Life

Consumers of health care, including long-term care, have expressed a desire for more choice in how and where they are cared for as a means of improving the quality of their lives. That often leads them to seek out community-based services. It has increased the demand for those services and also increased their expectations for the quality of those services. As an offshoot of the increased desire for consumer choice, more consumers are seeking alternative complementary forms of treatment such as acupuncture, therapeutic massage, and chiropractic care to bring comfort to patients who do not respond to traditional treatments. Such treatments are not currently covered by Medicare and most other reimbursement sources.

Olmstead Decision

On June 22, 1999, the U.S. Supreme Court held in *Olmstead v. L.C.* that the unnecessary segregation of individuals with disabilities in institutions may constitute discrimination based on disability. The court ruled that the Americans With Disabilities Act may require states to provide community-based services rather than institutional placements for individuals with disabilities. The court held that:

> unjustified segregation in institutions is discrimination not only because it perpetuates unwarranted assumptions that people with disabilities are incapable or unworthy of participating in community life, but also because confinement in an institution severely curtails everyday life activities, such as family relations, social contacts, work, educational advancement, and cultural enrichment. (O'Keeffe et al., 2010)

This has greatly increased the demand for, and reimbursement for, community-based services.

Technology

Increased availability and use of technology in the delivery of community-based services is possibly the most exciting trend in recent years and will continue to be in the near future. Advancements in technology have both increased the range of services that can be provided and improved the productivity of staff.

One ongoing aspect of technology is that it makes devices smaller at the same time their capabilities expand. Miniaturized wireless sensors and monitors can be used in the home much more easily than in the past. This has benefited home health and hospice care by making it possible to do in the home much of what had previously been possible only in hospitals or doctors' offices. Diagnostic tests can be conducted, with the results made available on site or transmitted electronically to test centers. Through telemonitoring, patients can be monitored at home either periodically or continuously, with the information transmitted to the care-providing agency or other high-technology center. The staff can review vital signs and other clinical data without having to actually visit the patient. It is even possible to "see" the patient with a telemetry unit or a simple computer video transmitter.

Emergency call devices are common for elderly individuals living alone. Such devices can be mounted in the home but are more often worn by the patient. Should the patient fall and be unable to get up, simply pressing a button on the emergency device alerts healthcare workers who can respond immediately. One such device alerts caregivers automatically if the patient fails to check in periodically or falls.

Many treatments can now be administered in the home, including kidney dialysis, intravenous feeding, and mechanical ventilation. Obviously, either the patient or an informal caregiver, such as a spouse or adult child, must be capable of administering the tests or treatments.

Technology also improves staff productivity. Instead of having to visit a patient each time a diagnostic test or a treatment is administered, home health nurses are able to keep in touch electronically, reducing the frequency with which they must travel to the home. It also assists supervisors in monitoring the work of home health and hospice staff working in patients' homes, checking on the results of what they do without having to do so in person. These productivity improvements reduce costs and help to offset staff shortages.

It also has great value for informal caregivers. Eight in 10 caregivers have access to the Internet, looking online for health information, such as looking up treatments and hospital ratings or information concerning end-of-life decisions. Caregivers often search online on behalf of someone else (Fox & Brenner, 2012).

As the technological revolution continues at a faster and faster pace, the potential benefits for home health care appear to be endless.

Managed Care

As is the case with other segments of the healthcare system, managed care had and is having a significant impact on community-based services. MCOs base their survival on being able to provide needed healthcare services at a lower cost. They have discovered that treating patients in their homes or in day care is more cost effective than keeping those patients in hospitals or long-term care facilities.

Wellness Programs

Some community-based services are beginning to create wellness programs for elderly individuals who are not yet in need of more traditional services. While this obviously does not apply to hospice (end-of-life care), it is a good fit with home health care and adult day care. Such programs do not qualify for funding from Medicare or other similar reimbursement sources. Thus, they are limited to patients (or their families) who can afford them. As people of all ages become more health and fitness conscious, wellness plans of many types are becoming more popular. Wellness programs extend these health and fitness opportunities to people who are otherwise unable to take advantage of traditional wellness programs.

■ Summary

Community-based services offer an alternative to institutional services for many long-term care consumers. Home health care, hospice care, and adult day care are three separate, but closely related, services that can delay or even prevent institutionalization. That means a higher quality of life and a lower cost of care. The latter is particularly attractive to third-party payers, both public (government) and private. As these community-based services have become more popular, there has been an increase in funding for them with attendant increases in regulation.

■ Cases

Because this chapter covers three somewhat different, although closely related, forms of community-based care (home health care, hospice care, and adult day care), we created three separate cases.

Home Healthcare Case: Joan and Jerry

Joan is 88 years old. She has suffered several small strokes over the past few years. Although the strokes were not catastrophic, each robbed her of a bit more of her independence. She eventually reached the point where she needed assistance with most ADLs. Once that happened, she was able to do little for herself. Her husband, Jerry, who is 85 and in surprisingly good health, took full-time care of her. He helped her bathe and assisted her in moving from chair to chair and into bed. Joan could walk a few steps with a walker or quad cane, but she was so unsteady on her feet that she used a wheelchair most of the time. She was able to eat by herself but needed some assistance in cutting her food.

Using the wheelchair, Jerry was able to get Joan out for rides in the car and even to dining in a restaurant occasionally. He did all of the cooking at home and all of the housework, including the laundry. He also did all of the shopping, either taking her with him to sit in the car while he shopped or leaving her alone for short periods of time.

Then, the situation got even worse. Although Joan's functional abilities deteriorated gradually, it was Jerry's own physical condition that changed their need for outside assistance. He had been experiencing an increasing amount of pain in his right hip. When it got so bad he could barely walk, much less take care of Joan without considerable suffering, he finally went to a doctor. He should have done so much sooner but was afraid of what he would learn. His worst fears were confirmed when the doctor told him he needed a total hip replacement. The idea of the surgery and necessary rehabilitation afterward did not worry him. What worried him was that he would not be able to continue caring for Joan by himself.

He finally had no choice and consented to the surgery. His only daughter lived several states away and came to live with them temporarily. She took over care of her mother while Jerry was in the hospital and of both when he returned home. Because she had a family and job of her own, she could only stay for a period of a few weeks. During that time, she worked with the hospital discharge team to arrange home health services for both Joan and Jerry.

Because they were both covered by Medicare, they were eligible for home health care. With a doctor's order, a nurse from the local home health agency arranged to visit while the daughter was there and conducted an assessment of the couple's needs. She determined that they would benefit from home visits by several other members of the home care team.

Following that assessment, they were visited by a physical therapist, who developed a therapy plan for Jerry to get his strength and movement back following the hip surgery. He also developed a care plan for Joan that involved exercises to help her maintain her range of motion and even regain some of her functional independence. In reality, she should have had such therapy much earlier but had not asked for it. A home health nurse came in once a week to check on their progress, but a home health aide provided much of the care received. The nature of the therapy was such that the aide was able to provide it as well as provide the nursing care needed. The aide also bathed Joan because Jerry was no longer able to do so.

A homemaker visited on a weekly basis to clean the house for them and do other minor chores as needed. The social worker from the home health agency also arranged for them to receive Meals on Wheels, providing them with one meal a day from an outside agency. Although not covered by Medicare, the Meals on Wheels program was inexpensive enough that Jerry was able to pay for it.

As Jerry recovered from his surgery, he became much more independent and no longer qualified for home care for himself. Thus, his services were discontinued. He was also able to assume more of the caregiving for Joan. However, while he was recovering, she had become more and more dependent, to the point where he could no longer bathe her by himself or get her into and out of the car. She clearly qualified for ongoing home health services and continued to receive them for several months. Then she suffered another stroke, a very serious one this time, and was admitted to a hospital where she died a week later.

A factor that is important to this case discussion is that Joan and Jerry are of a generation that developed an attitude that long-term care was something to be avoided because of the belief that was where you went to die. Joan had made Jerry promise that he would never put her away in a nursing home. He kept that promise but to the detriment of his own health. Had they accepted home health care earlier, the end result would probably not have been different, but the quality of both of their lives would have been improved during the last years of Joan's life. As it was, the services that their daughter eventually convinced them to get made their lives much better, at least for a time.

Hospice Case: Pierre

Pierre had generally been healthy throughout his life. Then, at the age of 68 years, he received the news none of us wants to hear. He was told that he had cancer. Although the cancer was located in his liver, which does not usually carry a very hopeful prognosis, the doctors recommended exploratory surgery to better determine the extent of involvement of the tumor. Pierre agreed, and the surgery was performed. Unfortunately, it confirmed what the doctors had suspected—that the tumor was so large it could not be removed surgically. In addition, there was considerable evidence that the cancer was spreading to other vital organs. Thus, neither radiation therapy nor chemotherapy was likely to improve his situation or significantly lengthen his life. He was told that he had less than 6 months to live. Naturally, Pierre and his family were devastated.

Hospital staff immediately put Pierre and his wife Alicia in touch with a well-respected hospice program affiliated with the hospital. At the initial meeting, Pierre and Alicia met with their family physician, the medical director of the hospice program (an oncologist), a hospice nurse, and a social worker. They had met the oncologist briefly before and after the surgery but did not know any of the others except the family doctor. They were nervous but soon realized that the others were there to help them. The purpose of the initial meeting was to meet one another, explain the services offered by hospice, and assess Pierre and Alicia's needs. (Note that both Pierre and Alicia are being treated as consumers here. This is because the surviving spouse or other family members need hospice services as well as the patient.)

Pierre did not need much in the way of nursing care at first, but the hospice team explained that they would provide it as his deteriorating condition required. However, the team stressed that other hospice services, particularly social services and counseling, should begin right away. The social worker helped them to put together a list of legal and financial steps that should be taken, such as updating Pierre's will. It was also decided that the family's pastor would be involved in Pierre's care.

In a matter of only a few weeks, the cancer had grown and spread to the point where it was sapping Pierre's strength and his ability to function, and the hospice services increased. A nurse visited periodically and helped Alicia with his care. He needed regular pain medication and had to be catheterized. Because he had little desire to eat, a nutritionist developed a menu that would be more attractive to him while providing him with better nutrition to give him as much strength as possible. In the meantime, the family's legal and financial matters were put in order, including, at Pierre's request, funeral arrangements. Pierre also created a living will that specified that there be no heroic life-saving measures, even after he lost the ability to communicate clearly concerning his wishes.

A hospital bed was rented and placed in the home to make Pierre more comfortable and to make it easier for Alicia or others to attend to him. At first, hospice staff and volunteers came for a short time each day to give Alicia some relief. However, toward the end, when Pierre needed more complete care and observation, hospice volunteers stayed all night, allowing Alicia to get some rest. The primary concern of the hospice team was making Pierre as comfortable as possible and assisting Alicia. When oral pain medication would no longer suffice, hospice nurses gave him injections to ease his pain.

In time, Pierre's end came. He died peacefully, with Alicia, the family pastor, and a hospice worker at his side. This did not end the work of the hospice team, however. They helped Alicia get through the funeral and assisted with the paperwork that is inevitably involved in such cases, including making sure the family lawyer got the estate settled. Although Alicia was very grateful for the services provided to her and to Pierre during his terminal illness, it was only when she was able to look back on it that she realized what a true godsend the hospice team had been for them.

Adult Day Care Case: Wilma and Karen

Wilma lives with her daughter and son-in-law and has for the past several years, since being widowed. Several events combined and led her to decide to accede to the wishes of her family and go to live with them.

When her husband died, she found herself unable to live alone, both because of her somewhat fragile health and because she could not afford to keep the house in which they lived for so many years. She also did not like living alone. Now, at the age of 78, she has diabetes that can be controlled with a combination of diet and insulin injections. However, her condition must be monitored regularly and carefully.

The move has worked out well, up to a point. Her daughter Karen is an only child and has always been close to Wilma, even though they lived two states apart. Her son-in-law, Lorenzo, is very attentive to Wilma, and she thinks of him as a son. Wilma's two grandchildren are away at college and come home when they can. Wilma enjoys being with them but wishes they were home more often.

However, as much as Wilma appreciates what her family is doing for her and loves them for it, the situation is not perfect. She finds the time that they are away at work to be increasingly lonely. Having moved from another state, she has few friends nearby except for those who are really friends of Lorenzo and Karen. They are nice, but she has found little opportunity to make friends of her own. Additionally, Wilma's diabetes requires not only careful monitoring but also that she eat properly and at the right times of day. When alone, she often neglects to eat right. Karen leaves lunch for her, but being alone, Wilma does not always eat it.

Faced with these problems, Lorenzo and Karen have tried a number of ways to spend more time with Wilma. Lorenzo is a teacher, so he can be at home during school vacations, but he has little flexibility in his schedule while school is in session. Karen is an investment counselor and tried working out of the house. It allowed her to be at home with her mother, but she found it to be a less-than-efficient way to conduct business. Besides, Wilma felt guilty for imposing on her daughter that way.

Seeking help, they looked around and found an adult day care center affiliated with the local senior citizen center. Wilma agreed to try it and soon found it to be just what she needed. She now goes to the center five days a week and loves it. To begin with, it meets her medical needs. At the center, she has someone to monitor her diabetes, make sure she takes her insulin appropriately, and gets lunch under the guidance of a nutritionist. Lorenzo and Karen had worried about the cost of the program because Wilma has very little money of her own, and they have two children in college. However, they discovered that Wilma is eligible for Medicaid, which covers the cost of the day care center.

The day program also meets her socialization needs. There are many activities available, both group and individual. Wilma participates in many of them but also appreciates the fact that she can choose not to participate if she wishes. She particularly enjoys some of the group exercise classes and feels better because of them. Since beginning to attend the day care program, she has made many new friends and has someone her own age to talk to. Although some day care programs cater particularly to people with varying degrees of cognitive impairment, this one focuses on individuals who are alert and can take part in stimulating activities.

Although the day care center provides transportation when needed, both Lorenzo and Karen go out of their way to transport Wilma back and forth whenever possible. Also, their flexibility overcomes one of the potential shortcomings of the day care program, which is only open from 8:00 a.m. to 5:00 p.m., Monday through Friday. Besides, Wilma is capable of being alone at home should her family not be available, at least at this time. Because Lorenzo has school vacations off, it was assumed that Wilma would not need to attend the day care center during those times. Although she may not need to attend, she insists on it. The program has become so important a part of her life that she would miss it were she to stay home. She would miss her friends, the staff, and the activities that have become so integral to her routine. As it is, she misses them on weekends but finds that she enjoys Karen and Lorenzo more for not being with them all the time.

For their part, Wilma's attendance at the day care center has allowed them to lead more normal professional lives without worrying about her. Because Wilma insists on attending, even during Lorenzo's school vacations, he has been able to resume the part-time job he previously held. All in all, it has benefited all concerned, including society, because the day care program has prevented, or at least delayed, Wilma's admission to a long-term care institution. Instead, she is living a happy and productive life, as are her family members. Given Wilma's fragile medical condition and advanced age, institutionalization may come eventually, but in the meantime she has found a form of long-term care that is just right for her.

■ Vocabulary Terms

The following terms are included in this chapter. They are important to the topics and issues discussed here and should become familiar to readers. Some of the terms are also found in other chapters but may be used in different contexts. Readers may wish to seek other supplementary definitions.

activities of daily living (ADLs)
adult day care
Balanced Budget Act
bereavement
capitation
caregiver
certified nursing assistant
dementia
functional independence
holistic
home health care
home care
hospice
informal caregivers
institutional care
managed care organizations (MCOs)
Medicaid
Medicare-certified home health agency

National Adult Day Services Association
occupational therapy
oncologist
Outcome and Assessment Information Set (OASIS)
pain management
palliative care
physical therapy
prognosis
Program of All-Inclusive Care for the Elderly (PACE)
prospective payment system
rehabilitation
skilled nursing services
social day care
speech pathologist
telemonitoring
United Way
visiting nurse association

■ Discussion Questions

The following questions are presented to assist you in understanding the material covered in this chapter. They tend to be general but lend themselves to detailed answers. The answers to these questions can be found in the chapter.

1. What are community-based services?
2. Who provides community-based services?

3. What are the patient services most commonly provided by each of the services discussed herein (home health care, hospice care, adult day care)?
4. How are each of the community-based services financed?
5. What are some of the human resource issues confronting community-based services providers?
6. What are some of the legal and ethical issues facing community-based services providers and consumers?
7. In reference to the home healthcare case at the end of this chapter, consider the following:
   a. Should Joan and Jerry have applied for home health care sooner, and, if so, who should have made them aware of the benefits of home health care?
   b. Given what you have learned about the accessibility and financing of home care services, are such services as readily available to other consumers as they were to Joan and Jerry?
8. In reference to the hospice care case described in the chapter, consider the following:
   a. The doctors were pretty sure that Pierre had less than 6 months to live, so he fell well within the guidelines for hospice coverage. Should hospice coverage be limited to those with 6 months or less to live, or should others be covered? Why?
   b. Volunteers played a large part in Pierre's care, even staying with him overnight toward the end. How can the hospice's management adequately supervise volunteer workers in such situations and ensure that they provide safe, appropriate care?
9. In reference to the adult day care case at the end of this chapter, consider the following:
   a. Although Wilma is clearly benefiting from day care, so are Lorenzo and Karen. Should society (Medicaid) be paying for something that benefits them, even though they are not poor?
   b. If there was not a day care center available for Wilma, do you think she would be able to continue living with Karen and Lorenzo? If not, to what type of long-term care facility would she likely be admitted?
   NOTE: There is no right answer. Part a of this question is intentionally argumentative, designed to get you thinking.

■ References

Administration on Aging. (2013, April 24). *What is home health care?* Retrieved from http://www.eldercare.gov/eldercare.net/public/resources/factsheets/home_health_care.aspx#what.

Benz, C. (2012, August 9). *40 must-know statistics about long-term care*. Retrieved from http://news.morningstar.com/articlenet/article.aspx?id=564139.

Bercovitz, A., Park-Lee, E., & Jamoom, E. (2013, May 20). *Adoption and use of electronic health records and mobile technology by home health and hospice care agencies.* Washington, DC: National Center for Health Statistics. Retrieved from http://www.ncbi.nlm.nih.gov/pubmed/24988819.

Community Health Accreditation Program (CHAP). (2014). *About CHAP.* Retrieved from http://www.chapinc.org/AboutCHAP.

Family Caregiver Alliance. (2014). *Caregiving.* Retrieved from http://www.caregiver.org/caregiver/jsp/content_node.jsp?nodeid=2313.

FamilyCare America. (2013). *What is adult day care?* Retrieved from http://www.caregiverslibrary.org/caregivers-resources/grp-caring-for-yourself/hsgrp-support-systems/what-is-adult-day-care-article.aspx.

Fox, S., & Brenner, J. (2012). *Family caregivers online.* Retrieved from http://www.pewinternet.org/Reports/2012/Caregivers-online.aspx.

Harris-Kojetin, L., Sengupta, M., Park-Lee, E., & Valverde, R. (2013). *Long-term care services in the United States: 2013 overview.* Retrieved from http://www.cdc.gov/nchs/data/nsltcp/long_term_care_services_2013.pdf.

Hospice Foundation of America. (2014). *What is hospice?* Retrieved from http://www.hospicefoundation.org/whatishospice.

The Joint Commission. (2014). *What is accreditation?* Retrieved from http://www.jointcommission.org/accreditation/accreditation_main.aspx.

Jones, C. (2012, April 8). *Characteristics and use of home health care by men and women aged 65 and over.* National Health Statistics Reports No. 52. Retrieved from http://www.cdc.gov/nchs/data/nhsr/nhsr052.pdf.

Kaiser Commission on Medicaid and the Uninsured. (2012). *Medicaid home and community-based service programs.* Washington, DC: Kaiser Commission on Medicaid and the Uninsured.

Levine, C., Halper, D., Peist, A., & Gould, D. (2010). Bridging troubled waters: Family caregivers, transitions, and long-term care. *Health Affairs.* 2010 Jan-Feb;29(1):116-24. Retrieved from http://content.healthaffairs.org/content/29/1/116.long.

Long Term and Post Acute Care and Health Information Technology Collaborative (LTPACHIT). (2012). *About long term and post acute care.* Retrieved from http://www.ltpachealthit.org/content/about-long-term-and-post-acute-care#top.

MetLife Mature Market Institute. (2012). *Market survey of long-term care costs.* New York, NY: MetLife.

National Association for Home Care and Hospice (NAHCH). (2010a). *Basic statistics about home care: Updated 2010.* Retrieved from http://www.nahc.org/assets/1/7/10HC_Stats.pdf.

National Association for Home Care and Hospice (NAHCH). (2010b, November). *Hospice facts & statistics.* Retrieved from http://www.nahc.org/assets/1/7/HospiceStats10.pdf.

National Association for Home Care and Hospice (NAHCH). (2012). *Who provides home care?* Retrieved from http://caring.org/consumer/home.html.

National Hospice and Palliative Care Organization (NHPCO). (2014). *CMS—Medicare hospice regulations.* Retrieved from http://www.nhpco.org/cms-medicare-hospice-regulations.

National Institutes of Health. (2013). *Long term care.* Retrieved from http://nihseniorhealth.gov/longtermcare/communitybasedservices/01.html.

O'Keeffe, L., Saucier, P., Jackson, B., Cooper, R., McKenney, E. C., & Moseley, C. (2010). *Understanding Medicaid home and community services: A primer—2010 edition.* Washington, DC: U.S. Department of Health and Human Services Office.

Singh, D. (2010). *Effective management of long-term care facilities* (2nd ed.). Sudbury, MA: Jones and Bartlett Learning.

Interaction Within the Continuum

Competition, Cooperation, and Integration

Learning Objectives

After completing this chapter, readers will be able to:

1. Understand the nature of the competitive forces acting on long-term care organizations.
2. Define various forms of cooperation and integration.
3. Discuss the benefits of the various forms of integration.
4. Identify the components of integrated systems and networks.
5. Discuss management, financing, and quality issues related to integration.

■ Introduction

It is probably a gross understatement to say that long-term care organizations have undergone tremendous change in the past several decades. They have been shaken from a complacency that existed because they had functioned for many years in a relatively benevolent environment. Gone are the days when a long-term care facility or agency existed as the sole provider of services in a community or neighborhood. No longer can they count on people coming to them for service with little or no effort on their part to advertise or even to market their services. Nor can they count on being reimbursed for all of their care-related expenses.

Instead, they find their organizations at risk of financial failure if they continue to ignore pressures to change. They do not automatically receive payment enough to cover their expenses but must examine and control those expenses. If they fail to do that adequately, their survival may be in jeopardy. If they are slow to recognize competition for their customers, they may lose those customers. They need to keep up with changes in the operating environment and how care is financed.

■ The Environment

Although some change has always been present in long-term care, never before has the operating environment changed so quickly and so dramatically. That environment has gone from static to very dynamic as the result of several specific developments. To begin with, society has responded to significant demographic changes, particularly the aging of the population. The growing number of elderly is such that the volume alone is affecting long-term care. According to the Federal Interagency Forum on Aging-Related Statistics (2013, p. 2), the number of elderly (defined as those older than 65 years) is projected to double by the year 2030, growing from 35 million to 72 million, representing nearly 20% of the total U.S. population, and the number older than 85 years will expand even more quickly. It is the group of those older than 85 who use long-term care most heavily. As impressive (or frightening) as these projections are, experience with previous forecasts suggests that they are probably quite conservative. They are based, in most cases, on current social and demographic situations and care delivery methods, yet new and innovative forms of long-term care delivery are developing all the time.

History has shown that increasing the availability of services usually results in greater-than-anticipated use. For example, original estimates of future demand for Medicare and Medicaid were almost ridiculously low. What the forecasters failed to include in their calculations was that people will go without many services until those services become realistically available. Skeptics say that they must not have really needed those services. However, regular physician visits, medication to control blood pressure, or vision and hearing examinations can all be postponed with little short-run harm if they are unavailable or not affordable, but the long-range effect of skipping them is another matter. Once services such as these became available through Medicare and Medicaid, use of them mushroomed.

Similarly, developments in long-term care delivery and financing over the next few years will almost certainly cause the demand for services to expand well beyond the current, already high projections. The increased demand for services caused by this growth is already straining the available resources and has stimulated several innovative new modes of delivery of long-term care. It is unclear at this time whether the Affordable Care Act will change this for better or for worse.

The impact of the growing number of potential consumers of long-term care is not based only on volume. Consumers today are better informed than ever before, expecting more from the organizations that serve them. The baby boomers, mentioned so often in this text, have already become a potent force in society and promise to be even more influential as they approach old age. They are more knowledgeable than previous generations about the types of services available to them and are not hesitant to demand those services. When, for some reason, services are not available to them, they are quite capable of taking action. These baby boomers and the others who are already among the elderly have learned to place more emphasis on quality of life, sometimes even when it means shortening their actual life spans. This philosophical evolution has created a demand for certain new types of long-term care services and has forced providers and payers alike to adapt existing services to better provide what their consumers want.

Long-term care consumers want to maintain their current lifestyles and are increasingly willing to shop around for providers that can accommodate them. They want to receive care at home whenever possible, resulting in more demand for home health care and other home-based services. Their desire for a homelike environment even when institutionalized has led to assisted living, congregate housing, and other similar modifications of the more traditional types of long-term care.

■ Financing Changes

There have also been developments in the financing of health care that have affected how and where long-term care is provided. The sudden transition from a retrospective payment system, which pretty much reimbursed providers for whatever they incurred by way of expenses, to one that sets payment rates prospectively forced providers to be far more efficient and cost effective than in the past. As a result, they learned to maximize those services that provide the best rate of return and to minimize others.

The financing of long-term care services has not experienced the magnitude of change that has revolutionized acute care. However, that change has affected long-term care both directly and indirectly. As hospitals and physicians' practices have been transformed by new financing mechanisms, they have shifted some types of care to other service providers, generally meaning those providing long-term care. Pressures to reduce healthcare costs have affected overall health care in several ways, including causing shorter lengths of stay in acute facilities, increased use of ambulatory care services, and earlier transfer to postacute care facilities and agencies. These changes in acute care have encouraged, and at times even caused, development of new forms of long-term care, such as assisted living and subacute care.

The introduction and rapid growth of managed care has been the most important factor in the financing of health care today. *Managed care* is

> a term used to describe a variety of techniques intended to reduce the cost of providing health benefits and improve the quality of care for organizations that use those techniques or provide them as services to other organizations. It is also used to describe systems of financing and delivering health care to enrollees organized around managed care techniques and concepts. (National Conference of State Legislatures, 2013)

Managed care organizations (MCOs) have quickly become significant players in the financing equation and, as such, have stimulated much of the change that is now taking place. Over the past 2 decades, managed care became the predominant form of health care in most parts of the United States. More than 70 million Americans have been enrolled in HMOs (health maintenance organizations), and almost 90 million have been part of preferred provider organizations. Overall enrollment in HMOs peaked in 2001 and generally remains a dominant type of health care and coverage (National Conference of State Legislatures, 2013). Enrollment in risk-based managed care is expected to further expand as millions gain Medicaid coverage under the Affordable Care Act (Howell, Palmer, & Adams, 2012).

These changes have forced long-term care provider organizations to get involved in some activities that had, in the past, been somewhat foreign to them: competition, cooperation, and integration. This chapter examines how they have dealt with the forces acting on them and the ways in which they have (or have not) embraced these concepts. The discussion begins with an examination of competition, both within the long-term care field itself and with other healthcare entities.

■ Competition

Historically, long-term care providers have not had to worry much about competition. They existed where there was enough demand for them, whether that demand was created by actual need or by the availability of reimbursement.

Conditions Required for Effective Competition

Several decades ago, Victor Fuchs identified five conditions that must be present for competition to be practical:

> (1) A large number of buyers and sellers, no one of whom is so big as to have a significant influence on the market price; (2) no collusion among the buyers or sellers to fix prices or quantities; (3) relatively free and easy entry into the market by new buyers or sellers; (4) no governmentally imposed restraints on prices or quantities; and (5) reasonably good information about price and quality known to buyers and sellers. (Fuchs, 1988)

These five conditions are still valid and provide a good framework within which to discuss why the long-term care system of the past was not market driven, as well as why and how it has moved much closer to a market orientation.

Influence of Individual Buyers or Sellers

A market approach requires that no individual buyer or seller be strong enough to influence market price. The long-term care system prior to the 1990s was about as far from meeting that requirement as it could be. Long-term care was essentially a government-financed system. Medicare and Medicaid were clearly the dominant, in fact almost the only, buyers. Thus, there was little reason for competition. Private insurance coverage for long-term care was virtually nonexistent. The number of people who could pay for their own long-term care was too small to have any significant impact on how or where care was delivered. Because the federal and state governments financed most long-term care, they played a much larger role in controlling it than would buyers in any form of market-based competition.

Although Medicare and Medicaid are still the most significant buyers of long-term care services, they are no longer the only buyers. Managed care has become a buyer with considerable influence in all of health care and is beginning to exert that influence in long-term care as well. In managed care, providers now have an additional option for reimbursement, giving them a bit more discretion in selecting the buyers to whom they will sell their services. The long-term care system still falls somewhat short of a market-driven system in this regard, with only a few major buyers. In most regions of the country, a few buyers, be they government agencies or MCOs, are still in a position to influence long-term care and the prices charged by providers. Private long-term care insurance is growing, but it is still not a key player. Only in those areas in which there are competing MCOs does the system approach a market-based orientation.

Single dominant sellers are much less common in long-term care, although they do exist in some areas. However, the very move toward market competition among buyers of long-term care services has been enough to force providers to be aware of their own need to be competitive in winning the business of those buyers.

Collusion to Fix Prices or Quantities

Not only have government buyers historically been in a dominant enough position to influence the prices paid for long-term care services through Medicare and Medicaid, but they actually have been able to set and dictate those prices through legislation and its accompanying regulations. This may not qualify as collusion in the usual sense of multiple entities getting together to inhibit competition, nor was there anything illegal about it, but the effect was the same. Sellers (providers) of long-term care services had no say in the prices set, nor were they able to influence them in any significant way.

Free and Easy Entry Into the Market

The long-term care market of the past was not very open, nor was entry into a particular segment of it always free and easy. Often, a nursing home (today called a nursing facility) was the only such facility in a small community or in a section of a larger community. For much of their history, these facilities were the only form of long-term care in many areas and provided a wide range of services. They may have been skilled nursing facilities, intermediate care facilities, intermediate care facilities for the mentally retarded, or a combination of these categories.

With the advent of Medicare and Medicaid, these facilities regularly experienced occupancy rates in excess of 90%. Whether they existed and the way in which they were categorized was usually determined by the government agencies responsible for paying them. It was not easy for a new provider organization to gain entry into a given market. It had to qualify for reimbursement according to government regulations and was somewhat at the mercy of the agencies administering those regulations. With the introduction of certificate-of-need legislation and its eventual application to long-term care facilities, the possible introduction of new providers was determined primarily by another government agency, not by competition.

Government-Imposed Restraints

As noted earlier, long-term care has long been subject to a variety of government-imposed restraints on both the prices they were paid and the quantity and type of services provided. The impact of these restraints on competition in long-term care has sometimes been incidental, such as when reimbursement rates have been insufficient to attract providers; yet many times that impact has been intentional. When the government attempts to divert resources away from one type of provider toward another—such as the effort to have more consumers cared for through home care instead of in nursing facilities—it is affecting the freedom of competition among those who provide and sell long-term care services. These restraints may take several forms. They can be accomplished, for example, through rule making and by determining eligibility. They can also be imposed through the way rates are set.

In either case, government has regularly restrained competition in long-term care and continues to do so. However, as nongovernment payment sources such as MCOs and private long-term care insurance have gained an increasing portion of the long-term care market, the ability of the government to impose those restraints is being eroded.

Information About Price and Quality

To be competitive, long-term care providers have to know where they stand in the market. That means that they need to know how they compare with their competitors and their relative strengths and weaknesses. It is something that most long-term care providers, until relatively recently, had not done well at all. In fact, most had not seen the need to gather such information and, as a result, made no effort to obtain it.

Pricing information has generally been available, given the dominance of public funding sources. Most similar providers were paid based on a common rate scale, so it was not that difficult to determine how much a competitor was being paid. Quality information, on the other hand, was not as easily obtained. Government surveys of nursing care and other long-term care facilities yielded some information that was publicly available. However, the results of those surveys have not been terribly consistent and, more important, only measure compliance with minimum standards. They fail to measure quality above that of minimally acceptable, nor are they designed to measure it.

In the noncompetitive system within which they formerly functioned, most long-term care providers made little attempt to know what their competitors were doing, how well they were doing it, or what changes they might have planned. Many could not accurately identify their actual competitors. They can no longer afford to be so blasé. The increasing competitiveness of their operating environment dictates that they plan and act strategically. If they are to successfully compete for the business of buyers with multiple provider options, they must understand what distinctive competencies they possess and must take the fullest possible advantage of those competencies.

Competition: What Has Changed?

Long-term care has not yet reached full status as a competition-driven system, but it is clearly moving in that direction. It has made some progress in satisfying each of Fuchs's conditions for competition, although that progress has been much better in some areas than in others. Probably the most change has come in the number of both buyers and sellers actively involved in health care in general and in long-term care specifically. As taxpayers and corporations, the ultimate sources of healthcare reimbursement, strive to reduce their costs simply to survive, they have created competition among both public and private buyers. Those buyers, including Medicare and Medicaid as well as MCOs and insurance companies, have, in turn, created a competitive environment for providers.

MCOs, in their combined role as both buyers and sellers, payers and providers, are operating in a very competitive environment. Survival for any individual MCO depends on securing a particular niche in the overall healthcare market. They rely on a relatively small number of contracts covering large numbers of people. One or two such contracts can make or break an MCO, increasing the importance of being competitive.

Few MCOs directly provide all of the services they cover, either because they do not have the ability or because they can achieve the same thing better and at lower cost by contracting with other providers. This is particularly true when it comes to long-term care. MCOs are more likely to provide acute and preventive care themselves, but they often contract for a variety of long-term care services. This opens up many opportunities for individual long-term care providers of all types. At the same time, it increases the need for them to become more competitive, because others will also be seeking to capitalize on those opportunities.

Public payment sources, particularly state Medicaid agencies, are learning from their private counterparts and are also examining the potential benefits of managed care contracting. Because Medicaid is a major—and, in many cases, still the largest—source of payment for long-term care, this new activity is further increasing the competitive nature of the field. Most states are experimenting with managed care for their Medicaid populations through federal waivers. They are contracting with private MCOs to run the programs. The MCOs, in turn, contract with providers. As that practice increases, it might mean that long-term care providers will not necessarily all have equal standing regarding a large portion of their potential market.

As this happens, even the public part of long-term care financing will become more competitive, and the government will be less able to fix prices or quantities. Also, as private payers become more of a factor in long-term care, picking up increasing numbers of consumers, many of whom are uncovered at present, both the types of services provided and the prices paid for them will be more subject to competitive forces.

The expansion of private payment sources into the field of long-term care demonstrates how much easier it is for new buyers to gain entry into the market than was the case in the past. Unfortunately for some of them, they are finding that it is easier to enter the market than to stay in it. The number of MCOs that fail is indicative of both the competitiveness of their environment and the relative immaturity of the managed care market, particularly in long-term care.

Entry into the market by providers is also easier than it has been. Recognizing that many MCOs are also providers, the opportunities for pure providers are also greater for a couple of reasons. First, the demand fueled by growth in the elderly population needing long-term care requires an enlarged supply of providers. Even without changes in delivery methods, there would be room for more providers in the future. Those who fill that gap will have a competitive edge over those that do not. Second, that increased demand and the highly dynamic nature of long-term care today have opened the door for new forms of care delivery (e.g., subacute, assisted living, high-tech home care). As these new provider types continue to develop, they create additional opportunities and also set the stage for competition among providers seeking to realize those opportunities.

That competition is additionally fierce because it occurs not just among like providers (e.g., home care agency versus home care agency) as has often been the case in the past, but also among different types of providers (e.g., skilled nursing facility versus assisted living facility). Long-term care organizations must now compete with a much broader field of contenders. They must satisfy consumers who now have multiple options available to them. No longer is the choice only among nursing facilities. Now it may include any of several other care modalities.

If providers are to compete successfully in this expanded arena, they must learn as much as possible about potential competitors, becoming familiar with segments of long-term care that may be foreign to them. They must also compete for the attention of payers who are seeking high-quality care provided in the most cost-effective manner. This might mean going to another type of provider. These payers are becoming very knowledgeable about their options. Providers wanting to compete should learn from them.

A truly competitive long-term care market would be subject to minimal, if any, government intervention to control the quantity of services or the prices charged for them. This has not happened, nor is it likely to. However, there have been changes in the types of restraints imposed by government. Repeal of most certificate-of-need laws and the relative impotence of those remaining have made it easier for new providers to enter the field, increasing competition. The goal of government restraints seems to have shifted from limiting the absolute number of providers to influencing the relative proportion of the field captured by different types of providers. There also appears to be a move by various governments to shift some of the limited financial resources available to them to particularly vulnerable populations or to those without adequate coverage.

The respective roles of government agencies and providers in the long-term care market have become interestingly interactive. As government eases some restrictions, the field becomes more competitive. In turn, as the field becomes more competitive and government agencies themselves become competitors, they find it in their interests to further ease restrictions. This is not to say that there will be any significant reduction of government restrictions or that pure competition will prevail, but it does indicate how competitive the field is becoming.

■ Competition From Other Healthcare Organizations

As great as competition has become within long-term care, it is also coming from other segments of the healthcare field. Hospitals have felt pressures of their own and see long-term care as one of the answers to those pressures. Competition has actually been a factor for hospitals for at least a decade longer than for long-term care organizations, and they have learned much more about how to deal with it and capitalize on it. This makes them competitors the long-term care field should watch and notice.

Pressure by payers for shorter lengths of stay, higher use of ambulatory care to avoid admissions, and development of less costly postacute care options all resulted in large numbers of empty beds in most hospitals. As was reported so widely in the popular press, insurance companies and MCOs imposed maximum lengths of stay for certain admissions or procedures, further reducing occupancy rates in most hospitals.

Many hospitals have closed in the past few years because they were unable or unwilling to adapt enough to be competitive when necessary. Others have sought new services to supplement acute care and to which they could apply overhead costs. For many, that has meant attempting to acquire a portion of the growing long-term care market. Some have even converted to long-term care completely. Futurist Russell Coile, in his 1990 book, *The New Medicine: Reshaping Medical Practice and Health Care Management*, predicted that:

> Every hospital and health system will own, manage, or control long-term care facilities in the future. Small hospitals will use swing beds, whereas larger hospitals may have extended-care units in house, own their own freestanding nursing home facility, or have nursing home beds available on contract. (Coile, 1990, p. 102)

That prediction has already been borne out to a great extent and will undoubtedly be true in its entirety in only a few more years, especially given the bundling provisions of the Affordable Care Act ("Obamacare").

Hospitals are powerful opponents in the competitive long-term care market. They tend to have sound infrastructures, both physically and organizationally. Converting beds from acute care to some form of long-term care is not all that difficult. Most already have systems in place that are more than capable of supporting that conversion. They have more than enough medical and nursing capability for the reduced needs of even skilled care. Other support departments and services—including maintenance, dietary, pharmacy, purchasing, housekeeping, and business office functions—are usually quite adequate. So are the physical facilities. Some service areas, such as patient (resident) assessment and activity programs, may have to be changed or even expanded a bit to meet the requirements of a nursing facility. Documentation in long-term care is considerably more detailed and intensive and probably requires more effort for most hospitals. If the hospital chooses to get involved in providing home health care, it may need to create outreach systems. However, those changes are minor compared to what would be needed for a new entrant into the field who would have to create an entire operational infrastructure.

Most hospitals also have other built-in advantages over either new organizations or existing long-term care organizations when it comes to changing their focus or moving into some aspect of long-term care. One of those advantages is their probable experience in planning. Although hospitals were much slower to get involved in strategic planning than many other industries, they are generally far ahead of most long-term care organizations. Most hospitals have already learned to plan strategically, due in part to the fact that their environment became competitive well before the long-term care environment did. They have had to be adaptive, to know their own strengths and weaknesses, and to find the market niche best suited to them. Not all hospitals were that farsighted or adaptable. Many were not, and the system in which they exist has been competitive long enough to eliminate most of these. Most of those remaining are survivors and have acquired the skills needed to compete in either their own system or in long-term care.

Hospitals were also quicker to adopt formal quality control measures than most long-term care organizations. This does not mean that quality is necessarily better in hospitals than in long-term care facilities and agencies, just that they implemented institutional quality programs such as total quality management or continuous quality improvement much earlier and much more completely than has been the pattern in long-term care. This process has not been totally voluntary or a result of hospitals being that much more farsighted than long-term care organizations. Rather, the greater involvement in formal quality assurance programs is likely related to their earlier involvement in accreditation. Organizations such as the Joint Commission have stimulated hospitals to adopt such quality measures and have even forced some hospitals to do so where they probably would not have otherwise.

Hospitals have generally participated in accreditation, whereas until recently, many long-term care organizations had not. However, long-term care organizations have caught up somewhat and are now much more involved in accreditation. The Medicare program recognizes Joint Commission accreditation as an acceptable substitute for state approval, granting deemed status to accredited hospitals, meaning that they do not have to undergo state inspection surveys. Long-term care organizations are not routinely given the same status, even when accredited. They therefore do not have the same incentive to seek accreditation or to participate in the formal quality control programs that go along with it. To their credit, many long-term care providers have embraced total quality management or continuous quality improvement, even without the same level of incentive. They simply are doing what is right in an effort to provide high-quality care to their consumers. They have also created several voluntary quality initiatives, the most prominent of which is Quality First, a commitment to performance excellence in quality of care and quality of life by the long-term care community. This voluntary initiative is "This voluntary initiative is an effort that builds upon the existing work of the long term and post-acute care field by setting specific, measurable targets to further improve quality of care in America's skilled nursing centers and assisted living communities" (AHCA, 2014).

Effects of Increased Competition

So what has this trend toward more competition in long-term care meant? How has it changed the system? It has meant, to put it as simply as possible, that long-term care providers have been forced to wake up and recognize that others are competing for some of their business. As such, those others are potential threats to them and their very survival. The changes in the system have also created new opportunities for those long-term care providers clever enough to see and take advantage of them. They must decide whether they should compete by themselves or join forces with others to strengthen their strategic position. In either case, they must develop a response to the environmental changes taking place around them. Doing nothing is not a valid long-term option.

One side effect of increased competition has been the increase in the number of multifacility chains and the corollary decrease in the number of single-site, privately owned, long-term care organizations. This has been particularly true for nursing facilities, but it has also occurred in other parts of the system. Individual facilities or agencies are finding it hard to go the course alone. The smaller of them, many of whom have served a limited population base for many years, now find it hard to keep up with the dynamics of today's long-term care field. Often referred to as mom and pop operations, they tend not to have the resources to compete with those that do keep abreast of changes in the field. When that happens, they either join with others to form a larger, stronger organization or sell to an existing organization already operating other facilities like theirs. They find ways to cooperate with others or to become part of an integrated delivery system, topics that we explore here.

However, while that trend toward nursing facilities affiliating with hospitals was strongest in the early 21st century, it has slowed some. A 2012 market survey of long-term care costs found that 86% of all nursing homes surveyed were freestanding facilities. The remaining were physically connected to or on the same grounds as an assisted living community (9%), hospital (5%), or both (< 1%). Eleven percent of nursing homes surveyed had an associated assisted living unit or wing, and 8% were part of a continuing care retirement community (MetLife Mature Market Institute, 2012, p. 1). It will be interesting to see if the requirements of the Affordable Care Act reverse the trend again.

■ Cooperation

The terms *cooperation* and *integration* have been separated in this discussion, although as they occur in health care, the differences between them are sometimes vague. Sometimes they are more than vague, they are irrelevant. However, these differences do exist, so they are examined briefly.

Types of Cooperation

Cooperation among healthcare or long-term care provider organizations, especially when stimulated by competition, usually involves some type of not-too-formal liaison that provides benefits for all involved. Integration, on the other hand, is more likely to be formalized, with the component organizations actually becoming part of a larger entity through merger, contracting, or some other form of affiliation. Thus, the differences are mostly a matter of degree and structure. However, those differences may be very important legally.

Some forms of voluntary cooperation have been in place for years. Most long-term care organizations have had transfer agreements with other types and levels of providers. They have had working arrangements providing them with a place to refer people no longer needing their level of care or, perhaps, needing a higher level. Hospitals have had agreements for placing their patients in nursing facilities or with home healthcare agencies. The two providers have worked out agreements to move consumers back and forth between them as care needs changed. At the same time, and sometimes of more importance, such arrangements have provided each of them with a source of consumers.

Transfer agreements serve several other purposes as well. Transfer agreements usually spell out such things as the clinical or functional conditions of patients for whom the receiving organization is prepared to care, which avoids inappropriate transfers. They signify agreement on the types of information to be shared, saving both providers and consumers potential grief and improving the quality of care. Discharge planners in one provider organization (e.g., an acute hospital) and admissions screeners in another (e.g., a nursing facility) exchange a variety of clinical, personal, and financial data about the person being transferred, easing the process.

Transfer agreements are not always restrictive. However, as the field becomes more competitive, there seems to be a trend toward increased exclusivity, giving the partners to such agreements an advantage over other providers. A home care agency, for example, would benefit greatly if it became the primary referral agency for the largest hospital in an area. Similarly, as hospitals face pressure to discharge their patients promptly, they need high-quality long-term care organizations to which they can send them. If one hospital developed a cooperative arrangement with a major nursing facility or home healthcare agency, it would have an advantage over other hospitals in its service area.

That type of cooperation has been encouraged (forced?) by the accountable care organization and bundling provisions of the Affordable Care Act. Accountable care organizations are networks of physicians and other providers who "contract with Medicare to improve the quality of health care services and reduce costs for a defined patient population" (Bassett, 2013). Under the bundling provision, Medicare would pay an entity for all covered services delivered during an episode of care. The episode of care must begin with a hospitalization and continues for 30 days after discharge. Bundled services can include inpatient hospital, physician, outpatient therapy, and postacute care services (Dummit, 2011).

Other types of cooperative arrangements among long-term care providers, or between them and other (e.g., acute) providers, sometimes include sharing a variety of support systems. Shared purchasing has long been popular because of the economy of scale it provides. As long-term care organizations have fallen increasingly under the spell of computer technology, expensive information systems are another likely area of shared cost and effort. Likewise, specialized professionals may be shared among several providers who could not afford them alone.

■ Moving From Cooperation to Integration

As healthcare providers move from relatively simple to quite formalized types of inter-organizational interaction, they eventually cross the somewhat indistinct line between cooperation and integration. As they experience more competitive pressure, they tend to move toward more formal integration. They go from being highly individual entities with limited areas of common interest to functioning more like components of an integrated delivery system.

The rapid growth of managed care has been the primary driver of that trend. MCOs rely heavily on organizational efficiency and effectiveness for their competitive survival. In attempting to achieve that goal, they often require a level of central control that will not work with a loosely formed cooperative arrangement. They must provide a full range of services to their constituents. Much of the time it is more cost effective for them to acquire many of those services through contractual agreements with existing providers. Because their environment is so competitive, they seek a high level of exclusivity in those contracts. They form service networks that are highly integrated.

■ Integration

Although some forms of integration of healthcare providers have been in existence for years, the concept of formal integration as a preferred operating methodology is relatively new. And as is so often the case with new (or newly discovered) ideas, the terminology used to describe them is confusing and inconsistent. Healthcare integration is no exception to that rule. Here is a list of the different terms used to describe integrated systems:

- Integrated health system (IHS)
- Integrated health network (IHN)
- Integrated care system
- Integrated care network
- Integrated delivery system
- Integrated delivery network
- Community care network
- Integrated healthcare organization (IHCO)

Note that with the exception of the last two, these names incorporate different combinations of the following common terms: *integrated*, *health*, *care*, *system*, and *network*. The name chosen does not automatically determine the nature of the integration, but there are some common themes.

System is likely to signify a single-ownership form of integration, whereas *network* is more apt to indicate a formal alliance among otherwise independent organizational entities. Similarly, the terms *delivery* and *care* imply that the integrated organization is limited to care delivery only. They suggest that it does not include financing as it would when MCOs are involved. The last term, *integrated healthcare organization*, is specifically designed to indicate a single-owner arrangement. It must be stressed here that even though there are common themes, the name does not necessarily indicate the organizational form chosen.

For the sake of simplicity, the term *integrated health system (IHS)* will be used when discussing integrated health organizations in an overall generic sense when those discussions include both vertically integrated, single-owner systems and formal networks or alliances among independent organizations. When the reference is specific to one or the other, it will be noted.

To further complicate discussion of IHSs, there are varying degrees of integration. It is acceptable to refer to an organization as an IHS even though it is somewhat less than fully integrated.

Horizontal and Vertical Integration

There are other commonly used terms that need definition and clarification before any further discussion of integration can occur; they are the terms *horizontal integration* and *vertical integration*. They have been around for a long time and are simple in concept, but they may be confusing if used improperly, as they often are.

Horizontal Integration

Horizontal integration denotes two or more organizations that provide similar services forming an alliance for their mutual benefit. In health care, the similarity of services generally refers to the level of care provided (e.g., home care, assisted living). The degree of formal affiliation may vary somewhat, but generally includes some common organizational oversight. The individual provider members may actually be owned by, or be under the full control of, an overall organization, or they may be separate entities who agree to joint management of a single function. A chain of nursing facilities owned by a national or regional firm would be an example of the former type of horizontal integration. A similar group of facilities, or any other like providers, who engage in shared purchasing or other limited interaction represent the latter. The organizations involved have common needs and unite to meet them.

Vertical Integration

Vertical integration involves an alliance of two or more organizations providing services that are dissimilar but that are interactive with, and may rely on, each other. In health care, vertical integration usually involves combinations of hospitals; nursing facilities; home care agencies; and perhaps other providers such as subacute care facilities, hospice organizations, and adult day care programs. They each provide a different level of care. Yet, as consumers move about within the continuum, the separate providers need each other for referrals or discharges.

The incentives for providers to combine vertically are quite different from those that spur horizontal integration. Vertical integration gives them better efficiency and coordination. It also provides a better position for bargaining with third-party payers. The organizations involved seek better, less costly interagency interaction. As noted earlier, they may also seek to gain a competitive advantage. Horizontal integration has been around for some time, but vertical integration is relatively new. It is the rise of vertical integration that has fueled the growing interest in IHSs.

Reasons for Joining an Integrated System or Network

A more detailed exploration of why a long-term care organization would want to become involved with either an IHS or an IHN is undertaken here. In either case, it usually begins with a desire or need on the part of an organization to join forces with other organizational entities to strengthen its own position in the long-term care field.

Economies of Scale

As the market for long-term care and other healthcare services has become more competitive, with more emphasis on cost-effectiveness and operating efficiency, many providers have realized that there are financial benefits to being part of a larger system. One of these benefits is the greater purchasing power of large groups. By banding together, they can secure group contracts for goods and services they need at prices that are more advantageous than those they could secure individually. Group purchasing was one of the earliest forms of organizational cooperation in health care. It has been well proven and has led to other similar efforts. For example, several state nursing home trade associations also provide group worker's compensation coverage and other kinds of insurance to their members, functioning as cooperatives.

These early and relatively simple forms of cooperation demonstrated to long-term care providers that they could benefit from group activities. It led to other more involved efforts that moved them closer to actual integration. As their services became more highly technical, the equipment and specialized manpower required became more expensive. Individual providers could not afford some of these services, nor did they have enough demand to utilize them fully and efficiently. Rehabilitation services are typical of those that many long-term care organizations found increasing need for but did not need on a full-time basis. Where they had acquired therapies from consultants previously, they began to band together to employ their own therapists. Because most long-term care facilities and agencies require numerous consultants, it soon became clear that there was potential for considerable benefit from future collaboration. The providers would have better control of their resources and, instead of having to rely on others for needed expertise, they would be in control, meaning more efficiency and cost-effectiveness and an opportunity to provide better services for their customers.

Economies of scale apply to both single-owner IHSs and IHNs. Single-owner, corporate systems are likely to carry the shared activities further, including virtually all aspects of their operations. As single organizations with multiple parts, it only makes sense for them to group like functions from their separate component entities. Such organizations usually centralize administrative support functions, including human resources, purchasing, in-service training, some financial services, and even maintenance. Professional services, although provided at the local level, are probably coordinated at the corporate level.

IHNs also benefit from economies of scale but usually in specific areas. Which services and functions are shared varies considerably from network to network, depending on the reason for formation of the network in the first place. If that reason was primarily to save money, collaboration probably focuses on shared product acquisition or use. If the component organizations band together to improve their ability to provide services, or to provide those services more efficiently, that is where the emphasis is likely to be. If, on the other hand, the reason for forming the network is broader—say, to better integrate the continuum of care for their constituent consumers—the range of collaborative efforts is apt to be broader as well.

Economies of scale can also be gained in organizations involved in both horizontal and vertical integration situations, although there are differences in the way those economies are realized. In horizontal integration, consisting primarily of segments providing similar levels of care, there is also much more commonality of products and services used. Most of their administrative and professional functions are similar as well. That gives them many more areas in which to collaborate.

When the integration is vertical in nature such that the organizational components provide different types and levels of care (e.g., consisting of a hospital, several nursing facilities, and a home care agency), there is less commonality and less opportunity to group services or functions. Although they can still participate in group purchasing, shared insurance, and so forth, it is more difficult than in a horizontal alliance. They do take advantage of these things, however, with some economies achieved by purchasing services from each other instead of from other unaffiliated organizations.

Gaining Market Share

Capitation and similar forms of managed care have greatly increased the need for long-term and other healthcare providers to capture particular segments of the market for these purchased services. This may mean diversifying in an attempt to cover more of the market. Conversely, it might involve identifying an individual portion of that market and focusing all efforts on it. In either case, there are demonstrated benefits to collaboration.

Joining an IHS gives a provider access to other types of services. If that provider's own services are highly specialized, such as those of a stand-alone adult day care program, integration helps to assure it of referrals from other provider types. It also secures needed services that the program's consumers might need that are beyond its ability to provide, such as care during an acute episode or professional dietary consultation.

A group of like providers (e.g., nursing facilities) might integrate among themselves to strengthen their hold on that portion of the market. Such integration would be horizontal, with the providers collaborating only among themselves for the shared benefits involved. However, they might also integrate vertically, joining as a group with providers above and/or below them in the continuum. By doing so, they will collectively enjoy the benefits inherent in that type of integration.

Increased Bargaining Power

Often, providers join together in an alliance or other form of integration for the purpose of increasing their bargaining power when contracting with MCOs or other group buyers. They recognize that they can negotiate better from a position of combined strength than from one of individual vulnerability. Providers who join the integration movement for this reason tend to do so relatively cautiously. They are more likely to begin with limited involvement, collaborating only in those areas where they perceive a need for support. They are somewhat reluctant to extend their participation into areas requiring more of a commitment. Some reach, and remain at, that initial level, but most move on to more involvement, recognizing the many benefits of integration.

Protection From Competitors

Most providers who integrate for the purpose of increasing their market share are acting proactively. However, others may do the same thing for purely defensive reasons. They may see their current position in the market threatened by other stronger providers. Often that threat comes from others who have already integrated. Joining with others for protection, to prevent deterioration of strategic standing, is a valid move. However, it may be indicative of a failure to adequately anticipate the dynamics of the field. In such cases, the organization joining out of a sense of survival does so at a disadvantage and may not get the best deal possible. Still, it is usually better than trying to go it alone without the necessary resources or talent.

In recent years, many hospitals, mostly small and/or rural facilities, have found themselves in just such situations. They were no longer able to provide a full range of services due to low volume and rising expenses. Many had been surviving marginally for years but eventually were faced with the decision of either ceasing to exist or joining forces with other, usually larger, hospitals. Even hospitals in stronger financial shape have recognized the dangers of remaining freestanding.

As has been true of so many of the changes occurring in health care, what the hospital industry experienced earlier happened later in long-term care. Marginal long-term care providers of all types are being threatened by their more aggressive competitors. Those competitors include others from within long-term care as well as some of those very hospitals who learned to integrate within the past few decades.

Whatever the type or level of integrated care, electronic health information systems are critical to providing integrated care. There must be a health information system that can collect patient-level data through an electronic health record and aggregate for evaluation and benchmarking (Essential Hospitals Institute, 2013).

Integration of the Continuum of Care

At this point, readers might have the impression that long-term care providers join integrated systems or networks for purely business reasons—to improve their competitive positions as a means of improving their financial situations. That impression would be unfair and is not intended here. Of course they seek financial success. They are not in business to lose money. Even not-for-profit organizations must at least break even. However, much of the integration we have seen has been for less selfish reasons. Providers know that the continuum is fragmented and that some consumers do not have full access to needed services. They also realize that integration is a promising means of overcoming at least some of those problems.

By joining forces, regardless of the precise format chosen, providers are able to increase the range of services offered. They can cooperatively provide services that might not be available otherwise. They can extend services to remote locations, taking advantage of their overall service volume to cover a much larger area. Their collective capabilities even make it possible for them to offer some services that would not be affordable for individual long-term care organizations to provide.

There are other benefits to those receiving long-term care services. Through integration, providers can coordinate referrals, smoothing the way for consumers moving about within the network or system. Through centralized information systems, integration makes it easier for consumers to get a variety of services provided by a variety of providers effectively and efficiently. Coordinated medical records avoid duplication of services and greatly reduce the possibility of missed treatments. Centralization of financial information saves consumers from much of the hassle involved with having to coordinate their own insurance coverage.

Few would disagree that there is a general lack of coordination of effort within the field of long-term care. There is a need for the system "to be planned and coordinated to reduce fragmentation and inefficiencies" (Saint Joseph's College of Maine, 1993, p. 3). Integration has emerged as a major way of achieving that coordination. In fact, a primary goal of integration is achieving seamless care for consumers. The degree to which an IHS achieves that is a good measure of the system's success.

Elements of an IHS or IHN

In her book, *The Continuum of Long-Term Care*, Dr. Connie Evashwick (2005, p. 9) identifies four integrating mechanisms required for an efficient, effective continuum of care: (1) interentity organization and management, (2) coordination of care, (3) integrated information systems, and (4) integrated financing. Given that such a continuum is a primary goal of any IHN or IHS, these four elements are now examined.

Interentity Organization and Management

Organizational structure is a prerequisite for the other integrating mechanisms. Managing an IHS is far more complex than managing a single provider. If it is to succeed, the individual entities involved must be coordinated in a fashion that provides true integration, not just an organizational coalition. This is true whether it is an integrated system under one corporate umbrella or an alliance of separate organizations tied together in a network. Whatever its form, integration requires that services be provided in a way that avoids duplication and/or gaps in availability and accessibility. It is the job of management to ensure that the organization is structured to ensure that integration.

Formation of an IHS usually requires some degree of subordination of autonomy by the individual organizations. Some or all of the members will find that certain of their interests are secondary to the interests of the whole. Each member organization has a set of goals and desired end results that have developed over a period of years. This is what makes them unique. As part of a larger organizational entity, however, some of these unique characteristics may be in conflict with the goals and desired end results of the integrated organization.

For example, if several home healthcare providers with overlapping service areas join an IHN, efficiency dictates that they eliminate that overlapping, meaning that some or all of them will have to give up portions of their previous consumer constituencies. Likewise, nursing facilities may have to accept the fact that not all can provide a full range of services.

The benefits of grouping together must outweigh the sacrifice of individual freedom, and usually do. Each of the member organizations has to balance the benefits and costs of interorganizational participation. Those negotiating from a position of relative strength often choose to participate in the less constricting network form of integration because it requires that they sacrifice less of their organizational independence. Others, seeing themselves as more vulnerable in a competitive environment, may find joining a more highly structured health system to be their best option, opting for the security of corporate involvement even though it may mean trading off some of their freedom of choice.

Achieving integration of services happens only when all involved plan jointly. They must work toward creation of an overall strategy. Strategic decision making at this level begins with a commitment by all parties to work collectively. Providers that have only recently learned to be competitive must now learn to share information about their organizations with others that may have been their competitors. Doing so is, to a large degree, an act of faith and is seldom easy.

Top management and members of the governing bodies of each member organization must commit not only to working collectively, but also to investing a considerable amount of their own time and effort. They must develop certain strategic competencies, including (1) articulating a common mission and vision satisfactory to all, (2) identifying short-term goals and communicating these to all members, (3) delegating implementation of these short-term goals to organization members, (4) intervening on behalf of the integrated organization, and (5) mediating internal disputes within the organization (Griffith, 1996). Achieving these competencies requires a lot of work and a significant amount of negotiation.

A sound strategic planning process is important to any organization, but it is absolutely critical for one that attempts to combine established diverse member organizations. It is a process that can result in development of common goals and agreement on implementation methods. These accomplishments will, in turn, lead to coordination of services. If those responsible for bringing the separate groups together fail to plan effectively or attempt to shortcut the process, they will be left with a collection of individual services that are integrated in name only. In reality, the members will still be competitors.

In a single-owner healthcare system, strategic decision making appears to be easier because dissident opinions can be overruled by the corporate powers. In an alliance of otherwise independent organizations, such as is commonly found in IHNs, reaching agreement on basic matters of mission, goals, and objectives can be more difficult because the independent members have the option, at least theoretically, of pulling out if disagreements become too heated. This simply increases the importance of an open, well-designed, and fairly implemented strategic planning process. Even when an optimum planning process is followed, however, there can still be barriers to effective management of an IHS. To begin with, all of the member organizations must shift from seeing themselves as individual entities to accepting that they are components of a larger one.

One of the most difficult decisions is determining which manager will emerge as chief executive officer of the system. Egos get involved (and bruised), and finding a solution that is agreed upon by, or is at least acceptable to, all parties can require a level of diplomacy somewhat akin to that needed for international statesmanship.

Beyond that, there are decisions to be made concerning which organizational members provide which services, how they interact with each other, and how they individually relate to the management of the governing entity. Given that the overall goals of the integrated system include coordination of services for consumers, efficiency of operation, and effectively reacting to changes in the operating environment, there is little room for competing interests from within. Some members may resist giving up any of their current markets to others even though those others may be better positioned to meet the needs of the consumers served by the larger organization.

Successfully melding these sometimes disparate providers into a coordinated, integrated whole depends on creation of a management organization that recognizes their individual needs in concert with the needs of the larger group. A key means of doing that is clearly separating and delineating the authority and responsibilities of the central office and the constituent members. In general, the larger management structure should be responsible for creating and implementing a common vision, establishing policies for the integrated organization, and providing support services for its members. It is not unlike the concept of strategic business units within a corporation. Each has its own purpose, its own distinctive competencies, and its own role as an integral part of the greater organization.

The members are responsible for providing the services that make the overall effort work. They do so within parameters set at the system level but must have the freedom to make operational decisions on a day-to-day basis to be successful. The front-line providers are the ones who must implement the short-term goals of the organization and must be free to make the decisions necessary to do that.

Balancing individual and collective organizational needs can be difficult, but it is necessary. The challenges to management are not that different in nature from those inherent in any business, but they do differ in the degree of complexity. Management involves accomplishing organizational objectives through coordinating the efforts of others. In the case of an integrated concern, those others are member organizations. Dealing with them and keeping them functioning well involves all of the management skills required for working with individuals. However, each member organization is itself made up of numerous individuals, adding to the difficulty of focusing them toward the larger organization's goals. When it comes to integration of both organizations and individual managers, there is increased emphasis on the skills pertaining to conflict resolution, negotiation, and consensus building.

Another challenge to managers of IHSs with any degree of vertical integration is the need to be knowledgeable about the separate types and levels of care involved. This may involve acute hospitals, subacute care, and the many forms of long-term care. Managers must know enough about how each of the other providers function to understand how each can best fit into the integrated system.

To date, most integrated systems have been built around a hospital or hospitals, with key managers experienced mostly in hospital administration. Few of them came with extensive knowledge of long-term care, yet they need to have such knowledge. They must have the knowledge and expertise to allow them to decide not only whether the system should offer a given service, but also how it should be integrated into the system. In the case of a single-owner health system, the decision is whether a particular service should be owned by the system or acquired through a contract with an outside provider. For less formal networks, the decision becomes whether the service in question should be provided by current members or by adding a new organization to the network. This situation presents an opportunity for experienced long-term care administrators to lend their expertise and knowledge to the system and even to move into top corporate administrative positions.

Coordination of Care

Coordination of care has been a major reason for the success of IHSs. They have shown that they can coordinate care for those they serve. Generally, but not always, they have access to a greater range of services, particularly in a vertically integrated system. They have the ability to organize those services in a manner to best meet the needs of a variety of consumers. Integration encourages efficient matching of resources to demand. Providing the right proportions of care at different levels of acuity avoids gaps or duplication in service. With careful planning, it is possible for an IHS to have most of the services its consumers need available when and where those services are needed, avoiding the inconvenience and expense of having to visit numerous providers or sites. This kind of planning requires a careful analysis of demographics and a good understanding of the population being served. Combining the resources of several member organizations makes it easier to support the costs of such analysis.

Integration can also improve use of manpower. Having several sites at which care is provided makes it possible to distribute personnel according to the requirements of the consumers. Balancing the numbers of clinical specialists at each site is cost effective. It is also critical to providing high-quality care and being responsive to actual demands. Having too many primary care practitioners at one site and not enough at another is more easily avoided when those sites are working together.

Because of their extensive resources, integrated systems have several service distribution options available to them. They may decide to apportion their services geographically, providing a relatively broad range of services at each of their sites, meeting most of the needs of a defined population group. On the other hand, they might decide to determine their service distribution on the basis of clinical specialization. In doing that, they provide limited services at designated sites, with specialty units and services each caring for certain illnesses or conditions or providing specialized treatments. For the long-term care portion of the system, this might include specialty units for such areas as Alzheimer's disease, subacute care, or hospice.

The advantages of geographic distribution center on convenience for consumers. These advantages are sometimes offset, however, by the higher costs to the system of duplicating services at several sites. Conversely, there are cost-efficiency benefits associated with clustering services and bringing consumers to them as needed. Each system decides whether to distribute its services according to geography or service specialty, depending on its own combination of demographics and resources and on related factors such as availability of transportation. Some systems find it advantageous to use a combination of the two approaches. In doing that, they must exercise caution to avoid invalidating the advantages of either.

An integrated system has more opportunity to reduce variations in care. In the overall healthcare field, significant variation in the amount and quality of care rendered has been well documented. Some clinical procedures (e.g., tonsillectomies, cesarean sections) are performed far more often in some geographic areas than in others and more often by some practitioners than by others. Because there are common standards for the practitioners in an integrated system, there is a better chance to reduce those variations. If the members of the system are operating within similar parameters, there is likely to be more control of clinical practices, resulting in more uniformity.

Integrated Information Systems

A major advantage of any integrated system, coalition, or network is the ability to share information among providers. They are able to coordinate both clinical and management information. Those without that ability are at a considerable organizational and competitive disadvantage. There is an old saying that information is power. In the case of IHSs, the ability to manage information does indeed seem to provide considerable competitive power.

Clinical Information Systems

Integrated clinical information systems typically address four specific areas: patient management, clinical guidelines, quality improvement, and clinical outcomes.

Patient Management—Being able to have information about all consumers available quickly at all provider sites is essential to integration. It avoids a great deal of duplicate questioning, something that not only is annoying to consumers but also takes a considerable amount of time for consumers and providers alike. Not having to repeat information about prior medical conditions and procedures makes it more convenient. It also helps prevent erroneous information from being given. When people are seriously ill, it is difficult for them to remember the details of medical tests or procedures they may have had in the distant past. The same can happen when they are apprehensive about the current visit to a healthcare provider. It is also true that long-term care's largest constituent group, the elderly, may have difficulty remembering such important bits of clinical information as allergies to medicines, long-ago surgical procedures, or even medication they are currently taking.

A coordinated clinical information system allows providers at any point in the integrated care system to have access to all of that information plus any recent tests or procedures that may have taken place at another site. By having complete, accurate information about those they serve, providers in an integrated system can also avoid procedures or treatments that could be potentially harmful if performed in ignorance of information that contraindicates them. In an IHS that effectively coordinates care, consumers find care to be seamless. Patients can schedule visits to other sites from their doctor's office, and their electronic medical records can move freely throughout the entire system.

This kind of coordination can also prevent one of the greatest problems with advanced directives such as living wills or durable powers of attorney. Advanced directives specify certain limitations on what procedures can be performed on a person if that person is unable to make his or her wishes known at the time. The problem is that advanced directives are often not transferred from one provider to another, resulting in actions being taken that are contrary to the wishes of the consumer who created the documents. In an integrated information system, there is a mechanism for alerting all providers to the existence and contents of those documents.

Clinical Guidelines—As noted earlier, care can be coordinated better if all providers are working within a common set of clinical guidelines. This is not to say that they must all provide care in exactly the same manner as all other providers, only that there are parameters to guide them. In most cases, those guidelines are developed by the providers themselves. The clinical information system gives them the data they need to create the guidelines and to identify and make changes to them as needed.

Quality Improvement—Healthcare providers, including all segments of the long-term care field, are very concerned about providing high-quality care. In recent years there has been much attention paid to improving quality using any of the several processes available to the healthcare providers. Quality management processes such as total quality management and continuous quality improvement require a great deal of data to be successful. An integrated information system can provide those data, not only for individual providers, but for all providers in the system. That broader scope allows system members to compare quality indicators with each other, enhancing their individual ability to make improvements.

Clinical Outcomes—In an integrated system, outcomes of care can be more easily measured. Sharing of clinical information enables the system members to compare the results of their clinical care. Because they are working toward common goals and are not in competition with each other, there is more willingness to share data about their work. Accurate measurement of outcomes is critical to development of realistic clinical guidelines. It also provides information for the integrated system to use in bidding for or negotiating contracts with MCOs or other consumer groups.

Management Information Systems

The value of a well-developed management information system (MIS) has been proven many times over in a variety of businesses. The more complex the business is, the more sophisticated its MIS must be. IHSs represent one of the most complex business forms. Thus, development of a sound MIS is critical to their success. It can handle the more traditional areas of cost control and billing of charges, including providing data needed for negotiating contracts with purchasers of the services of the IHS. It can also serve as the basis for operational control and for making improvements in a variety of nonclinical functions.

The MIS can provide valuable demographic information about the population served—information needed to allocate services and manpower effectively and efficiently. An IHS with multiple providers and service sites may be dealing with several distinct constituent groups, each with its own needs. Coordinating services for them requires knowledge of those needs, which are apt to change frequently. Thus, the MIS must be kept current.

Development of an adequate information system can be very expensive, making it difficult for fledgling systems to compete with those that are more established. This seems to be, in part at least, because integration—as we now know it—is still fairly new. Some new systems have attempted to develop their own information systems, in effect reinventing the wheel. Fortunately, others have learned from this and have relied more on established, proven systems. It is still a major undertaking.

Integrated Financing

As noted earlier in this chapter, the growth of capitation and other forms of managed care has spurred the development of IHSs. Large-group purchasers of health services have shown a desire to contract with a single-provider organization, looking for one-stop shopping, if you will. This places a premium on the ability of the sellers to provide a full range of services and penalizes those who cannot.

IHSs are best designed when they can accommodate both large contractors, such as MCOs, and smaller insurers and other purchasers of services. The large contractors probably account for the vast majority of their income, but relying too heavily on one or two of them can be perilous. There should also be other, perhaps smaller, buyers in the mix to ease some of the impact of losing a major contract.

The buyer of services may actually be a partner in an IHS, taking the system concept beyond the mere provision of care. In most such cases, the relationship is in the form of an alliance, leaving the member organizations less committed organizationally. However, because our focus here is on long-term care and the effects of integration on providers, we treat purchasers of care as entities outside of the integrated system.

Governance Issues

IHSs are not the same as individual providers in many ways. One of the most significant ways is in how they are governed. The system board must oversee a conglomeration of member organizations, each with its own unique strengths and weaknesses. Whether it is a corporate structure with all subsidiary organizations under the same ownership umbrella, a network of legally separate organizations, or a combination of the two, the systemwide governing board has to look at the big picture. Its primary responsibility is to the whole, not to the individual parts. Yet, the interests of those parts—the member organizations of which it is composed—must also be considered. The governing board must constantly balance these competing interests. It is very similar to the balancing act required of system managers but at a slightly different organizational level.

The board of an IHS functions as the ultimate authority. It coordinates the subordinate boards, mediates disputes among them, and ensures that the subordinate boards act in line with the interests of the system board. Failure to do so effectively can result in problems between member agencies or difficulty in creating an overall strategy.

Although an ownership-based IHS usually consists of subsidiaries that are all for profit or all not for profit, the members of an IHN may include a combination of both types. This increases the difficulty of representing them equitably and coordinating their efforts toward the interests of the overall system. The for-profits and not-for-profits come to the table with different operating philosophies. Most have lengthy experience providing care in one format or the other but little knowledge of how their counterparts operate. There may be strong policy differences. Yet, the benefits of consolidation, or at least collaboration, are too great to keep them from participating.

Another area that boards of integrated networks must think about is the possibility of antitrust violations. There has been some concern that networks may be vulnerable to antitrust considerations. That vulnerability comes from the fact that the networks are made up of providers that could also be seen as competitors. Therefore, any affiliation agreements between them must avoid any suggestion of price fixing or monopoly. Obviously, developers of any form of IHS should have advice from legal counsel experienced in such matters.

Role of Long-Term Care in Integrated Systems

Long-term care providers in most parts of the country have increasingly become involved in IHSs. Managed care now plays a larger role for most of them. In their early stages, IHSs tended to focus on acute and preventive care, with some secondary thought given to long-term care. That has changed—and the shape of the future is clear. Integration is not a fad, nor is it going to go away. It makes sense both organizationally and as a means of improving the continuum of care.

However, integration is far from mature as a business. That relative immaturity presents many opportunities for long-term care providers of all types. They would be wise to look closely at the many forms of integration, learn about them, and determine which is most advantageous for their organizations. As is so often the case in business, those organizations that get involved early run some risks but, if successful, reap great rewards. Of perhaps more importance in this increasingly competitive field, they establish themselves and their claim to a segment of the market.

■ Summary

Long-term care is going through a major evolution. It has gone from an industry in which competition was scarce to one in which competition has become the rule rather than the exception. This competition has emerged both within the field and without, forcing providers to pay attention to what is going on around them. Like the other healthcare providers before them, long-term care organizations have found ways to cooperate among themselves and with others to provide services better and more efficiently. This has led to their increased involvement in IHSs.

Early integration was generally limited to acute care providers and MCOs or health maintenance organizations (HMOs). As the movement has grown, there has also been growing understanding and acceptance of the role of long-term care in any comprehensive system. That realization has begun to create opportunities for long-term care organizations as participants in a variety of systems, networks, alliances, and coalitions. These opportunities will continue to expand, and proactive long-term care organizations will find ways to take advantage of them.

■ Vocabulary Terms

The following terms are included in this chapter. They are important to the topics and issues discussed here and should become familiar to readers. Some of the terms are also found in other chapters but may be used in different contexts. They may not be fully defined herein. Readers may wish to seek other supplementary definitions.

affiliation
Affordable Care Act
bargaining power
bundling
clinical information systems
collusion
competition
continuous quality improvement
continuum of care
cooperation
distinctive competencies

economies of scale
health maintenance organization
 (HMO)
horizontal integration
infrastructure
integrated delivery system
integrated health network
 (IHN)
integrated health system (IHS)
integrating mechanisms
integration

management information system
   (MIS)
merger

strategic business unit
transfer agreement
vertical integration

■ Discussion Questions

The following questions are presented to assist you in understanding the material covered in this chapter. They tend to be general but lend themselves to detailed answers. The answers to these questions can be found in the chapter.

1. Why has the long-term care field not been subject to strong competition in the past? Why has that changed?
2. What is the difference between cooperation and integration?
3. What is an integrated health network?
4. What is an integrated health system?
5. Under what circumstances might a long-term care organization choose to join an integrated system? An integrated network?
6. What are some of the potential economies of scale resulting from integration?
7. What are some of the benefits of integration for long-term care consumers?
8. How are management and governance of an integrated system or network different from management and governance of an individual organizational entity?
9. Why are information systems so important to integration efforts?
10. Why is planning so important to integrated networks or systems?

■ References

AHCA. (2014). *The AHCA/NCAL Quality Initiative*. Retrieved from http://www.ahcancal.org /quality_improvement/qualityinitiative/Pages/default.aspx.

Bassett, B. (2013, Oxtober 8). *Accountable care organizations and long term care: ACOs are changing the health care payment game*. Retrieved from http://healthcare-executive-insight.advanceweb.com /Web-Extras/Long-Term-Care-Feature/Accountable-Care-Organizations-and-Long-Term-Care.aspx.

Coile, R. (1990). *The new medicine: Reshaping medical practice and health care management*. Rockville, MD: Aspen Publishers.

Dummit, L. (2011, March 28). *Medicare's bundling pilot: Including post-acute care services*. Issue brief No. 841. Retrieved from http://www.nhpf.org/library/issue-briefs/IB841_BundlingPostAcuteCare _03-28-11.pdf.

Essential Hospitals Institute. (2013). *Integrated health care literature review*. Washington, DC: America's Essential Hospitals.

Evashwick, C. (2005). *The continuum of care* (3rd ed.). Clifton Park, NY: Thomson Delmar Learning.

Federal Interagency Forum on Aging-Related Statistics. (2013, July 31). *Older Americans 2012.* Hyattsville, MD: Federal Interagency Forum on Aging-Related Statistics. Retrieved from http://www.agingstats.gov/agingstatsdotnet/Main_Site/Data/2012_Documents/Docs/EntireChartbook.pdf.

Fuchs, V. (1988). The "competition revolution" in health care. *Health Affairs* 7, no.3, 5–24.

Griffith, J. (1996). Managing the transition to integrated health care organizations. *Frontiers of Health Services Management* 12, no.2, 4–50.

Howell, E., Palmer, A., & Adams, F. (2012). *Medicaid and CHIP risk-based managed care in 20 states.* Washington, DC: U.S. Department of Health and Human Services.

MetLife Mature Market Institute. (2012). *Market survey of long-term care costs.* New York, NY: MetLife. Retrieved from https://www.metlife.com/assets/cao/mmi/publications/highlights/mmi-market-survey-long-term-care-costs-highlights.pdf.

National Conference of State Legislatures. (2013, June 17). *Managed care, market reports and the states.* Retrieved from http://www.ncsl.org/research/health/managed-care-and-the-states.aspx.

Saint Joseph's College of Maine. (1993). *Criteria for designing or evaluating a long-term care system.* Standish: Saint Joseph's College of Maine.

External Control of Long-Term Care

After completing this chapter, readers will be able to:

1. Understand why there is need for external control of long-term care and the problems inherent in such control.

2. Discuss the ways in which quality and cost are controlled and by whom.

3. Identify and discuss the respective roles of federal and state governments in regulating long-term care.

4. Understand which individual long-term care practitioners are subject to specific controls and by whom.

5. Identify and define nongovernment controls, such as accreditation and certification.

▪ Introduction

As the long-term care system grows, both in numbers and in types of services offered, public and private agencies are increasingly attempting to control costs and provide protection for consumers. This chapter discusses the background and current types of cost and quality control. It also offers some insight into where the system is likely going in this area. It focuses on long-term care organizations and efforts by external agencies to ensure that costs are controlled and that the quality of care is acceptable, rather than on what those organizations are doing to control their own costs and quality.

External controls can be divided into two categories: public and private. Public controls result from passage of laws. They are nonvoluntary and are imposed by government agencies. Private controls are provided by nongovernment agencies and organizations, and compliance is voluntary. However, in some situations in which these private controls substitute for government inspections, they take on the importance of mandated oversight. Although there is some overlap from category to category, there are significant differences, and they are discussed separately.

■ Public (Government) Control Mechanisms

Public controls include regulation of long-term care providers and licensure of individuals working in the field. They are similar and both have the same general origin: the desire of the government to protect consumers of long-term care services and those (particularly the government itself) who pay for the services.

To study regulation and licensure, we must first understand the basis of the legal system of which they are a part. A system of law has been called "a system of principles and rules devised by organized society to set norms for conduct" (Showalter, 2012, p. 3). Or, saying it a bit differently, "laws are general rules of conduct that are enforced by government, which imposes penalties when prescribed when laws are violated" (Pozgar, 2013, p. 158). This set of rules has several sources, all emanating from various branches and levels of government, whether they are legislatures, courts, or administrative agencies at federal, state, or municipal levels. All of these rules, whether referred to as laws, regulations, or court decisions, have several common characteristics.

First, they are (usually) not enacted without a hearing of some type having been held to explore the need for a decision in the matter. This is true whether it is a congressional hearing, a regulatory agency hearing, a hearing before a state legislative body, or a court hearing. These hearings have the purpose of allowing interested parties to present their views and evidence to a governmental body that has the power to resolve the matter. Also, these rules, once enacted by a governing body, must be implemented with discretion on the part of the rule enforcers. This discretion is nothing more than a term meaning "good-faith judgment" to efficiently, fairly, and honestly accomplish the mandate of the rule.

A law created by legislation affects all within the jurisdiction of the legislative body. A court decision affects the parties to the legal disagreement, but it may also have broader effect as a rule because other courts will tend to follow that rule, which was established by the decision of the judge in that case, when they themselves face similar cases. Regulations created and enforced by government agencies are much more specific and affect only certain specified groups or individuals. They are the focal point of the interaction between the long-term care system and the legal system.

Regulation

Regulations vary from laws primarily in their specificity. A legislative body enacts a law, and an agency enacts regulations to implement that law. The law is usually a very broad general mandate to accomplish a certain objective. An agency is created to carry out the intent of the law and develops regulations to make that happen. Agency-implemented regulations, as they affect long-term care, often get very much into the specifics of eligibility, levels of care, and payment. The regulations themselves are, of course, subject to hearings and input from interested parties. They are also subject to court review, where they may be deemed to be in violation of the constitutional rights of individuals or groups. Courts, however, are not quick to overturn the decision of an agency, particularly when due process has, in fact, been followed in terms of hearings, rule-making procedures, and so forth.

Who Regulates and Why

Regulations are imposed by a government unit—federal, state, or local (including county and municipal)—because of the responsibility of that unit to protect the welfare of the public, particularly those that the government judges to be unable to protect themselves. This protection covers two primary areas: quality and payment. Most regulation of long-term care, and of other industries as well, is either to maintain the level of quality in the goods or services produced or to minimize the level of payment for those goods or services. In long-term care, regulations set minimum levels of staffing, cleanliness, and safety to ensure that those persons needing care are treated properly and receive the necessary services. Various government agencies also set revenue and spending limits to prevent those paying the bills from being overcharged. In long-term care, that payer is primarily the government, through Medicare and Medicaid. Thus, the government has another motive for regulating payment other than purely the protection of individuals. Some question whether this is a conflict of interest, but it is not something that is going to change.

Long-term care regulations cover both organizational providers and individuals who work in the field. Although there is some overlap between the two, there are also significant areas of divergence, including often having different agencies responsible for implementing and enforcing the regulations. Thus, they are discussed separately here, but they are also included in the section dealing with the pros and cons of regulation.

Long-term care has a great deal of regulation, more than many other fields of endeavor. There are several reasons for the relatively heavy regulation of long-term care. First, its history has been one of service to those who have had no other recourse. There has, from the very beginning, been a close relationship between long-term care and welfare. Like many other segments of health care, long-term care facilities began as almshouses or homes for the poor who could not care for themselves, and a large portion of those using long-term care services were formal or informal wards of the state, meaning that they were the responsibility of the government. That heritage of helping the less fortunate fostered a large role for government in protecting their interests.

Second, long-term care has been subjected to heavy regulation because of the vulnerability of the users of its services and the potential damage that might be caused by poor quality. Lack of sufficient quality in most manufacturing industries means selling an inferior product, leading to future sales slumps. In long-term care, as in all of health care, poor-quality services mean a reduction in the quality of life of the consumer at the very least. At worst, it means physical harm, even death. Because of the seriousness associated with the need for quality, government has determined that it has to play a strong oversight role.

Third, long-term care consumers are particularly at risk because they are often unable to judge quality for themselves. This may be because they are elderly, frail, or not fully competent mentally because of illness or advanced age. They also may have difficulty judging quality of care because it is somewhat technical and foreign to them.

This concern on the part of the government has not been without justification, which brings us to the fourth reason for regulation of long-term care. The record of early long-term care, in the form of nursing homes, is full of incidents of abuse, fraud, and just plain poor care. Such is not the case today, and those charges of impropriety did not apply to all nursing homes, even in early days. But they did apply to far too many of them. As a result, they were subjected to a much tighter scrutiny than other parts of the healthcare industry. To a large extent, they still are.

Although there were scattered earlier attempts at regulation in long-term care, the first national regulation came with the 1950 amendments to the Social Security Act. These amendments mandated that any facility caring for more than four unrelated individuals receiving Social Security income had to be licensed by the state in which the facility was located (Shore, 1994, p. 2). Later federal programs, most notably Medicare and Medicaid, created in 1965, added new levels of regulations.

The most sweeping regulations pertaining to long-term care were passed as part of the Omnibus Budget Reconciliation Act (OBRA). Some key provisions include the following:

- The right to freedom from abuse, mistreatment and neglect;
- The right to freedom from physical restraints;
- The right to choose a personal physician;
- The right to access medical records;
- The right to be treated with dignity and to exercise self-determination;
- The right to accommodation of medical, physical, psychological and social needs;
- The right to participate in resident and family groups;
- The right to communicate freely and voice grievances without discrimination or reprisal;
- The right to appropriate resident discharge and transfer;
- The development of a comprehensive resident assessment process;
- The development of preadmission and annual screening for residents with mental illnesses and other chronic conditions that might not be appropriately addressed in nursing homes. (Pioneer Network, 2013, OBRA 87 Key Provisions section)

Since it was first passed in 1987, it has commonly been known as OBRA '87, or simply OBRA, although the final enforcement rules did not take effect until much later, and additional regulations continue to be added.

Regulations governing long-term care are much too voluminous to discuss in detail here. They also change so frequently that any detailed review would soon be outdated. Therefore, the objective of this chapter is only to present an overview in hopes of imparting a basic understanding of the what, who, why, and how of those regulations. For a more detailed, current examination of them, there are several excellent texts and, of course, the regulations themselves.

Regulation of Quality

Ensuring quality of care is the primary reason for regulation of long-term care. Consumers have a right to receive care that is of high quality. Regulations are designed to guarantee that right, but how difficult is that to do? How can government agencies oversee all of the many aspects of long-term care to ensure that it is delivered properly? To do so, they must first define quality, measure the degree to which there is compliance, and then take actions to correct any deficiencies. It is a tall order. Quality in long-term care is looked at herein from a regulatory perspective.

Defining and Measuring Quality

Quality is difficult to define because it means different things to different people. We could go on at great length attempting to define quality in long-term care, but the focus here is on how it is regulated. Let us agree that quality of care is subjective, includes both technical and personal components, and varies from individual to individual and situation to situation. Having done that, it is time to move on to talking about measuring and guaranteeing quality and the role of regulation in doing so.

If quality is so hard to define, how can it be attained and its success measured? Who should do the measuring? Is there more than one correct approach? These questions begin to get at the key policy issues as they relate to quality and regulation.

Just as there are many definitions of quality, there are also many methods of measuring it. Most of them fall into three categories: process, structure, and outcomes. These terms were originated in the 1960s and have since become standard terminology. Process-based measurement looks at how tasks are accomplished and whether they follow accepted procedures. Structure-based measurement focuses on the capacity of the organization to provide care (e.g., staff-to-client ratio, size of facility). Neither looks at what is accomplished, which is what outcomes measurement does. Outcomes measures relate to the result of treatment or care. They measure changes in the functional status accruing from the care given.

A major fault found with most current long-term care regulations is the emphasis of regulators on process and structure, not outcomes. They seldom measure what is accomplished, but focus rather on how it is accomplished, or worse, how it is documented. This kind of focus only stifles innovative approaches to solving problems. It also opens the door for fraud and/or deception by those clever (and dishonest) enough to document actions that never happened as though they had.

Most people feel that outcomes-based measurement is a superior method, but they also recognize the difficulty of using it in a field as complex as long-term care. Still, an outcomes-based approach is a desirable end. Some regulatory agencies have seriously attempted to shift their focus from process and structure documentation to measurement of outcomes and have advertised that change widely. Yet these attempts have had only limited success. Over the past 10 years, the Joint Commission (formerly the Joint Commission on Accreditation of Healthcare Organizations) audits have begun to examine outcomes, and some states have developed methodologies for measuring outcomes, but the results are still somewhat controversial. Outcome measures in different contexts can be controversial because inferences are sometimes difficult to make (AHRQ, 2014). As honorable as the agencies' intentions are, they seem to find it difficult to let go of the old way of inspecting. Outcomes measures will be effective when they replace process and structure measures, not when they are simply an add-on.

The most common argument for emphasizing outcomes is that it judges the end result, leaving providers free to find the best way to attain that result. With the rapid advances in technology and delivery methodology expected over the next few years, innovation is both possible and desirable. Anything that stifles that innovation is undesirable.

Who Should Measure Quality?

The debate over how quality is measured is not nearly as heated as is the debate over who should do the measuring—the providers (internal) or regulators (external). Historically, most quality measurement has been external, in the form of mandatory licensure surveys and reimbursement-driven regulations. As the government became more involved in paying for health care through Medicare and Medicaid, it also began to demand a certain level of quality in the services for which it was paying. It did so by setting standards against which providers were compared. Those standards have been heavily oriented toward measurement of process and structure, not outcomes. They also aim at maintaining a minimum level of quality beneath which providers may not slip but do little to stimulate any effort beyond the minimum.

Types of Quality Regulations

Regulations addressing quality of care come from all levels of government, from federal budget oversight agencies to local health departments. They each have their own areas of concern, their own sets of rules dealing with those concerns, and their own methods of enforcement. Their common goal is protecting their constituents—in this case, consumers of long-term care—from harm or neglect. Providers of long-term care must be cognizant of all of these agencies and must comply with all of their regulations.

Federal Regulation—Most regulation of quality of care in long-term care organizations originates at the federal level. More often than not, it is contained in legislation appropriating funds for long-term care reimbursement or is attached to the federal budget. As could be expected, Medicare and Medicaid account for a large proportion of federal regulations dealing with quality of care, even though they are primarily payment programs. These programs include detailed and stringent requirements that must be met by providers to qualify for reimbursement from them. For nursing facilities, an entirely new level of federal regulation was imposed in 1987 when OBRA not only added specific standards for those facilities, but also extended the coverage of the regulations to all nursing facilities, regardless of whether they receive Medicare or Medicaid funds.

These acts (Medicare, Medicaid, and OBRA) and the regulations emanating from them govern virtually all aspects of care in long-term care organizations. They set staffing levels that must be met, both in terms of the number of staff required and in the mix of healthcare professionals needed for each level of care provided. They mandate certain levels of coverage by nurses, nursing assistants, therapists, dietitians, and social workers. They spell out the minimum amount of coverage by physicians, dentists, and pharmacists. They also establish minimum amounts of care to be received each day by each consumer.

Regulations associated with these acts require providers to follow a number of specific procedures designed to ensure the quality of care rendered. Providers must conduct preadmission screening according to procedures included in the regulations. They must carry out regular assessments of the functional status of the consumer and adjust care plans accordingly. There must be internal quality assurance mechanisms in place to monitor how care is given. Each provider must develop and implement a bill of rights, outlining the rights of consumers and ensuring that those consumers understand how to exercise those rights.

Long-term care providers are also subject to numerous other federal regulations relating to quality of care. The Patient Self-Determination Act of 1990 required that all healthcare consumers be made aware of their right to determine the amount and type of care to be received in end-of-life situations and to create advanced directives, such as living wills and durable powers of attorney, to hold providers accountable to their wishes. Other federal laws, such as the Civil Rights Act and the Americans With Disabilities Act, relate to quality of care by guaranteeing equal access and treatment for all.

State Regulation—The primary role of state government in regulating long-term care quality is as the designated agency administering federal programs. These programs require that each state have a single agency charged with oversight of Medicare and Medicaid. That agency, often a state health department or department of regulation, inspects long-term care provider organizations and certifies them for Medicare and Medicaid. They also, in most cases, license providers not involved with Medicare or Medicaid. The state agencies may impose additional rules, and they routinely survey providers to ensure compliance with federal and state regulations. An important role of states in regulating quality in long-term care is in licensure of individual healthcare professionals.

Local Regulation—Local, meaning municipal or county, agencies also have an interest in ensuring the quality of care received by consumers of long-term care. They are usually represented by health departments, who also have other areas of interest besides long-term care. Their regulations cover a variety of public health areas, such as sanitation, food preparation and service, and avoidance of epidemics. Providers of long-term care fall within those parameters and must comply with local regulations just as would any other business or individual.

Regulation of Payment

The primary purpose of any healthcare regulations is to ensure quality. Yet, nearly as much attention (some would say more) is given to avoiding excessive payments, saving money for government agencies, and preventing fraud and abuse in government funding programs. Again, as is the case with quality control, Medicare and Medicaid are the preeminent sources of regulations when it comes to controlling payment for long-term care. The two programs represent huge sums of taxpayer money, and government agencies administering them are responsible for stewardship of that money. These programs also represent a major source of reimbursement for long-term care provider organizations. As such, the impact of seemingly minor changes in reimbursement rates or eligibility regulations can be enormous.

These programs historically paid on the basis of reasonable costs incurred by providers. However, what the government agencies determined to be reasonable and what providers saw as reasonable bore little resemblance. Under this payment mechanism, providers had to submit detailed cost reports showing how and where they incurred expenses. Within the scope of the regulations these expenses were subject to review and could be disallowed or reduced. They were also subject to limits set by regulation. The goal of the regulations was to prevent providers from reaping excessive profit at the expense of the taxpayers.

A new prospective payment system has been implemented for those segments of long-term care reimbursed by Medicare. The system regulates payment by setting a predetermined rate for certain services.

Another way in which government agencies regulate payment is by channeling it from provider groups that they see as high expense to those that are less costly. This has been the background motivation for the recent emphasis on home-based services. By changing eligibility regulations for nursing facilities and other institutional providers, the government seeks to divert consumers to home healthcare or other community-based services. Even something as seemingly innocuous and beneficial as creating regulations making it easier to access hospice services comes with a background motive of changing the balance of payments for the overall system.

Health Insurance Portability and Accountability Act

One of the most significant pieces of legislation, with its accompanying regulations, to affect health care in recent years is the Health Insurance Portability and Accountability Act (HIPAA) of 1996. The purposes of HIPAA are threefold: to provide consumers with greater access to healthcare insurance, to protect the privacy of healthcare data, and to promote more standardization and efficiency in the healthcare industry. Thus, its various parts affect different constituencies differently. It does not focus primarily on control of quality or cost but has elements of each. They are looked at briefly next.

Consumer Access to Healthcare Insurance

Title I of HIPAA is designed to protect health insurance coverage for workers and their families when they change or lose their jobs. By placing certain restrictions on healthcare insurance plans and employers, HIPAA provides protection for those workers and their families. Among its specific protections in this regard, HIPAA:

1. Limits the use of preexisting condition exclusions.
2. Prohibits most group health plans from discriminating by denying coverage or charging extra for coverage based on a covered person's past or present poor health.
3. Guarantees certain small employers, and certain individuals who lose job-related coverage, the right to purchase health insurance.
4. Guarantees, in most cases, that employers or individuals who purchase health insurance can renew the coverage regardless of any health conditions of individuals covered under the insurance policy. (U.S. Department of Labor, 2004)

Although this may be the most important part of the law as far as individual consumers are concerned, it is not the one with the most impact on long-term care services.

Protecting the Privacy of Healthcare Data

The administrative simplification section of HIPAA addresses the security and privacy of health data. It limits the release of patient protected health information without the consent of the patient for the purpose of guarding personal information.

Protected health information is information, including demographic information, which relates to:

- the individual's past, present, or future physical or mental health or condition,
- the provision of health care to the individual, or
- the past, present, or future payment for the provision of health care to the individual, and that identifies the individual or for which there is a reasonable basis to believe can be used to identify the individual. Protected health information includes many common identifiers (e.g., name, address, birth date, Social Security Number) when they can be associated with the health information listed above. (HHS, 2013)

This means that providers of long-term care and other health services must not reveal personal information about consumers unless the consumers give written permission. It excludes from this rule any information that is necessary for the provision of care, such as sharing medical test results with another provider who must have them to provide the proper care.

This provision has resulted in the most visible aspect of HIPAA and is responsible for what has made it somewhat of a household term, even if many consumers are not really sure what it means. That most visible aspect manifests as a flood of paper to consumers and yet another form to sign when receiving healthcare services. This is because all covered entities under HIPAA (healthcare providers, health plans, and healthcare clearinghouses) must develop their own privacy policies in keeping with HIPAA requirements, must provide all consumers with copies of those privacy policies, and must have written proof that all consumers have received them. They must also get permission from consumers to release information about their health care. The idea of more carefully guarding private information is admirable, and HIPAA has gone far toward that goal, but, like most such regulations, it has created a great deal of paperwork for all who fall under its jurisdiction.

Promoting Standardization and Efficiency

HIPAA requires everyone covered by the regulations to use standard formats for processing claims and payments. It also adopts transaction standards for several types of electronic health information transactions, as well as for the maintenance and transmission of electronic healthcare information and data. HIPAA requires every provider who does business electronically to use the same healthcare transactions, code sets, and identifiers. HIPAA has identified certain standard transactions for electronic data interchange for the transmission of healthcare data. These transactions are: claims and encounter information, payment and remittance advice, claims status, eligibility, enrollment and disenrollment, referrals and authorizations, coordination of benefits, and premium payment (CMS, 2013b).

These regulations benefit everyone involved since they have been implemented, but the first few years of adapting to them were very time and effort intensive for providers and others covered by HIPAA.

Other Regulations

Quality and payment command most of the attention when it comes to regulations affecting long-term care providers and consumers. However, there are many other government agencies overseeing them, and each has its own set of regulations. Many of these are not specific to long-term care but still require compliance.

Employees of long-term care organizations are protected by the same laws and regulations as are employees of any other business. Their employment rights are protected by several different agencies, including the Equal Employment Opportunity Commission, which enforces regulations addressing issues such as conditions of employment, equal pay, sexual harassment, age discrimination, nondiscrimination on the basis of handicaps, and other civil rights. They are also covered by the Fair Labor Standards Act and a variety of other labor relations acts. The Occupational Safety and Health Administration monitors businesses to ensure a safe and healthy workplace.

Its regulations cover areas such as safety programs and infection control. All of these and more protect workers in long-term care organizations, indirectly protecting the consumers for whom they care.

Providers must also adhere to regulations addressing life safety and protection of the environment, as well as state and federal tax codes and other financial regulations. In most cases, they are treated much as are other businesses. These regulations are sometimes seen as secondary to those directly affecting long-term care and only long-term care, but their purposes are valid and are every bit as important in the overall scheme of protecting the industry, its consumers, and society.

Licensure of Individuals

Just as long-term care organizations are regulated, so are individuals who work in long-term care or, for that matter, in any segment of health care. They are licensed by the states rather than by the federal government. Licensure can be defined as "the process by which some competent authority grants permission to a qualified individual or entity to perform certain specified activities that would be illegal without a license" (Pozgar, 2013, p. 298). It ensures that they are properly qualified and conduct themselves in a professional manner. In most cases, there is a mechanism for them to transfer a license from one state to another through a process of reciprocity, sometimes called endorsement.

Healthcare Professionals

Professionals in a variety of healthcare specialties are licensed to practice (in most cases) throughout the continuum of care, not just in long-term care. Physicians, dentists, nurses, therapists, dietitians, social workers, and other similar professionals are each licensed individually by a state agency. In some states there is a single board of registration responsible for licensing all of them. In others, there are separate boards, either for each specialty or for subcategories of specialties. For example, one board might license physicians while another might license registered nurses, and so on.

These boards are responsible for determining the qualifications of candidates for initial licensure, usually including certain required levels of formal education. Often, there are experiential requirements as well, demonstrating that the practitioner is able to put his or her formal education to practical use. The licensing boards also monitor each healthcare professional's practice and take disciplinary action when needed. Some type of formal continuing education is usually required to maintain or renew a professional license.

As is so common throughout other areas of health care, the terminology regarding licensure is far from uniform and can be confusing. The terms *licensure* and *registration* are sometimes used interchangeably. Registration usually refers to the process by which individuals are listed as eligible to provide a regulated service. Registration does not necessarily require demonstration of competency in that service.

A third term that is also used, *certification*, usually refers to voluntary, nongovernmental testimony of qualifications. In some cases, it may refer to government processes. It involves recognition that an individual's expertise meets the standards of that group. The standards established by the professional associations generally exceed those required by government agencies (Pozgar, 2013). Unlike licensing authorities, certification organizations lack the authority to limit incompetent or illegal practice.

The licenses, registrations, or certifications issued to healthcare professionals are not specific to the institution, agency, or other organization where they work. They are carried as individual credentials. However, it is up to the organizations to determine (and document) that the credentials of all professionals working for them are legitimate and are kept up to date. This is true whether the professionals are employees or contractors. The organizations are subject to legal penalties if they fail in this.

Practitioners Specific to Long-Term Care

Although the healthcare professionals discussed in the previous section are not licensed specifically for work in long-term care organizations, federal and state regulations governing those organizations do specify certain standards that must be met by staff working in them. Generally, those standards refer to other licensure, registration, or certification processes. For example, the Centers for Medicare and Medicaid Services (CMS, 2013a) says that "skilled nursing services can only be performed safely and correctly by a licensed nurse." Standards for employment of other professionals are worded similarly.

There are several categories of healthcare practitioners who work specifically in long-term care and are regulated as such.

Certified Nursing Assistants

First are certified nursing assistants (CNAs) working in nursing facilities. OBRA includes regulations, implemented in 1990, that require all nursing assistants working in nursing facilities to be certified. Those regulations state "CNAs are trained and certified to help nurses by providing non-medical assistance to patients, such as help with bathing, dressing, and using the bathroom" (CMS, 2013a). It does not include anyone who is a licensed healthcare professional, a registered nurse, a registered dietitian, or someone who volunteers to provide such services without pay (Townsend & Davis, 2010). The purpose is to ensure that these unlicensed staff members have at least a minimum amount of training to do their jobs properly and safely.

This is an interesting combination of public regulation and private certification. Technically, nursing assistants are certified by training programs that may be public or private. The government (through OBRA) does not license them as such. However, it does set standards for their training and must approve all certification training programs, even those that are private. Each state must also, through its Medicaid agency, keep a register of certified nursing assistants (nurse aides). This register keeps track of the qualifications of the CNAs in the state, and only those registered with it may be employed in nursing facilities.

Similar training standards have been set by the federal government for home health aides working in Medicare-certified home health or hospice agencies.

Long-Term Care Administrators

It has not been customary for healthcare administrators to be licensed, with one notable exception: administrators of nursing facilities (formerly called nursing homes). Landmark legislation passed in 1967 required that all nursing home administrators be licensed. That particular legislation, and the resulting regulations, speak to the state of (or the perception by the government of) nursing homes. Hospital administrators have never been required to be licensed, nor have most other long-term care administrators. Only those running nursing homes were singled out for licensure. This inconsistency is largely the result of the feeling that nursing home administrators needed to be controlled more than did hospital administrators.

Contributing to this sentiment was the fact that hospital administrators, even in the late 1960s, were being trained for their profession at the college level. (Today, although there is no formal requirement that they possess a college education, a master's degree is the accepted norm.) Conversely, long-term care managers, including nursing home administrators, did not generally need to have such education.

The federal government mandated that each state license nursing home administrators. Unfortunately, it gave the states little guidance or structure for determining licensure requirements. Each state set standards for the education and experience required for licensure. As a result, the education requirements varied greatly, ranging from a high school diploma in some states to a degree from a college or university in others. Even those requiring a college degree varied greatly. In some states it could be any degree; others required a specialized degree in long-term care. The individual states also determined for themselves how much, if any, continuing education would be needed to maintain or renew a license. Again, the requirements differed greatly, from no continuing education needed at all to as much as 60 hours every 2 years.

Even today, there is little consistency from state to state. While nearly all states require a college degree for a nursing facility administrator, many accept any bachelor's degree, regardless of whether it relates to long-term care or administration. This is changing gradually, with more movement toward establishing a long-term-care-related bachelor's degree as the standard. Federal officials have also talked about imposing a minimum education requirement as a regulation.

Another area of inconsistency is the amount of hands-on experience required prior to licensure. Some states mandate a formal practicum experience commonly known as an administrator-in-training program. As with nursing facility administrators, the required length of the administrator-in-training program varies from none in some states to as much as 2 years in others. Several states make the required length of the administrator-in-training variable depending on the educational preparation of the candidate. Other states require the same amount of administrator-in-training experience regardless of education.

Other long-term care administrators are subject to varying, usually less strict, licensure standards than those in nursing facilities. Federal and state standards require any long-term care organization that is licensed by the state or certified to provide care under the Medicare or Medicaid programs to have a qualified administrator. However, in most cases, they do not require that administrators themselves be licensed. This is also true of home healthcare agencies, hospice organizations, and adult day care programs.

The area in which licensure is changing most is in institutional services that may be provided under the same roof or within the same organizational entity. For example, assisted living and subacute care are often provided in and by nursing facilities. When that happens, they require a licensed administrator. As those services have grown and become more clearly delineated, government agencies have rushed to catch up with them and create new licensing categories to cover them. As of this writing, numerous states have created licensure regulations to cover assisted living administrators, and others are looking to do so. Some have developed separate licensure categories for care variations such as assisted living and congregate housing, while others are all inclusive.

It is not usually easy to create new licensure categories and to develop the regulations to govern those covered by them. It often means passing new legislation or adding to existing legislation. This requires that state agencies go through a formal regulation-development process, including hearings and solicitation of public comment. In at least a few states, there has been heated competition between state agencies to determine which will be authorized to cover these new provider categories.

Efforts to Resolve the Confusion Over Licensure

There has been significant progress toward increasing the uniformity of state licensing regulations, removing some of the confusion, duplication, and fragmentation. In some cases, it is also making them more strenuous. This progress has primarily been the result of efforts by several organizations, including both government and private, federal and state.

One of the more intensive efforts is under way at the National Association of Long-Term Care Administrator Boards (NAB). NAB, which consists of representatives of the respective state long-term care administrator licensing boards, has developed a national licensing exam that is required for nursing facility administrator licensure in all of them. The exam is updated continually to keep pace with changes in nursing facility administration. The exam is based on the following five domains of practice, which are determined by NAB to be areas of knowledge or skill required of long-term care administrators:

- Resident-centered care and quality of life
- Human resources
- Finance

- Physical environment and atmosphere
- Leadership and management (NAB, 2012)

These domains were developed, in part, from the *Standards of Practice for Long-Term Care Administrators* developed originally by the American College of Health Care Administrators (ACHCA). They are updated regularly by NAB members.

NAB has also taken the initiative in other areas, including education and transferring licenses from state to state. In the area of education, NAB has developed a formal academic accreditation program designed to ensure that college and university programs training administrators of nursing facilities teach what is necessary to produce qualified graduates. Although the number of such programs has been growing rapidly, not all are accredited by NAB, and there has been little similarity in their curriculum requirements. They have offered degrees ranging from business administration to gerontology. Yet studies have clearly shown the value of degrees that focus specifically on long-term care administration.

By reviewing education programs and accrediting those meeting their rigid standards, NAB has established minimum standards of education for future nursing facility administrators. Accreditation by NAB gives those educational institutions the credibility of having a seal of approval from a national organization overseeing licensure. It also makes it easier for colleges with students in multiple states. Although states do not have to accept NAB accreditation as automatically meeting their education requirements, most will. This relieves the colleges of the necessity of negotiating with individual state licensing boards for acceptance.

In 1997, NAB took another step toward expanding the educational opportunities for nursing facility administrators when it granted its first academic approval to a college-based distance education program. Distance education programs allow students to study through correspondence and/or electronic media. They are designed to meet the needs of working adults who find traditional campus-based college programs inconvenient or unavailable. Saint Joseph's College of Maine, which provides degree and certificate programs in long-term care administration through a distance education mode, met NAB's standards and was accredited, signaling NAB's recognition of the value of education programs for current administrators and other adult learners who work full-time. The bachelor's degree in long-term care administration was reaccredited in 2002, 2007, and 2012. The master of health administration program was initially accredited in 2007 and reaccredited in 2012.

Another way that NAB is working toward uniformity in the licensure of nursing facility administrators involves transferring licenses from one state to another (also known as reciprocity or endorsement). Historically, there has been little commonality among state licensing boards concerning what they require from an administrator licensed in one state and wishing to be licensed in another. Because the requirements for initial licensure have varied so greatly, prospective administrators often went to the states with the least stringent requirements for licensure, then attempted to transfer those licenses to other states where the rules were tougher. NAB has worked toward uniformity in this area, encouraging state boards to require that anyone seeking endorsement meet licensing requirements at least equal to their own state regulations. NAB has also encouraged its members to accept certification by the ACHCA as a way to meet endorsement requirements. This will provide another means of ensuring quality and uniformity.

NAB has been active in the area of residential care/assisted living as well. The organization began preparing for licensure of residential care administrators several years ago by conducting a detailed study of the skills and knowledge required by these administrators. Working with several national professional and trade associations, NAB identified areas in which the skills inherent in residential care/assisted living administration are the same as those in administration of nursing facilities and where different skills and knowledge are needed. From this information, it developed a national examination similar to the one it uses for nursing facility administrators. Recently, it has begun to explore coverage of home- and community-based care administrators.

The examination is not mandatory for those states choosing not to create separate licensure categories at this time, but it is available to them when they do. It provides a uniform measure of qualifications for administrators who are licensed in states where regulations are diverse. Should other subcategories of licensure of long-term care administrators emerge, NAB is in a good position to address them as well.

The Pew Commission

Citing concerns about the problems inherent in the current workforce regulatory system in this country, the Pew Health Professions Commission and the University of California at San Francisco's Center for Health Professions created a task force on healthcare workforce regulations. That task force, supported by grants from the Pew Charitable Trusts, issued a report outlining a series of recommendations for improving the existing regulatory system. The task force developed a vision statement as a foundation for its recommendations:

Based on The Following Principles for The Regulatory System

1. Promoting effective health outcomes and protecting the public from harm;
2. Holding regulatory bodies accountable to the public;
3. Respecting consumers' rights to choose their health care providers from a range of safe options;
4. Encouraging a flexible, rational, and cost-effective health care system which allows effective working relationships among health care providers; and
5. Facilitating professional and geographic mobility of competent providers.

The Task Force Envisions a System For State Regulation of The Health Care Workforce Which is:

1. Standardized where appropriate;
2. Accountable to the public;

3. Flexible to support optimal access to a competent workforce; and
4. Effective and efficient in protecting and promoting the public's health, safety, and welfare. (Finocchio, Dower, McMahon, & Gragnola, 1995, p. 3)

Among the suggestions of the task force: (1) improving uniformity among regulatory agencies and among professions, (2) having licensure and certification based on demonstration of competency, (3) broad recognition of the interdisciplinary nature of the healthcare workforce, (4) improved accountability of regulatory agencies, and (5) consumer education.

In the decades since the release of this report, the efforts of the Pew Commission task force have resulted in increased interaction and discussion among a variety of workforce regulatory agencies and organizations. To the degree its recommendations were followed, it has had a positive impact on licensure of professionals in health care, including in long-term care.

State Efforts

Several states have also taken action to improve their workforce regulatory systems. However, there has been limited success from these efforts. These state and national projects are important for the recommendations they produce, but their ultimate value may be the discussions they have fostered among regulators, professionals, and consumer advocates. All of these groups seek to improve the system, and the ongoing dialogue among them is the most promising method of doing that. The results of these talks will be felt well into the future.

Regulation: Pros and Cons

As you have probably guessed by now or already knew, regulation of long-term care has its supporters and its critics. Those who favor regulation cite the need to protect consumers from historic abuses. They also maintain that there is a need to protect those who pay for long-term care from excessive costs. The latter argument covers both private organizations and individuals paying for care and taxpayers supporting government programs such as Medicaid and Medicare.

Critics argue that the current system of regulation is ineffective. They see long-term care regulations as uncoordinated and duplicative, based on the government's habit of reacting—often overreacting—to crisis situations. As the National Commission for Quality Long-Term Care, in its 2007 report, *From Isolation to Integration: Recommendations to Improve Quality in Long-Term Care*, noted:

Regulatory agencies are routinely too understaffed to enforce regulations meant to protect and improve the lives of individuals receiving long-term care. Even those regulations that are enforced often have little impact on low-performing providers. Instead, the mediocre survive and those who would innovate in the name of high quality receive few incentives or rewards for their efforts. Regulators and providers alike lack a consistent understanding of long-term regulations and guidelines, and both need training to develop consistent expectations. (National Commission for Quality Long-Term Care, 2007, p. 6)

Regulatory oversight has other weaknesses. Singh (2010, p. 124) reports that:

Monitoring for compliance is based on periodic inspections and complaint investigations. Inspections of a nursing home may take place as much as 15 months apart. This sporadic system of monitoring does not guarantee that compliance with standards is continuous. Complaint investigations can be conducted any time, but they take place only when a complaint is filed against the nursing home by someone, such as a patient, family member, friend, or employee.

The practice of imposing regulations on all to control a few violators has resulted in regulations that are seen by most in the industry as punitive measures that restrict their ability to be innovative.

Both sides of the argument over the benefits and shortcomings of regulation are well represented by advocates who are both ardent and eloquent. Those who are proregulation see healthcare regulations as desirable, even necessary. Many others also favor government regulation as a means of controlling health care. They have some support in the public arena. A poll by the Henry J. Kaiser Family Foundation (2007) found that:

many adults believe the government is not doing enough to regulate the quality of nursing homes. In that poll, about 6 in 10 adults (64 percent) agree that there is not enough government regulation of the quality of nursing homes.

They argue that decisions concerning medical care purchases are not made in the usual manner of a rational consumer of goods. Their point is well taken. Those decisions are not typical of other purchases. Consumers often make the decision during times of emotional and/or physical crisis, negatively affecting their objectivity. They are seldom fully informed about their options and choices.

On the other side of that argument are critics of regulation in health care. They counter that healthcare consumers are capable of making those choices if given the needed information that consumers are more capable than government gives them credit for being.

Proregulation forces contend that competition, or a market-based system, cannot provide true equity, that some are better served than others. They credit government with helping to maintain that equity, ensuring access to care to the poorest consumers, those least capable of looking out for themselves. They argue that without government intervention, many healthcare consumers would not receive appropriate care, and some would receive no care at all.

The procompetition camp, on the other hand, maintains that in doing so the government lowers the overall standard, reducing the level of quality and the efficiency of the system's providers by constraining their ability to innovate. Some even argue that while regulation raises the weakest sections of the system to a higher level, it also lowers the top to a common level of mediocrity. They also see consumer choice as a foundation for a successful healthcare system, and they call for government to remove, or at least reduce, barriers to innovation and customer service.

Both sides of this dialogue make sound arguments for their respective positions. They discuss regulation of health care in general, not long-term care specifically. However, the essential arguments apply well, and they provide us with an excellent view of the debate.

Actually, they do not disagree completely. Neither claims that health care can get along without any regulation, nor do they see the present mix of regulations as working ideally. Both agree that there is much fragmentation and overlap among the many regulations governing health care and that a better solution needs to be found. The differences are in the degree of change needed and the methods chosen for reform.

Problems Associated With Uncoordinated Regulations

An acquaintance of your author, a former head of a large hospital trade association, used to delight in shocking his hospital administrator colleagues by saying that the healthcare industry is not overregulated. As they would start to protest, he would quickly add, "It just has too many regulations." His point, and one well taken, was that an abundance of individual, uncoordinated, often conflicting regulations did not necessarily add up to a regulated industry. Instead, it usually adds up to frustration on the parts of both those being regulated and those doing the regulating.

One major problem with long-term care regulations is that they have been created at many different times, by many different agencies, for many different purposes. All too seldom is there any effort to coordinate them. All long-term care facilities and organizations are subject to regulation by numerous government agencies. As a result, they find compliance to be expensive and time-consuming. Interestingly, their primary complaint is not the cost of meeting regulatory requirements (e.g., installing a fire alarm system or creating a new resident-monitoring system). They often agree that those costs are justifiable. Their biggest criticism is that in addition to those costs, providers have the added expense of documenting compliance with the regulations. The record keeping can become extremely burdensome and onerous.

Another lament by long-term care providers is that they are frequently put in the position of having to choose among conflicting regulations. It is not uncommon to find rules issued by different arms of government making conflicting demands. When that happens, the provider has to meet the strictest interpretation, usually at greater cost. One of the more common examples of such conflict concerns fire safety regulations. Federal and state regulators have very strict regulations concerning fire safety in long-term care facilities. Yet, local fire officials often have their own, different, regulations. It is up to the facility to comply with both.

None of this is intended to suggest that regulations are not needed or that those devising them do not have reasons for doing so. It does demonstrate the results of lack of coordination. Much of the frustration of providers is not directed at regulations as such but at the resources they may take away from meeting the needs of long-term care consumers.

Finding a Happy Medium

On one hand, this chapter has discussed why regulation is necessary in long-term care and, on the other hand, has discussed all the problems that regulations cause for providers. If we could create a perfect long-term care system, what would it look like? Would we get rid of all regulations or add more? Anyone thinking, at this point, that they have an easy answer to these questions is (1) overly optimistic, (2) not paying enough attention to the complexities revealed by this discussion, or (3) very intelligent and about to become very rich upon revealing the solution! It is an extremely complicated and difficult issue that does not lend itself to quick fixes.

Policy Issues

Given this brief overview of regulation, some of the more critical policy issues surrounding it are now addressed.

Balance Between Regulation and Innovation

How does the long-term care system achieve a minimum acceptable level of quality while encouraging efforts to exceed that minimum level by as much as possible? Somehow policy makers must find a way to protect those who cannot protect themselves without burdening those who do not need such protection or making it unnecessarily difficult for providers to do their jobs. Providers repeatedly cry out for more flexibility to innovate than current regulatory approaches allow. These approaches, focused as they are on deficiencies and enforcement, do little to encourage superior performance. The American Association of Homes and Services for the Aging, in its AAHSA Public Policy Priorities 2008, said:

> Regulatory reform is essential to accommodate the culture change that is making nursing homes more home-like for residents and better workplaces for staff. We support federal quality standards, but the prescriptive nature of some regulations can act as barriers to innovation and quality of care. (AAHSA, 2008)

That sentiment continues today.

Those providers make a strong case for shifting more of the responsibility for quality assurance to providers. At the same time, there are questions about how ready providers (particularly nursing facilities) are to assume this responsibility. Although they seek flexibility to innovate, their willingness and ability to undertake such a massive change are far from unanimous.

Is government willing to trust providers to deliver quality without external oversight? It is doubtful. There is simply too long a history of regulation and reacting to regulation for this to happen all at once, or perhaps even for it to happen at all. Government represents society and has a responsibility to protect its constituents. Providers will have to prove themselves over a long period of time before government will release much of that responsibility.

There is also the matter of regulatory turf. The many different regulatory agencies, and the fragmentation and overlap of their jurisdictions, have been discussed at some length. They are not likely to give up any of their authority without a fight. Only with some unified, integrated national policy will there be significant improvements in this area.

Shifting Focus to the Consumer

How can our society shift from a regulatory system that focuses on services and providers to one that focuses on the consumer? Consumers have become more and more diverse. If long-term care is to be successful, we must find a way to identify the needs of these diverse consumers and adapt the system to meet those needs.

How can this be done without losing sight of the goals of the system as a whole? An outcomes-based approach to regulating quality clearly moves the system in that direction—but only if those outcomes are relevant to what individuals need and want. Traditional healthcare outcomes address technical competency and access. To make the long-term care system truly responsive to individual needs, another factor must be added: patient satisfaction. This is a measurement of how well care is provided in keeping with the personal values of consumers. In a consumer-driven long-term care system, this is an essential dimension of quality.

Although a system that focuses on the consumer/client might require providers and reimbursers to make significant changes to adapt their way of doing things, it would remove the fragmentation, overlap, gaps, and general confusion for consumers as they attempt to use the services.

Doing all of this is possible, but not without its difficulties. There will be inherent conflicts between what is identified as high technical quality and what the consumers want. Consumers' perceptions of quality will affect the choices they make. An individual consumer's perception of quality of life may preclude accepting certain treatments, even though there is valid clinical reason for those treatments. One such conflict that comes to mind is an elderly person needing a hip or knee replacement. He or she might opt not to go through the surgery and rehabilitation even though it would improve ambulation.

Management of Care

There has been much discussion about managing the care received by individuals. Managed care is a method of trying to manage quality, access, and cost. Case management, an unfortunately similar name, is also a system that coordinates the provision of care to groups of consumers for the same purposes. It tends to be used for groups of people with catastrophic or high-cost medical conditions. The concepts are noble, but they run into several problems. The first involves balancing access, quality, and cost. It is not always possible to accomplish all three. So, where should the emphasis be put? This is the issue.

If quality is to be put above all else, it is the same as saying, "at all costs." Do we really mean that? Are we willing to pay whatever it costs to get the highest possible quality, or do we settle for good quality that is somewhat less expensive? If the latter, how is *good* defined? Where do we draw the line? If access is to be the top priority, meaning that everyone, ideally, can find their choice of services whenever they need them, we again run up against the question of cost—and sometimes of quality.

So, do we put cost control as the primary goal, settling for less access and quality? The easy answer is that we do the best we can in all three areas, but that is not really an answer. Decisions have to be made. If we each paid for our own care and had unlimited funds, we could get excellent access and quality, but for the majority of us, we either have limited funds or rely on third-party payers for our care, and they do not have unlimited funds. This is where it becomes a policy issue. Government must set rules to attempt to find the right balance. This means regulation, like it or not.

A subissue related to regulation of managed care and/or case management is the question of who will do the managing. Who will be the gatekeeper who determines how much and what type of care is received by an individual? There are several possibilities. Historically, the provider has been the gatekeeper. Physicians ordered tests, procedures, and treatments for patients. In long-term care, other healthcare professionals have assumed some of those decisions. However, with the advent of care management, it is often the payer who has become the gatekeeper, making many of the decisions by determining what services will be allowed or disallowed. Note that *disallowed* does not mean that the service cannot be received, but that the payer will not pay for it. In many cases, with the high cost of services, this is the same thing as saying that it cannot be received.

Ideally in a consumer-driven system, the person receiving the services would be the gatekeeper. However, that consumer may not have the necessary information and/or contacts to do so effectively. In some situations, the consumer is represented by a family member or other advocate. Thus, they also must be educated to fulfill the role optimally.

When providers are gatekeepers, payers and consumers accuse them of ordering unnecessary services just to make more money. When payers (including government agencies) are gatekeepers, providers and consumers accuse them of skimping on services to save money. When consumers are their own gatekeepers, providers and payers accuse them of demanding excessive services at the expense of someone else.

Management of care does not always involve government regulation, but it is increasingly seen as a way to better manage programs like Medicare and Medicaid, so it has become a public policy issue.

■ Private Control Mechanisms

In addition to external control of long-term care providers by government agencies, there are several private organizations involved with controlling those providers. When comparing the public and private control mechanisms, there are both similarities and differences.

They are different in that the public agencies have a dual purpose—to control both quality and costs—while the private organizations have a single purpose—to measure, evaluate, and ensure the quality of care. The two are also different because the government programs seek to ensure a minimum level of quality or competency; anything below that level is not acceptable. The private organizations set standards that measure and ensure more of an optimum level, usually quite a bit above the minimum.

They are similar in one way: They focus on both long-term care organizations and individuals within those organizations. When the private control agencies look at an overall provider organization, it is usually called accreditation, the counterpart of institutional regulation on the public side. When addressing individual competencies, the private mechanism is commonly known as certification, relating to the government's licensure of professionals.

Accreditation

There are several characteristics that distinguish the accreditation process, whether it be dealing with long-term care providers or other healthcare organizations. First, private accreditation bodies are typically made up of organizations representing the providers that are covered by that process. Second, it is a voluntary process. Providers are not required to participate unless they choose to. As will become apparent, there are some pretty strong incentives to do so for some providers, although not for others. Third, private accreditation evaluates providers against predetermined performance standards. These common characteristics are examined briefly.

Because accreditation represents an attempt by providers of long-term care and other healthcare segments to monitor their own quality, the agencies doing the accrediting are usually composed of representatives from several provider-related associations. This does not mean that it is not still an external form of control. The accrediting agencies do not answer to any individual providers, but rather to professional and trade organizations.

Accreditation is not required by any law, nor is there any mandated penalty for providers who do not participate. In fact, any healthcare provider organization wishing to be accredited must formally request to be included. They must also pay for the privilege. The accrediting agencies are funded by the fees paid by individual providers to participate. In fact, although the charges are tailored to the type of provider organization, they typically run to several thousand dollars for a survey.

There is an aspect of some types of accreditation that gives them more importance than might be inferred from the description of them as voluntary. For hospitals, subacute care units that are part of hospitals, and home healthcare agencies, accreditation by the Joint Commission provides deemed status for Medicare. This means that they are deemed by the CMS to be in compliance with Medicare conditions of participation. This status was given to hospitals in 1965, when the act was originally passed, and to home healthcare agencies in 1993. It means that they do not have to be surveyed separately by Medicare or its fiscal and regulatory intermediary. The savings in time and hassle are significant. Most states also recognize Joint Commission accreditation as meeting or exceeding their standards for licensure, in effect granting deemed status. Such status is not available to other long-term care organizations, at least at this time, although some states have explored the possibility of at least conducting joint surveys with accreditation organizations.

The Joint Commission

The Joint Commission on Accreditation of Healthcare Organizations (JCAHO), or the Joint Commission as it is now known, has long been involved with hospitals. Its influence is representative of the efforts by hospitals and their national organizations to self-inspect for quality of care and to provide public assurance of that quality. Long-term care organizations did not do so, an omission that led, in part at least, to the more intense government regulation of them. By the time the Medicare program was created, the Joint Commission, then operating as the JCAHO, had established itself as a credible, independent process for evaluating the quality of care in hospitals, resulting in granting of deemed status for those facilities.

One reason for the success of the Joint Commission is the make-up of its governing body. It consists of physicians, administrators, nurses, employers, a labor representative, health plan leaders, quality experts, ethicists, a consumer advocate, and educators. It is significant that the Joint Commission board decided in 2012 to make the three field representatives for long-term care, behavioral health care, and home care full voting members. Previously, the field representatives voted on board committees, but not at the full board level (Eaken Zhani, 2012).

The Joint Commission began its long-term care accreditation program in 1966. However, at that time, nursing homes were the predominant providers of long-term care. Without the incentive of deemed status, few of those facilities chose to participate. Many considered the expense to exceed the value, even though Joint Commission accreditation would give them a significant marketing advantage. There was simply not enough competition among them to convince them of the need to market their services very much. As the long-term care field became increasingly competitive, more and more nursing facilities began to seek accreditation. They must now compete with home care agencies for some of their consumers and with hospital-based subacute care units for others. Because both of those provider groups have deemed status, they are more likely to seek accreditation and use it as proof of their high-quality care. Additionally, the Joint Commission now accredits provider networks. As long-term care organizations of all types become more intricately involved with such networks, accreditation is seen in a more favorable light by them. As of 2014, the Joint Commission accredits and certifies more than 20,000 healthcare organizations and programs in the United States (Joint Commission, 2014).

As attractive as Joint Commission accreditation has become for some long-term care providers, it is still not overwhelmingly accepted by them. Hospice care is included in the home healthcare standards of the Joint Commission.

The Joint Commission, like other private accreditation agencies, measures performance of provider organizations against standards that are intentionally set higher than most licensure requirements. Accreditation seeks high-quality care, not a minimum acceptable level. Although there are slight variations among the standards for differing provider types, recognizing differences in their constituents and care methods, there are several key areas that are common:

1. Consumer rights
2. Admission and assessment
3. Care and treatment
4. Continuity of care
5. Organizational leadership
6. Human resources management
7. Information management
8. Environmental safety
9. Infection control
10. Quality assessment and improvement

The Joint Commission has striven to be more focused on outcomes in recent years. A long-standing complaint of providers was that the Joint Commission measured what was documented more than what was done. In response to that complaint, the Joint Commission has shifted its standards to be more resident-centered and performance focused. They are designed to measure how well the organization being surveyed accomplishes its care objectives, with somewhat less emphasis on how it goes about doing it.

CARF International

Founded in 1966 as the Commission on Accreditation of Rehabilitation Facilities, CARF International is an independent, nonprofit accreditor of health and human services in the following areas:

- Aging services
- Behavioral health
- Opioid treatment programs
- Business and services management networks
- Child and youth services
- Employment and community services
- Vision rehabilitation

- Medical rehabilitation
- Durable medical equipment, prosthetics, orthotics, and supplies (CARF International, 2014)

Its impact on long-term care is generally limited to subacute care services, which are included under medical rehabilitation. However, as that service category has grown, and as other long-term care providers have become more involved in providing mental health services and/or become integrated into multilevel organizations, the influence of CARF International in long-term care has grown.

CARF International is different from the Joint Commission in several ways. First, it focuses on specific programs whereas the Joint Commission covers whole facilities. Second, CARF accreditation carries no deemed status, although it is recognized as a sign of excellence. Lastly, and of most significance, CARF International has a long history of outcomes-based program evaluation. Although it covers a variety of management and treatment processes, its primary focus is on outcomes measurement, much more so than that of the Joint Commission.

CARF International standards address initial evaluation of the functional disabilities, capabilities, and needs of a consumer. Organizations receiving CARF International accreditation must have systems in place to evaluate these areas as preparation for treatment. They must then develop and implement treatment plans designed to meet the needs. The true uniqueness of the approach is its emphasis on postdischarge follow-up planning. Accredited programs must have formalized systems to follow their discharged patients to measure the degree to which they maintain the level of functional independence achieved during treatment. For the purpose of improving its internal systems, CARF International requires detailed record keeping of program success through monitoring of individual patients.

CARF International is made up of a large number of member associations, similar to those of the Joint Commission in that they are professional associations. The list of participating members is too long to repeat here, but it includes representation of all interested parties, including organizations representing professionals and consumers.

Other Accreditation Organizations

There are other organizations providing private accreditation of healthcare and long-term care providers. Most are very specific in their focus and, as such, have limited impact on the system as a whole. One such is the Community Health Accreditation Program. Originally developed by, and a part of, the National League of Nursing, it accredits community and home care agencies. Like the Joint Commission, it also provides those agencies with Medicare deemed status.

Private Certification

There are numerous private organizations involved in certifying the competency of individual healthcare professionals and practitioners. They range from professional boards certifying physicians in their specialties to the National League for Nursing and the National Association of Social Workers. As is the case with private accreditation of healthcare organizations, these certification organizations measure against standards set well above minimum acceptability. They ensure that certified professionals are competent in their areas of specialization and are well qualified to practice their professions. Their value to individuals is the possession of a credential attesting to that competency. Thus, certification becomes more than just a source of personal and professional pride. It has worth in the job market, increasing the value of the individual for employment.

Most certification covers professionals working in all segments of health care, although there are some exceptions. One of these is certification of long-term care administrators. The ACHCA has undertaken certification of administrators in several specific areas. The ACHCA certification programs

> have the goal of defining excellence in the profession. They include Nursing Home Administration and Assisted Living Administration and certify professionals who have demonstrated the knowledge, skills and values consistent with the high standards of management necessary to provide quality care to residents, families and communities. They also provide visible and tangible evidence of public accountability for the efficient delivery of quality health care. (ACHCA, 2014)

The ACHCA has taken other steps to improve and ensure the quality of its members. In 1986, the organization developed a set of standards of practice for long-term care administrators. These standards became the basis on which many state nursing home administrator licensing boards developed licensing regulations. NAB built the domains of practice it uses in evaluating long-term care administrators, in part at least, on the ACHCA standards. The ACHCA has also developed a code of ethics for long-term care administrators. Although it carries no regulatory or other authority, it serves as an ethical foundation on which administrators can voluntarily base their work.

■ Summary

Because long-term care is so important to those needing it, there is a considerable amount of oversight of its providers by external agencies. Because the care is ongoing, lasts for many years in most cases, and is so intimately involved with the very lives of its consumers, it is necessary for those external agencies to have some type of assurance that the care received is of high quality. Because most long-term care is paid for by third-party organizations, those organizations have a legitimate interest in avoiding any unnecessary expenses associated with provision of the care.

For all of these reasons, the long-term care system is subjected to a variety of laws, regulations, and rules. Both provider organizations and their personnel are often required to be licensed. The amount of care given and the manner in which it is provided are prescribed. As might be expected, providers complain about the lack of coordination, and sometimes the lack of fairness, of these regulations. Yet, many of them are willing to submit to voluntary assessment through accreditation and/or certification. The two forms of external control—legislated regulations and voluntary accreditation—seem destined to come together. Meaningful progress in that area will be slow, however.

■ Vocabulary Terms

The following terms are included in this chapter. They are important to the topics and issues discussed here and should become familiar to readers. Some of the terms are also found in other chapters but may be used in different contexts. They may not be fully defined herein. Readers may wish to seek other supplementary definitions.

accreditation
American College of Health Care
    Administrators (ACHCA)
CARF International
Centers for Medicare & Medicaid
    Services (CMS)
certification
code of ethics
deemed status
domains of practice
endorsement
Equal Employment Opportunity
    Commission
external controls
gatekeeper
Health Insurance Portability and
    Accountability Act of 1996
Joint Commission
law

legislation
licensure
National Association of Long-Term
    Care Administrator Boards (NAB)
National Commission for Quality
    Long-Term Care
Occupational Safety and Health
    Administration
Omnibus Budget Reconciliation Act
    (OBRA)
Patient Self-Determination Act of
    1990
Pew Commission
private controls
public controls
quality assurance
regulation
Social Security Act

■ Discussion Questions

The following questions are presented to assist you in understanding the material covered in this chapter. They tend to be general but lend themselves to detailed answers. The answers to these questions can be found in the chapter.

1. Why are long-term care providers subject to so much external control by government agencies?
2. What is the difference between a law and a regulation?
3. What is the difference between licensure and accreditation?
4. What problems are identified (by providers) with government regulation of long-term care?
5. How do the three usual quality measurement methods (process, structure, and outcomes) differ?
6. Why are government programs such as Medicare and Medicaid so concerned with regulating cost?
7. What other types of regulation (not specific to long-term care) apply to long-term care providers and their employees?
8. What groups of long-term care practitioners are subjected to specific controls, such as licensure?
9. What are the most common accreditation agencies, and what provider organizations do they accredit?

▪ References

Agency for Healthcare Research and Quality (AHRQ). (2014). *Selecting health outcome measures for clinical quality measurement.* Retrieved from http://www.qualitymeasures.ahrq.gov/tutorial/HealthOutcomeMeasure.aspx.

American Association of Homes and Services for the Aging (AAHSA). (2008). *AAHSA public policy priorities 2008.* Washington, DC: American Association of Homes and Services for the Aging.

American College of Health Care Administrators (ACHCA). (2014). *Professional certification handbook.* Retrieved from http://www.achca.org/content/pdf/CertificationHandbook__130926_temp.pdf.

Centers for Medicare and Medicaid Services (CMS). (2013a, May 14). *Glossary.* Retrieved from http://www.cms.gov/apps/glossary/default.asp?Letter=C&Language=English.

Centers for Medicare and Medicaid Services (CMS). (2013b, December 11). *HIPAA transaction and code set standards—Overview.* Retrieved from http://www.cms.gov/Regulations-and-Guidance/HIPAA-Administrative-Simplification/TransactionCodeSetsStands/index.html?redirect=/TransactionCodeSetsStands.

Commission on Accreditation of Rehabilitation Facilities (CARF International). (2014). *Quick facts about CARF.* Retrieved from http://www.carf.org/About/QuickFacts.

Eaken Zhani, E. (2012, January 11). *The Joint Commission and JCR announce 2012 board appointments.* Retrieved from http://www.jointcommission.org/nr_2012_board_appointments_/.

Finocchio, L., Dower, C., McMahon, T., & Gragnola, C. (1995). *Reforming health care workforce regulation: Policy considerations for the 21st Century.* San Francisco, CA: Pew Health Professions Commission.

Joint Commission. (2014). *About The Joint Commission.* Retrieved from http://www.jointcommission.org/about_us/about_the_joint_commission_main.aspx.

Kaiser Family Foundation. (2007, December). *Views about the Quality of Long-Term Care Services in the United States*. Retrieved from Henry J. Kaiser Family Foundation: http://kaiserfamilyfoundation.files.wordpress.com/2013/01/7718.pdf.

National Association of Long-Term Care Adminstrator Boards (NAB). (2012). *NAB study guide—How to prepare for the nursing home administrator's examination* (5th ed.). Washington, DC: National Association of Long-Term Care Adminstrator Boards.

National Commission for Quality Long-Term Care. (2007). *From isolation to integration: Recommendations to improve quality in long-term care*. Washington, DC: National Commission for Quslity Long-Term Care. Retrieved from http://www.allhealth.org/briefingmaterials/out_of_isolation-914.pdf.

Pioneer Network. (2013). *The basics of promising practices: The history and key provisions of OBRA '87*. Retrieved from http://www.pioneernetwork.net/Providers/PromisingPractices/OBRA87.

Pozgar, G. (2013). *Legal and ethical issues for health professionals* (3rd ed.). Burlington, MA: Jones & Bartlett Learning.

Shore, Herbert (1994). History of long-term care. In Seth Goldsmith (Ed.), *Essentials of long-term care administration*. Gaithersburg, MD: Aspen Publishers.

Showalter, J. S. (2012). *The law of healthcare administration* (6th ed.). Chicago, IL: Health Administration Press.

Singh, D. (2010). *Effective management of long-term care facilities* (2nd ed.). Sudbury, MA: Jones & Bartlett Learning.

Townsend, J., & Davis, W. (2010). *The principles of health care administration*. Bossier City, LA: Professional Printing and Publishing, Inc.

U.S. Department of Health and Human Services (HHS). (2013). *Guidance regarding methods for de-identification of protected health information in accordance with the Health Insurance Portability and Accountability Act (HIPAA) privacy rule*. Retrieved from http://www.hhs.gov/ocr/privacy/hipaa/understanding/coveredentities/De-identification/guidance.html#protected.

U.S. Department of Labor. (2004, December). *Fact sheet: The Health Insurance Portability and Accountability Act (HIPAA)*. Retrieved from http://www.dol.gov/ebsa/newsroom/fshipaa.html.

Long-Term Care Reimbursement

Learning Objectives

After completing this chapter, readers will be able to:

1. Understand how long-term care services are reimbursed.

2. Identify and define key public sources of reimbursement, including Medicare and Medicaid.

3. Identify and define private reimbursement sources, including private pay and private long-term care insurance.

4. Understand how managed care works and its impact on long-term care.

5. Understand the trends affecting long-term care reimbursement.

■ Introduction

The long-term care (LTC) system in the United States is reimbursement driven, meaning that the way care is provided is highly dependent on the way it is financed. Access to care, the availability of specific services, and even the quality of care provided are all dictated by the type and amount of reimbursement. It is unfortunate that such vital services are not universally and uniformly available, but the fact is they are not. Each of the provider segments along the continuum of care has its own unique mix of payment sources. Providers must understand what the various reimbursement agencies require of them. They have to understand the many different eligibility rules, the extent of coverage allowed, and the type and amount of documentation involved. It can be both bewildering and time consuming.

The situation is even worse for consumers. As they move from one type or level of care to another, or even from one provider to another within the same provider category, they encounter a reimbursement system that must seem to them to be designed to be as confusing as possible. Long-term care reimbursement comes from a confusing combination of public and private sources. This chapter presents an overview of current reimbursement options and methodologies, and it examines the trends and forces affecting the future of long-term care financing.

■ Origins and Development

The long-term care system has followed much the same pattern of development as the acute hospital system, although each stage seems to have developed somewhat later. Both systems began as charity-based care for all except the very wealthy. Most people needing health or custodial care received it at home, if there was someone available to provide it. As the need grew and families found themselves less able to care for the sick or disabled, private charitable organizations, often religious, took over some of the care in institutions operated and financed by them.

In time, state and federal governments began to get involved in protecting the welfare of the poor and needy. In 1935, following the Great Depression, Congress passed the Social Security Act, which included certain categorical assistance programs to help with care of the elderly, those who were blind, and families with dependent children (Goldsmith, 1994). This began serious government involvement in the financing of health care, including long-term care. During the next several decades, private coverage for hospital care became more available through the formation of Blue Cross/Blue Shield plans and the growth of private health insurance. In the 1960s, with the creation of the Medicare and Medicaid programs, government involvement in reimbursing health care was greatly expanded.

Yet with the exception of Medicaid, which requires individuals to become medically indigent to be eligible, little of this coverage applied to long-term care. Medicare reimbursement remained very limited. Private long-term care insurance was virtually nonexistent. Those with private financial resources had to use them to pay for their care. That situation remained pretty much the same up to the 1990s, when several factors forced the government, the long-term care industry, and society in general to reconsider how the system should be financed.

First, the number of elderly needing ever-larger amounts of long-term care was large and growing exponentially. In part because of this, the costs associated with providing long-term care were escalating. This made it more difficult for individuals to pay for their own long-term care, which, in turn, increased the burden on state governments funding Medicaid to the point where they were in desperate need of new financing sources, or at least new reimbursement methodologies.

These pressures have led to a considerable amount of examination of existing ways of reimbursing for long-term care services. They have also stimulated some reimbursement initiatives, which are discussed later in this chapter, but there has not been any significant improvement in either methods or results. The abortive Clinton healthcare financing reform effort in 1994, even had it passed, would have done little to change reimbursement of long-term care. The Affordable Care Act of 2010 has more impact on long-term care reimbursement, but only indirectly, through provisions such as bundling and accountable care organizations, discussed later herein.

■ Current Reimbursement Options

An overview of the options that are currently available for financing of the long-term care system in general and for reimbursing the individual segments begins this discussion. These options can be broken into three categories for easier study: public sources, private sources, and public/private partnerships.

Public Reimbursement Sources

Medicare and Medicaid are by far the most prominent sources of public funding of long-term care and other types of health care. They were both created in 1965 as amendments to the Social Security Act. A centerpiece of President Lyndon B. Johnson's Great Society, the two programs provided first-time healthcare coverage for millions of Americans. They have been amended many times in the past 3 decades, most often clarifying eligibility rules or tightening enforcement of provider regulations. Now, they are being reviewed with major change in mind. New payment methods are being tried, and the very structure of the programs is under review.

Medicare

The Medicare program was created as Title XVIII of the Social Security Act. Its primary purpose was to provide healthcare coverage for the elderly, who were defined at that time as anyone 65 years of age or older. In 1972, provisions were added to the act to include people who were permanently disabled and those with kidney disease.

The four main elements of the program are Part A, which provides hospital insurance, including some sections of long-term care (skilled care, home health care, hospice); Part B, which provides supplementary medical insurance that covers physician care; Part C, the so-called Medicare Advantage plans that deal with managed care organizations; and Part D, which covers medications. Parts A and B are the sections most closely related to long-term care, so we concentrate on them in our discussions in this chapter.

Part A is automatic for anyone meeting the eligibility criteria. Part B is purchased by beneficiaries with payment of a small premium. That separation pretty well defines the major thrust of the program. It is oriented to the acute care, medical model. Although some limited forms of long-term care coverage have been added over the years, this was not the original intent of the Medicare program.

Medicare is an entitlement program, meaning that anyone belonging to a particular population group is entitled to coverage. There is no requirement that recipients demonstrate financial need (as there is with Medicaid). The wealthiest retiree has the same rights to Medicare coverage as the poorest. This has become a major issue in recent years as the program struggles to provide coverage for a population that has grown many times faster than was predicted. In fact, the funding source for the program, the Medicare trust fund, is currently in considerable jeopardy. The Social Security and Medicare boards of trustees (2013, p. 1) project that "the financial condition of the Social Security and Medicare programs remains problematic and that projected long-run program costs are not sustainable under current financing arrangements." For the seventh consecutive year, the trustees issued a Medicare funding warning. When the Affordable Care Act was passed in 2010, it was proposed that it would be paid for, in large part, by reductions in Medicare. Just what those reductions are to be has not yet been revealed.

There is widespread disagreement about what should be done to solve the problem, but there is virtually complete agreement that there is a problem.

Why does this situation exist? When Medicare was developed in the 1960s, it adopted the retirement age built into the Social Security Act in 1935. At that time (1935) the average life expectancy was far shorter than today. However, from 1900 through 2004, life expectancy at birth increased from 46 to 75 years for men and from 48 to 80 years for women (NCHS, 2007, p. 50). Sixty-five was chosen initially as a retirement age on the assumption that a relatively small number of people would take advantage of it and would not live for many years thereafter. Because the life span has increased steadily to where it is today, many more people now qualify for Medicare. What is more significant is the number of years each of them can expect to continue qualifying and continue to collect benefits.

Longer life is not the only factor not adequately anticipated by the framers of the Medicare program. They also failed to realize that increased availability of coverage would lead to increased usage. The frequency with which people visited their doctors or were admitted to hospitals was part of the equation used to predict the rate at which Medicare funds would be needed in the future. Although there was undoubtedly some consideration of inflation, there appears to have been no realization that many of the elderly were not availing themselves of medical services for the simple reason that they could not afford them. Once the Medicare program made those services available, the rush was on. Pent-up demand for needed, although postponable, care resulted in considerably more usage of health care than had been expected.

The politicians and others responsible for developing Medicare (probably innocently) contributed to the use, and even overuse, of Medicare when they touted it as being much more inclusive than it actually was. As they got caught up in the euphoria of having taken such a major step toward helping the elderly with their medical needs, they were not above implying that it would meet most, if not all, of those needs. In fact, it was never intended to do that. This erroneous public perception led many of the elderly, and their families, to expect much more from Medicare than it could provide.

During the 5 decades of Medicare's existence, medical technology has also developed and expanded at an unprecedented rate. That technology has created new treatments, the ability of which to save lives and improve the quality of life could hardly be denied by a public entitlement program. An example of the extent of the problem that introduction of such technological improvements has caused is treatment for end-stage renal disease. Patients who would have died can now live prolonged, useful lives through the wonders of renal dialysis. As beneficial as these treatments are, they are also ongoing and expensive. Finding it difficult to deny such life-saving treatment and anticipating a relatively small volume of usage, the Medicare program added it to the list of categories of eligibility, regardless of the age of the patient. Kidney transplantation soon became a viable alternative to dialysis. Although very expensive initially, it eliminated the need for very costly, thrice-weekly treatments, although it did require lifelong use of extremely expensive medications. It, too, was allowed as a Medicare-reimbursable procedure.

It is not hard to guess what happened next. The technology continued to improve, and large numbers of patients became medically eligible for dialysis, transplantation, or both. As with most medical technology, it became more expensive, not less so. Also, those receiving such treatments lived for years, and the cost to Medicare for this one category mushroomed; yet once it had been given as an entitlement, it could not easily be taken away.

This example represents much of what has happened to the overall Medicare program. It is, in many ways, suffering from its own success. It is worth noting here that, as other types of organ transplantation (e.g., heart, lung) became medically feasible, the Medicare program did not rush to include them, having learned from its experience with kidney transplants. Even in that, there has been criticism from those people needing such transplants because they feel discriminated against.

What does all of this have to do with long-term care? It is indicative of the systemic problems facing Medicare in the next few years. It is also why adding any new coverage is difficult. As noted earlier, long-term care was not intended to be a major component of Medicare. Attempts to find less costly alternatives to hospitalization and other institutionalization have led the program to add coverage for some types of long-term care, including subacute care, home health care, and hospice care. In many cases, however, experience is showing that the elderly using these services are not necessarily those who would otherwise be institutionalized. When this is the case, those services become added, rather than replacement, costs. Nevertheless, providing coverage of more forms of care does give Medicare a more prominent role in the reimbursement of long-term care than has been traditional. It is likely that it is a role that will continue to grow as the system experiences further pressures to reduce costs.

Medicare: What Is Covered?

The Medicare coverage situation is changing so rapidly that it is not feasible to attempt to describe it in detail here, because any such description would soon be outdated. However, the following is a brief summary of the long-term care services Medicare does cover at this time.

Skilled Nursing Services—Medicare covers what it defines as skilled nursing care in nursing facilities or units in hospitals:

> Skilled nursing facilities (SNFs) may be freestanding, or they can be units in hospitals or nursing facilities. Skilled care is health care given when individuals need skilled nursing or rehabilitation staff to treat, manage, observe, and evaluate their care. Examples of skilled care include intravenous injections and physical therapy. Care that can be given by nonprofessional staff is not considered skilled care and is not covered by Medicare. (CMS, 2014a)

Skilled services must be certified as necessary by a physician, be related to a hospital admission (occur within 30 days of a hospital stay of at least 3 days for the same condition), and be needed on a daily basis. Coverage of SNF care by Medicare is limited to 100 days per benefit period, with the patient paying a portion of the cost from day 21 through day 100. A benefit period is defined as beginning when the Medicare beneficiary first enters the hospital until there has been a 60-day break in hospital or SNF services.

Medicare reimbursement for skilled nursing services has historically been retrospectively determined based on a combination of costs and per diem payments. However, payment by Medicare to provider organizations is in the middle of a drastic change of methodology. In 1997, Congress passed legislation creating a prospective payment system (PPS) for Medicare-funded postacute care. Similar to the payment system used to reimburse hospitals for acute services, it began on July 1, 1998, and was phased in completely over a 3-year period. The basic premise is that providers be given an incentive to operate more efficiently. Instead of being paid for costs already incurred, they are given a set rate for certain services and must find ways to provide those services within that rate. If they are able to save more than that, they get to keep the remainder. If they fail to do so, they must absorb the difference between their costs and the PPS rate.

The PPS is designed to reduce cost inflation to Medicare. There had been a steady increase in skilled nursing care payments by Medicare for years. At the beginning of the new system, average Medicare payments to nursing facilities were reduced by 17%, an amount that Congress determined to be the inefficiency rate. This change created a great deal of concern among providers, as might be expected. It also resulted in as much confusion for nursing facilities as the original PPS did for hospitals when it began. Routine, ancillary, and capital costs were all included in one payment instead of separately as in the past. Payment was and is based on a formula that takes into consideration the mix of residents, their acuity levels, and the amount and type of care those residents receive—similar to the resource utilization groups used in an earlier PPS demonstration project. The new system required facilities to develop new resident management and cost-tracking systems, in many cases meaning acquiring and learning to use new technology. Hospital-based SNFs would appear to have somewhat of an advantage, given the head start their parent organizations had with PPS.

Recognizing the magnitude of the change for nursing facilities, the Centers for Medicare & Medicaid Services (CMS), formerly the Health Care Financing Administration (HCFA), developed a phase-in period for some of them—namely, those that were receiving Medicare payments prior to 1995. That phase-in process gradually changed the balance from a facility-specific rate to a federally set rate.

As is usually the case with any major change in payment methodology, the regulations governing PPS are still, several years later, undergoing some revision and refinement, including some changes based on challenges by providers.

Subacute Care—Subacute care is not a separate category under Medicare. It is covered under the category of postacute care, is generally provided in Medicare-certified SNFs or units, and is reimbursed through the SNF mechanism. However, subacute care may be provided in other settings. When this is the case, the reimbursement mechanism of that licensure category governs the reimbursement. For example, Medicare allows some hospitals to participate in a swing-bed program under which small rural hospitals may use certain beds interchangeably at a hospital, SNF, or nursing facility level of care as needed. The reimbursement for those beds is based on the type of care provided for the patient in the bed.

Home Health Care—Medicare embraced home health care as an alternative to institutionalization early on and is the primary provider of reimbursement for home healthcare services. To receive that reimbursement, these services must be provided by agencies certified by the Medicare program. As was the case with Medicare skilled nursing coverage, the former retrospective payment system was changed to a PPS as the result of the Balanced Budget Act of 1997. It was phased in over 3 years, during which home health providers were reimbursed on the basis of an interim payment system. With the PPS, Medicare pays for each 60-day episode of care. The amount paid for that 60-day period is a set amount based on a standard rate adjusted for the type and intensity of care provided in what is known as a case-mix formula.

The original intent of Medicare was that it would cover home health care only after discharge from a hospital. This has been broadened to allow consumers to choose home health care as another option, including as an alternative to hospital care. Medicare beneficiaries must (1) be confined to home; (2) be under the care of a physician; (3) be in need of skilled services; (4) be under a plan of care; and (5) receive the services from, or under arrangements made by, a participating home health agency.

Hospice—Medicare covers hospice care for people who are certified to be terminally ill, with 6 months or less to live. The care must be palliative rather than curative and, as with other types of Medicare coverage, must be delivered by a provider organization that is certified by that program. The care may be provided in a healthcare facility or in the patient's home. It generally includes services such as pain management, nursing services, and some therapies.

Other Long-Term Care Services—Medicare does not regularly provide coverage in settings such as assisted living or adult day care. However, under some Medicaid waiver programs (discussed later herein), these services may be included.

Medicaid

At the same time that the Medicare program was developed to provide health care for the elderly, Congress also created Medicaid as a program to provide health care for the poor. Enacted as Title XIX of the Social Security Act, Medicaid is different from Medicare in several very specific ways. First, it has no age limitations but covers people of all ages. Second, it does have income restrictions, covering only those who are medically indigent and who cannot pay for their own health care or do not have insurance. Third, Medicare is funded and operated by the federal government, but Medicaid is jointly funded by the federal and state governments and is run by the states under federal guidelines. In theory, Medicaid is funded half and half by the state and federal governments, but in practice some states receive as much as 75% of their Medicaid funding from the federal government. Finally, whereas Medicare coverage is limited in terms of the types of services covered and the length of time they are covered, Medicaid essentially covers most services needed by its beneficiaries. This is not to say that it covers everything. In fact, the states have considerable flexibility in determining which healthcare services are covered by their state programs. They must cover certain basic services but may choose not to cover services beyond that. However, in most states, Medicaid coverage is extensive in long-term care. It is the principal payer of long-term care, accounting for nearly two thirds of LTC reimbursement (O'Shaughnessy, 2011). Medicaid also serves as a backup to Medicare, paying for services for low-income elders beyond those covered by Medicare.

Because Medicaid is a welfare-type program, it is not intended as a reimbursement source for anyone with other resources. This means that consumers must not be eligible for other forms of health insurance, public or private. They must also use up all of their available resources before becoming eligible for Medicaid.

Medicaid: What Is Covered?

Like Medicare, Medicaid coverage for long-term care services ranges from none at all for some providers to being the primary funding source for others. Also, like Medicare, there are several changes, some experimental, in the works. Several of these changes are tied to the Medicaid waiver program. This program, included in the 1987 Omnibus Budget Reconciliation Act, allows states to apply for a waiver from Medicaid rules to allow them flexibility in operating their Medicaid programs. The waiver programs give the CMS authority to:

- Approve projects that test policy innovations likely to further the objectives of the Medicaid program.
- Grant waivers that allow states to implement managed care delivery systems or otherwise limit individuals' choice of provider under Medicaid.
- Allow long-term care services to be delivered in community settings (CMS, 2014a).

Since passage of that act, which has been expanded twice, many states have been granted waivers. Working within those waivers, they have found ways to fund services other than the traditional medical-related services found in nursing facilities. They can also use waivers to change their focus from care in nursing facilities to home- or community-based care. This has had some effect on the funding of those services to date, and those services will probably expand.

Nursing Care Facilities—Medicaid accounts for nearly half of nursing care facility reimbursement (Benz, 2012). There are a couple of reasons for this. To begin with, other sources of reimbursement for these facilities are very limited. As was noted earlier, Medicare coverage for nursing care is limited to skilled nursing care and does not include residents whose care needs fall below that level. Private sources of reimbursement are also very limited, although that seems to be changing. Given the lack of other payment sources, Medicaid is often left to fill the resultant coverage gaps.

A second, closely related, reason for the prominence of Medicaid as a reimbursement source for nursing facilities is its role as a safety net. Nursing care facility residents are often institutionalized for years, usually the last years of their lives. By that time, they have generally incurred heavy expenses, including hospitalization. They have used up any insurance coverage they may have had, as well as their personal savings.

Assisted Living—Medicaid is also a provider of reimbursement for assisted living facilities and programs (called "residential care facilities" in some states). That coverage is far from universal, varying from state to state, but it is growing. Much of the Medicaid coverage of assisted living has resulted from waiver programs. One of the primary goals of many of these states is to reduce the number of beds in nursing facilities. They see shifting payment to assisted living and residential care as one way of doing that.

Home Health Care—Medicaid is the largest source of funding for home healthcare agencies (CMS, 2014b). The Medicaid portion has grown as states have sought cost savings through waivers and have tried to move more of their Medicaid recipients from institutions to home-based care. Medicaid is often used to supplement Medicare coverage for low-income seniors.

Other Long-Term Care Providers—Other forms of long-term care, such as subacute care, hospice, and adult day care, are generally not covered by Medicaid, but may be covered as a supplement to Medicare or under some of the waiver innovations.

State Efforts to Reduce Medicaid Expenses

In the past several years, both federal and state governments have found their Medicaid budgets rising to levels that threaten their ability to fund them. In 2006, total spending for Medicaid was $331 billion (Kaiser Family Foundation, 2008). By 2013, total Medicaid spending had grown to $415 billion (Kaiser Family Foundation, 2014). More than one third of that amount was being spent on long-term care. The portion funded by the states has grown just as fast. Many states have seen their portion of Medicaid grow to being one of the top two or three most expensive items in their budgets. This has led to a number of efforts to lower expenses.

One of the most common ways of doing so is by reducing the amount of care received by Medicaid recipients in nursing facilities. A method used by some states to accomplish this is raising the eligibility requirements. One of the primary criteria for admission to a nursing facility is the number of activities of daily living (ADLs) with which a person needs help. After increasing the minimum requirement from two to three ADLs, a significant portion of the Medicaid long-term care population was no longer eligible for admission. Several states have also reduced the allowed number of licensed beds in nursing facilities, arguing that they are excessive and expensive to operate. A third method of reducing state Medicaid expenses is through managed care, a topic that is discussed further later in this chapter.

Medicaid Spend-Down Requirements

There has been a great deal of concern recently about one of Medicaid's most basic rules—or at least about reactions to it. That rule specifies that no one can qualify for Medicaid benefits if he or she has other resources available, such as money in the bank, real estate, or other property. Before consumers can become eligible, they must use up all such resources, hence the term, *spend down.*

The rule is logical in and of itself. After all, Medicaid is a welfare-type program intended for those who have no other funds. However, enforcement of this restriction (and efforts to circumvent it) has generated much controversy. The situation has caused battle lines to be drawn, creating opposing camps. First are the consumers and their families. In another camp are the state and federal agencies charged with funding Medicaid. They identify Medicaid as a safety net for those who need help and find it unfair for taxpayers to provide healthcare coverage for people who have resources of their own that could be spent. Both sides have valid arguments, and it is a dispute that will not be solved easily.

Add to these two groups a couple of other not-so-innocent bystanders—providers and estate planners, both of whom have stakes in this argument and have something to gain or lose, depending on its outcome. The providers want to get paid for their services and fear that the Medicaid program will become insolvent, or at least cut reimbursement rates to below where they are already. Estate planners and tax lawyers have found a profitable business advising their clients on ways of avoiding the spend-down rule. They show how to create trusts and other financial mechanisms that protect funds from being taken.

A note of caution here: as much as picking on lawyers has become somewhat of a national pastime, we should not assume that all tax lawyers and estate planners seek to circumvent the Medicaid rules. Most do not. Even those that do so, do it within the letter of the law, so they cannot be criticized for illegal acts. Perhaps the saddest part of this situation is that the really wealthy are usually able to find a way to avoid spending down, while those in the lower- and middle-income categories are far less likely to know how to do that. The latter groups are the ones caught in the middle.

Both sides, providers and estate planners, have taken steps to solidify their positions, with neither clearly winning; however, there have been some interesting results. For example, in 1996, Congress made it a criminal act to willfully dispose of assets for the purpose of gaining eligibility for Medicaid. This was the first time there had been any legal sanction for such acts. Suddenly, anyone caught transferring or otherwise disposing of personal assets to avoid having to spend down would be subject to fines and possible imprisonment. It seemed like a good idea at the time, but Congress failed to anticipate the degree of concern and opposition it would generate. Amid a great deal of publicity claiming that the legislation would result in jailing Granny, Congress did an about-face and, as part of the 1997 budget act, repealed that provision. In its place was put a new section that provided for criminal actions against those who advise consumers—attorneys and estate planners. Early interpretations of the change tended to deem it only slightly more enforceable.

Other suggested remedies for the spend-down problem range from tighter enforcement of existing laws and regulations to providing incentives for consumers to provide their own coverage. The enforcement advocates have had a weapon in place since 1982. It is the Tax Equity and Fiscal Responsibility Act, parts of which allow states to (1) restrict asset transfer within 2 years of Medicaid nursing home eligibility, (2) place liens on the property of living recipients, and (3) recover from the estates of deceased recipients. Despite the time that has elapsed since the act was passed, it appears that states have either had little success implementing these provisions or have not really tried. The 1993 Omnibus Budget Reconciliation Act did go a step further by actually requiring states to recover the costs of nursing facility and other long-term care services from the estates of Medicaid beneficiaries. The Omnibus Budget Reconciliation Act does not appear to have made a significant difference in the states' success, at least to date.

Among the incentives that have been tried or proposed to reduce spend-down avoidance are several forms of public/private partnership demonstration projects, which are discussed in more detail later.

Payment Bundling

The newest (at least at the time of this writing) approach to healthcare reimbursement by the federal government is bundling of payments. As described by the American Hospital Association (2010):

> bundling is designed to align payment incentives and encourage efficiencies between acute and post-acute providers. Currently, the Medicare fee-for-service system has unique payment rules and amounts for each provider type. Under a bundled payment, a single entity would receive a sum of money to cover the costs of an episode of care spanning two or more providers. (p. 13)

This will be accomplished, in most cases, through accountable care organizations—networks of providers who work together to cover a defined patient population.

Created under the Affordable Care Act, the concept of payment bundling is to pay for more comprehensive episodes that may encompass multiple provider types. Its supporters see it as "one alternative to fee-for-service payment that has the potential to promote more efficient, coordinated care across providers or settings" (Linehan, 2012, p. 1). Others caution that unless proper quality safeguards are put in place, bundled payments could lead to withholding needed care (Mechanic & Altman, 2009).

Other Public Funding Sources

While Medicare and Medicaid are by far the largest public reimbursers of long-term care, there are several other smaller sources of public funding for long-term care services. They include the Supplemental Security Income program, the Department of Veterans Affairs, and the Older Americans Act. These programs serve limited populations, and, although they are very important to their recipients, their impact on the overall long-term care system is not great.

Private Reimbursement Sources

In addition to public payment for long-term care services, there are several private (meaning nongovernment) methods of reimbursing providers for those services.

Managed care, which includes a variety of prepayment options, is becoming a major force in health care, primarily as a private reimbursement source. However, because it is also increasingly being applied to public sources such as Medicare and Medicaid, and because of its large current and potential impact, it is discussed separately.

Out-of-Pocket Payments

Historically, the largest private reimbursement source for long-term care has been out-of-pocket payments by individuals and their families. As recently as 1993, this represented slightly more than one third of all long-term care payments, public or private (Meiners, 1996). The other primary sources, private long-term care insurance and managed care, have begun to have some impact. The growth of these two sources is at least partly responsible for the fact that out-of-pocket payments dropped to 28.3% in 2010 (Genworth Financial, 2013).

Private Long-Term Care Insurance

Private long-term care insurance has grown very slowly as an option until the past several years, when its availability and popularity increased considerably. Currently, about 8 million Americans are protected with long-term care insurance. A report released by the American Association for Long-Term Care Insurance (AALTCI) showed that over 264,000 individuals received a total of $6.6 billion in LTC insurance benefits in 2012 (AALTCI, 2014b). By definition, *long-term care insurance* is insurance sold by insurance companies specifically to pay for long-term care services. Some long-term care insurance is purchased through group plans, including employers and organizations, but most such insurance is sold to individuals.

Although most Americans get their health insurance through group plans offered at their places of work, until quite recently few employers offered long-term care insurance to their employees. This seems to be changing with more employer groups offering a form of employer-sponsored long-term care. However, the severe economic downturn experienced in recent years across the country most likely caused many firms to forgo adding this benefit. Hopefully, that will change when the economy rebounds.

There have been a number of reasons given for the reluctance of businesses to add long-term care insurance to their employee benefits. Most are concerned that it is too expensive and that the costs to them will be overwhelming when added to already high health insurance premiums. They find themselves caught in a dilemma. If they provide employer-funded long-term care insurance for all employees, their total premiums may well be prohibitive. However, if they make it optional, they run the risk of adverse selection—only those most likely to use it will take advantage of the option, and the company's premiums will escalate accordingly. If it is offered as part of a company plan but paid for by individual employees, the likelihood of adverse selection becomes even greater, raising premium rates beyond the ability of most employees to pay.

Perhaps the biggest reason companies are not offering long-term care insurance more regularly is that their employees have not demanded it, at least not in large enough numbers to convince them. Interest in long-term care insurance is still not high among people of working age. They have enough to worry about financially without thinking about something that may (or may not) occur several decades in the future. They have also been conditioned to believe that the government will provide for them when they get old. They, like many of the elderly of today, believe that Medicare will cover the bulk of their healthcare needs when they reach the age of 65. The result is that younger people, those of working age, are not convinced of the necessity for purchasing long-term care insurance, yet it is for this group that long-term care insurance is most cost-effective.

There is, however, a countering force that is prodding some younger people to look seriously at buying long-term care insurance, and that is their experience as members of what has come to be known as the sandwich generation. They are caught between taking care of their own children and also taking care of their parents when those parents become elderly and dependent. As these young and middle-aged adults struggle to make sure that their parents receive long-term care services, they learn just how difficult it can be to get reimbursement for them. They are now much more likely to seek ways to avoid putting their own children through the same hassle in future years. Long-term care insurance is one solution that has begun to catch on. The average buyer of LTC coverage is younger than ever before. The findings of a recent survey show an emerging trend.

- In 1999, the average age of LTC Tree's long-term care insurance buyer was 67.3 years old.
- By 2006, that age had dropped 6.09% to 63.2 years old.
- By 2013, that age had dropped a staggering 21.09% to 56.1 years old. (PRWeb, 2013)

One of the complaints from the elderly and their advocates, such as AARP (formerly called the American Association of Retired Persons), is that long-term care insurance is too expensive. It is—for anyone who anticipates using it relatively soon. As might be expected, most individuals receiving benefits from their long-term care insurance policies are older. Approximately a quarter (25.4%) of new claims in 2012 began for individuals between 70 and 79. Nearly two thirds (63.7%) began for those aged 80 or over. However, 10.6% were for those between 50 and 69 (AALTCI, 2014b).

One of the basic precepts of any type of insurance program is that the longer a person pays premiums before collecting benefits, the lower those premiums will be per annum. According to a 2012 national price index, a 55-year-old couple considering long-term care insurance protection can expect to pay $2,700 a year, while the premiums would rise to $3,335 at age 60 and $4,333 at age 65 (NPR, 2012). This is clearly too expensive for many seniors. However, younger workers can find good coverage for as low as around $400 per year. For many of them, this is the equivalent of one month's payment on a car loan or a fraction of a monthly home mortgage payment.

Long-term care insurance, when first offered, was quite restrictive and gave individuals few options from which to choose. As it has developed, insurance companies have added benefit choices that allow purchasers to tailor their benefits to correspond to the amount they are willing to pay for premiums. Long-term care insurance policies are nearly always indemnity-based, meaning that they pay a certain dollar amount of covered services per day. Buyers usually have several dollar amounts on which to base their policies. They may also choose to have their insurance cover nursing facility care, home care, other selected services, or any combination of these services, and they can select the amount of coverage for each. While most people associate long-term care insurance with nursing home care, quite the opposite is true. Most benefits paid today cover care at home or in an assisted living community.

They also may have the option of determining the length of coverage, generally defined in years. Policies most commonly offer choices ranging from 1 to 5 years in nursing facilities and/or home care. Another option is an inflation provision that is designed to anticipate increases in service costs, keeping the same proportional coverage for the insured.

Long-term care insurance is destined to play a much larger role in the reimbursement of long-term care services in the future. There are too few other alternatives for that not to happen. It will not be effective, however, unless the public accepts both its necessity and its value. One factor that will help in gaining that acceptance is the increasing concern over the future viability of Medicare and Medicaid. The possible insolvency of these programs and some of the options suggested for saving them (e.g., raising the eligibility age for Medicare, converting it to a means-based program, and reducing benefits for both Medicare and Medicaid) are beginning to scare the public and shake their complacency. They are starting to realize that they have some responsibility to provide for their own future care needs to the extent they can, and they see long-term care insurance as one alternative.

The willingness of the public to invest in long-term care insurance would be greatly enhanced if there were some tax incentives to do so. One survey showed that the single most important step government could take to encourage the purchase of LTC coverage is to offer tax incentives. According to that survey, more than 80% of those who currently forgo purchase of LTC insurance would be more interested in buying a policy if they could deduct premiums from their taxes (AHIP, 2007b). Several states already allow credits or deductions for the premiums of long-term care insurance. At the national level, the Health Insurance Portability and Accountability Act of 1996 (HIPAA) provided some favorable tax treatment of long-term care insurance premiums. Individual taxpayers can treat long-term care insurance premiums as a personal medical expense subject, however, to the limitations on medical expenses (AALTCI, 2014a). There has been some discussion of national tax incentives, and there will need to be more if private long-term care insurance is to be a significant factor in the near future (AALTCI, 2014b). (See "Significant Trends and Their Impact on Long-Term Care Reimbursement" later herein for a more detailed discussion.)

Partnership Programs

One of the most promising initiatives to come along in long-term care reimbursement in recent years attempts to take advantage of the willingness of many people to accept social responsibility and to facilitate fulfillment of that willingness. It is the concept of developing public/private partnerships. Public/private partnership programs seek ways to provide incentives for individuals to purchase long-term care insurance. The primary incentive is asset protection in return for meeting some of the cost of long-term care. Individuals purchasing private LTC insurance policies are assured that Medicaid will cover LTC costs incurred beyond the terms of the private coverage.

Public/private partnerships began with a program sponsored by the Robert Wood Johnson Foundation. That program, titled Partnership for Long-Term Care, provided financial support for innovative state initiatives that would encourage the purchase of private long-term care insurance by individuals, thus reducing the drain on their Medicaid budgets. Several states participated in the program, using different methods to make the purchase of long-term care insurance more attractive to consumers.

The program was so successful, the government endorsed it. In 2006, Congress approved legislation clearing the way for expanded, nationwide public–private LTC insurance partnerships. The law allows individuals to purchase private LTC insurance that coordinates with Medicaid. In states adopting the partnership program, people with private insurance are not required to spend down their remaining assets to qualify for Medicaid (AALTCI, 2014c).

Partnership programs hold benefits both for consumers and for state and federal governments. The addition of the programs in other states would create financial incentives to purchase private LTC coverage, which would create an improved market for private LTC insurance, which would, in turn, help to limit growth in Medicaid spending (AHIP, 2007a).

■ Managed Care

Few innovations, movements, or trends have affected health care in the United States as much as managed care has in the past several decades. The National Conference of State Legislatures (2013) defines managed care as

> a term used to describe a variety of techniques intended to reduce the cost of providing health benefits and improve the quality of care for organizations that use those techniques or provide them as services to other organizations. It is also used to describe systems of financing and delivering health care to enrollees organized around managed care techniques and concepts.

However, Peter Kongstvedt, who has written several texts dealing with managed care, calls *managed health care*

> A regrettably nebulous term. At the very least, it is a system of health care delivery that tries to manage the cost of health care, the quality of that health care, and access to that care. Common denominators include a panel of contracted providers that is less than the entire universe of available providers, some type of limitations on benefits to subscribers who use non-contracted providers (unless authorized to do so), and some type of authorization system. (Kongstvedt, 2007, p. 657)

He goes on to urge his readers to formulate definitions of their own.

The definitions do, however, identify several basic components of managed care plans. First, managed care integrates, in some fashion, the financing and delivery of health care. Second, its purpose is to manage cost, quality, and access for a defined group of consumers. Third, it manages the behavior of both consumers and providers through financial and administrative mechanisms. Fourth, providers, and sometimes consumers, share the financial risk.

There are many variations of managed care plans or organizations, but there are three prominent types:

- Health Maintenance Organizations (HMO) usually only pay for care within the network. You choose a primary care doctor who coordinates most of your care.
- Preferred Provider Organizations (PPO) usually pay more if you get care within the network. They still pay part of the cost if you go outside the network.
- Point of Service (POS) plans let you choose between an HMO and a PPO each time you need care. (MedLinePlus, 2013)

It is not the purpose of this book to present a comprehensive discussion of managed care, nor would it be feasible to do so herein. The intent is to discuss managed care as it affects long-term care organizations. With that limitation, there are some points for the reader to keep in mind.

One is that it is recognized that managed care is more than just a reimbursement mechanism. It is a combination of reimbursement and delivery. Yet, to keep the discussion in proper perspective, managed care is approached here as a reimbursement source for long-term care. Also, managed care is still largely oriented to physicians and hospitals, and its impact is being felt by long-term care organizations to differing degrees. Rather than attempt to describe all aspects of this very extensive topic, that impact is the focus here.

Managed Care: How It Works

What is now called managed care began with HMOs, a type of provider/reimbursement organization that delivered health care to a specified group of members on a fixed-rate basis, regardless of how much service they required. Enrollment was generally in groups, by employers or other distinct membership organizations. They prepaid the HMO an amount per member per month or per year; thus these were also known as prepaid health plans. It was a direct reversal of the traditional fee-for-service payment mechanism. The HMO employed physicians directly or contracted with groups of physicians. These physicians either received a salary or were paid on a capitation basis, meaning that they received a rate based on the number of enrollees for whom they were responsible, not on the amount of service rendered.

These early HMOs evolved over time, and several new variations have emerged. The changes include expanding the ways they charge their enrollee organizations, their financial relationships with their providers, and how they control costs. Actually, managed care includes several types of plans that vary in their ability to balance access to care, cost, quality control, benefit design, and flexibility (Wagner & Kongstvedt, 2007). Today, they range from managing care for an insurance company or employer on an indemnity basis to constituting a fully integrated health system.

Managed Care and Long-Term Care

Managed care has taken hold much more in some parts of the country than in others. This is particularly true when it comes to long-term care. One early study found that more than 75% of long-term care facilities involved with managed care were in a few states: Arizona, California, Florida, Massachusetts, Minnesota, Oregon, Pennsylvania, and Washington (Fisher, 1997). That has certainly changed significantly, but the distribution is still uneven.

An important development in managed care is its use by public agencies. States, attempting to lower their costs through waiver programs, began contracting with managed care organizations (MCOs) to manage care for their Medicaid and Medicare beneficiaries. They found it to be a good way to reduce their costs or to minimize ongoing growth in those costs. The number of such states has grown significantly. The American Health Care Association found in 2014 that 28 states were using such approaches (AHCA, 2014). Managing care for public programs has already increased the involvement of long-term care organizations beyond the level it occupied when managed care was primarily private.

Institutionalized long-term care, including facilities that provide skilled nursing care, subacute care, nonskilled care, and/or assisted living services, are on the verge of having to become heavily involved with MCOs if they are not already involved. As the long-term care provider closest to acute hospitals, subacute care is leading the pack. The MCOs, in seeking less costly alternatives for hospital care, find nonhospital subacute care attractive. Being able to add that level of care to their comprehensive service packages makes them more competitive. As Medicare makes more use of managed care, this will only increase.

Facilities that do not provide subacute or skilled care are more likely to be influenced by the increasing desire of state Medicaid agencies to contract for management of their caseloads. As the largest source of reimbursement for nursing care and assisted living, the incursion of Medicaid into managed care will force those facilities to join as well.

Home healthcare organizations have also found themselves attractive to MCOs. Where they had relied mostly on Medicare for funding in the past, they are now finding MCOs, both public and private, becoming more important as buyers of their services. These MCOs need to offer a full spectrum of care, including community-based services. They generally do not have the capability to offer those services directly within their own organizations, so they must acquire the services on a contract basis.

Hospice care would seem to be a natural choice for managed care involvement. It already relies heavily on Medicare for reimbursement and has proven itself a less costly alternative during the final months of life. However, the rate of utilization of hospice by MCOs is still relatively low. This may be caused by several factors, including the complexity of MCO transfer rules. However, some hospice providers blame a lack of understanding of the benefits of hospice care on the part of MCO staff and blame themselves for not educating MCOs adequately. They note that hospice care is cost effective, in addition to providing terminally ill patients and their families more freedom and support.

Types of Managed Care: Provider Arrangements

The possible forms of interaction between an MCO and a long-term care provider are almost endless. However, there are several general categories into which most tend to fall, including: (1) per diem, (2) discount from charges, (3) case rates, and (4) capitation (Gleckman, 2012). The simplest and most common is the per diem contract, in which the provider agrees to accept referrals from the MCO. Discounts are just what they sound like: agreed-upon reductions in charges. A case rate contract involves the provider in a bit more risk, because the payment is the same for all cases with a given diagnosis or all cases that require a particular type of treatment. Capitation involves guaranteeing coverage for a given population.

Medicaid and Medicare Managed Care

While long-term care organizations may be involved in private (nongovernment) managed care, the largest impact for them is Medicaid and Medicare managed care, simply because those two are the largest sources of LTC reimbursement.

Medicaid—In the past 15 years, states have increasingly relied on managed care for Medicaid benefits. Almost 50 million people receive Medicaid benefits through some form of managed care (Medicaid.gov, 2014). While this has benefited the state governments, it has not been as beneficial to long-term care providers. Actually, it has just continued the problem of Medicaid underfunding providers. In 2012, state Medicaid programs, on average, reimbursed nursing facilities only 88.9% of their projected allowable costs for Medicaid residents (Eljay, LLC, 2012). LTC providers have also expressed concern about the impact of managed care arrangements on the quality of care. The American Health Care Association has called on state and federal agencies to "carefully weigh and consider the needs of older adults as they implement new payment structures under Medicaid." Specifically, the association "is concerned that long term services and supports (LTSS) will be managed by groups with little-to-no experience in the vastly complex needs of Medicaid's older adult population in nursing centers" (AHCA, 2014).

Medicare—Medicare managed care is found in the form of Medicare Advantage plans through which Medicare benefits are managed by private organizations. In 2012, about 13 million seniors participated in Medicare Advantage plans—about 27% of the Medicare population, and twice as many as were enrolled just 7 years earlier (Gleckman, 2012). Since the inception of the Affordable Care Act in 2010, there have been repeated suggestions that Medicaid Advantage plans would see their benefits reduced as a means of paying for the Affordable Care Act. Should that happen, the impact on long-term care (and all of health care) could be severe.

Managed Care: Making the Transition

In looking at the need for long-term care organizations to embrace managed care or at least become an active participant in it, there are three questions that should be asked.

1. How big a step is it for a long-term care provider to become involved in managed care?
2. What capabilities must it have in its operations to be successful?
3. How ready is it?

The short answers to those questions are:

1. It is a big step.
2. Many specific capabilities are needed.
3. It is generally not very ready.

These questions and answers are now explored in a bit more depth.

Taking the Big Step

Getting involved with managed care is a significant undertaking for most long-term care organizations. Granted, there are many who have already taken the step—and have done so successfully—but all indications are that the vast majority have not. Changing from traditional fee-for-service reimbursement to capitation or other managed care payment method means giving up some of its own control over its residents or clients. The MCO will have its own cost and quality control mechanisms, often different from those of the long-term care provider both in format and in focus. Given the traditional retrospective payment to which most long-term care providers have been accustomed, many were and are not nearly as cost-conscious as are MCOs. The PPS has changed that, making most long-term care organizations quite cost conscious. MCOs are interested in quality of care but make their purchasing decisions based on price.

Even with the most at-arms-length arrangements, the MCO becomes another organization with which to work. This requires the provider to understand how the MCO works and what it is looking for in a relationship. Depending on how deeply involved the provider becomes with the MCO, the arrangement may interfere with, or even replace, relationships with other payers or acute care providers.

Capabilities Needed

MCOs look for providers that can meet their needs completely and efficiently. They choose providers able to demonstrate their experience in providing high-quality care and that are able and willing to adapt as necessary. There are also certain financial and administrative capabilities that a long-term care provider needs to have to interact successfully with an MCO. Perhaps the most important is a working case management function. This is also the area in which many of them fall short. Their existing utilization review programs, while meeting current needs, may not be stringent or detailed enough to satisfy the MCO.

A second major capability that providers must have is a highly sophisticated information system. To begin with, that system must make it possible for the provider to identify and manage costs. MCOs expect their contractors to have a sound grasp of where and how they are spending their money. That information system also prepares the provider for future negotiations with the MCO. The information system must also be capable of providing the data needed for measuring clinical outcomes. MCOs will look for outcomes-measurement capability on the part of contracting providers.

They want measurement of utilization, length of stay, and use of quantitative outcome measurement tools.

State of Readiness

Most observers agree that much of the long-term care field is not adequately prepared for managed care. On the whole, the degree of involvement of long-term care organizations in managed care runs the gamut from highly involved to not interested. Some recognize the value of participation; others are not yet convinced. Some are in areas of the country where MCOs have made few inroads. Others are working on developing the capabilities needed.

Managed Care: A Tarnished Image

It is assumed here that managed care is here to stay and that long-term care organizations cannot afford to ignore it. There would appear to be plenty of justification for that assumption. However, all is not sweetness and light with managed care. From its inception, it has taken hits from all sides because of the perception that MCOs put cost control ahead of quality of care or the interests of consumers. The news media have been full of stories of MCOs denying tests and procedures to save money. Individual physicians and physician groups have complained of having their medical decisions overturned by nonmedical MCO staff. Public and teaching hospitals fear that they will be left to care for only the sickest and poorest patients while, through selective enrollment, MCOs skim off those patients who are less expensive to handle. Consumers who are enrolled, often by their employers, in managed care plans tell of losing their ability to choose their physicians and other providers.

These and other similar complaints have generated a great deal of consumer and political backlash against MCOs. Consumer advocacy groups such as AARP and Families USA work hard to protect the rights of their constituents, including providing them with the information needed to judge the care they are getting. This concern from healthcare professionals and the public has led to creation of a presidential commission. The 1997 President's Advisory Commission on Consumer Protection and Quality in the Health Care Industry developed a consumer bill of rights and responsibilities. Although it addresses the entire healthcare system, it was clearly stimulated by worry about the direction that the system seemed to be taking as managed care became ever more influential.

This bill of rights addresses a number of consumer rights, focusing directly on the complaints heard about managed care. These rights include the rights of consumers "to receive accurate, understandable information; to choose their healthcare providers; to have emergency care reimbursed; to participate in treatment decisions; to be treated respectfully and in a nondiscriminatory manner; and to appeal differences with providers and health plans" (President's Advisory Commission, 1997, p. 2). At the same time, several states have also developed their own managed care consumer assistance legislation. Several states have considered bills aimed at helping people more easily navigate the often confusing world of managed care. These bills are designed to support the national bill of rights and fill perceived gaps in the national bill.

The backlash against MCOs by both consumers and physicians caused some long-term care providers to question whether they want to become involved. It gave others an excuse to remain distant from a part of the system that they saw as changing their operations too radically. Managed care will weather this storm, will make some changes as a result of it, and will emerge as an even more important mechanism for providing and reimbursing health care. For that reason, long-term care organizations will continue to become more involved with it, although some will do so reluctantly.

■ Significant Trends and Their Impact on Long-Term Care Reimbursement

There are several changes taking place in long-term care reimbursement that will continue to have impact on providers and consumers alike. They include (1) the growing influence of private MCOs; (2) the degree to which public reimbursers, such as Medicare and Medicaid, use managed care; (3) the ongoing impact of the change from retrospective payment to a PPS; (4) an emphasis on noninstitutional forms of care; (5) the provision of incentives for consumers to purchase private long-term care insurance; and (6) efforts to reduce the cost of liability insurance through tort reform. These developments are, not surprisingly, closely interrelated. They share a common goal of containing the rising cost of providing care.

These changes have been initiated primarily by public and private organizations responsible for paying for care. However, the stimulus actually comes from their customers, who are seeking financial relief. For private MCOs, the customers are the companies and others who contract for healthcare coverage for the members of their groups. They are looking for ways to reduce the expenses associated with providing that coverage. For the public agencies administering Medicare and Medicaid programs, the ultimate customers are taxpayers, who are also feeling the need for relief.

Private Managed Care

Managed care, in spite of the questions that have been raised about it, will continue to be a major player in the area of long-term care reimbursement for the foreseeable future. It experienced some growing pains, as happens with just about any new business concept. These growing pains are shaping it into a more stable entity. Trying to predict what shape that entity will ultimately take is risky, but it is likely to be somewhat less extreme than some of the earlier versions. The competing forces of cost containment and consumer choice are working to eliminate some of the provisions and characteristics most objectionable to each, which will result in a product both can live with.

Government, acting in its regulatory mode, has already responded to some of these forces and has established some parameters within which managed care can operate.

Long-term care organizations are, and will be, faced with the reality of private managed care as a serious source of reimbursement. The percentage of their funding received from that source has grown slowly in most cases and, with some exceptions, will not exceed public reimbursement. However, the relationships between long-term care providers and other segments of the continuum may well hinge on how willing and able those providers are to embrace managed care. The influence of an organization's other stakeholders, particularly referring hospitals, will be significant. The importance of managed care is much greater for those hospitals than for most long-term care organizations. They are looking for long-term care partners who can help them as they compete for the business of the MCOs.

Public Managed Care

As was noted earlier, both the Medicare and Medicaid programs have actively increased their use of managed care. Like the private sector, they see it as a way of managing their costs. Because of their much larger role in long-term care reimbursement, their managed care involvement is affecting long-term care providers significantly.

The CMS, which administers the Medicare program, has experimented with a number of managed care formats. The agency has contracted with private MCOs to develop and pilot a variety of different plans and options. These projects generally focus on acute care for Medicare recipients, but most include some long-term care elements as well. State Medicaid agencies are also trying managed care as an option for reducing, or at least containing, their growing costs. As trials or demonstration projects, the formats have varied considerably in structure and coverage and continue to do so. In most cases, Medicaid agencies also contract with private MCOs to develop and administer their plans, rather than attempting to create their own MCOs.

The long-range impact of these efforts on long-term care organizations is not yet clear. In areas in which demonstration projects have taken place, the impact has been significant, particularly with Medicaid projects. In others, it has not been felt yet. However, the necessity of finding solutions to the financial problems of Medicare and Medicaid make managed care look very attractive to those agencies. Add in the still unknown factor of the Affordable Care Act, and the potential impact on long-term care organizations could be much greater than anyone would have guessed.

Although changes in Medicare eligibility rules tend to get most of the spotlight, it is a safe bet that there will also be a continued and expanding search for ways to reduce expenses for coverage of those who are eligible. It is these actions, many of which are already under way, that will most significantly affect providers of long-term care services. The CMS has stepped up its efforts to reduce fraud in Medicare billing. Many state Medicaid agencies, with assistance from the CMS, have done the same. Case-mix payment programs, where providers (primarily nursing facilities) are paid according to the proportion of their residents needing certain levels of care, have been tried. And, finally, the various managed care experiments mentioned here will have the most impact in the long run.

Prospective Payment

As Medicare completed the change from a retrospective payment system to one that is prospective for providers of long-term care services, many of these providers have had to make significant changes in their record keeping and operating practices. They have had to develop case management systems, if they did not already have them in place. There has been, and will continue to be, pressure on them to reduce their costs even further. For those providers whose primary service is subacute or skilled care, these changes have already been made or are at least under way. For others, such as the large and growing number of nursing facilities with small skilled care components, it is much more difficult. They must adopt a highly complicated billing and record-keeping system for a small part of their facilities, one that is very different from what they use for the rest of their residents.

Most long-term care providers accepted the changes but expressed a number of concerns. Some expressed concerns about how the new program would be implemented, fearing delays and confusion about reporting requirements. Opinions were mixed concerning how it would affect their competitive position with hospital-based subacute care units. On one thing, however, there seemed to be consensus: The intent of the PPS was to lower costs; therefore, providers could expect to receive less. In general, their concerns were realized, but most likely not to the degree they had anticipated.

Emphasis on Community-Based Care

As reimbursers of long-term care services, both public and private, begin to look for more ways to ensure that their constituents receive appropriate care at the lowest possible prices, there has been a very clear and well-documented shift of reimbursement resources from institution-based care to that which is home or community based. This has obviously been a boon for home health and hospice organizations and a concern for nursing care, assisted living, and residential care providers. The shift is likely to continue, although some of the policy makers most enamored of the idea have come to realize that it does not work in all situations. Studies have shown that the population of consumers, particularly the elderly (who are the majority), who can best make use of home-based services are not necessarily the same ones who reside in nursing care or other residential facilities. Therefore, to some degree, the effect of shifting resources from institutional care to home-based care has been to create additional demand. This is good for those consumers who benefit from the added coverage and for the organizations providing the care. It has also forced institutional providers to be more cost conscious and competitive. However, it has not had the overall effect on the reimbursement system anticipated by some.

Incentives for Purchasing Private Long-Term Care Insurance

Because of the historic lack of interest of many consumers in purchasing private long-term care insurance, there needs to be, and will be, continued pressure for better incentives for them to do so. As noted earlier, there have been some efforts to provide tax incentives for consumers paying premiums for long-term care insurance.

One question that stirs a lot of controversy today—and will in the future no matter what financing system we develop—is who should be the gatekeeper? Someone has to make healthcare decisions for each individual. Who should it be? In an ideal system, it should be the consumers, but they are often not sufficiently well informed. The players in this game do not trust each other. Providers and payers suspect that the consumers will want too much if they have control. If the providers are the gatekeepers, the payers are afraid they will prescribe too much expensive care. Yet, if the payers are the gatekeepers, both the consumers and providers accuse them of putting cost ahead of quality. There is no easy answer, and this question will only continue to get in the way as new systems develop.

Liability Costs and Tort Reform

In the past few years, all of health care, including long-term care, has been beset by increasing numbers of multimillion-dollar lawsuits. Without attempting to judge the validity of such lawsuits, it is easy to see that the effect on both providers and reimbursement organizations (including Medicare and Medicaid) has been nearly devastating. Although most of the costs have been borne directly by liability insurance companies, they pass that cost on to providers in the form of higher premiums. They, in turn, pass the cost on to their sources of reimbursement and, eventually, to the consumers. In several states, physicians have had to retire from practice or move to other states because they could not afford to pay their liability insurance premiums. Although the costs associated with this phenomenon are often higher in acute care, a recent study of the impact on long-term care revealed the following information:

- Long-term care loss rates are increasing by 5% annually.
- The overall forecasted 2014 long-term care general liability/professional liability loss rate is $1,940 per bed.
- Long-term care claim frequency is increasing by 2% annually.
- The 2014 long-term care general liability/professional liability frequency is 0.91 claims per 100 occupied beds.
- Long-term care claim severity is increasing by 3% annually.
- The forecasted 2014 long-term care general liability/professional liability severity is $213,000 per claim. (Aon Risk Solutions, 2013, p. 5)

That same report showed that there has been significant improvement in states that have enacted tort reform in the past several years.

It is perhaps the fact that so much of the money is going to lawyers that is most disturbing. Few would deny injured consumers fair compensation. However, much of the liability settlement money is paid to their attorneys.

There has been a call for reform of current tort laws to address this problem. As with most such issues, this one is hotly contested in the political arena, and little has been accomplished. Even the Affordable Care Act, which addresses healthcare reform, does not include tort reform in any substantive manner.

Financing Reform

There has also been much talk about reforming the overall U.S. healthcare system, which really means reforming the healthcare financing system. The debate, which culminated in the Affordable Care Act of 2010, centers on providing coverage for people needing acute and preventive care. There has been little attention given to providing more coverage for long-term care. The one provision of the Affordable Care Act that would have directly impacted long-term care was a voluntary insurance program known as the Community Living Assistance Services and Supports program (CLASS Act). The CLASS program was described by the Henry J. Kaiser Family Foundation as "designed to expand options for people who become functionally disabled and require long-term services and supports" (Kaiser Family Foundation, 2010). Unfortunately, the CLASS Act was repealed in 2013 after the Department of Health and Human Services determined it was unworkable.

There seem to be several reasons for this lack of focus on long-term care. First, long-term care financing does not have the urgency of acute care. The public sees it as something that can be put off—unless they are already involved with it. Acute care, on the other hand, affects them now and in dramatic fashion. Lack of access to it can be immediately and permanently devastating. People unable to pay for emergency or preventive care, especially children, evoke a great deal of concern. They should—and they should receive the highest priority. However, the gap in public interest between that top priority and the somewhat lower priority of long-term care is far too great. Efforts by the elderly and their advocates have begun to raise public consciousness and close that gap, but it still exists.

A second reason long-term care financing is given low priority in reform talks is that it is so hard to get a handle on it. As has been demonstrated throughout herein, long-term care takes many forms, is constantly evolving into new forms, and is subject to many separate, uncoordinated methods of reimbursement. Politicians and other policy makers—those who must make reform happen—are having a hard enough time reforming the less complex acute care financing system. They find it exceedingly difficult to grasp a system that is not purely health care but is inextricably interwoven with other social systems. They are reluctant to attempt reforming the way long-term care is financed when that may require also reforming other social systems such as welfare, housing, and transportation.

The third, and probably most important, factor preventing meaningful reform of how long-term care is reimbursed is the cost. Most discussions of financing reform begin with an assumption that it means significantly greater government involvement, which means a level of public spending that would be unpalatable to most taxpayers. Even the most conservative estimates show that increased public spending on long-term care would mean a major increase in the burden on taxpayers. Given our history of underestimating such things, the actual result would be much higher.

Still, in spite of these barriers, reform is happening. It is not happening all at once or in dramatic fashion but incrementally. Changes are taking place. New ideas are being tried. The evolution of managed care, in both the public and private sectors, is one example. Another is the testing of public/private partnership innovations. Those tried so far have demonstrated that it is an appropriate approach to follow. Further experimentation should provide additional evidence of this and a refinement in methodology. One element that will contribute greatly to the success or failure of any public/private partnership attempt is consumer education. It will require an intensive, ongoing effort—one that may not pay off for many years—but one that is absolutely essential.

The growth of private long-term care insurance, although slow, can also have some impact. It is unlikely to become a major source of reimbursement, but it can be significant. What is needed to make that happen are more incentives for individuals and/or employers to invest in it. These incentives might take the form of tax credits or even subsidies. Tax incentives are already in place to a limited degree and show promise. The idea of the government subsidizing the purchase of private insurance premiums has been floated. It is attractive to those advocating more choice by consumers, but it is looked on with skepticism by others concerned about losing control.

Other reform discussions, particularly as they affect public programs, are taking place. Again, however, the direct involvement of long-term care is very limited. The discussions address the Medicare and Medicaid programs primarily, aimed at preserving the programs and the services they cover. The impact on long-term care reimbursement and on long-term care providers may be significant, but it is usually secondary to concerns for the programs themselves.

■ Summary

This chapter attempted to present a broad overview of how long-term care is reimbursed. It is far too complex a topic to do justice to in a single chapter, and there are some excellent books available that cover it in more appropriate detail. It is a topic that is, and probably always will be, in a state of constant evolution, meaning that even the best text on the subject is quickly out of date.

That complexity and dynamism are among the factors contributing to the increased importance given to the role of specialists in long-term care reimbursement. It is difficult for many administrators to keep up with the details of reimbursement and manage their organizations as well. A secondary, but directly related, result is the incentive for long-term care providers to become involved in integrated networks or systems where such specialists are more likely to be available. However, all administrators of long-term care organizations and anyone seeking an understanding of the continuum of care must understand, at least, the essentials of reimbursement.

■ Vocabulary Terms

The following terms are included in this chapter. They are important to the topics and issues discussed herein and should become familiar to readers. Some of the terms are also found in other chapters but may be used in different contexts. They may not be fully defined herein. Thus, readers may wish to seek other, supplementary definitions of them.

Affordable Care Act

beneficiary

case management

consumer bill of rights and
   responsibilities

entitlement program

health maintenance organization
   (HMO)

Medicaid

medically indigent

Medicare

Medicare trust fund

managed care

Part A

Part B

payment bundling

private long-term care insurance

prospective payment system

public/private partnerships

reimbursement driven

spend down

waiver programs

■ Discussion Questions

The following questions are presented to assist you in understanding the material covered in this chapter. They tend to be general but lend themselves to detailed answers, which can be found in the chapter.

1. What do we mean when we say that the long-term care system is reimbursement driven?
2. Who is covered by Medicare? Medicaid?
3. What long-term care services does Medicare cover? What restrictions are placed on them?
4. What long-term care services does Medicaid cover? What restrictions are placed on them?
5. What is the spend-down provision of Medicaid, and why is it controversial?
6. What is the purpose of waiver programs?

7. What are public/private partnerships?
8. Why has managed care taken hold more slowly in long-term care than in other segments of health care?
9. What are the most common forms of managed care organizations?
10. What is the managed care consumer bill of rights, and why is it needed?

■ References

American Association for Long-Term Care Insurance (AALTCI). (2014a). *Long-term care insurance tax-deductibility rules - LTC tax rules.* Retrieved from http://www.aaltci.org/long-term-care-insurance/learning-center/tax-for-business.php#individual.

American Association for Long-Term Care Insurance (AALTCI). (2014b). *Long-term care insurance facts—Statistics.* Retrieved from http://www.aaltci.org/long-term-care-insurance/learning-center/fast-facts.php.

American Association for Long-Term Care Insurance (AALTCI). (2014c). *Long term care insurance partnership plans added protection ideally suited for middle-income Americans.* Retrieved from http://www.aaltci.org/long-term-care-insurance/learning-center/long-term-care-insurance-partnership-plans.php.

American Health Care Association (AHCA). (2014, January 16). *Surge of Medicaid managed care is fraught with problems unless root concerns are addressed.* Retrieved from http://www.ahcancal.org/News/news_releases/Pages/Surge-of-Medicaid-Managed-Care-is-Fraught-with-Problems-Unless-Root-Concerns-are-Addressed.aspx.

American Hospital Association. (2010, November). *Maximizing the value of post-acute care.* Retrieved from http://www.aha.org/research/reports/tw/10nov-tw-postacute.pdf.

America's Health Insurance Plans (AHIP). (2007a). *Long-term care insurance partnerships: New choices for consumers—potential savings for federal and state government.* Washington, DC: America's Health Insurance Plans.

America's Health Insurance Plans (AHIP). (2007b). *Who buys long-term care insurance?* Washington, DC: America's Health Insurance Plans.

Aon Risk Solutions. (2013). *2013 long term care general liability and professional liability actuarial analysis.* Retrieved from http://www.ahcancal.org/research_data/liability/Documents/2013%20Liability%20Analysis.pdf.

Benz, C. (2012, August 9). *40 must-know statistics about long-term care.* Retrieved from http://news.morningstar.com/articlenet/article.aspx?id=564139.

Centers for Medicare and Medicaid Services (CMS). (2014a). *Chapter 1—Inpatient hospital services covered under Part A.* Retrieved from https://www.cms.gov/Regulations-and-Guidance/Guidance/Manuals/downloads/bp102c01.pdf.

Centers for Medicare & Medicaid Services. (2014b). *National Health Expenditures 2012 Highlights.* Retrieved from CMS.Gov: http://www.cms.gov/Research-Statistics-Data-and-Systems/Statistics-Trends-and-Reports/NationalHealthExpendData/Downloads/highlights.pdf.

Eljay, LLC. (2012). *A report on shortfalls in Medicaid funding for nursing center care.* Washington, DC: American Health Care Association.

Fisher, C. (1997, October). Unprepared for managed care? *Provider*, pp. 9–10.

Genworth Financial. (2013). *Genworth 2013 cost of care survey.* Retrieved from https://www.genworth.com/dam/Americas/US/PDFs/Consumer/corporate/130568_032213_Cost%20of%20Care_Final_nonsecure.pdf.

Gleckman, H. (2012, December 26). *The promise and risks of Medicare managed care.* Retrieved from http://www.forbes.com/sites/howardgleckman/2012/12/26/the-promise-and-risks-of-medicare-managed-care/.

Goldsmith, S. (1994). *Essentials of long-term care administration.* Gaithersburg, MD: Aspen Publishers.

Kaiser Family Foundation. (2008). *Dual eligible beneficiaries as a share of Medicare and Medicaid population and spending, 2008.* Retrieved from http://kaiserfamilyfoundation.files.wordpress.com/2013/06/duals-as-a-share-of-medicare-pop-and-spending-2008-medicare.png.

Kaiser Family Foundation. (2010, April 28). *Health care reform and the CLASS Act.* Retrieved from http://kff.org/health-costs/issue-brief/health-care-reform-and-the-class-act.

Kaiser Family Foundation. (2014). *Distribution of Medicaid spending by service.* Retrieved from http://kff.org/medicaid/state-indicator/distribution-of-medicaid-spending-by-service.

Kongstvedt, P. (2007). *Essentials of managed health care* (5th ed.). Sudbury, MA: Jones and Bartlett.

Linehan, K. (2012, April 20). *Bundled payment in Medicare: Promise, peril, and practice.* Retrieved from http://www.nhpf.org/library/details.cfm/2890.

Mechanic, R., & Altman, S. (2009). Payment reform options: Episode payment is a good place to start. *Health Affairs.* http://content.healthaffairs.org/content/28/2/w262.full.

Medicaid.gov. (2014). *Managed care.* Retrieved from http://www.medicaid.gov/Medicaid-CHIP-Program-Information/By-Topics/Delivery-Systems/Managed-Care/Managed-Care.html.

MedLinePlus. (2013, September 23). *Managed care.* Retrieved from http://www.nlm.nih.gov/medlineplus/managedcare.html.

Meiners, M. (1996). The financing and organization of long-term care. In R. Binstock, L. Cluff, & O. Von Mering (Eds.), *The future of long-term care: Social and policy issues* (pp. 191–214). Baltimore, MD: Johns Hopkins University Press.

National Center for Health Statistics (NCHS). (2007). *Health, United States, 2007 with chartbook on trends in the health of Americans (2007).* Hyattsville, MD: National Center for Health Statistics.

National Conference of State Legislatures. (2013, June 17). *Managed care and the states.* Retrieved from http://www.ncsl.org/research/health/managed-care-and-the-states.aspx.

NPR. (2012, May 8). *Long-term-care insurance: Who needs it?* Retrieved from http://www.npr.org/2012/05/08/151970188/long-term-care-insurance-who-needs-it.

O'Shaughnessy, C. (2011, February 1). *National spending for long-term services and supports (LTSS), 2011.* Retrieved from http://www.nhpf.org/library/details.cfm/2783.

President's Advisory Commission. (1997). *President's Advisory Commission releases consumer bill of rights and responsibilities.* Washington, DC: President's Advisory Commission on Consumer Protection and Quality in the Health Care Industry.

PRWeb. (2013, August 27). *Long term care insurance buyer's age drops dramatically.* Retrieved from http://www.prweb.com/releases/2013/8/prweb11062582.htm.

Social Security and Medicare Boards of Trustees. (2013). *A summary of the 2013 annual reports.* Retrieved from http://www.ssa.gov/oact/trsum/.

Wagner, E., & Kongstvedt, P. (2007). Types of managed care plans and integrated healthcare delivery systems. In P. Kongstvedt (Ed.), *Essentials of managed care* (5th ed., pp. 19–40). Sudbury, MA: Jones and Bartlett.

Long-Term Care Quality

Learning Objectives

After completing this chapter, readers will be able to:

1. Understand the concept of quality improvement and how it applies to long-term care.

2. Identify the similarities and differences between quality assurance and continuous quality improvement.

3. Discuss and compare outcomes-based measures and process-based measures and the advantages of each.

4. Discuss the value of a systemwide approach to management of quality.

5. Identify government and private resources available to assist providers in developing and maintaining quality improvement programs.

■ Introduction

Long-term care managers must be dedicated to providing care that is of the highest possible quality. This means constantly striving not only to maintain quality, but to improve it. Today there is much emphasis on quality in all of health care, particularly in long-term care. Some is the result of a public that is concerned about the quality of long-term care services; some is the result of elected and regulatory officials expressing that concern. Politicians and advocacy groups such as AARP are demanding that the federal government exercise more oversight over the long-term care field. Lawyers are openly advertising in some states with ads that read something like, "Have you or a loved one been mistreated or harmed in a nursing home?"

The concern over quality in long-term care has resulted in several major studies by the National Institute of Medicine (IOM). First was the report of the IOM Committee on Nursing Home Regulations, Improving the Quality of Care in Nursing Homes. It was the basis for the Nursing Home Reform Act, passed as part of the 1987 Omnibus Budget Reconciliation Act, which imposed significant new regulations on long-term care providers. More recently (2001), the IOM released two additional reports concerning quality. One, entitled *Crossing the Quality Chasm: A New Health System for the 21st Century*, reported on the findings of the IOM Committee on Quality of Health Care in America. It addressed the topic of quality in all of health care, including long-term care.

The other report focused directly on long-term care. It covered the work of the IOM Committee on Improving Quality in Long-Term Care. Entitled *Improving the Quality of Long-Term Care*, it contained significant conclusions about the level of quality found in long-term care services, along with recommendations for improvement. The committee found that since implementation of the Omnibus Budget Reconciliation Act, the quality of care has generally improved, even though nursing homes are serving a more seriously ill population, and that quality of life for nursing home residents has also shown some improvement, but to a lesser extent (Wunderlich & Kohler, 2001). The committee noted that information about the quality of care for long-term care other than nursing homes is scarce and inconsistent, making it difficult to evaluate.

There have been a number of quality initiatives aimed at long-term care and other segments of the healthcare field. In part, it is because of this kind of pressure. However, it is also because quality is important to providers. Organizations tend to embark on quality improvement for a variety of reasons, including accreditation requirements, cost control, competition for customers, and pressure from employers and payers (McLaughlin & Kaluzny, 2006). They recognize the benefits of establishing a comprehensive quality agenda that becomes part and parcel of daily operations—high-quality resident care, improved workforce retention, increased organizational effectiveness, better use of available resources, and a positive impact on the success of the operation (Schiverick, 2008). We discuss both government and private quality measurement a bit later in this chapter, but first, let us look at how quality is defined.

■ Defining Quality

Just about anyone involved with any form of quality assurance (QA) or quality measurement agrees that the first step to accomplishing anything is determining what is meant by quality. It is also the most difficult step. Quality means different things to different people and different things in different situations.

The most commonly cited, perhaps easiest to use, definition comes from Dr. Avedis Donabedian of the University of Michigan, one of the earliest to teach and write about quality assessment in health care. He defines healthcare quality as "a judgment about the goodness of both technical care and the management of the interpersonal exchanges between client and practitioner" (Donabedian, 1991, p. 61). This definition, while covering all of health care, has excellent application to long-term care. It is also brilliant in its simplicity. He describes the definition as "rather broad, but not so broad as to be crippling" (1991, p. 61). Let us examine some of the key words and phrases in that definition:

1. *Judgment:* There is no absolute measure of quality. It depends on many inconstant factors, as well as the perception of the person making the judgment.
2. *Goodness:* Although that term seems to be pretty subjective and difficult to quantify, most of us have our own understanding of what goodness is.
3. *Technical Care* and *Interpersonal Exchanges Between Client and Practitioner:* This includes quality of life.

Quality is a multifaceted concept. Quality in a nursing facility can be defined as the consistent delivery of services that maximizes the physical, mental, social, and spiritual well-being of all residents, produces desirable outcomes, and minimizes the likelihood of undesirable consequences (Singh, 2010). These factors are even more important in long-term care than in acute settings because of the very nature of the relationship between consumer and provider. That relationship is ongoing and long-standing. It involves very personal, day-to-day interactions. Long-term care consumers are being cared for, not cured. Care for them means more than treatment of a disease or alleviation of a temporary medical condition. They rely on their caregivers for the quality of every aspect of their lives.

Quality of Life

Quality of life refers to the total living experience, which results in overall satisfaction with one's life. Technology that enables people to live independently generally enhances the quality of life. Quality of life is a multifaceted concept that recognizes at least five factors: lifestyle pursuits, living environment, clinical palliation, human factors, and personal choices. Quality of life can be enhanced by integrating these five factors into the delivery of care (Singh, 2010). Although many elements have a bearing on quality of life, each individual places different degrees of importance on each of them. It is hard for outsiders—that is, anyone other than the person directly involved—to measure the quality of life of that person. For this reason, measurement of quality in long-term care has moved toward including more input from consumers. Where it had historically been based largely on empirical data (number of falls, infections, etc.), recent efforts have begun to add an element of consumer satisfaction. Although often overshadowed by measures of clinical process and outcomes, consumer satisfaction is also an important indicator of quality. Long-term care consumers are now asked what is important to them and whether they are satisfied with the care they get.

Consumer satisfaction is only one element of quality measurement, and as important as it is, it is not always easy to measure. Many long-term care consumers have limited cognitive ability or are unable to communicate their thoughts clearly, making their input either impossible to get or of questionable validity.

There is still one more definition of quality that perhaps says it even better, although the quality it defines may not be as easy to measure or regulate. Someone once told a group of administrators that "Your customers may not know what quality is, but they know when they don't get it." On a practical basis, this says it well.

Whatever means are chosen to measure (and therefore ensure) quality, it probably involves one or more of three generally accepted measurement types: structure, process, and outcomes (Donabedian, 1966). Structure measurement deals with the makeup of the organization where the care is provided, including organizational structure, resources provided, and so on. Process measurement refers to how the care is delivered. Outcomes measurement focuses on the end result—the effect the care has on the individual. An outcome is an actual result obtained from medical, nursing, and other clinical interventions. An increase in positive outcomes indicates that quality has improved (Singh, 2010).

Historically, most quality measures have focused more on structure and process than on outcomes, in large part because structure and process are easier to measure than outcomes. It is easier to document what was done and how it was done than what the resultant effect on the consumer was. Measurement of outcomes is more difficult in long-term care than in acute care settings. In acute care, successful outcomes often mean restoring patients to their level of functioning before the onset of illness. In long-term care, successful outcomes are usually aimed at maximizing quality of life and physical function in the presence of permanent, and sometimes worsening, impairment. They often focus on such things as overall health status, presence or absence of specific conditions (e.g., pressure sores), social and psychological well-being, and satisfaction with care (Wunderlich & Kohler, 2001). More recently, there has been an increased emphasis on achieving such outcomes, difficult though they may be to measure.

Yet outcomes depend in large part on both process and structure, and the three are invariably linked. Process (how care is delivered) depends on the structure of the delivery organization (staffing, equipment). As important as outcomes are, it is also necessary to measure process and structure as indicators of the reasons the outcomes may be less than optimal.

For example, a high rate of nosocomial infections (those contracted while in the facility) is definitely an undesirable outcome, yet the only way to deal with it is to examine the structure and processes involved in care of residents. Did poor infection control techniques cause the high rate? If so, that is a process issue. Did lack of resources resulting in overcrowding of residents or understaffing (structure issues) contribute to the high infection rate? As you can see, the outcomes are important in measuring results, but it is likely structure or process (usually process) that causes these outcomes, and only by focusing on the structure or processes can the outcomes be improved.

■ Total Quality Management/Continuous Quality Improvement

Although sometimes called by other names, continuous quality improvement (CQI) is the most common name for what is essentially total quality management as applied to health care. Total quality management was created by Dr. W. Edwards Deming. It has been used extensively in business and industry for years, but its acceptance by long-term care and other healthcare organizations has been quite recent. As they have adapted its principles to their organizations, they have generally chosen to call it continuous quality improvement. This slight difference in terminology is important because it better defines what they seek to accomplish.

CQI (also called quality improvement) is a proactive and continuous study of processes with the intent to prevent or decrease the likelihood of problems by identifying areas of opportunity and testing new approaches to fix underlying causes of persistent/systemic problems. CQI in nursing homes aims to improve processes involved in healthcare delivery and resident quality of life. It can make good quality even better (CMS, 2013a).

The basis of CQI is that quality is not separate from other aspects of the organization's operations. It is a holistic approach that is based on a desire by the staff and administration to achieve excellence in what they do—provide care to the residents who rely on them. Deming based his approach to quality improvement on a set of principles known as his fourteen points. They are not covered in depth here, nor are they all identified. Instead, the overall aspects of CQI and how they apply to long-term care is discussed. It is worth noting, however, that these principles recognize the inherent goodness of individuals and their desire to work, as well as the contributions they can make toward improving quality and reducing costs. As a result, CQI encourages their active involvement. Another definition of CQI (or total quality management) is that it is "a structured organizational process for involving personnel in planning and executing a continuous flow of improvements to provide quality health care that meets or exceeds expectations" (Sollecito & Johnson, 2013, p. 4).

■ Quality Initiatives

As noted at the beginning of this chapter, there are many initiatives and/or efforts aimed at measuring and improving quality in long-term care. Some of these are internal in nature in that they are administered by the provider organization primarily for the benefit of that organization and its consumers. Others are developed and administered by some entity external to any individual provider organization and are meant to ensure quality for the overall system or at least for major segments of the system. Although these separate types of quality initiative are generally quite well defined, the distinction is not always clear because some of the systemwide quality initiatives involve grouping several of the programs used by providers. These situations are pointed out as the discussion continues.

■ Systemwide Quality Programs

In addition to the internal quality improvement efforts of providers, there are several external initiatives in place that attempt to improve the overall quality of the long-term care system. Some of them are managed by government agencies, and others are operated by private organizations.

Government Programs

Much of what we have seen in the way of standardizing quality measurement and assurance has been dictated by government regulation. The government has, when paying for care through programs such as Medicare and Medicaid, a responsibility to ensure both the quality and cost-effectiveness of the care for which they pay. Unfortunately, the two aspects often become confused. In some cases, the idea of quality has taken on more of a focus on medical necessity—is the care provided medically necessary? Ideally, medical necessity should mean neither more nor less than is appropriate. In the past, the pressures to achieve cost-effectiveness seem to have tilted that equation toward ensuring that the government does not pay for more than it must. To be fair, it may only seem that such is the focus, but the evidence has been pretty strong and consistent. The requirement for utilization review was focused more on cost saving than on quality. You should not assume that government agencies are not concerned with quality. They certainly are. It is just much harder to measure and ensure. Government concern with quality is shown by requirements that providers create and maintain QA programs and, more recently, quality improvement programs.

There is a major difference in emphasis in externally mandated quality requirements and in internal, provider-administered, quality improvement. Typically, externally mandated requirements do not focus on improving the average performance of providers over time. They are aimed at weeding out poor performers and ensuring that providers meet minimal standards. Internal quality improvement, on the other hand, is designed to sustain and improve quality within the organizations.

Federal and state governments are concerned with quality of care, particularly for consumers covered by government-run eligibility plans such as Medicare and Medicaid. Government attempts at ensuring quality fall into three distinct approaches: regulation of quality, public information initiatives, and quality-related research.

Regulation of Quality

Government regulation of long-term care covers both regulation of quality and regulation of cost. Regulation of quality takes the form of measuring providers against minimally acceptable levels and punishing those providers who fall below those levels. It mostly involves setting standards, designing survey processes to monitor compliance, and determining sanctions for noncompliance. Because of the dominant role of Medicare and Medicaid in reimbursement of nursing facilities, subacute care, home health care, and hospice care, the federal government is the major source of quality regulations for these providers. For others not generally covered by Medicare and Medicaid (most notably assisted living/residential care), the states determine the quality regulations. This is changing somewhat as states increasingly use Medicaid waivers to cover some residential care consumers.

History of Government Quality Regulations

While government entities, particularly the federal government, have long regulated quality in long-term care, that regulation has evolved through several different formats and initiatives.

Quality Assurance—Quality assurance was one of the early forms of quality regulation required by the Medicare and Medicaid system. QA is a process of meeting quality standards and assuring that care reaches an acceptable level. Nursing homes typically set QA thresholds to comply with regulations. They may also create standards that go beyond regulations. QA is a reactive, retrospective effort to examine why a facility failed to meet certain standards. QA activities do improve quality, but efforts frequently end once the standard is met (CMS, 2013a). Because it was required for several decades, it was long seen as the primary method of measuring and ensuring quality in long-term care organizations. It is regulation driven, and, as with many regulations, much of the focus was on documentation of compliance rather than on the actual quality itself. Many long-term care managers and staff saw it as a requirement, not something they do by choice, which limited its effectiveness. QA relied on reviews of reports of infections, accidents, transfer of residents (utilization review), and administration of medications to identify any real or potential problem areas. It was focused as much on cost savings as it was on quality.

CQI—CQI, also called performance improvement (PI), has been discussed earlier. It is a proactive and continuous study of processes with the intent to prevent or decrease the likelihood of problems by identifying areas of opportunity and testing new approaches to fix underlying causes of persistent/systemic problems. CQI/PI in nursing homes aims to improve processes involved in health care delivery and resident quality of life. It can make good quality even better (CMS, 2013a).

QAPI—QAPI is the merger of quality assurance and performance improvement, and it has replaced them. Both involve seeking and using information. QAPI is a data-driven, proactive approach to improving the quality of life, care, and services in nursing homes. The activities of QAPI involve members at all levels of the organization to identify opportunities for improvement, address gaps in systems or processes, develop and implement an improvement or corrective plan, and continuously monitor effectiveness of interventions (CMS, 2013a). Nursing home providers will be required to implement a QAPI program as prescribed by Section 6102(c) of the Affordable Care Act (Fosco, 2013).

Minimum Data Set for Long-Term Care—In 1998, the federal government mandated use of a minimum data set (MDS) as a means of structuring the assessment of long-term care (nursing home) residents. The long-term care MDS is a standardized, primary screening and assessment tool of health status that forms the foundation of the comprehensive assessment for all residents in a Medicare- and/or Medicaid-certified long-term care facility. The MDS contains items that measure physical, psychological, and psychosocial functioning. The items in the MDS give a multidimensional view of the patient's functional capacities and help staff to identify health problems (CMS, 2012a).

Using information collected from these assessments, the government provides the facility with a list of identified deficiencies when compared with the standards.

OASIS—The Centers for Medicare & Medicaid Services (CMS) uses a similar assessment tool for home health care, called the Outcomes and Assessment Information Set (OASIS). OASIS is a key component of Medicare's partnership with the home care industry to foster and monitor improved home healthcare outcomes and is proposed to be an integral part of the revised conditions of participation for Medicare-certified home health agencies. OASIS is a group of data elements that:

1. Represents core items of a comprehensive assessment for an adult home care patient; and
2. Forms the basis for measuring patient outcomes for purposes of outcome-based quality improvement (CMS, 2012b).

Quality Improvement Organizations—The CMS now contracts with one organization in each state, as well as the District of Columbia, Puerto Rico, and the U.S. Virgin Islands, to serve as that state/jurisdiction's quality improvement organization (QIO) contractor. QIOs are private, mostly not-for-profit organizations staffed by professionals, mostly doctors and other healthcare professionals, who are trained to review medical care and help beneficiaries with complaints about the quality of care and to implement improvements in the quality of care available throughout the spectrum of care. QIO contracts are 3 years in length.

By law, the mission of the QIO program is to improve the effectiveness, efficiency, economy, and quality of services delivered to Medicare beneficiaries. Based on this statutory charge and the CMS's program experience, the CMS identifies the core functions of the QIO program as:

- Improving quality of care for beneficiaries
- Protecting the integrity of the Medicare trust fund by ensuring that Medicare pays only for services and goods that are reasonable and necessary and that are provided in the most appropriate setting
- Protecting beneficiaries by expeditiously addressing individual complaints, such as beneficiary complaints; provider-based notice appeals; violations of the Emergency Medical Treatment and Labor Act; and other related responsibilities as articulated in QIO-related law (CMS, 2013b)

Pay-for-Performance—As part of its overall quality initiative, the CMS also began several pay-for-performance programs, with a goal of improving quality and lowering costs. The pay-for-performance (also known as P4P) programs involve identifying procedures for which providers will not be reimbursed such as procedures resulting from facility-acquired infections. Other preventable conditions might include falls, catheter-based urinary infections, and pressure ulcers. While the concept sounds good, not all agree with its effectiveness. Some have suggested that it is more effective as a cost-control measure, but dispute the relationship between payment and quality. For example, one study that compared P4P-participating hospitals and similar ones (both in a large multihospital system) showed no significantly different rates of improvement in the quality of care provided by the P4P-participating facilities (Grossbart, 2008). Providers object to the implication that they will improve quality—or decrease provision of poor quality—if they are paid more.

Public Information Quality Initiatives

In recent years, government agencies have increasingly attempted to provide the public with information about healthcare quality with the intent of creating more knowledgeable consumers capable of judging quality for themselves. The most ambitious such project occurred in late 2002, when the CMS announced a nationwide quality initiative for nursing care facilities.

Nursing Home Compare—Under the initiative, the CMS released comparative data for all nursing facilities serving residents covered by Medicare and/or Medicaid. The approach was to identify certain quality measures and to show how individual facilities compared with the preset standard and with each other. Among the first quality measures chosen were the number of residents with loss of ability in daily tasks, residents with pressure sores, residents with pain and infections, and residents in physical restraints.

CMS makes information about these measures and how providers rate available on its website in a section titled, "Nursing Home Compare." On this site, consumers can get information about individual nursing homes, including number of beds and type of ownership; data on the selected quality measures; results of state surveys; and information about staffing. Although this initiative is quite different in nature from internal quality improvement programs, there is a relationship. The CMS initiative relies on reports submitted by the facilities through the MDS information that all must file with the government agency. The initiative uses numerical data in much the same way as was described earlier in the "Quality Assurance" paragraph. The CMS does not attempt to improve quality but strives to pressure the facilities to do so.

Similar initiatives concerning hospitals, home health providers, dialysis facilities, and physicians are also in place. There is at this writing no compare program for assisted living (not covered by Medicare).

Five-Star Ratings—In June 2008, the CMS announced the launch of a ranking system of America's nursing homes, giving each a star rating. The CMS anticipated that its new Five-Star Quality Rating system "will provide a composite view of the quality and safety information currently on Nursing Home Compare to help beneficiaries, their families, and caregivers compare nursing homes more easily" (CMS, 2008, p. 11).

A recent analysis of the impact of the five-star quality rating system determined that "Nursing Home Compare" has increased consumer awareness and improved facility performance. All but three states (Hawaii, Montana, and Idaho) showed an increase in four-star or five-star nursing facilities, while there was an 8% increase in facilities earning four or five stars, with five states posting the greatest increase in five-star ratings: Delaware, nearly 23 percent; Tennessee, about 16 percent; Georgia, nearly 15 percent; Indiana and Oregon around 14 percent (Hoban, 2013).

There have also been numerous efforts by state governments to publish report card–type information about providers in their state jurisdictions.

Quality-Related Research

There are several government agencies involved in quality-related research. They fund research studies and disseminate the results. They also serve as a valuable source for quality improvement guidelines, measurement tools, quality indicators, and other data.

Agency for Healthcare Research and Quality—Foremost among these resources is the Agency for Healthcare Research and Quality (AHRQ). Formerly known as the Agency for Health Care Policy and Research, this organization is a source of many studies concerning healthcare quality. It regularly produces reports documenting research studies it has funded. It has developed quality indicators (quality improvements) that serve as valuable measures used both by researchers and by individual provider organizations. The Agency for Healthcare Research and Quality also maintains the National Guideline Clearinghouse, a centralized source of information about clinical practice guidelines that provides recommendations for how care should be given.

National Library of Medicine—The National Library of Medicine, on the campus of the National Institutes of Health in Bethesda, Maryland, is the world's largest medical library (NLM, 2012). It collects materials and provides information and research services in all areas of biomedicine and health care and works closely with the AHRQ to produce and disseminate data, guidelines, and other information for researchers and practitioners.

Private Quality Programs

Not all systemwide quality improvement efforts come from the government. Several private organizations and coalitions of organizations have produced their own quality programs. In fact, there has been such a proliferation of quality programs it is difficult to list them without omitting some. A good effort is made to do so, but apologies are in order in advance for any that were inadvertently missed.

Quality First

In 2002, several leading long-term care professional organizations created a voluntary five-year initiative designed to improve the quality of nursing home care and other long-term care services. That initiative, called Quality First: A Covenant for Healthy,

Affordable, and Ethical Long-Term Care, was developed by the American Association of Homes and Services for the Aging, the American Health Care Association (AHCA), and the Alliance for Quality Nursing Home Care. These organizations signed a covenant that reads as follows:

Through Quality First we are collectively and individually committed to healthy, affordable, and ethical long-term care. We commit to achieving excellence in the quality of care and services for older persons and strengthening public trust. We recognize that confidence on the part of consumers and policy makers is lacking and must be restored. We are committed to taking bold and deliberate steps, embedded in the principles of this Covenant to ensure quality. We believe that by doing so, there will be measurable improvements in defined outcomes as well as in ethical, compassionate, and resident-centered practices in the provision of care for those who are frail, elderly, or disabled. (AHCA, 2007)

The covenant is rooted in the following seven principles, designed to "cultivate and nourish an environment of continuous quality improvement, openness and leadership" (AHCA, 2007, p. 1):

1. Continuous quality assurance and quality improvement
2. Public disclosure and accountability
3. Patient/resident and family rights
4. Workforce excellence
5. Public input and community involvement
6. Ethical practices
7. Financial stewardship (AHCA, 2007)

Quality First represented a major commitment by long-term care providers to assure consumers, consumer advocacy organizations, and government that they will provide high-quality care. It is the most significant such initiative to date, in part because of the many providers represented by these organizations and because they are committing to going beyond what may be required by government regulation. In doing this, they are accepting their individual and collective responsibility to gain the trust and confidence of the public. The Quality First organizations originally outlined several specific outcomes to be achieved:

1. There will be continued improvement in compliance with federal regulations.
2. There will be demonstrable progress in promoting financial integrity and preventing occurrences of fraud.
3. There will be demonstrable progress in the quality of clinical outcomes and prevention of confirmed abuse and neglect.
4. There will be measurable improvements in all CMS continuous quality improvement measures.

5. High rates on consumer satisfaction surveys will indicate improved consumer satisfaction with services.
6. There will be demonstrable improvement in employee retention and turnover rates (AHCA, 2007).

Although Quality First is a private initiative, the participating organizations have pledged to work with the government, particularly the CMS. They use the quality improvement measures adopted by the CMS and report on their progress to government officials on an annual basis. They also point out that Quality First and the CMS share several common goals:

- Achieve excellence in the quality of care and services
- Emphasize continuous quality improvement
- Publicly report results to strengthen public confidence and trust (AHCA/NCAL, 2004)

AHCA/National Center for Assisted Living Quality Award

The American Health Care Association/National Center for Assisted Living is a nonprofit federation of state health organizations, together representing more than 10,000 nonprofit and for-profit assisted living, nursing facility, and subacute care providers, as well as providers of services to the developmentally disabled. Together, these organizations care for more than 1.5 million elderly and disabled individuals nationally.

To assist its members in achieving the goals of Quality First, the AHCA developed the AHCA/National Center for Assisted Living Quality Award: a criteria-based program that recognizes a commitment to performance excellence by member facilities. Quality award recipients demonstrate their commitment to deliver ever-improving value to residents and other customers, to improve overall organizational effectiveness and capabilities, and to champion organizational and personal learning. Facilities may apply for recognition and awards at three levels, each of which requires a more detailed and comprehensive demonstration of systematic quality. Facilities must receive a quality award at each level to progress to the next level. Since launching its quality initiative in February 2012, the AHCA announced that nationwide, 6,206 member skilled nursing care centers have achieved one or more of the initiative's four goals. Among the achievers are 68 skilled nursing centers that have accomplished all four goals. The Quality Initiative Recognition Program recognizes AHCA nursing center members that demonstrate the attainment of one or more of the following four AHCA quality initiative goals:

- Safely reduce hospital readmissions within 30 days during a skilled nursing stay by 15%
- Increase staff stability by reducing nursing staff turnover by 15%

- Increase customer satisfaction by having 90% of residents and families willing to recommend their center to others
- Safely reduce the off-label use of antipsychotics by 15% (Advance Healthcare Network, 2013)

Advancing Excellence in America's Nursing Homes

Advancing Excellence in America's Nursing Homes is an ongoing, coalition-based campaign concerned with how we care for the elderly, chronically ill, and disabled, as well as those recuperating in a nursing home environment.

The mission of the Advancing Excellence in America's Nursing Homes campaign is to help nursing homes achieve excellence in the quality of care and quality of life for the more than 1.5 million residents of America's nursing homes by:

1. Establishing and supporting an infrastructure of local area networks for excellence.
2. Strengthening the workforce.
3. Improving clinical and organizational outcomes.

The campaign works to achieve its mission by:

1. Helping nursing homes make a difference in the lives of residents and staff by focusing on nine goals related to its mission.
2. Providing free, practical, and evidence-based resources to support quality improvement efforts in America's nursing homes.
3. Providing support to those on the front lines of nursing home care.
4. Promoting open communication and transparency among families, residents, and nursing home staff.

The campaign works closely with other national nursing home quality initiatives to streamline efforts and to prevent duplication of efforts. National quality initiatives include Quality First, the Nursing Home Quality Initiative, the Culture Change movement, and the Quality Improvement Organization (QIO) (Advancing Excellence in America's Nursing Homes, 2014).

Alliance for Quality Nursing Home Care

The Alliance for Quality Nursing Home Care was the third major organization involved in the creation of Quality First to sign on to the Quality First covenant. The alliance is a coalition of 14 national provider organizations that care for elderly and disabled patients. In 2013, the alliance and the AHCA agreed to join their organizations and operate under the AHCA name.

Although there is undoubtedly some cross-membership among these three organizations, it is clear that they represent the vast majority of providers of institutional long-term care. Their commitment to actively work toward the goals of the covenant and to work with government and other long-term care stakeholders is a major step toward achieving a high level of confidence in the quality of long-term care received by consumers.

American Health Quality Association

The American Health Quality Association is a charitable, educational, not-for-profit national membership association dedicated to healthcare quality through community-based, independent quality evaluation and improvement programs. It represents QIOs and professionals working to improve healthcare quality and patient safety. American Health Quality Association member organizations assist federal and state agencies and provider organizations by providing technical support. They work with long-term care providers such as nursing facilities and home healthcare agencies, providing them with guidelines, procedures, and hands-on assistance as needed.

Through participation both nationally and at the local level, the American Health Quality Association and the QIOs support Advancing Excellence in America's Nursing Homes, an initiative to make nursing homes better places to live, work, and visit. QIOs serve as coordinators of local Advancing Excellence activities and incorporate the initiative's resources into their work with nursing homes. Tools and resources to support improvement on nine organizational and clinical topics can be found on the Advancing Excellence website (AHQA, 2013).

National Quality Forum

The National Quality Forum (NQF) is a private, not-for-profit membership organization created to develop and implement a national strategy for healthcare quality measurement and reporting. The mission of the National Quality Forum is to improve the quality of American health care by setting national priorities and goals for performance improvement, endorsing national consensus standards for measuring and publicly reporting on performance, and promoting the attainment of national goals through education and outreach programs (NQF, 2008). The NQF develops and implements quality measures, working with government and private agencies. The NQF is a nonprofit, nonpartisan, public service organization. NQF reviews, endorses, and recommends use of standardized healthcare performance measures. Performance measures, also called quality measures, are essential tools used to evaluate how well healthcare services are being delivered. The NQF's endorsed measures are often invisible at the clinical bedside but quietly influence the care delivered to millions of patients every day (NQF, 2013).

Accreditation Organizations

There are several private accreditation organizations involved with long-term care, including the Joint Commission, the Commission on Accreditation of Rehabilitation Facilities (CARF International), the Continuing Care Accreditation Commission, and the Community Health Accreditation Program. It is important to note that all these organizations require a strong emphasis on quality improvement in the provider organizations they accredit.

Private Foundations

Numerous private foundations provide funding for quality-related research and project implementation. Among the largest and best known is the Robert Wood Johnson Foundation, which has a mission to improve the health and health care of all Americans. Its efforts focus on improving both the health of everyone in America and their health care—how it's delivered, how it's paid for, and how well it does for patients and their families (RWJF, 2014). Because the Robert Wood Johnson Foundation has long had an interest in chronic care, it is a very valuable source of information for long-term care providers. The Robert Wood Johnson Foundation is not the only private foundation supporting this type of research. There are too many others to list all of them here.

College and University Research Institutes

Many colleges and universities maintain research institutes or other organizational divisions addressing quality of care. They generally rely on private and/or government grant funds to conduct research and disseminate the results. They are valuable sources of needed information.

A Combination of Efforts

These quality resources, both private and government sponsored, serve several purposes. First, they bring a great deal of emphasis to the topic of quality care, giving it the prominence it deserves. As noted by both the CMS and the signatories to Quality First, consumers of long-term care have a right to expect high-quality care and to have access to enough information to adequately judge whether the care they receive meets those expectations.

Second, these initiatives make it easier for individual providers to develop and maintain quality improvement programs. It can be difficult for small provider organizations to allocate the staff and other resources needed for a good quality improvement program. By taking advantage of the processes, guidelines, standards, and quality indicators available from these sources, they can avoid the necessity of creating their own.

Finally, they help bring a high degree of uniformity and commonality to quality programs across the continuum. As providers become better at quality improvement in their own organizations, the level of quality in the long-term care system becomes better—and consumers are able to have a higher level of confidence in that system.

Other Organizations

There are many other organizations, associations, and coalitions working to improve long-term care—too many to list here. All strive for the same goals: the best possible care for consumers.

■ Provider-Administered Quality Improvement Programs

There are several programs used by long-term and other healthcare providers to ensure quality of care within their organizations. The term *quality improvement* is used here to cover them in general terms.

Quality improvement began in the acute care sector of health care and has more recently been adapted to long-term care. This has something to do with the fact that the Omnibus Budget Reconciliation Act now requires providers to implement and maintain quality improvement programs, but to be fair to those providers, many had embraced the concept well before that happened. Another impetus for development of quality improvement programs, both in acute care and in long-term care, has come from accrediting agencies such as the Joint Commission. Healthcare organizations seeking accreditation must have such programs in place. Even though these programs may be in place primarily because of regulations or encouragement from external entities, they fit the definition of *internal* because they are facility based or organization based and are implemented by staff of the organization.

Although several different types of quality improvement in long-term care are discussed, there are two that are most prominent: QA and CQI.

Developing a Quality Improvement Program

Creating an effective quality improvement program for a long-term care facility is not simply a matter of copying one developed for an acute care hospital. The focus is different, and the quality improvement plan must reflect that difference. In acute care, quality improvement focuses on episodes of care and ensuring the quality of care during those episodes. In long-term care facilities, the focus must be more on quality of life and must include ongoing monitoring and evaluation of physical, functional, and psychological indicators over a longer period of time (Cohan, 1997). The time period may include several acute episodes, but the overall objective of the quality improvement program is focused on the quality of life of the individual. What follows is a brief description of some of the important elements of a quality improvement program.

Top-Level Support

To begin with, a quality improvement program must have support from the very top levels of administration. In long-term care facilities, this includes the chief executive officer of the facility and, if part of a larger corporation, the corporate officers. Studies have shown a correlation between involvement of senior management and successful quality improvement. One such study found five significant roles and/or activities of senior management that are of most importance:

1. Personal engagement, characterized by advocacy for quality improvement efforts, participation in quality improvement teams, and dissemination of quality improvement data

2. Relationship with clinical staff, characterized by perceived understanding of clinical/professional staff activities and skill at negotiating with clinical/professional staff
3. Promotion of a quality improvement organizational culture, characterized by goal setting consistent with quality improvement, and consensus-driven interdepartmental and/or multidisciplinary norms
4. Support of quality improvement with organizational structures, characterized by the existence of quality improvement teams and linkages of quality improvement teams to central decision makers
5. Procurement of organizational resources, characterized by procuring and allocating adequate staffing and information technology capability (Larson, 2003)

This does not necessarily mean that the chief executive officer must be involved in day-to-day quality improvement activities, but he or she must stay on top of the program. In most facilities, the program director will be someone who has other clinical duties, because many cannot afford to designate a full-time position for quality improvement. In multifacility organizations, a full-time quality director may be designated by the corporate offices and shared among facilities. In either case, there should be a quality steering committee or council that oversees the work of other committees and individuals. That committee or council should include the top clinical and administrative staff members, including the chief executive officer, the director of nursing services, the medical director, and any others who are in charge of major divisions or service areas.

Mission Based

Ideally, the quality improvement program should be an integral part of the mission of the organization. Most organizational mission statements include some, usually vague, reference to providing quality of care. If an organization has such a statement and really means it, then it can develop a quality improvement program based on the intent of the mission statement.

Defining the Customers

To improve quality, the organization must define who its customers are—those residents or other individuals served by the organization. If it already has a good strategic planning process in place, such data are probably available. However, a special effort should be made to be sure the data are up to date because such information can easily become obsolete.

Standards

Having defined its customers, the organization then needs to identify what it wants for them in terms of quality. Although there are many ways of defining that quality, there are some good benchmarking tools available to use, including predetermined quality standards. Standards represent levels of quality against which the care given in an organization can be measured. Some organizations develop their own, but there are many good quality standards that have been set by various regulatory, accrediting, and professional organizations. These standards may represent an optimal level of quality, but more often they are set at the acceptable level, recognizing that the optimum may not be achievable, at least not at first. As such, standards become dynamic, continuously moving higher toward an optimal level as each standard is achieved (Larson, 1997). When standards developed by someone else are used, they should be evaluated carefully to see how closely they match the outcomes desired for the organization's own customers. If needed, the standards can be adapted to better serve their needs. However, in most cases, that will not be necessary until the quality improvement program becomes more mature.

Measurement

Once an organization has determined the standards against which its quality will be measured, it is time to move on to the measurement itself. Much of the measurement of quality is accomplished by monitoring certain key indicators, such as the number of residents with physical restraints, number of medication errors, or infection rates. Determining which indicators to use takes some effort, but once they have been chosen, the actual measurement is relatively uncomplicated. However, it can be time consuming. Staff may need to organize into teams to measure the key indicators against the standards that have been chosen. Most likely, structure, process, and outcomes measures will all be used.

Evaluation

When measurement has taken place, producing a volume of data sufficient to draw conclusions, it is up to the quality improvement steering committee to evaluate how well the organization is doing. Initially, this probably involves comparing its performance in key indicator areas against standards set by outside agencies. As the program grows, the committee will increasingly want to compare current results with earlier results to determine how much progress has been made.

Improvement

Because the ultimate purpose of a quality improvement program is to improve quality in specific areas, the next step is to identify appropriate corrective steps to take to improve the quality level in a particular area. This may include changing procedures, reassigning resources such as staff or equipment, education and/or training of staff, restructuring of organizational responsibilities, or other similar steps. In some cases, the solutions may be difficult and expensive. For example, excessive use of physical restraints might indicate that there are not enough staff available, leading to a need to increase the staffing complement. On the other hand, it may simply involve retraining of staff, at little expense. Each quality area will have its own method of improvement, often a combination of several.

Ongoing Measurement and Evaluation

Once corrective steps have been taken, measurement against the standards must be ongoing. If measurement over a period of time indicates that significant progress has been made, the quality improvement team may determine that further steps are not needed. However, they may instead decide to raise the standard and attempt to reach it. Quality improvement is an ongoing program that continues to move on to new areas while keeping track of previously studied areas to make sure there has not been slippage back to an unacceptable level.

■ Quality Teams

Quality improvement borrows another philosophy from Deming's total quality management—namely, that the people involved in doing a job are usually best suited to solving problems related to that job. Instead of an individual or small committee doing all of the measurement and improvement, quality improvement usually involves teams consisting of staff closely involved with the area being evaluated. They do report to a steering committee, but the individual teams deal directly with identifying and solving the problem. For instance, staying with the example used earlier of a high nosocomial infection rate, the team would include at least representatives from the medical staff, nursing, others involved in hands-on care, and possibly outside consultants with expertise in infection control. A facility may have several quality teams at work at any given time, with some overlap in the personnel assigned to them. For that reason, the number of teams should not be too high.

■ Technology

Omission of a discussion about how valuable technology can be to a quality improvement plan would be remiss. Much of the work of the quality teams, the designated quality director, and the steering committee relies on getting access to data that are current and accurate. Although much of that record keeping was handled manually in the past, it can now be computerized. The result is not only less to do but much more accurate and usable information. There are some excellent commercial software packages available that do much of the work, although the quality improvement team will still need to interpret it and act on it.

■ Summary

Quality in long-term care is of highest importance to everyone involved. There has been much improvement in quality in recent years, but there is more to be done. The most significant development has been the widespread acceptance of formal quality improvement programs as essential for good care. The number of such programs, both public and private, has grown and they continue to evolve into ever-improving entities.

It is vital that any long-term care administrator understand that and understand how quality improvement is accomplished. Although the techniques of quality improvement are still being developed in many areas, particularly in long-term care, there is already enough information and technical support available for any long-term care organization to develop and implement an effective quality improvement program.

■ Vocabulary Terms

The following terms are included in this chapter. They are important to the topics and issues discussed here and should become familiar to readers. Some of the terms are also found in other chapters but may be used in different contexts. They may not be fully defined herein. Thus, readers may wish to seek other supplementary definitions.

Advancing Excellence in America's
   Nursing Homes
American Health Quality
   Association
CARF International
continuous quality improvement
   (CQI)
Five-Star Quality Rating System
Joint Commission
National Quality Forum (NQF)

outcomes measures
quality
quality assurance (QA)
Quality First
quality steering committee
quality teams
standards
total quality management
utilization review

■ Discussion Questions

The following questions are presented to assist you in understanding the material covered in this chapter. They tend to be general but lend themselves to detailed answers, which can be found in the chapter.

1. Why is quality difficult to define?
2. Why is quality of life of particular importance in long-term care?
3. What are the purpose and functions of a quality assurance (QA) committee?
4. How do process, structure, and outcomes measures differ?
5. What are the differences between QA and continuous quality improvement (CQI)? The similarities?
6. What are quality indicators?
7. What incentives are there, if any, for individual long-term care providers or groups of providers to think in terms of the overall system when focusing on quality?

8. What disincentives exist in the payment system when it comes to improving quality? How can they be overcome?

■ References

Advance Healthcare Network. (2013, November 1). *More than 6,200 member centers reach AHCA quality initiative goals.* Retrieved from http://healthcare-executive-insight.advanceweb.com/News/Long -Term-Care-News/More-Than-6200-Member-Centers-Reach-AHCA-Quality-Initiative-Goals.aspx.

Advancing Excellence in America's Nursing Homes. (2014). *Program & description.* Retrieved from https://www.nhqualitycampaign.org.

American Health Care Association (AHCA). (2007). *Quality First: The covenant.* Washington, DC: American Health Care Association.

American Health Care Association/National Center for Assisted Living (AHCA/NCAL). (2004). *The quality connection: Bridging Quality First and the CMS.* Washington, DC: American Health Care Association/National Center for Assisted Living.

American Health Quality Association (AHQA). (2013). *Quality improvement organizations: Partners.* Retrieved from http://www.ahqa.org/quality-improvement-organizations.

Centers for Medicare & Medicaid Services (CMS). (2008, June 18). *Improving the Nursing Home Compare Web site: The Five-Star Nursing Home Quality Rating System.* Retrieved from Centers for Medicare & Medicaid Services: https://www.cms.gov/Medicare/Provider-Enrollment-and-Certification/ SurveyCertificationGenInfo/Downloads/ImprovingNHCompare.pdf.

Centers for Medicare & Medicaid Services (CMS). (2012a, February 27). *Long term care minimum data set (MDS).* Retrieved from http://www.cms.gov/Research-Statistics-Data-and-Systems/Files -for-Order/IdentifiableDataFiles/LongTermCareMinimumDataSetMDS.html.

Centers for Medicare & Medicaid Services (CMS). (2012b, March 5). *Outcome and Assessment Information Set (OASIS) background.* Retrieved from http://www.cms.gov/Medicare/Quality-Initiatives -Patient-Assessment-Instruments/OASIS/Background.html.

Centers for Medicare & Medicaid Services (CMS). (2013a, June 5). *QAPI description and background.* Retrieved from http://cms.gov/Medicare/Provider-Enrollment-and-Certification/QAPI/qapidefinition .html.

Centers for Medicare & Medicaid Services (CMS). (2013b, October 13). *Quality improvement organizations.* Retrieved from http://www.cms.gov/Medicare/Quality-Initiatives-Patient-Assessment -Instruments/QualityImprovementOrgs/index.html?redirect=/QualityImprovementOrgs/.

Cohan, M. A. (1997). Improving quality in long-term care. In C. Meisenheimer (Ed.), *Improving quality: A guide to effective programs* (2nd ed., pp. 507–520). Gaithersburg, MD: Aspen Publishers.

Donabedian, A. (1966). Evaluating the quality of medical care. *Milbank Memorial Fund Quarterly,* (44), No. 3, Part 2. Pp. 166–203.

Donabedian, A. (1991). Reflections on the effectiveness of quality assurance. In H. D. Palmer (Ed.), *Striving for quality in health care: An inquiry into policy and practice* (59–128). Ann Arbor, MI: Health Administration Press.

Fosco, C. (2013, October 18). *QAPI: Insights from the experts—Experts in the field offer some practical advice for the QAPI-averse.* Retrieved from http://www.providermagazine.com/columns/Pages /QAPI-Insights-From-The-Experts.aspx.

Grossbart, S. (2008, Spring). *Effectiveness of pay for performance as a quality improvement strategy. Prescriptions for excellence in health care,* pp. 2–4.

Hoban, S. (2013, July 11). *Nursing home quality improves under Five-Star Quality Rating System, study finds*. Retrieved from http://www.ltlmagazine.com/news-item/nursing-home-quality-improves-under-five-star-quality-rating-system-study-finds.

Larson, S. (1997). Standards: The Basis of a Quality Improvement Program. In C. Meisenheimer (Ed.), *Improving Quality: A Guide to Effective Programs* (2nd ed., pp. 33–41). Gaithersburg, MD: Aspen Publishers.

Larson, S. (2003). The roles of senior management in quality improvement efforts: What are the key components? *Journal of Healthcare Management*, Vol. 348, No. 1, p. 20.

McLaughlin, C., & Kaluzny, A. (2006). Defining quality improvement. In C. A. McLaughlin (Ed.), *Continuous quality improvement in health care: Theory, implementations, and applications* (3rd ed., pp. 3–40). Sudbury, MA: Jones and Bartlett.

National Library of Medicine (NLM). (2012, February 25). *Fact sheet National Library of Medicine*. Retrieved from http://www.nlm.nih.gov/pubs/factsheets/nlm.html.

National Quality Forum (NQF). (2008). *About us: Mission*. Retrieved from http://www.qualityforum.org/story/About_Us.aspx.

National Quality Forum (NQF). (2013). *Who we are*. Retrieved from http://www.qualityforum.org/who_we_are.aspx.

Robert Wood Johnson Foundation (RWJF). (2014). *Our mission*. Retrieved from http://www.rwjf.org/en/about-rwjf/our-mission.html.

Schiverick, B. (2008, October). An evidence-based quality agenda should be part of the everyday game plan. *Provider*, pp. 2–7.

Singh, D. (2010). *Effective management of long-term care facilities* (2nd ed.). Sudbury, MA: Jones and Bartlett Learning.

Sollecito, W., & Johnson, K. (2013). Defining quality improvement. In C. A. McLaughlin (Ed.), *McLaughlin and Kaluzny's continuous quality improvement in health care* (4th ed., pp. 1–48). Sudbury, MA: Jones & Bartlett Learning.

Wunderlich, G., & Kohler, P. (2001). *Improving the quality of long-term care*. Washington, DC: National Academies Press.

Ethical Issues in Long-Term Care

After completing this chapter, readers will be able to:

1. Understand the social and emotional impact of changes caused in the lives of individuals when long-term care is needed.

2. Discuss the ethical aspects of access to care, including rationing.

3. Define and discuss autonomy and the relationship between independence and self-determination.

4. Identify end-of-life issues and discuss their ethical and legal implications.

5. Understand the magnitude of the day-to-day needs of long-term care consumers and the efforts of providers to accommodate them.

6. Discuss management ethics and its role in a long-term care organization.

■ Introduction

> It has been said that the moral heart of a society can be judged by how well it provides for those at the dawn of life, those in the shadows of life, and those in the twilight of life. Nursing facilities are places of lengthening shadows at twilight. By and large they are the last refuge in our society's broader system—if such a tattered, patchwork arrangement of overlapping and conflicting programs can be called that—of social support and provision for the elderly, the frail, and those with chronic illness and disability. (Collopy, 1991, p. 1)

This statement, the introductory paragraph of a report dealing with nursing facility ethics, eloquently establishes the ethical responsibility of nursing facilities to meet the needs of some of society's most needy individuals. It applies equally well to other types of long-term care.

Yet describing the responsibilities of the long-term care field and knowing how to properly fulfill those responsibilities are two entirely different matters. The changes in long-term care discussed earlier have raised some very serious, difficult-to-answer ethical questions throughout the field. Needed changes in the delivery system or the financing system cannot be made without making some major changes in how long-term care and those who use it are viewed.

The discussion of necessity tends to focus on specific situations, such as those involving autonomy and informed consent, and their solutions, such as the use of ethics committees. However, before even getting into that kind of detail, a brief look at the larger overriding ethical issues associated with the provision and financing of long-term care is in order. If specific problem areas are to be addressed, the reader must first have a basic foundation of understanding on which to build. What is needed is what the Hastings Center calls

> A guiding moral vision ... to focus the efforts of individual caregivers, families, support groups, advocacy organizations, and local communities. It is needed to make the growing presence of chronic illness in our midst an occasion for strengthening the ties of mutual respect, benevolence, and caring between young and old, sick and well, in families and communities. (Jennings, 1988, p. 3)

An understanding of chronic illness and functional disability and the types of ethical conflicts these conditions and their treatment pose is crucial. Ethical questions are easily answered if everyone agrees and if everyone approaches them from the same viewpoint, yet it is the nature of ethical questions that such consensus seldom occurs. Most ethical dilemmas occur when there are strongly held beliefs on both sides of the question or when people have little ability to change their positions.

■ Emotional Impact on Consumers

It is important that the emotional impact on consumers of long-term care be considered. With the onset of a chronic illness or disability, people find that the most intimate aspects of their lives are changed. They can no longer do the things that have been so important to their way of living. If they have been employed, they are no longer, or at best have to find other, less strenuous forms of work.

Most of the elderly of today grew up during and immediately after the Great Depression of the 1930s. They have a strong work ethic, and many do not retire until forced to, usually by some physical disability. Hobbies or avocations that have stimulated them physically and mentally are no longer possible. Whether they played golf or bridge, were gardeners or seamstresses, they may now have to abandon those activities, resulting in a feeling of emotional loss that few fully appreciate until it happens. If the disabling condition is such that a person needs to be admitted to a nursing care or other long-term care facility, it may mean separation from a husband or wife of many years—perhaps the greatest change that person has ever experienced. It also represents a significant loss of personal freedom (Agich, 2009). Whether these changes come on suddenly, as can happen with occurrence of a stroke, or gradually, the disruption they cause in previously orderly lives can be devastating.

Even worse than the dislocation that so often accompanies the need for long-term care is the emotional strain caused by the lack of ability to perform even the most basic functions without assistance. People in this situation must bear the indignity of having someone else, usually a stranger, feed them, bathe them, and even help them with their toileting needs. That kind of dependency is an affront to their sense of independence, to say nothing of any modesty they may possess. The emotional reaction to changes of this magnitude can range from passive compliance to anger, from a sense of relief and gratitude for the help to a feeling of great loss. It also often results in depression, one of the most common problems of the elderly.

Because people afflicted by disabling conditions seldom have the option of fully overcoming those conditions, they must struggle to readjust their very lives to living with the condition in the best way they can. Their standing in society changes, often for the worse. Individuals who have been accustomed to making their own decisions are no longer able (or allowed) to do so. For someone who has always been strong and relied on by others, having to rely on those others can be difficult and frequently degrading.

One of the more subtle, but no less devastating, aspects of chronic illness is the diminution of a person's perceived role as an active contributor to society. We all need to be needed, to feel that we are doing our part. When elderly or handicapped people lose the ability to provide for themselves or others, they lose some of their pride. The perception of such loss, whether factual or not, can be equally devastating.

Living with these dramatic changes in their lives requires a process of negotiation in which people attempt to adjust their way of doing things with minimum loss of purpose, coherence, and meaning in their lives (Collopy, 1991). It is the ethical responsibility of all who are in any way involved with long-term care to help them make these adjustments as easily and smoothly as possible.

The focus of this discussion is about ethical issues in long-term care, not ethical and legal issues in long-term care. There is no question about the interrelationship between ethical and legal matters, and certain legal topics are discussed. In fact, they are often difficult to separate. However, the legal issues, while closely related, are (or should be) based on the ethical issues. By focusing on the ethical dimensions, this discussion tries to avoid getting overly involved in the details of the legal system, which is a complex, highly technical topic area, one about which there are numerous relevant texts.

■ Access to Long-Term Care

Any discussion of ethical issues relating to long-term care must start with the issue of getting that care in the first place. Access to long-term care is far from universal. It is closely related to financing, but there are ethical implications that go well beyond mere payment or nonpayment.

In the current reimbursement-driven long-term care system, access is usually determined by availability of reimbursement. The efforts by Medicare and Medicaid to reduce their costs and to pay for care in the most cost-effective setting and manner has had a major effect on how and when the constituents of those plans can access long-term care. In the private sector, insurance companies and managed care organizations also play a much more direct role in determining when and how care is provided. They are reacting to higher healthcare costs and to pressures from their constituents, mostly employers with their own cost-cutting needs.

The result is that long-term care consumers often have little real choice in deciding when, how, and where they receive their care unless they are wealthy and do not have to rely on the approval of others. As has been discussed in earlier chapters, even people with private financial resources usually end up exhausting them and eventually having to rely on the public system. When they do, their access to long-term care services becomes limited and, to a large degree, under the control of others.

The issue of access goes beyond merely the question of whether a person gets long-term care services. More often it focuses on the types of services received. Determination of whether care is received in an institutional setting (such as a nursing care, subacute care, or residential care facility) or at home with supportive services (such as home care, hospice, or day care) is supposedly made on the basis of which type of care would be most appropriate. However, in reality, the decision often depends on financing, regulations, or even politics. For example, the Affordable Care Act of 2010 combines aspects of all three. The actual consumer and his or her family have only limited say in the decision.

We tend to assume that all individuals prefer to continue to live in their own homes. Is that assumption really based on what we feel is good for the consumer, or is it sometimes influenced by the comparatively lower costs associated with home-based care? Whatever the reason for believing it, the assumption is not necessarily valid in all cases. Moving to an institution may, in some circumstances, be welcomed. It may provide a better quality of life than an individual is capable of achieving at home, even with sporadic assistance. It may also represent escape from the loneliness, isolation, and danger of a solitary house or apartment (Collopy, 1991). We have an ethical responsibility to accede to the wishes of the consumer if at all possible.

Few individuals can afford to pay for their long-term care out of pocket. The costs are just too high and last for too long. Long-term care is not a sudden catastrophe from which one recovers quickly and then, after the fact, looks for ways to pay for it. It is ongoing and well beyond the means of all but the wealthiest, meaning that most consumers of long-term care must rely on third-party sources for coverage. Even in those cases where financial coverage is not an issue, access may be limited by a lack of available services. In many geographic locations, the number of long-term care organizations providing appropriate types and levels of care may be limited or even entirely unavailable. Those that are available may have waiting lists. When the need is for a nursing facility or some other type of full-time institutionalization, the only available services may be a considerable distance away. Even when the consumer could get along with home-based care, adequate services may not be available, sometimes leaving institutionalization as the only remaining option. For many who need long-term care, particularly the elderly, being institutionalized in a facility far from home, family, and friends makes them feel as though they have been exiled. No wonder they see it as an undesirable, unacceptable alternative. Yet it may be the only one they have.

In fact, the very act of determining which level and type of care is needed by an individual has ethical overtones. For example, families will often care for a vulnerable family member at home as long as possible. Almost inevitably, the time comes when the family can no longer cope or provide safe, adequate care. When that happens, the question may come up as to whether they are looking after the interests of the family member or themselves. Even if, as is usually true, they really are thinking about what is best for their loved one, a lot of guilt is engendered. Society and the long-term care system need to develop an outlook that will support informal caregivers, encouraging their participation in the care of loved ones, but one that will release them from those responsibilities when appropriate.

So, what is the obligation of society when it comes to guaranteeing access to long-term care? When the idea of an ideal long-term care system is explored, one of the things most commonly discussed as characteristic of such a system is universal access. Yet in any such discussion, the difficulty of meeting the ideal must be recognized. There are many reasons universal access to long-term care poses a significant challenge. First is the magnitude of the problem—the large numbers of people who need long-term care or are expected to need it in the near future. Couple that volume of services needed with the ever-rising costs of providing those services and you have expense projections that appear to be beyond any hope of realization.

The ethical issue under discussion here is not whether we have an obligation to provide long-term care but how we balance that obligation with the reality of limited resources. It also involves balancing that ethical obligation with the countervailing obligation to meet other, equally compelling needs in our complex society. There is little question that the need for long-term care is great, but financing just hasn't been there, nor is the likelihood of such financing becoming available. The most oft-discussed solution is a new or expanded government program such as the Affordable Care Act. However, half a decade after that act was passed, it is still to be seen how much it will actually increase access to long-term care.

Ethics of Rationing

One outcome of these competing obligations is the question of the rationing of health care. The question of whether rationing of such a vital commodity as health care is ethical is one of the most divisive, hotly debated issues today. It is complicated by other related questions. What is rationing? How does it apply to health care? These questions, although framed as matters of ethics, always seem to end up as political discussions. Those favoring a free-market approach charge that any government intervention in the allocation of health care is, in fact, rationing. Their opponents, those advocating a universal government-run healthcare system, argue that health care is already rationed, although implicitly.

In an attempt to bring some sense to this discussion, a definition of rationing is needed. It means "a method of distributing resources outside the market system" or "allocation of scarce resources" (Hackler, 2009, p. 356). While it usually involves government, that is not always the case. It is most often used in terms of more routine, but essential, consumer commodities such as fuel or food. Although not everyone will agree (do they ever?) on the basis for the rationing of such commodities or the portions allocated, they generally accept the need for rationing and the concept of giving everyone an equal share.

With health care, it is much more difficult to determine what equal really means. Most agree that everyone deserves and has a right to a basic level of health care, but attempting to identify that level is where the discussion falls apart. Do we all have a right to whatever health care we want or only to emergency or life-saving care? Does it include treatment to artificially prolong life? Should it go so far as to include elective treatments? It is relatively easy to rule out the need for some treatments, such as plastic surgery for purely cosmetic reasons. How about surgery that is not absolutely essential to preserve life but that will give a person greater independence by eliminating a functional disability? Where do we draw the line?

When the question concerns explicit rationing of health care—meaning the government mandates by law who gets what type and what amount of health care—most people have a position on one side of the argument or the other. There are many valid arguments on both sides. However, the question of implicit rationing is much more difficult and controversial. Care is rationed in many ways that are much less easily identifiable. Reimbursement (referred to by some as green rationing) determines whether someone gets an equal share; so does availability of services. If a needed long-term care or other healthcare service is available to some but not others, has it not in effect been rationed?

When government implements a policy designed to divert consumers from one form of care to another, is that not also a form of rationing? Efforts by state and federal governments to emphasize home health care as a desirable (meaning less costly?) alternative to nursing facilities is a not-so-subtle means of influencing what portions of the overall resources of the long-term care system are allocated to certain segments of the population. Is the government rationing long-term care? If it is, is this ethical? The answer, as is the case with just about all ethical issues, is not definitive, but depends on the outlook of the observer.

Transfer of Assets: Spending Down

Another side product of the quandary caused by conflicting societal obligations is an ethical issue that has been gaining considerable attention. Related to financing, and therefore to access, it is the issue of spending down one's resources to qualify for Medicaid coverage. It has also produced one of the most urgent and pervasive ethical debates associated with long-term care.

To what extent does the government owe each of us coverage for our care, regardless of our ability to pay for it? Consumers faced with spending down ask why they, who have been paying their taxes all these years, have to lose all they have saved just to be eligible for long-term care? After all, is it not the same care that is covered for those who were not so farsighted and prudent? Should coverage not be an entitlement as so many other government benefits are? They argue that the savings that they put away over many years were meant to be passed on to children and grandchildren. They say that it is unfair to take all of that away from them, in effect penalizing them for being frugal, and point to others who either spent all they had frivolously or never bothered to provide for themselves in the first place. Where is the incentive to save if it is to be taken away by the government? Countering arguments, primarily coming from government entities that are hard-pressed to finance Medicaid programs, center on the unfairness of providing coverage to those who have their own resources.

Which is more (or less) ethical: to take away an individual's savings or to force government to pay for someone who has those savings? The issue also affects the children and grandchildren of the individual consumers of long-term care. If asset transference is not allowed, they may not receive the inheritance that they, and their parents, had anticipated. On the other hand, if today's elderly are allowed to collect Medicaid while transferring their assets to their children and grandchildren, these later generations may not have a public system on which to fall back.

Although this issue is far from resolved, ethically or legally, all is not negative. There have been several notable attempts to reach a compromise. The more successful of these are public/private partnership demonstration projects.

■ Autonomy

Virtually all other ethical issues in long-term care somehow seem to revolve around the question of how much autonomy a person has in deciding how he or she will live and be treated. Autonomy can be defined simply as "self-determination, or the right of an individual to make his or her own independent decisions" (Pozgar, 2010, p. 25). The philosophy of allowing people to have control and autonomy over their own lives and respecting the choices that people make is not new—it is consistent with basic humanistic values that have been articulated in cultures all over the world for hundreds of years (Geron, 2000). The word *autonomy* derives from the Greek word for *self* (*auto*) and *rule* (*nomos*) (Summers, 2009). In this context, it means recognizing an individual's right to make decisions about what is best for himself or herself (Pozgar, 2010) and, in doing so, to direct the course of his or her care. It is the overriding concern of long-term care consumers, whether in a nursing facility or when receiving some other form of service. They want to determine their own actions because that gives them a feeling of self-worth and respect. Autonomy is also related to, and a contributing factor in, a person's individual identity (Agich, 2009).

At the very core of long-term care is the concept of functional independence. Long-term care services assist people by helping them (1) maintain a given level of independence, (2) achieve (or regain) a higher level of independence, or (3) substitute services for independence that has been irrevocably lost. People need long-term care services precisely because they can no longer perform basic functions as well as they once could. Those functions, especially the ones known as activities of daily living, represent the degree of their independence or lack thereof. Once a person's ability to perform any or all of those functions is diminished, full autonomy is impossible to attain.

The challenge for the long-term care system is finding ways to optimize the independence level of every consumer and, in turn, their ability to be autonomous. This optimum level is different for each individual, making it even more difficult to achieve. For some, being able to live in their own homes with the assistance of home healthcare or other related services is the highest form of self-dependence possible. Others may have to settle for being institutionalized but still have the ability to perform some functions for themselves. In both cases, the more they can do for themselves, the more they have the ability to make key decisions about the care they receive.

A person's independence may be compromised by functional disabilities, but it may also be limited because of attitudes. Historically, healthcare consumers have relied on doctors and other professionals to tell them what is good for them. The judgment of professionals was seldom questioned. The medical model on which the acute care system was built was characterized by physicians making all key decisions. These decisions focused on clinical outcomes, with social factors being secondary in most cases. Over time, however, technology and new modes of delivery have made more care options available. This increased availability has compounded the process of choosing the one best option for any individual. Making those choices, particularly in long-term care, is an enormously complex process. The decisions are not made all at once, but over time, and include various combinations of medical, social, and personal factors. These factors must all be considered, with medical factors sometimes receiving lower priority than the social or personal ones.

There has also been an awakening on the part of consumers to their legal right to participate in their own decisions. They have readily embraced the idea of consumer choice and have come to demand a say in how, when, and where they receive long-term care and even whether to receive that care at all. No longer are they content to let others decide for them. This growing insistence by consumers on more decision-making power has forced most healthcare providers, particularly physicians, to reexamine how they interact with their patients. Unfortunately, there are still some who have not accepted these changes and who cling to outdated attitudes and techniques. Over time, these providers will experience great pressure to adapt, but until they do, some consumers may not have true autonomy.

It is not only the providers who are sometimes slow to change. As strong as the move toward greater decision-making freedom is, there are still many consumers who are more comfortable being told what to do. Many elderly, having lived their entire lives in a society that did not expect them to take part in healthcare decisions, are understandably reluctant to exert their independence at this point in their lives. Nor are many of them equipped to do so effectively. However, as younger adults move into the age groups most likely to need long-term care, overall attitudes will change even more rapidly.

This trend toward greater self-determination has occurred in all of health care, but it is particularly evident in long-term care. This is true largely because long-term care represents a change in lifestyle, not just a short-term inconvenience. It goes beyond medical decision making and includes other elements with lasting impact on people's lives. Long-term care consumers are increasingly expressing concern for the quality of the lives they have left. Quality of life is not necessarily more important in their particular lifestyles than in any other, but it is more easily compromised by the acts of others. Thus, it becomes more of a concern for them. It is also defined differently by different people.

The long-term care system "should be consumer driven and those consumers should make their own decisions about the care they receive as much as possible as a means of promoting quality, dignity, and self-improvement for them" (Saint Joseph's College of Maine, 1993). In accomplishing this, the long-term care system needs to recognize individual choice. Increasingly, providers have come to agree with that position.

Culture Change

In the late 1980s, a national grassroots effort known broadly as the culture change movement started in isolated pockets of the nursing home industry, driven by a variety of independent organizations. Gaining formal status in 2000, it has continued to grow in recent years (Grant, 2008). As defined by the Pioneer Network (2013):

> Culture change is the common name given to a national movement for the transformation of older adult services, based on person-directed values and practices where the voices of elders and those working with them are considered and respected. Core person-directed values are choice, dignity, respect, self-determination, and purposeful living.

It has occurred mostly in nursing homes but is also happening in other long-term care settings and is clearly a response to the well-documented desire by long-term care consumers for more of a voice in the care they receive.

In the culture change model, residents enjoy much of the privacy and choice they would experience if they were still living in their own homes. Their needs and preferences come first; facilities' operations are shaped by this awareness. A nursing home is a place residents call "home." A place where someone lives and calls "home" should nurture the human spirit as well as meet medical needs. Culture change seeks to create an environment that follows the residents' routines rather than those imposed by the facility; it encourages staff assignments with a team focus. It allows residents to make their own decisions and encourages residents to be treated as individuals (NORC, 2014).

Today, more and more long-term care leaders have changed their workplace practices, deinstitutionalizing their physical environments, and embracing person-directed care. They do it in order to get to the next level in terms of quality. As person-directed care gains widespread acceptance as an alternative to more traditional, institutional frameworks, there is a general consensus that it is more than just the right thing to do (Farrell & Elliot, 2008). The Eden Alternative movement, which preceded the culture change movement, paved the way for person-centered environments and settings (Jurkowski, 2013).

Autonomy–Beneficence Conflict

The increased decision-making role of long-term care consumers, while an important step toward granting them as much independence as possible, complicates the provision of care. In assessing autonomy, the fundamental consideration is an older person's decision-making capacity. This capability involves understanding what is being considered as well as appreciating the consequences of the decision (Williams, 2006). Autonomy in long-term care may conflict with the more traditional concept of beneficence: the responsibility of the provider to act in the best interests of the patient. The term *beneficence* "describes the principle of doing good, demonstrating kindness and helping others" (Pozgar, 2010, p. 44). How far must the provider go in allowing a long-term care consumer to make his or her own care decisions when those decisions may be against the professional judgment of the provider? This difficult question and its implications for providers and consumers alike are explored here.

Allowing consumer autonomy in an institutional setting can be particularly troublesome. It is appropriate to focus somewhat on nursing facilities here, although the issues do apply to other types of long-term care, because it is in these facilities that the conflict between care and lifestyle is most likely to occur. The residents have less functional independence and require more care or they would not be there.

At the heart of the autonomy–beneficence problem is the obligation of providers to protect those in their care. The training and experience of individual providers leads them to favor clinical interventions that they know hold potential benefits for those in their care. On the other hand, the consumer may not always wish to receive that care. In such cases, the decision often involves weighing the long-range benefits of the proposed treatment against the short-term inconvenience and discomfort that accompanies many clinical procedures.

For example, should a very elderly man, with multiple disabilities and medical conditions, choose to undergo renal dialysis? With dialysis, he would probably live longer, but the process itself is uncomfortable and would significantly diminish the quality of his life during the extra time the procedure would give him. More important to the discussion is whether the provider should attempt to influence him in favor of undergoing dialysis. There was a time in the not-too-distant past when providers would have felt ethically bound to push for whatever treatment would prolong life. This has changed as they recognize that more long-term care consumers are opting for quality of life over extension of life with lesser quality. Equally important ethical discussions such as those covered here have made healthcare professionals aware that they have options beyond merely saving lives and that their responsibility is to the whole person, not just to the person as patient.

In another case, an elderly woman with chronic arthritis needs a double hip replacement if she is to walk again. She chooses not to have the surgery at first, then her condition deteriorates to the point where she can no longer sit in a wheelchair because of the pain, and she is even in considerable pain when in bed. At this point she accepts the corrective surgery. She had decided that it was not worth going through the surgery and lengthy rehabilitation process just to be able to walk when she got around as much as needed in her wheelchair. However, she did find it worthwhile to endure it to relieve her of the terrible pain.

In both of these cases, the consumers took command of the situation and made decisions in their own best interests. Yet, in both cases, some of the providers felt an obligation to recommend the more aggressive treatment.

Providers have an obligation to give consumers as much information as possible on which to base their decisions. Then, to the extent their decisions do not jeopardize others or put the providers in a position of liability, those decisions should be honored. However, the right of the consumer to decide is not absolute and may be affected by other factors. Inherent physical, mental, or functional limitations have to color any decision about how much self-determination to allow. The responsibility of providers to look out for the well-being of consumers is not invalidated by the rights of consumers to make their own decisions. To the contrary, long-term care professionals have an obligation to use their expertise to influence important care-related decisions.

This may involve protecting consumers from their own choices if those choices are not in their best interests. The issue becomes involved with the question of paternalism—"making decisions for others without their consent" (Summers, 2009, p.11)—and determining the degree of influence that is compatible with maintaining respect for the consumer's autonomy (Agich, 2009). Providers must attempt to achieve a balance that best serves those for whom they care, helping them decide wisely but stopping short of inappropriate influence or anything that might be construed as coercion. It may also mean challenging the ability of the consumer to make a meaningful decision.

Other Autonomy-Related Conflicts

The duty of providers to act in the best interests of their consumers is not the only area of potential conflict created by the desire for increased autonomy. Another is the difficulty of meeting the wishes (demands) of the consumer within the resources of the provider. A resident in a long-term care facility may want to do things that the facility is not prepared to support, such as having a private room when there are none available or demanding food that is beyond the ability of the facility to provide. Some resident requests go beyond the seemingly mundane.

A more common source of conflict is the need to balance the autonomy of an individual and the societal requirements of a community of nursing facility residents all living together. As with any other group living situation, individual desires sometimes have to be subordinated to the needs of the whole. It is a major problem for provider and consumer alike, one that is discussed in more depth later in this chapter.

Attempting to respect the consumer's right to autonomy can result in asking long-term care professionals to take actions that they see as unethical, creating a somewhat different ethical issue. As one author put it, "It is not possible to practice in the health-care profession for long without encountering some kind of ethical dilemma because different principles of ethics or different virtues conflict" (Summers, 2009, p. 12). Providers may be asked to do things that are in violation of their professional judgment or that are simply against their beliefs. The most obvious situation that comes to mind involves removal of life-sustaining equipment. Even if doing so is clearly in compliance with the wishes of the consumer and all legal requirements have been met, it is not ethical to require an individual staff member to perform the actual act if she or he strongly objects. Others who do not disagree should be selected to do it.

Sometimes consumer requests may be considered unacceptable by the organizations themselves, usually because of religious ties. In such cases, organizations have two clear obligations to the consumers. First, they should make their position clear right up front. This is usually done through an organizational mission statement or a statement of their philosophy. Second, they have an obligation to do everything possible to assist the consumer in transferring to another facility or service provider if there is one willing to accede to the request.

Informed Consent

The right of consumers of long-term care to make their own decisions is based on the doctrine of informed consent, meaning that they have the right to have enough information to make intelligent decisions about the care they receive. As defined by Pozgar (2010), informed consent is "a legal concept that provides that a patient has a right to know the potential risks, benefits, and alternatives of a proposed procedure" (p. 352). Underlying the concept of informed consent is the principle of respect for individuals and demonstrating that respect by providing them with the information they need to make sound decisions. This reflects an even more basic doctrine: that a person cannot be treated without his or her consent, regardless of the good intentions of those administering the treatment. To give that consent, the person must be fully informed of all aspects of the treatment, its potential benefits and drawbacks, and even possible negative results. The consumer is also entitled to an explanation of the alternatives to a proposed course of treatment (Showalter, 2008). The person involved must have a good understanding of the alternatives involved, including the alternative of doing nothing. Given all of this, it is possible to make an informed decision and to grant consent in a way that is legally and ethically acceptable.

One of the more common problems with informed consent is affirming that the consumer is truly informed and actually understands what he or she is being told. The provider representative who is doing the informing has an obligation to verify that the consumer has a full understanding of that to which he or she has consented (Pozgar, 2010). Professionals have a responsibility to explain fully without being overwhelming or using unnecessarily technical language.

In practice, informed consent has come to mean that consumers must be told what is to be done to them or on their behalf, by whom, and any possible side effects or consequences of the treatment. Although it is based on an ethical right to know, informed consent has been molded in the legal arena. Consumers have sued providers, claiming (often with justification) that they did not know that there were potential side effects to certain procedures. Providers have countered by overinforming and overdocumenting in many cases, to the point where the consumer may find it even more difficult to make a sound decision.

An example of this that most of us have seen is the practice of commercial pharmacies that are required by law, in most cases, to accompany every prescription with a lengthy list of possible side effects. Because of the threat of liability, doctors feel it necessary to document that they told their patients everything that might possibly go wrong, doing it as much to protect themselves as the patients. The result may be that the consumers are so overwhelmed by the possible disadvantages that they forgo a beneficial treatment.

In acute care, informed consent often revolves around choosing which method of treatment, such as surgery, medication, or other active intervention, to receive. In long-term care, informed consent is more likely to center less on which treatment to receive and more on whether a resident or client wishes to receive a treatment at all. When informed consent is mentioned, most people think of end-of-life issues such as these, but it applies equally, and probably more often, to everyday care decisions.

The actual process of securing informed consent—the necessary consent forms and the required content of those forms—is pretty well defined by state and federal laws and regulations. Because they are essentially legal requirements and may vary considerably from one long-term care setting to another, they are not discussed further here. Readers are encouraged to check on laws and regulations applicable to them, including accreditation requirements.

Having established consumer choice as the overriding ethical issue affecting long-term care, we will now examine some of the more specific issues, starting with end-of-life treatment issues, then moving on to more routine everyday life issues.

End-of-Life Treatment Issues

Long-term care providers must confront several issues affecting life itself, issues involving patients accepting or rejecting treatment. These are certainly the most urgent issues to the individual consumer and the provider involved, and are covered here in some detail.

In an acute hospital setting, such decisions usually involve high-technology treatments designed to prolong life or at least to delay the onset of death. Treatments such as cardiopulmonary resuscitation, ventilator-assisted breathing, and tube feeding are regular occurrences, usually related to sudden or emergency episodes. In long-term care, the eventual need for these treatments may be foreseen farther ahead of time. Thus, individuals may have more opportunity to express their wishes, including a wish to refuse the treatments. If they are mentally and physically competent and able to express themselves, they clearly have such rights.

Competency and Decision-Making Capacity

Many long-term care consumers cannot exercise autonomy in decision making because of some mental and/or physical incapacity. In these cases, someone else must make critical decisions on their behalf. In this situation, several questions must be answered. How do we know the consumer is incapable? Who determines that incapacity? Who decides on his or her behalf? How do we ensure that the consumer's best interests are represented?

The first question, which deals with the determination of capacity to make one's own medical decisions, is primarily a legal issue. A person is considered competent to make medical decisions regarding his or her care unless a court determines otherwise (Pozgar, 2010). It is based on previous court cases and current law, although the details do vary somewhat from state to state and will undoubtedly be subject to future refinements. However, there are ethical questions involved as well. The determination of competency is usually made by the courts, but the actual basis for making that determination is far from clear.

Defining competency is a subjective process at best. It is "essentially the ability to make a decision and usually involves answering one question: should we allow this person to make this decision under these circumstances?" (Chell, 2009, p. 113). To begin with, it is not all inclusive. A person can be deemed competent to make some decisions but not others. For example, an individual might be considered incapable of making decisions concerning personal finances but able to decide whether to accept a particular clinical treatment.

In most cases involving determination of competency, particularly in situations where decisions center on life and death, emotions are involved. If there are family members available to participate in the determination process, they almost inevitably have a hard time separating their own emotions from those of the loved one under scrutiny. Guilt can be nearly overwhelming. They may feel guilty for "letting Dad die" by allowing him to refuse treatment, even though it is clearly what he wants. There may be religious beliefs involved, further complicating the situation. Sometimes there is guilt caused by a feeling that they did not do all they could to prevent the current state of affairs or that they did not make more of an effort to know what the consumer would have wanted.

Keep in mind that this is not a discussion of the actual decision making, just the process of determining whether a person is competent to make her or his own decisions. Yet this often becomes the most complex, emotion-ridden, and contentious part of the process, because whoever "wins" at this stage gets to make the actual decisions without further interference from others.

Finally, competency is often confused with rationality, although it should not be. Competency refers to the capacity to make decisions. It in no way has anything to do with the rightness or wrongness of the decision itself. Rationality, on the other hand, is a measure of the decision, not one's ability to make it. Rational, in this context, means "having the capacity to think logically" (Pozgar, 2010, p. 410). In judging someone else's decision-making capability, it becomes extremely difficult to exclude the rationality of the proposed decision, for to do so would mean completely bypassing one's own feelings. If we think, based on our own convictions, that no rational person would choose to refuse treatment that would probably extend his or her life, yet someone close to us makes that choice, it becomes hard for us to escape the conclusion that such a person is therefore irrational.

Determining whether a particular long-term care consumer is competent to exercise his or her right to make decisions may be a legal matter, but it also determines the degree of that person's right to autonomy and thus becomes an ethical issue. It should be noted here that disagreements over competency do not always involve family members seeking to restrict the ability of a loved one to refuse treatment, although this seems to be the most common scenario. There are many others as well. There may be a disagreement between a spouse and children of the individual around whom the storm centers or among multiple siblings. Or the contention could be between family members and clinical providers who question the family's judgment or motives. In cases in which there is no immediate family, healthcare professionals sometimes get involved on behalf of consumers if they feel that the consumers are not making the right decisions.

If the determination is that the person is competent to make decisions, the issue is generally put to rest. However, if that person is declared incompetent, further questions remain. The most important, and sometimes most contentious, is the question of who should be appointed as guardian or conservator, the person who will make the decisions on behalf of the consumer declared incompetent. In most cases, it is a relatively easy decision. Someone who clearly has the best interests of the consumer in mind is appointed, sometimes subject to further restrictions by the court. But what if there are several relatives who want the appointment? Which should be chosen? Do they have ulterior motives, consciously or unconsciously? It can be difficult to determine who would best protect the consumer. What if there is no one at all? In such a case, the court appoints an independent guardian to act on behalf of the patient.

The last question (How do we ensure that the best interests of the consumer are represented?) is a critical ethics issue to be considered. All involved—including the official guardian, the courts, the providers, and family members—are concerned with what is best for the consumer, so what is the issue? It would seem easy enough to agree on this, but usually it is not. Where we run into difficulty is in our different interpretations of what is best for someone else.

The debate centers on whether we (the system) should provide what we identify as best for the consumer or what the person would have preferred, even if the two philosophies are in conflict. There has been increased interest in, and emphasis on, the rights of long-term care consumers. That is good, but is not always appropriate. As Agich (2009) puts it, "advocating the rights of nursing home residents frequently overlooks the strikingly dependent and fragile nature of many of these people" (p.191). The doctrine of informed consent holds that the consumer cannot legally and ethically consent to treatment unless he or she is fully informed concerning the nature of the treatment and possible outcomes. In the case of the incapacitated consumer, this means a substituted judgment, sometimes called proxy consent, by a person who must then be informed. Several developments in recent years have helped clarify how that substitute judgment is to be made. The following is a brief description of them.

Advance Directives

One of the ways in which long-term care consumers can protect their rights to have their wishes carried out is by creating an advance directive. Advance directive is the general term for a variety of documents designed to enable competent adults to make healthcare decision-making plans in advance of possible future incapacity, including terminal illness (Clarke, 2009). Through advance directives, individuals are able to make clear their wishes concerning treatment, particularly life-sustaining treatment, in the event they are not able to express those wishes at the time.

The most common forms of advance directive are living wills and durable powers of attorney. They are both forms of a declaration by a person who is physically, mentally, and legally competent to make decisions about his or her health care, anticipating the possibility that he or she may, at some future time, be incompetent to do that. Such incompetence may be physical, such as being comatose and unable to speak or otherwise communicate. Or, it might be caused by diminished mental capacity resulting from Alzheimer's disease, senile dementia, or some other condition resulting in an inability to make sound decisions. Fearing that eventuality, many people have chosen to spell out their feelings about various types of treatment in a document known as a living will, with the expectation that those wishes will be honored.

Living wills—also known as instructional directives or terminal care documents (Clarke, 2009)—have done much to assist family members and healthcare providers in knowing what the individual would have wanted done or not done on his or her behalf, describing those treatments he or she wishes or does not wish to receive should he or she become unable to communicate treatment decisions (Pozgar, 2010). They substitute for an actual conversation with the person such as would occur during the process of informed consent. However, living wills do not necessarily carry the weight of law, nor do they automatically ensure that the wishes contained in them will be honored. Some states have passed legislation giving living wills some legal standing, but many have not. Even where there is such legislation, there are many avenues of exception available. For example, in most cases, family members may challenge the legality of the document.

Although it is very possible for a living will to express the wish that all possible clinical interventions be used to prevent death, most specify the opposite. The reason most people create living wills is to prevent extraordinary actions on their behalf. They do not wish to linger in a near-vegetative state, nor do they want to become a burden on their families and loved ones. They clearly prefer a shorter, but higher, quality of life to extending life with less quality.

One of the most common situations in this regard is when the author of the living will specifies that there are to be no heroic actions (e.g., cardiopulmonary resuscitation or use of a ventilator) taken to prolong life when death is inevitable in the near future. A spouse or child of the patient might challenge the document because of an unwillingness to let the loved one die. When this happens, the issue is usually left for the court to settle.

The discussion here is less concerned with the legal recourse available and more with the ethical issues involved. Should family members, even when they feel that they are acting in the best interests of the patient, have the right to overturn the stated intent of that person? On the surface, the answer would seem to be a clear negative. It is the individual's life, and his or her wishes should be paramount in keeping with the precept of individual autonomy. However, as we have seen with other ethical issues, things are seldom as simple as they seem.

Living wills have been challenged on a number of bases. It is argued that healthy, competent people cannot possible know how they would actually react in a life-threatening situation, that what they think now might not apply when faced with such a critical decision. This becomes even more of a question when lengthy periods of time, up to many years, pass between the creation of the living will and its application. Much can happen that might change a person's feeling about certain acts or procedures.

What if a middle-aged widower with grown children expresses in a living will that he does not want to extend his life artificially should the situation arise? His wife has already passed on and, as much as he loves his children, they are grown and secure enough to get along without him. What if, in the intervening years, several grandchildren are born, with whom he becomes very close? Would he still feel the same about not trying everything possible to extend his life? What if someone adopts a new religion after drafting a living will, with different proscriptions concerning end-of-life choices, but neglects to change the document? What if she or he makes oral statements to family members that appear to be in conflict with the written document? Which should be honored?

The answer to some of these questions and concerns would seem to be not the invalidity of living wills as statements of personal intent but rather the importance of keeping such documents updated. If they are to truly reflect a person's views and preferences, they should be reviewed at least every several years and modified as needed. They should also be discussed freely with family members, clergy, and even legal counsel. After all, the purpose of a living will is to make one's wishes known. Yet some people are uncomfortable discussing matters of life and death, particularly with close family members. Far too often, living wills are simply documents that are created and filed away, with key people unaware of their existence or contents.

A second type of advance directive is the durable power of attorney—also known as a proxy directive (Clarke, 2009). It is similar in its purpose of protecting the interests of the individual consumer. However, it is different in how that is accomplished. A living will spells out, in a person's own words, what that person would want to happen in certain future circumstances. A durable power of attorney, on the other hand, specifies someone else to make those decisions as a surrogate. It gives another person the legal authority to act on one's behalf in the event of future incapacity. It assumes that the person who will be acting as an agent of the consumer fully understands the wishes of the one giving the power of attorney.

Much has been said here, and justifiably, about the obligations of providers and others involved in long-term care to assist consumers in exercising their rights to make decisions about the care they receive, but consumers also have some responsibilities in this regard. Among these responsibilities is providing for possible future incapacity by making their feelings known through a living will or appointing someone to make decisions for them by means of a durable power of attorney. In doing so, they can avoid many of the problems identified here, can save loved ones a great deal of grief, and can give long-term care providers the information needed to do their jobs.

Patient Self-Determination Act

Consumer choice and informed consent received a significant boost in 1990 when the Patient Self-Determination Act was passed. It was passed as a section of the Omnibus Budget Reconciliation Act and became effective late in 1991. The Patient Self-Determination Act provided, for the first time, a national standard spelling out how healthcare providers, including long-term care facilities and organizations, should go about making consumers aware of their rights. It mandated that everyone admitted to a hospital or nursing facility be advised of their right to make life-and-death decisions and that they be provided with advance directive forms and information.

The act specifies that all consumers admitted must be asked whether they have a living will or other advance directive that spells out their wishes concerning treatment, particularly extraordinary life-extending measures. They must also be made aware that they have the right to create such documents and that they will not be discriminated against if they do or do not. The act requires provider facilities to have written policies regarding implementation of these rights and that they share those policies with all consumers.

Although the Patient Self-Determination Act clearly established the responsibility of providers to assist consumers in exercising their rights of self-determination, it was not taken seriously at first by some of those providers, as demonstrated by a couple of situations your author experienced.

At one point, I was presenting a day-long seminar on the new act, accompanied by several highly knowledgeable attorneys. The audience was made up of nursing facility administrators. At the end of the day, after we explained all of their obligations and the penalties involved with noncompliance, one of those administrators complimented us on our presentation but said it did not apply to him. He never explained why he felt that way, but he obviously had heard little of what we had said.

On another occasion, I was admitted to a hospital overnight for surgery. During the admission process, the admitting clerk thrust a packet of materials (related to advance directives) at me, saying, "I guess I'm supposed to give you these." As it happened, the chief executive officer of that hospital was an acquaintance of mine. Needless to say, he heard from me about his admitting department's approach to the Patient Self-Determination Act. Fortunately, most long-term care and other healthcare providers have accepted the intent of the law and now actively participate in making consumers aware of their rights.

Although most people involved in long-term care see advance directives as a very positive development and a means of ensuring that the desires of an individual are followed in difficult situations, not all agree. Several highly respected ethicists have questioned whether advance directives really serve as well as intended, contending that there is a danger that these written declarations might take the place of more productive doctor–patient dialogue or other more meaningful discussions and thus be used to limit needed or desired care. Their concerns are valid. There is always a danger that form will replace substance and that documents meant to clarify will, instead, result in oversimplification. However, the problem is not the documents. It is in how they might be used. It was never intended that advance directives take the place of interpersonal conversations or that they be used to invalidate the stated wishes of a frail elder or other dependent person. They are a vast improvement over the near total lack of information available prior to their introduction. Any information vehicle that improves the amount of understanding between consumer and provider is better than no vehicle at all.

These questions about advance directives and their intended value and potential misuse can only improve the status quo. By enlarging on existing knowledge and assisting in clarification of difficult ethical issues, they make us all more aware of the many complex, sometimes conflicting, aspects of seemingly simple ethical issues. Such concerns foster and stimulate further discussion of these issues, a valuable service indeed, but let us not discard what works now, admittedly somewhat less than perfectly, until a better replacement is found.

Ethics Committees

Many long-term care facilities have formed ethics committees to assist in ensuring that life-and-death decisions are made properly and in accordance with the wishes of the resident. Such committees have been in existence longer in hospitals but are becoming increasingly popular in long-term care. The committees determine the process for making ethical decisions, educate staff and residents, and provide professional consultation.

The first duty of an ethics committee is to formulate policies on which the organization will rely in addressing difficult ethical issues. Organizational policies are not designed to answer questions in advance, nor do they necessarily provide decisions for every possible ethics situation. What they do provide is a set of ground rules that reflects the overall mission and philosophy of the organization as well as applicable laws and regulations. The policies created by ethics committees anticipate difficult situations and set parameters within which the provider's staff must operate. From these policies come specific procedures that are to be followed, an important component of a consistent policy.

Another duty of ethics committees is to provide consultation to healthcare providers about specific problems. They do not make the actual decisions but offer consultation to those who must. By providing an array of medical experts, ethicists, clergy, and other involved staff, they make sure that all aspects of any given decision are covered. They also ensure that the established process is followed fairly and equitably, guaranteeing that the many difficult decisions to be made are at least made in a consistent manner.

The third major role of the ethics committee is education. It starts by educating its members concerning the committee's legal and ethical authority and responsibility. Then, it becomes the source of education for the remainder of the organization's staff and, when appropriate, for involved consumers and their families.

Ethics committees serve a most valuable function in helping long-term care providers make some of their most difficult ethical decisions. They do so through a process of discussions and informed interaction with all who are involved. It is a process that might well be used in other types of ethical decision making.

While ethics committees traditionally deal with consumer-related issues, there is also a role for them in management ethics, a topic we discuss in depth later in this chapter.

Futile Care

One of the more difficult care-related situations facing long-term care providers is having to provide life-extending care regardless of the previously stated wishes of the resident when there is no hope of recovery or improvement in the patient's condition. It is called "futile care" or "futility of treatment" and occurs "when the physician recognizes that the effect of treatment will be of no benefit to the patient" (Pozgar, 2010, p. 137). This is a common problem in acute care settings that often carries over to long-term care. There are many situations in which the care goes beyond the wishes of the resident but is either required by transfer arrangements with other institutions or because the long-term care facility is not made aware of the presence of an advance directive. As a person's condition worsens, or in times of medical crisis, communication between the long-term care facility and hospitals or ambulance services often breaks down. Even when interagency communication is adequate, the advance directive may be too specific to apply to the new setting. In these situations, the provider must go on providing care that is considered by everyone to be useless or futile. One thing that is quite clear both legally and ethically is that providers have an obligation to treat unless told otherwise. How long must they do so? There are legal remedies, including appointment of a guardian, and the courts will sometimes make the decisions, but these processes are lengthy, cumbersome, and expensive.

Autonomy: How Far to Go

As the right of the individual to refuse or to withhold life-prolonging treatment has become generally accepted, we are now faced with an even more difficult question: Does that individual have the right to take actions to actually end life (euthanasia)? Do providers have a right to assist consumers in such actions? One should not be too quick to answer that. A short while ago, those questions would not even have been asked, but no longer. Euthanasia originated from the Greek word, *euthanatos*, meaning "good death" or "easy death," and was accepted in situations in which people had what were considered to be incurable diseases. From its inception, euthanasia has evolved into an issue with competing legal, medical, and moral implications, which continue to generate debate, confusion, and conflict (Pozgar, 2010). The efforts of Dr. Jack Kevorkian to assist terminally ill patients to commit suicide are well known, although controversial. In 1995, the state of Oregon passed the first right-to-die law in the nation, allowing physician-assisted suicide. Although that law is under attack, other states have also debated the issue. Is this the right way to go? What other options are there? These may well be the most difficult, but most important, ethical issues of the foreseeable future.

■ Everyday Life Issues

Everyday life issues are also important to long-term care consumers. Because these everyday life issues involve the very basis for how long-term care is provided, a substantial portion of this chapter is devoted to them.

In several studies, nursing facility residents have been asked what decision-making issues they consider important. Somewhat to the surprise of everyone, the residents rarely said anything about living wills or other right-to-die issues. Instead, they worried about their autonomy in day-to-day issues such as leaving the facility, access to phones and mail, and deciding when and what to eat.

We have begun to realize that the long-term care institution is, to the residents, primarily a place to live. Traditional ethical perspectives have made the mistake of regarding nursing facility care as an extension of hospital care (Collopy, 1991). It is not. It requires a care, not cure, philosophy. The nursing facility becomes family and community for its residents. That they (the residents) must also receive care is a fact that they must tolerate and about which they can do little. However, the circumstances of their living arrangements and lifestyles are something they can influence. The degree to which they are allowed to exert that influence contributes to their feeling of independence and self-worth. It can alternately lead to a feeling of dependence and frustration. The difference is, to a large measure, up to the providers to decide.

Daily decisions that most of us take for granted, those concerning food, social activity, sleep habits, even sexual activity, are sometimes denied long-term care consumers. The importance to nursing facility residents of making these decisions should not be underestimated. What might seem to be an unimportant matter, such as being allowed to decide when to retire for the night or whether to participate in group activities, can be a major event for people confined in an institutional setting where they must conform to rules designed for the overall facility population. Nor should the difficulty providers have in allowing them to make those decisions be discounted.

Readers are urged to try to imagine what it would be like to live in a nursing facility and to have your freedom restricted. I once saw a number of nursing facility administrators involved in role-playing in which they experienced what it is like to be residents. When they were debriefed following the role-play, they had some interesting observations to make: "I felt as though I had no control at all over my own life." "They took away what little dignity I had." "Everyone talked about me as if I wasn't there." "No one talked to me." The experience was a real eye-opener for most of these experienced administrators and made them more willing to listen to and act on consumer concerns. It would be a valuable exercise for all providers of long-term care.

Privacy

Individual privacy is a critical component of a feeling of self-worth and independence. We all demand it to some degree, some more than others. Maintaining that privacy while living in an institution or other group setting can be extremely challenging to say the least. Having to share your only private space with a roommate, eat in a communal dining room, and even bathe in a shared facility are the very antithesis of personal privacy, yet these situations are a reality in much of long-term care, particularly in institutions. Even when long-term care is delivered at home, the need for professional caregivers to come into that home and assist in the most intimate daily functions imperils much of what we have come to know as privacy. That privacy is one of the most important factors in what we call quality of life. We go to great lengths to protect it, yet we are not always successful.

Long-term care consumers, particularly those residing in nursing facilities, have limited freedom to exercise their personal right to privacy, so someone else must assist them in protecting and exercising that right. It is usually the providers who are faced with the responsibility and challenge of providing as much privacy as possible for those in their care. How do they do that?

Numerous studies have proven what most of us already knew: that most residents in long-term care institutions would like to have private rooms. Their rooms are, after all, the closest thing they have to homes. Many elderly, particularly those who have been able to live alone in the past, find having to live with someone not of their own choosing to be an intrusion on their privacy. This can lead to embarrassment, anger, frustration, and even a sense of futility and hopelessness (Coons & Mace, 1996). Some would rather have roommates for companionship and social interaction, but more would like to have some place to which they can retreat or simply be alone for a while. Their rooms are also spaces that can be furnished or decorated to match their individual tastes and personalities. They are spaces that may be the only thing these people have to remind them of their former lives. Private living spaces are an important link to the past. Turning these rooms into personal living spaces is usually accomplished by hanging family pictures, furnishing with family heirlooms, or simply decorating in a familiar fashion. As simple as this may seem, it becomes much more difficult when two residents must share a room and must attempt to agree on the room's decor.

Given existing reimbursement and regulations, few long-term care facilities can provide private rooms, with the exception of those whose clientele are mostly private pay. It is important, however, that long-term care providers recognize the need for some private space for residents in their institutions, even when private rooms are not possible. Many providers have found innovative ways of creating that space. It is sometimes accomplished by designing public areas so that individual residents can gain some feeling of seclusion from others. Scheduling of events and use of space can also provide opportunities for them to be alone for a while.

There are other ways of providing individual privacy that long-term care providers can, and do, use. One of these is providing privacy in bathing and toileting facilities and practices. Recognizing that a large number of long-term care consumers are unable to accomplish these basic activities by themselves, providers owe them as much privacy and personal dignity as possible, given the institutional setting. Some go to great lengths to do so and have been very creative in finding solutions to this problem. It is, however, something on which all providers must continually focus.

Shared Space

As much as residents value their privacy or their individual space, they cannot and should not be confined to their rooms if they are at all able to move around or to be moved. Long-term care facilities by their very definition include a considerable portion of public space, such as living rooms, dining areas, and areas for watching television or performing other activities. These spaces are an important part of the residents' environment, shared though they may be.

In recent years, long-term care providers have made admirable progress in making these public spaces part of a homelike atmosphere. They have created areas that lend themselves to specific activities, each designed to meet a proven need of their residents. These public spaces may include rooms for games such as bingo or cards, or quiet areas for reading or just contemplation. There may be some outside areas where residents can pursue an interest in gardening and other areas simply for relaxing. The biggest challenge for providers has been finding ways to allow residents their privacy while still maintaining the needed care and supervision.

Confidentiality

Respecting privacy also means respecting confidentiality. We all have a right to keep information of a personal nature to ourselves as long as doing so does not adversely affect others. Our ability to decide what others know about us is a major element of our control over our own lives. For those of us not in an institution, it is relatively easy to regulate the amount of information given out to others. In long-term care, however, much of that control rests with others. For example, most elderly are uncomfortable having their bathing or toileting abilities discussed with others, yet staff are inclined to see that information as clinical and part of the care plan. Providers have an obligation to protect the privacy and confidentiality of those for whom they care. Most caregivers would not intentionally violate that obligation, but they can cause just as much embarrassment and emotional distress for residents through carelessness as through deliberate actions.

Food

It is true of all long-term care facilities, just as it is true of any other type of communal living situation (e.g., colleges), that food is one of the easiest targets for complaints and criticism. No matter how good the food may be in an institution, it probably differs from what a person has been accustomed to eating. Even if it is technically of better quality and is prepared more attractively, it is still seen as inferior by most people if it is different from that to which they are accustomed. We may not be able to accurately evaluate the clinical care we receive, but we do know whether we like the food served to us. Food tastes are not unlike that old claim by would-be art lovers: "I don't know much about art, but I know what I like." The ability of long-term care consumers to control, or at least have input into, decisions concerning what they eat is a critical component of their overall control of their lives. It is an easily understood, tangible means of exerting their autonomy.

Again, many providers have been ingenious in responding to that need. They may give residents menus from which they can select their meals or serve buffet-style meals, allowing more individual choice. Some regularly hold theme-based dining sessions, breaking the monotony of cyclical menus. When residents are able to eat without assistance, they are often allowed to eat some meals, such as breakfast, in their own quarters. Doing all of this is not easy given the need to serve a large number of people each day, to say nothing of the necessity of meeting special dietary needs of residents with medical conditions, but it is very important in defining long-term care consumers as individuals.

Activities

One of the ways in which long-term care facilities recognize and reinforce the individuality of residents is through well-designed activity programs. The staff find creative, innovative ways to include as many residents as possible in activities that are interesting and stimulating. This becomes difficult, given the many different physical and mental abilities of the residents. Activity planners must find a variety of activities that are not overly difficult for some yet not overly simplistic for others. Activities that are beyond a person's capabilities can result in frustration, withdrawal, and probable refusal to participate. At the other extreme are activities that are seen by some residents as childish and demeaning.

A corollary of the responsibility to provide interesting, challenging activities for long-term care residents is an equal responsibility to allow them to not participate if they so choose. The line between supportive encouragement of residents to be active and coercing them to participate can be a very fine one. Respect for them as individuals and for their right to control their own lives as much as possible requires that they be allowed to say no when appropriate.

■ Restraints

One issue that illustrates the difficulty of providing care while abiding by ethical principles is the use of physical and chemical restraints. Individuals who need to be protected from injuring themselves have historically been restrained for their own good. In most cases, the restraints were physical, usually some form of tying the resident down. Others were chemical restraints, use of medications such as psychotropic or antipsychotic drugs to reduce the desire or ability of residents to move around, possibly injuring themselves or other residents.

Unfortunately, restraints have also been used for less noble reasons: controlling troublesome residents, freeing up staff to do other tasks, and to keep track of residents inclined to wander. The Omnibus Budget Reconciliation Act severely restricted the use of restraints in long-term care facilities, although some states had already taken similar actions. Changes in care practice, particularly regarding use of restraints, have been necessitated by the new rules. Those changes limited when restraints could be used and how often they must be removed or relaxed. It can be difficult to determine whether individuals are being restrained for their own good or to make it easier for others to provide care.

Restraints, even when used appropriately as they are in most instances, are a very tangible restriction on the autonomy of a long-term care consumer. They prevent movement, which is so important to a sense of functional independence. If an individual is unable to move around independently because of a physical disability such as paraplegia, we seek ways to increase that person's functional independence. Yet, in using restraints, we actually create a similar functional limitation and often do little to help the consumer adapt to it.

The other aspect of restraints that should be considered here is the emotional effect they have on those who are restrained. Restraints strip people of both their autonomy and their dignity. The frustration that usually goes along with being restrained is destructive by itself, but it can also engender other harmful feelings such as depression or agitation. There has been improvement in the use of restraints in recent years.

■ Abuse

Abuse in long-term care can be defined as "Conduct by responsible caregivers or other individuals that constitutes 'abuse' under applicable state or federal law" (Williams, 2006). Any form of abuse of long-term care residents or clients is, of course, both unethical and illegal. It is not, however, that easily defined or identified. Consumers of long-term care depend on providers for assistance in meeting many of the everyday demands of life and are, therefore, highly vulnerable to anyone who might be inclined to take advantage of them. When that happens, it constitutes abuse. There are many types of abuse of the elderly or others who are disabled and dependent. It may be overt or subtle. It may also be intentional or unintentional. Whatever the nature of the abuse, the results are the same, and everyone connected with the long-term care system has an obligation to prevent it whenever and wherever possible.

When discussing abuse, we tend to think first of physical abuse, which can take many forms. Any action that results in physical harm or pain is clearly inexcusable, including striking or otherwise handling the consumer with unnecessary roughness. Unreasonable restraint is also a type of physical abuse. So is denying any care that would prevent pain or suffering. For example, allowing a bedridden resident to lie in soiled linens for an unreasonable length of time is clearly a form of abuse, as is failure to provide needed pain medication as ordered. Taking sexual advantage of a dependent consumer is a definite form of abuse, to say nothing of being a reprehensible act, but how about more subtle acts such as not providing adequate privacy while bathing or dressing? Could they not also be considered forms of sexual abuse?

In many ways the worst form of abuse, particularly of the frail elderly, is emotional abuse. It is also the most difficult to identify and thus to prevent. Emotional abuse can include a caregiver yelling, saying hurtful words, threatening, or repeatedly ignoring an older person. Keeping an older person from seeing close friends and relatives is another form of emotional abuse (National Institute on Aging, 2013). Because long-term care consumers are so dependent on their caregivers, they often have little ability to defend themselves against such treatment. Because they may need help with chores that younger, healthier people take for granted, it is easy to see them as unresponsive children and to treat them accordingly. Nevertheless, such treatment, which might include talking to them as though they were babies or not having the patience to allow them to do as much as they can at their own speed, is demeaning and often insulting. It denies them the respect and dignity that they deserve and as such is a form of emotional abuse.

Unfortunately, some abuse of long-term care consumers is intentional. It occurs at the hands of individuals who achieve some twisted form of satisfaction by abusing others who cannot defend themselves. Fortunately, it is very infrequent—reports in the public press notwithstanding—and is usually dealt with promptly and appropriately. More often, however, abusive behavior is not intentional, and the perpetrator may not even be aware that what is happening is inappropriate. Caring for the needs of physically and emotionally dependent adults involves dealing with unpleasant situations, and it can be frustrating. When staffing is short, that frustration grows and can be manifested in many ways. Rushing a resident through a meal because there are so many others to feed, taking too long to respond to a request for a bedpan, or even speaking too harshly are all minor incidents that can be blamed on lack of adequate help. They are still forms of abuse and constitute unacceptable behavior. Providers have an ethical obligation to prevent them through adequate staffing and/or training of staff.

Another form of abuse in long-term care facilities, although not usually the first that comes to mind, is what is sometimes referred to as fiduciary abuse: failure to demonstrate appropriate stewardship of the finances of consumers or, even worse, theft of money or belongings. This can include forging checks, taking retirement and Social Security benefits, or using another person's credit cards and bank accounts. Financial abuse includes changing names on a will, bank accounts, life insurance policies, or the title to a house (National Institute on Aging, 2013).

Noninstitutional long-term care, such as home health care, presents its own problems concerning abuse of the consumers served. In fact, because the care is provided in the consumer's own home, with little direct supervision, the opportunities for inappropriate behavior are greater. It is often very easy to take advantage of an elderly person living at home, because that person must rely on a home healthcare professional on a regular basis. Thus, the provider organization must take additional steps to prevent any staff actions that might be unsuitable. Of equal importance is avoiding any perception or accusation of such actions. The organization should have clearly stated policies concerning interaction between staff and consumers and concerning how staff is supervised. Sharing those policies with consumers can help minimize the possibility of staff being accused unfairly or of consumers perceiving that something inappropriate has happened.

This lengthy discussion of types of abuse and identification of the many chances for it to occur is not meant to indicate that abuse of long-term care consumers is rampant. There are many legal protections against it, including requirements that healthcare professionals report it or be subject to criminal action. Ombudsmen and other consumer advocates are valuable sources of abuse prevention. Training requirements of long-term care providers have been greatly increased in recent years, including training in how to prevent and avoid resident or client abuse. In addition to all of this is the good-faith commitment of providers to treat their charges with respect and dignity. Yet the ethical responsibility to prevent abuse in any form cannot be overstated.

In closing this discussion of abuse, it should be noted that abuse is not caused only by providers. Family members, friends, and acquaintances of the consumer can also be responsible for inflicting all of the types of abuse mentioned here. This is more likely to occur at home because there is less scrutiny of their actions there, but it can also happen in a nursing facility or other institutional setting. Whatever the setting, providers have an obligation to be diligent in detecting it and taking whatever actions they can to stop it.

■ Other Long-Term Care Settings

Throughout much of this chapter, the discussion has focused on nursing facilities, largely because it is in those facilities that consumer autonomy and protective care are most likely to clash. Nursing care residents are sicker or have more functional limitations than do most other long-term care consumers. Unlike those receiving home care or other community-based services, they have been uprooted from their homes and their familiar lifestyles and thrust into living situations not of their choosing. However, this does not mean that the ethical issues discussed here do not apply to other types of long-term care.

Other institutional settings, such as boarding homes or assisted living facilities, share many of the same issues resulting from potential conflicts between respecting individual autonomy and the group needs of other residents. Because people living in these settings may not have the same functional limitations, they may be even more demanding of their decision-making rights. The problem is not always related to placing an individual in an institution. Home-based services also face problems in balancing personal choice and good care practice. Individuals living at home have more independence and are freer to accept or ignore recommendations of the healthcare professionals who serve them, yet they must accept someone else coming into their home and telling them what to do. Issues of privacy and confidentiality are every bit as important when dealing with home care consumers.

■ Management Ethics

Throughout this chapter, we have focused on ethical issues directly related to caring for consumers. Let us look as well at ethical issues concerning the management of the provider facilities and agencies. They are closely related and equally important in the long run, but with different effect and a different focus. Management-related ethical issues may not affect consumers as directly, but can have the same long-term impact.

What is management ethics? In business generally, the concept has come to mean various things to various people, but generally it's "coming to know what is right or wrong in the workplace and doing what's right" (McNamara, 2014). Management ethics is a key element in leadership.

There are three essential components of managing ethically: integrity, morality, and principle. Integrity as a manager involves developing and maintaining trust and mutual respect between the manager and those managed. Integrity involves

> a steadfast adherence to a strict moral or ethical code and a commitment not to compromise this code. A person with integrity has a staunch belief in and faithfulness to, for example, his or her religious beliefs, values, and moral character. (Pozgar, 2010, p. 15)

Morality is a bit broader term and is based on a foundation of ethical goals, motives, and standards. Morality is "a code of conduct. It is a guide to behavior that all rational persons should put forward for governing their behavior" (Pozgar, 2010, p. 3). A moral manager views laws as a minimum standard of conduct, accepting no deviation from that standard. Principles are taught to us early. They are the values that affect our personality and behavior. These three components are integral to ethical management of any organization. Given the service nature of long-term care and the vulnerability of those served, it takes on even more importance.

Is it difficult to manage ethically? It need not be, but over time any long-term care manager faces many difficult situations, including:

- Making decisions in situations that are seldom black or white, clearly right or wrong. It means sometimes having to choose between less-than-perfect options. For example, when an organization must make staffing cuts, deciding which staff members to lay off can be easier said than done.
- Dealing with staff (and consumers) with diverse backgrounds and values. The manager owes it to those others to understand them and to deal with them fairly and appropriately.

- Dealing with personal relationships at work that might compromise the manager's integrity or that of the organization.
- Staying away from conflict of interest situations, particularly where the manager might have a personal or fiduciary interest that could involve (or be seen as involving) objective decision making.
- Avoiding wrongful use of resources, such as taking organizational property for personal, nonwork use.

These are only a few of the situations in which a manager must work to avoid being seen as unethical—or actually being so. All will occasionally make mistakes. The job is too tough to always avoid that. However, striving to do the right thing and staying continuously aware of the potential pitfalls will serve managers well.

There are a number of tools that managers can use to create and maintain an ethical environment, including ethics management programs, codes of ethics, and codes of conduct.

Ethics Management Programs

An organization can manage ethics in its workplace by establishing an ethics management program. Ethics programs "are designed to ensure that there is no deviation from the standards laid down and also to ensure that employees are fair and honest in their conduct to the organization" (MSG, 2013). Brian Schrag, executive secretary of the Association for Practical and Professional Ethics, described ethics management programs as follows: "Typically, ethics programs convey corporate values, often using codes and policies to guide decisions and behavior, and can include extensive training and evaluating, depending on the organization. They provide guidance in ethical dilemmas" (McNamara, 2014). Ethics management programs spell out an organization's values, set guidelines for behavior, train employees, and provide guidance in difficult situations. Their structure and how they work vary from organization to organization. Some function by committee, while others appoint an individual in charge. An ethics management program can be used to oversee other ethics programs such as a code of ethics, a code of conduct, and compliance programs, both internal and external.

Codes of Ethics

A code of ethics is a description of the organization's values and the ethical rules by which it operates—a list of "thou shalts and thou shalt nots" (McNamara, 2014). Such codes are a part of good management and part of a values-based culture. They serve as a solid foundation for operation of the organization. Pozgar (2010) says:

> an organization's code of ethics should provide guidelines for behavior that help carry out an organization's mission, vision, and values. Organizational codes of

ethics build trust, increase awareness of ethical issues, guide decision making, and encourage staff to seek advice and report misconduct. (p. 262)

A code of ethics has to be more than some fancy printed words to which every new employee affixes his or her signature. A well-written code of ethics should also give guidance to employees on how to deal with certain ethical situations (Magloff, 2014).

One of the first—and sometimes difficult—steps in creating a code of ethics is identifying the values on which to base it. The *Complete Guide to Ethics Management* (McNamara, 2014) recommends seeking values that are:

- Related to laws and regulations
- Most treasured by the overall organization
- Prized by your customers
- Related to workplace issues

From organizational values come organizational norms, codes of conduct, and policies and procedures that prescribe appropriate kinds of behavior by employees in particular situations and control the behavior of organizational members toward one another (Chand, 2014). Such values often come from the results of a strategic planning process. Once finalized and distributed to all employees, a code of ethics becomes an integral part of the organization's culture.

Codes of Conduct

Codes of conduct support the code of ethics by identifying behaviors that are acceptable (and those that are unacceptable). They also identify consequences for improper behavior. This gives employees a concrete understanding of the code of ethics and the values on which it is based.

Policies and Procedures

Policies and procedures support the codes of ethics and conduct by spelling out the details of what is expected.

The ethics of management and the ethics of direct care may seem to have different emphases, but should be based on the same premise: doing what is right. Both require a bit of work and effort to accomplish, but both are achievable and rewarding.

■ Summary

A variety of issues that focus on the ethics of long-term care have been explored in this chapter. As noted early on, many of these issues revolve around the question of how much choice individual consumers have in directing their lives and the care they receive. In recent years, there has been a major shift toward allowing them to have much more choice, recognizing their rights as individuals.

This change, while most welcome, is not without its share of difficult-to-answer questions, and far more questions have been raised here than have been answered. This is because the answers vary so much depending on the circumstances. The issues relating to consumer choice and autonomy are most problematic in long-term care institutions, where providers and residents face problems concerning how to implement the new philosophy of consumer choice while acting in everyone's best interest. To their credit, both groups have begun to work together to find solutions. Many nursing facilities have formed resident councils or have found other innovative means of getting the residents involved in group decision making. Newer types of long-term care institutions, such as assisted living, life care communities, and congregate housing, are being designed in ways that provide residents with more autonomy.

The momentum toward more noninstitutional service (e.g., home care, adult day care, respite services) recognizes the desire of individuals to remain as independent as possible and to stay in their own homes as long as they can. Yet as we have seen, these services have their own sets of ethical issues that must be resolved.

Giving consumers more choice in long-term care means giving them respect, dignity, self-worth, and independence. It is not easy and cannot be absolute for all consumers, but accepting it as a philosophy provides a sound basis for development of a long-term care system that is truly ethical.

At the same time, a conscious effort to manage long-term care organizations ethically has gained increasing importance. That is not to say that most long-term care managers are not or have not been managing ethically. They have. It is just that there is a new degree of attention paid to the topic—probably because of so many high-profile corporate ethical failures in the news.

■ Vocabulary Terms

The following terms are included in this chapter. They are important to the topics and issues discussed here and should become familiar to readers. Some of the terms are also found in other chapters but may be used in different contexts. They may not be fully defined herein. Thus, readers may wish to seek other supplementary definitions.

abuse	competency
access to long-term care	confidentiality
activity programs	consumer choice
advance directive	decision-making capacity
autonomy	dependency
beneficence	durable power of attorney
code of conduct	end-of-life issues
code of ethics	ethics committee

ethics management program
explicit rationing
functional disability
functional independence
futile care
guardian
implicit rationing
incompetent
informed consent
living will

management ethics
Patient Self-Determination Act of
  1990
physician-assisted suicide
quality of life
rationality
restraints
right-to-die law
transfer of assets

■ Discussion Questions

The following questions are presented to assist you in understanding the material covered in this chapter. They tend to be general but lend themselves to detailed answers, which can be found in the chapter.

1. What are the most common problems faced by consumers when suffering disabling conditions or otherwise needing long-term care services?
2. What is rationing (explicit and implicit), and what are some of the ways in which it occurs?
3. What does the Patient Self-Determination Act of 1990 do for consumers? What does it require of providers?
4. What is meant by the autonomy–beneficence conflict?
5. What is the difference between competency and rationality, and how does that difference affect decision making in long-term care?
6. What is informed consent, and whose responsibility is it?
7. What are the functions of ethics committees in long-term care?
8. What are the most common types of ethical issues relating to daily life in a long-term care facility?
9. What constitutes abuse in a long-term care setting? How might it be avoided?
10. How is management ethics different from other types of long-term care ethics? How is it similar?

■ References

Agich, G. (2009). Respecting the autonomy of old people living in nursing homes. In E. Morrison (Ed.), *Health care ethics: Critical issues for the 21st century* (2nd ed., pp. 184–200). Sudbury, MA: Jones and Bartlett.

Chand, S. (2014). *Organizational culture: Meaning, structure and other details*. Retrieved from The Next Generation Library: http://www.yourarticlelibrary.com/organization/organizational -culture-meaning-structure-and-other-details/29504/.

Chell, B. (2009). Competency: What it is, what it isn't, and why it matters. In E. Morrison (Ed.), *Health care ethics: Critical issues for the 21st century* (2nd ed., pp. 111–122). Sudbury, MA: Jones and Bartlett.

Clarke, D. (2009). The Patient Self-Determination Act. In E. Morrison (Ed.), *Health care ethics: Critical issues for the 21st century* (2nd ed., pp. 123–166). Sudbury, MA: Jones and Bartlett.

Collopy, B. E. (1991, March–April). *New directions in nursing home ethics.* Garrison, NY: Hastings Center.

Coons, D., & Mace, N. (1996). *Quality of life in long-term care.* New York, NY: Haworth Press.

Farrell, D., & Elliot, A. (2008). Investing in culture change. *Provider*, Aug; *34*(8). Pp. 18–30.

Geron, S. (2000, Fall). *The quality of consumer-directed long-term care.* Retrieved from http://www .questia.com/library/journal/1P3-64938894/the-quality-of-consumer-directed-long-term-care.

Grant, L. (2008). *Culture change in a for-profit nursing home chain: An evaluation.* New York, NY: The Commonwealth Fund.

Hackler, C. (2009). Is rationing of health care ethically defensible? In E. Morrison (Ed.), *Health care ethics: Critical issues for the 21st century* (2nd ed., pp. 355–364). Sudbury, MA: Jones and Bartlett.

Jennings, B. (1988, February–March). *Ethical challenges of chronic illness.* Garrison, NY: Hastings Center.

Jurkowski, E. (2013). *Implementing culture change in long-term care: Benchmarks and strategies for management and practice.* New York, NY: Springer Publishing.

Magloff, L. (2014). *Examples of a code of ethics for business.* Retrieved from http://smallbusiness.chron .com/examples-code-ethics-business-4885.html.

Management Study Guide (MSG). (2013). *Ethics management programs.* Retrieved from http:// managementstudyguide.com/ethics-management-programs.htm.

McNamara, C. (2014, January 31). *Complete guide to ethics management: An ethics toolkit for managers.* Retrieved from http://managementhelp.org/businessethics/ethics-guide.htm.

MSG. (2013). *Ethics Management Programs.* Retrieved from Manaagement Study Guide: http:// managementstudyguide.com/ethics-management-programs.htm

National Institute on Aging. (2013, October 17). *Elder abuse.* Retrieved from http://www.nia.nih.gov /health/publication/elder-abuse.

National Long-Term Care Ombudsman Resource Center (NORC). (2014). *Culture change.* Retrieved from http://www.ltcombudsman.org/issues/culture-change.

Pioneer Network. (2013, February 13). *What is culture change?* Retrieved from http://www.pioneernetwork.net/CultureChange/Whatis/.

Pozgar, G. (2010). *Legal and ethical issues for health professionals* (2nd ed.). Sudbury, MA: Jones and Bartlett Learning.

Saint Joseph's College of Maine. (1993). *Criteria for designing or evaluating a long-term care system.* Standish: Saint Joseph's College of Maine.

Showalter, J. (2008). *The Law of Healthcare Administration, 5th ed.* Chicago: Health Administration Press.

Summers, J. (2009). Theory of health care ethics. In E. Morrison (Ed.), *Health care ethics: critical issues for the 21st century* (2nd ed., pp. 3–40). Sudbury, MA: Jones and Bartlett.

Williams, M. (2006, May 2006). *The ethical challenges of elder abuse.* Retrieved from http://www .medscape.org/viewarticle/532943.

Managing in the Long-Term Care System

Governance and Administration

After completing this chapter, readers will be able to:

1. Understand the nature of governance in long-term care organizations.
2. Identify the elements that make up governance.
3. Discuss the differences in governance in profit, nonprofit, and government organizations.
4. Identify and discuss the roles and responsibilities of governing boards.
5. Identify and discuss the roles and responsibilities of administration.

■ Introduction

In earlier parts of this text, the discussion covered the long-term care system, its consumers and providers, and how they interact with each other and with others outside the system. Now it is time to look at what it takes to manage within that system. Governance and administration are discussed first, and then in this and the following chapters the specific skills required of such managers are examined.

■ Definitions

The first step is to begin clarifying and defining several terms that are often confused and misused. Effective governance and administration depend on everyone who is in any way connected with them having a clear, unambiguous understanding of what the terms mean and using them correctly. Many people, however, including those directly involved, lack that understanding.

Governance. In its simplest definition, governance means governing, overseeing, presiding over. It is a broad term identifying the overall operation of the organization. As generally used, it includes both the governing body and the administration, although some feel that it should apply only to the governing body.

Governing Body. The governing body is the policy-making arm of the organization. *Governing body* is generally used as the generic term, although most governing bodies carry other, more specific names such as governing board, board of directors, board of overseers, or board of governors. Throughout this discussion, the terms *governing body* and *board* are generally used interchangeably.

Chief Executive Officer. The chief executive officer (CEO) is just what the title suggests—the top administrative official (executive) in the organization. She or he is the direct link between the governing body and the other employees, including those involved in administration. Although CEO has become the accepted title, the CEO may have other official titles, including administrator, executive director, or president.

Administration. Made up of those employees of the organization who manage the day-to-day operations of the organization, the administration carries out the policies of the governing body. It includes the top levels of administration such as the CEO, chief financial officer, and, in the case of long-term care organizations, the director of nursing services and medical director.

Administrator. This term can be used in reference to any member of the administrative team but most commonly is used synonymously with CEO.

Management. *Management* is also a generic term that refers to all who supervise the work of others. In fact, the generally accepted definition of management is accomplishing the objectives of the organization through others or, more simply, getting work done through the efforts of others. It includes various levels of the organization, depending on its size and complexity, from front-line supervisors, such as charge nurses and department heads, to the CEO.

Each of these terms/concepts is examined in much more detail, showing how they exist in different types of long-term care organizations and how they interact.

■ Organization Types and Who Governs Them

Before getting into specifics concerning the governing body and administration, let us take a brief look at the different types of ownership of long-term care organizations and how that ownership affects the nature and role of the governing bodies. There are three types of long-term care organizations: for profit, nonprofit, and public. The duties of their governing bodies are essentially the same, although their makeup may be quite different.

For-Profit Organizations

For-profit, long-term care organizations are those companies owned by individuals, partnerships, or corporations that generate (hopefully) a profit for those owners. Historically, individuals or families owned many long-term care provider organizations, particularly the more traditional nursing homes. As the system has become more complex and the demands on providers have grown, such organizations have largely given way to corporations.

The term *corporation* refers to a legal form of ownership. It means that the owners divide the profits of the organization among them. They are investors or stockholders (even if no stock is traded publicly), and their financial liability is limited to the extent of that investment. Even if the organization should go bankrupt, the individual investors would lose only the amount they had specifically invested.

When we think of long-term care corporations, we usually think of large regional or national corporations owning many facilities, and they are indeed becoming a more common form of ownership. However, the two or three owners of a small corporation have the same governance responsibilities as the stockholders of a much larger organization. So how does this difference in size affect the nature of the governing body? In smaller for-profit long-term care organizations, the governing board may include all of the owners. In a large corporation, the board is generally elected by all of the owners, or stockholders, to represent them.

Nonprofit Organizations

Nonprofit (also called not-for-profit) organizations exist to serve a community or sometimes a religious group. No individuals receive any share of the profit from the activities of the organization. All such profits (called "return on assets" in financial parlance) are reinvested in the organization. This form of organization has long been the most common in some other segments of health care, particularly acute hospitals. This is mostly the result of the way those facilities developed, quite differently from the way long-term care developed. There are, however, a significant number of nonprofit long-term care organizations providing care today. The American Health Care Association, an organization representing nursing care facilities, reported that in 2013, 68% were for profit, 25% were nonprofit, and a small number (6%) were government owned. Fifty-five percent were owned by national, multifacility chains (AHCA, 2013). Similarly, the majority of assisted living facilities are owned and operated by for-profit organizations. A 2011study found that approximately 82% were for profit and the remainder were not for profit or were owned by government entities (Park-Lee, 2011). Ownership of home healthcare, hospice, and adult day care agencies is a bit more difficult to put percentages on because many of them are combined with other organizations.

The owners of nonprofit long-term care organizations are the members of the community they serve, and the governing body is made up of individuals who represent that community. It should be noted here that the term *community* does not always refer to a municipality or geographic locality. The service community of a particular long-term care organization may be determined by a variety of demographic characteristics. For example, one nursing facility may have a mission to serve the members of a religious or ethnic group and tailor its services to meeting their needs. Another may be organized to serve a rural area covering several towns or a small segment of a large city.

The governing body of a nonprofit organization may be chosen in any of several ways, depending on its mission; however selected, that body is charged with representing the community served, just as the board of a for-profit corporation represents its owners.

Public Organizations

Public is simply another term for government owned. Public long-term care organizations are owned and operated by city, county, or national (e.g., the Department of Veterans Affairs) entities. Their owners are the voters in that jurisdiction, and the governing body is usually made up of elected or appointed government officials.

■ Governing Body and Administration: Roles and Responsibilities

The governing body and administration have numerous responsibilities. Some are independent, meaning that the responsibilities are assigned to either the board or the administration. However, most of their responsibilities are codependent, meaning that they are shared between the two groups. This discussion begins with a review of the responsibilities of the governing body, and then goes to the administration, before moving on to how they interrelate.

Governing Body

The governing body of any organization, including those engaged in providing long-term care, is the group of people legally responsible for the way that organization functions. They determine its overall direction by establishing and maintaining its mission. They represent the owners, and in the case of for-profit organizations, may actually be the owners.

Governing Body: Regulatory Requirement

Medicare and Medicaid require that organizations receiving funds from them have a governing body. There are separate definitions of the governing body and what it does for nursing care facilities, home care agencies, and hospice agencies, most likely resulting from the fact that they were written at different times by different people. However, they essentially require the governing body (1) to be legally responsible for the operation of the facility or agency and (2) to hire a qualified administrator. Some state facility licensing regulations go into much more detail concerning the requirements for governing bodies.

Governing Body: Responsibilities

The governing body, or board, of any organization has a number of specific responsibilities. The following discussion was compiled from several sources (Furr & Furr, 2013a, 2013b; Pozgar, 2010; Singh, 2010) using portions from each to develop a comprehensive list. It applies to long-term care organizations, whether for profit or nonprofit, and, generally, to public organizations, although there are occasional differences. Where such differences occur, they are explained.

1. Develop and Maintain the Mission and Operational Strategies of the Organization

Because the board has overall responsibility for the direction of the organization, it is critical that the board be directly involved in establishing the organization's mission, vision, goals, and operational strategies.

- The mission identifies and defines what the organization is all about and what it does.
- The vision identifies and defines what the organization would like to be.
- The goals are benchmarks by which progress toward the vision can be measured.
- The strategies are the way the organization sets about achieving those goals.

In some cases, particularly with public organizations, the mission may be well defined by legislation and difficult to change. In such cases, the role of the board is to make certain that the current goals of the organization and the policies created to implement the goals, are within the scope of the legislated mission. Usually, the board still has opportunities to determine what kinds of services the organization provides.

The planning process by which the mission, vision, goals, and strategies of an organization are determined is dynamic and ongoing, not static and set. Each piece must be reviewed, evaluated, and (if necessary) changed on a periodic basis. Although the CEO and other administrators may coordinate much of the planning effort, it is ultimately the responsibility of the board to ensure that it happens and that it is effective. A study of board members from a variety of businesses and industries showed that boards are beginning to realize that they need to take a much more active role in strategic planning, plan implementation, and evaluation (Furr & Furr, 2013b). It can be a very time-consuming task, but it gives everyone involved a much better grasp of the purpose of the organization. Strategic management/planning is fundamental in leading organizations in dynamic environments. It provides the momentum for change (Swayne, Duncan, & Ginter, 2006).

Strategic planning must be an ongoing process to be effective. In fact, most experts believe that the planning process is usually of more value than the resulting plan. This is because all involved, including board members, learn so much about the organization and about their roles in that organization. The process itself—collecting and analyzing data, evaluating the strengths and weaknesses of the organization, and developing strategies—contributes to informing and educating them. This makes them better participants in the governing body. Although this kind of education is valuable for all, including the administration and staff involved, it may mean more to board members. They are not full-time employees and have limited interaction with operational details of the facility or agency. Seldom do they have such a good opportunity to learn how it functions and who its constituents are.

2. Determine the Programs and Services of the Organization and Monitor Them

One very tangible result of these planning activities is determination of which programs and services should be offered by the organization. Will it offer only skilled nursing services, or will it be a multilevel organization providing other services such as assisted living and/or home care? Will it find a service niche and concentrate on it or attempt to serve a broader constituency of consumers? Questions like these are critical to the long-range success of any business, including those in long-term care. Such questions apply even when the mission is somewhat limited, such as those of the public facilities referenced earlier. For example, a county facility with a mission of caring for the poor that has always provided only traditional nursing home care (skilled nursing care) might decide that it could better serve its constituents if it converted part of that facility to assisted living.

The board has the final say on whether services are added, continued, or discontinued. These decisions are seldom easy and usually have great impact on the organization, its staff, and customers. Some boards let the CEO and other members of the administrative staff make such decisions, but those on the board are accountable and should be involved in making the decisions. This involvement means monitoring the performance of the various services to stay abreast of how well they are doing. By reviewing performance data regularly, the board and administration should be able to anticipate serious changes in either the volume or quality of services provided and be prepared to act accordingly.

3. Select a CEO and Evaluate His or Her Performance

Many argue, with considerable justification, that the most important role of the board is the selection of a CEO. The functions of the CEO are far reaching and critical, making the selection of the CEO an extraordinarily demanding board decision (Griffith & White, 2010). Because the CEO is the primary agent in accomplishing the purposes of the organization, the board must take every action possible to ensure that the CEO is qualified for the position.

In small, for-profit long-term care organizations, one of the owners often serves as CEO. As the business of long-term care has become more complex and the organizations have become larger, there has been a definite trend away from owner-administrators. More and more, long-term care organizations are hiring an outside or professional administrator. Quickly, lest anyone interpret these words as indicating that owner-administrators are not professionals, let us explain that they are. The term *professional* as used here is more in keeping with the concept of hired help. In such cases, the CEO is much more similar to the CEOs of nonprofit or public organizations.

Having hired the CEO, the board has an ongoing responsibility to evaluate her or his performance. Failure to do so raises all kinds of possibilities for disaster for both the board and CEO. The corporate scandals of recent years in other businesses often pitted boards and CEOs against each other, with each side pointing fingers at the other. Failure by the board to know and understand what the administration is doing is no excuse for poor performance, nor is the CEO saying, "I thought that was what they wanted."

A good, board-driven CEO evaluation process provides good feedback, guides the CEO in continuous improvement of his or her own performance, clarifies expectations that address ineffective behavior before it becomes a crisis, and enhances board–CEO communication (Furr & Furr, 2013b). It can avoid misunderstandings and the resultant strained relations between these two most important segments of the governance structure of the organization.

The evaluation process should include a clear statement of the board's expectations of the CEO, as well as a list of goals that are jointly developed and mutually acceptable. These goals must relate to, and be in concurrence with, the goals of the organization. Both parties must understand how the evaluation will be conducted, and by whom. Generally, it will be board officers (e.g., chair or executive committee) or a small committee convened specifically to handle the evaluation process. As with any other personnel evaluation, it should focus on accomplishments and areas of potential improvement, rather than on failures. Finally, the evaluation should be tied to the CEO's compensation.

4. Advise the CEO

Boards are made up of people with experience and expertise in areas such as finance, human resources management, marketing, planning, and building construction. These board members have a responsibility to provide such advice and assistance as they can. However, they must not cross the line into interference in the actual operation of the organization, as discussed in the "Potential Problem Areas" section later herein.

5. Plan for Management Succession

Just as the board has a duty to hire a qualified CEO, it also has a responsibility to provide for other members of the administrative staff, including ensuring that there is someone capable of moving into the top position should the current CEO leave. This does not necessarily mandate that the other person will be guaranteed the job, only that there will be someone capable of maintaining continuity. There must also be some assurance that the other members of the administrative staff are capable of operating the organization during any unanticipated absence of the CEO, such as illness. The board shares these responsibilities with the administration but is ultimately accountable for their fulfillment.

6. Provide Adequate Resources and Oversee Their Effective Management

The board has a responsibility to provide the administration with the resources needed to accomplish the objectives of the organization. This includes providing adequate finances and staffing. It does not mean that there will be unlimited funding, but it does mean that the board will make every effort to ensure that the administration has the necessary tools to do what is expected of it. A well-thought-out operating budget that is developed jointly by the board and administration will go far toward promoting agreement on the appropriate level of funding.

Providing adequate resources carries with it the need to ensure that those resources are used wisely. This involves active board oversight of spending. Members receive and review monthly financial and staffing reports to keep tabs on expenses and revenues. They also need to ensure that adequate information systems are in place to produce needed reports.

7. Ensure the Legal and Ethical Integrity of the Organization

The board is the body responsible for ensuring that the organization adheres to all legal and ethical standards. It must take steps to guarantee that no laws are broken and no ethical norms are violated. This is best accomplished by creating and enforcing well-thought-out policies in several areas. First, members of the board must see that employees are treated fairly and equitably. It is up to them to ensure that all financial practices, including reporting to regulatory authorities, are honest and in accordance with accepted practices. Most of all, they must ensure that the organization's customers (patients, residents, clients) receive care of the highest possible quality and are treated with dignity and respect. As with many of the responsibilities of the board, the work is shared with the administration, but the board must take final accountability for the end result.

8. Serve as a Link to the Owners and the Community

The board exists as a group representing the owners of the organization. As discussed earlier, these owners may be the members of the community served. The board has a responsibility to carry the message of the organization to the community. It is in an excellent position to articulate the organization's mission to the public, let the public know of its accomplishments, and gain support of key individuals and groups outside of the organization (Ingram, 2010).

9. Organize Themselves to Effectively Carry Out Their Responsibilities and Evaluate Their Performance

Boards are in the somewhat unique position of setting their own rules for how they manage their own responsibilities. These rules must be in keeping with all legal and regulatory requirements, but other than that there is no other body telling them how to organize. This has its pluses and minuses. On the plus side, it gives boards considerable freedom to find the way that works best for them. On the minus side, it has allowed many boards to muddle along in relative inefficiency and ineffectiveness.

The board establishes how it will deal with each of its responsibilities. It sets up committees and reporting mechanisms. It determines how the CEO and other members of the administrative staff interact with it. For the board to be effective, these decisions should be formalized. Creating governance mechanisms is not a one-time task. It must be ongoing, and the board should continually evaluate itself and its performance. A formal board self-evaluation process can demonstrate areas in which the board is doing very well and areas in which it could use improvement. A board that is willing to hold itself up to such scrutiny becomes stronger and more effective. It learns its relative strengths and weaknesses and is able to act to capitalize on the strengths and overcome the weaknesses. A board undergoing self-evaluation should ask the following questions:

- Are we getting the information we need to fulfill our responsibilities?
- Are our meetings effective and designed to create an environment for honest expression of views from everyone?
- Is the composition of the board such that it has the breadth and depth of competencies needed?
- Are we accountable? (Furr & Furr, 2013b)

10. Ensure Board Succession

Good governance involves incorporating policies to make certain that it will continue beyond the tenure of individual board members. This includes practices such as setting term limits for board members, creating a mechanism for bringing new members to the board periodically, and providing ongoing training and education of all board members. When boards take these responsibilities seriously, as most do, its portion of organizational governance will be effective.

Administration

Having defined the role and responsibilities of the board or governing body, let us examine the other principal player in the governance of long-term care organizations—the administration. Whereas the role of the governing body is to develop policies and oversee the way the organization operates, it is up to the administration to carry out these policies and see to the day-to-day functioning. The authority of the administration is delegated by the board, and whatever actions the administration takes are on behalf of the board.

Members of the Administration

The term *administration* generally refers to the top level or levels of staff within the hierarchy of the organization. It always includes the CEO and usually includes several other administrative staff such as the chief financial officer, the director of nursing services, and the medical director. Other titles, such as assistant administrator, may be used in addition to or in place of the other titles listed here. Regardless of the exact titles used, the members of the administration have in common that they all supervise other staff.

Functions of the Administration

Perhaps the easiest way to cover what the administrative staff do is to show how they fit into the most commonly accepted functions of administration (management): planning, organizing, staffing, leading, and controlling.

Planning

The planning function involves identifying and defining the desired ends to be achieved and determining appropriate means to achieve those defined ends (Gibson, Ivancevich, & Konopaske, 2012). It includes both formal and informal planning activities. Formal planning is generally referred to as strategic planning or strategic management. It is the process of identifying the mission and goals of the organization, analyzing internal and external factors affecting the ability of the organization to achieve its mission and goals, evaluating alternatives, developing strategies based on that analysis, and implementing the chosen strategies. It is an ongoing process that involves the board and all levels of administration. However, the administration is usually expected to organize the strategic planning process and produce the information needed.

Informal planning also takes place in day-to-day administration. It is an integral part of making management decisions. The planning portion of dealing with any problem or situation follows the same basic steps as formal strategic planning, although it usually boils down to identifying a problem and deciding what should be done to resolve it. An example of this type of informal planning would be the CEO determining that a new employee orientation program is needed based on a growing list of problems with recently hired employees, including a high turnover rate.

This type of everyday strategic planning is part of a broader concept known as strategic thinking. Strategic thinking is "an individual intellectual process, a mindset, or method of intellectual analysis that asks people to position themselves as leaders and see the 'big picture'" (Ginter, Duncan, & Swayne, 2013, p. 13).

Organizing

The organizing function of leadership controls the overall structure of the organization. It involves designating tasks and responsibilities to employees with the specific skill sets needed to complete the tasks. Organizing also involves developing the organizational structure and chain of command within the company (Roberts, 2014). The organizing function also involves developing or applying organizational structures to translate the plans into action. It includes determining which people and activities will be involved, assigning roles, and delegating authority to act. It can be very complex, such as creating a new organizational structure to integrate a new service (e.g., adult day care) into the overall configuration of the organization. On the other hand, it may be very simple, dealing with a routine day-to-day issue. As in the example cited earlier, developing and implementing a new employee orientation program requires organization—deciding what, how, and by whom things will be done.

Staffing

Staffing involves providing the needed staff to accomplish the objectives of the organization. The main purpose of staffing is to hire the right people for the right jobs to achieve the objectives of the organization (Roberts, 2014). Many experts do not list it as a separate function of management but include it as part of organizing. However, many long-term care organizations are small enough that the top levels of administration are much more involved in staffing issues than they would be in larger, more complex organizations. Therefore, it is listed here as a separate function. In its broadest sense, staffing includes all of the activities normally associated with personnel management or human resource management: recruitment, development of personnel policies and procedures, wage and hour administration, orientation, and training. With less complicated management situations, staffing simply means assigning the right staff to the right jobs.

Leading

The leading function is also called "directing" by some. However, the change of name is indicative of the change in management philosophy away from dictating and ordering people to leading them. Thus, the term *leading* is used throughout this discussion. Leading, or leadership, is such an important subject, and such a huge one, that full textbooks have been written about it. Obviously there is not room for that kind of detail here; however, there are some basic leadership skills required of all managers, particularly those who reach the CEO position.

Leadership is a process of social influence that maximizes the efforts of others toward the achievement of a goal (Kruse, 2013). It is about enabling those others to do their jobs to the best of their abilities or, as one leading leadership text put it, "Leadership is ultimately about creating a way for people to contribute to making something extraordinary happen" (Kouzes & Posner, 2007, p. 3).

The leadership function is very much concerned with the way administrators interact with their staff members. It is the way in which they (the administrators) relate to others and get those others to willingly follow their lead. Leadership requires that the CEO and other members of the administrative team serve as examples for all other staff members. This means that they must establish a high moral and ethical tone. They must also make clear what their expectations are in terms of work ethics and customer service. A knowledgeable management/leadership expert can identify quite well how top management (the CEO) functions by observing how other members of the staff function. If there is a general feeling that the organization's employees enjoy their work and enjoy serving their residents or clients, it is a pretty good sign that the CEO is doing a good job and is exercising good leadership.

Controlling

Many people think of controlling as having power over or manipulating others. This is not at all how the term is used in describing management functions. The controlling function of management is one of determining whether intended outcomes are achieved and, if not, why not (Gibson et al., 2012). It is how an administrator checks to determine whether tasks were completed and how well. The controlling function is essential to management effectiveness in that it provides crucial information needed to make changes for the better. Requiring a periodic report of certain activities is a form of controlling, as are monthly financial reports. Again using the example of a new employee orientation program, the CEO would fulfill the controlling function by comparing the problems that existed before implementation of the new program (including the high turnover rate) to similar information gathered after implementation to determine whether the program was successful.

These functions of administration have been presented here linearly, suggesting that one follows another in an orderly manner, which they sometimes do. However, that is not always the case. In practice, administrators are usually balancing (juggling?) several projects, problems, and situations at the same time, and the functions are bound to overlap. It is the need to deal with several sets of circumstances at once that makes administration both difficult and challenging. With few exceptions, most facilities do not have separate positions of human resource manager, financial officer, marketing director, and quality control manager. Thus, a typical nursing home administrator wears several different hats (Singh, 2010).

Other Responsibilities

Although most activities of administration fall within these functional categories, there are other, more specific responsibilities of the administration. Some portions of them may be delegated to assistants, but the final answerability rests with the CEO. In fact, the CEO usually performs most of these tasks himself or herself.

Keeping the Governing Body Informed

If the governing body (board) is to fulfill its responsibilities, it must have a sufficient quantity of high-quality information. For instance, to evaluate the quality and financial effectiveness of services provided by the organization, the board needs access to quality and financial information such as quality assurance committee reports, state surveys, cost reports, and periodic financial statements. To carry out its planning responsibilities, it needs a detailed analysis of both internal strengths and weaknesses and external factors affecting the organization. Information such as this is supplied to the board by the CEO. Some is given to them regularly, such as staffing and financial reports handed out at board meetings. Other kinds of information may be requested by the board on an ad hoc basis. It is the responsibility of the CEO to keep the board informed and to provide it with whatever data it needs. In recent years, the expanding use of information technology has made it easier to do so, but this has also increased the sheer volume of information available. It is up to the CEO to sort through it to avoid overwhelming the board with too many, sometimes useless, statistics.

Educating the Governing Body

In addition to providing the board with the information it needs to function, the CEO also has a duty to keep the board educated concerning developments in long-term care. This includes developing an orientation program for new board members and presenting them with current facts about regulations, legislation, and other issues affecting the organization. They should receive regular briefings about what is happening in the state and nation, trends such as shortages of particular types of staff, and what competitor organizations are doing. Because the board has legal liability for their actions, the CEO, with assistance from legal counsel, should ensure that all board members understand that liability. Keeping in mind that the board members serve the organization on a part-time basis, the full-time CEO is in a position to be more up to date on such issues. It is up to him or her to pass that knowledge on to the board.

Overseeing Use of Resources

Just as the board has an obligation to oversee the way resources (funds, staff, etc.) are used, so does the CEO. The board is responsible for overall oversight, but the CEO, aided by others in administration such as the chief financial officer and director of human resources, is responsible for managing those resources in a hands-on manner. This means setting up procedures for the approval of expenditures and the hiring of staff. It also means monitoring both expenses and revenues to maintain a proper balance. Although the board approves all budgets, the administration develops them for approval.

Ensuring the Integrity of the Organization

The administration, particularly the CEO, has a responsibility to ensure that all actions taken by the organization or on its behalf are legal and ethical. Long-term care CEOs spend a great deal of their time and effort complying with regulations and documenting such compliance. Some of the detailed work involved in compliance can be delegated to others, but the CEO must be personally involved to ensure that the end result is appropriate because she or he is ultimately responsible—and is liable—for doing so. Similarly, the CEO has a duty to ensure that everything done by or within the organization is done in an ethical manner. The organization's relations with consumers, staff, and outside agencies must be handled ethically and with a sense of social responsibility.

Maintaining Good Community Relations

It is important that all long-term care organizations maintain good relations with the communities they serve. The CEO is often the most visible member of the administration in the outside environment and must continually look for ways to foster good community relations. This may mean involvement in other social or service organizations, participation in charity events, or simply interacting one-on-one with the leaders of other healthcare organizations. It often involves open houses and other means of letting the community see what the organization does and the services it provides.

Creating a High Level of Administrative Capability

The CEO is assisted in her or his duties by a varying number of other members of the administrative team. An effective CEO works at developing a team of managers who are highly qualified and well trained in their specific areas of expertise. The CEO has an ongoing responsibility to help these others grow professionally, both for their own good and for the good of the organization.

By now, readers have recognized many areas of overlap between the duties of the governing body and those of the administration, especially the CEO, demonstrating how interdependent they really are in their joint governance roles. For the organization to succeed there must be a synergistic relationship between the two; they should work together and be moving in the same direction with common goals and objectives.

■ Potential Problem Areas

The relationship between the governing body and administration is not always smooth. There are many areas of potential difficulty and conflict, caused in part because they have similar responsibilities and because the ways those responsibilities are fulfilled are so closely aligned.

Board Interference in the Administration

One of the most common reasons for conflict occurs when the board, or an individual board member, becomes too involved in the day-to-day operations. Whenever CEOs get together with their counterparts from other organizations, the conversation often turns to the topic of board interference. Stories abound of ways in which boards get in the way of administration—at least as seen by administrators. The following are some of the more frequently heard examples of board member interference:

- Seeking to have a friend or acquaintance hired by the organization, although the friend may not be the best qualified person, bypassing the usual hiring policies and practices.
- Seeking to have a friend or family member admitted to the services of the organization, again bypassing the usual (and usually regulatory) processes.
- Getting involved in a disciplinary situation involving an employee.
- Allowing employees to go directly to the board with complaints about the administration.
- Becoming involved in purchasing or other financial decisions.
- Second-guessing management decisions (not the same as holding management accountable).

These are examples of board members forgetting or ignoring the distinct roles of the governing body and the administration. If the administration is to be held accountable for fulfilling its responsibilities, the board must let it do so without interference. Although each example seems relatively innocuous, taken together they can seriously undermine the authority of the administration. What is worse, they jeopardize the all-important relationship between the CEO and the board. Such actions are usually not intended to create problems, but the end result is that they do.

Overstepping Administrative Authority

Role violations are not solely on the part of the board; there are also potential problems caused by the administration exceeding its authority. Such transgressions can include:

- Failure to keep the board informed of situations that could potentially have a negative impact on the organization, such as failure to comply with regulations.
- Making or approving expenditures in excess of the amount previously authorized by the board.
- Not implementing board-approved policies.
- Implementing policies or procedures without board approval.
- Negotiating with other organizations without board approval.

Conflict of Interest

Both the board and administration have an obligation to avoid any situations constituting conflict of interest. Any time members of the governing body or the administration take actions that serve their own welfare instead of the good of the organization, there is a conflict of interest. Some examples of possible conflict of interest could include a situation in which the board contracts with a business owned by a board member for such items as fuel, supplies, or insurance coverage without going through a competitive bidding process. Another would occur when the CEO or a member of the administrative staff works a second job for a competitor.

It is worth noting here that the appearance of a conflict of interest can be just as damaging as the actual actions. All who are involved in governance have an obligation to avoid even the appearance of misdeeds. Long-term care providers are under constant scrutiny by regulatory bodies, consumer advocacy groups, their owners, and the public. Any perceived or actual violation of ethical principles can be costly to the individuals and to the organization. The reason conflict of interest promotes disunity is that it almost always puts another member of the governance team in a difficult spot. If the board or a board member creates a conflict-of-interest situation, the administration has an ethical duty to report it. When the administration gets involved in a conflict-of-interest situation, the board loses trust in it.

As shown by these examples, most problems between the governing body and administration result from one of them impinging on the authority of the other. It is often unintentional but can be very damaging to the ongoing relationship between them. Problems such as these can best be avoided by clearly defining their respective roles, developing unambiguous policies and procedures, and working hard at abiding by those policies and procedures. It is really a matter of having mutual respect for each other.

■ What's Different About Long-Term Care?

As a general rule, governance and administration are not all that different from one type of business to another. However, there are some areas deserving of a bit more discussion, including licensing of administrators, management structure, corporate relationships and their impact on individual facilities or agencies, and legal liability.

Licensing of Administrators

Long-term care is somewhat unusual in that many of its administrators must be licensed. Throughout other industries, and even throughout other segments of health care, top administrators do not have to meet such a legal condition. Licensing requires long-term care administrators to acquire specific education and experience in order to be allowed to do their jobs. This does not mean that unlicensed administrators of other businesses are in any way less qualified, only that the way in which their performance is monitored is different. Although other administrators may lose their jobs for poor performance, licensed nursing facility or assisted living administrators would not only be fired but also might lose their licenses, meaning that they could not be employed by another similar facility.

Management Structure

By nature, long-term care organizations are lean with a relatively flat hierarchy. The layers of management found in many other types of organizations are mostly absent from their organizational structures. A flat structure means that the administrator has a broader span of administrative responsibilities compared with other types of organizations with taller hierarchical structures (Singh, 2010). Acute hospital administrators have numerous specialists as department heads dealing with areas such as human resources, finance, planning, marketing, and social services, while long-term care administrators have to handle many of these subjects themselves. It means that they must have some expertise in several areas without the availability of specialists in some of them.

Corporate Relationships

The roles and responsibilities of governing bodies and administrators have been discussed with an eye toward overall organization. When the organization is a single facility or agency, those relationships are relatively clear and straightforward, but what about the more complex relationships involved when a larger corporation with multiple facilities or agencies is being discussed, as happens so often in long-term care? It is not totally different, but it probably needs some clarification.

The overall corporation has a governing body and administration, including a CEO. It is also responsible for the multiple business units it operates. Each of those facilities or agencies has an administrator. That person performs the functions already described for administration, applying those functions to the individual facility or agency. Most such facilities do not have a local governing body, although some may have an advisory board. Thus, the CEO of that unit reports to corporate headquarters. Depending on the size and complexity of the overall organization, that reporting line may be to a corporate vice president or to a regional administrator. For the local administrator, corporate headquarters takes the place of a governing body.

Corporate policies are set by the overall board and passed along to local administrators through the corporate administration. In most cases, corporate headquarters also determines many of the procedures and operating rules for the local administrators. This gives them more uniformity of operation and also gives the local administrators access to all of the resources of the larger organization. This does help them overcome the shortcomings of the flat organizational structure described earlier. However, it does place some limits on the freedom of local administrators to innovate or adapt to the needs of their units.

Legal Liability

All governing bodies and administrators have liability for any actions that negatively affect those they serve—their customers. That liability is not unique to long-term care.

However, the liability situation in health care, including long-term care, has reached a near-crisis situation. Nursing facilities have become particular targets of high-priced lawsuits, in part because their residents are so vulnerable and so dependent on the facilities for their very lives and the quality of those lives. The responsibility of both governing bodies and administrators to protect residents has been discussed. When these entities fail to do that adequately, they are liable for damages.

Long-term care administrators are subject to two types of liability: professional liability and general liability. Because of their administrative oversight capacity, they may be liable for injuries to a patient caused by breach of duty on the part of a healthcare professional they supervise (professional liability). All other claims—claims regarding the failure of the facility to provide safe, appropriate care—are considered general liability. Because they are licensed, some long-term care administrators fall into both categories.

Most long-term care organizations now carry both general and professional liability insurance to cover the governing board, administration, and professional staff members (e.g., the medical director). In some cases, the administrators must carry their own professional liability insurance. Because of the growing number of gigantic settlements, the cost of that insurance has skyrocketed.

■ Summary

Governance of long-term care organizations is of the highest importance in the success of those organizations. It is the governing bodies and administrators who determine the direction the organization will take and how it will get there. It is they who identify the mission, vision, and goals and do what is needed to accomplish them. The relationship between governing board and administration is sometimes strained, although it need not be. Each has its own role to play and its own responsibilities. The degree to which they understand those responsibilities and work together, in large part, determines the success of the organization.

■ Vocabulary Terms

The following terms are included in this chapter. They are important to the topics and issues discussed here and should become familiar to readers. Some of the terms are also found in other chapters but may be used in different contexts. They may not be fully defined herein. Thus, readers may wish to seek other supplementary definitions.

accountability	controlling
administration	goals
board	governance
chief executive officer (CEO)	governing body

leadership	organizing
leading	planning
management	staffing
mission	strategies
organization	vision

■ Discussion Questions

The following questions are presented to assist you in understanding the material covered in this chapter. They tend to be general but lend themselves to detailed answers, which can be found in the chapter.

1. What is governance? How can it apply to both governing boards and administrators?
2. How does governance differ depending on ownership of the organization (for profit, nonprofit, government)?
3. What are some of the potential difficulties between governing bodies and administration? How can they be avoided?
4. What are the board's responsibilities concerning hiring the CEO?
5. What are some of the ways governance is different in long-term care?

■ References

American Health Care Association (AHCA). (2013, June). *LTC stats: Nursing facility operational characteristics report*. Retrieved from http://www.ahcancal.org/research_data/oscar_data/Nursing%20 Facility%20Operational%20Characteristics/LTC%20STATS_PVNF_OPERATIONS_2013Q2 _FINAL.pdf.

Furr, L., & Furr, R. (2013a). *Getting it right the first time with your first board*. Retrieved from http:// www.furrresources.com/article_board_of_directors.asp.

Furr, R., & Furr, D. (2013b). *Your board's approach to its responsibilities: Resting on laurels or raising the bar*. Retrieved from http://www.furrresources.com/article_board_responsibilities.asp.

Gibson, J., Ivancevich, J., & Konopaske, R. (2012). *Organizations: Behavior, structure, processes* (14th ed.). Boston, MA: McGraw-Hill.

Ginter, P., Duncan, W., & Swayne, L. (2013). *The strategic management of health care organizations* (7th ed.) San Francisco, CA: Jossey-Bass.

Griffith, J., & White, K. (2010). *The well-managed healthcare organization* (7th ed.). Chicago, IL: Health Administration Press.

Ingram, T. (2010). *What are the basic responsibilities of nonprofit boards?* Retrieved from http://www .uic.edu/cuppa/gci/programs/profed/online/courses/bd/week1/ten_basic_responsibilities_of _nonprofit_boards.pdf.

Kouzes, J., & Posner, B. (2007). *The leadership challenge* (4th ed.). San Francisco, CA: Jossey-Bass.

Kruse, K. (2013, April 9). *What is leadership?* Retrieved from http://www.forbes.com/sites /kevinkruse/2013/04/09/what-is-leadership/.

Park-Lee, E. (2011, December). *Residential care facilities: A key sector in the spectrum of long-term care providers in the United States.* NCHS data brief No. 78. Retrieved from http://www.cdc.gov/nchs /data/databriefs/db78.pdf.

Pozgar, G. (2010). *Legal and ethical issues for health professionals* (2nd ed.). Sudbury, MA: Jones and Bartlett Learning.

Roberts, C. (2014). *Five functions of management & leading.* Retrieved from http://smallbusiness.chron .com/five-functions-management-leading-56418.html.

Singh, D. (2010). *Effective management of long-term care facilities* (2nd ed.). Sudbury, MA: Jones & Bartlett Learning.

Swayne, L., Duncan, J., & Ginter, P. (2006). *Strategic management of health care organizations* (5th ed.). Malden, MA: Blackwell Publishing.

Leadership in Long-Term Care

After completing this chapter, readers will be able to:

1. Discuss the role of leadership in long-term care.
2. Identify the components of leadership.
3. Identify the characteristics of successful leaders.
4. Identify and understand the skills needed by successful leaders.
5. Understand how to gain or improve leadership skills.

■ Introduction

It would be a huge understatement to say that leadership is one of the most important building blocks in the foundation of successful long-term care delivery. As the field of long-term care evolves, so must the profession transform itself to keep pace. Leadership is required now more than ever to continuously look for ways to maintain or bolster organizational creativity and innovation (Dana & Olson, 2007). As one group of authors stated:

> An organization's leadership sets the tone for the entire system. Leaders' visibility makes them uniquely positioned to define the organization's quality goals, communicate these goals and gain acceptance from staff, make learning a priority, and marshal the resources necessary for the vision to become reality. (Smith, Saunders, Stuckhardt, & McGinnis, 2013, p. 257)

■ Leadership

What is leadership, anyway? It is a term we use regularly, but not always accurately. It means different things to different people and different things in different situations. We each have our own concept of what it is and how it is demonstrated.

There are many excellent and time-tested theories about leadership and an equal number of books, articles, and websites discussing those theories, including:

- Transformational leadership
- Transactional leadership
- Strategic leadership
- Participative leadership
- Collaborative leadership
- Servant leadership
- Situational leadership

It is not within the scope or intention of this text to discuss and elaborate on each of these theories, but rather to look at leadership as it applies to long-term care.

There are also many scholarly definitions of leadership. Most are arbitrary and subjective. Some are more useful than others, but there is no single, correct definition of leadership (Yuki, 2006). The one thing the various definitions have in common is that they all involve purposeful influence in a group or organization (Dana & Olson, 2007).

One definition that captures the essence of leadership particularly well came not from a scholarly journal, but from a popular novel of the 1960s. In *The Pyramid Climbers*, author Vance Packard noted that leadership "appears to be the art of getting others to want to do something that you are convinced should be done" (Packard, 1962, p. 13). The beauty of that definition is that it separates leadership into three distinct components:

1. Influencing others (getting others to do something)
2. Providing direction (something you are convinced should be done)
3. Getting voluntary acceptance (getting them to want to do it)

Should any of these three components be missing, effective leadership will not be possible. Keep this definition in mind; it is the basis for our discussion of leadership skills.

■ Leaders: Who Are They?

Who are the leaders in long-term care (or other) organizations? There are a number of questions, assumptions, and misunderstandings about who leaders are. Let us look at some of them with the goal of understanding leaders better.

Are Leaders Born or Created?

The question has long been asked whether leaders are born or made. Actually, what is really being asked is whether anyone can be a leader or only a few. James Kouzes and Barry Posner, authors of the highly successful text, *The Leadership Challenge*, answer the question emphatically and definitively, saying, "It's just pure myth that only a few can ever understand the intricacies of leadership. Leadership is not a gene, and it's not a secret code that can't be deciphered by ordinary people" (Kouzes & Posner, 2007, p. 145). Leadership is not only for a few.

Granted, leadership comes more easily to some than others, but it is a set of skills that can be learned. Anyone can have the fundamental requirements necessary for the leadership role. It has been said that there's only one thing that a person needs to actually be born with in order to be a leader later in life: intelligence. A leader needs to be smart *enough*, but effective leaders aren't necessarily the smartest people. They do have to know enough to do the job. We discuss those skills and how they are acquired and applied in considerable detail later in this chapter.

Leaders Are Prescient Visionaries

Are leaders more farsighted than others? Can they foretell the future? Do they know what tomorrow will bring? The answer to all of these questions is no. They are obviously intelligent enough to look at trends and try to proactively anticipate what may happen, but they have no special prophetic gifts. They study the past and learn from it. They apply skills such as strategic thinking and planning, which we explore later.

Leaders Are Charismatic, Possess a Special Gift

Leaders have the ability to convince others to follow them, but is that a special gift? Is it charisma—defined as "a personal magic of leadership arousing special popular loyalty or enthusiasm for a public figure (as a political leader) or a special magnetic charm or appeal" (Merriam-Webster, 2014)? Leaders certainly have charm and appeal that arouse loyalty, but again, it's not something special that only a few have.

Leadership Is Associated With a Superior Position

Leadership does not automatically relate to a position as supervisor or boss. In an ideal situation, all managers will be leaders, but that is not always the case. Some managers are unable to make the transition to leader. Similarly, not all leaders are managers. In any organization or work group, there will likely be one or two individuals to whom others routinely turn for advice or counsel, regardless of their job or position. They are leaders.

Leadership Is a Matter of Control

There was a time (long ago) when managers were taught that they had to control those they supervised, meaning to dominate, manipulate, or rule them. It implied that those supervised could not be trusted to do what is right. That is not leadership. Leadership means getting those others to want to do what is needed. A leader "is one who converts followers to leaders" (Bennis & Nanus, 1985, p. 3).

Leaders Are Remote and Distant

Another outdated management belief is that managers must be detached from their subordinates; they must be remote and distant. The idea was that they had to be seen as superior and could not break down the barrier between them and their employees. Actually, all that demonstrated was the insecurity of the managers. Leadership requires just the opposite—that leaders be seen as approachable by their followers.

■ Common Characteristics of Leaders

People look for certain things in their leaders, whether they are in long-term care or some other business. Research by Kouzes and Posner (2007) demonstrated that the top characteristics they look for are honesty, forward-looking, inspiring, and competency.

Honesty

Honesty goes beyond simply not committing crimes (although that is important). It also means being sincere. Followers want their leaders to be genuine. They want to know that what they see is what they get, and they reject phoniness, artificiality, and hypocrisy. Honesty means being fair and treating all equally. If some are treated differently from others—or are perceived to be treated differently—the leader will lose his or her followers' respect. If the leader is seen as honest, followers will understand it even when things do not go as they might wish.

Honesty also implies being trustworthy. It means saying what you mean and meaning what you say. Leaders should be willing to admit their mistakes and their faults. Followers must know that they can trust their leader. As leadership icon Warren Bennis puts it, "Leadership without mutual trust is a contradiction in terms" (Bennis, 2003, p. 131). Such trust takes a long time to develop but can be lost in an instant. A single failure of trust can invalidate many prior successes. Engendering trust is a competency that can be learned, applied, and understood. It is something that you can get good at, something you can measure and improve, something for which you can "move the needle." You cannot be an effective leader without trust (Covey, 2009).

Another aspect of honesty that is sometimes overlooked is being unselfish. Leaders must be secure enough in their roles to take blame for mistakes, even when those mistakes were the fault of others, and to give credit to others, even when the leader might properly deserve some of the credit. Being unselfish requires that a leader have patience with those who do not know as much as she or he does. There is a good feeling in knowing that you know—that should be enough.

Forward-Looking

People expect their leaders to be forward-looking. We have already said that they are not prescient, nor do they have special visionary powers. People expect leaders to have a sense of direction and a concern for the future of the organization. They must know where they are going if they expect others to willingly join them on the journey (Kouzes & Posner, 2007). A leader is not satisfied with the status quo.

Inspiring

Individuals want their leaders to be inspiring. The term *inspiring* is not used here in the religious sense, although most religious leaders are indeed inspiring. Rather, it means that a leader takes people where they did not think they could go. The leader makes them believe they can do things they had previously thought they could not. They "breathe life into people's dreams and aspirations, making those people much more willing to enlist in the movement" (Kouzes & Posner, 2007, p. 34). To better understand *inspiring* in this context, readers are urged to look the term up in a thesaurus (it can be done very easily online). It matches terms such as invigorating, enlivening, encouraging, motivating, energizing, and stimulating.

Competency

Leaders are expected to know what they are doing—to be competent. Their followers must believe in them and their ability to lead. In a field such as long-term care, there are two kinds of competence. First, the leader must be competent in the profession being practiced, such as nursing, rehabilitation, or management. That does not mean that the leader has to know as much as all of the technical professionals supervised, but he or she must know enough about them to "speak their language" and know whether they are performing well or not. A leader must know what he or she can do and what she or he cannot. He or she should not show off (as opposed to demonstrating competence). Others will see through it quickly and lose respect.

A second kind of competence is leadership competence. As we discuss later, there are specific leadership skills, and a person's ability to practice those skills is all too observable to subordinates or followers.

These characteristics are only a few of those common to successful leaders, but they are the ones most often cited.

■ Leadership Skills

Do you remember the Vance Packard definition we discussed at the beginning of this chapter? It identified three components of leadership: (1) influencing others, (2) providing direction, and (3) getting voluntary acceptance. There are specific leadership skills involved in mastering each of these components. Readers should recognize some of them as representing the basic foundation of management. That is true, but the use of these skills by leaders goes well beyond routine management.

Before moving on to the specific skills required for effective leadership, let us review several assumptions about leadership that will help to put it into perspective:

- Leadership means influencing the behavior of others.
- Leadership effectiveness relates to how successfully you influence others.
- Leadership in management involves facilitating subordinate performance.
- Leadership is a function of perception.
- Leadership in management implies a mutual dependency.
- Leadership is largely behavioral in nature.
- Leadership behavior can be learned (Management Research Group, 2002).

Keep these statements in mind as we look at specific leadership skills and how they are implemented.

■ Influencing Others

Influencing others is essential, because how can one lead if others do not follow? A leader accomplishes his or her goals through the following of others. Leadership effectiveness relates to how successfully you influence those others. As an individual contributor, you just have to decide to work harder, longer, or smarter to improve performance. When you're responsible for the performance of a group, the group is your destiny. They choose whether to act or not. When you become a leader, your influence goes up. The people who work for you pay attention to what you say and do. They adjust their behavior accordingly (Bock, 2006).

Skill: Managing Power/Influence

Influence is another term for *power*. To be effective, a leader must understand the uses and limitations of power. There are two primary types of power that leaders can use: position power and personal power (Management Research Group, 2002).

Position Power

Position power is that power or influence a person has by virtue of holding a particular position. It may be a management position or a position to which he or she is elected or appointed. There are four distinct types of position power.

Coercive Power—This is the power a person holds because he or she can affect another's life negatively. He or she can fire that person, deny a pay raise, or deny a desired position within the organization. It can be seen as the "Do what I want or I'll punish you" type of power.

Reward Power—The opposite of coercive power, this is the power a person holds because of his or her ability to reward another for doing what is wanted. The reward may be a pay raise, a promotion, or simply an elevation in status within the organization. Think of it as the "Do what I want and I'll reward you" form of power.

Legitimate Power—The power that goes along with the official position. The boss can order others to do his or her bidding because "I told you to." Use of this form of power should always be a last resort, because it does not produce willing followers.

Connection Power—It is possible to have influence over others because of a connection with someone in a position of power. People are apt to follow a person because of that person's connections, or who they know (and the perception that these connections give a person influence).

Personal Power

Personal power is power that an individual possesses that is not directly connected to any organizational setting, although it can be used in such settings. There are three types of personal power.

Expert Power—Others will follow a person if that person is seen as an expert in a particular topic area. For example, a person who is not very computer literate is likely to defer to someone who is.

Information Power—It has long been recognized that having information that others do not have gives one influence over them. Knowing the financial status of an organization gives one an advantage over others in budget negotiations.

Referent Power—This is the least recognized, but often the most important, reason individuals follow a leader. It is because they wish to be like that leader, who is a role model for them. As highly visible members of the leadership team, executives are uniquely positioned to serve as role models (Robertson & Johnson, 2010). It is why individuals buy the same athletic shoes as their athletic heroes or why novices pattern themselves after their mentors.

Having any of these types of power carries a great deal of responsibility. It is incumbent on a leader to avoid abusing power at all times. To do that the leader must understand the power he or she has, its impact on others, and its limitations. While it would sometimes be tempting to overuse power, in the long run it is self-defeating.

Leaders must also be aware of the role perception plays in the use of power and influence. If the followers think that a leader has a certain type of power, that is the same as having the power. The degree of influence on the followers is the same. Many a manager has expressed an off-the-cuff opinion about something and been surprised later when subordinates took it as an order.

Skill: Motivation

To influence others—get them to do something—a leader must be able to motivate. That includes understanding and mastering motivation techniques. There are many such techniques, but to be successful a leader does not have to be a motivational speaker (such as those often seen at conventions and meetings), nor are high-powered pep talks necessary. Day-to-day interaction with those one seeks to motivate is much more important.

The most important aspect of motivating any group of people is knowing what motivates each of them. That means knowing them as individuals! Some respond favorably to an official approach, while others prefer a simple private word from the leader. While some need continual urging and even pushing, others work better if left alone. It is up to the leader to understand what motivates each one and then to address each one appropriately. It requires work and effort, but it will pay off.

A key element of successful motivation is knowing how and when to use rewards. There is an old saying that what gets rewarded gets repeated. Just as individuals respond differently to different types of rewards, they also respond differently in different situations. Formal recognition ceremonies have their place, but much of the time a simple thank you is more effective.

Lastly, motivation must be sincere and passionate. If followers do not perceive that the leader is motivated, they will not be. They look to the leader for guidance and energy and want her or him to exhibit passion and enthusiasm.

Skill: Communication

A leader cannot influence others without being able to let them know what is wanted. She or he must understand how to communicate with them. There are many means of communicating, including person-to-person; written communications; and, in this age of technology, electronic communications. To be effective, a leader needs to know which of them to use in any given situation and with any specific individual or group.

The leader must also understand when to communicate, including how often. Too little communication runs the risk of leaving followers unsure of the leader's wishes. It also leaves them feeling uncertain and insecure. On the other hand, too much communication can be just as confusing. Nearly everyone has had the experience of receiving so many bits of communication that they either ignore them or take them less seriously than they should. It used to be some people sent too many memos. Today, it seems to be some send too many emails. It is human nature to tend to ignore them after a while.

Communication must be two-way to be effective. The leader must communicate with his or her followers but must also listen to them. It is not possible to know what is going on without feedback from the folks on the front line. Too many would-be leaders fail to recognize the importance of listening. That sends a signal to their followers that they do not value the input from others and/or do not care about anyone but themselves.

■ Providing Direction

Providing direction requires that the leader understand what it is that is desired. It demands knowledge of the goals to be attained. If the leader does not know where he/she wants to go, how can the followers? Leadership has the ability to align activities to ensure that individuals have the necessary resources, time, and energy to accomplish the organization's goals. By defining and visibly emphasizing a vision that encourages and rewards learning and improvement, leadership at all levels of the organization "prompt its disparate elements to work together toward a common end" (Smith et al., 2013, p. 257). There is a passage in the story of *Alice in Wonderland* by Lewis Carroll where Alice asks the Cheshire cat which path to take. He asks where she wants to go, and she says that she doesn't know, to which the cat replies that it doesn't matter which path she takes. Any group of people, particularly in a work situation, look to their leaders for direction. They want to be comfortable knowing that there is a reason for what they do and that someone in a position of authority has a vision.

Skill: Strategic Thinking

A leader must be able to see the big picture. That often means separating oneself from the day-to-day activities and visualizing a larger scenario. It is not always easy, given the many seemingly urgent events that occur every day. However, the leader must find a way to do so. In the case of a long-term care administrator, it means understanding the goals of the overall organization and making decisions within that context.

Strategic thinking can be thought of in terms of two dimensions, forward and sideways. Forward strategic thinking involves understanding what the long-range implications are of any decisions made today. What will those decisions mean 3 or 5 years in the future? Have all contingencies been considered? Sideways strategic thinking involves understanding what the implications of a decision are on others within or without the organization. Will a seemingly positive decision have negative consequences for other organizations or other units within the organization? All possible repercussions should be considered.

A successful leader needs to be able to understand abstract concepts. For example, the concept of aging in place has become generally accepted within long-term care. However, in its infancy, it was a pretty abstract concept. Those who were able to understand and embrace it easily had an advantage over those who could not. The phrase *thinking outside the box* has been much overused, but it applies in this case. A leader needs to be able to accept and understand unconventional ideas.

A leader must have a vision for the organization, work group, or other group of people over which he or she has influence. There are myriad definitions of an organizational vision. James Kouzes and Barry Posner (2007), in their outstanding book, *The Leadership Challenge*, describe a vision as "an ideal and unique image of the future" (p. 105). Another classic leadership text refers to a vision as "a target that beckons" (Bennis & Nanus, 1985, p. 89). It is not a mission statement (which says what the organization is), nor is it a prediction of what the organization is going to be. In its simplest terms, a vision is the leader's concept of where the organization should be going.

The leader must not only have a clear vision, but be able to communicate that vision to others. If that is done well, the others in the group will adopt the leader's vision as their own. That kind of buy-in goes a long way toward realization of the vision. Each vision is unique to both the leader and the organization, taking into account all of the internal and external factors affecting it. The leader must also realize that any vision has limitations. Unrealistic expectations can cause it to fail.

Skill: Planning

Leadership of an organization requires an ability to plan effectively. Strategic planning is not the same thing as strategic thinking, although they are obviously closely intertwined. Strategic thinking is an overall approach to leadership or management, while planning involves specific activities and skills. Planning entails understanding the environment in which the organization operates. It requires an ability to objectively assess the strengths and weaknesses of the organization.

Planning results in a written plan for the organization, clearly describing a direction for it. The plan can be seen as a blueprint for future actions and decisions. However, anyone who has been through a formal strategic planning process understands that the process is, in many ways, more important than the final plan. The process brings all of the organization's stakeholders together and demands that they come to consensus concerning the future of the organization.

While the leader needs to guide the planning process, he or she should not get overly involved in the details of the process. The ultimate focus should be on outcomes, not the process itself. If designed properly, the process will largely take care of itself.

Skill: Managing Change

Nothing is as inevitable as change. Over time, particularly in a field as dynamic as long-term care, much change will occur. A successful leader must be able to manage that change as much as possible. Managing change does not necessarily mean avoiding or even controlling it. That may not be completely possible. However, a skillful leader can influence change and sometimes direct it to the advantage of the organization.

First, the leader must be able to recognize change as it happens, or preferably well before it happens. Most change affecting long-term care administrators comes from other sources—regulators, third-party payers, competitors, or even demographic changes. There is usually little that can be done to prevent such changes, even if they are unfavorable. However, much can be done to anticipate them and their impact. That means understanding the environment (see the preceding "Skill: Planning" section) and accepting that change will happen. A successful leader has the skill to take advantage of opportunities offered by external change and to position the organization accordingly.

Managing change requires that the leader make it a part of an overall strategy. Attempting to manage change without integrating it into an overall organizational strategy is risky in that it may lead to a fragmented response, or even the wrong response. Integrating change into strategy requires having a strategy that, in turn, means understanding the organization.

While most change comes from external factors, it can actually come from within. Occurrences such as reorganization, merger or other forms of cooperation with other organizations, or creation of new services all involve change. Generally, this type of change comes about as the result of planning efforts, but not always. Whatever its origin, internally initiated changes are easier to manage than external changes, meaning that the leader has more opportunity to control them.

The leader may sometimes want to actually create change for reasons other than the change itself. It can be a way of shaking up a group of followers—eliminating complacency, motivating them, or focusing their attention. A departmental reorganization might be an example of such created change.

Skill: Decision Making

Leaders are expected to make decisions. It is an elemental part of the role. Yet, many managers who would like to be considered leaders have difficulty doing so. There are many reasons for such reluctance to commit. They may not feel that they have enough information to make a decision, or that they have the authority to. Usually, however, it represents an unwillingness to take a stand and be held accountable. They fear making a mistake or being seen as wrong. That fear can spring from personal and professional insecurity or may be because the person involved recognizes the impact of his or her decisions on others and does not want to be responsible for that impact.

Whatever the reason, a leader cannot dodge making decisions and still be successful. A leader must be decisive. Inaction is like a vacuum. If the leader or manager does not make a decision, someone else will. Procrastination can undermine all leaders have built. That does not, however, mean that leaders must always make quick decisions. A successful leader understands the need to gather information and input to support the decision to be made. He or she also understands the implications of any decision. Most decisions affect some people more favorably than others and may negatively affect some. Thus, the decision may not be popular. Still, it must be made. A no-decision leaves everyone unhappy in most circumstances. Making decisions requires the leader to be a bit of a risk-taker. Successful leaders are comfortable making decisions and standing by them.

■ Getting Voluntary Acceptance

The third component of leadership is getting voluntary acceptance. It may be the most difficult of all, in that it requires convincing others to follow willingly, not by force or coercion. There are several separate, but related skills involved.

Skill: Enabling

Leadership in management involves facilitating subordinate performance. The job of a leader or manager is to accomplish organizational objectives through others. That is done more easily and effectively by enabling those others to do their jobs rather than controlling how they work. The first step in enabling is to set clear expectations—letting them know what is wanted and how it is to be measured. Paraphrasing the Cheshire cat quote referenced earlier, we might ask: "If you don't know where you're going, how will you know when you get there?"

Once expectations have been spelled out, it is time for someone to go to work. The leader cannot do it all, but must rely on others to perform most tasks. That involves delegation. It has been said that delegation is the sincerest form of trust (Pratt, 1997). Enabling others necessitates trusting them to do what is needed and to do it well, or at least adequately. Many would-be leaders are afraid to delegate (enable) for fear of having to live with the inadequate work of others. They do not trust them to come through.

Even though the leader has clearly set expectations, he or she should not micromanage the work processes by telling the others exactly how to do the work. While the need for such direction can vary, depending on the tasks and the abilities of workers to do them, a true leader encourages the staff to be creative and innovative. They are the ones most directly knowledgeable about the work they do and often have suggestions for improvement—if someone just asks them. It has been proven over and over that individuals grow both personally and professionally when given tasks that challenge them. A culture must be created where all employees can challenge something that does not make sense to them. This requires a high level of trust, communication, and freedom.

An important part of enabling others is providing them with the necessary support, which may range from simple moral support and encouragement to providing resources to assist them. It is the leader's job to make those others successful.

Lastly, part of enabling others is staying out of their way. Be an enabler, not a barrier. Too often, managers inhibit the ability of their staff members to be creative and successful by placing barriers in their way. Whether those barriers are created by the enforcement of regulations and rules, failure to provide adequate resources, or simply micromanagement, they need to be avoided for a leader to be a successful enabler. We noted earlier that leadership in management implies a mutual dependency. What we mean by that is that managers or leaders and those they lead or manage must rely on each other. A failing of many managers that keeps them from becoming true leaders is that they are reluctant to depend on their followers or subordinates. They are afraid those others will not meet their expectations. It is something they need to get over if they are to be successful and effective as leaders.

Skill: Providing Feedback

Even if the leader or manager has followed all of the preceding enabling steps, the process is not complete without giving workers feedback telling them how well they have performed. They deserve to know if they have met expectations, and if not, why. That is how they will grow and improve. Giving feedback is the process of providing them with that information. It comes in two forms: positive feedback and negative (euphemistically called "constructive") feedback. Positive feedback consists of telling them what they did right and praising them for it. Constructive feedback tells them what they can do better next time. Both are equally important. Most managers are more comfortable giving one than the other, but to be successful they must be able to do both.

Most prefer to give good news rather than bad news because they do not want to face the other person in a difficult situation. That is simply not fair to the person who wants to know how to improve on the job. However, there are those who are uncomfortable praising others, often because they are uncomfortable receiving praise. It is something they need to get over if they are to be successful leaders.

Skill: Problem Solving

Leaders are faced with problems to be solved. Without such problems, there often would be no need for leaders. Problem solving involves three steps, each with its own skill set. First, the leader must learn to recognize problems. The sooner potential problems can be identified, the sooner they can be solved, but that can be difficult. It means that the leader must be aware at all times of what is going on around him or her. Recognizing problems also entails knowing when a situation is not a problem. Understanding when to not act can be as important as knowing when to act. What may seem to be a problem—or is seen as a problem by someone else—may not really necessitate the involvement of the leader. A little benign neglect is sometimes a good thing.

Once problems have been recognized and identified, the next step is prioritizing them. Not all problems are of equal gravity, nor do they require equal actions. Some may be urgent but not serious, others serious but not urgent, and some both urgent and serious. The latter group obviously requires higher priority.

The final step is solving the problems. If the first two steps have been conducted properly, it may be the easiest step of all. Then, again, it may not. Few problems present single, obvious solutions. Rather, there may be several solutions with varying degrees of desirability. It is the leader's job to seek the optimal solution—and hope it was the right one.

Many problems can be forestalled, at least at the level of involvement of the leader, if others in the organization are taught how to problem solve. It enables them and frees the leader up to deal with more important matters.

Skill: Conflict Resolution

At first glance, problem solving and conflict resolution might seem to be the same. They are similar but not necessarily identical and may require different skills. Whereas problem solving may include choosing among multiple solutions, there may not be actual conflict involved. Conflict occurs when there are two divergent forces at work. That may mean two or more individuals with differing views or separate work units with conflicting interests or agendas. No matter how legitimate the positions of those involved, there is a potential for discord, tension, and even hostility.

As with other forms of problem solving, the first step is to identify the nature of the conflict. This is particularly important in conflict resolution because many conflict situations grow out of misunderstandings. It is up to the leader to clarify what is at stake and where each of the opponent's interests lies. That is a huge step toward resolving the conflict.

The most difficult part of conflict resolution is that it is usually unpleasant. It is likely that one party will be less than satisfied with the resolution chosen. It is the role of the leader to gain acceptance from them, at least to the degree possible, and to explain to all involved why a particular resolution was chosen.

Skill: Negotiation

Whereas conflict resolution usually involves resolving differences between two other parties, negotiation is the process of reaching an amicable agreement when there are differences between the leader and another party. It often comes into play when the leader or manager is representing the organization in interaction with another organization, but it may involve individuals in some instances.

The skill of negotiation requires understanding two key elements: what both parties want and what they are willing to give up. One of the most common situations requiring negotiation is wage and salary talks between an employer and an employee bargaining group (labor union). Each side attempts to estimate how far they can push the other. The better they can calculate the other party's limits, the stronger their negotiating position. Another, usually less contentious, example of negotiation would include sharing of services by two or more organizations or facilities.

The goal of negotiation is to arrive at an agreement that is good for both parties. While both parties may not be equally satisfied with the final agreement, the negotiation is a success if both are comfortable living with it. Negotiation is a skill that can be best learned and refined through experience, although there are classes that can be taken to learn the basics.

Skill: Mentoring

An effective leader is a mentor or coach. He or she understands the importance of developing those around him or her, creating new leaders. It is a critical part of enabling them as well as getting and maintaining their commitment. Mentoring takes time and effort, but it is highly rewarding. It involves being able to recognize potential talent and expertise—and finding ways to develop that talent and expertise.

The goal of mentoring is to bring out the best in people and help them reach their full potential. Many organizations have implemented formal mentoring programs, whereby new or junior staff members are joined with more experienced colleagues to assist them and to help them to grow. However, informal mentoring can be every bit as successful and rewarding. Simply taking an interest in subordinates and their careers is a good start. People are a leader's most valuable asset. Leadership success depends on an ability to surround oneself with an inner core of competent people who complement one's particular leadership style and goals (Pollice, 2008).

Skill: Team Building

By definition, a leader needs a group of followers (or employees in the case of an administrator). However, converting that group into a team requires certain skills. One text defines a team as "a high-performing task group whose members are actively interdependent and share common performance objectives" (Francis & Young, 1992, p. 9). That definition nicely fits leadership within the context of management. It highlights the important aspects of an effective team: high-performing, actively interdependent, and sharing common objectives.

One of the responsibilities of a leader is to motivate the team members to all work together toward the common objective. This can be a daunting mandate because a team often comprises diverse members, each with their own strengths, weaknesses, and work styles. The team dynamics are also often complicated by internal disagreements and personal conflicts, making creation of team dynamics difficult.

Team building takes skill. The team leader must provide direction to the team and facilitate its activities toward common goals. If that is done well, the team members will see themselves as a team and take pride in being part of it. They will identify with the team as much as with their own separate roles. They will collectively share the challenges facing the team and celebrate its successes as a group. It is important here to note that the leader must fulfill dual roles, both as the leader of the team and as a team member. Balancing them may be difficult at times, but neither role can be ignored.

Skill: Managing Stress

Being a leader can be stressful. It goes with the position. Managers who cannot accept this concept are not likely to succeed as leaders. Yet, stress can be managed. Doing so begins with recognizing where the stress is coming from. It may be from the need to make difficult decisions, experiencing pressures on one's time and activities from multiple sources, or the responsibilities of the position. In long-term care, as in other segments of health care today, much of the stress comes from having to do one's job with inadequate resources.

The best way to manage such stress is to do the best you can and understand that you may not be able to please everyone or accomplish all that is expected of you. A leader should try to avoid expending time, worry, or effort on those things that he or she cannot control. There are plenty of other things to deal with. Also, a leader should try not to dwell on what has already happened. Look ahead. If a leader can do those things, he or she can relieve a lot of the stress in the job.

A leader needs to recognize that other members of the staff also experience stress. He or she needs to acknowledge that and do everything possible to help them deal with it.

■ Gaining and Improving Leadership Skills

The list of essential leadership skills given herein is lengthy and may, at first glance, appear to be difficult to achieve. That does not have to be the case. As noted earlier, leadership skills are not all that different from good management skills. They simply take those management skills to a higher level.

Remember the assumptions about leadership discussed earlier? Two of those assumptions were:

- Leadership is largely behavioral in nature.
- Leadership behavior can be learned.

These assumptions are important because they demonstrate first that people judge a leader's skills by the actions they observe (how the leader behaves) and second that leaders can change the way they are seen (learning new behaviors and skills). Leadership behaviors are primarily learned and are often categorized as task oriented, relations oriented, and participative (Dana & Olson, 2007).

These skills can be learned in numerous ways. One can attend classes or seminars, read books and articles, and/or learn them through practice on the job. Actually, a combination of these methods is usually most effective and most practical. However, prior to embarking on a process of gaining or improving one's leadership skills, there are a couple of steps that must occur: recognizing the need for improvement and assessing current skills.

Recognize the Need for Improvement

Before improvement can occur, there must be a realization that it is needed and possible. No one possesses leadership skills so completely that there is no room for improvement. Anyone can get better at some or all of the leadership skills we have discussed. Yet, there are always a few managers who think they are as good as they can get. They are destined to fail. If a leader wants to improve his or her leadership skills, he or she must make it a goal to go to the next level.

Assess Current Skills

Leaders must objectively assess their natural tendencies, behaviors, and how they approach people. Leadership is about being proactive, and that means continually testing one's ideas and ideals (Llopis, 2013). Even when one has recognized that improvement is possible, it is difficult to assess one's own skills and the areas where there is room for improvement. It is highly recommended that an independent, professional analysis be completed. There are many different ones available. While they vary in how the assessment is accomplished, most rely on some form of data input—a questionnaire or form—completed by the manager or leader. Some simply give the individual a format for self-assessment.

However, it is recommended that anyone sincerely interested in skills improvement look for a process that:

1. Involves input both from the individual being assessed and from others within the workplace (boss, peers, subordinates). While self-assessment is valuable, a process that involves others has the advantage of balancing how the individual thinks she or he leads and how those others see her or him.
2. Is conducted by a professional or organization with experience and expertise at conducting such assessments. The result—a foundation for self-improvement—is too important to trust it to an inadequate process.
3. Is confidential and private. The assessment results should be intended for the use of the person being assessed, not for other purposes such as hiring or promotion. While the individual may choose to share the results, it should not be mandatory. Even when others have input into the process, confidentiality can be maintained if their contributions are summarized anonymously and presented in the aggregate. This is where an independent professional conducting the assessment is a big advantage.
4. Goes beyond simply assessing skills and includes an individualized action plan for skills improvement.
5. Provides individualized assistance and tutoring for each person who completes the process.

An assessment process that includes all of these elements will be more expensive than some others, but it will be money well spent. And believe it or not, this initial assessment is often the most difficult part of a self-improvement program. If conducted well, it can lead to specific actions for skills development.

While there has been ongoing discussion and disagreement about whether leaders are born or made, there is much evidence supporting the latter. Nearly anyone can lead. Some will do it better than others—and will be more successful—but that is relative. Leadership skills can be developed, maintained, or improved. It just requires a bit of commitment and effort.

■ Summary

Leadership is critical in any organization. This is particularly true in long-term care organizations, given the fast-paced nature of the field. As has been so well documented throughout this text, it is a field that is undergoing nearly continual transformation. It is a situation crying out for leadership (that is not to imply that there is currently no leadership, just that more will always be needed). If providers are to be competitive, they need leaders who can carry them to the next level of success.

■ Vocabulary Terms

The following terms are included in this chapter. They are important to the topics and issues discussed here and should become familiar to readers. Some of the terms are also found in other chapters but may be used in different contexts. They may not be fully defined herein. Thus, readers may wish to seek other supplementary definitions.

charisma	legitimate power
coercive power	managing change
communication	managing stress
competent	mentoring
conflict resolution	motivation
connection power	negotiation
decision making	personal power
enabling	planning
expert power	position power
feedback	power
forward-looking	problem solving
honest	referent power
influence	reward power
information power	strategic thinking
inspiring	team building
leader	vision
leadership	

■ Discussion Questions

The following questions are presented to assist you in understanding the material covered in this chapter. They tend to be general but lend themselves to detailed answers, which can be found in the chapter.

1. What are the basic components of leadership?
2. What are the characteristics of leaders most commonly desired by people?
3. What skills are needed to be a successful leader?
4. How does one go about learning or improving leadership skills?
5. Why is managing organizational change important?
6. What are some barriers to successfully changing an organization's culture?

■ References

Bennis, W. (2003). *On becoming a leader.* Cambridge, MA: Perseus Books.

Bennis, W., & Nanus, B. (1985). *Leaders: The strategies for taking charge.* New York, NY: Harper & Row.

Bock, W. (2006). *Simple leadership basics.* Retrieved from http://agreatsupervisor.com/articles/simpleleadership.htm.

Covey, S. (2009, May 12). *How the best leaders build trust.* Retrieved from http://www.leadershipnow.com/CoveyOnTrust.html.

Dana, B., & Olson, D. (2007). *Effective leadership in long term care: The need and the opportunity.* Alexandria, VA: American College of Health Care Administrators.

Francis, D., & Young, D. (1992). *Improving work groups: A practical manual for team building* (Rev. ed.). San Diego, CA: Pfeiffer & Co.

Kouzes, J., & Posner, B. (2007). *The leadership challenge* (4th ed.). San Francisco, CA: Jossey-Bass.

Llopis, G. (2013, December 2). *5 ways to refresh your leadership style.* Retrieved from http://www.forbes.com/fdc/welcome_mjx.shtml.

Management Research Group. (2002). *LEA facilitator's guide.* Portland, ME: Management Research Group.

Merriam-Webster. (2014). *Merriam-Webster's online dictionary.* Retrieved from http://www.merriam-webster.com/dictionary/charisma.

Packard, V. (1962). *The pyramid climbers.* New York, NY: McGraw-Hill.

Pollice, N. (2008, April 28). *The five levels of leadership.* Retrieved from Pollice Management Group Inc.. http://pollicemanagement.com/doc/The_Five_Levels_of_Leadership.pdf.

Pratt, J. (1997). Delegation: The sincerest form of trust. *Home Health Care Management & Practice,* 9(6), 81–87.

Robertson, J., & Johnson, K. (2010). Rounding to influence. Leadership method helps executives answer the "hows" in patient safety initiatives. *Healthcare Executive,* 215(5), 72–75.

Smith, M., Saunders, R., Stuckhardt, L., & McGinnis, L. (2013). *Best care at lower cost: The path to continuously learning health care in America.* Washington, DC: The National Academies Press.

Yuki, G. (2006). *Leadership in organizations* (6th ed.). Upper Saddle River, NJ: Prentice Hall.

Culture Change in Long-Term Care

After completing this chapter, readers will be able to:

1. Understand the nature of culture change.

2. Identify the benefits of culture change.

3. Understand the role of culture change in long-term care.

4. Identify the components of culture change and how it is implemented.

5. Understand the difference between resident-centered culture change and organizational culture change.

■ Introduction

Culture change has become one of the hot items in long-term care in recent years. It has, in fact, been important for much longer than that—although not necessarily by that name. We should note here that the term *culture change* is used in two separate, but closely related, ways. The two ways in which *culture change* is used herein are as follows:

- As it applies to long-term care consumers (particularly nursing home residents).
- As it relates to changing organizational (corporate) culture in long-term care and other businesses and its impact on the organizations' employees.

Successful organizations, whether in long-term care or some other enterprise, need to be dynamic and constantly changing. An organization that is overly stable is also stagnant.

■ Culture Change and Long-Term Care Consumers

What Is Culture Change?

Defining culture change begins with defining culture. Culture is "how different aspects of human conduct—roles, norms, values, customs, likes, dislikes, symbols, language, priorities and more—dovetail and turn a group of disparate individuals into a community with a distinct identity" (Planetree, 2014). As defined by the Pioneer Network (2013), "Culture change is the common name given to the national movement for the transformation of older adult services, based on person-directed values and practices where the voices of elders and those working with them are considered and respected." Note: Culture change can apply to all forms of long-term care but has largely been applied to nursing facilities (nursing homes), and that will be the focus here. Where appropriate, we will note how it affects other providers and consumers. Another source defines it as follows:

> Culture change is a movement that seeks to create an environment for residents, which follows the residents' routines rather than those imposed by the facility; encourages appropriate assignments of staff with a team focus to make deep culture change possible; allows residents to make their own decisions; allows spontaneous activity opportunities; and encourages and allows residents to be treated as individuals. (NORC, 2014)

Yet another says "Culture change is not about change for its own sake. It is about de-institutionalizing services and individualizing care" (Consumer Voice, 2011, p. 1).

Culture change can also be described as "resident-centered care." This means settings where people can live comfortably and feel at home, as opposed to feeling like they are in an institution (Caulkins & Brush, 2009). It transforms the long-term care medical model to one that nurtures the human spirit as well as meeting medical needs. Culture change is not a finite destination—it is a work in progress, always evolving to meet the needs of the residents (MANHR, 2008).

Benefits of Culture Change

While culture change is primarily about the residents, there are benefits for the provider organization and its staff:

Resident benefits: reduces loneliness, helplessness and boredom; improves physical and mental health (e.g. reduces depression and behavioral problems); reduces unanticipated weight loss, reduces mortality, etc.

Staffing benefits: reduces employee turnover, eliminates temporary agency staffing and mandatory overtime, reduces workers' compensation claims/costs, etc.

Additional benefits: significantly improves employee, resident, and family satisfaction; increases involvement with the outside community including children, students, clubs, and religious organizations, etc. (MANHR, 2008)

Culture Change Programs

The Eden Alternative movement, which preceded the culture change movement, paved the way for person-centered environments and settings (Jurkowski, 2013). Other key players have included Wellspring, the Green House Project, and the Pioneer Network. Each has approached culture change a bit differently. Let us look at them:

The Eden Alternative

The Eden Alternative is a small, not-for-profit organization that is based on the core belief that aging should be a continued stage of development and growth, rather than a period of decline. It was created in 1991 with the mission of

> transforming institutional approaches to care into a community "where life is worth living." Awareness and adoption of some components of culture change have gained considerable momentum in the past two decades and made even greater strides in the past several years. (Eden Alternative, 2009, p. 2)

The Wellspring Model

Wellspring Innovative Solutions for Integrated Health Care was formed in 1994 as an independent, not-for-profit organization. The Wellspring model combines resident-directed care concepts, staff empowerment, and clinical training modules (Commonwealth Fund, 2004). Its facilities provide its frontline workers with training in best practices concerning nutrition, feeding, palliative care, leadership, and pain management. That training is based on problem-solving techniques and helps managers translate ideas into everyday practices. It also gives frontline workers a voice in how their work should be performed (Commonwealth Fund, 2004). The Eden Alternative and Wellspring merged their operations in 2012, enhancing their progressive approach to long-term care.

The Green House Project

One model of culture change that is gaining momentum at a fairly rapid rate is the Green House Project. The Green House Project model breaks the mold of institutional care by creating small homes for 6 to 10 elders who require skilled nursing or assisted living care. The homes are designed for the purpose of offering "privacy, autonomy, support, enjoyment, and a place to call home" (Pawloski, 2011). This model is a departure from traditional skilled nursing facilities. Each resident lives in a private room, designed to receive high levels of sunlight and easy access to all areas of the house, including the kitchen, laundry, outdoor garden, and patio (LaPorte, 2010).

Pioneer Network

The Pioneer Network was formed in 1997 by a small group of prominent professionals in long-term care to advocate for person-directed care. It advocates for elders across the spectrum of living options and is working towards "a culture of aging that supports the care of elders in settings where individual voices are heard and individual choices are respected, whether it is in nursing homes, transitional care settings or wherever home and community may be" (Pioneer Network, 2013).

Components of Culture Change

One group of authors has identified five areas within an organization that are transformed by culture change: decision-making, leadership, staff roles, the physical environment, and organizational design (Haran, 2006). Their categorization is a useful way to examine these components.

Decision Making

Giving residents more say in how they live and in the care received is at the heart of culture change. This is becoming particularly important as the baby boomers make up a larger portion of the long-term care consumer base. It has been well documented that they are better educated and more demanding and expect to play a significant role in care decisions. Culture change transformation "supports the creation of both long and short-term living environments as well as community-based settings where both older adults and their caregivers are able to express choice and practice self-determination in meaningful ways at every level of daily life" (Pioneer Network, 2013). Increasingly, nursing homes are working to be more like assisted living facilities, which emphasize privacy, dignity, and choice (Caulkins & Brush, 2009).

Leadership

It is not enough for providers to state a desire for culture change. The organization's leadership must be committed to it—particularly the ownership and administration. The administrator and other managers must be strong advocates. They should be role models that exemplify caring. When they all consistently support the culture, then the staff naturally follows (Gerber, 2012).

Staff Roles

Greater control is given to the nurse aides who handle much of the day-to-day care of residents. They are assigned to a group of residents as members of a self-directed work team. Rather than working in a single department, such as nursing, housekeeping, or food service, staff functions are blended so that all can help residents with their personal care, can lead activities, and can do cooking and light housekeeping (Haran, 2006). This gives a sense of permanence, consistency, and increased familiarity between residents and staff. The experiences of those who live and work in these settings are intricately interwoven, and "there is no greater influence on the life of a long-term care community than the relationships between residents and staff" (Planetree, 2014).

While some worry that a resident-centered care approach will make life harder for staff while deemphasizing the quality of clinical care provided, the evidence so far suggests the opposite (Haran, 2006). Clinical care is, and must be, a critical component of care. It cannot be compromised.

Educational programs are important in achieving staff acceptance of culture change. Most providers already have many educational programs for staff. However, caring behaviors can be integrated into existing educational experiences (Gerber, 2012).

The Physical Environment

While the Green House Project probably takes changes to the physical structure of nursing facilities further than most, the concept of creating homelike living units has caught on with many providers. The physical and organizational structure of the facilities becomes less institutional. Instead of nursing units or resident units, the facility is divided into "neighborhoods" with their own names and even their own entrances. Each household has its own kitchen and living room (Haran, 2006). The changes are not just structural. The language has changed as well in an effort to become less institutional. For example, the lobby or common area becomes the living room, parlor, or foyer. The nurses' station becomes a work area. The facility itself "is no longer an institution or a nursing home. It is a home, life center or living center" (Schoeneman, 2014). Your author's favorite is renaming the tub room the *spa* as one facility did.

Organizational Design

Culture change involves making significant (often previously unheard-of) changes in the way services are provided. Generally, this means organizing staff into teams and giving them more responsibility for care such as decisions about assigning tasks, scheduling, and monitoring of performance. One organization went so far as to dismantle its formal leadership group of traditional department heads. The new team established in its place includes the former department heads as well as frontline workers, such as nursing assistants and housekeeping staff (Haran, 2006).

Other Aspects of Culture Change

In addition to the basic structural changes that are necessary for successful culture change, there are other elements that are also important.

Creating a Sense of Community

Many, if not most, of the services offered in the nursing home can be provided through home-based care. What sets some facilities apart is the opportunity for residents to socialize with each other. The community atmosphere can be a selling point to potential residents (Feldman Barbera, 2014).

Amenities

Amenities can be an important component of cultural change in a long-term care facility and can be keys to creating a pleasant place to live. Thoughtful planning, design, and management of common areas can transform residents from passive observers to active participants (Koch, 2012).

Amenities could include laundry facilities on each floor, flat linen service, monthly housekeeping, and maintenance. Other amenities may include a hair salon; bank; and gift shop; social, recreational, spiritual, fitness, and wellness programs; a computer room; meditation room; library; craft room; game room or wood shop; religious services; nature areas; gardens; and footpaths (O'Brien, 2014).

Using amenities to advance social engagement supports residents' comfort and acceptance of the housing choice by the resident and family members and increases the value of the housing environment (Koch, 2012).

Transportation

Today's seniors are more mobile than generations before. While some nursing home residents have limited ability to venture outside the facility, others are able to. They need and want to get out into their communities. Getting residents where they need to go is important to keep them and their families satisfied. It also helps convince potential residents to choose the facility (LaVecchia Ragone, 2013).

Social Media

Social media is a term that covers an array of computer platforms, the most popular platforms today being Facebook, YouTube, MySpace, Twitter, LinkedIn, and Flickr (Lourde, 2010)—and probably several new ones by the time you read this. Today's long-term care consumers can be involved in social media to an extent that surprises many. Providers have found truly exceptional ways of integrating social media into their programs.

■ Organizational Culture

Every organization has its own unique culture. That culture

> is made up of the values, beliefs, underlying assumptions, attitudes, and behaviors shared by a group of people. Culture is the behavior that results when a group arrives at a set of—generally unspoken and unwritten—rules for working together. It is made up of all of the life experiences that each employee brings to the workplace. Culture is particularly influenced by the organization's founder, executives, and other managerial staff because of their role in decision making and strategic direction. (Heathfield, 2014c)

Put more simply, an organization's culture "is the collection of self-sustaining patterns of behaving, feeling, thinking, and believing, the patterns that determine 'the way we do things around here'" (Katzenbach & Aguirre, 2013). Healthcare organizations have a culture that is very different from the typical business enterprise in that they provide a service unique in society and because they are humanitarian in nature. Their managers manage in the special context of the organization's culture (Longest & Darr, 2014).

Culture is one of those terms that is difficult to express distinctly, but everyone knows it when they sense it (MacNamara, 2014). However, there is universal agreement that (1) it exists, and (2) it plays a crucial role in shaping behavior in organizations. There is little consensus on what organizational culture actually is, never mind how it influences behavior and whether it is something leaders can change (Watkins, 2013). An organization's culture can be a key to the organization's success.

Organizational culture is

the workplace environment formulated from the interaction of the employees in the workplace. It is defined by all of the life experiences, strengths, weaknesses, education, upbringing, and so forth of the employees. While executive leaders play a large role in defining organizational culture by their actions and leadership, all employees contribute to the organizational culture. (About.com, 2014)

John Griffith, a noted healthcare expert, says that an organizational culture of service excellence has five key characteristics:

1. *Respect for All Individuals*—This includes associates (employees), patients (residents), and visitors. The organization is free of any form of harassment, discrimination, or activity that creates unnecessary discomfort.
2. *Responsiveness to Questions*—Any associate, patient, or guest is entitled to the best possible answers to questions.
3. *Freedom From Blame*—It is understood that most failures in organizations are related to process rather than individuals; reporting failures is rewarded to create a culture of safety.
4. *Honesty*—The truth is expected in all transactions.
5. *Respect for Scientific Evidence*—Empirical data and established science are the gold standards for resolving questions and debates (Griffith & White, 2010).

Culture depends on relevance. Members of an organization soon come to sense the particular culture of an organization. They look for values within the organization that mean a lot to them personally. Those values must include ethical standards. Values-based leadership provides an environment that raises the ethical bar by bringing clarity to what is important and creating a stronger, more ethical culture (Switzer, 2009). Employees are able to relate it to themselves and, in turn, can relate to it. They need to feel good about the organization's policies, rules, regulations, and ethics. They need to have opportunities to advance; otherwise they will feel stuck, which can lead to negative feelings, lack of self-esteem, and a lack of empowerment. Negative perceptions by employees can affect their productivity. They need to be motivated to do their best.

One trend that is changing organizational behavior is a more relaxed work environment. It is occurring because as organizations relax the setting, the employees are becoming more productive. Leaders know the old axiom: "Happy employees mean good customer service; good customer service means happy customers; happy customers mean happy employees."

But culture is not all about the relationship between bosses and employees. Coworkers have a great deal of influence on the culture of a workplace as well. Different people in the same organization can have diverse ideas about organization's culture, especially between the top and bottom levels of the organization (MacNamara, 2014). That can both affect the organization's culture and be affected by it. The behaviors described previously can also be affected by the organization's leadership.

Changing the Culture

First, we need to remember that any culture can be changed. Changes to the organization's culture are constantly happening—both for the better and for the worse. Culture is not sacred. In many instances, it develops by accident. All organizational cultures need to be intentionally changed occasionally. Or, put another way: "Cultures are like fruit trees. If you want them to be more bountiful, they need to be reshaped, and sometimes they need a hard prune. But here's the thing: They won't prune themselves" (Beckham, 2008). Just as needing to be aware of the need for cultural change is important, so is the need to understand that any change to corporate culture will redefine the organization's identity. Changing the organizational culture may well be the toughest task a leader will ever take on. An organization's culture was formed over years of interaction among the participants in the organization (Heathfield, 2014a). An organization's culture "comprises an interlocking set of goals, roles, processes, values, communications practices, attitudes and assumptions. The elements fit together as a mutually reinforcing system and combine to prevent any attempt to change it" (MacNamara, 2014).

Implementing Organizational Cultural Change

Once the need for cultural change is recognized, how does a leader go about achieving it? There are four primary ways to influence the culture of an organization.

1. Emphasize what's important.
2. Reward employees whose behaviors reflect what's important.
3. Discourage behaviors that don't reflect what's important.
4. Model the behaviors that you want to see in the workplace (MacNamara, 2014).

Building coalitions and bolstering allies—creating a critical mass of supporters—is also important. That means knowing those around you well enough to appreciate what they believe in. It also means communicating clearly to them what you want to accomplish and what it means to the organization—and to them.

In communicating the need for change, focus on the positive. It is always more helpful to focus on what can be gained and the positive outcomes of change than to play on the fears of what is potentially being lost. Being positive can result in less resistance.

Change Takes Time

The relationship between change and performance is not something that produces an instantaneous result. It took time for the current culture to develop. It will take time to change it. While actually making a change will take time, it is also likely to take an unexpected amount of time to see results. Most cultural change involves changing how people behave and how they interact with each other and with those they serve. They will need to learn how to change.

Provide Resources

As with anything else as important as cultural change, the organization will usually have to provide resources—people, funds, training. Expecting change to happen (or telling the people in an organization to change) without giving them the resources to do so is a fool's errand.

Change Opportunities

Times of transition in a business or corporation can provide good opportunities to make changes to the overall corporate culture. Mergers, introduction of new products or services, or when individuals are being promoted or changing positions—especially when a new chief executive takes over—are all good times to change the culture.

Role of the Leader

There is usually a driving force in changing a culture. That person is the leader. The leader sets the tone, leading by example. Hopefully, the chief executive officer has the necessary leadership skills. Understanding the importance of organizational culture is not the same as being an effective cultural chief executive. The chief executive officer's direct engagement in all facets of the company's culture can make an enormous difference not only in how people feel about the company, but in how they perform (Katzenbach & Aguirre, 2013).

In any given situation, one of the responsibilities of a leader is to motivate the team members to all work together toward the common objective. This can be a daunting mandate, because it is very often the situation that a team comprises very diverse members, each with his or her own strengths, weaknesses, and work styles. The commitment of team members to work together effectively is a critical factor in team success. The relationships they develop out of this commitment are keys in team building and team success (Heathfield, 2014b).

Culture change depends on behavior change. Members of the organization must clearly understand what is expected of them and how to execute the new behaviors (Heathfield, 2014a). It requires members, especially leaders, to acknowledge the impact of their behavior on the organization's culture. Organizational culture is possibly the most critical factor determining an organization's capacity, effectiveness, and longevity.

There are several frequent mistakes in trying to change culture, including:

- Overuse of the power tools of coercion and underuse of leadership tools.
- Beginning with a vision or story, but failing to put in place the management tools that will cement the behavioral changes in place.
- Beginning with power tools even before a clear vision or story of the future is in place (Denning, 2011).

■ Summary

As we noted at the beginning of this chapter, there are two ways in which culture change is used in long-term care:

1. As it applies to long-term care consumers (particularly nursing home residents).
2. As it relates to changing organizational (corporate) culture in long-term care and other businesses and its impact on the organizations' employees.

Both have been recognized as critical to success for a long-term care provider. While the latter is important, it is the former that has the most impact on the consumers. It goes a long way toward meeting their needs.

■ Vocabulary Terms

The following terms are included in this chapter. They are important to the topics and issues discussed here and should become familiar to readers. Some of the terms are also found in other chapters but may be used in different contexts. They may not be fully defined herein. Thus, readers may wish to seek other supplementary definitions.

amenities	Green House Project
communications	organizational culture
community	Pioneer Network
culture	resident-centered
culture change	social media
Eden Alternative	Wellspring model

■ Discussion Questions

The following questions are presented to assist you in understanding the material covered in this chapter. They tend to be general but lend themselves to detailed answers, which can be found in the chapter.

1. What is culture change, and why is it important in long-term care organizations?
2. What are the similarities between resident-centered culture change and organizational culture change?
3. What are the differences between resident-centered culture change and organizational culture change?
4. What are the benefits of culture change? For residents? For staff? For the organization?
5. What are some barriers to successful culture change in an organization?

■ References

About.com. (2014). *Organizational culture: Corporate culture in organizations.* Retrieved from http://humanresources.about.com/od/organizationalculture.

Beckham, D. (2008, September 16). *The power of culture.* Retrieved from www.beckhamco.com/40articlescategory/107_powerofculture.doc.

Caulkins, M., & Brush, P. (2009, December 1). Improving quality of life in long-term care. *Perspectives on Gerontology,* 14, 37–41.

Commonwealth Fund. (2004, August 6). *Improving the quality of nursing home care: The Wellspring model.* Retrieved from http://www.commonwealthfund.org/publications/tools/2004/aug/improving-the-quality-of-nursing-home-care--the-wellspring-model.

Consumer Voice. (2011, August). *Consumer fact sheet.* Retrieved from http://theconsumervoice.org/uploads/files/advocate/Culture-Change-in-Nursing-Homes.pdf.

Denning, S. (2011, July 21). *How do you change an organizational culture?* Retrieved from http://www.forbes.com/sites/stevedenning/2011/07/23/how-do-you-change-an-organizational-culture.

Eden Alternative. (2009). *About the Eden Alternative.* Retrieved from http://www.edenalt.org/about-the-eden-alternative.

Feldman Barbera, E. (2014, February 20). *How to better foster community among long-term care residents.* Retrieved from http://www.mcknights.com/how-to-better-foster-community-among-long-term-care-residents/article/335001.

Gerber, D. (2012, December). *Create a caring culture.* Retrieved from http://www.providermagazine.com/archives/archives-2012/Pages/1212/Create-A-Caring-Culture.aspx.

Griffith, J., & White, K. (2010). *The successful health care organization* (7th ed.). Chicago, IL: Health Administration Press.

Haran, C. (2006, April 7). *Transforming long-term care: Giving residents a place to call "home."* Retrieved from http://www.commonwealthfund.org/Publications/Other/2006/Apr/Transforming-Long-Term-Care--Giving-Residents-a-Place-to-Call--Home.aspx.

Heathfield, S. (2014a). *How to change your culture: Organizational culture change.* Retrieved from http://humanresources.about.com/od/organizationalculture/a/culture_change.htm.

Heathfield, S. (2014b). *Role of team commitment in team building.* Retrieved from http://humanresources .about.com/od/teamworksuccess/qt/team_commitment.htm.

Heathfield, S. (2014c). *What is culture?* Retrieved from http://humanresources.about.com/od /organizationalculture/g/what-is-culture.htm.

Jurkowski, E. (2013). *Implementing culture change in long-term care: Benchmarks and strategies for management and practice.* New York, NY: Springer Publishing.

Katzenbach, J., & Aguirre, D. (2013, May 28). *Culture and the chief executive.* Retrieved from http:// www.strategy-business.com/article/00179?gko=6912e.

Koch, R. (2012, February 14). *Senior living amenities that boost resident satisfaction.* Retrieved from http://www.providermagazine.com/columns/Pages/Senior-Living-Amenities-That-Boost-Resident -Satisfaction.aspx.

LaPorte, M. (2010, May). *Culture change picks up speed in LTC.* Retrieved from http://www.provider-magazine.com/archives/archives-2010/Pages/0510/Culture-Change-Picks-Up-Speed-IN-LTC.aspx.

LaVecchia Ragone, G. (2013, October/November). Need a ride? *Long term living.* Retrieved from http:// mydigimag.rrd.com/display_article.php?id=1533319&id_issue=179121.

Longest, B., & Darr, K. (2014). *Managing health services organizations and systems* (6th ed.). Baltimore, MD: Health Professions Press.

Lourde, K. (2010, March). *Social media in long term care: Everybody's talking about it.* Retrieved from http://www.providermagazine.com/archives/archives-2010/Pages/0310/Social-Media-In-Long-Term -Care-Everybody's-Talking-About-It.aspx#magazine-article.

MacNamara, C. (2014). *Organizational culture and changing culture.* Retrieved from http:// managementhelp.org/organizations/culture.htm.

Massachusetts Advocates for Nursing Home Reform (MANHR). (2008). *Culture change FAQ.* Retrieved from http://www.manhr.org/culture_chng_faq.aspx.

National Long-Term Care Ombudsman Resource Center (NORC). (2014). *Culture change.* Retrieved from http://www.ltcombudsman.org/issues/culture-change.

O'Brien, S. (2014). *How to find the right nursing home.* Retrieved from http://seniorliving.about.com /od/housingoptions/ss/findnursinghome.htm.

Pawloski. (2011, January 15). *The Green House Project: Tangible Results from Empathetic Design.* Retrieved from dot.nic: http://blog.lib.umn.edu/toll0076/dotnic/065781.html.

Pioneer Network. (2013, February 13). *What is culture change?* Retrieved from http://www .pioneernetwork.net/CultureChange/Whatis.

Planetree. (2014). *Creating dwellings of possibilities.* Retrieved from http://www.residentcenteredcare .org/Pages/creatingdwellingsofpossibilty.html.

Schoeneman, K. (2014). *The language of culture change.* Retrieved from http://www.pioneernetwork .net/CultureChange/Language,

Switzer, M. (2009, April). *The role of ethics in the 21st century: A call for values-based leadership.* Retrieved from http://webapps.icma.org/pm/9103/public/pmplus1.cfm?title=The%20Role%20of%20 Ethics%20in%20the%2021st%20Century%3A%20A%20Call%20for%20Values-Based%20 Leadership&subtitle=&author=Merlin%20Switzer.

Watkins, M. (2013, May 15). *What is organizational culture? And why should we care?* Retrieved from http://blogs.hbr.org/2013/05/what-is-organizational-culture.

Technology in Long-Term Care

After completing this chapter, readers will be able to:

1. Identify and define potential applications of an information technology system.
2. Discuss issues dealing with privacy and access to information.
3. Understand how technology can benefit long-term care providers, consumers, and the system as a whole.
4. Identify barriers to the successful use of information technology.
5. Identify and define options for acquiring and using information technology.

■ Introduction

As has been noted so often in previous chapters, the field of long-term care has changed rapidly in the past several decades and will continue to do so well into the foreseeable future. Providers have learned to adapt to payment systems such as the prospective payment system in government programs and capitation in managed care. They are also trying to keep up with changes in regulations, such as the Health Insurance Portability and Accountability Act (HIPAA) and those included in the Affordable Care Act. They are experiencing increased competition, both from within long-term care and from without. Finally, long-term care providers are finding new ways to provide high-quality care and are more willing than ever to work with government agencies and consumer advocates to ensure that quality.

One very visible aspect of these changes is the increased use of and reliance on technology. Research shows that technology has the potential to play a critical role in launching a new model of geriatric care that "allows older people to live independently for as long as possible, supports family caregivers in the important work they do and gives healthcare providers the tools they need to deliver high-quality care at a reasonable cost" (Alwan & Nobel, 2008, p. 2). Computerized record keeping, electronic reporting to reimbursement and regulatory agencies, and integrated management information systems are becoming commonplace. Of perhaps more significance are the ways in which technology improves the quality of life of the consumers of long-term care. In this chapter, all of these technological tools and how they work are explored. Readers will not become technology experts, but the information in this chapter should raise awareness of the importance of technology, particularly health information technology (HIT), to the long-term care field.

First, however, it should be noted that while hospitals have embraced HIT to improve their patient service, long-term care organizations have been slower to adopt technology (Hioban, 2013). This is in part because they have not had to, at least until relatively recently. Acute care, meaning hospitals and physician practices, rely much more heavily on high technology to treat their patients and to keep up with the vast amounts of information needed to fulfill their tasks. Their patients are in and out of their systems more quickly and often require immediate results. Long-term care, on the other hand, deals with chronic illnesses and interacts with its consumers over a long period of time. Its focus is on caring, not curing.

Another reason long-term care has not embraced technology as quickly or as completely as acute care is the investment cost. Although using technology actually saves money in most cases, the initial cost of investing in technology can be high. Long-term care providers often have not had the capital needed to make such an investment.

Readers should not rush to the conclusion that long-term care providers are not using technology. Most are. They use electronic documentation in many ways to be more efficient in their operation and more effective in providing care. We discuss the types of programs they use as this chapter progresses.

Although long-term care providers have not jumped on the technology bandwagon as speedily as have some other segments of the healthcare system, they are now doing so. It is clear that providers who ignore the benefits—and necessity—of technology jeopardize their very survival. As the field of long-term care has become ever more competitive, technology offers huge advantages to those using it over those who do not. Also, government programs are now requiring that reporting be electronic.

The ways in which technology can be used in long-term care fall into two broad categories: applied technology and health information technology (HIT).

■ Applied Technology

Of the two ways in which technology can apply to long-term care, the first is applied technology. A primary goal of most long-term care services is maintaining or improving a person's functional independence. Technology has much to offer in achieving that goal, although future developments will undoubtedly make the achievements of today look pretty basic. The Center for Aging Services Technologies (CAST) says:

Aging-services technologies can be broadly defined as technologies that can influence the aging experience for seniors, including their quality of life, health outcomes, satisfaction and/or the quality of care they receive. These include technologies that can be used by seniors, caregivers (both professional and informal), health care providers and aging services providers to improve the quality of care, enhance the caregivers' experience, efficiencies and cost-effectiveness. These technologies broadly include assistive, telemonitoring, telehealth, telemedicine, information, and communication technologies that intend to improve the aging or care experience. (Center for Aging Services Technologies (CAST), 2011, p. 3)

The Long-Term and Post-Acute Care (LTPAC) Health Information Technology (HIT) Collaborative says, "Emerging information, monitoring, diagnostic, communications, coordination and assistive technologies dramatically empower consumers and their caregivers to pursue personal health, wellness and independence goals" (LTPAC HIT Collaborative, 2012, p. 14). A few of the ways technology can be applied to improve the functional status of individuals follow.

Artificial Functioning

For years, our society has taken for granted that some human functions can be improved or even replaced with artificial devices. Perhaps the most common is the electric wheelchair. Patients with virtually no physical range of motion can control such devices by blowing on a tube or, in some cases, even with eye movement. Artificial limbs and other prosthetics have come a long way as well, thanks to technology. They are lighter and have a much improved range of function, and much progress has been made in using sensors to send messages to the artificial limbs from the nervous system.

However, that is just the beginning. Artificial functioning has become so sophisticated, it can support long-term care consumers in just about any task they need to undertake. For example, the controller of one such appliance will anticipate that an individual using a wheelchair is approaching a closed door, and it will recognize the door, identify the door handle, automatically move its robotic arm to grasp it, and then coordinate the movements of both the arm and chair to allow quick entry into a room.

Remote Monitoring/Telehealth

With remote monitoring, residents and their living spaces are outfitted with sensors to detect movement, monitor sleep quality, and collect other information about day-to-day activities. The information is transmitted via a secure Internet site to a registered nurse, who compares the data with a client's usual patterns of daily living. With telehealth, the consumer measures his or her own vital signs such as blood pressure and heart rate using equipment provided to him or her, and the information is sent electronically to a collection point where it is analyzed by a nurse (Connole, 2012).

Emergency Notification

Several systems that allow the elderly and other dependent individuals to live alone with the knowledge that they can reach help in an emergency are now readily available. Such systems usually involve a simple panic button worn on the body (e.g., as a necklace). Should that person need help, even if he or she falls and cannot get up, help can be reached with the mere pressing of a button. Other systems involve more active monitoring of the individual, prompting a response if a regular pattern of activity is broken. Fall detection, fall prevention, and location tracking technologies monitor patients in terms of their location, balance, and gait. Such devices allow caregivers and other parties to assess patient mobility and safety (Center for Technology and Aging, 2012). Devices of this type, although technologically quite simple, bring a great deal of peace of mind to both the consumers and their families.

Telemedicine

The American Telemedicine Association defines telemedicine as "the use of medical information exchanged from one site to another via electronic communications to improve a patient's clinical health status" (ATA, 2012). Telemedicine and telehealth are often used as interchangeable terms, covering a wide range of remote healthcare. Telemedicine includes numerous forms of telecommunications technology including two-way video, email, and smartphones. Perhaps even more significant, according to the ATA, "patient consultations via video conferencing, transmission of still images, e-health including patient portals, remote monitoring of vital signs, continuing medical education, consumer-focused wireless applications and nursing call centers, among other applications, are all considered part of telemedicine and telehealth" (ATA, 2012). Telemedicine involves providing some forms of care to consumers at locations remote from those delivering the care with the use of technology. Among the most common applications are remote monitoring of a consumer's condition, conferencing among healthcare professionals, and consultation with specialists. Home health agencies are beginning to make good use of technology to monitor vital signs (blood pressure, pulse, temperature) without having to actually visit an individual's home. Some use television with Web cameras to see the consumer face to face. It is also a valuable tool in patient–client education.

Telemedicine has been used for some time in enabling healthcare professionals to interact over distance. Hospitals and long-term care facilities can send diagnostic information such as X-rays, electrocardiograms, and laboratory tests to remote centers for interpretation. They are able to get input from specialists at major medical centers who would otherwise be unavailable to them. Healthcare professionals in several different locations can conference using telemedicine tools.

These applications of technology, and many others like them, are capable of greatly improving the functional capacity of many long-term care consumers.

However, these options are not used to their fullest potential, in part because many reimbursement sources do not cover them. There are also a number of regulatory and reimbursement issues that long-term care providers will need to overcome in order to see more widespread utilization of telemedicine. For example, while the Centers for Medicare & Medicaid Services says that "States are encouraged to use the flexibility inherent in federal law to create innovative payment methodologies for services that incorporate telemedicine technology" (CMS, 2014), there is little uniformity in either the types of services covered or the extent of coverage. These obstacles have hindered widespread adoption of telehealth. They still exist, but there are signs of improvement, including less restrictive Medicare reimbursement rules (Pittman, 2013). As the value of these technologies becomes better known, we should see greater acceptance of them. When we combine a growing consumerism and preference for personal choice and control with the emergence of a wide array of technologies, that value becomes better recognized (LTPAC HIT Collaborative, 2012).

■ Health Information Technology

Although the types of applied technology just described are of utmost benefit and importance to individuals, the area in which technology does most for providers and for the overall system is HIT. The Alliance for Health Reform defines HIT as "Information processing using both computer hardware and software for the entry, storage, retrieval, sharing, and use of health care information. Two common components of HIT are electronic medical records and computerized physician order entry" (Takvorian, 2007).

Indirectly, as the system and providers benefit through HIT, the consumers also benefit. HIT is simply the application of certain types of technology to the collection and use of information. All information systems, including health information systems, are built on the foundation of three processing phases: data input (data acquisition and verification), data management (data storage, classification, update, and computation), and data output (data retrieval and presentation Quality Management, 2013). Although such data can be collected and manipulated manually, use of technology makes it immeasurably faster and more accurate.

Providers are beginning to participate in many of the nation's health information exchange initiatives, and calls are being made to expand HIT meaningful-use incentives to long-term and postacute care (LTPAC HIT Collaborative, 2012). The American Health Care Association/National Center for Assisted Living (AHCA/NCAL) issued a statement saying that it "strongly supports a high quality, safe, and efficient health care system. Health information technology (HIT) plays an integral role in the operation of such a system" (AHCA/NCAL, 2013).

■ Clinical Applications

There are many potential ways that HIT can improve the care that is delivered. It allows the provider organization to control and manage the care given, the records kept, and the scheduling of care elements. Some of the more common uses follow.

Admission, Assessment, and Care Planning

The process of accepting a consumer into any of the various forms of long-term care is of great importance because it creates a foundation on which all subsequent care is delivered; yet, historically, it has often been a process that was lengthy, confusing (at least to the consumer and family members), and time consuming. Worse, it was sometimes less than effective because information was not always obtained or coordinated among the members of the provider team.

With the assistance of HIT, the process of intake and assessment can become more efficient, with fewer opportunities to miss (or misplace) vital information. Programs collect the vital data from different sources (e.g., referring organization, patient and family interviews, potential reimbursement sources) and collate it into a comprehensive, usable format. The medical history of the consumer can be made readily available as can eligibility for coverage by Medicare, Medicaid, or other insurance.

The assessment information collected is used to develop an individual plan of care for each consumer. The information system simplifies the process of care planning by allowing staff to access a menu of predetermined care plan elements, selecting those that best meet the needs of the individual. Because several different specialists (physicians, therapists, nurses, social workers) are usually involved in care plan development, a centralized system integrates their individual contributions and produces a care plan for all to use. It also makes it easier to update the care plan as needed and ensures that all members of the provider team are working with the same information, avoiding many potential mistakes.

For billing, electronic interaction between the provider and agencies such as Medicare and Medicaid provides quick and accurate coding to expedite the process. Medicare and Medicaid require that providers use a system of assigning a code to each consumer based on that person's primary diagnosis. A computerized information system allows the providers to quickly and correctly identify and assign the appropriate code.

The Centers for Medicare & Medicaid Services (CMS) also requires that certified skilled nursing providers (including subacute care providers) complete an assessment tool called a minimum data set (MDS) on each consumer served. An MDS is a data set composed of core elements and common definitions regarding care provided to residents of nursing facilities. The MDS includes standard demographic data for identification, such as resident name and birth date, and also contains data elements that describe the resident's health status in areas such as customary routines, cognitive patterns, and disease diagnoses. All facilities certified to participate in Medicare and/ or Medicaid are required by law to encode and transmit the information contained in the MDS to the state survey agency. The data are collected with a resident assessment instrument designated by the CMS; the state is subsequently required to transmit the data to them. Home healthcare providers certified by the CMS have a similar requirement, although a data collection instrument called the Outcome and Assessment Information Set (OASIS) is used. In either case, a computerized information system makes it easy to transmit that information quickly and accurately.

Many computerized systems are available, making it possible for a provider organization to find one that fits its particular circumstances and needs.

Consumer Safety

When each caregiver has access to the same integrated record, there is less opportunity for errors. One way technology can do this is with use of bar codes similar to those used in retail stores. Originally, bar codes were used to ensure accurate billing for procedures and supplies. However, providers have learned that bar codes can also help them avoid confusion and mistakes. Some healthcare providers have carried it to the point where each patient wears a wrist band with a bar code on it. When a caregiver administers a medication or begins a treatment procedure, the patient's bar code is checked against the record. In long-term care, particularly in nursing facilities where many residents have some degree of cognitive impairment and cannot always be counted on to respond coherently or accurately, bar codes can eliminate many potential mistakes.

The information system allows staff to schedule and track ancillary services such as therapies and consultations using a master schedule, avoiding time conflicts. It also tracks such services for billing to ensure that they are in keeping with the individual's care plan.

Record Keeping

A computerized information system greatly simplifies other forms of record keeping. It allows providers to keep track of all clinical records in an organized manner, making them more readily available when needed. Most such systems have simple-to-use electronic recording processes, often allowing staff to check items off on a menu, eliminating much writing by hand. It also eliminates many errors caused by illegible handwriting.

Professionals on the staff of the provider organization can enter care-related information from wherever they are: at the bedside, in a therapy setting, or even in a less formal setting that is more conducive to interacting with the consumer and/or family members (e.g., a lounge or dining area). The information is immediately entered into the central information database and is available to others needing to use it. Caregivers can see the resident's care plan instantly either on a handheld device or by logging in at a terminal in or just outside of the resident's room. This cuts down on errors such as medication errors and nearly eliminates missed treatments or other resident activities.

One extension of this concept has gained a lot of popularity in home health care. Because home healthcare staff have most of their client interaction in an individual's home, record keeping can be difficult. In the past, they had to keep notes and then transcribe those notes when back at the home health agency. With the right information system, and some relatively inexpensive computer hardware, they can enter information at the site and have it transmitted electronically to the central database, saving time, mileage, cost, and effort.

Quality Measurement

Long-term care providers are deeply involved in quality improvement. Not only does a computerized information system make it easier for them to measure quality, but it would be very difficult and less effective for providers to attempt to implement a good quality improvement program without it. Quality improvement programs rely on data collection and the measuring of the performance of one organization against quality indicators and other standards. Whether providers develop their own measurement standards or use some that are readily available from other sources, the information system quickly and easily handles the measurement process, producing results that are both valid and usable.

The ability to enter care-related information quickly and accurately via electronic means and to retrieve it just as quickly has benefits for both the providers and consumers. It avoids mistakes and delays and saves the provider time and money. It avoids inconvenience for consumers, lessening frustration and improving their satisfaction with the care received. It speeds communication among caregivers and helps to ensure accuracy. Reporting and quality monitoring are important to ensure consistent quality of care. They support quality assurance and internal quality improvement. Both of these activities benefit from robust, IT-supported analysis of data from many sources (MITRE Corporation, 2012).

■ Administrative Applications

In addition to the preceding clinical applications, many of which are rarely used outside of health care or long-term care, there are numerous administrative applications of HIT. They tend to be more similar to applications found in other fields.

Staffing

Computerized staffing is common in larger enterprises and has many benefits for them. Managers are able to schedule staff easily and more equitably using HIT tools. Keeping track of payroll, payroll taxes, and benefits for the staff is easier and much more accurate. Personnel files can easily be kept up to date. Yet many smaller long-term care organizations still feel that they are not big enough to benefit from such tools. They are wrong. Even a very small provider can do a better job with a good information system. Staff scheduling may be easy to do manually with a few employees, but the other aspects of staff record keeping can be handled so much better with an automated system.

Financial Management

Few businesses attempt to practice financial management today without some degree of assistance from HIT. There are many excellent, easy-to-use systems available. The need for accuracy in financial record keeping makes it nearly imperative that such a system be used. A computerized financial management system makes the process of budgeting much less time consuming. It can keep track of billing, accounts receivable, and accounts payable. It can be used to manage capital assets and investments. Moreover, a good information system will integrate all of these separate aspects of financial management into an overall program that produces useful, accurate information.

In long-term care, it is necessary to keep detailed records for reporting to reimbursement and regulatory agencies such as Medicare and Medicaid. Cost reports, case-mix reports, and other types of financial data are required by these agencies. The ability of an organization to generate that data in the right format and transmit it is vital. Providers must be able to collect a great deal of information that they may not have had to collect in the past. Similarly, with the increasing popularity of capitation as a payment method for managed care, much of the same data is needed but in a different format. An information system can do both with little difficulty.

■ Strategic Support Applications

The importance of strategic management in all healthcare organizations, including those in long-term care, has never been greater. Organizational executives must be prepared at all times to make strategic decisions—decisions that will affect the future direction of their organizations. Without good information, there can be no good decision making. There are several ways in which an information system can assist executives to lead their organizations toward success.

Planning

Strategic planning is undertaken to make thoughtful decisions about an organization's future in order to ensure its success. It involves clearly defining the organization's mission and conducting an assessment of its current state and competitive landscape (Lebeaux, 2012). It relies heavily on the availability of information. Planning involves collection and analysis of information about the internal capabilities and weaknesses of the organization and the external environment in which it functions. Such data collection used to be tedious, time consuming, and sometimes of questionable accuracy. With HIT, such data can be collected and analyzed much more quickly and with more accuracy. An added benefit is that an information system can rapidly integrate new or changing information. Because any strategic planning process is dynamic, this is a very valuable advantage.

Another way that HIT can be an asset to planning is in developing scenarios. Scenarios, as part of a planning process, are lists of potential occurrences that might affect an organization and proposed responses to those occurrences. For example, if the U.S. Congress and the administration are looking at two different plans for reforming the Medicare program, each with significant potential impact on the long-term care system, providers would need to be prepared for each of them. Using this planning approach, a long-term care organization would develop three different scenarios—one for plan A, one for plan B, and one for the status quo. For each, it would try to anticipate the impact on the organization and develop plans for dealing with that impact. Although such scenarios can be created manually, use of a computerized information system can make it much easier.

Operational Decision Making

As important as strategic planning is for the long run, long-term care executives also have to make many short-term decisions. Having a good source of reliable information is as important in this as it is for planning purposes. Operational decisions cover such areas as resource allocation, purchase of equipment, and recruitment of staff.

Performance Measurement

IT can assist management by providing tools to measure how well the organization is performing. Other industries have relied on formal performance measurement systems for years. In health care, primarily in acute care, some performance measurement processes have been in place, but these have mostly been limited to financial performance. The possibilities for performance measurement in long-term care include quality of care, allocation of staff, and customer satisfaction. With the use of HIT, performance can easily be measured against preset standards and criteria.

Marketing

Marketing has assumed a high degree of importance in long-term care as the field has become more competitive. Each provider organization needs to know who its customers are and needs to look at other potential customer populations with an eye toward attracting them to its services. Although marketing and planning have much in common, including the data used, each has a slightly different focus. Marketing requires a more detailed analysis of demographic information. Also, if marketing outreach is to be successful, it also requires an evaluation of what consumers in the service area see as important to them. Some of the information needed for development of a marketing plan is available within the organization and some is available from external sources. A good information system can collect and integrate information from these different sources. It can make it much easier to create marketing strategies and to evaluate them over time. It is important that an organization track its marketing efforts to know which are productive and which are not. Technology can be a useful tool as long-term care providers develop strategies to make themselves more attractive to hospitals (Cheitlin Cherry, 2013).

■ Networking Applications

Long-term care provider organizations are increasingly becoming involved in integrated health systems (IHSs). These systems bring multiple providers together into a single system, although the degree to which there is central control varies. The benefits are many, including economies of scale, gains in market share, increased bargaining power, and protection against competitors. To do all of this, the IHS needs a strong information system to coordinate the activities of its members. The HIT-related functions that can be integrated effectively include a master patient index and clinical data repository, central financial and business office applications, a patient scheduling function, decision-support and outcomes applications, and management service operations. This is often not easy because each organizational member may have had a different system or no system at all. Whatever the type of IHS, one of the most pressing issues is upgrading and integrating the separate information systems of the providers and creating a centralized system. Well-designed information systems strengthen internal planning and quality control to enhance management and clinical functions (Shi & Singh, 2008). It is not uncommon for the IHS to encounter considerable difficulty and cost when attempting such integration of multiple information systems, but it is well worth it when finished.

Another type of networking for long-term care providers is involvement with managed care organizations. Although contracting with a managed care organization does not usually entail the same form of actual system integration as is the case with an IHS, there are still likely to be many different players involved, each with different information systems. They need common data collection and transmittal processes to interact successfully.

■ Systemwide Applications

Thus far the discussion has focused on the use of technology as it applies to individuals and provider organizations. However, there are broader applications that affect the entire healthcare system. It is a system that is complex, diverse, and badly fragmented.

There are many ways in which IT can make it better. In fact, a far-reaching report issued in 2001 by the Institute of Medicine Committee on Quality of Health Care in America said that IT "holds enormous potential for transforming the health care delivery system" (IOM, 2001, p. 5), and "must play a central role in the redesign of the healthcare system if a substantial improvement in healthcare quality is to be achieved during the coming decade" (IOM, 2001, p. 165). While there has been some improvement, that goal has not been achieved. However, there are several HIT applications that can move the system in that direction: automated patient records, quality measurement and improvement, and consumer information and education.

Electronic Health Records

One of the most discussed systemwide applications of HIT is an electronic health record (EHR). EHRs come in two forms: an electronic health record (EHR) system and a personal electronic medical record (EMR). In common usage, *EHR* and *EMR* are used interchangeably to refer to a patient's medical record in digital format (Takvorian, 2007). In either case, the goal in creating electronic health records is better communication between providers, regulatory agencies, and consumers.

Automated patient records allow quick and easy access to patients' clinical history and information concerning medications taken, current providers, and insurance coverage. This improves communication among providers, saves a considerable amount of time and money, and greatly simplifies movement of patients through the many levels and segments of the healthcare system. For consumers of long-term care, such records would cut down on much of the tedium associated with the process of intake and assessment. Because many long-term care consumers have an extended length of stay and their care has become increasingly complex, providers realize that they need electronic records to review and compile information in real time.

There has been progress toward a system of EHRs. The Agency for Health Care Research and Quality developed a HIT initiative as part of the nation's strategy to put information technology to work in health care. That initiative found that by developing secure and private electronic health records for most Americans and making health information available electronically when and where it is needed, HIT can improve the quality of care, even as it makes health care more cost effective (AHRQ, 2008). A major step forward occurred in 2004, when President George W. Bush signed an executive order calling for the widespread adoption of EHRs for most Americans within 10 years. He also established incentives for the use of HIT and created the position of the national coordinator for health information technology (Martin, Brantley, & Dangler, 2007). Continuing the federal focus on health information technology, the secretary of health and human services in 2005 established the American Health Information Community (AHIC), which was created to advise the secretary, recommend specific actions to achieve a common interoperability framework for HIT, and serve as the focal point for prioritizing the federal agenda around HIT adoption and coordination (Martin et al., 2007). However, while the American Health Information Community formed seven workgroups to address specific topic areas, there was none directly related to long-term care, nor have long-term care representatives been very involved with the workgroups, a fact lamented by numerous long-term care organizations.

Those organizations took some actions to help themselves, including convening the third annual Long-Term Care Health Information Technology Summit in Chicago, Illinois, in June 2007, to establish and advance a road map for long-term care IT. Cosponsors included the following:

- American Association for Homes and Services of the Aging
- American Health Care Association
- American Health Information Management Association
- American Medical Directors Association
- Center for Aging Services Technology
- National Association for the Support of Long Term Care
- National Association of Home Care and Hospice
- National Center for Assisted Living (Martin et al., 2007)

The Affordable Care Act of 2010 gave new impetus to the electronic health record. The transition to electronic records underpins many of the goals of the Affordable Care Act, such as curbing hospital readmissions and encouraging the development of accountable care organizations (Allard Levingston, 2013). The impact of that on long-term care providers is yet to be determined, as many of them are not eligible for the Medicare and Medicaid EHR incentive programs' EHR technologies, causing them to lag behind healthcare providers who may participate in the EHR incentive programs (i.e., eligible professionals and eligible hospitals) (Dougherty, Williams, Millenson, & Harvell, 2013).

Quality Measurement and Improvement

Another systemwide HIT application would be collection of data for the purposes of measuring quality, developing practice guidelines, and sharing data among researchers and policy makers. There has been some progress in this area through provisions of the Affordable Care Act. The information collected by the CMS has added to the store of common knowledge about healthcare providers and consumers. Although it is far from universal, covering only those providers certified by Medicare and Medicaid, these providers represent such a large portion of all providers that the system is producing some very useful data. There are three such systems at the national level involved with long-term care: the Online Survey, Certification and Reporting (OSCAR) system, Resident Assessment Instrument/minimum data set (RAI/MDS), and OASIS.

OSCAR

According to the American Health Care Association, OSCAR is

> a data network maintained by the Centers for Medicare and Medicaid Services (CMS) in cooperation with the state long-term care surveying agencies. OSCAR is a compilation of all the data elements collected by surveyors during the inspection survey conducted at nursing facilities for the purpose of certification for participation in the Medicare and Medicaid programs. OSCAR is the most comprehensive source of facility level information on the operations, patient census and regulatory compliance of nursing facilities. (AHCA, 2014)

This collective information has great value in systemwide planning.

RAI/MDS

By federal law, all nursing home residents are to have an interdisciplinary, individualized assessment upon admission to the nursing home, and at a minimum, reassessed quarterly or if there is a significant change. This assessment is referred to as the Resident Assessment Instrument (RAI) and consists of three components:

1. MDS
2. Care area assessment process
3. RAI utilization guidelines

The utilization of the three components of the RAI provides information about a resident's functional status, strengths, weaknesses, and preferences (University of Minnesota, 2014). Although these assessment tools are essentially clinical and designed to improve resident care in nursing facilities, they also provide nationwide data about nursing facilities and their consumers. Some states have developed their own assessment systems for residential care providers not certified by Medicare and Medicaid, based on the RAI and MDS used in nursing facilities.

OASIS

A third data collection tool involved with long-term care is OASIS for home health care. Intended as a quality measurement system, it also produces data that can be used systemwide. OASIS is a key component of the Centers for Medicare & Medicaid Services (CMS) partnership with the home care industry to foster and monitor improved home healthcare outcomes. The Outcome and Assessment Information Set-C (OASIS-C) is a group of data elements that:

- Represents core items of a comprehensive assessment for an adult home care patient
- Forms the basis for measuring patient outcomes for the purposes of outcome-based quality improvement (CDPH, 2014)

As valuable as these three data sources are, there is still no single data collection tool that covers all of long-term care, which leaves considerable gaps in knowledge about how care is delivered and to whom. If such a tool was created, using HIT to collect, coordinate, and disseminate the information broadly, its potential uses would be many.

Consumer Information and Education

A third systemwide application of HIT is making information available to consumers. More and more, consumers are turning to the Internet for information about health care and how to access it. They are using HIT whether they know it or not. Any long-term care system even approaching the ideal would include an education component. It is a constant complaint from consumers and consumer advocates that there is not enough information available for them to make sound decisions. Yet contrary to what some think, the problem is seldom too little information, but rather too much information that does not produce significant meaning to those who need it. The available information is not coordinated and is often difficult to find. HIT has the capability to provide such coordination, allowing individuals to access the information they need, when they need it.

There has been some progress in this area as well, again initiated by CMS, which has created consumer information sections on its website called, "Nursing Home Compare" and "Home Health Compare." Using information collected from multiple sources, including OSCAR, OASIS, and the MDS systems, it makes it possible for consumers to get detailed information about any nursing facility or home health agency that is certified by Medicare and Medicaid. Anyone can go to the website and look up a particular provider organization to get information such as ownership, number of beds by level of service, staffing, and deficiencies resulting from state surveys. Information of this type goes far toward providing consumers (and potential future consumers) with what they need to know in choosing a long-term care provider.

These and other systemwide applications yet to come are all valuable in and of themselves. However, they will only be successful if developed and applied in an overall systemwide manner.

■ Privacy Concerns and HIPAA

There has long been concern about the privacy and confidentiality of personal medical information. Consumers have raised concern about any type of system that allows individuals or organizations other than their primary physician or provider to have access to their medical histories or records of care received. As HIT has made it easier for that information to be shared, the concerns have increased. Numerous studies have documented the fact that, although consumers welcome the benefits of an IHS, they are apprehensive about possible invasions of their privacy.

Congress took a major step toward addressing these concerns in 1996 with passage of the Health Insurance Portability and Accountability Act (HIPAA), which has two major purposes: (1) to assure consumers that they will have better access to health insurance and (2) to protect the privacy of their health information. It is this second purpose that pertains to HIT.

HIPAA encourages the use of HIT in transactions involving health information, such as exchange of clinical data among providers and healthcare professionals, billing, and confirmation of eligibility for coverage. At the same time, it creates a set of national standards governing such electronic transfers to protect the privacy and confidentiality of consumers.

The impact on consumers is that they can now feel more confident that their personal health information is protected, even while it is shared for their benefit. The impact on providers has been considerable as well. HIPAA requires health plans, pharmacies, doctors, and other covered entities to establish and implement policies and procedures to protect patient privacy. HIPAA directed the U.S. Department of Health and Human Services (HHS) to promulgate a regulation—the Privacy Rule—to protect and enhance the right of consumers to control how their personal health information is used and disclosed. Specifically, the Privacy Rule:

- Stipulates the individual rights of consumers to control their personal health information, including guaranteed access to their medical records and a clear avenue of recourse if their medical privacy is compromised
- Outlines the procedures organizations must adopt to enable patients to exercise their privacy rights, including proper notification of how their personal health information is used and shared
- Establishes the conditions under which individuals or organizations may use and/or disclose personal health information
- Sets an industry standard for disclosing only the minimum amount of information necessary to satisfy an authorized request for patient information
- Requires organizations to appoint a privacy officer to conduct privacy assessments, create policies to protect patient privacy, train staff, and establish an internal grievance process (Burns, 2003)

Although HIPAA applies to all kinds of transfers of confidential information, whether delivered electronically, in paper form, or through verbal interaction, much of the emphasis is on electronic transactions. Thus, it has a great impact on the use of HIT. It has caused providers to review their HIT systems, if they had any, to ensure compliance. It has also encouraged many who were not using HIT extensively, such as many long-term care providers, to think seriously about doing so. The transformation has been fraught with many difficulties and more than a little added expense for such providers, but the end result has been positive for all concerned. HIPAA has not resolved all concerns about privacy and confidentiality, but it has been a good start. Perhaps as important as what HIPAA does cover is the fact that it has forced those involved in all of health care, including consumers, to think about privacy issues and to work toward their resolution.

■ Cyber Security

It is a sad but salient fact that all entities relying on computer systems (and what organization does not?) must today be concerned about cyber security. After the terrorist attacks on September 11, 2001, our nation became aware that our information systems are potentially vulnerable to outside attack. Although many in the field of health care, especially in long-term care, may think they are far removed from such threats, this is not necessarily true. As we move closer to the systemwide information infrastructure described earlier in this chapter, we must realize that each part of that infrastructure is important to the success of the whole. Loss of either personal or organizational information could greatly disrupt the ability to provide high-quality care to those who rely on the healthcare system. The answer would appear to be a separate and distinct authentication number assigned to each individual healthcare consumer. The issue of cyber security is of enough concern that a national Computer Science and Telecommunications Board issued a 2002 report titled, *Cybersecurity, Today and Tomorrow: Pay Now or Pay Later.* The report warned all health care organizations about the threat to cyber security. To a large extent, that warning has been heeded, but the threat continues to grow and expand. Constant attention must be paid to it.

■ Benefits of HIT

Although several of the benefits of increased use of HIT have been noted in this chapter, they are listed more specifically here. There are benefits for the system as a whole, for individual provider organizations, and for individual consumers.

Benefits for the Long-Term Care System

Innovative healthcare technologies offer the potential to lower costs while enhancing clinical outcomes, while expanding the reach of care to at-risk populations. High-value technologies are underused and held back by systemic barriers that hinder technology adoption and innovation (Bartolini & McNeill, 2012). A 2007 report by the National Commission for Quality Long-Term Care noted:

> The good news is that computer-based technologies already exist that could allow care providers in long-term care, acute care, and home-based settings to efficiently collect, manage, and share vital information about their clients' medical histories and care regimens. New technology products are continually being developed and many of these products have the potential to improve the quality

of long-term care services and help older people remain independent for longer. (National Commission for Quality Long-Term Care, 2007, p. 60)

Sharing of best clinical practices, the use of clinical guidelines, and quality measurement tools enhance the delivery of care.

Second, the more timely and accurate exchange of financial information saves money and avoids waste. A third benefit is the ability to improve research into both clinical and administrative methods through HIT, again improving the way care is delivered. Last, but certainly of equal importance with the other benefits for the system, is the increased ability to provide consumers with the information they need to make care-related decisions. The better informed consumers are, the better they will be able to use the services available, improving the overall system.

Benefits for Providers

Long-term care provider organizations appear to benefit most directly and immediately from the use of HIT. HIT can help them operate more efficiently and effectively. Better information assists them in both long-range planning and short-range decision making. It produces cost savings by avoiding duplication and waste and allows them to optimize their resources. Electronic billing, production of cost reports, computerized staffing, and tracking of physical resources all contribute to overall administrative efficiency. When providers are part of IHSs, HIT makes it possible for them to network with each other.

Benefits for Consumers

The benefits that HIT offers to the overall system and to providers extend to consumers as well, although at times indirectly. While some seniors have limited awareness of new technologies that could help them, an increasing number are willing to use them. As both individual provider organizations and the entire system become more efficient through HIT and offer more and better services, the consumers of those services benefit. However, there are benefits that apply primarily to consumers.

Applications such as assistive devices, telemonitoring, telehealth, and telemedicine have been discussed herein earlier. There are other valuable applications that can benefit consumers as well. They include social networking, physical and mental stimulation, and education. Social networking allows older people to connect, share knowledge, provide support to others, and relate to others in similar circumstances. Social networking also helps to overcome social isolation, which is a major problem with negative health consequences (International Federation on Ageing, 2012).

Some of these technologies include:

- *Tablets and iPads*—Seniors can view photos, listen to music, and read.
- *Video games*—Video games can improve cognition, mental agility, and physical health.

- *Skype*—Communicating with family long distance allows seniors to view their loved ones in real time.
- *Wireless Internet*—Most of the technologies available to seniors work better with wireless Internet.
- *Smartphones*—Cell phones are becoming more senior friendly, with models that have larger buttons and readouts to make usage easier (Stevensen, 2013).

The benefits of social networking apply both to consumers in nursing homes or other long-term care facilities and those living at home.

Consumers in Long-Term Care Facilities

Residents of senior living facilities benefit from using technology to gain access to the Internet's wealth of information and stay in touch with family and friends (Watt, 2014). Most nursing homes and assisted living communities already have Wii sports games and other similar exercise devices. They often have wireless capability for use by their residents. They may provide computers or tablets or accommodate those provided by family members. With the large numbers of baby boomers reaching age 65, it makes sense to work at meeting the demands of these consumers (Connole, 2012). As has been well documented, the baby boomers want (demand) access to the technologies that have become such an important part of their everyday lives, and they will continue to do so as they become long-term care consumers.

Consumers Living at Home

Technology cannot take the place of in-person human interaction, but services such as Skype or email and social media can supplement seniors' social interactions when in-person visits with friends and family aren't possible (Home Instead, 2014). They can reap the same benefits from technology as institutionalized residents. In fact, technology can make it not only easier to live at home, but in some cases, make it possible where it would not be otherwise. The interconnectivity provided by technology allows them to function much as other, younger people.

Technology also benefits caregivers of long-term care consumers. A study by Family Caregivers Online has shown that

eight in ten caregivers (79%) have access to the internet. Of those, 88% look online for health information, outpacing other internet users on every health topic included in our survey, from looking up certain treatments to hospital ratings to end-of-life decisions. Caregivers are significantly more likely than other internet users to say that their last search for health information was on behalf of someone else: 67% vs. 54%. (Fox & Brenner, 2012, p. 2)

As the push for community-based care continues to grow, the market for elder-care technology and services is expected to grow exponentially (Connole, 2012).

Consumers living at home benefit by being able to access information about providers, services, and eligibility using the Internet. It allows them, in some cases, to get detailed statements showing services rendered and charges applied. In many cases, they can schedule appointments online, just as they order merchandise, do their banking, or schedule appointments with nonmedical service providers such as beauty shops and automobile repair centers.

The potential benefits of HIT are enormous and include many we simply cannot conceive of today. A primary characteristic of all technology is that it grows exponentially in terms of both quantity and quality. Each new breakthrough in technology builds on previous developments. The future promises to be exciting.

■ Barriers to Use of HIT

The field of long-term care has barely begun to make optimal use of HIT. If it is to take even modest advantage of the benefits HIT offers, there must be a concentrated effort to learn about its uses and to put HIT to work. However, there are barriers to doing so.

Lack of Commitment

Any organization, whether in long-term care or some other field, venturing into the area of HIT must do so with a full commitment to doing it right. Far too often organizations try to use HIT as little as possible or only use it because they are forced into it by some other entity. In long-term care, requirements by Medicare and Medicaid and most state survey agencies make it mandatory that all providers have some HIT capability. However, this is not enough. If they are going to invest in HIT, they would find it far more cost effective to invest in a system that will provide them with a full array of benefits.

It is also essential that the commitment come from the top. The chief executive officer and governing body must demonstrate that commitment. Not only must they provide the needed resources, but they must also make it clear to all staff that they are indeed committed to taking full advantage of HIT.

Lack of Understanding

The first step to making that commitment is understanding what it is all about. Top management must understand what HIT has to offer, how it works, and what its limitations are. This sounds straightforward, but many long-term care managers do not find it to be all that easy.

There are several reasons some current long-term care administrators are uncomfortable with HIT. First, it is something that many of them did not learn in their formative years. For the middle-aged executive, having to learn a new technology can be scary. Although a younger generation of administrators and all generations to follow will have grown up with computers and see them as an integral part of their lives, there are still many long-term care administrators who have not had that advantage. It is tempting here to fall back on that old adage "you can't teach an old dog new tricks," but this is simply not true. Many an old dog (and lest any reader be offended by the term, your author is including himself when using it) has proven that new concepts and skills can be learned. The difficult part is often getting the learners to understand the need to learn.

Second, lack of understanding can cause a certain degree of fear. Fear of the unknown is often accompanied by fear that one will lose control. It can be intimidating to have to base decisions on information that was produced by a machine or by someone who has a better understanding of how it was generated. There is also the fear of failure. Many an administrator has voiced the concern, "What if I'm not able to learn this? What will others think of me?"

First, there must be possession of contemporary skills, the ability to use today's computer applications, enabling an individual to apply HIT immediately. This does not mean being a technology expert, but merely having basic skills, which are not that difficult to learn. Second, fluency in HIT requires that one understand the basic principles and ideas of computers, networks, and information. Again, an administrator does not have to know all of the technical details but must understand how the parts of the system fit together. Third, administrators must have the intellectual capacity to apply HIT to their organizations. Few administrators would have achieved their current positions without such capacity.

These three types of knowledge are not difficult to acquire, but will entail some effort and time. Also, please note that while there are definitely long-term care administrators without this knowledge, they do not represent the majority, and their number is shrinking constantly.

Financial Investment

HIT pays for itself in a surprisingly short time, but the initial investment is considerable and may seem prohibitive to many, particularly small provider organizations. They will need to invest in some, if not all, of the components of a good HIT system, including hardware, software, system changes, and personnel. This means finding enough investment capital to cover the up-front costs. Cash is not always easy to come by for long-term care providers, particularly when they rely heavily on reimbursement from government programs such as Medicare and Medicaid. In part because of this, IHSs seem to have an advantage over individual providers. They are more able to access the cash needed and can usually get more for the money spent through the economies of scale concept.

Need to Upgrade Old Technology

Although the relative lack of HIT in most long-term care organizations has been commented upon here, it must be noted that many of them have had some data collection and processing systems in place for some time. However, most of them are rudimentary and generally not compatible with state-of-the-art systems. Such existing systems, often called "legacy" systems, are apt to be made up of hardware and processing systems that are not based on relational technology, meaning they will not interact with other hardware or systems. Organizations tend to find it difficult to scrap systems and hardware that required a considerable investment.

Changing Operational Systems

Creating a workable information system in a provider organization requires more than simply purchasing a computer. It demands that the organization review all of its procedures and make the changes needed to adapt to a new way of doing things. These changes can include revising who does what as well as how it is done. Unfortunately, many organizations, not just those involved in health care, attempted to skip this step and computerized paper-based systems. The result was that they not only failed to get the improvements in efficiency they wanted, but they sometimes made their situation worse by retaining both their paper systems and the new electronic systems. Converting to a system based on HIT requires that they replace many policies and procedures.

Obtaining HIT Expertise

HIT and development of information systems necessitate the acquisition of staff with specialized knowledge. Few long-term care provider organizations have it, and most of those that do have not had it for long. They must commit to finding such expertise and providing the resources needed to take full advantage of it. For some this will mean development of a separate department or unit headed by a chief information officer. For others, it may be less formal, with HIT staff integrated into other departments. In either case, there will need to be someone in the organization with the required expertise.

■ Options for Acquiring HIT

Long-term care providers have several options available to them when they decide to acquire new HIT or upgrade existing systems. These options range from developing an entirely in-house system to contracting with an outside firm to provide and manage the system, with several possible alternatives in between. Few providers, except perhaps the largest corporate chains, will opt for a large, central mainframe computer. Such computers have largely been replaced by networks of personal computers, which have the advantage of more flexibility. However, it is an attractive option for some providers. The investment in staff with system development expertise, in system development costs, and in hardware is usually higher than with other options, but it may prove worth it in the long run.

Instead of developing its own information system, an organization has the option of purchasing software for its own hardware (personal computers, data-entry terminals, etc.). There is so much excellent software available it would be foolish to try to reinvent it. Software that has been developed by others and tested in other organizations saves much of the development cost and time for the organization purchasing it. Such software may not be quite as capable of meeting the particular needs of each organization as would an in-house system designed particularly for it, but with so many software applications available, this should not be a major obstacle.

A third option is to outsource the entire system development and maintenance to a contract firm. The benefit is the simplicity of having someone else handle everything, but the disadvantage may be further loss of control over the system.

In choosing one of these options, a long-term care provider organization needs to evaluate three categories of costs: system development costs, operating costs, and maintenance costs. Development costs include programming, training of personnel, writing of procedures, system testing, and conversion of existing data. Operating costs include labor, materials, and a prorated share of computer time used for the new system, while maintenance costs generally include keeping qualified staff available for system evaluation and improvement (Austin & Boxerman, 2003).

■ Guidelines for Selecting a HIT Vendor

Whatever system is chosen, there are several recommended steps to follow when selecting a vendor.

1. Analysis of the business requirements
2. Vendor search
3. Request for proposal and request for quotation
4. Proposal evaluation and vendor selection
5. Contract negotiation (Bucki, 2014e)

Let's look at those steps in a bit more detail.

1. Analysis of the business requirements
   a. Assemble an evaluation team
   b. Define the product, material or service
   c. Define the technical and business requirements
   d. Define the vendor requirements
   e. Publish a requirements document for approval (Bucki, 2014a)
2. Vendor search
   a. Compile a list of possible vendors
   b. Select vendors from whom to request more information
   c. Write a request for information
   d. Evaluate responses and create a short list of vendors. (Bucki, 2014f)

3. Request for proposal. The request for proposal should contain the following sections:
   a. Submission details
   b. Introduction and executive summary
   c. Business overview and background
   d. Detailed specifications
   e. Assumptions and constraints
   f. Terms and conditions
   g. Selection criteria (Bucki, 2014d)
4. Proposal evaluation and vendor selection
   a. Preliminary review of all vendor proposals
   b. Record business requirements and vendor requirements
   c. Assign importance value for each requirement
   d. Assign a performance value for each requirement
   e. Calculate a total performance score
   f. Select the winning vendor (Bucki, 2014c)
5. Contract negotiation
   a. List rank your priorities along with alternatives
   b. Know the difference between what you need and what you want
   c. Know your bottom line so you know when to walk away
   d. Define any time constraints and benchmarks
   e. Assess potential liabilities and risks
   f. Confidentiality, noncompete, dispute resolution, changes in requirements
   g. Do the same for your vendor (i.e., walk a mile in their shoes) (Bucki, 2014b)

■ Summary

Technology, particularly HIT, has gone from being something with considerable potential benefit to an indispensable tool for all long-term care providers. Its applications are many and growing in importance, covering all aspects of long-term care. As technology grows, it continues to become more flexible, easier to use, and usually less expensive. Potential future applications include further improvements in the quality of care provided; in the effectiveness and efficiency of how that care is provided; and in providing needed information for consumers, policy makers, and researchers. Technology is and will be central to many of the positive developments seen in coming decades.

■ Vocabulary Terms

The following terms are included in this chapter. They are important to the topics and issues discussed herein and should become familiar to readers. Some of the terms are also found in other chapters but may be used in different contexts. They may not be fully defined herein. Thus, readers may wish to seek other, supplementary definitions of them.

application	Internet
artificial functioning	mainframe computer
automated patient records	network
chief information officer	personal computer
electronic health record	request for proposal
hardware	software
health information technology (HIT)	technology
infrastructure	vendor
integration	

■ Discussion Questions

The following questions are presented to assist you in understanding the material covered in this chapter. They tend to be general but lend themselves to detailed answers, which can be found in the chapter.

1. Why is information technology of such importance to long-term care organizations?
2. What are some ways in which technology improves the type and quality of care received by long-term care consumers?
3. What are some of the benefits of information technology for providers? For consumers? For the long-term care system?
4. Why is commitment by top management important to success in using information technology?
5. What are some of the likely barriers to implementing an information technology system?
6. How should a long-term care organization go about selecting an information system?
7. Why are there concerns about the privacy and confidentiality of information, and how are those concerns being addressed?

■ References

Agency for Health Care Research and Quality (AHRQ). (2008). *Decision maker brief: Telehealth.* Washington, DC: Agency for Health Care Research and Quality.

Allard Levingston, S. (2013, November 14). *Electronic health records' 'Make-or-break year.'* Retrieved from http://www.businessweek.com/articles/2013-11-14/2014-outlook-electronic-health-records-make-or-break-year.

Alwan, M., & Nobel, J. (2008, March). *State of technology in aging services: Summary.* Retrieved from http://www.leadingage.org/uploadedfiles/content/about/cast/resources/state_technoloy_summary.pdf.

American Health Care Association (AHCA). (2014). *What is OSCAR data?* Retrieved from http://www.ahcancal.org/research_data/oscar_data/pages/whatisoscardata.aspx.

American Health Care Association/National Center for Assisted Living (AHCA/NCAL). (2013, August 7). *Issue brief: Health information technology.* Retrieved from http://www.ahcancal.org/advocacy/issue_briefs/Issue%20Briefs/IBHITFacilityAdoption.pdf.

American Telemedicine Association (ATA). (2012). *What is telemedicine?* Retrieved from http://www.americantelemed.org/about-telemedicine/what-is-telemedicine#.UxYbvP-YZHw.

Austin, C., & Boxerman, S. (2003). *Information systems for healthcare management* (6th ed.). Chicago, IL: Health Administration Press.

Bartolini, E., & McNeill, N. (2012, June). *Getting to value: Eleven chronic disease technologies to watch.* Cambridge, MA: NEHI.

Bucki, J. (2014a). *Analyze business requirements: Step #1 in the vendor selection process.* Retrieved from http://operationstech.about.com/od/vendorselection/a/VendorSelectBusinessReq.htm..

Bucki, J. (2014b). *Contract negotiation strategies: Step #5 in the vendor selection process.* Retrieved from http://operationstech.about.com/od/vendorselection/a/VendorSelect-ContractNegotiation.htm.

Bucki, J. (2014c). *Proposal evaluation and vendor selection: Step #4 in the vendor selection process.* Retrieved from http://operationstech.about.com/od/vendorselection/a/VendorSelectEvaluation.htm.

Bucki, J. (2014d). *Request for proposal (RFP) and request for quotation (RFQ): Step #3 in the vendor selection process.* Retrieved from http://operationstech.about.com/od/vendorselection/a/VendorSelect-RFP-RFQ.htm.

Bucki, J. (2014e). *The successful vendor selection process.* Retrieved from http://operationstech.about.com/od/vendorselection/a/VendorSelectionHub.htm.

Bucki, J. (2014f). *Vendor search: Step #2 in the vendor selection process.* Retrieved from http://operationstech.about.com/od/vendorselection/a/VendorSelectVendSearch.htm.

Burns, R. (2003). *Privacy standards for individually identifiable health information.* Retrieved from http://www.nga.org/files/live/sites/NGA/files/pdf/HIPAA_PRIVACY.pdf.

California Department of Public Health (CDPH). (2014, April 5). *Information for health care providers—OASIS.* Retrieved from http://www.cdph.ca.gov/PROGRAMS/LNC/Pages/OASIS.aspx.

CAST. (2011, September 12). *State of Technology in Aging Services Report.* Retrieved from Leading Age Center for Aging Services /technologies: http://www.leadingage.org/State_of_Technology_in_Aging_Services_Report.aspx

Center for Technology and Aging. (2012). *Fact sheet: Highlights from the remote patient monitoring position paper.* Retrieved from http://www.techandaging.org/rpmfactsheet.pdf.

Centers for Medicare and Medicaid Services (CMS). (2014). *Telemedicine.* Retrieved from http://www.medicaid.gov/Medicaid-CHIP-Program-Information/By-Topics/Delivery-Systems/Telemedicine.html.

Cheitlin Cherry, J. (2013, October). *Technology and readmissions.* Retrieved from http://www.providermagazine.com/archives/2013_Archives/Pages/1013/Technology-And-Readmissions.aspx.

Connole, O. (2012, March). *Facilities tap fresh ideas, new technology.* Retrieved from http://www.providermagazine.com/archives/archives-2012/Pages/0312/Facilities-Tap-Fresh-Ideas-New-Technology.aspx.

Dougherty, M., Williams, M., Millenson, M., & Harvell, J. (2013). *EHR payment incentives for providers.* Washington, DC: U.S. Department of Health and Human Services.

Fox, S., & Brenner, J. (2012). *Family caregivers online.* Washington, DC: Pew Research Center.

Hioban, S. (2013, April 23). *Long-term care is slow to adopt health information technology.* Retrieved from http://www.ltlmagazine.com/news-item/long-term-care-slow-adopt-health-information-technology.

Home Instead. (2014). *5 benefits of technology to share with seniors and their caregivers.* Retrieved from http://www.caregiverstress.com/geriatric-professional-resources/5-benefits-of-technology-to-share-with-seniors-and-their-caregivers.

Institute of Medicine (IOM). (2001). *Crossing the quality chasm: A new health system for the 21st century.* Washington, DC: National Academies Press.

International Federation on Ageing. (2012, May 28). *2012 senior government officials meeting long term care and technology.* Retrieved from http://www.ifa-fiv.org/wp-content/uploads/2012/11/som-2012-ltc-and-technology-final-report.pdf.

Lebeaux, R. (2012, November). *Definition strategic planning.* Retrieved from http://searchcio.techtarget.com/definition/strategic-planning.

Long-Term and Post-Acute Health IT Collaborative (LTPAC HIT Collaborative). (2012). *A roadmap for health IT in long term and post acute care (LTPAC).* Retrieved from http://www.ahcancal.org/facility_operations/hit/Documents/RoadMap20102012.pdf.

Martin, R., Brantley, D., & Dangler, D. (2007). *Essential but not sufficient: Information technology in long-term care as an enabler of consumer independence and quality improvement.* McLean, VA: BearingPoint, Inc.

The MITRE Corporation. (2012). *Information technology for bundled payment.* McLean, VA: The MITRE Corporation.

National Commission for Quality Long-Term Care. (2007). *From isolation to integration: Recommendations to improve quality in long-term care.* Washington, DC: National Commission for Quality Long-Term Care.

Pittman, D. (2013, September 16). *Barriers to telemedicine slowly dropping.* Retrieved from http://www.medpagetoday.com/PracticeManagement/Reimbursement/41629.

Quality Management. (2013, March 4). *Data validation to ensure that good, useful data have been collected.* Retrieved from http://mrpalsmy.wordpress.com/2013/03/04/data-validation-to-ensure-that-good-useful-data-have-been-collected.

Shi, S., & Singh, D. (2008). *Delivering health care in America: A systems approach* (4th ed.). Sudbury, MA: Jones and Bartlett.

Stevensen, S. (2013, September 17). *10 pieces of technology seniors should embrace.* Retrieved from http://seniornet.org/blog/10-pieces-of-technology-seniors-should-embrace.

Takvorian, S. (2007, December 13). *A reporter's toolkit: Health information technology.* Retrieved from http://www.allhealth.org/publications/health_information_technology/health_information_technology_toolkit.asp#it.

University of Minnesota. (2014). *Resident assessment instrument (RAI): An overview.* Retrieved from http://www.nursing.umn.edu/prod/groups/nurs/@pub/@nurs/documents/asset/nurs_asset_403026.pdf.

Watt, T. (2014, January 14). *More seniors use technology to learn, stay in touch.* Retrieved from http://www.sunriseseniorliving.com/blog/january-2014/more-seniors-use-technology-to-learn-stay-in-touch.aspx.

Marketing and Community Relations

After completing this chapter, readers will be able to:

1. Understand marketing and community relations, how they differ, and how they apply to long-term care.
2. Understand the relationship between strategic planning and market planning.
3. Identify and define how a marketing strategy is developed.
4. Understand the role of market research in creating a marketing plan.
5. Define the resources and skills needed to implement and maintain a marketing plan.

◼ Introduction

Marketing and community relations are critical to the success of any long-term care organization for several reasons, including:

1. Increased competition among long-term care providers and between them and other segments of the healthcare field.
2. Growing awareness on the part of consumers of their rights to choose among facilities and services.
3. The financial uncertainty of being a long-term care provider organization.
4. Increasing impact of managed care organizations on long-term care.
5. The need for long-term care providers, both individually and collectively, to improve an image that has been poor in the past and is even now under attack from some quarters.

These and other related factors mandate that all long-term care providers develop sound marketing and community relations programs and devote the needed resources to make them work. In addition, providers must understand what it takes to be successful.

■ Defining Marketing and Community Relations

Although most of this chapter focuses on marketing, it is intentionally titled, "Marketing and Community Relations" because both are elements of a successful overall program. It should be noted here that *public relations* and *community relations* are often used synonymously, and they do indeed share many characteristics. Therefore, the discussion begins with definitions of these terms, to show how they are similar, how they are different, and where they overlap.

Marketing is defined by the American Marketing Association as "the activity, set of institutions, and processes for creating, communicating, delivering, and exchanging offerings that have value for customers, clients, partners, and society at large" (American Marketing Association, 2014). It is specifically focused on getting consumers to choose and purchase the products or services the organization has to offer. The marketing process involves conducting market research, developing a marketing strategy, and implementing that strategy.

To understand community relations, public relations must first be defined. Public relations is "a strategic communication process that builds mutually beneficial relationships between organizations and their publics" (Public Relations Society of America, 2014). Simple and straightforward, this definition focuses on the basic concept of public relations—as a communication process, one that is strategic in nature and emphasizing mutually beneficial relationships (Public Relations Society of America, 2014). It is much broader in scope than marketing and focuses more on creating a positive image for the organization than on selling its services. It usually contains some element of getting good publicity and avoiding, or at least managing, bad publicity.

Community relations, on the other hand, involve positive interaction with the community served. This includes public relations as a means of creating a favorable image with that community—but goes a bit further. It involves participation in community activities; providing certain services that the community needs, such as free clinics; and being considered a good neighbor by the community it serves.

It is easy to see how the terms *marketing*, *public relations*, and *community relations* can be confused because they each rely on the others. It is not necessarily important that they be considered separately as long as the role of each is understood. The way that each fits into an organization's overall marketing plan is explored later in this chapter.

■ Organizing for Marketing

Although they may not identify it as such, all long-term care organizations are engaged in marketing activities. However, do they do so effectively, efficiently, and in an organized manner? The sad fact is that many do not. With market competition increasing within long-term care, successful marketing campaigns have become essential aspects of doing business even for smaller LTC organizations. Despite the size of the organization, the quality of the customer service it provides in addition to the efforts put into establishing relationships are key components for marketing long-term care services (Keefer, 2014). Some long-term care provider organizations continue to attempt to attract customers on somewhat of an ad hoc basis. Others have developed formal marketing plans and have integrated marketing concepts into their overall operations. Organizations in this latter group have a far better chance of survival and prosperity in the long-term care system. They have developed a marketing mentality.

Developing a marketing mentality means understanding the value of having a good marketing plan. A marketing plan is a road map that your organization will be following to achieve its goals and objectives for revenue growth. In other words, a marketing plan is a description of the activities you and your team will execute to grow or maintain your organization's goals (Fannon, 2013). It also means knowing that marketing is an integral part of the overall success of the organization. The reason to create a marketing plan could be any or all of the following:

- To provide greater discipline in the planning process
- To provide strategic direction for an organization or business unit
- To provide an action plan for marketing-related activities
- To provide a formal record of marketing-related decisions
- To request budget
- To request internal resources
- To create dialogue with senior management
- To communicate marketing priorities to other parts of the organization
- To obtain buy-in from other parts of the organization (Lee & Hayes, 2007)

A marketing strategy or plan can answer the following questions:

- What economic and business environment are you experiencing?
- What opportunities and problems are you facing?
- What business objectives do you expect to achieve?
- What exactly do you sell?
- Who are your customers?
- Why should they buy your product or service rather than your competitors'?
- How will you communicate your product or service to your customers?
- Who will do what, when?
- How are you going to measure your progress so you can learn from the experience (Lee & Hayes, 2007)?

An organization with a marketing mentality recognizes that it must allocate the necessary resources for development and implementation of the marketing plan. This does not necessarily mean devoting huge amounts of money. A marketing strategy doesn't necessarily mean an expansive budget. It does, however, mean that your organization's marketing program must be focused on driving revenue by targeted resident opportunities and not only through branding efforts (Tromczynski, 2013). The marketing plan can be simple or complex, depending on the size and complexity of the organization, with corresponding costs. A marketing plan and associated materials should highlight the benefits and qualities of your services (Hawthorne, 2014). What is more important than the amount of resources is having a budget specifically dedicated to marketing, rather than treating it as a secondary activity.

■ Market Planning Versus Strategic Planning

There has long been an ongoing discussion about whether market planning is a subset of strategic planning or strategic planning is a subset of market planning. As one might expect, the point of view usually depends on the role of the person holding that view. Strategic planners tend to see the market plan as an offshoot of the larger strategic plan; marketers like to think of the strategic plan as merely a tool for use in developing a market plan. In fact, they are both right and neither is right. The two aspects of planning overlap a great deal, rely on essentially the same information, and contribute to the larger goal: success of the organization.

The purpose of the strategic plan is to develop a strategy that will help the organization thrive and prosper. The purpose of the marketing plan is to develop a (marketing) strategy that will help the organization thrive and prosper by selling more of its services or products. The analysis and strategy selection elements of the strategic planning process build the foundation on which the marketing plan is created, while the marketing plan is one of several ways in which the goals of the strategic plan are realized.

■ The Planning Process

The strategic planning process consists of several well-defined steps:

- Self-assessment
    - Evaluation of the mission and vision
    - Internal analysis
- External assessment
    - Environmental analysis
    - Stakeholder analysis
    - Competitor analysis
- Strategy development
    - Identification of alternative strategies
    - Selection of strategy
- Implementation
- Evaluation

The information collected in the early stages (self-assessment, external assessment, and the identification of alternative strategies portion of strategy development) serves both the strategic and market planning goals. As it pertains to marketing, the assessment is also known as a marketing plan audit. A marketing plan audit is a comprehensive review used to evaluate marketing strategy, gauge return on investment, and ensure meeting an organization's objectives. Simply, the audit will identify strengths and weakness, enabling the organization to recommend changes in processes and resources to increase effectiveness and efficiency (Markovich, 2014). It is after completion of these steps that the market plan really begins to take shape. These steps are now explained in a bit more detail, showing how this occurs.

Self-Assessment

The first step in developing a strategic plan is assessing the organization, including its mission and vision, as well as its strengths and weaknesses. To try to put this in perspective, it has been said that strategic planning consists of answering three questions: Where are we? Where do we want to go? How do we get there?

The self-assessment is the first part of answering the question, *Where are we?* It consists of two parts: (1) evaluation of the organization's mission and vision to determine whether they accurately portray the desires of those representing the organization and (2) identifying and analyzing the organization's internal capabilities—its strengths and weaknesses.

Evaluation of the Mission and Vision

To look at how the strategic planning process evaluates the mission and vision of the organization involves making an assumption that the organization has already identified them. However, in reality, many long-term care organizations have not done so. For them, it means creating a statement of mission and vision for the first time. They will have to start from scratch in developing mission and vision statements. For the rest, it means reviewing those statements to see whether they are still valid or need revision. To clarify for the uninitiated, the mission describes what the organization is and the vision describes what it wants to be. They are vital to the success of any planning process. As the Cheshire cat told Alice in Wonderland, "If you don't know where you're going, it doesn't matter which way you go" (Carroll, 1966, p. 49). Another way of stressing the importance of mission and vision is the statement, "If you don't know where you want to go, how will you know when you get there?" The mission statement identifies what the organization is, what services it provides, and of importance to the marketing effort, who it serves. The vision statement identifies what the organization wants to be, who it would like to serve, and what services it would have to provide to serve them. At first, it may be difficult to see the relevance of the mission and vision evaluation process to a discussion of marketing. However, it is very relevant in that it identifies an ideal destination for the marketing plan to attempt to reach.

Internal Analysis

The internal analysis consists of an introspective assessment of the strengths and weaknesses of the organization. In terms of strategic planning, it involves review of major operational areas including, at the least, administration and governance, staffing, services provided, financial viability, and the state of the physical plant (Pratt, 2000). In terms of market planning, however, this review includes assessment of the success or failure of previous marketing efforts, trends in the volume of products or services delivered, and changes in the types of products or services provided. The success of a marketing plan depends on strong and accurate data. Reliable information is obtained through situational analysis, which is an essential aspect of establishing your organization's operating climate (English, 2014). Most of this information (services or product provided, trends) can be collected as part of the overall planning process, whereas some (evaluation of marketing efforts) may require additional data collection efforts.

Perhaps the most difficult part of conducting an analysis of strengths and weaknesses is keeping it honest and objective. Because the primary purpose of the internal analysis is to better understand the organization, the process should not be used to tell the planners what they want to hear, but to tell them what they need to hear. The results of the analysis may not be what was expected (Pratt, 2000). Scrutiny of services may show that some are not cost effective or have declined markedly in volume. It may indicate that certain services are still being provided although they are being subsidized by other services. When the analysis of services produces such results, the organization must decide whether to continue providing them. Keep in mind that in health care, it is not uncommon to provide some services that do not pay for themselves but that are important to the community of consumers served. When this is the case, the organization attempts to keep the subsidy to a minimum.

Analysis of the relative success of previous marketing efforts can be even more difficult, particularly for the marketers involved. It is important that other members of top management be involved in such an analysis. They might also want to bring in outside consultants to assist them.

The result of the internal analysis, both for strategic planning and for market planning, should be a sound evaluation of the capabilities and shortcomings of the organization, backed up by credible data. Without such information, the strategy development phase will not produce the desired outcome.

External Assessment

The external assessment is aimed at defining those factors that affect the organization but are out of its direct control. It can be broken into three segments: (1) environmental analysis, (2) stakeholder analysis, and (3) competitor analysis (Pratt, 2000).

Environmental Analysis

The environment in which a long-term care organization exists is influenced by legislative/political, economic, social/demographic, technological, and competitive factors (Swayne, Duncan, & Ginter, 2006). Any or all of these factors can affect how the organization functions and how successful it is. They need to be identified and evaluated.

As for market planning, the environmental analysis looks specifically at the market in which the organization competes. There are several ways of defining that market. It may be defined geographically, covering a town or city, multiple towns or cities, or perhaps only a portion of a larger city. It may also be defined by demographic factors such as age, income level, ethnicity, or religion. For example, an assisted living facility might be competing within a market composed of middle- to high-income elderly people belonging to a specific religious group. Another may be in a market made up of lower-income, perhaps Medicaid-eligible, elderly. Understanding the market may involve asking questions such as:

- How is the market structured? Is it highly regulated or relatively unstructured?
- How big is the market?
- Are there segments in the market?
- What are the overall trends and developments in the industry?
- What is the rate of market growth or shrinkage over time?
- What are the key factors for success in this particular market? (Lee & Hayes, 2007)

Stakeholder Analysis

Stakeholders are any individuals or organizations that are affected by, or have the ability to affect, the organization. They may include staff and management within the organization, referral sources, reimbursement agencies, community groups, regulatory bodies, or—most important of all—consumers and potential consumers. Although all need to be considered in the larger planning process, market planning needs to pay particular attention to the last group of stakeholders: consumers and potential consumers. They are the ones who will ultimately make use of the organization's services.

Note that the term *consumers* is used here rather than *customers*. Patients, residents, and/or clients are all consumers (meaning they actually use the services) and customers (meaning that they are potential purchasers of the services). However, other entities, such as managed care organizations, employers, and government agencies, are also potential customers. They may be the object of marketing as well. Market planning defines those customers and potential customers in terms of who they are, how many of them there are, how likely they are to use the services of the organization doing the planning, and what influences their choice of providers. How can an organization hope to attract new customers or maintain its current customers if it does not know who they are?

Competitor Analysis

Because marketing is focused on making an organization competitive in its market, that organization must understand who its competitors are. They may be other similar provider organizations, or they may be from a different segment of the long-term care system or even from outside the system. There may be new competitors entering the market that were not there a short time ago. The market planning process needs to identify who the competitors are, what services they offer, and how they compare in terms of strengths and weaknesses. Competition is also analyzed with a concentration on their perceived strengths and weaknesses, oversaturation of the market, profitability, and market share (Markovich, 2014).

Market Research

To conduct the external assessment, and to some degree the self-assessment, the organization needs to conduct some level of market research. Market research is the process by which the organization identifies the consumers it serves, potential future consumers, and issues of importance to them through the collection and use of data. It also can be used to evaluate the effectiveness of previous or current marketing efforts or to test the public's knowledge of, and acceptance of, its services. Market research might involve compilation and analysis of information collected specifically for this purpose. Consumer surveys are a popular method of ascertaining how consumers and their families feel about the organization. They can also be used to test potential new service ideas. Focus groups serve the same purpose but bring people together to answer questions as a group rather than in individual surveys.

Some market research involves analysis of information already available. For instance, data concerning referrals from individual hospitals or other sources can identify which of those sources are producing the most referrals and which might produce more if approached properly. Other data are available from outside sources. The U.S. Census Bureau can be a gold mine of demographic data. Trade associations produce information about similar providers, providing benchmarks and identifying trends that might be of importance to the marketing effort. Some firms exist for the sole purpose of collecting and disseminating market data (for a price). The Internet has become a primary source of data for market research, as well as for most other types of inquiries.

In collecting data for market research, there is a certain risk of becoming overwhelmed by the volume of data available. This is why it is so important that the organization identify what it wants to know before starting to collect information. Erroneous data, or data that are not relevant, can send the market planning process off in the wrong direction. Market research is a highly skilled undertaking, and most organizations would be wise to use the services of research experts, either as employees or consultants. Many such experts are available.

Analysis of the research data is as important, and as full of potential hazards, as is collection of those data. Such analysis needs to be conducted carefully and by individuals skilled at it. At some point, final decisions based on the data collection and analysis must be made by the top management and probably the governing body of the organization. They will need to know what the data mean and what they do not mean. Again, it would be wise for them to seek guidance from an appropriate expert.

Strategy Development

Once the self-assessment and external assessment have been completed and all of the information needed has been collected, the organization has the answer to the first of the three questions asked earlier (*Where are we?*). Now it is time to begin developing a strategy or strategies to answer the other two questions (*Where do we want to go? How do we get there?*). The strategy formulation process is difficult and time-consuming but all-important to the success of the organization. The organization should establish an overall strategy to guide it toward its vision and goals. In most cases, it supports this with plans for the supporting functional areas of marketing, finance, human resources, and operations (Berkowitz, 2011). Because the focus of this chapter is on marketing, the other three functional areas are not discussed here, but the reader should recognize that each is equally important.

Identification of Alternative Strategies

The planning process, at this stage, involves gaining a full understanding of all of the market strategy alternatives available and choosing from among them. There are numerous strategies from which to select. The final determination of what is best for the organization may be a combination of more than one single strategy. Marketing strategies are generally categorized as growth strategies or consolidation strategies.

Growth strategies are those designed to expand the organization into new markets or gain additional customers in existing markets. There are four basic growth strategies:

1. *Market Penetration*: Expanding the current services to current customers.
2. *Market Development*: Also called market expansion; finding new markets for existing services.
3. *Product Development*: Offers new services to current customers.
4. *Diversification*: Also called product innovation/market expansion; developing new services for new customers (Berkowitz, 2011).

Consolidation strategies are designed to focus on a smaller set of markets, products, or services and include:

- *Divestment*: Selling a business or product line that is unprofitable or noncompetitive.
- *Pruning*: Reducing the number of services offered to the market.
- *Retrenchment*: Withdrawing from certain markets.
- *Harvesting*: Gradually withdrawing support from a service until there is little or no demand left for it (Berkowitz, 2011).

Selection of Strategy

There are several models and/or formulas available to help the organization determine whether it should adopt a growth strategy or a consolidation strategy and which of the specific market strategies within those two categories is best for it. They are not detailed in this discussion because the purpose here is to provide an overview of market planning, not to get involved in the actual planning.

A long-term care organization that provides more than one service or type of service may want to adopt different strategies for each, as long as they fit within the overall organizational strategy. For each of its services, it should identify a market strategy consisting of a selected target market and development of a marketing mix to appeal to that particular target market (Bearden, Ingram, & LaForge, 2001).

Selection of Target Market(s)

Strategy formulation utilizes the concepts of market segmentation and target marketing to determine and evaluate which of its constituencies (consumers/stakeholders) to interact with and which of its offerings to promote to them.

Market segmentation uses information from the stakeholder analysis to divide the market into potentially distinct groups of consumers who might merit separate products and/or marketing mixes. Long-term care subgroups might be permanent residents or short-term rehabilitation clients or those who require supportive care at home. A nursing home chain might segment its clients by payment type (private/public) or geographic, demographic, or lifestyle/behavior characteristics. The organization then prioritizes these market segments into a few primary and secondary target audiences. It could decide to serve several (differentiated) markets or elect to concentrate on the most promising (niche) market segment and develop a competitive product/service positioning and marketing mix strategy for each (Lane, 1999).

For example, a provider might identify consumers with mental illness or mental retardation as an underserved market and decide to capture that market segment. Before doing so, the provider would want to know how many potential customers were in the group, sources of reimbursement, and what special services it might have to create to serve them. If successful, serving the mentally ill and mentally retarded would become that provider's niche.

In determining which groups or segments of the market to target, the organization needs to ask the following four questions:

1. What do customers want or need?
2. What must be done to satisfy these wants or needs?
3. What is the size of the market?
4. What is its growth profile? (Peter & Donnelly, 2004)

For some providers, the choice of market segment is pretty easy because they have few options from which to choose. Others have more options and must choose carefully.

Although some may decide to serve all markets, their number is diminishing. Successful marketing is focused, seldom trying to be all things to all consumers.

Marketing Mix

The marketing mix is the particular mixture of marketing tools selected to strengthen the competitive position of the organization with a specific target market. It has come to be widely accepted that the marketing mix contains four elements: product, price, place, and promotion, often called "the four Ps." These four elements are combined differently for each target market segment.

Product is the service provided. In developing a marketing mix for a specific target market group, the organization would seek to provide that combination of services most needed and valued by the targeted consumers. Price refers to the setting of a competitive price for a specific service. Place represents the manner in which goods or services are made available for use by consumers (Berkowitz, 2011). In long-term care, it relates to how accessible the service is and may include the characteristics of service distribution, modes of delivery, location, transportation availability, hours and days open, parking, waiting time, and other access considerations. Promotion is the combination of methods of communicating with the target market and might include advertising, public relations, community relations, and publicity.

The way in which these elements are combined determines the marketing mix for each target market. Obviously, there will be overlap and similarities in development of these marketing mixes.

Implementation of the Marketing Strategy

In spite of the seemingly endless work that goes into development of a marketing plan, it is worth absolutely nothing unless successfully implemented. Implementation involves the application of the selected marketing mixes for the targeted market segments. A look at how this occurs follows.

Product

Throughout much of this chapter, the discussion has focused on services rather than products because long-term care is a service industry. However, marketing professionals use the term *product* much more widely. As used by them, it is more generic, referring to any goods, services, or other outputs provided by the organization. However, this discussion continues to center on services, because marketing them is not the same as marketing products.

Eric Berkowitz, a leading expert in the field of healthcare marketing, notes that marketing of services is more challenging because they are not tangible. Services differ from products in five components, which he refers to as "the 5 I's": intangibility, inconsistency, inseparability, inventory, and interaction (Berkowitz, 2011).

Intangibility: Services are intangible in that the consumer cannot feel, touch, see, or hear them prior to encountering them. They need to be shown how the services will benefit them.

Inconsistency: Long-term care services are delivered by people, as opposed to a product that comes off an assembly line. Thus, they will vary at times.

Inseparability: Services depend on the individual providing the service and, to some degree on the person receiving the service.

Inventory: Inventory refers to the volume of services available. Unutilized services, such as having therapists available who are not being used, constitute inventory.

Interaction: Delivery of services involves interactions between customers and providers. Such interactions are potential sources of good or bad marketing. (p. 258)

Each of these characteristics of what constitutes a service holds both challenges and opportunities for marketing staff. A good marketing plan capitalizes on them to the degree possible and minimizes any potential negative results from them. For example, a good customer service program can improve the interaction, inseparability, and inconsistency characteristics, giving the marketers something to sell to future consumers. Similarly, innovative scheduling can reduce the inventory problems, again providing a marketing opportunity.

Price

In marketing parlance, price is "the formal ratio that indicates the quantities of money goods or services needed to acquire a given quantity of goods or services" (American Marketing Association, 2014). The price set for a service can be either a positive or negative factor in terms of marketing that service. In some segments of long-term care, the price is largely determined by the reimbursement agencies and their accompanying regulations. However, there are areas in which the provider has some flexibility in setting the prices for services rendered. There are three major approaches for establishing prices for healthcare services: cost based, negotiated, and market driven (Neumann, Clement, & Cooper, 1999).

1. Cost-based pricing is most common because it relates to the various government reimbursement mechanisms. Whether a long-term care provider is reimbursed on a retrospective or prospective basis, government rates are based on their determination of reasonable costs for delivery of services.
2. Negotiated pricing is becoming more common. For example, a provider may negotiate with a managed care organization to provide services to its members. In such a negotiation, the provider has to seek a balance in setting prices that are low enough to be competitive but high enough to return an adequate profit.

3. Market-driven pricing assumes that there are multiple providers and that consumers are sensitive to differences in price. This has not been as common an approach, but it is growing. An example would be assisted living facilities that rely primarily on private payment and compete with each other for the same pool of customers.

Place

Where and how the service is delivered can be a very important aspect of marketing. Because long-term care services are provided to consumers directly, those consumers tend to place high value on this element. Services, however, generally involve a convenience factor. The more accessible they are and the easier it is for consumers to get them, the better the consumers like them.

Quality of care is obviously of high importance to consumers of long-term care services. However, they are not able to judge clinical quality as well as they can judge convenience and ease of access. In recent years, providers have done much to improve this characteristic, but they can do more. A nursing care facility cannot do a great deal in terms of where the resident receives care because that person is already there in the facility. However, it can make it more convenient for the resident to receive therapy or other ancillary services by bringing them to the resident rather than making the resident travel to a remote location. It can also improve access to family members by extending visiting hours, providing transportation, and so forth.

Assisted living facilities regularly market the lifestyle services they make available to their residents. This is a form of place marketing. Home healthcare organizations already take services to the client's home. They can improve the place rating, and thus its marketability, by changing when they visit, by combining multiple services into single visits, and so on.

Aging in place is a form of place-related service. It brings the services to the consumer instead of making the consumer go to the services. Organizations providing several levels of care have a distinct advantage over single-level organizations when it comes to marketing the convenience factor.

Promotion and Types of Promotion

Promotion is how the organization gets its message out to potential consumers, informing them of what it has to offer. It also must differentiate itself from its competitors. Successful differentiation can give a facility the competitive edge (Keefer, 2014). Some long-term care facilities have used the differentiation strategy to concentrate on a single market segment through a high degree of specialization in a particular service. Examples include Alzheimer's care facilities, rehabilitation facilities, and noncertified upscale facilities that cater to wealthy clients (Singh, 2010). Promotion consists of different combinations of advertising, community relations, public relations, and publicity. Because of the importance and complexity of promotion, each element is dealt with separately; then we show the way they are integrated.

Advertising—Advertising is

the placement of announcements and persuasive messages in time or space purchased in any of the mass media by business firms, nonprofit organizations, government agencies, and individuals who seek to inform and/or persuade members of a particular target market or audience about their products, services, organizations, or ideas. (American Marketing Association, 2014)

Not that long ago, most managers in long-term care or other aspects of health care reacted negatively to the concept of advertising. They saw it as crass and too "Madison Avenue" for a service provider. This was particularly true of nonprofit organizations. Often, they equated advertising with selling of consumer products and considered it somehow beneath the dignity of healthcare providers. Even the term *customer* brought negative reactions. That has all changed.

Today, most long-term care providers engage in some form of advertising. Advertising is distinguished from other forms of promotion in that it is both paid and nonpersonal (Berkowitz, 2011). It consists of purchasing space in newspapers, magazines, or on billboards; commercial time on radio or television, banner ads or pop-up ads on the Internet, or even placing an ad on the side of a blimp flying overhead. Advertising is a very direct form of promotion. It can be accurately targeted. Ads are developed to convey a specific message to a specific target population. For example, long-term care organizations frequently place ads in magazines whose readers are elderly. They match television advertising with certain shows regularly watched by the targeted population. You are not likely to see any long-term care commercials associated with MTV or Sesame Street. Viewers of that kind of programming are simply not the demographic groups they want to reach. Similarly, because elderly and middle-aged consumers are more likely to watch local news programs than are younger individuals, that is a good place for television ads for long-term care services.

Advertising has the potential to reach a large audience. It can also repeat the same or complementary messages over a period of time, reinforcing that message in the minds of potential customers.

Although advertising is a powerful marketing promotion tool, it does have a couple of drawbacks. First, it is very expensive and may be beyond the financial capabilities of some small provider organizations. That does not necessarily mean that it is the most used form of promotion, just that it is responsible for large expenditures. Another potential drawback is the negative reaction some consumers have to advertising by healthcare providers. Remember that most of them are of an age to have the same biases against advertising by professionals and service organizations that were mentioned earlier. Providers wishing to use advertising must be very careful to make it tasteful, professional, and subtle; otherwise, they run the risk of creating the opposite impression of what they intended.

The primary purpose of advertising—the desired outcome—is to make potential customers aware of the services available from the organization doing the advertising and to leave a favorable impression with them. It needs to paint a picture of competency, caring, and compassion. Most consumers of long-term care are concerned with quality-of-life issues. They do not want to be customers of long-term care providers. They are usually giving up some portion of their independence. In most cases, with the possible exception of assisted living, they resent having to rely on such services. It is not, then, the job of marketing to convince them to purchase the service, as is true in most other business transactions. Instead, what marketing should focus on is convincing them that one provider is better able to meet their needs than another. It should make them think, "If I have to go to a facility, or rely on home health services, this is the organization I want taking care of me."

One growing form of advertising is less direct than the traditional methods of newspapers, magazines, and radio or television ads. It can best be described as consumer education. An ideal long-term care system would have an education component. Providing that information is a good marketing tactic for a provider organization. Doing so will gain it credit for doing a good deed, a public service. It will also familiarize potential customers with the organization's services and its reputation. Education about long-term care and answers to frequently asked questions by consumers and their families can be provided in numerous ways. However, the one that is becoming most common is the Internet.

More and more, consumers and their families are searching the Internet when they seek information. Once they learn how and get over the fear of the technology involved, they find it is fast, easy, and productive. Developing a website that provides information and educational material is relatively inexpensive and is an excellent way of reaching customers. Such a site can be created so that it will appear when Web surfers search for a particular term, such as *long-term care*.

Web-based education should be just that—education. It cannot be heavy handed in pushing its services or in proclaiming its superiority. Such tactics will quickly cause people seeking information to go elsewhere. However, the provider organization should be clearly identified on the website, with a link to its more commercial messages. If consumers find it to be a good source of fair, objective information, they will likely remember who provided that information when the time comes that actual service is needed.

Social Media—Just as consumers are turning more to the Internet for education and information, so are they turning to social media. Web-based social networking allows older people to connect, share knowledge, provide support to other older people, and relate to others in similar circumstances. Social networking also helps to overcome social isolation, which is a major problem with negative health consequences (International Federation on Ageing, 2012). Facilities should have a Facebook business page for a more powerful marketing tool than a personal page. Business pages let administrators track more data about their customers and their website. Twitter allows administrators to send regular messages to customers and allows those administrators to respond quickly to important events (Ashe-Edmunds, 2014).

Community Relations—As noted earlier, community relations is all about building a good relationship with the community served. An important first step for any provider in developing community relations is identifying its service community (see the "Environmental Analysis" section under "External Assessment"). For example, a nursing facility might serve the Jewish population in its area, complying with all of the religious traditions of that group. Another might serve a highly bilingual ethnic population, again recognizing and meeting the requirements of that group for certain language and traditions. Identification of an organization's service community should be accomplished during the assessment portion of the planning process. Once that has been done, it can then design a community relations program specifically for that community. For example, an urban community and a rural community have different transportation requirements for long-term care services such as home healthcare and hospice.

Community relations has several elements, including public relations, publicity or media relations, and involvement in community activities. Although these activities overlap considerably, each has its own distinct focus. How the organization blends them together and blends them with its marketing and advertising may well determine how successful it will be.

Public Relations—Public relations is designed to create a positive image of the organization. It assists the marketing effort by helping to develop relationships with its stakeholders. These stakeholders include customers and potential customers, as well as other community groups who are in a position to influence how the organization is seen by the public in general.

Public relations develops and maintains the positive image of the organization in many ways. It gains attention through news releases and other media tools. It may do so through a distinctive corporate logo that has a clear association with the organization. It builds brand identity, which is discussed shortly, making the public aware of the organization and what it does without (or in addition to) paid advertising. It involves keeping its positive image in front of the community. Public relations is not something that happens successfully overnight. It takes time, commitment, and patience.

Publicity—Although a part of public relations, publicity is not all there is to public relations, yet many organizations have limited their public relations to attempts to gain good publicity. Publicity is "the non-paid-for communication of information about the company or product, generally in some media form" (American Marketing Association, 2014). It consists of news stories, press releases, and other similar means of gaining some positive media coverage for the organization. The media are very important stakeholders, so much so that the terms *public relations* and *media relations* are sometimes used interchangeably. This is not totally accurate. Media relations is more closely identified with publicity as a method of influencing public opinion through the media. Public relations does that but also goes beyond it. Most long-term care providers seek publicity by issuing news releases about events or situations that they consider favorable to their image. Such releases may focus on residents or clients who have an interesting story to tell. One of the most common is the resident who reaches 100 years of age. Others may include individuals with unusual hobbies or talents, such as the 90-year-old who can still play a mean piano.

Sometimes providers get news coverage of special or creative ways of meeting the needs of their consumers. In one case, an elderly resident of a nursing care facility had been an airplane pilot most of his life. His greatest wish was to take one more airplane ride. The facility arranged it and got excellent publicity as a result. Other publicity opportunities involve staff and the organization itself. Hiring a new chief executive officer or medical director qualifies as news. So does receiving a deficiency-free state survey or achieving accreditation or reaccreditation.

In seeking publicity, organizations need to realize that what they see as important news is not always seen that way by the news media or the public. Too many news releases without adequate news value can do more harm than good. The media representatives understand that the organization is trying to promote itself, but promotion that is too flagrant will not be used. In submitting a publicity release to the media, the representatives of the organization should ask two questions: "What message do we want to convey?" and "Why is this newsworthy?" They should attempt to look at it from the public's viewpoint and see whether it would be of interest to them.

Unfortunately for providers, not all publicity they receive is favorable. The historic and ongoing image problem that long-term care providers have has been discussed at length here. One important aspect of the public relations function is preventing or minimizing bad publicity. Unfavorable publicity can happen no matter how hard the organization tries to do a good job and avoid problem situations. An unsatisfied consumer or family member, a disgruntled former employee, a publicity-seeking lawyer, or an unhappy neighbor, are all potential sources of negative publicity. Obviously, the first step is to anticipate and avoid such problems, but if that fails the organization needs to counter the negative publicity quickly and effectively. The best way to do so is to already have a good relationship with the community, especially the media. If the provider's public relations representative and top management have developed a reputation for being honest and forthright with the media and the public, they will be more credible. If they have not always answered questions from the media honestly—or have avoided answering them at all—there may already be a built-in bias and a willingness to believe the worst about them.

Community Involvement—If a provider organization wants to maintain a good image in its service community, it must become a valuable and recognized member of that community. This means being involved in community activities. Representatives of the organization should be members of, and highly visible in, social and civic organizations such as the Rotary and Kiwanis clubs. The organization itself will probably want to be part of a local chamber of commerce or similar group and participate in community fund-raising efforts such as the United Way. One community participation endeavor that would seem a natural is participating in fund-raising efforts sponsored by groups representing people who might be some of the organization's own consumers (a bicycle tour for multiple sclerosis or the annual Muscular Dystrophy Association telethon). Such involvement lets the community know that the organization is working with it. Some long-term care provider organizations also sponsor Little League teams or similar community groups.

Another form of community involvement is providing free services for the community. This does not mean giving away the long-term care services that are the organization's primary revenue source, but smaller things such as letting a community group use a function room for their meetings or letting them use one of the organization's vehicles to transport their members. Any such assistance makes the community more familiar with the provider's service capabilities and with the people who work there.

All of these activities are valuable methods of improving the organization's relationship with its community. That relationship should be ongoing—and requires an ongoing effort. It is also important that all members of the organization's staff be seen as community/public relations representatives. The effort cannot be left solely in the hands of a public relations department or even with top management alone. Every person who comes into contact with consumers, consumers' families, referral sources, or the general public can help improve or diminish the organization's image. They should all consider themselves ambassadors to the community.

Finally, most long-term care providers rely heavily on referrals from other organizations, such as hospitals, physicians, social service agencies, and other long-term care providers. These referral organizations need to be seen as customers and courted.

Branding—One form of marketing that has become very prevalent in recent years is a concept called "branding." It consists of creating a specific identity for the organization and its services that is quickly and easily identified with them. It is any names, terms, colors, or symbols that distinguish one seller's product or services from another (Berkowitz, 2011). The legal term for *brand* is *trademark*. A brand may identify one item, a family of items, or all items of that seller (American Marketing Association, 2014). The purpose of an organizational brand is to develop brand equity, which is defined as "the value of the loyalty between a consumer and the organization. The equity exists in the minds of the organization's constituencies and is the collection of perceptions associated with the organization—good or bad" (Speak, 1996, p. 41).

Although only a few healthcare organizations, and fewer long-term care organizations, have done much in the way of developing brand recognition, other industries have done it for years and have done so very successfully. Logos, such as those used by Mercedes-Benz, the United Way, and Merrill-Lynch, have become quickly recognizable and present a distinctive image to consumers. Names such as the Mayo Clinic, Coca-Cola (or just Coke), or Life Care Centers are also recognizable. The colors green and yellow are readily associated with John Deere products. Some companies create symbols to help the public connect to their products, such as Tony the Tiger and the Michelin

Man. Many organizations have developed highly recognizable slogans or jingles. Even the U.S. Army gave us a slogan, and one of the best, in its "Be All You Can Be" slogan.

Long-term care providers do not necessarily need to be that creative, but they can benefit from anything that will bring them brand recognition. Organizations that provide highly successful services should have a strong brand to set them apart from their competitors in the eyes of potential consumers (Center for Healthcare Governance, 2008). They should, however, be careful that the brand truly represents the image they want to project. It should be based on the organization's mission, vision, and strategies. As a service provider, a long-term care organization wants to project an image of competence, caring, and customer service. Any branding that it does should reflect those qualities. Any attempt at a hard sell could be disastrous because that is not what their consumers expect from them.

Who Does the Marketing?

We have discussed how a marketing and/or community relations strategy is developed, some examples of such strategies, and how the marketing plan (strategy) is implemented—but who does the actual marketing? That varies considerably from provider to provider, depending on the size, complexity, and marketing budget of the organization. Some hire marketing managers and perhaps several assistants to do the marketing. Others combine marketing with public relations and even with other administrative functions. Still others contract with a marketing firm to either advise them or actually do the marketing. Regardless, marketing and community relations must be seen as a priority of top management. They cannot pass it all off to subordinates or outside contractors, no matter how good those others may be. The marketing function is to coordinate efforts and implement strategies, but others in the organization need to be involved.

Evaluation of the Plan

The marketing plan needs to be monitored and evaluated on an ongoing basis. In a field as dynamic as long-term care, the elements affecting the plan and its success are constantly changing. Thus, the plan needs to be kept up to date. This is not something that can be done now and then, but continuously.

■ Summary

Marketing and community relations are very important to long-term care providers and are becoming more so as the field becomes more competitive and consumers become better informed and more discriminating. Neither marketing nor community relations is the primary job of a provider organization, but they are valuable tools for advancing the organization's goals.

■ Vocabulary Terms

The following terms are included in this chapter. They are important to the topics and issues discussed herein and should become familiar to readers. Some of the terms are also found in other chapters but may be used in different contexts. They may not be fully defined herein. Thus, readers may wish to seek other, supplementary definitions of them.

branding
community relations
constituencies
external assessment
internal analysis
market expansion
market penetration
market planning
market segmentation
marketing

marketing mentality
place
price
product
promotion
public relations
self-assessment
stakeholders
strategic planning
strategy formulation

■ Discussion Questions

The following questions are presented to assist you in understanding the material covered in this chapter. They tend to be general but lend themselves to detailed answers, which can be found in the chapter.

1. Why is marketing appropriate for long-term care organizations? Why have such organizations not embraced it more quickly and fully in the past?
2. How do public and/or community relations differ from marketing?
3. What is the relationship between strategic planning and marketing?
4. What is involved in conducting a self-assessment as part of market planning? An external assessment?
5. What are the four growth strategies identified in the chapter, and when might they be used?
6. What are the four consolidation strategies identified in the chapter, and when might they be used?
7. What are the four elements (the four *P*s) of the marketing mix?
8. What is meant by *branding*?

■ References

American Marketing Association. (2014). *Definition of marketing.* Retrieved from https://www.ama .org/resources/Pages/Dictionary.aspx.

Ashe-Edmunds, S. (2014). *Marketing tools and techniques*. Retrieved from http://smallbusiness.chron .com/marketing-tools-techniques-42705.html.

Bearden, W., Ingram, T., & LaForge, R. (2001). *Marketing: Principles & Perspectives*. New York, NY: McGraw-Hill/Irwin.

Berkowitz, E. (2011). *Essentials of health care marketing* (3rd ed.). Burlington, MA: Jones & Bartlett Learning.

Carroll, L. (1966). *Alice's adventures in Wonderland and through the looking glass*. New York, NY: MacMillan.

Center for Healthcare Governance. (2008, September/October). The far-reaching power of the brand. *Healthcare Executive*, 64, 66–67.

English, D. (2014). *Key elements of a marketing plan situation analysis*. Retrieved from http:// smallbusiness.chron.com/key-elements-marketing-plan-situation-analysis-65457.html.

Fannon, L. (2013, January 11). *3 ways to measure marketing tactic effectiveness*. Retrieved from http:// www.ltlmagazine.com/blogs/luke-fannon/3-ways-measure-marketing-tactic-effectiveness.

Hawthorne, M. (2014). *How to develop a marketing plan for a nursing home*. Retrieved from http:// smallbusiness.chron.com/develop-marketing-plan-nursing-home-26293.html.

International Federation on Ageing. (2012, May 28). *Long term care and technology: 2012 senior government officials meeting*. Retrieved from http://www.ifa-fiv.org/wp-content/uploads/2012/11 /som-2012-ltc-and-technology-final-report.pdf.

Keefer, A. (2014). *About the best marketing tools for a nursing home*. Retrieved from http:// smallbusiness.chron.com/marketing-tools-nursing-home-40052.html.

Lane, S. (1999). Marketing/Community Relations. In J. Pratt, *Long-Term Care: Managing Across the Continuum* (pp. 510–530). Gaithersburg, MD: Aspen Publishers.

Lee, L., & Hayes, D. (2007, April 30). *Creating a marketing plan*. Chicago, IL: American Marketing Association.

Markovich, M. (2014). *Marketing plan audit*. Retrieved from http://smallbusiness.chron.com /marketing-plan-audit-19317.html.

Neumann, G., Clement, J., & Cooper, J. (1999). *Financial Management: Concepts and Applications for Health Care Organizations*, 4th ed. Dubuque, IA: Kendall-Hunt.

Peter, J., & Donnelly, J. (2004). *Marketing management: Knowledge and skills*. New York, NY: McGraw-Hill.

Pratt, J. (2000). A common sense approach to strategic planning. *Home Health Care Management & Practice*, 13(2), p. 31.

Public Relations Society of America. (2014). *What is public relations?* Retrieved from http://www.prsa .org/AboutPRSA/PublicRelationsDefined/#.VD_hyrl0xHx.

Singh, D. (2010). *Effective management of long-term care facilities* (2nd ed.). Sudbury, MA: Jones and Bartlet Learning.

Speak, K. (1996, April). The challenge of health care branding. *Journal of Health Care Marketing*, Winter, 40–43.

Swayne, L., Duncan, J., & Ginter, P. (2006). *Strategic management of health care organizations* (5th ed.). Malden, MA: Blackwell Publishing.

Tromczynski, T. (2013, August 20). *A strategy for success: Focus on marketing*. Retrieved from http:// www.mcknights.com/a-strategy-for-success-focus-on-marketing/article/309427/.

The Future:
Continuing Change

PART

V

Into the Future: Trends To Watch

Learning Objectives

After completing this chapter, readers will be able to:

1. Understand the forces that have brought the long-term care system to its current state and how those forces continue to act on it.

2. Identify ways in which the challenges resulting from the forces have been met and to what degree.

3. Identify challenges that have not been met.

4. Identify changes that have been brought on by the solutions to earlier challenges.

5. Identify and discuss the trends that will affect the long-term care system in the future.

■ Introduction

As has been said often, the field of long-term care has gone through, and is still experiencing, a time of great change. It has been, as such times tend to be, both trying and exciting. It has presented challenges to providers, consumers, payers, and regulators alike. Some of these challenges have been met, at least in part. Others have not. The desire of consumers to receive care in the most appropriate setting and the desire for a high quality of life have led to development of more and better alternative services such as hospice and adult day care. They have also stimulated more home- and community-based care. This has improved access to care for many.

Institutional care providers have done much to make their facilities more home-like and conducive to a high quality of life. The increased practice of including several levels of care in one facility or facility complex has made it easier for consumers to move with relative ease from one level of care to another. Also, the move toward more integration of long-term care and other healthcare organizations and the services they provide has improved the way in which care is delivered. Integrated health services and networks have affected how care is delivered, the cost of delivering it, and the way it is used by consumers.

There has been progress in allowing consumers to have more say in their care. The Patient Self-Determination Act of 1990 lent credence to advance directives and made it more feasible for consumers to state their wishes for end-of-life treatment in advance of the need for such treatment.

We have also seen a move toward culture change.

> Culture change—as used in the context of providing care—supports the creation of environments where residents and their caregivers are able to express choice and practice self-determination in meaningful ways at every level of daily life. Culture change transformation may require changes in organization practices, physical environments, relationships at all levels, and workforce models—leading to better outcomes for consumers and direct care workers. (Pioneer Network, 2008)

It has to start with a shift in thinking from regulatory compliance to a real focus on meeting the expectations of the customer (defined as the resident and the resident family) (Farrell & Elliot, 2008, p. 20). Bruce Yarwood, former president and chief executive officer of the American Health Care Association/National Center for Assisted Living, said in an interview published in *Provider* magazine:

> The marketplace is demanding that the type of service we provide be driven by their expectations. To stay in business, we have to do more than the "old" nursing home stuff. We need to create a culture and environment of positive experiences for the residents—all the way from the food they eat, to the staff that serve them, to the therapy they receive. Not only is the culture changing in terms of what people are demanding, but the marketplace is forcing change through economics. (Farrell & Elliot, 2008, p. 20)

Culture change is based, in large part, on improved relationships between staff and those they serve. Where nursing homes have traditionally grouped residents by floor with 40 to 50 people, they are now creating households with 10 to 16 people to create a more intimate environment. In this more personal environment, residents see the same faces—of other residents and caregivers—and build stronger connections (Proctor, 2014). Staff stability and consistent assignment have a tremendous impact on quality and overall performance. The benefits of consistent assignment have been described by Barbara Frank, cofounder and consultant, B & F Consulting, as follows:

> Consistent assignment supports caring relationships between staff and residents. These caring relationships are what draws staff to this work and keeps them. Stability and consistency allow staff to work better with each other, which reduces

stress and allows staff to provide more consistent care to residents. This consistency improves care outcomes (Farrell & Elliot, 2008, p. 23)

Many nursing facilities have found that seemingly small efforts on their part can have a substantial impact on the quality of life of their residents. For example, nursing units have become neighborhoods. The bathing area (formerly called by the inglorious name of *tub room*) has become the spa.

Some of the solutions created new challenges. For example, as the government and private corporations began to experience healthcare expenses beyond their ability to cover, they sought relief. They found some of that relief in the form of managed care. Yet, at the same time, the rise of managed care presented the long-term care system with other problems. Providers have been forced to make major changes. They have had to pay much more attention to cost-effectiveness while trying to maintain high quality and have had to face complaints that managed care organizations put cost savings ahead of choice or quality.

Integration of services has been a positive step overall, but it has been fatal for some providers. Those who have not been able to adjust to integrated care or competition from within and without their own spheres of operation have generally fallen by the wayside. This has sometimes forced consumers to change how and where they received care. Although integration and competition may have been the forces that triggered the loss of these providers, their demise was probably inevitable.

Creation of new services has created additional demand. As more consumer-friendly services have become available and consumers have become more knowledgeable about them, there has been an increase in use of those services. This is good news for both consumers and providers but not necessarily for those who must pay for the added services out of a funding pool that has not grown accordingly.

Other challenges of the recent past still show little, if any, resolution. Many of those also deal with financing, a difficult subject to address, to say the least. The long-term care system is still essentially reimbursement driven. The services received depend somewhat on the reimbursement available. There is still more demand for service than there is money to pay for it. Access to and availability of long-term care services continue to be areas of shortcoming. Services are not distributed equitably for a variety of reasons.

■ Future Directions

Let us now look at where the long-term care system is likely going and why. Anyone can predict the future, and many do. The following identification of trends is not the result of special psychic powers, nor does it represent any particular knowledge that others do not have. What it does represent is a careful review of the history of the long-term care system, analysis of current events, and an understanding of how that system is likely to react to those events. It represents what one author calls "estimates of the probabilities of possibilities" (Bauer, 2006, p. 15). It also represents the personal views, insights, and opinions of your author, for better or worse.

Some of what follows is based on a keynote talk presented by your author at a conference in New Orleans, Louisiana in 1997. The conference was titled, "Health Care in the Next Millennium: Integration Strategies for Organizational Success," and my keynote talk was called, "The Future of Health Care in America." At the time, the idea of forecasting trends that would occur in the next millennium was both attractive and daunting. The thoughts presented at that time have been updated and expanded here in an effort to accurately reflect the changes that have taken place since then. Actually, it is interesting how many of the trends predicted more than a decade ago are still in play, as well as how many new ones have burst onto the scene.

In the following sections are some of the trends that can be expected to continue, or to develop, in long-term care over the next few years.

■ Changing Consumer Demographics

The demographics of long-term care consumers have been changing faster than the system has been able to adjust. The number of elderly is growing. They are staying alive longer and using more long-term care services. Plus, the baby boomers are no longer coming—they are here! They are already beginning to join the ranks of the elderly, the largest users of long-term care services, further multiplying existing problems. There has been a lot of talk about addressing these demographic changes, but not much has been seen in the way of solutions to date.

The consumers of long-term care have changed in recent years and will continue to do so. Those changes fall into two general categories: (1) the aging of society and (2) greater cultural and ethnic diversity.

The Aging of Society

Just as the growth in the number of elderly has been a major factor in the development of the continuum of care to its present state, so will it be a driving influence on the system for years to come. In fact, the influence of the elderly will be felt even more in years to come than has been the case in the past. The number of elders in American society is growing at an amazing rate. The number of elderly (65+) is projected to mushroom to 70 million by the year 2030. By that time, the youngest baby boomers will have reached retirement age (Melnyk, 2012). By 2050, one fifth of the total U.S. population will be elderly (that is, 65 or older), up from 12% in 2000 and 8% in 1950. The number of people age 85 or older will grow the fastest over the next few decades, constituting 4% of the population by 2050, or 10 times its share in 1950 (Congressional Budget Office, 2013).

The elderly have steadily gained years of life expectancy in the past several decades. By 2004, life expectancy at birth reached a then record high of 77.8 years (National Center for Health Statistics, 2007). Since then, it has kept on rising, with an estimated life expectancy of 79 years in 2015 (CantyMedia, 2014).

They are living longer for a number of reasons and will continue to do so. First, the longer life is due, in large part, to the improved quality of the medical care they have received during their lives. Many of the diseases that once killed people as children or as young adults have been effectively eradicated. Also, two of the greatest killers in recent years—heart disease and cancer—have declined. An American Cancer Society report finds "steady declines in cancer death rates for the past two decades add up to a 20 percent drop in the overall risk of dying from cancer over that time period" (ScienceDaily, 2014). Over the past 10 years, the death rate from heart disease has fallen about 39% (American Heart Association, 2013). Second, longer life can also be attributed to changes in people's lifestyles. As tomorrow's seniors have progressed through middle and advanced age, improvements in public health and preventive medicine have extended their average life spans even further. Better nutrition, conscious efforts to get more exercise, and the slow but increasingly successful fight against smoking will all lead to longer, healthier lives.

It may seem a bit paradoxical to equate preventive services—generally seen as being at the front end of the continuum—with long-term care, which is at the other end, but we are beginning to understand that there is a direct correlation between the two.

Preventing or delaying the onset of chronic conditions, along with effective management after diagnosis, can lower the demand for healthcare services (Hibbard & Hayes, 2008). An ideal system would put more emphasis on, and provide reimbursement for, illness prevention efforts as an integral part of that overall system (Saint Joseph's College of Maine, 1993). As society realizes the long-range value of preventive health care, to say nothing of its cost-effectiveness, there will be a more intensive effort to improve these services and their availability to consumers of all ages.

A third reason for the growth in numbers of elderly is the aging of the baby boomers of whom we have heard so much. They are just beginning to swell the ranks of the elderly. Their impact over the next couple of decades will be more significant than any other population cohort seen to date. Since 2011, 10,000 (yes, ten thousand!) people have been turning 65 every day (Boling, 2007). The sudden influx of so large a group will provide challenges and opportunities enough for all segments of the long-term care system. Born in the 2 decades following World War II, these baby boomers are now in, or beyond, middle age. They are often finding themselves in a position of caring for, or arranging care for, their parents. In this role, they are experiencing both the benefits and shortcomings of the current system of care. In many cases they are becoming determined to save their own children from the worst parts of that experience. As a result, they are more likely to be open to better education about the system and learning how to use it wisely. These younger generations may be more aware of the need to plan for long-term care (LTC) needs and may be more risk averse (Melnyk,

2012). They represent a previously unheard-of opportunity for consumer education. It is an opportunity that will pass unseized if it is not acted on in the very near future.

The impact of the aging of society on the continuum of care, particularly on long-term care, will be twofold. According to a study by the U.S. Department of Health and Human Services, more than 70% of Americans over the age of 65 will need long-term care services at some point in their lives. If that doesn't open eyes, consider the following HHS statistic: Anyone reaching the age of 65 years has a 40% chance of entering a nursing home, with a 20% chance of staying there for at least 5 years (Banham, 2010). It will, as pointed out earlier, extend the time over which the elderly will require long-term care services. The elderly will continue to use acute care services, but not significantly more than at present. The need for acute services will simply come at a later age. However, long-term care may be needed for many years. The federal Administration on Aging estimates that by 2020, 15 million seniors will require LTC, 50% more than in 2012 (Melnyk, 2012). This will result in a continuation of the current shift of focus from acute to long-term care services. Second, it will probably shift some of society's limited financial resources away from institutional to noninstitutional long-term care providers. This means that those providers must plan ever more carefully to focus their efforts on the most needed and most cost-effective services to provide.

Increase in Chronic Conditions

There will be an increase in chronic conditions as society ages. The number of people with chronic conditions is rapidly rising. By 2030, the number of Americans with one or more chronic conditions will increase 37% from 2000 levels, an increase of 46 million people. By 2030, half the population will have one or more chronic conditions. Some 28% of Americans have two or more chronic conditions (Anderson, 2010).

The prevalence of multiple chronic conditions increases with age. While 1 in 15 children have multiple chronic conditions, almost 3 out of 4 people ages 65 and older have multiple chronic conditions (Anderson, 2010). In addition to the impact on the individual consumers who have to live with and manage these multiple chronic conditions, there is an impact on the system as a whole. The more chronic conditions one has, the more expensive the care is. Even today, two thirds of Medicare spending is for beneficiaries with five or more chronic conditions (Anderson, 2010).

The increase in elderly with chronic conditions will result in a similar increase in people with functional and cognitive limitations. Functional limitations are physical problems that limit a person's ability to perform routine daily activities, such as eating, bathing, dressing, paying bills, and preparing meals. Cognitive limitations are losses in mental acuity that may also restrict a person's ability to perform such activities. On average, about one third of people aged 65 or older report functional limitations of one kind or another; among people aged 85 or older, about two thirds report functional limitations. A study by the Congressional Budget Office (2013) estimates that more than two thirds of 65-year-olds will need assistance to deal with a loss in functioning at some point during their remaining years of life. The Congressional Budget Office goes on to say, "If those rates of prevalence continue, the number of elderly people with functional or cognitive limitations, and thus the need for assistance, will increase sharply in coming decades" (Congressional Budget Office, 2013).

The healthcare system is not well designed to meet the needs of people with chronic conditions. Their care is not coordinated, which leads to unnecessary service use. Consumers may receive conflicting advice from different providers and report difficulty accessing services. Because they have difficulty paying out of pocket for health care, people with chronic conditions frequently rely on others for financial support and personal assistance (Anderson, 2010). It is up to the professionals in the system to help them.

There will be an increase in "new" diseases—actually, existing diseases with new prominence: Alzheimer's disease, macular degeneration, osteoarthritis, osteoporosis, dementia, cardiovascular disease, and diabetes. Although these chronic conditions can reduce an individual's independence, they can be controlled in most cases outside of institutions.

Greater Cultural and Ethnic Diversity

The coming generation of older adults will be the most diverse the nation has ever seen with more education, increased longevity, more widely dispersed families, and more racial and ethnic diversity, making their needs much different than those of previous generations (National Academy of Sciences, 2008). They bring with them different languages, cultural practices, and some unfamiliar diseases. While most healthcare providers are already providing interpreters to accommodate consumers who speak a different language or dialect, they need to do more. As one might expect, in those parts of the country where such cultural diversity has become more common, providers have learned much about meeting their needs. However, in other places—often rural or geographically remote—there is still work to be done.

Cultural diversity is also bringing a need for providers to be more sensitive to different cultural practices. For example, Muslim women object to the lack of privacy afforded by the traditional hospital "Johnny." As a result, some providers have designed one that better meets their needs. Other examples include different ways in which family members participate in a consumer's care.

This increasing diversity will result in very different rates of major illnesses and the appearance of many diseases that are unfamiliar (Bauer, 2006). Diseases that have been largely eradicated in the United States, such as polio and tuberculosis, have begun to appear as people emigrate from other parts of the world.

A Consumer-Driven System

The most important descriptor of the future healthcare system is that it will be a system that is consumer driven. Not consumer oriented or consumer focused, but consumer driven! Consumers are demanding more choice in both the care they receive and in how their dollars are spent, and they will continue to do so (Pratt, 1996). This is not only the most important element of an ideal system, but it is the prediction for the future in which we can have the most confidence.

Unlike previous generations, baby boomers want to be informed and educated. As a result, they are better able to make choices. All who are involved in health care in one form or another have an opportunity—and an obligation—to provide them with the information they need. It is clearly in everyone's best interests to do so. They are more technologically savvy and will expect to get that information largely from the Internet.

They will have more disposable income. Because they will be more conscious that they are paying for their care, either directly or indirectly, consumers will want the ability to shop around. This does not mean that they will always have a choice among providers. Such choice is not going to be possible in many rural areas, but they will want to have as much choice as possible in the types and levels of care they receive and in the locations where that care is delivered. We are all used to the attitude, "Someone else is paying for it, so I don't care how much it costs." Maybe these people are not being given enough credit.

Study after study has shown that informed healthcare consumers make better choices about the quality of care they receive. Researchers who have examined regional differences in how health care is provided have found that when consumers understand the comparative value of various options, they tend to opt for less or cheaper treatment or shorter stays, even when they are not paying for it directly. And, as long-term care consumers become better informed, they will lose some of their fear of the system. Today, that system is still dealing with several generations of people who grew up thinking of hospitals and nursing homes as places to go to die. Today's consumers want more control of their lives and are willing to look around until they find it, or, as one author puts it:

> seniors in nursing homes are not waiting to die—they just need a bit of help to live a purposeful, happy life. The culture change of nursing care reflects this shift in thinking, not only in the places offered for senior living, but in the very core of the nursing care system. Even the vocabulary is changing by focusing on the senior as a whole and vital person, rather than a number on a chart. (Lee, 2011)

Younger generations have been more exposed to the various types of care and accept them more readily. They are relatively free of the fears of their parents and grandparents. This will make the jobs of long-term care providers easier. It will, however, remove some of the mystique that has surrounded the system and will force providers to let consumers be more involved—whether they, the providers, like it or not. No longer will they be able to dictate to their patients/residents/clients what care will be given.

A variety of polls have shown that (1) a majority of people feel that there is something seriously wrong with the healthcare system, (2) they are not optimistic about the future of health care, and (3) they believe that quality of care is often compromised to save money. There is reason to be skeptical of too much reliance on polls and surveys, but there is a message here that cannot be ignored: as providers, payers, regulators, and policy makers strive to reengineer, restructure, and revolutionize how long-term care is delivered, they had better be very aware at all times of what the consumers want. We hear a lot about consumerism. Now that the sleeping giant of consumerism has been awakened, it will allow no less than that we meet their expectations. There is already backlash against changes that consumers perceive to be placing cost savings above quality. They object to things such as the so-called drive-through deliveries, the term some have applied to limiting mothers giving birth to 48 hours in the hospital. There will be a lot more of that backlash against perceived infringements on consumer choice. Consumer attitudes are changing, and the system must change with them. They have learned to say, "I won't stand for it anymore." Nowhere will that consumerism be felt more dramatically in the years to come than in health care. The long-term care segment of the field can expect to experience the consumer movement more than most because of the long-range, intimate relationship between long-term care providers and consumers.

It is important for all providers in the continuum of care to recognize these changes because people who have adapted their lifestyles over the course of many years will want to continue those lifestyles as much as possible in their later years. Consumers will look for care that is flexible and adaptable to their particular lifestyles, even extending to alternative medicine and self-care. End-of-life care will be more important to them than was the case with previous generations, because they will be accustomed to making their own decisions.

Providers and payers will need to accommodate their desires. They have begun to do so, but the future will bring even more necessity for them to provide the types of services wanted by consumers. For example, there are already a few highly successful wellness programs for the elderly, even in long-term care facilities. There will be more in the next few years.

■ Focus on Quality and Outcomes

Although cutting costs has dominated much of the debate surrounding health care in the past several decades and will continue to do so into the next several, quality is equally important to all concerned. Consumers of long-term care are learning how to judge quality as it pertains to them and will continue to as they become better informed. They will judge the system and its providers by how they are affected. Although many of those consumers may not even understand what the term *outcomes* means, that is really the measure they will be using.

Quality

Quality concerns fall into three distinct but related categories: (1) quality of care, (2) patient safety, and (3) quality of life.

Quality of Care

There are several reasons for the concerns about quality of care. First, various studies have shown that quality of care is not equitable across the United States (RWJ Foundation, 2010). Second, there is the ongoing media hype focusing on examples of poor care—while seldom mentioning examples of outstanding care quality. Add to that the frequent number of lawsuits in the news and concerns about the effects of cost-cutting, and it is no wonder consumers have their doubts.

Patient Safety

Patient safety will assume new prominence, both in acute care and in long-term care. This will be because of several factors. First, as consumers learn to demand more of a role in their care, they will become less and less forgiving of clinical errors or lapses in care. Second, payers will continue to insist on fewer errors. Medicare and Medicaid have already begun to do that with their "never events" list of serious reportable adverse events for which they will not pay (CMS, 2008). While they started with hospital procedures (e.g., wrongful surgery), they have moved toward long-term care. Third, providers have become more concerned with patient safety—not that they were not before—but with renewed enthusiasm. They realize the need to do so, and have more tools to work with, such as technology that can help them collect and manage relevant information to avoid errors (Applied Management Systems, 2008).

The government has taken several steps to ensure safety, including requiring that all skilled nursing facilities have sprinklers as part of their fire prevention and control systems.

Another approach to ensuring patient/resident safety is the concept of risk management. As defined by the American Academy of Family Physicians (2013):

> risk management refers to strategies that reduce and minimize the possibility of an adverse outcome, harm, or a loss. The systematic gathering and utilization of data are essential to loss prevention. Good risk management techniques improve the quality of patient care and reduce the probability of an adverse outcome or a medical malpractice claim. (p. 2)

Some see risk management as a means of avoiding lawsuits or other costs to the organization. That is an element of risk management—and in many cases, a prime motivator. However, it is essentially a means of avoiding threats to the safety of those who use the services.

A new concern for long-term care—at least newly realized—has come about because of the damage caused in recent years by hurricanes such as Katrina and Rita. Although all long-term care facilities had disaster plans, as did other healthcare facilities, most found them to be woefully inadequate for natural disasters such as those hurricanes. For example, in at least one location, all healthcare providers had the required agreement with a transportation company to provide buses to move their patients/residents out of harm's way. The only problem is that they all had agreements with the same company, which obviously could not handle all of them. In other situations, long-term care administrators and staff were unable to get to their facilities because they did not have proper identification and could not get through the lines of emergency personnel.

They have learned from these problems and are far more prepared than in the past.

Quality of Life

Quality of life has come to assume a high priority with today's long-term care consumers and will become even more important in the future. Long-term care consumers want care that is either provided in their homes or in familiar surroundings and in a manner that is as close to home as possible. As the culture change in long-term care takes hold, the lives of seniors are changing for the better. These are not the nursing homes your grandmother knew—and as the trend continues, more seniors may experience the philosophy of the Pioneer Network, the Eden Alternative, and the Green House Project as the rule, rather than the exception (Lee, 2011). Institutional providers have responded with amenities such as à la carte menus, homelike living settings, and flexible treatment regimens. Other adaptations include more flexible outpatient care and remote monitoring and safety call systems that allow more elders to actually stay in their homes.

The future will include many more such attempts and efforts to improve the quality of life of all long-term care consumers. Those consumers want more control of their lives and are willing to look around until they find it. Aging baby boomers will require programming and facilities to exceed current standards in meeting the needs of all seven aspects of wellness, including the emotional, intellectual, physical, environmental, social, occupational, and spiritual aspects (Golden & Schneider, 2014).

Outcomes

Payers and regulators have begun to understand outcomes measurement and to rely on it. They are gradually moving from judging how care is delivered to assessing it based on what it accomplishes. To do so is in their best interests and will be, coincidentally, in concert with the interests of those they serve. However, there is a need to achieve agreement on quality standards and metrics in long-term care, including what patient outcomes to strive for in a population that is not expected to be cured of their disabling conditions (Raphael, 2008).

Both government regulators and private accreditation agencies are moving toward outcomes-based quality measurement systems. They have not become especially proficient at it yet, but this will improve greatly in the future. They will demand that providers follow suit. This will not be a problem for most long-term care providers as long as the system measures outcomes as a substitute for process measurement and does not simply add another layer of documentation. A successful outcomes-based system will include more flexibility to allow providers to find better methods of achieving desired results. It will also have built-in incentives for innovation in improving those outcomes. To do this, payers and regulators will have to set minimum standards below which performance is unacceptable and above which there are some benefits accruing to the providers.

Quality is difficult to judge. This is particularly true in a field such as long-term care in which most such measurements are subjective. What providers see as high quality, based on clinical standards, may not be seen by consumers as high quality, based on how it affects their lifestyles. Individuals view quality-of-life issues through their own combination of personality, culture, and experiences. They may not be able to describe what quality means to them very precisely, but they know what they like and what they dislike. As time passes, providers will lean toward the consumers' point of view. They will, as they are doing now, change how care is delivered to make it more homelike, more comfortable for the consumer to accept. This does not mean that providers will relinquish their responsibility to provide safe, clinically sound care. It simply means that they will be more receptive to some of the more subtle nuances of what consumers see as their preferred quality of life.

One area of confusion about past, and some current, quality measurement and assurance tools is the close ties between quality and cost. Utilization review, introduced with Medicare and Medicaid, was often presented as being designed to guarantee that patients received the most appropriate care. In reality, it was designed to ensure that the government did not pay any more than necessary. Similarly, quality assurance programs have also tended to mix quality and cost.

■ Changes in the Workforce

The long-term care workforce will change dramatically in the future. The trends to watch in relation to the workforce are growth in demand, aging of the workforce, staff shortages, and blending of professional roles. Let us look at them.

Growth in Demand

Health care (including long-term care) is already one of the largest and fastest growing occupations. Yet, even that rate of growth will not meet future needs. The

Paraprofessional Healthcare Institute (2008) projected a need for 1 million more healthcare workers by the year 2016, many of them in long-term care. This results in a dramatic shortage of all types of healthcare workers, especially those in long-term care settings.

Aging of the Workforce

The workforce is getting older, paralleling the aging of society in general. Many of them are baby boomers, because that is the largest age cohort we have. The post–baby boomers are a smaller group, providing fewer people for the workforce. Baby boomers tended to have smaller families.

- In 1960, the average woman had 3.6 children.
- In 2010, the average woman had 2.1 children.
- Low fertility eventually results in fewer working-age people per retiree.
- In 1930, there were 10.3 working-age people per retiree.
- In 1960 there were 5.6 working-age people per retiree.
- In 2010 there were 4.6 working-age people per retiree.
- In 2030 there will be 2.8 working-age people per retiree (Melnyk, 2012).

One report defines a caregiver support ratio as the number of potential caregivers aged 45–64 for each person aged 80 and older. The report uses this support ratio to estimate the availability of family caregivers during the next few decades. That report states that

in 2010, the caregiver support ratio was more than 7 potential caregivers for every person in the high-risk years of 80-plus. By 2030, the ratio is projected to decline sharply to 4 to 1; and it is expected to further fall to less than 3 to 1 in 2050, when all boomers will be in the high-risk years of late life. (Redfoot, Feinberg, & Houser, 2013, p. 1)

As more baby boomers leave the working group and move to the group needing long-term care, the situation will worsen.

Staff Shortages

As is clearly shown by the growth in the number of people expected to need long-term care in the future, and the expectation that each of them will need services for a longer time, we are facing a serious shortage of staff to care for them. The Bureau of Labor Statistics (2014) projects that demand for the paraprofessional healthcare workers will increase faster than overall demand for workers, but slower than demand for health-care workers in general. In contrast, it projects that demand for home health aides and personal care aides will increase substantially more than overall labor demand

(McCarthy, 2013). This is particularly true when it comes to health personnel trained and willing to care for America's rapidly aging population. Finally, the overall healthcare workforce is inadequately trained to care for older adults (National Academy of Sciences, 2008). Direct-care workers (nursing assistants, home health aides, and personal care aides) provide an estimated 70% to 80% of the paid hands-on long-term care and personal assistance received by Americans who are elderly or living with disabilities or other chronic conditions. The majority of direct-care workers are now employed in home and community-based settings, and by 2020, home and community-based direct-care workers are likely to outnumber facility workers by more than two to one (PHI, 2013). In 2007, less than 1% of nurses were certified in geriatrics, while 7,128 physicians were certified in geriatric medicine as of 2007—a level that may grow by another 700 physicians by 2030. Yet the Alliance for Aging Research has estimated that the nation will need 36,000 geriatricians by 2030 (Blumenthal & Davenport, 2008).

The impact on long-term care will be great. The Bureau of Labor Statistics (2014) suggests that as a result of the growing elderly population, many healthcare paraprofessionals will be needed in long-term care facilities. In 2010, the Bureau of Labor Statistics projected that total demand for these workers would grow by 20% from 2010 to 2020, faster than the 14% average for all occupations. However, the Bureau of Labor Statistics also noted that demand for these workers may be constrained by the fact that many nursing homes rely on government funding, which tends to increase slower than the cost of patient care. The Bureau of Labor Statistics projected that the growth in healthcare-related occupations taken as a whole would be 34% during this period. It also projected that demand for personal care aides and home health aides would rise 70% and 69%, respectively, during this period. In addition, as the population ages, there will be an increasing number of people with disabilities.

The workforce of the future will also need to be properly sized to respond to the population's healthcare needs. It must contain the correct mix of personnel: physicians, nurses, other professionals and nonprofessionals, generalists, and specialists. The workforce must be prepared for continual changes in the organization of the U.S. healthcare system; for increasing demands for accountability regarding their performance; and for changes in the demography of the U.S. population, including its older age, increasing burdens of chronic conditions, and growing racial and ethnic diversity (Blumenthal & Davenport, 2008).

While most observers recognize the pending staff shortages, little appears to be happening to solve the problem. One organization, called the Center for American Progress, has recommended a new focus on the burgeoning need for direct care workers by launching a new program specifically targeting long-term care workers—in essence, a long-term care worker investment act. The original Worker Investment Act of 1998 provided federal workforce training funds for worker training, job placement, and retention activities (Blumenthal & Davenport, 2008). The Workforce Investment Act of 2013 amends the Workforce Investment Act of 1998 (WIA) to include long-term care workers. As of this writing (late 2014) the 2013 WIA is in congressional committees.

The Workforce Investment Act of 2013 amends the Workforce Investment Act of 1998 to revise requirements and reauthorize appropriations for: (1) WIA title I, workforce investment systems for job training and employment services; and (2) WIA title II, adult education and family literacy education programs.

Blending of Professional Roles

If the kind of changes in organization and delivery that are foreseen here are going to be accomplished, there will have to be some breaking down of the artificial barriers created by healthcare professionals. This means moving from the traditional medical model toward more of a holistic model of care. The entire healthcare system, but long-term care in particular, will shift its emphasis from disease- or condition-related treatment to person-centered care. The emphasis will be on the consumers, not on the professionals caring for them.

To accomplish this shift, providers will have to be more flexible in staff assignments, taking staff to the consumers rather than bring the consumers to the staff. Long-term care is relationship centered, and training to develop the skills required to care for older adults is crucial to providing quality care (Raphael, 2008).

Regulators and payers will also have to show increased flexibility. Their rules will have to permit providers to be innovative if they are to respond to the needs and desires of consumers. It also means an increased blurring of the lines among professional disciplines to permit more working together and less contesting of professional turf. This will not be easy.

Nonlicensed staff play a major role in long-term care and influence the consumer's quality of life for better or worse. They are often the first to observe change or to receive important information from or about consumers, yet their jobs carry little discretionary authority (Kane, 1993). These paraprofessionals, be they certified nurse aides, food service workers, or other nonlicensed staff, are critical to the future success of long-term care providers. Yet, turnover among these workers is very high due to factors such as low pay and lack of benefits. It will be necessary to improve their lot by providing them with more input in and respect for the work they do, higher wages and improved benefits, training and educational opportunities, and safer working conditions (Novelli, 2007). The way they are included in, or excluded from, the caregiving process will affect the success of the system in improving both efficiency and effectiveness. There will be increasing need for the system to make better use of them than at present.

Recruitment and retention efforts will have to be better than they are now in many cases. There will need to be an increased focus on innovative efforts, including seeing staff as customers and meeting their particular needs, sponsoring scholarships, recruiting minorities, using volunteers, and other yet-to-be-determined initiatives.

■ Changes in the Organization and Delivery of Long-Term Care

There will be many changes in the way long-term care is organized and delivered in the future. Let us look at some of the changes we can expect.

Toward a Seamless System of Care

There has already been significant movement toward a more seamless system of care. By now, *seamless system* has become one of the catchphrases just about everyone uses, but there really is movement in that direction. Seamless means a system that is coordinated, accessible, user friendly, and efficient. A seamless system is one that recognizes individual needs, rights, and responsibilities. It is a system characterized by more consumer choice and autonomy, by integration of services, and by a blending of the healthcare system and the social care system. Both the pressures on the system and its accomplishments are leading toward this ideal. The place managed care has found in the continuum in the past few years is testimony to the importance of coordinating care to make it more cost effective. Increased demand and strain on resources that are already stretched to the breaking point will continue to emphasize efficiency. The demands of consumers for more choices in the types of care available to them will lead to a continuum that is more user friendly, reducing much of the fragmentation and confusion that exists today.

One of the most important elements of a seamless system of care is the melding of what are now essentially separate systems of health care and social support services. If true seamlessness is to be attained, consumers will no longer have to access those systems separately. They will, in a better system, not even realize it when they move from one to another. There are many examples of where the two systems overlap, but perhaps the most common is in the area of housing. The line between a retirement community and an assisted living facility is subtle. As more and more long-term care providers move into multiple levels of services or offer aging in place, that separation becomes even less clear. There is a well-accepted movement toward increasing the availability of home-based healthcare services, but this is not possible without a home of some type in which to deliver those services. Thus, housing policies and programs will have a major influence on the long-term care system.

Making the continuum of care more seamless will require effort by all facets of the system, not just providers but payers, regulators, policy makers, and even consumers. Not all are moving in that direction at the same rate. To date, service providers are achieving seamlessness much faster than some of the payers of care, although there is some progress on that front. Private managed care organizations seem to be combining services and payment in a way that is better coordinated and thus more seamless. Government reimbursement agencies, encumbered as they often are by rules and regulations, still tend to maintain some of the barriers between payment categories.

Still, they are also trying to do their part to make the continuum of care more seamless. Primarily, that effort has been directed toward contracting with managed care organizations to manage segments of care for their constituents. It is a start.

The degree to which the system of care becomes seamless will depend, as will much of our future, on advances in technology. Russell Coile, probably the best-known healthcare futurist, predicted 2 decades ago that "The future of health care is a network of relationships overlaid by a computer-linked information system which integrates the hospital, physician's office, and purchaser" (Coile, 1993, p. 8). As long-term care providers become more intricately involved in the continuum, they are rapidly learning to be part of, and to rely on, these information-based relationships. It is not beyond reason to think of consumers of the future playing a greater role as contributors to the information system, not just being beneficiaries of it.

Please note that the phrase *moving toward a seamless system* is used here because no one really knows how long it will take to achieve that end. We can safely predict that we will get there, but we dare not predict how fast. A reasonable projection, however, is that significant progress will continue to be made in the next few years.

Consumer-Directed Care

As we indicated earlier, consumers of the various forms of long-term care will expect to direct their own care as much as possible. Providers will continue to find ways for them to do so, without jeopardizing that care in any way. This movement gained a major boost in November 2008 when the Centers for Medicare and Medicaid Services published a final Medicaid rule that permits Medicaid recipients to self-direct their own healthcare and supportive services (Smith, 2008). Self-direction, with the benefit of counseling, puts the individual back in control. This raises expectations and demands greater personal responsibility on the part of the Medicaid recipient. But properly understood, that in itself adds value and quality as well as expands access to services. This Medicaid rule will take effect only in states that accept it, but it is a noteworthy step forward.

New Living/Housing Options

As we have noted herein, long-term care providers have made significant strides toward meeting the needs of consumers for convenient, homelike living situations. We can expect more in the future, including cohousing, small house design, and sustainable design practices.

Cohousing—Currently considered a niche market, cohousing is a form of collaborative housing, where residents actively participate in the design and operation of their neighborhood. This type of housing will likely increase due to affordability. Cohousing promotes both social contact and individual space. Although not technically considered a long-term care facility, certain "neighborhood" design practices and ideas of cohousing can be implemented to shift the focus to resident-directed care. Examples include promoting resident individuality while developing a sense of community, adding outdoor common spaces (e.g., patios, courtyards), and establishing a designated social hub/community room.

Small House Design—Small house design skilled nursing (10-bed residences) eliminates the institutional feel often associated with long-term care facility design and fosters a more homelike setting, reminiscent of the homes residents once lived in.

Sustainable Design Practices—An increasing number of providers are incorporating practical environmental practices to develop energy-efficient communities that are sustainable in ways that contribute meaningfully to the lives of their residents. Implementing practical sustainable programs could include programs such as establishing a resident-directed recycling program or planting a vegetable garden to cut food costs and encourage residents to engage in participatory activities (Golden & Schneider, 2014).

Improved and Enhanced Amenities

Assisted living facilities and postacute providers such as continuing care communities have led the way in providing amenities aimed at meeting the needs of their consumers. Nursing care facilities have learned from them and have greatly increased the amenities offered and will continue to do so. Such amenities could include a hair salon, a bank, and a gift shop; social, recreational, spiritual, fitness and wellness programs; a computer room, a meditation room, and religious services; and a library, a craft room, a game room, or a wood shop (O'Brien, 2014).

■ Technological Advances

Perhaps the most significant and unpredictable factor in determining the shape of health care in the future will be the continued dramatic expansion of technology. The goals of bringing high-tech capacity and innovation to the nursing facility level are to make life better for residents, make work less arduous for staff, and provide facilities with easier methods to report outcomes to state and federal governments, which are radically shifting reimbursement payment by making accountability king. Many long-term care providers are already finding it difficult to make optimum use of the technology now available. As that technology expands, their task will be no easier. It presents an interesting dilemma for them. The new technology will make their jobs easier, but keeping up with it will make those same jobs more difficult, at least during the interim learning stages. Technology that enables people to live independently generally enhances the quality of life.

Technology will also dominate how the healthcare system is organized and managed. As important as clinical advances will be, two of the most important aspects of technology will be in integrating system components and providing information for consumers. Technology has the potential to integrate a fragmented system, and providers should be encouraged to use technology as one tool to create innovative and affordable long-term care (Raphael, 2008). The capacity of an integrated care system to be competitive is going to depend in large part on its ability to provide care to patients anywhere in the system. That ability may well depend on how readily and accurately it can access clinical and financial data. Good information will also be needed to measure both the efficiency of the system and the effectiveness of care given.

The need for consumers of the long-term care system to be informed if they are going to make good choices and use the healthcare system wisely has already been discussed. With certain exceptions, informing consumers is not something the system has done very well in the past. Health information technology provides an opportunity for healthcare providers to share health information in a timely and secure manner across care settings to support patient-centered care, particularly during transitions from one care setting to another (HealthIT.gov, 2013). It can do the same for long-term care. Information technology holds tremendous promise in this area. In fact, the cell phone has already become the all-around technological device of the current decade and will possibly become the only tool needed in the future to support higher quality care, protecting consumer privacy and cutting costs (Applied Management Systems, 2008).

The current generation of adults has had to learn to use computers and will probably never use them as well as will successor generations. However, they have been misrepresented. Research shows that many of the assumptions about the baby boomers and technology are incorrect. Neither slow to pick up new concepts, nor resistant to the ever-changing digital world, baby boomers and the elderly are a quickly growing group of media and technology users. Nearly half of all people age 50–64 have at least one online profile, and most of them (90%) use email. Americans age 50+ are the fastest growing sector of social media users, especially Facebook (Koeppel, 2013). Almost all seniors say that technology is important in helping them stay in touch with family and friends (87%), keep up with the world (84%), learn new things (80%), and stay mentally sharp (79%) (National Council on Aging, 2013).

Our children are growing up with advanced technology and accept it as a given. Most parents will reluctantly admit that their children are better able to use the family's media devices than they are. As these children grow up, they are going to be very comfortable using technology for a lot of things, including making them better informed consumers of long-term care. They will expect the system to make the necessary information available to them.

Technology has already had an impact on education. Medical schools now routinely teach future doctors to use and rely on computer-based records. Colleges already teach online courses, and they are just crawling. In the near future, they will all be running just to keep up with each other and with the demands of consumers—in this case, students.

Information technology will also help healthcare workers in the future. They will need vastly improved systems for supporting decision making in real time—bringing improved information to bear in a usable form at the point of decision making. Some technologies to watch in the near future include:

Extended care e-visit technologies enable physicians to consult with nursing home patients who require physician services. Most physicians are unable to make routine visits to extended care facilities as they are often seeing patients at many facilities and maintain a community practice as well. As a result, most patients receive physician care in a hospital setting, often resulting in overuse of the emergency department among the elderly.

Home telehealth technology provides a tool for patients to take an active role in the management of their diseases. Home telehealth works by allowing patients to transmit vital health data from their home to physicians' offices and, in turn, receive health coaching from their providers based on the clinical data they transmit. Home telehealth tools include audio and video conferencing capabilities (Bartolini & McNeill, 2012).

As noted by the American Telemedicine Association (2012):

telemedicine includes a growing variety of applications and services encompassing a wide variety of remote healthcare. Patient consultations via video conferencing, transmission of still images, e-health including patient portals, remote monitoring of vital signs, continuing medical education, consumer-focused wireless applications and nursing call centers, among other applications, are all considered part of telemedicine and telehealth.

Many more methods of telemedicine have not yet been conceived or implemented.

■ More and Better Clinical Applications

Over the next decade or 2, there will be new clinical procedures that we cannot even begin to imagine today. These procedures, whatever they may be, are going to keep long-term care providers scrambling to remain at state-of-the-art levels and to stay ahead of their competitors.

■ Innovative Delivery Methods

Coming decades will see a continuation and escalation of the changes that have occurred lately in how care is delivered. There are now mobile screening labs going from community to community providing services that were previously not available. Urgent care centers and ambulatory care units located in shopping malls have improved access and, at the same time, have taken some of the strain off emergency rooms, leaving them freer to do what they were intended to do. Long-term care has also seen considerable innovation in delivery methods, as described earlier. New forms of care, changes in assessment methods and care planning, and efforts to become more consumer oriented have all improved the lot of the consumer of long-term care.

Special Care Units

It is likely that there will be an increase in special care units designed to treat people needing highly specialized care. Although this may seem at first to be at odds with the trends toward multilevel, all-inclusive care providers, it is not necessarily incompatible. As we are learning more about how to care for consumers with very special needs, we are finding that it can often be done best in special units, as opposed to blending them on general care units. Special care units for consumers with cognitive disabilities are the most common. Alzheimer's disease, mental illness or retardation, traumatic head injury, and deterioration of cognition resulting from other diseases all make it difficult to mix consumers together. Advocates for people with these conditions argue that they need to be mainstreamed as much as possible to preserve the highest level of normality in their lives. They are right, but involving people who have cognitive limitations with those who do not can be unfair to both.

This difficulty supports the case for more home- and community-based care, where the interaction between individuals is not as frequent and opportunities for problems are less likely. However, limited cognitive functioning makes it very difficult for people to receive care at home. In many cases, the reason they can no longer be cared for by family members is that they cannot be trusted not to hurt themselves if left without supervision.

Informal Caregivers

Last, but certainly not least, the long-term care system will find ways to make better use of informal caregivers. It has been estimated that 78% of the elderly in need of long-term care receive that care from family members and friends, and 34 million caregivers provide care to someone age 50 or over (Benz, 2012). There will finally dawn a recognition that this vast, generally unorganized group of caregivers is vital to the success of the long-term system. At the same time the emphasis is swinging toward home-based care, the number of family and/or friends available to provide that care is shrinking. This means that formal home care providers must pick up more of the care. However, we cannot ignore the informal caregivers who continue to serve. The future system will learn to use them more efficiently and effectively. To do that, there will have to be financial rewards for these informal caregivers and backup services to supplement their efforts.

In addition to better integrating informal caregivers into the healthcare team, we will see attempts to also make better use of the patients/residents themselves. While not all will be able to do so, some will be capable of learning self-management skills, allowing them to improve their health and reduce their need for formal care (Institute of Medicine, 2008).

There will also be dramatic changes in the way healthcare providers are organized over the next few years. Although some futurists have said that the trend toward integration is temporary and will only last a few more years, they are wrong. It will continue. The many examples of integration of services have shown how much better organized care can be. Yet we have only just begun to explore the possible variations of integration. We can expect to see many more. Integration methodology is far from mature, but it is well on its way.

■ New Organizational Relationships

Competition among providers has already produced many improvements. Competition has inspired much of the change. There is no question that the demands of consumers for more options in the future will foster even more competition. This will, in turn, lead to more change. In trying to secure their share of a particular market, long-term care providers will find many new and innovative ways to deliver care.

Among Providers

Integrated care systems will dominate because they will have the ability to provide more of the seamless system of care mentioned earlier. Integrated systems will also have the organizational ability to adapt and to withstand bumps in the road. Providers not affiliated with an integrated network or system in some way or other may find themselves in a very difficult position.

Along with the integration phenomenon will be a corollary move toward niche marketing. Long-term care providers realize that they cannot be everything to everybody. The system is becoming much too big and complex for that. They will identify those services that are best for them and will focus on them. They will take advantage of their own distinctive competencies, those characteristics or services that set them apart from the competition. At the same time, because they are no longer competing for the same customers but need related services, there will be increased incentives to cooperate, both formally and informally. Providers of different types and levels of long-term care services will get together to meet consumer needs. Both within integrated networks and in individual facilities, we will see new organizational practices that will make what many current administrators, and your author, studied in school look like something from the 19th century.

Because of the complexity of the system, there will be more internal organization along the lines of strategic business units than there has been in the past. Instead of the traditional hierarchical organization, something more closely resembling a matrix form of organization will become more common, although it will be a vastly improved form and will probably be called something else.

One unfortunate prediction is that managers and those who teach them will feel obliged to find new names for what they do. They will become all too hung up on the names and formats and will not pay enough attention to the end results. That will make it difficult for students to understand the basic principles of management, as they devote unnecessary time and effort attempting to understand the different names and formats. Every new management system, from MacGregor's scientific management to Deming's total quality management, is essentially a new name for old-fashioned good management. Whatever their form, these organizational innovations are going to require long-term care providers to be open to new ways of doing things and to unlearn much of what they now know. If it is any consolation, it will pose as great a challenge to those who teach management as to those who practice it.

Between Providers and Payers

Providers will find new ways to work more closely in partnerships with payers, an extension of what is already happening in some areas. Both care management and case management will continue to grow, although they too will evolve. There are currently too many unanswered questions for either to succeed unchanged. The conflicts between service providers and payers over control of care will work themselves out, probably resulting in new, quite different variations of what exists today.

Institutional to Noninstitutional Care

The shift that has been taking place from institutional to community-based or noninstitutional care will continue as the long-term care system tries to find ways to deliver only the amount of care needed and no more. It is a positive trend, but it is likely that the pendulum will swing back a bit as there is realization that not everyone can be cared for at home and that combinations of delivery methods are often best, as some providers are discovering. In the meantime, the result is that some of the more sick and needy consumers are being cared for in institutional settings, which, in turn, raises the average acuity level of the residents in those facilities. Long-term care providers will continue to venture further into the social care system. They will, in attempting to meet the demand for one-stop care, blend health care and social services even more than at present. Congregate housing and continuing care retirement centers are examples of these ventures. They will also find it beneficial, both for them and for the consumers, to include a full range of amenities, either in one facility or in one that is easily accessible. Payers, particularly managed care organizations, will also find this trend attractive, simplifying their contracting.

Efficiency

Some of the experiments described earlier will fail, and others will be modified so much that the original idea will be largely unrecognizable, but in the end we will see delivery methods that are more efficient—that are more responsive to the needs of consumers—without significant loss of quality. Efficiency of operation has become a prime focus for today's providers and will become even more important in the future as costs rise and resources become more limited.

Providers will utilize technology to increase efficiency, including streamlining of admission and discharge practices and workforce management.

These changes will not take place easily if not properly supported. Regulators and payers, especially the federal government, should provide compelling incentives to encourage providers to become part of organizations, and then achieve the efficiencies that will enable them to reduce costs (Lee & Berenson, 2008). In its classic report, *Crossing the Quality Chasm: A New Health System for the 21st Century*, the Institute of Medicine called for payment and regulatory environments that allow providers to improve performance (Institute of Medicine, 2001). The need for those supportive environments has grown rather than diminished in recent years.

■ Changes in Financing and Reimbursement

By this point, readers of this text recognize the critical role financing plays in the delivery of long-term care. That will not only continue, but will intensify as we go forward. Just how that plays out is hard to predict, but the following are several financing and reimbursement trends to watch.

Increase in Overall Healthcare Spending

For several decades, healthcare spending has increased as a percentage of the national gross domestic product. Health spending is projected to grow at an average rate of 5.8% from 2012 to 2022, 1.0 percentage point faster than expected average annual growth in the gross domestic product, and is projected to be 19.9% of the gross domestic product by 2022 (CMS, 2013). Given that increase in spending, it can be anticipated that both public and private reimbursement sources will find it difficult to keep up. The impact of that will be a need to find a balance that will meet the needs for care without bankrupting those payment sources. To achieve that balance—or hope to—payers will make better use of technology to save costs. We will also see more involvement by payers in how care is delivered. They will expect concessions from providers in both the amount of reimbursement and how that money is spent. While many providers now think the payers are overly intrusive in their operations, it will get worse (from their view). As noted earlier, those providers will be under great pressure to become even more efficient.

Decrease in Employer-Sponsored Insurance

Although the majority of Americans receive their health insurance through an employment-based health plan, that number is declining. The share of Americans under age 65 covered by employer-sponsored health insurance eroded for the 10th year in a row in 2010, falling from 59.4% in 2009 to 58.6% (Gould, 2012). The future is likely to bring a continuing decrease in the degree to which employers provide health insurance for their employees. It has become a significant portion of the costs those employers bear. In February 2014, the Centers for Medicare and Medicaid Services predicted that the Affordable Care Act (ACA) could cause premiums to increase for nearly two thirds of small- to medium-sized businesses (Roy, 2014). All employers will need to be more efficient as well just to survive. It is to be expected that they will seek to reduce their obligations for health insurance, either by reducing the amount provided or expecting their employees to share a larger portion of the cost. Employees are already paying an ever-increasing share. Roughly 11 million individuals' premiums are estimated to be higher as a result of the ACA (Roy, 2014). There are two reasons this will impact long-term care.

1. We had begun to see an increase in employers offering long-term care insurance. However, as employers faced an increasingly unstable economy, long-term care insurance was an extra that they could not afford. It has been reported that LTC insurance is becoming hard to afford—and even to find, as private insurers pull out of the market. In part, this development is because low interest rates make it hard for insurers to build up reserves to cover benefits, forcing them to raise premiums, which discourages potential buyers (Butler, 2012). That appears to be a trend that will continue.
2. A significant drop in employer-sponsored coverage can have a major impact on public programs on which long-term care relies, such as Medicaid.

Public Payers Continue to Struggle

There is much talk of late that Medicare is going broke. The argument seems to be not if, but when this will happen. There are many reasons for this, not the least of which is the unanticipated number of people who are living longer. Today, the number of people who can expect to live to the age of 90 years is far greater than it was in the 1960s when Medicare was conceived, and it is projected to grow even more in the next several decades.

At the same time, Medicaid, the other largest funding source, is among the top areas of expenditure in most states. Those states have to choose between funding Medicaid or maintaining their transportation infrastructure, replacing crumbling highways and bridges. States have looked for ways to slash Medicaid as one way to reduce steep budget shortfalls for the coming year. Yet as important as those things are, the healthcare safety net has to be maintained for those who need it. In many ways, it is long-term care that is breaking the backs of these programs: Government programs currently account for 63% of LTC funding, with Medicaid paying for 40% and Medicare paying for 23% of postacute care (Calmus, 2013).

The result of this struggling by these public reimbursement sources is and will be an emphasis on ways to reduce their financial commitments. Many states are trying to cut

Medicaid costs by reducing benefits, paying providers less, and/or tightening eligibility, even as the federal government, through the ACA, prepares to expand Medicaid by adding as many as 17 million more people (Galewitz & Fleming, 2012). That will take the form of changes in regulations to move consumers toward less expensive forms of care such as home and community-based services and tightening of reimbursement regulations. It will also mean a continuation of the current prominence of managed care within those programs.

Providers Continue to Struggle

Long-term care providers are also struggling to survive and will continue to do so. In part, that is due to the difficulties their most significant payer sources are having as noted earlier. It is not uncommon for providers to be owed large amounts of money by Medicare and Medicaid in particular.

They are also subject to the vagaries of the economy with rising costs for staff, supplies, and equipment. For example, between 2004 and 2014, the nation experienced a rise in the price of gasoline of more than 100% (GasBuddy.Com, 2014). At first glance, it might appear that the price of gasoline would not have an impact on long-term care, but it did. Everything that is either made of petroleum (e.g., plastic medical supplies) or is transported by gasoline-burning vehicles (just about everything) became more expensive. Any such repeat of that or a similar crisis will test an already vulnerable system.

Innovative Financing

The future will also bring innovations in healthcare financing. It has to. There is no way we can achieve what we want if the healthcare system continues to be driven by fragmented financing. Regardless of whether there is one source of payment or dozens, there must be some coordination.

Everyone has seen or experienced the fragmentation caused by the way health care is financed, meaning that the care one gets is often determined by reimbursement, something that has to change if the healthcare system of the future is to adequately use its limited resources. Managed care, with all of its strengths and shortcomings, will probably be the primary vehicle of coordination within the continuum of care. Because of this, it is fast becoming the dominant form of care delivery and financing.

The current trend toward capitation and other prepaid group contracts will continue and grow. Providers must keep in mind that employers are their customers too. These corporate customers have begun to exercise their growing clout. Negotiations between these employers and providers, particularly integrated care networks, will produce some surprisingly innovative financing schemes over the next few years.

Prospective payment of one sort or another has become the dominant form of payment for long-term care providers. Regardless of what the actual payment scheme is, the concept of both purchaser and provider knowing up-front what to expect will endure and grow.

We can expect a significant expansion of pay-for-performance initiatives. While they will primarily be used to improve quality of care, they also serve as cost-cutting tools. These value-based payment program rules will continue to gain favor with both public (Medicare and Medicaid) payers and private insurers. It means that providers need to learn a whole new set of coding rules and procedures.

Public/Private Partnerships

The key to future financing of the healthcare system may well be public/private partnerships, such as those financed by the Robert Wood Johnson Foundation and through an increasing number of the state Medicaid waiver programs. The Heritage Foundation describes these programs as follows:

> to provide an incentive to purchase LTCI, these partnerships offer Medicaid eligibility after the exhaustion of LTCI coverage even when the policyholder's assets would otherwise make them ineligible. At its core, the incentive for the individual to purchase a partnership LTCI policy is to protect assets and increase personal control over care. The public policy intent is to decrease reliance on Medicaid by encouraging middle-income individuals to cover a portion of their LTC, with Medicaid providing catastrophic coverage if care needs far exceed the average. The program began as a four-state experiment, but the Deficit Reduction Act of 2005 expanded the program. As of July 2011, 40 states have such partnership programs. (Calmus, 2013)

The best of these experiments need to be replicated and expanded. The reason public/private partnerships will prevail is that the system has failed to come up with any other successful way to meet the costs involved.

Long-term care consumers have responsibilities as well as rights, including the responsibility to contribute to the cost of their care and to use that care wisely. This is not as naive as it sounds. Most people are willing to pay their share if they can be assured it is fair. Already, some have purchased long-term care insurance, not just to protect their families and themselves but because they feel an obligation to pay for that protection if they can, leaving the public pay safety net for those who legitimately need it. Of course, the safety net is there for them as well if the time comes when they can no longer pay.

Some would go so far as to make Medicare needs-based as a way of saving it. After all, why should taxpayers continue to pay for health care for millionaires? However, that may well prove to be too controversial. If we expect people to contribute more to their healthcare financing, we have to provide them with some incentive other than a pat on the back. One way to provide those incentives is through expanded use of public/private partnerships.

Another is through tax breaks. There has been some small progress, with several bills being filed in Congress and in state legislatures to provide tax incentives for consumers paying premiums for long-term care insurance. However, as much as tax breaks will help, other incentives will have to be found in the future if consumers are to be expected to participate in financing of their care. Along these same lines, we are already seeing more co-pay provisions in healthcare contracts, although their effectiveness is the subject of some debate.

■ Ethical Dilemmas

We can safely predict an increase in both the number and scope of ethical issues that will arise and need to be resolved. Those issues are of increasing concern to consumers of long-term care.

Life-and-Death Issues

The system now has the clinical ability to save life in ever-more-extreme circumstances. As shown by the cloning of a sheep and monkeys, we may soon have the ability to produce human life artificially. (Some already claim to have done so.) This raises some massive ethical questions. Many agree that there should be, at least temporarily, a ban on cloning of humans, but almost everyone also agrees that such a ban would be almost impossible to enforce, increasing the level of ethical difficulty. Closer to home, the ability to extend life, often beyond the point of personal dignity and quality, is forcing society to balance quality of life with life itself. Whether one admires Dr. Jack Kevorkian or despises him, the publicity and controversy surrounding him are evidence of how difficult and important this issue is.

Although these life-and-death issues primarily affect the individuals involved, they also affect providers of care, both individually and organizationally. These providers are going to have to try to guarantee their patients' rights of self-determination while, at the same time, protecting the rights of their employees to not participate in activities with which they do not agree. As long-term care providers look to aligning their organizations with others or to joining integrated care networks, they need to set parameters within which they can comfortably participate. For example, in one northeastern city, two of the three major hospitals merged as the beginning of a network of providers, one that will probably dominate the local healthcare scene. The third hospital, a Catholic institution, chose not to join, largely because the others would be doing abortions. There is little question that they would have enjoyed many benefits of participation in the larger network, but they decided what was and was not within the bounds of their mission. As the players in the healthcare game continue to form alliances, they will be faced with many ethical questions of this type, many of them not as clearly defined as the one just described.

Allocation of Resources

Not all of the ethical issues faced deal directly with life and death. Many of them will involve balancing cost, quality, and access. Healthcare-related organizations—including not only providers but payers, regulators, and policy makers as well—will be faced with ever-more-difficult decisions concerning the allocation of resources. It is doubtful that those resources will ever be sufficient to cover everything, so how are they to be allocated?

The ACA of 2010 promised to extend insurance coverage to millions of Americans who did not have such coverage. By the target date of 2014, when anyone without coverage had to sign up for policies or face a financial penalty, the Obama administration reported that 7 million had signed up for a plan on the government-sponsored exchanges, meeting their target. However, many of these enrollees had previously had coverage until their policies were invalidated by the rules of the ACA.

There has been a lot of focus recently on social responsibility. Actually, the healthcare system, including long-term care, has long been more socially responsible than it is sometimes given credit for being. However, this was also easier in the more benevolent era of the past, and even then there were major gaps in the system. In the near future, some very tough choices will have to be made between spending money on prevention or spending it on heroic measures. How much of available financing should be allocated now to preventing illness in years to come as opposed to caring for those already ill? How much should be spent on those with no hope of improvement? At what point does society tell the mother of an anencephalic child that it—society—can no longer afford to provide care—what some have called "futile care"—for her child, a child who is going to die soon anyway? These questions are not only difficult (if not impossible) to answer, they are unpleasant to even contemplate. Yet contemplate them we must.

The healthcare system is going to continue to have to choose between cost-effectiveness and patient convenience. Over the past several decades many communities have had to face the painful reality of not having their babies born in the local maternity unit. Now many of those same communities are facing loss of the local hospital completely. One of the most difficult problems they will face in the future will be balancing the efficiency and economy of dealing with an integrated care system against loss of choice because that system is the only one in their area. This will be particularly true of rural or geographically isolated areas that simply cannot support multiple providers.

There has been, and will continue to be, emphasis on the rights of individuals to receive good health care when they need it. However, the future will bring more focus on the responsibility of those individuals to care for themselves. The next several years will bring many situations requiring individuals to decide the extent of their duty to take care of themselves and will bring some very difficult questions for all to answer. Will society be willing to deny expensive care, such as a liver transplant or ongoing long-term care, to the person who has caused the problem with alcohol and drugs?

How will it balance the rights of individuals against the larger rights of society? This issue, like many others, is not confined to long-term care or even to health care, but it will have an impact on the future of the system and on how we all function within it.

For those involved in providing care, there will be some very practical ethical issues to be faced. They will have to provide some services and care for some people even knowing that they will lose money on them. This is nothing new, but the ease with which they could pass those costs on to others is a thing of the past. They are going to find it much more difficult to balance social responsibility with organizational efficiency.

■ Regulation

What can we say about future trends in regulation of long-term care except to predict that it will continue and that it will have an ever-greater impact on how that care is delivered? Various levels of government will keep on asserting their responsibility to protect the public—and particularly consumers of care.

They will regulate access to care by mandating coverage for those they believe to be underserved at present. This has already happened with the ACA, which mandates certain coverages in all insurance policies. They will regulate the cost of care by allocating resources to those segments of the system they favor and support and limiting resources to others that they see as too expensive—such as favoring community-based care over institutional care. They will regulate quality through pay-for-performance measures and quality indicators that providers must meet.

Providers will continue to complain about what they see as the unnecessary intrusion of government into their organizations and about the onerous requirements imposed upon them. This often-confrontational interplay between the government and the governed is not necessarily a bad thing in that it ensures an active and ongoing dialogue between the two.

■ Health System Reform

As we have discussed earlier, when we talk about healthcare reform or health system reform, we really mean healthcare financing reform.

A better way to finance health care, including long-term care, must be found. Until recently, most bets would be that it was unlikely that there would be a single, all-inclusive reform of healthcare financing such as was attempted in 1994. That effort failed for a number of reasons, including its lack of flexibility, its all-or-nothing approach, and the staggering costs involved. However, in 2010, President Barrack Obama succeeded in passage of the ACA. Half a decade later, its impact—particularly on long-term care—is still developing.

One other solution that has been suggested in the past, and will undoubtedly be suggested in the future, is to move toward two separate and distinct care systems: one for people with private coverage and one for those covered by public programs. Even though this only means separate financing systems, not separate care systems, it goes against everything we have been taught about fairness. The challenge, if it should come to that, will be to ensure that quality and access are equal in the two systems. No one really knows whether this is possible. As is the case now, financing the care of those with the greatest needs—the elderly, children with special care needs, the physically and mentally handicapped—will continue to be the most difficult part of the problem.

A study published in the *New England Journal of Medicine* revealed some interesting—and seemingly contradictory—facts about public opinion and healthcare reform. Americans regularly rank health care among the top four most important problems facing the country and believe that the system is in a state of crisis. However, they tend to oppose a single government-run plan. Support for the ACA has been divided from its inception and remains so. A Quinnipiac University poll conducted March 26–31, 2014, showed that 41% supported the law, 55% opposed it, and 5% were unsure or did not answer. Similar polls by the Gallup organization produced similar results (PollingReport.com, 2014).

■ Summary

If the future of long-term care had to be summed up in one word, that word would obviously be *change*. The system can anticipate an era of change in coming years that will dwarf all that has gone before. It will be, as Dickens would describe it, the best of times and the worst of times. The trends outlined here will play themselves out over a relatively short period and be replaced with others. The continuum of care is so complex and intricately interrelated, a major shift in any one segment can result in significant, often unanticipated, changes in the rest of the system. Still, those who do the best job of anticipating coming changes will be the ones who are most successful. Providers who are proactive will prosper. Payers who are able to respond to changing demographic and economic conditions will survive while others do not. Regulators may have the most difficulty anticipating and dealing with change because of the built-in statutory rigidity of their roles. Policy makers, who will probably include representatives from all segments of the continuum, may have the largest role to play in shaping the future. They are the ones who design new systems, create new regulations, and determine how other members of the long-term care system function. Their ability to anticipate and prepare for changes will be critical to the system as a whole.

It has been a bit difficult here to separate predictions from wishful thinking, to identify trends that are likely to occur, not those that we would like to see occur. However, there is a sound basis for the trends discussed in this chapter. None of them is dramatically different from what is happening at present. Most are continuations of current trends. The big differences for the future will be found in the degree to which one trend overshadows another and in the speed with which that takes place.

■ Vocabulary Terms

The following terms are included in this chapter. They are important to the topics and issues discussed herein and should become familiar to readers. Some of the terms are also found in other chapters but may be used in different contexts. They may not be fully defined herein. Thus, readers may wish to seek other, supplementary definitions of them.

aging in place	integration
consumerism	outcomes-based system
demographics	public/private partnerships
ethical dilemmas	seamless system of care
forecasting	social responsibility
informed consumers	strategic business units
institutional providers	trends

■ Discussion Questions

The following questions are presented to assist you in understanding the material covered in this chapter. They tend to be general but lend themselves to detailed answers, which can be found in the chapter.

1. What are the major challenges that have faced the long-term care system in recent years?
2. How successfully has the system responded to those challenges?
3. What challenges remain unmet?
4. What types of new problems have been created by the solving of current problems?
5. What impact will the predicted increase in consumers' involvement in their care have on providers?
6. What changes can be expected in terms of long-term care financing?
7. What will changes in technology mean to long-term care providers and consumers?
8. What are the most likely ethical challenges to be faced in the near future?

■ References

American Academy of Family Physicians. (2013). *Risk management and medical liability*. Retrieved from http://www.aafp.org/dam/AAFP/documents/medical_education_residency/program_directors/Reprint281_Risk.pdf.

American Heart Association. (2013, December 18). *Heart disease and stroke continue to threaten U.S. health*. Retrieved from http://newsroom.heart.org/news/heart-disease-and-stroke-continue-to-threaten-u-s-health.

American Telemedicine Association. (2012). *What is telemedicine?* Retrieved from http://www.americantelemed.org/about-telemedicine/what-is-telemedicine#.VEP4g7l0xHx.

Anderson, G. (2010). *Chronic care making the case for ongoing care*. Washington, DC: Robert Wood Johnson Foundation. Retrieved from http://www.rwjf.org/en/research-publications/find-rwjf-research/2010/01/chronic-care.html.

Applied Management Systems. (2008). *The AMS top ten trends in healthcare management*. Burlington, MA: Applied Management Systems.

Banham, R. (2010). Facing the future: When it comes to accepting the need for long-term care down the road, many opt for denial. *The Wall Street Journal*. Retrieved from http://online.wsj.com/ad/article/longtermcare-future#top.

Bartolini, E., & McNeill, N. (2012, June). *Getting to value: Eleven chronic disease technologies to watch*. Cambridge, MA: NEHI. Retrieved from NEHI: http://www.slideshare.net/blueeyepathrec/getting-to-value-eleven-chronic-disease-technologies-to-watch.

Bauer, J. (2006, September/October). The future of healthcare: Forecasts, implications and responses. *Healthcare Executive*, pp. 13–20.

Benz, C. (2012, August 9). *40 must-know statistics about long-term care*. Retrieved from http://news.morningstar.com/articlenet/article.aspx?id=564139.

Blumenthal, D., & Davenport, K. (2008). Workers, tools, and knowledge: The infrastructure for delivery system reform. In C. F. Progress (Ed.), *The health care delivery system: Blueprint for reform* (pp. 15–31). Washington, DC: Center for American Progress.

Boling, P. (2007). Managing the impact of advanced chronic illness in the elderly by the year 2030. In Genworth Financial (Eds.), *The future of long term care in America* (pp. 71–83). Richmond, VA: Genworth Financial.

Bureau of Labor Stistics. (2014, April 3). Nursing assistants and orderlies. *Occupational Outlook Handbook* (2014–15 ed.). Retrieved from http://www.bls.gov/ooh/healthcare/nursing-assistants.htm.

Butler, S. (2012, September 27). *Confronting the problem of long-term care*. Retrieved from http://www.heritage.org/research/commentary/2012/09/confronting-the-problem-of-long-term-care.

Calmus, D. (2013, February 6). *The long-term care financing crisis*. Retrieved from http://www.heritage.org/research/reports/2013/02/the-long-term-care-financing-crisis.

CantyMedia. (2014). *The world: life expectancy (2014)—Top 100+*. Retrieved from http://www.geoba.se/population.php?pc=world&type=015&page=2.

Centers for Medicare & Medicaid Services (CMS). (2008, August 4). *CMS improves patient safety for Medicare and Medicaid by addressing never events*. Retrieved from http://www.cms.gov/Newsroom/MediaReleaseDatabase/Fact-Sheets/2008-Fact-Sheets-Items/2008-08-042.html.

Centers for Medicare & Medicaid Services (CMS). (2013). *National health expenditure projections 2012–2022*. Retrieved from http://www.cms.gov/Research-Statistics-Data-and-Systems/Statistics-Trends-and-Reports/NationalHealthExpendData/downloads/proj2012.pdf.

Congressional Budget Office. (2013, June 26). *Rising demand for long-term services and supports for elderly people*. Retrieved from http://www.cbo.gov/publication/44363.

Coile, R. (1993). Future trends, health care reform and the outlook for long-term care. *Journal of Long-Term Care*, 21(3), 6–12.

Farrell, D., & Elliot, A. (2008, August). *Investing in Culture Change*. Retrieved from Provider: http://safehavenpch.com/wp-content/uploads/2010/08/Article-3-Investing-in-Culture.pdf.

Galewitz, P., & Fleming, M. (2012, July 4). *13 states cut Medicaid to balance budgets*. Retrieved from http://www.kaiserhealthnews.org/Stories/2012/July/25/medicaid-cuts.aspx?p=1.

GasBuddy.Com. (2014). *Historical price charts*. Retrieved from http://www.gasbuddy.com/gb_retail_price_chart.aspx.

Golden, G., & Schneider, L. (2014). *Future trends in long-term care: What can you do now to prepare?* Retrieved from http://prarch.com/docs/default-source/White-Papers/future-trends-in-long-term-care.pdf?sfvrsn=0.

Gould, E. (2012, February 23). *A decade of declines in employer-sponsored health insurance coverage*. Retrieved from http://www.epi.org/publication/bp337-employer-sponsored-health-insurance.

HealthIT.gov. (2013, March 15). *Health IT in long-term and post acute care: Issue brief*. Retrieved from http://www.healthit.gov/sites/default/files/pdf/HIT_LTPAC_IssueBrief031513.pdf.

Hibbard, J., & Hayes, K. (2008). Second generation consumerism. In C. F. Progress (Ed.), *The health care system: A blueprint for reform* (pp. 81–95). Washington, DC: Center for American Progress.

Institute of Medicine. (2001). *Crossing the quality chasm: A new health system for the 21st century*. Washington, DC: National Academies Press.

Institute of Medicine. (2008). *Retooling for an aging America: Building the health care workforce*. Washington, DC: National Academies Press.

Kane, R. (1993). Ethical and legal issues in long-term care: Food for futuristic thought. *Journal of Long-Term Care Administration*, 21(3), 66–74.

Koeppel, P. (2013, April 19). *Baby boomers & seniors in the digital era*. Retrieved from http://visual.ly/baby-boomers-and-seniors-digital-era.

Lee, S. (2011). *Investigating the culture change in nursing home care*. Retrieved from http://www.eldercarelink.com/Nursing-Homes/Investigating-the-Culture-Change-in-Nursing-Home-Care.htm.

Lee, T., & Berenson, R. (2008). The organization of health care delivery: A road map for accelerated development. In C. F. Progress (Ed.), *The health care delivery system: A blueprint for reform* (pp. 31–49). Washington, DC: Center for American Progress.

McCarthy, K. (2013, November 13). *Long-term care workforce issues*. Retrieved from http://www.cga.ct.gov/2013/rpt/2013-R-0365.htm.

Melnyk, A. (2012, November 28). *Demographic trends and demand for long-term care services*. Retrieved from http://www.naic.org/documents/committees_b_senior_issues_2012_fall_nm_ltc_hearing_presentations_melnyk.pdf.

National Academy of Sciences. (2008). *Retooling for an aging America: Building the health care workforce*. Washington, DC: Institute of Medicine National Academy of Sciences.

National Center for Health Statistics. (2007). *Health, United States, 2007 with chartbook on trends in the health of America*. Hyattsville, MD: National Center for Health Statistics.

National Council on Aging. (2013). *The United States of aging*. Washington, DC: National Council on Aging.

Novelli, W. (2007). The boomers: Igniting a revolution to reinvent long term care. In Genworth Financial (Ed.), *The future of long term care in America* (pp. 3–12). Richmond, VA: Genworth Financial.

O'Brien, S. (2014). *How to find the right nursing home*. Retrieved from http://seniorliving.about.com/od/housingoptions/ss/findnursinghome.htm.

Paraprofessional Healthcare Institute. (2008, May 27). *America faces caregiving crisis: One million new direct-care workers needed by 2016*. Retrieved from http://phinational.org/sites/phinational.org/files/wp-content/uploads/2008/07/job-projections-release-final-5-27-08.pdf.

Paraprofessional Healthcare Institute (PHI). (2013, November). *America's direct-care workforce*. Retrieved from http://phinational.org/sites/phinational.org/files/phi-facts-3.pdf.

Pioneer Network. (2008). *What is culture change?* Retrieved from http://www.pioneernetwork.net /CultureChange/Whatis.

PollingReport.com. (2014). CBS news/*New York Times* poll. Retrieved from http://www.pollingreport .com/health.htm.

Pratt, J. (1996). Taking turns at the crystal ball: Long-term care leaders foretell the future. *Nursing Homes, 45*(2). 10-19.

Proctor, S. (2014, April 1 25). *Transforming communities with the household model of care.* Retrieved from http://www.mcknights.com/transforming-communities-with-the-household-model-of-care /article/343352.

Raphael, C. (2008, July 21). *Long-term care: Preparing for the next generation.* Retrieved from http:// www.commonwealthfund.org/publications/publications_show.htm?doc_id=695882.

Redfoot, D., Feinberg, L., & Houser, A. (2013, August). *The aging of the baby boom and the growing care gap: A look at future declines in the availability of family caregivers.* Retrieved from http://www .aarp.org/content/dam/aarp/research/public_policy_institute/ltc/2013/baby-boom-and-the-growing -care-gap-insight-AARP-ppi-ltc.pdf.

Roy, A. (2014, February 25). *The next shoe to drop: Obamacare will increase the cost of employer- sponsored insurance.* Retrieved from http://www.forbes.com/sites/theapothecary/2014/02/25 /the-next-shoe-to-drop-obamacare-will-increase-the-cost-of-employer-sponsored-insurance.

RWJ Foundation. (2010, July). *Quality & equality in U.S. health care: Message handbook.* Retrieved from http://www.rwjf.org/en/research-publications/find-rwjf-research/2010/06/latest-from-aligning -forces-for-quality-communities/quality---equality-in-u-s--health-care.html.

Saint Joseph's College of Maine. (1993). *Criteria for designing or evaluating a long-term care system.* Standish: Saint Joseph's College of Maine.

ScienceDaily. (2014, January). *Cancer statistics 2014: Death rates continue to drop.* Retrieved from http://www.sciencedaily.com/releases/2014/01/140107102634.htm.

Smith, D. G. (2008, November 13). *Consumer direction in Medicaid and opportunities for states.* Retrieved from http://www.heritage.org/Research/HealthCare/wm2129.cfm.

Managing for the Future

After completing this chapter, readers will be able to:

1. Understand the challenges and opportunities facing managers in the long-term care system of the future.

2. Understand the skills managers will need to successfully meet those challenges and opportunities.

3. Understand the need to interact proactively with other segments of the long-term care system and with the community.

4. Understand the need for all long-term care providers to operate effectively and efficiently.

5. Understand why each manager must act as a change agent for the good of the overall system.

■ Introduction

If the predictions made in this text prove reasonably accurate and actually come to pass, how should the long-term care system prepare for the future? How do long-term care managers prepare their organizations to deal with the changes? The future contains both challenges and opportunities. However, dealing with them will take skill and preparation. There will be little room for those who are unprepared. Herein we present some of the ways managers of long-term care organizations can get ready for whatever the future brings. We also examine steps the overall long-term care system will need to take.

■ Actions for Managers

Managers who want to deal with the future proactively will need to address all of these challenges and opportunities. It is assumed that many readers of this book are either currently managers in some type of long-term care or plan to be in the future. Therefore, the following suggestions are directed at them. For others, they present a good overview of what managers face and how they should act. The actions are not presented in any order of priority but are of generally equal importance.

Listen to the Customers

Long-term care organizations must listen to their customers. It cannot be emphasized enough how important this will be. Successful organizations will know who their customers are and what those customers want. This may sound easy, but it is not. First, the customer population of any long-term care organization is changing. No longer are customers limited to a narrowly defined, easily identified constituency. The customer mix can change almost monthly. The changes can come from evolution of the consumer population. For example, the aging of the population and increase in chronic conditions both increase the need for services (Benz, 2012). The changes can also come from alterations in services by the provider. As providers create new types and levels of services in response to demands of the consumers, they create new customers for those services. This, in turn, can create new demand, and so on. Although the actual consumers of care are the ultimate customers, they are not the only ones long-term care organizations need to consider. Their customers will also include employers, organizations that contract for services, and others who pay the bills. Managed care organizations will clearly be important customers. Several of these categories may also include various levels of government. Even other providers with whom an organization affiliates are its customers, as are a variety of social agencies.

Once the customers have been identified, the process of knowing what they want from the organization begins. Customers, including the individual consumers, will all have their own agendas, their own needs, and their own demands. How well each provider understands those agendas and how well it responds to those needs will determine the success of the organization over the long run.

One valuable way of reaching the customers of a specific organization is through groups representing them. Those groups might include consumer advocacy organizations such as AARP, business organizations such as local chambers of commerce, or trade organizations. By contacting and working with these groups, a long-term care provider can learn more about what particular customer groups want. Contact with customers also presents a good opportunity to spread the word about the services offered.

Long-term care organizations are also advised to develop social contracts with their customers. They should think of those customers as partners, clearly identifying respective roles and expectations. If they do this, they will find many mutual interests and benefits. This means meeting with their customers to discuss what they want and what the organization has to offer. It also involves some negotiating.

Be Knowledgeable

Beyond their customers, long-term care managers must be knowledgeable in several other areas. To succeed in the future, they will need to be constantly aware of their environment, knowing it well enough to be able to act or react quickly and effectively. They will need to know themselves, their organizations, and other organizations that are possible competitors or allies. Both strategic planning and market planning are valuable tools (Berkowitz, 2011).

Know the Organization

To begin with, managers will have to know themselves, organizationally. They must honestly evaluate their capabilities and weaknesses. This means understanding what distinctive competencies the organization has. It means accepting that it is no longer possible to do everything equally well and that every organization has areas of weakness. Each must accept that there will always be services that someone else provides better or at a lower cost. The smart thing to do is to let them; just make sure the organization's consumers have access to the services they need. Each organization has to find its niche and focus on excelling in the areas where it has the most expertise. This kind of self-examination is not easy, but it can be done. More than anything else, it takes commitment to doing whatever is needed for success and survival.

Know the Community

Successful long-term care managers will know their communities. This begins with knowing what makes up the community. It used to be easy. An organization served a well-defined community, usually a geographically identifiable locale. There was little competition. Each organization had its own service area, with minimal overlap. Those days when the community served by a facility or agency was neatly defined by municipal boundaries are long gone in most cases. Service communities of the future will be determined by a mix of factors, including such things as demographics, financing mechanisms, availability of transportation, and competitors. These factors will be constantly changing, and managers must understand them well if they are to survive. There will not be a single factor defining the service community. It will be quite likely that each long-term care organization will have several service communities for some of its different services, each defined by its own unique combination of environmental factors.

Knowing the community is an important first step to serving that community. The next is finding ways to meet the needs of that community. This may mean giving less emphasis to or even eliminating a current service and focusing on others that are more in demand. It will require a great deal of flexibility and a willingness to adapt as needed.

Know the Full Continuum

The long-term care managers of tomorrow will need to know about all types of health-care services, not just those they provide. Until recently, most providers focused on one type of care without bothering to learn much about others, something they cannot afford to do in the future. This does not mean that each manager has to be expert in all areas of the continuum—acute care, subacute care, nursing facilities, assisted living, home health care, adult day care, hospice, and whatever else comes along. It does mean that each needs to know enough about these areas or have access to enough information about them to be aware of how they are changing. They will keep changing, and those changes are potential sources of impact for each organization.

It is clearly important to stay abreast of developments that have the potential to be either very beneficial or very harmful to an organization. Involvement in professional or trade organizations or civic clubs can also help managers to stay up to date, as can faithful reading of news reports and professional journals. It requires some effort but can easily become a habit.

Get Involved With Integrated Care

If an organization is not involved with an integrated care system now, it should get involved. Integration is where the action is going to be. Integrated systems or networks have the best chance of succeeding in the unsettled times yet to come. They will have the best ability to meet the diverse challenges ahead. Through a combination of efforts, they will be in a position to provide a wide range of coordinated services and to cover large geographic areas. Administrators should form partnerships that will improve their service capabilities. Partnering with key community organizations (e.g., hospitals/ clinics, schools, health clubs, restaurants, hospice providers, etc.) will increase awareness of the facility.

This does not mean that all long-term care organizations have to be full partners in formal systems or networks, or that they have to form their own. However, they do need to be involved with, affiliated with, or contracted with, such a system or systems in one way or another. They do not have to go all out, nor should they think they have to do it all themselves. What every manager should do is decide what his or her organization has to offer to such a system, what the system has to offer them, and what opportunities exist for mutual benefit.

Maintain Roots in the Community

As valuable and necessary as it is to branch out and actively integrate with others, it is of critical importance that long-term care organizations retain their ties to the community. As healthcare providers get ever larger—joining with others to cover a larger service area and working more closely with payers and large employers—they are going to find it more and more difficult to maintain the roots to the community that characterized their history. One of the strengths of the healthcare system is that providers, including those in long-term care, have always been key, valuable members of the communities in which they resided. They must try to avoid losing that relationship.

If they do lose touch with what is happening locally or are perceived to have done so, there is a very real danger that regulators at various levels of government will react negatively, seeing it as a sign of social inefficiency and unresponsiveness, and they might be right. If government officials do feel that way, they may well move toward a more restrictive—perhaps a public utility—form of regulation that will make the jobs of long-term care managers far more difficult. Experience has shown that the most powerful stimulus for most people to change is the fear that someone else, usually government regulators, will do it for them. Managers of long-term care organizations are the ones who can forestall such a move by making sure that they do respond to the needs of their communities, however those communities may be defined in the future.

Build a Solid Foundation

As managed care continues to grow, both in size and in influence on the continuum of care, the long-term care organizations that succeed will be those that understand capitation and have a large enough base of prepaid or capitated contracts to provide organizational stability. Providers, be they individual facilities or integrated care systems, will not be allowed to care for only the lowest risk patients. All will also have to care for some of the more fragile populations, ones needing special, expensive care. We have already seen the effect of piecemeal legislation that mandates certain benefits. Much of the impetus for passage of that legislation comes from the inability of certain population groups to access adequate care. To the degree that access remains uneven and inequitable, additional special interest regulations can be expected. People such as those with diseases or physical conditions resulting from mental illness and AIDS often need that additional assistance and protection.

Each provider organization is going to have to take on some of the financial risk involved in delivering good care, whether as part of an integrated system or operating independently. This type of financial risk is a foreign concept to some, particularly in long-term care, because of the way they have been able to operate in the past. They have not always had the same financial risk as payers or even consumers. They, the providers, usually got paid. Yet, to succeed in an era of integrated systems and competition, willingness to assume some of the risk will be necessary. This means understanding that failure to produce the desired level of quality for the identified customer population at the contracted cost will result in financial penalties. This is a scary prospect, but it goes along with the related prospect of great success in the system of tomorrow. It is one of the realities of the changes in how health care, including long-term care, will be financed in the future. Hospitals and managed care organizations understand this, even though they also see the dangers. Some hospitals with experience dealing with managed care organizations have found that entering into risk-sharing arrangements required them to learn a whole new set of skills. Yet, they find it in their best interests to continue to do so. Long-term care organizations cannot afford to be far behind.

To do all of this, successful providers will need a large enough customer base to balance high-risk patients with the less expensive, healthier populations. Individual organizations will find it hard to do that on their own, another reason for joining with others in integrated systems or networks.

Organize for Effectiveness and Efficiency

We can all agree that the future will bring dramatic innovations in how healthcare-related businesses are organized. Managers who are out there on the leading edge (it has also been called, with some justification, the "bleeding edge") of such innovation will be the ones who are most successful. Their efforts will not be without risk, but there is often a correlation between risk and reward. The dynamics of the healthcare system in this new era will demand new and different ways of organizing resources. Provider organizations, including all those in long-term care, will have to be both efficient and effective in everything they do. Those who are slow to change as required will be left behind.

As is so often the case in organizational life, it is not only the manager who must change but the entire organization. Everyone from the governing body to line workers will have to demonstrate an ability to organize and work in new and different ways. However, it is usually the job of top-level administrators to stimulate that willingness. It takes time and a great deal of effort, but when handled well, it is almost always worthwhile.

Be Skillful

Managers in all forms of long-term care must understand the details of how their services are provided. They need knowledge of the type of care provided and what it takes to deliver that care successfully. They have to understand a great deal of detailed information about their facilities and staffs. However, effective long-term care managers of the future will also have to possess solid management skills. Developing those skills will require more than reading a few chapters in this book. It will require additional study and considerable hands-on practice. Good managers, like any leaders, are not born. They are made. Through a well-designed program of study and experience, it is possible for every long-term care manager to improve. That program of study may include formal college or university courses. A surprising number of long-term care administrators have come up through the ranks and never received a college degree. Newer standards for administrators are moving toward requiring such a degree. Although existing administrators are sometimes grandfathered in their licenses, even they would be wise to continue their education. It is never too late for formal management education. In fact, adult students with a solid base of experience get more out of their classes than those without. They find it easier to relate management theories and concepts to their own work situations and usually have the maturity and discipline to get the most out of their courses.

Fortunately, just when the need for formal education is at its greatest, there are more learning options available than ever before, including both traditional, classroom-based courses and distance-learning programs (Pratt, 1998). These options make it possible for anyone to enroll in college, even while maintaining a full-time job. Many have already done so. Fortunately one does not have to enroll in a degree program to gain valuable management education. Many colleges and universities offer management certificates or other means of taking only those courses deemed necessary. Long-term care administrators should also participate in continuing education seminars and programs designed to keep them abreast of changes in this dynamic field. Administrators of nursing facilities are required by many states to obtain a certain number of continuing education units to retain their licenses. Administrators of other long-term care organizations may or may not have to meet such requirements but should participate for their own betterment.

Again, as with college degree programs, there is an ever-growing variety of ways to obtain continuing education. Professional and trade organizations regularly provide seminars designed for that very purpose. Self-study and faculty-directed study courses are becoming much more available than they were a few years ago. Their quality has improved to the point where they are acceptable to licensing and other oversight agencies such as the National Association of Long-Term Care Administrator Boards. For the electronically adept, both continuing education and college degree courses are available online. The availability of these different methods of study leaves administrators little excuse for not improving and maintaining their management skills.

Manage Ethically

We would like to think that all managers are ethical, but it is too important a matter to be taken lightly. The term *management ethics* has come to mean various things to various people, but generally it is "coming to know what is right or wrong in the workplace and doing what's right" (McNamara, 2008). The three essential components of managing ethically are integrity, morality, and principle. Successful managers understand that managing ethically requires commitment and continual effort. Simply wanting to do what is right is not enough.

Create a Learning Organization

It is not just the top managers who need to develop and maintain skills for an organization to survive in the future. Peter Senge, in his classic text, *The Fifth Discipline:*

The Art and Practice of the Learning Organization, describes learning organizations as "organizations where people continually expand their capacity to create the results they truly desire, where new and expansive patterns of thinking are nurtured, where collective aspiration is set free, and where people are continually learning how to learn together" (Senge, 1990, p. 3).

In such an organization, it is possible to unleash the creativity of all staff members. In the new organizational forms anticipated, there will be room for input from everyone on the organization's staff. Yet, without enlightened guidance from top administration, this will not happen. It will require leadership, direction, and patience. Most of all, it will require an attitude of willingness to be creative and innovative from the bottom of the organization to the top—particularly at the top.

Plan

To succeed in the future, managers have to plan for the future. Many readers will remember an old cartoon showing the written words, *plan ahead* in a box with the last couple of letters crammed in because the writer obviously failed to plan ahead. Managers in long-term care are going to have to do much better than that. Long-term care managers have only recently learned to plan the way most other businesses have for years. Whether it is called strategic planning, strategic management, or some catchy new name, these managers and their organizations are going to have to invest both time and resources in planning if they are to survive and prosper.

This planning should begin with defining the essential purpose of the organization and then developing goals and objectives for achieving that purpose and a strategy for implementing the goals and objectives. Planning will be critical for long-term care organizations because they are going to have to be flexible and be able to respond to both anticipated and unanticipated events. Changes in the business environment can come from a multitude of directions. These changes may be global or local. What if treatment of AIDS or Alzheimer's disease patients is one of the cornerstones of an organization's service delivery system and a cure is found for the disease? The organization might still have patients for a while, but how rapidly can it change direction? It could be affected by the arrival in the area of a new, well-financed competitor or a sudden demographic shift such as that caused by a plant closing. The future direction of a long-term care organization or of the entire system could also be changed by the advent of a new disease or a new funding source.

Good managers must be ready to react when events such as these occur. They will certainly be far more ready if they attempt to anticipate those events. This means keeping good data so they can predict trends. One highly successful tool is use of what-if scenarios. No one can anticipate everything that will happen, but a proactive organization can prepare alternative plans for what it will do if certain situations or events occur. They can vastly increase their options if they have some idea of possible changes and what they would do if those changes take place.

For example, during the various national healthcare reform debates of 1994 and 2010, smart organizations developed hypothetical scenarios showing what they would do if the proposed plan should pass and what they would do if it did not. The same thing can be done on a very local level. Suppose an organization is competing for a major contract with a large employer. Most would plan for getting it, but how many would have planned what they would do if they failed to get it? Changes will happen with such rapidity in the future that it will be difficult to react to them swiftly enough to take full advantage, but proactive planning might just be the edge needed for success.

Be a Change Agent

Planning for the future as a means of preparing for coming changes is valuable, but it is not enough. The long-term care administrators of tomorrow need to go a step beyond that. They need to become personal agents of change. They have a responsibility to actively seek ways to improve their organizations, their communities, and the long-term care system.

Administrators of long-term care organizations are in positions of considerable authority. They are the ones who shape the attitudes and work habits of their employees. Thus, they are the ones who can implement change for the better of their organizations. Change can be frightening, but it can also be a valuable tool for any manager. Change will happen, with or without leadership, but it will not necessarily be the change desired. With leadership, the manager can manage the change. Without leadership, change manages the manager (Pratt, 1997).

Being a true change agent also involves extending one's efforts beyond the boundaries of the organization. It means having an impact on the community and on long-term care in general. Many long-term care administrators hold positions of influence in their communities. If they wish to see long-term care in those communities continue to improve, they need to provide leadership there as well.

Finally, they can be change agents in the overall long-term care system. Through active membership in professional and trade associations, they can have an impact on state and national policy making. Through involvement in politics, they can have a say in development of the laws and regulations that govern them. This does not necessarily mean running for elected office, although that works also. It is possible to have meaningful involvement by paying attention to what is happening in government circles, directly or through advocacy organizations. It is far too easy to sit back and complain about the changes occurring in long-term care, but getting involved in those changes—being a change agent—is far more rewarding.

Be Technology's Master, Not Its Slave

Another way in which a long-term care manager can prepare for the future is to make sure the organization is technology's master, not its slave. In particular, that preparation will include using clinical and management information systems as an integral part of how the organization functions. We have pointed out how important these systems are, but it is easy to be overwhelmed by both the sheer volume of information and by the many new methods of collecting and using it. Managers must learn how to separate out the information and tools that best serve them. Even those who consider themselves or their organizations to be doing that already should avoid getting too comfortable or they may find themselves suddenly out of touch. An organization that masters technology will stand out from the pack (Connole, 2012).

Strive for Quality

Nothing will better position a long-term care organization for success in the future than a well-deserved reputation for providing high-quality care. Achieving that reputation will require an ongoing, carefully planned effort. It will not happen accidentally but must be intentional. It will require a significant commitment of time, effort, and resources. Most of all, it will require a commitment of attitude on the part of all within the organization. The processes of ensuring quality are well documented and not that difficult to follow. However, they will succeed only if quality is given top priority.

Lead

Lastly, but perhaps of most importance, long-term care mangers must lead! Leadership is critical to the success of any business venture. That is particularly true of long-term care, with its changing demographics, regulations, and payment schemes. If long-term care managers are to thrive, they must also be leaders. That does not happen automatically, nor is it a birthright. Managers can, however, become leaders with some effort and guidance. Leadership is based on behavior—and behavior can be learned (Bock, 2006).

■ Actions for the System

The actions defined here for individual organizations and those who manage them will help them deal effectively with the future, but what of the overall long-term care system itself? How can it prepare for what is to come? The following are some suggested actions for the collective system to take. They are not necessarily new and generally represent continuation or intensification of current actions. However, this does not lessen their importance or their potential impact on the future.

Stop Infighting

Just as individual provider organizations will find it beneficial to work more closely with each other, formal provider groups should also learn to cooperate more than at present. This will usually mean that state and national trade associations will need to show more accord and less rivalry as well. They have common adversaries, if that is not too strong a word for those other elements of the long-term care system—regulators, payers, and consumer advocates. We do not like to think of the working of the system as adversarial, but in reality it often is. There is an ongoing tug of war over control of those key aspects of the system: cost, access, and quality.

Actually, that contesting of power is not all bad. It tends to keep some semblance of balance among the competing elements and probably creates innovation through constructive conflict. However, the providers weaken their collective positions by squabbling among themselves. Probably the most visible example is the well-documented shift of resources and influence from institutional to noninstitutional providers. It is no secret that payers, particularly state and national governmental agencies, play the groups of providers against each other (O'Keeffe et al., 2010). To the extent that these provider groups, through their representative organizations, attack and criticize each other, they both lose. Similar situations have also developed in recent years between nursing facilities and hospitals and among the various levels of residential care with regard to subacute care.

It would be naive to think that there will be no competition. However, little good is done by allowing that competition to reach levels of excess. Nor would it be fair to indicate that there is no ongoing cooperation among provider entities at the present. There is. However, if the continuum of care is to even approach a state of seamlessness, there must be less bickering among provider groups and more collaborative effort.

Collaborate More Closely With Providers and Consumer Groups

Just as contention among provider groups can be unproductive, so can be the lack of cooperation between those providers and consumer advocacy organizations. National organizations such as the AARP have a great deal of influence on long-term care policy. That influence will continue to grow. The same is true of state and local organizations such as councils of senior citizens and area agencies on aging. Yet it is not uncommon for some of these groups to consider providers as their foes, concentrating their efforts on overcoming what they see as the inadequacies of the providers. When the providers fall into the trap of responding in kind, no one is well served.

Government officials also tend to see the two groups as adversaries, further compounding the differences. For example, several years ago the governor of Maine appointed a long-term care steering committee to advise him on issues relevant to the field and to offer suggestions for improvements in the system. He specifically excluded providers from serving on the committee. Only consumers were allowed. To the surprise of very few, the focus of that committee was decidedly antiprovider. There are many similar stories in other states and at the national level. It is occurrences such as these that make it hard for providers and consumers to work well together.

Yet there are also many examples of how they can collaborate cordially and productively. Again using the state of Maine as an example, an organization—consisting of all segments of the system—was created, demonstrating that they can work well together. The Continuing Care Council was formed for the purpose of improving the long-term care system in that state. The stated mission of the Continuing Care Council[1] was "to bring together a diverse group of individuals for the purpose of advancing a consumer-driven system of long-term care" (Saint Joseph's College of Maine, 1998, p. 1). That diverse group of individuals includes consumers, consumer advocates, providers from across the continuum, payers, and academics. Meeting monthly, they developed a series of issue papers, affected proposed regulations concerning assisted living and congregate housing, and provided information to other organizations. Perhaps their greatest contribution has been the interaction and self-education that took place among the members. They came to understand, and gained an increased appreciation for, each other and the positions of others. This new level of understanding definitely carried over to their constituencies and is only one example of many. It is, however, the kind of thing that needs to become even more common in the future.

Be Proactive

The long-term care system has undergone turbulent times and continues to do so. It is only fitting that we discuss that turbulence here and what the system should do about it.

The answer, while not simple or easy, is straightforward. The issues and problems facing the long-term care system should be met proactively. Far too often in the past there has been a failure to anticipate what was coming, with the result that it was treated reactively. This has not always been effective. Again, it would be unfair to make a blanket statement indicating that there is no proactivity. There is, but much more is needed.

Some of the trends on which change will be based, such as the aging of America, are well documented, and it is widely known that the demand for long-term care services will continue to grow and that expenses associated with providing that care will grow at least as fast. What are we doing about it? Are we doing enough?

We also know that improvements in technology and the way care is provided will continue to create additional ethical problems, as will conflicts between demand and supply. There needs to be a formal dialogue among all concerned (and it concerns us all) in an attempt to resolve some of these extremely difficult issues and to head off others. Such a dialogue is happening only in small, scattered pockets, and then usually more reactively than proactively.

Be Innovative

There are actually two parts to the statement, "Be innovative." First, the long-term care system, and all of its components, must find as many ways as possible to be creative and innovative in solving problems and in doing things ever better. Second, it must take those innovations that work and replicate them as widely as possible.

---

[1] The Continuing Care Council has since been incorporated into a larger organization with similar goals.

The first part is already happening to a surprising degree. Experimental modes of delivery, methods of financing, and organizational structures are being developed and tested regularly. This needs to continue and probably accelerate. Also needed for the future are better ways to seize upon successful ventures and to make them available across the continuum and across organizational, geographic, and demographic boundaries. At this, we have not done nearly as well.

Prototype methods and projects that have proven themselves should be copied by others. They, in turn, become prototypes for the next generation of innovation. The barriers to such replication are often regulatory, but it is too easy to always blame the regulators. Providers, payers, and even consumers may erect barriers of their own, including self-interest and apathy.

■ Summary

In spite of recognizing the turbulence and change in the long-term care system and the many risks ahead, there has purposely been no reference here to the crisis in health care—a topic that seems to pop up regularly around election time. We are not in the midst of a crisis. Rather, we are in the midst of a period of unprecedented, challenging, and (at times) traumatic transformation. It is not unlike what many other industries have already experienced.

The long-term care system has major problems, but as has been documented, many of them are because of our successes. We are doing some very good things and are capable of doing even more. The system will survive, will continue to meet the ever-increasing requirements placed on it, and will make the continuum of care more of a reality.

■ Vocabulary Terms

The following terms are included in this chapter. They are important to the topics and issues discussed herein and should become familiar to readers. Some of the terms are also found in other chapters but may be used in different contexts. They may not be fully defined herein. Thus, readers may wish to seek other, supplementary definitions of them.

AARP	high-risk patients
advocacy organizations	innovation
challenges	integrated care
change agent	learning organization
continuum	managed care organizations
effectiveness	proactive
efficiency	social contracts
environment	trade organizations

■ Discussion Questions

The following questions are presented to assist you in understanding the material covered in this chapter. They tend to be general but lend themselves to detailed answers, which can be found in the chapter.

1. What challenges and opportunities are future long-term care managers likely to face?
2. What skills will those managers need, and how can they acquire such skills?
3. What is meant by an organization's service community, and how can long-term care organizations best deal with that community?
4. Why should long-term care providers become involved with integrated systems or networks? What are some of the possible types of involvement?
5. What is meant by a learning organization, and how can a manager move toward achieving such an organization?
6. What is a change agent, and how can a manager become one?
7. What are some of the ways in which long-term care managers can act proactively to improve the overall system?

■ References

Benz, C. (2012, August 9). *40 must-know statistics about long-term care.* Retrieved from http://news.morningstar.com/articlenet/article.aspx?id=564139.

Berkowitz, E. (2011). *Essentials of health care marketing* (3rd ed.). Burlington, MA: Jones & Bartlett Learning.

Bock, W. (2006). *Are leaders born or made?* Retrieved from http://ezinearticles.com/?Are-Leaders-Born-or-Made?&id=366710.

Connole, P. (2012, March). Facilities tap fresh ideas, new technology. *Provider.* Retrieved from http://www.providermagazine.com/archives/archives-2012/Pages/0312/Facilities-Tap-Fresh-Ideas-New-Technology.aspx.

McNamara, C. (2008). *Complete guide to ethics management: An ethics toolkit for managers.* Retrieved from http://managementhelp.org/businessethics/ethics-guide.htm#anchor26548.

O'Keeffe, L., et al. (2010). *Understanding Medicaid home and community services: A primer—2010 edition.* Washington, DC: U.S. Department of Health and Human Services Office.

Pratt, J. (1997). Managing change. *Home health care management & practice*, 10(1), 75–77.

Pratt, J. (1998). Back to school! Distance learning offers alternatives for administrators. *Balance*, 2(1), 9–13.

Saint Joseph's College of Maine. (1998). *Continuing care council mission statement.* Standish: Saint Joseph's College of Maine.

Senge, P. (1990). *The fifth discipline: The art and practice of the learning organization.* New York, NY: Currency Doubleday.

Criteria for Designing or Evaluating a Long-Term Care System

These criteria have been developed by the Continuing Care Council and the Long-Term Care Management Institute of Saint Joseph's College for use in designing a new long-term care system or for evaluating any current or proposed long-term care system. Although each of the criteria is important in its own right, it is only when taken as a whole that they represent an optimum system. It is recognized that there is some duplication and overlapping of criteria, but this serves to emphasize the importance of certain aspects of long-term care. The criteria are stated as general precepts against which a long-term care system should be measured. Each criterion is accompanied by several statements identifying what benchmarks a system must accomplish to meet that particular criterion and a brief explanation of why and how those benchmarks are met.

I. **The long-term care system should be based on recognition of the needs, rights, and responsibilities of individuals. It should**

   A. **Be consumer driven.**
   Availability and utilization of long-term care services should be based on the needs (not necessarily the wants) of consumers of those services, rather than on the needs of providers or reimbursement agencies.

   B. **Meet the needs of the consumers.**
   The long-term care system should address the full range of consumer needs, rather than meeting only some of them. Otherwise, it will be neither complete nor effective.

   C. **Focus on the individual, recognizing that individuals have unique needs.**
   It should be flexible enough to recognize those needs, including the psychological, social, and financial limitations of recipients of services.

   D. **Respect different cultures and cultural values.**
   The system should recognize these differences and attempt to accommodate them.

E. **Promote quality, dignity, and self-improvement for consumers. In doing this, it should**
   1. Value older adults and those with chronic disabling conditions.
   2. Promote a positive approach to living with chronic illness and dependency.
   3. Allow care recipients to continue to contribute to life and society.
   4. Promote the highest achievable level of functioning.
F. **Balance consumer rights and responsibilities.**
   Consumers of long-term care services and their families should be allowed and encouraged to participate in the continuum of care, including making care-related decisions and taking responsibility for lifestyle choices and financing when appropriate.
G. **Offer consumers a choice of service providers and service delivery modalities.**
   The consumer's right to choose should be respected and encouraged.

II. **The long-term care system should be easily accessible. It should**
A. **Be universally accessible.**
   Services should be available to all who need them, based on uniform functional criteria.
B. **Be user-friendly.**
   The long-term care system should be uncomplicated for the consumer to access and use, with minimal paperwork, simplified financing and approval processes, and no excessive delays in service.
C. **Provide care in the least restrictive environment.**
   The long-term care system should facilitate the provision of care in the setting and service modality that will provide the best combination of appropriate care, quality of life, and cost-effectiveness.
D. **Encourage single-site care availability.**
   The system should be designed to provide, to the degree possible, all necessary services without requiring the consumer to access multiple sites and/or providers.

III. **The long-term care system should coordinate professional, consumer, family, and other informal caregiver resources. It should**
A. **Integrate professional, community, family, and other informal caregiver efforts.**
   The various sources of support should be coordinated to take fullest advantage of their availability.
B. **Evolve from the current medical model to a holistic model of service delivery.**
   The system should encourage broader involvement of nonmedical personnel in problem solving.
C. **Involve families in case management and care delivery.**
   The system should facilitate caring at home by providing resources to family caregivers.

IV. The long-term care system should be an integral part of the health and social system to promote integration, efficiency, and cost effectiveness. It should
   A. **Include a full continuum of services.**
   Those services should meet the needs of all with chronic illness, not just the elderly.
   B. **Include a full and uniform assessment (initial and ongoing) of the consumer's needs.**
   The assessment should reflect an understanding of chronicity.
   C. **Provide emphasis on, and reimbursement for, illness prevention efforts as an integral part of the overall system.**
   Although preventive services are not usually seen as part of a long-term care system, their impact on such a system must be considered.
   D. **Be planned and coordinated to reduce fragmentation and inefficiencies.**
   The system should integrate systemwide coordination with local and regional autonomy.
   E. **Be based on outcome-oriented accountability.**
   To attain this accountability, the system must include
   1. Elimination of unnecessary paperwork.
   2. A focus on results as they affect quality of life rather than a focus on documentation.
   3. Incentives to improve quality of services rather than inspecting for quality.
   4. Consistent development and application of standards.
   5. Outcome-oriented versus process-oriented accountability.
   6. Flexibility that encourages innovation and change.
V. **The long-term care system should be adequately and fairly financed. It should**
   A. **Utilize public and consumer resources to ensure universal access to services.**
   All available resources, public and private, should be considered in providing services for current and future consumers.
   B. **Provide incentives for consumers to use services in an appropriate and cost-effective manner.**
   The overall cost of the system can be controlled by avoiding excessive and unnecessary use.
   C. **Provide incentives for consumers to self-finance their care.**
   Consumers and their families should be encouraged to pay for their own care when possible.
   D. **Avoid causing impoverishment of consumers and families.**
   Although consumers and families should be encouraged to contribute to the cost of their care, that contribution should be limited to prevent causing undue hardship.
   E. **Provide incentives for providers to develop cost-effective measures.**
   Providers of long-term care services can improve the cost-effectiveness of the system, given incentives to do so.

F. Develop payment mechanisms that allow efficient providers to adequately compensate staff and to allow for appropriate operating surplus and/or return on investment.

    Both the for-profit and not-for-profit sectors should continue to have significant roles in the long-term care system.

G. Operate within the limits of a well-conceived budget.

H. Provide significant flexibility to enable consumers to meet long-term care needs as each consumer defines those needs.

    The financing of the system should reflect the needs of individuals (as reflected in Criterion I).

I. Be based on uniform financial eligibility criteria.

VI. The long-term care system should include an education component to create informed consumers, providers, reimbursers, and regulators. It should

A. Include community education.

    The public should be informed about long-term care, including available service options, limitations, and access methods.

B. Include education for providers.

    The system should provide for more geriatric education for physicians and others dealing with the elderly.

C. Educate young healthy persons to better prepare them to cope with chronic illness.

    A better understanding of chronicity will lead to better acceptance of chronic illness in individuals and family members and more effective, efficient use of available resources.

Reprinted with permission: Saint Joseph's College of Maine.

Glossary

AARP (American Associate of Retired Persons) A nonprofit organization committed to the welfare of the U.S. elderly population. AARP originally stood for American Association of Retired Persons.

abuse As the term relates to the long-term care setting, any violation of the terms that a care provider has accepted in agreeing to meet the everyday demands of a client or resident, who due to his or her vulnerable situation is highly dependent upon that care provider.

access to long-term care The ability of a person to secure the care that he or she needs. It is often dependent on availability of reimbursement.

accountability An organization's sense of responsibility for its actions.

accountable care organizations (ACOs) Organizations participating in a model of care that involves coordination by physicians, hospitals, and long-term care providers. The goal is to reduce hospital readmissions, reduce quality variations, and manage risk.

accreditation Recognition conferred by a respected professional entity that a service provider meets predetermined performance standards. Accreditation is a voluntary process.

activities of daily living (ADLs) The functions that a person must perform on an ongoing basis to maintain health and hygiene. Examples include cooking meals and brushing one's teeth.

activity programs In residential care settings, programs aimed at engaging residents in interesting, stimulating activities that are appropriate for their functional level.

acuity levels Parameters used to describe the severity of an illness.

administration The component of an organization made up of the employees who manage day-to-day operations. The administration carries out the policies of the governing body.

adult day care A type of community-based care that provides relief for family members who provide long-term care for relatives in their homes.

advance directives Legally binding documents through which individuals describe their treatment wishes in the event of future inability to express those wishes themselves. Healthcare providers must abide by these desires to the best of their ability, even when they disagree. Advance directives usually take the form of a living will or power of attorney.

Advancing Excellence in America's Nursing Homes An ongoing, coalition-based campaign concerned with how we care for the elderly, chronically ill, and disabled, as well as those recuperating in a nursing home environment.

advocacy organizations Groups formed to represent and promote specific causes.

affiliation A professional relationship between organizations or providers in which they agree to conform to certain standards, possibly with the oversight of a governing body, and to share defined responsibilities and resources.

Affordable Care Act (ACA) Legislation, signed into federal law in 2010, designed to improve access to affordable health coverage for U.S. citizens to regulate the practices of health insurance providers.

age-restricted communities Communities that are restricted to people usually 55 years of age or older, or 62 and older. They often involve purchase of property or condominiums. To be competitive and attractive to a retirement lifestyle, age-restricted communities usually offer amenities, activities, and services that cater to residents.

aging and disability resource centers One-stop locations designed to provide comprehensive information and assistance to people of all income levels and all types of disability.

aging in place An approach to care that provides recipients with long-term care in a stable, homelike setting that is familiar and comfortable.

AIDS Abbreviation for acquired immune deficiency syndrome. AIDS, if preventive methods are not properly maintained, could become one of the leading causes of long-term care disability.

Alzheimer's disease A degenerative disorder of the brain that can require intensive long-term care.

amenities See *service amenities*.

American College of Health Care Administrators (ACHCA) A professional association for healthcare administrators that has developed both a code of ethics and a set of standards of practice for long-term care administrators.

American Health Care Association (AHCA) A nonprofit collaboration of state health organizations, represented by both nonprofit and for-profit organizations, that provide various types of care to the elderly, including assisted living, nursing facility care, developmental disability services, and subacute care.

American Health Quality Association A charitable, educational, not-for-profit national membership association dedicated to healthcare quality through community-based, independent quality evaluation and improvement programs.

Americans with Disabilities Act Legislation intended to prohibit discrimination against people with disabilities in employment, transportation, public accommodation, communications, and governmental activities.

application As the term relates to information technology, a program or method designed to allow users to achieve a specified goal electronically, such as remote monitoring of a consumer's condition, conferencing among healthcare professionals, and consultation with specialists.

Area Agencies on Aging A source of information on local long-term care services, among other topics relating to elderly care.

artificial functioning The use of technological devices in place of functions that are normally biologic in nature.

asset recovery The process by which a state recovers Medicaid long-term care payments by claiming the deceased recipient's assets.

assisted living/residential care An approach to care that provides relatively independent seniors assistance and limited healthcare services in a homelike atmosphere.

automated patient records Electronic health records that allow quick and easy access to patients' clinical history and information concerning medications taken, current providers, and insurance coverage.

autonomy The ability to live in accordance with one's own wishes.

baby boomers Individuals born in the period following World War II, between 1946 and 1964. As this large segment of the U.S. population continues to age, they will place unprecedented demands on the healthcare system.

Balanced Budget Act Legislation passed in 1997 an effort to produce a balanced federal budget by 2002.

Balancing Incentive Payments Program A provision of the Affordable Care Act designed to keep long-term care consumers out of costly institutions. It is aimed at removing barriers to providing long-term care in people's homes and communities.

bargaining power The strength of an organization during contract negotiations. An organization may integrate with other organizations to increase its bargaining power.

beneficence The responsibility of the provider to act in the best interests of the patient.

beneficiary An individual who receives services or funding (e.g., Medicare) by meeting predefined eligibility requirements, or an individual who is designated as the recipient of another person's assets upon a specified event, such as the person's death.

bereavement The period of grief and adjustment that occurs after the death of a loved one.

board See *governing body*.

brain injury units Units designed to provide specialized, often long-term, care for individuals who have suffered traumatic brain injury. These individuals are often young adults and may suffer from a unique combination of physical and behavioral disabilities.

branding The process of creating a specific identity for the organization and its services that is quickly and easily identified with them.

bundling An arrangement by which payment is made to a single entity for a defined episode of care rather than individual payments to individual service providers.

capitation A set rate paid to providers for each person covered rather than on a fee-for-service basis.

care management An element in managing the provision of subacute care concerned with the type and quality of care received.

care planning The process of assessing each patient's needs, developing a care plan to meet those needs, and constantly reviewing the care plan and adjusting it as needed.

caregiver Any person, whether a trained professional or not, who attends to the needs of another person.

CARF International A program evaluation system that offers processes for measuring functional outcomes in services provided. Formerly known as the Commission on Accreditation of Rehabilitation Facilities.

case management An element in managing the provision of subacute care concerned with the cost-effectiveness of the care given.

case manager A member of the interdisciplinary team focused on the degree of efficiency with which care is given. This individual manages the utilization of resources expended in providing care.

Center for Excellence in Assisted Living (CEAL) An organization formed to continue the work of the Assisted Living Workgroup and serve as an ongoing source of information and guidance to states regulating assisted living.

Centers for Medicare & Medicaid Services (CMS) The federal agency that oversees Medicare and Medicaid.

certificate of need (CON) A federal mandate designed to reduce the amount of expansion of healthcare facilities by requiring approval before any new construction or expansion can take place.

certification Recognition that a service provider's expertise meets the standards of that profession. Certification is usually conferred in a voluntary, nongovernmental capacity, but sometimes involves government processes. The standards established by the professional associations generally exceed those required by government agencies.

certified nurse assistants (CNAs) Nonlicensed paraprofessionals who provide most of the hands-on care in a nursing facility. They represent the largest category of staff in most nursing facilities.

challenges Forces that impede, or threaten to impede, an organization's success.

change agent A person who seeks to improve his or her organization and community, and the long-term care system in general.

charisma The ability to motivate or inspire the followership of others. It is often difficult to describe specifically what makes one person more charismatic than another person, and this quality is often associated with a sense of "magic."

chief executive officer (CEO) The top administrative official (executive) in the organization. She or he is the direct link between the governing body and the other employees, including those involved in administration.

chief information officer The individual in charge of an organization's information system.

chronic care See *long-term care*.

chronic subacute care Care for patients with serious chronic conditions requiring services such as ventilator or intravenous therapy. The average stay is longer than in the transitional or general subacute care units, but most patients stay only about 60 to 90 days before they are transferred to a lower level of care or before they die.

chronicity The duration or frequency of a disorder's recurrence.

CLASS program A proposed initiative of the Affordable Care Act by which an individual would contribute to long-term care insurance for 5 years before being eligible to receive benefits. The CLASS program was suspended indefinitely on October 14, 2011.

clients As the term relates to long-term care, individuals receiving services in the community-based setting.

clinical information systems Information management systems that typically address four specific areas: patient management, clinical guidelines, quality improvement, and clinical outcomes.

co-payment A fee paid by the patient/consumer, as defined by his or her health insurance policy, to receive a service or prescription.

code of conduct Guidelines that support the code of ethics by identifying behaviors that are acceptable (and those that are unacceptable).

code of ethics A description of the organization's values and the ethical rules by which it operates.

coercive power The power a person holds because of his or her ability to affect another's life negatively.

cognitive disability A functional disability defined by dementia or a simple inability to understand and follow directions.

cohousing A type of collaborative housing in which residents participate in the design and operation of their own neighborhoods.

collusion Cooperation between organizations that is often illegal and aimed at creating an unfair competitive advantage or saving money.

communication As the term relates to leadership, the process of conveying to others what is expected of them. There are many types of communication, including person to person, written, and electronic. The leader must know which type to employ and when. Effective communication is a two-way process, so leaders must be willing to listen to others.

communications The means of and distinct instances of communicating. See *communication*.

community In the long-term care setting, a facility or living environment that presents the opportunity for residents to socialize with each other and that represents the residents' values.

Community First Choice Option An incentive of the Affordable Care Act that provides a 6% increase in federal Medicaid matching funds to states for providing community-based attendant services and supports within their Medicaid program.

community relations Actions that an organization undertakes to create a favorable image with the community. This effort involves participation in community activities; providing certain services that the community needs, such as free clinics; and being considered a good neighbor by the community it serves.

community-based care Care that is delivered in the community, not in institutions. The most prominent types of community-based care services are home health care, adult day care, and hospice care.

community-based services Services that are delivered in the community, not in institutions. The most prominent types of community-based care services are home health care, adult day care, and hospice care.

competency The ability to make informed decisions for oneself.

competent In professional terms, the ability to complete one's job effectively. In patient terms, the mental, physical, and emotional abilities required to make sound decisions.

competition The contest between two or more parties to secure consumers' business.

confidentiality The right to keep information of a personal nature to oneself as long as doing so does not adversely affect others.

conflict resolution A type of problem solving in which two or more parties with conflicting interests or agendas are brought to an agreement or functional arrangement.

congregate housing A form of independent living that usually provides convenience or supportive services like meals, housekeeping, and transportation.

Congressional Budget Office An agency that provides Congress with nonpartisan analyses for economic and budget decisions and with estimates required for the congressional budget process.

connection power Influence over others gained through a connection with someone in a position of power.

constituencies The consumers and stakeholders that an organization serves.

consumer bill of rights and responsibilities As the term relates to managed care, rules developed by the 1997 President's Advisory Commission on Consumer Protection and Quality in the Health Care Industry to ensure consumers receive accurate, understandable information about services; receive informed, affordable, nondiscriminatory treatment; and have the ability to appeal decisions made by providers and health plans.

consumer choice The right of consumers to participate in decisions that affect themselves. In the long-term care setting, consumers have readily embraced the idea of consumer choice and have come to demand a say in how, when, and where they receive care and even whether to receive that care at all.

consumer responsibilities As the term relates to developing long-term care plans, the commitments that care recipients and their caregivers are willing to make to ensure a positive outcome.

consumer rights As the term relates to developing long-term care plans, the assurances that care recipients and their caregivers will receive a level of care and assistance that will ensure a positive outcome.

consumer-driven Care in which the consumer is the primary focus of services and in which the consumer plays a major role in determining which services to access, and when.

consumerism The impact of consumers' demands on the manner in which a service or product is delivered and marketed.

Continuing Care Accreditation Commission The organization responsible for accrediting continuing care retirement communities.

continuing care retirement communities (CCRC) According to the Assisted Living Federation of America (2013), "a community that offers several levels of assistance, including independent living, assisted living, and nursing home care" in providing a continuum of care, "often all on one campus or site."

continuous quality improvement (CQI) A proactive and continuous study of processes with the intent to prevent or decrease the likelihood of problems by identifying areas of opportunity and testing new approaches to fix underlying causes of persistent/systemic problems.

continuum The culmination of all of the areas involved in long-term care, including acute care, subacute care, nursing facilities, assisted living, home health care, adult day care, hospice, and more.

continuum of care According to Connie Evashwick, author of *The Continuum of Long-Term Care*, "an integrated, client-oriented system of care composed of both services and integrating mechanisms that guides and tracks clients over time through a comprehensive array of health, mental health, and social services spanning all levels of intensity of care."

controlling As the term relates to management functions, the process of determining whether intended outcomes have been achieved and, if not, why not.

cooperation An arrangement among healthcare or long-term care provider organizations, especially when stimulated by competition, that usually involves some type of not-too-formal liaison that provides benefits for all involved.

cost offsets Reductions in the cost of a service. Cost offsets are important in funding the Affordable Care Act.

culture As defined by Planetree (2014), the ways in which "different aspects of human conduct—roles, norms, values, customs, likes, dislikes, symbols, language, priorities, and more—dovetail and turn a group of disparate individuals into a community with a distinct identity."

culture change As defined by the Pioneer Network (2013), "the common name given to the national movement for the transformation of older adult services, based on person-directed values and practices where the voices of elders and those working with them are considered and respected."

decision making The process of considering all of the options and potential outcomes involved in a situation and choosing the one that best meets the individual's or organization's needs.

decision-making capacity The ability to understand what is being considered and to appreciate the consequences of the decision.

deemed status Recognition conferred by a respected professional entity that a provider's services meet certain effectiveness criteria. This term is often applied in the context of becoming eligible to receive payment from Medicare or Medicaid programs.

deinstitutionalization The transfer of individuals from institutional to noninstitutional care settings.

dementia A degenerative disorder of the central nervous system marked by deteriorated cognitive functioning.

demographics The unique characteristics of a population, including such factors as age, sex, religious affiliations, ethnicity, health status, and educational level.

dependency The inability, and therefore reliance upon others, to perform basic daily functions.

diagnosis-related groups A system of financially reimbursing providers based on the general care involved in treating an episode of a particular illness. This system led to imprecise reimbursement and in turn efforts by providers to minimize the services rendered.

distinctive competencies The unique skills and services that a provider possesses that set the provider apart from the competition.

domains of practice The areas in which a service provider must be competent in order to receive licensure. The National Association of Long-Term Care Administrator Boards has determined that the following five areas of knowledge or skill are required of long-term care administrators: resident-centered care and quality of life, human resources, finance, physical environment and atmosphere, and leadership and management.

Dual-Eligible Initiative An initiative of the Affordable Care Act designed to coordinate care for individuals who are eligible for both Medicaid and Medicare.

durable power of attorney Legal authorization given to another person to act on one's behalf in the event of future incapacity. Also called proxy directive.

economies of scale The competitive advantages created by providing services on a larger scale. Generally, as the scale of services increases, the associated costs decrease.

Eden Alternative A small, not-for-profit organization that is based on the core belief that aging should be a continued stage of development and growth, rather than a period of decline.

effectiveness A measure of an organization's success in achieving an objective.

efficiency A measure of the amount of resources—whether money, time, personnel, or other resources—required to achieve an objective.

electronic health record A means of centralizing all information pertaining to a patient's care within a computer system. Electronic health records (EHRs) are readily accessible by any qualified professional with access to the system and are transferrable to other providers' systems should the need arise.

employer mandate A requirement of the Affordable Care Act that all businesses with over 50 full-time equivalent employees provide health insurance for their full-time employees or pay a penalty.

enabling A leadership skill that involves delegating responsibilities and trusting employees to do what is needed.

end-of-life issues The legal and ethical considerations relating both to medical/care decisions and to practical personal affairs as a person approaches the end of his or her life.

endorsement In the long-term care setting, the transfer of a license from one state to another through a process of reciprocity.

entitlement program A healthcare program in which anyone belonging to a particular population group is eligible to receive coverage.

environment As the term relates to long-term care, the context in which a service is provided. It can refer to factors ranging from physical to financial to emotional.

Equal Employment Opportunity Commission A federal agency that promotes fairness in employment through administrative and judicial enforcement of the federal civil rights laws and through education and technical assistance.

ethical dilemmas Challenges that an organization may face in ensuring fair, unbiased delivery of services to all potential consumers or in ensuring fair, unbiased hiring processes and work practices for all employees.

ethics committee A committee dedicated to determining the process for making ethical decisions, educating staff and residents, and providing professional consultation.

ethics management program A program that spells out an organization's values, sets guidelines for behavior, trains employees, and provides guidance in difficult situations.

expert power The power that one holds because he or she is considered to be an expert in a particular area.

explicit rationing The government mandating, by law, of who gets what type and what amount of health care.

external assessment A type of assessment aimed at defining those factors that affect the organization but are out of its direct control. It can be broken into three segments: (1) environmental analysis, (2) stakeholder analysis, and (3) competitor analysis.

external controls The means used to ensure that care facilities/professionals are qualified to provide a particular service. External controls can be divided into two categories: public and private. Public controls result from passage of laws. They are nonvoluntary and are imposed by government agencies. Private controls are provided by nongovernment agencies and organizations, and compliance is voluntary.

Fair Labor Standards Act Legislation that establishes minimum wage, overtime pay, recordkeeping, and youth employment standards.

Family Medical Leave Act Legislation that allows eligible employees to take unpaid, job-protected leave for specified family and medical reasons.

fee-for-service contract A contract specifying that residents of the continuing care retirement community will pay separately for all health and medical services and for long-term care.

feedback The process of telling employees how well they have performed—that is, whether they have met expectations and, if not, where they have

fallen short. Feedback enables employees to grow and improve.

Five-Star Quality Rating System A ranking system of America's nursing care facilities aimed at providing a comprehensive review of the facilities' services that consumers can use in selecting a care provider.

forecasting The process of anticipating consumer demands so that providers can meet those demands as they arise. Effective forecasting can give an organization a competitive advantage.

forward-looking As the term relates to management, having a sense of direction and a concern for the future of the organization.

functional disabilities Disabilities that limit an individual's ability to function independently.

functional independence The ability of an individual to live according to his or her own standards with little or no assistance from others.

futile care Care provided, regardless of the previously stated wishes of the resident, when there is no hope of recovery or improvement in the patient's condition.

gatekeeper The person who controls access to care.

general subacute care Care for patients whose need for ongoing therapy or monitoring requires a longer stay than in transitional units.

geriatrician A medical doctor who specializes in the healthcare needs of older adults.

goals Benchmarks by which progress toward an organization's vision can be measured.

governance The process of governing, overseeing, or presiding over. It is a broad term identifying the overall operation of the organization.

governing body The policy-making arm of the organization. *Governing body* is generally used as a generic term, but most governing bodies carry other, more specific names such as governing board, board of directors, board of overseers, or board of governors. A governing body may also be referred to as a *board*.

Green House Project A long-term care model that attempts to break the mold of institutional care by creating small homes for 6 to 10 elders who require skilled nursing or assisted living care. The homes are designed to promote privacy, autonomy, and social activity.

guardian A person who makes decisions on behalf of a consumer declared incompetent.

hardware As the term relates to computers, components and devices that have a physical presence, such as a computer mouse or keyboard.

health homes As described by the Kaiser Family Foundation (2011), "person-centered systems of care that facilitate access to and coordination of the full array of primary and acute physical health services, behavioral health care, and long-term community-based services and supports."

health information technology (HIT) The application of certain types of technology to the collection and use of healthcare-related information.

health insurance exchanges Online marketplaces for health insurance.

Health Insurance Portability and Accountability Act of 1996 Legislation designed to provide consumers with greater access to healthcare insurance, to protect the privacy of healthcare data, and to promote more standardization and efficiency in the healthcare industry. The act is often abbreviated HIPAA.

health maintenance organization (HMO) A managed care structure that oversees health care for individuals by coordinating payment and treatment options with providers. Health Maintenance Organizations (HMOs) usually pay only for care within the network. Consumers choose a primary care doctor who coordinates most of their care.

high-risk patients Patients who are likely to require more frequent or expensive health services.

holistic Concerned with providing care that takes all aspects of the individual into account, including personality traits and health considerations unique to the individual.

holistic philosophy of care A care philosophy in which healthcare consumers are viewed as individuals defined by distinctive personalities, strengths, weaknesses, and varying degrees of functional disability or limitation. In caring for them, long-term care providers should not focus on the clinical causes of disabilities, but rather must attempt to develop an overall care plan that overcomes or minimizes the disabilities.

home care Services provided to recovering, disabled, and chronically or terminally ill persons to enhance their ability to live at home. Home care typically includes chore and housecleaning services and is different than *home health care*, which involves helping seniors recover from an illness or injury.

home health care A type of community-based care that provides services to the client in a homelike setting, thereby avoiding institutionalization.

honest A leadership trait marked by consistent adherence to the facts at hand and absence of personal agenda or biases. Leaders who are honest are considered genuine and trustworthy.

horizontal integration The formation of a mutually beneficial alliance between two or more organizations that provide similar services.

hospice care A type of community-based care that provides emotional and physical support for persons with terminal illness. It is usually provided in the home, often by volunteers.

hospital readmissions reduction program (HRRP) A function of the Affordable Care Act intended to assess penalties on hospitals with high readmission rates for patients with certain medical conditions.

implicit rationing The determination of who will receive services or be reimbursed for services that is built into the nature of some healthcare plans. Implicit rationing often does not allow for exceptions or situational decision making that might be perceived as fair.

incompetent A person who is not physically, mentally, and legally able to make decisions about his or her health care.

independent lifestyle As the term relates to senior housing, the freedom of residents to choose whether to participate in a facility's services or programs. Residents are given the opportunity to engage in a lifestyle filled with recreational, educational, and social activities among other seniors.

independent living A residential living setting for elderly or senior adults in which residents require minimal or no extra assistance and lead an independent lifestyle filled with recreational, educational, and social activities among other seniors. Residents usually have complete choice in whether to participate in a facility's services or programs.

individual mandate A provision of the Affordable Care Act requiring most individuals to purchase health insurance or pay a penalty.

influence See *power*.

informal caregivers Long-term care providers who are not formally trained healthcare professionals. Examples include family members and friends, religious organizations, and community groups formed specifically to help those less fortunate than themselves.

information power The power that one holds because he or she has access to information that others do not have.

informed consent A decision made with access to sufficient information to anticipate possible outcomes and understand the dynamics relating to the decision.

informed consumers Consumers who understand the options available to them and can demand a certain type, price, or quality of service.

infrastructure The personnel and resources (e.g., facilities, information technology systems) needed to provide a service.

innovation As the term relates to long-term care, a recent and usually dramatic improvement in the way care is delivered or in service efficiency.

inspiring A term used to describe leaders who are talented at leading people where they did not think they could go. An inspiring leader makes individuals believe they can do things they had previously thought they could not do.

institutional care An approach to long-term care in which care is provided in facilities developed for that purpose. Nursing care, assisted living care, subacute care, and housing services are usually considered to be institutional care.

institutional providers Providers who provide long-term care in facilities designed specifically for that purpose. Consumer demands are causing these providers to incorporate such amenities as à la carte menus, homelike living settings, and flexible treatment regimens.

integrated care Care that incorporates a broad range of services.

integrated delivery system A system in which two or more organizations formally coordinate their efforts (as opposed to simply cooperating with one another or acting as completely individual entities) to provide the most competitive and efficient services possible.

integrated health network (IHN) An alliance of integrated health providers. See *integrated health systems (IHSs)*.

integrated health systems (IHSs) Organizational models that are able to better serve the needs of their customers by uniting the various services relating to their care. They represent an important step toward achieving a true continuum of care. The term is used generically to describe vertically integrated, single-owner systems and formal networks or alliances among independent organizations.

integrating mechanisms The means by which organizations will find success in integrating their services. As described in her book, *The Continuum of Long-Term Care*, Dr. Connie Evashwick (2005, p. 9) identifies four integrating mechanisms required for an efficient, effective continuum of care: (1) interentity organization and management, (2) coordination of care, (3) integrated information systems, and (4) integrated financing.

integration The unifying of related services through communication and collaboration of the involved professionals. Integration, as compared to *cooperation*, is more likely to be formalized, with the component organizations actually becoming part of a larger entity through merger, contracting, or some other form of affiliation. As the term relates to information technology, it refers to the unification of multiple information systems.

interdisciplinary team The various individuals involved in a patient's care who bring unique assessment skills and knowledge of specific treatments to the ongoing care planning process.

intermediate care facility A term formerly used to describe a nursing facility providing less advanced services than those of a skilled nursing facility.

internal analysis A type of assessment that consists of an introspective assessment of the strengths and weaknesses of the organization. In terms of strategic planning, it involves a review of major operational areas, including, at the least, administration and governance, staffing, services provided, financial viability, and the state of the physical plant.

Internet A network of computer systems connected to one another electronically in order to exchange information through data protocols.

Joint Commission A nonprofit organization that accredits healthcare organizations and programs, including assisted living facilities.

law A formally defined rule of conduct that is enforced, through predefined penalties, by a governing body.

leader An individual with the unique character traits required to inspire the followership of others and the knowledge and skills required to help them reach an intended destination.

leadership The individual(s) in charge of leading the organization. See *leading*.

leading The process of influencing the efforts of others toward the achievement of a goal. The purpose of leadership is to enable others to do their jobs to the best of their abilities.

learning organization An organization in which members actively seek out educational opportunities that will allow them to improve care delivery.

legislation The process or outcome of a governing body's efforts to define rules of conduct.

legitimate power The power that goes along with an official position. For example, the boss can order others to do his or her bidding because "I told you to."

licensure The process by which individuals are deemed eligible to provide a regulated service. It does not necessarily require demonstration of competency in that service. This term is often used interchangeably with *registration*.

life care community According to Episcopal Homes (2013), "a form of [continuing care retirement community] that offers an insurance-type contract and provides all levels of care. It often includes payment for acute care and physician's visits. Little or no change is made in the monthly fee, regardless of the level of medical care required by the resident, except for cost of living increases."

life care/extensive contract A contract requiring that the continuing care retirement community provide unlimited long-term nursing care at little or no additional cost for as long as the nursing services are necessary.

Life Safety Code A standard published by the National Fire Protection Association aimed at ensuring that occupancies are designed and constructed so as to limit risk to life in the event of a fire.

living wills Documents through which individuals communicate the medical care they wish to receive should they become unable to make decisions for themselves. Also known as instructional directives or terminal care documents.

long-term care An approach to care that is required over extended periods, with temporary, short-term breaks, but typically lasting for the remainder of the recipient's life. Also referred to as *chronic care*.

long-term care insurance Health insurance that is personally funded by the recipients, often while the recipients are still young, in expectation of one day funding their long-term care needs. Some long-term care insurance is purchased through group plans, including through employers and organizations, but most such insurance is sold to individuals.

long-term services and supports The broad range of services and infrastructures to help frail older people and younger people with disabilities remain independent.

long-term transitional subacute care Care (usually hospital-based) for patients with more complex medical problems who need more intensive, but still not acute, care over a longer time before transitioning to home or another level of care.

mainframe computer A central computer used by an organization to control large quantities of data and to disseminate those data to various users and sources.

managed care A relatively new form of healthcare financing and delivery in which the recipient's care is overseen by a third party to ensure that the most cost-effective practices are being used.

managed care organizations (MCOs) Healthcare organizations designed to closely assess the recipient's care to ensure that the most cost-effective and medically advisable practices are being used.

management A generic term that refers to those who supervise the work of others. In fact, the generally accepted definition of management is accomplishing the objectives of the organization through others or, more simply, getting work done through the efforts of others.

management ethics Efforts to determine what is morally right and to conduct business accordingly. There are three essential components of managing ethically: integrity, morality, and principle.

management information system (MIS) A means of gathering and interpreting data used for cost control and the billing of charges. As the MIS relates to integrated health systems, it can serve as the basis for operational control and for making improvements in a variety of nonclinical functions.

managing change The process of influencing changes within an organization to the advantage of the organization. Managing change involves recognizing that a change is occurring and then embracing it and finding a functional manner of incorporating it into operations.

managing stress The process of embracing unavoidable sources of stress relating to a job and finding ways to be as efficient as possible, with the understanding that it may not be possible to please everyone or accomplish all job demands.

market expansion Also called *market development*, the process of finding new markets for existing services.

market penetration The process of expanding the current services to current customers.

market planning A planning process that involves defining customers and potential customers in terms of who they are, how many of them there are, how likely they are to use the services of the organization doing the planning, and what influences their choice of providers. The purpose of the marketing plan is to develop a (marketing) strategy that will help the organization thrive and prosper by selling more of its services or products.

market segmentation The use of information from a stakeholder analysis to divide the market into potentially distinct groups of consumers who might merit separate products and/or marketing mixes.

marketing Efforts specifically focused on getting consumers to choose and purchase the products or services the organization has to offer. The marketing process involves conducting market research, developing a marketing strategy, and implementing that strategy.

marketing mentality An appreciation for the value of having a good marketing plan.

Medicaid A program that serves the medically indigent—those unable to pay for their own health care.

medical device tax A revenue-raising provision intended to help fund the Affordable Care Act. Most medical devices become subject to a 2.3% excise tax collected at the time of purchase as long as they are being sold to medical providers, including such items as examination gloves and catheters that are used in long-term care.

medical versus social model A care model that takes into account both the medical needs and the social needs of individuals living in long-term care facilities. Care for these individuals is often not focused purely on curing a disorder but on providing a comfortable and financially sustainable environment that meets the full range of their personal and medical needs.

medically indigent An individual who does not have the financial means to pay for healthcare services. Medical indigence is an eligibility requirement for receiving Medicaid benefits.

Medicare A program that serves the elderly, the blind, and certain categories of the permanently disabled, without regard to ability to pay.

Medicare Advantage plans As defined by Medicare (Medicare.gov, 2014), "a type of Medicare health plan offered by a private company that contracts with Medicare to provide all [of a consumer's] Part A and Part B benefits."

Medicare trust fund The monetary source for the Medicare program. It is currently in jeopardy due to an aging U.S. population that is exceeding the funding allotted to Medicare and the lack of legislative progress in increasing funding.

Medicare-certified home health agency A home healthcare agency that meets state licensure and/or Medicare requirements in order to receive Medicare reimbursement.

medication management An initiative of assisted living services to ensure that residents properly take their medications.

mentoring The close guidance, or coaching, of inexperienced employees by more experienced, knowledgeable employees in hopes of bringing out the best in employees and helping them reach their full potential. Mentoring can be a formal job function or a more informal interest that an employee takes in the development of colleagues.

merger The absorption of one business entity into another, usually larger or more profitable, business entity.

mission A statement of what the organization is all about and what it does.

modified/continuing care contract A contract requiring that the continuing care retirement community provide long-term health care or nursing services for a specified period of time. After the specified care period, the resident is responsible for the additional cost.

Money Follows the Person program A provision of the Affordable Care Act intended to help transition Medicaid beneficiaries living in institutions back to the community.

motivation The drive one feels to complete a task.

multidisciplinary approach to care An approach to care that coordinates the efforts of medical, social, residential, and other allied professionals to develop and implement care plans for individual consumers.

multilevel facilities Long-term care facilities that provide several different levels of care in the same location.

multiple entry points The many different points at which consumers enter the system and the different steps required to reach services from those multiple points.

National Adult Day Services Association An organization devoted to advancing the national development, recognition, and use of adult day services.

National Association of Long-Term Care Administrator Boards (NAB) An organization that coordinates the process of testing administrators of nursing facilities and that administers a national licensure examination.

National Commission for Quality Long-Term Care A nonpartisan regulatory body devoted to improving long-term care in the United States.

National Committee for Quality Assurance (NCQA) A nonprofit organization dedicated to improving healthcare quality by accrediting and certifying a wide range of healthcare organizations.

National Quality Forum (NQF) A private, not-for-profit membership organization created to develop and implement a national strategy for healthcare quality measurement and reporting.

negotiation The process of reaching an amicable agreement when there are differences between the leader and another party.

network As the term relates to information technology, a system for connecting computers and electronic devices in order to efficiently transfer data.

No Wrong Door system State efforts to streamline access to long-term services and simplify access to long-term care services for the elderly and individuals with disabilities.

noninstitutional care An approach to long-term care in which care is provided in the consumer's home. Home care, adult day care, and hospice care are considered noninstitutional (community-based) care.

nursing facilities Healthcare facilities licensed by the states offering room, board, nursing care, and some therapies.

nursing home A facility that provides residents with a room, meals, personal care, nursing care, and medical services. Residents may be individuals with chronic conditions requiring long-term care or individuals needing a shorter-term acute recovery period after hospitalization.

Obamacare A nickname given to the Affordable Care Act by its opponents that has since gained general popularity.

Occupational Safety and Health Administration The federal agency charged with the enforcement of safety and health legislation of work environments.

occupational therapy Therapy aimed at helping patients to overcome limitations with the use of assistive devices and techniques.

Older Americans Act Legislation authorized in 1965 to ensure the welfare, including nutritional, financial, and medical needs, of older adults.

Omnibus Budget Reconciliation Act of 1987 (OBRA) A law specifying Medicare and Medicaid standards for care in the nursing home setting.

oncologist A doctor who specializes in the treatment and prevention of cancer.

organization A structure of individuals and resources working toward a common goal of providing services or goods and operating in accordance with defined standards.

organizational culture The qualities of a work environment produced as a culmination of the values, skills, experiences, education, upbringing, personality traits, and other attributes of the organization's members.

organizing A leadership function that involves controlling the overall structure of the organization. Organizing involves designating tasks and responsibilities to employees with the specific skills needed to complete the tasks. It also involves developing the organizational structure and chain of command within the company.

Outcome and Assessment Information Set (OASIS) A method of collecting and monitoring data to improve outcome measures in home health care.

outcomes measures Indicators of the end result of care delivery—the effect the care has on the individual.

outcomes-based system A system that measures, first and foremost, the results of a service. A successful outcomes-based system will include more flexibility to allow providers to find better methods of achieving desired results. It will also have built-in incentives for innovation in improving those outcomes.

pain management Care focused on providing medication and other symptom relief.

palliative care Care focused on providing pain and symptom relief. For patients who are terminally ill, providing comfort often becomes the top treatment priority.

Part A The component of the Medicare program that provides hospital insurance, including some sections of long-term care (skilled care, home health care, hospice).

Part B The component of the Medicare program that provides supplementary medical insurance that covers physician care.

Patient Self-Determination Act of 1990 Legislation designed to ensure that individuals are given the opportunity to determine the course of their own medical care, such as through advance directives, and that these decisions are protected. This national standard spells out how healthcare providers, including long-term care facilities and organizations, should go about making consumers aware of their rights.

pay-for-performance (P4P) A system of financial incentives awarded to providers in an effort to improve the quality and efficiency of healthcare services.

payment bundling See *bundling*.

personal computer A computer with relatively modest capacity (as compared to a mainframe computer) that can be used by an individual for daily work or personal functions and connected to a network for greater data access.

personal power Power that an individual possesses that is not directly connected to any organizational setting, although it can be used in such settings. There are three types of personal power: expert, information, and referent.

Pew Commission A regulatory committee administered by the University of California at San Francisco, Center for the Health Professions, devoted to assisting health professionals, workforce policy makers, and educational institutions in responding to the challenges of the changing healthcare system.

physical therapy Therapy aimed at restoring or maintaining the mobility and strength of patients who are limited by physical injuries, using techniques such as exercise and massage.

physician-assisted suicide The termination of one's own life with the approval or indirect assistance of a physician. In 1995, the state of Oregon passed the first right-to-die law in the nation, allowing physician-assisted suicide.

Pioneer Network A long-term care model created by a small group of prominent professionals in long-term care to advocate for person-directed care. It advocates for elders across the spectrum of living options and promotes "a culture of aging that supports the care of elders in settings where individual voices are heard and individual choices are respected, whether it is in nursing homes, transitional care settings or wherever home and community may be" (Pioneer Network, 2013).

place The manner or context in which goods or services are made available for use by consumers. In long-term care, it relates to how accessible the service is and may include the characteristics of service distribution, modes of delivery, location, transportation availability, hours and days open, parking, waiting time, and other access considerations.

planning The process of identifying and defining the desired ends to be achieved and determining appropriate means to achieve those defined ends.

position power The power or influence a person has by virtue of holding a particular position. It may be a management position or a position to which he or she is elected or appointed. There are four distinct types of position power: coercive, reward, legitimate, and connection.

power The ability to produce an outcome, or to cause others to produce an outcome.

power of attorney Legal authorization that individuals give to another person to make decisions in accordance with their wishes should the individuals become unable to make informed decisions for themselves.

price The monetary value placed on a specific service or product. To succeed, the organization must ensure its pricing is fair and competitive.

private controls Governing bodies that are independently funded and operated and that are focused on measuring, evaluating, and ensuring the quality of care provided by long-term care organizations.

As compared to public (governmental) controls, these bodies are not focused on the cost of services.

private long-term care insurance See *long-term care insurance.*

proactive Self-motivated to improve oneself or one's organization before the need for such improvements may be evident to others.

problem solving The process of finding a solution to a source, or potential source, of dysfunction within an organization. It involves first recognizing, then prioritizing, then resolving the problem.

product As the term relates to long-term care, the service provided. In developing a marketing mix for a specific target market group, the organization would seek to provide that combination of services most needed and valued by the targeted consumers.

prognosis The anticipated course of an illness or disease. In the case of terminal illness, it may refer to the amount of time that a patient is expected to live.

Program of All-Inclusive Care for the Elderly (PACE) A community-based government healthcare program that features a comprehensive service delivery system and integrated Medicare and Medicaid financing.

promotion The combination of methods of communicating with the target market, possibly including advertising, public relations, community relations, and publicity.

prospective payment system (PPS) A system for paying long-term care facilities in which rates are adjusted for case mix and geographic variation in wages and cover costs of furnishing Medicare-covered skilled nursing facility services.

public controls Governing bodies that are government-funded and that are focused on both the quality and the costs of services provided by long-term care organizations.

public funding sources Funding provided through government provisions.

public relations Efforts made by organizations to communicate and interact with the public segments that they serve, with the goal of achieving a mutually beneficial relationship.

public/private partnerships Programs that seek ways to provide incentives for individuals to purchase long-term care insurance. The primary incentive is asset protection in return for meeting some of the cost of long-term care.

quality The degree of success a provider achieves in delivering care.

quality assurance (QA) Measures taken to prevent or decrease the likelihood of problems by identifying areas of opportunity and testing new approaches to fix underlying causes of persistent/systemic problems.

quality assurance and performance improvement (QAPI) A proactive and continuous study of processes with the intent to prevent or decrease the likelihood of problems by identifying areas of opportunity and testing new approaches to fix underlying causes of persistent/systemic problems.

Quality First A voluntary five-year initiative designed to improve the quality of nursing home care and other long-term care services through improving quality assurance measures and strengthening the bond between providers and consumers.

quality of life A measure of an individual's ability to live in accordance with his or her desires, whether unassisted or with the help of caregivers.

quality steering committee A committee or council that oversees the work of other committees and individuals. It should include the top clinical and administrative staff members, including the chief executive officer, the director of nursing services, the medical director, and any others who are in charge of major divisions or service areas.

quality teams Staff members closely involved with the area being evaluated who work as a unit to deal directly with identifying and solving problems.

quicker and sicker discharges The practice of transferring patients from acute care to long-term care as expeditiously as possible, often before the patient is physically ready for this transfer, to limit the costs associated with acute care.

rationality A measure of the correctness of a decision. This term is often confused with *competency*, which refers only to a person's capacity to make informed decision, not whether the decision is correct.

reconciliation A promise made by House Democrats to fix points of contention should the Affordable Care Act be passed.

referent power The power a person holds because others wish to be like him or her. A leader who serves as a role model to others can hold great power.

regulation A specific guideline or requirement created by an agency to ensure compliance with a law. A law is usually a very broad general mandate to accomplish a certain objective; a regulation helps define and carry out the intent of the law.

rehabilitation The process of recovering from an injury or illness.

reimbursement driven As the term relates to long-term care, the nature of care that is delivered in accordance with the way it is financed. Access to care, the availability of specific services, and even the quality of care provided are all dictated by the type and amount of reimbursement.

request for proposal A solicitation made to potential vendors that they compete for a defined job by specifying the conditions and prices of their services.

resident-centered Care that prioritizes the quality of residents' lives, creating settings where people can live comfortably and feel at home, as opposed to feeling like they are in an institution.

residential care facilities Facilities that, prior to modern assisted living practices, provided services in small homes caring for one or several seniors. Commonly referred to as boarding homes or boarding care facilities, they primarily provided nonmedical care and supervision and were often based in the private homes of the service providers.

residents As the term relates to long-term care, individuals receiving services in the long-term institutional setting.

respite care Relief given to the primary caregivers from their duties for short periods of time, while maintaining the level of care.

restraints Measures, whether physical or chemical, used to prohibit individuals from causing harm to themselves or others.

reward power The power a person holds because of his or her ability to reward another for doing what is wanted. The reward may be a pay raise, a promotion, or simply an elevation in status within the organization.

right-to-die law A law designed to give terminally ill individuals the ability to legally end their own lives in a manner that they feel will preserve their dignity and reduce the suffering associated with the final stages of their illness.

sandwich generation A nickname for the baby boomer generation, the members of which are often simultaneously responsible for the care of their children and their parents.

seamless system of care A system that is coordinated, accessible, user friendly, and efficient and that recognizes individual needs, rights, and responsibilities. This type of system is characterized by more consumer choice and autonomy, by integration of services, and by a blending of the healthcare system and the social care system.

Section 202 A program operated through the U.S. Department of Housing and Urban Development, formally titled the Supportive Housing for the Elderly Program, that allows for limited federal subsidization of senior housing.

self-assessment The first stage of strategic planning, concerned with answering the question, "Where are we?" It consists of two parts: (1) evaluating the organization's mission and vision and (2) identifying and analyzing the organization's internal capabilities.

Senate Special Committee on Aging A Senate committee that convened a meeting of assisted living stakeholders to request that they work together and make recommendations to ensure high-quality care and services for all assisted living residents.

senior apartments Age-restricted multiunit rental housing available to older adults who are able to care for themselves.

senior housing A general term used to describe living accommodations that meet the functional and personal needs of the ever-growing elderly population in our society. Many seniors are not able to live in their traditional homes but do not require institutional care.

service amenities Services offered by a senior living community that go beyond the meeting of residents'

basic needs. Examples include massage therapy, indoor swimming, banking services, concierge services, fitness centers, and movie theaters.

single-site care availability The ability of a system to provide all of a patient's care, rather than requiring the patient to seek out multiple sites and/or providers.

skilled nursing facility (SNF) A facility that provides short-term care, serving as a means of transitioning from highly intensive hospital units while maintaining the availability of acute care if needed. As such, transitional units are usually located at or near hospitals and operated by those hospitals.

skilled nursing services Advanced nursing practices typically carried out in skilled nursing facilities.

social contracts The partnerships that long-term care organizations form with their customers. Organizations should think of their customers as partners, clearly identifying respective roles and expectations.

social day care A type of adult day care that provides a safe and secure environment for people without significant healthcare needs but who may have some minor limitations in performing activities of daily living.

social media Internet-based computer platforms that allow individuals to easily communicate and share personal information with others. Popular platforms include Facebook, YouTube, MySpace, Twitter, LinkedIn, and Flickr.

social responsibility The sense of obligation that an organization has to its consumers and the community in which it operates.

Social Security Act of 1935 The act establishing welfare programs for society's needy, particularly the aged, blind, and families with dependent children. It has been identified as the indirect beginning of the nursing home industry.

software As the term relates to computers, programs and procedures that enable a computer to operate. Software exists as data communicated between devices.

special care units (SCUs) Care units designed to meet the unique needs of specific resident populations. Examples include Alzheimer's disease units and brain injury units.

speech pathologist A clinician who works with individuals whose ability to properly use the apparatus of the mouth and throat has been impaired.

spend down A term used to describe the requirement that before consumers can become eligible for Medicaid benefits, they must deplete all personal resources.

spousal impoverishment protections Provisions of the Affordable Care Act designed to prevent financial hardships to spouses of people receiving home- and community-based services.

staffing The process of providing the needed staff to accomplish the objectives of the organization. The main purpose of staffing is to hire the right people for the right jobs to achieve the objectives of the organization.

stakeholders Individuals or organizations that are affected by, or have the ability to affect, the organization.

standards Measures of success that are established by an authoritative entity and generally agreed upon by all parties within the field.

strategic business unit An integral part of the greater organization that has its own purpose, its own distinct competencies, and its own role.

strategic business units The elements of a matrix-like organizational structure in which relatively small, specialized units address the distinct functions of a much larger, more complex system such as health care. This structure stands in contrast to traditional hierarchical organizational structures.

strategic planning A planning process that involves assessing the organization, including its mission and vision, as well as its strengths and weaknesses. Strategic planning consists of answering three questions: Where are we? Where do we want to go? How do we get there? The purpose of the strategic plan is to develop a strategy that will help the organization thrive and prosper.

strategic thinking The process of understanding what the long-range implications are of any decisions made today (i.e., forward strategic thinking) and understanding what the implications of a decision are on others within or outside of the organization (i.e., sideways strategic thinking).

strategies The methods by which the organization sets about achieving its goals.

strategy formulation The stage of strategic planning concerned with answering the questions, "Where do we want to go?" and "How do we get there?" The organization should establish an overall strategy to guide it toward its vision and goals.

subacute care An approach to care that provides highly skilled nursing care, therapies, and more medical supervision than nursing facilities. It is highly focused care designed to bridge the gap between acute and long-term care, with a relatively short length of stay.

Supportive Housing for the Elderly Program See *Section 202*.

team building Selecting and guiding team members to work together toward a common objective. The team leader must provide direction to the team and facilitate its activities toward common goals.

technology The practical application of knowledge and ideas that enables a given function.

telemonitoring The remote monitoring of patients who are at home through electronic transmission of vital signs and other clinical data to the care-providing agency or other high-technology center.

total quality management An approach to quality assurance created by Dr. W. Edwards Deming. See *continuous quality improvement (CQI)*.

trade organizations Associations formed by members within a given profession in hopes of learning from one another and improving the overall quality of the profession.

transfer agreement Cooperative efforts made by long-term care organizations to help consumers transition to a different level of care or a different service provider.

transfer of assets The depletion of one's assets in order to qualify for Medicaid. It is associated with the concept of *spending down*.

transitional subacute care Care that is usually short term, serving as a means of transitioning from highly intensive hospital units while maintaining the availability of acute care if needed. As such, transitional units are usually located at or near hospitals and operated by those hospitals.

trends The prevailing, often quite temporary, demands or desires of consumers, or practices of an organization.

uniform assessment A single-review process that takes all of the individual's needs into account, rather than several different, uncoordinated processes.

uniform financial eligibility criteria The standards used in determining the type and amount of payment received from a consumer. These standards must be comprehensive enough to apply to all consumers fairly.

United Way A charitable organization that, among other services, helps fund hospice services for needy individuals.

universally accessible Available to all who need them, not limited to certain groups.

utilization review A review process designed primarily to ensure that the government does not pay more than necessary for healthcare services.

vendor A professional or organization that provides a specified service.

vertical integration An alliance of two or more organizations providing services that are dissimilar but that interact with, and may rely on, each other.

vision A statement of what the organization would like to be.

visiting nurse association A service that developed in the late 1800s as a means of supplementing the work of physicians, who at the time regularly made house calls.

waiver programs Programs designed to allow exceptions to Medicaid rules so that states may better operate their Medicaid programs.

Wellspring model An independent, not-for-profit organization that promotes resident autonomy in the long-term care setting and empowers staff members to proactively improve the quality of care for residents, providing training in best practices concerning nutrition, feeding, palliative care, leadership, and pain management.

Index

C

capitation, 212–213

care. *See also* continuum of care; specific types of care and care services
- alternatives to nursing facilities, 160–161
- coordination of, 71–72, 252–253
- delivery methods, innovative, 502–504
- informed consent for, 355

care management, 131

care needs, special units based on, 99

care planning services
- of HIT, 436–437
- at subacute care units, 128–129

caregivers, 214. *See also* family caregivers; informal caregivers
- dedication of, 25–26
- pediatric day care for, 27
- respite for. *See* adult day care

CARF. *See* Commission on Accreditation of Rehabilitation Facilities

CARF International, 129, 136–137, 285–286

case management, 310, 314
- family involvement in, 66
- at subacute care units, 131–132

case managers
- external, 131
- as gatekeepers, 132
- internal, 131
- in MCOs, 131

case-mix formula, 210

case-mix payment programs, 313

case studies
- adult day care, 224–226
- assisted living, 173–174
- home healthcare, 222–223
- hospice care, 223–224
- nursing facilities, 115–116
- senior housing, 188–189
- subacute care, 146–147

CAST. *See* Center for Aging Services Technologies

categorical assistance programs, 292

CBO. *See* Congressional Budget Office

CCAC. *See* Continuing Care Accreditation Commission

CCRC. *See* continuing care retirement community

CEAL. *See* Center for Excellence in Assisted Living

Center for Aging Services Technologies (CAST), 432–433

Center for American Progress, 496

Center for Disability and Aging Policy, 42

Center for Excellence in Assisted Living (CEAL), 163

Centers for Medicare & Medicaid Services (CMS), 24, 45, 124, 135, 328, 435, 436, 444
- managed care, 313
- minimum data set (MDS), 327–328
- "Nursing Home Compare," 329
- phase-in period for some Medicare services, 297

certificate of need (CON)
- regulations, 10
- for subacute care facilities, 135

certification. *See also* licensure
- of assisted living administrators, 95, 107, 171, 287
- certified nursing assistants, 272–273
- of healthcare professionals, 210, 271–272
- private, 286–287

certified nursing assistants (CNAs), 69, 92, 107, 108, 215
- certification of, 272–273
- definition of, 272

challenges, 520

CHAMPUS. *See* Civilian Health and Medical Program of the Uniformed Services

change
- leadership for, 408–409
- managing for, 3

change agent, manager as, 527

CHAP. *See* Community Health Accreditation Program

charisma of leaders, 401

chemical restraints, 367

Cheshire cat, 407, 410

chief executive officer (CEO)
- definition of, 380
- governing body responsibilities for advising, 385
- evaluation process, 384–385
- selection of, 384–385

responsibilities of, 390
- creating high level of administrative capability, 392
- educating the governing body, 391
- ensuring integrity of the organization, 391–392
- informing the governing body, 391
- maintaining good community relations, 392
- overseeing use of resources, 391

chief information officer, 452

children
- of assisted living residents, 161
- long-term care use by, 16

choice of care, 62, 114, 133–134
- of assisted living residents, maximizing, 154
- demand for, 114, 133
- market forces affecting, 206–207

choice of service delivery modalities, 62

choice of service providers, 62

chronic care, definition of, 6

chronic conditions, increase in, 488–489

chronic subacute care, 127

chronicity, 83

Civil Rights Act, 267

Civilian Health and Medical Program of the Uniformed Services (CHAMPUS), 210

CLASS Act. *See* Community Living Assistance Services and Supports Act

clients, definition of, 13

clinical applications of HIT, 436–438
- admission, assessment, care planning, 436–437
- consumer safety, 437
- quality measurement, 438
- record keeping, 437–438

clinical applications of information technology, future trends in, 502

clinical information systems
- clinical guidelines, 254
- clinical outcomes, 254–255
- patient management, 253–254
- quality improvement, 254

Internal Revenue Service, exceptions for "homes for the aged," 177
Internet, 433, 445, 449, 450
intravenous therapy, 140
IOM. *See* Institute of Medicine
IOM Committee on Nursing Home Regulations, 321
iPads, 448
IRFs. *See* inpatient rehabilitation facilities

J

JCAHO. *See* Joint Commission on Accreditation of Healthcare Organizations
Jennings, Bruce, 56
Johnson, Lyndon B., 293
Joint Commission on Accreditation of Healthcare Organizations (JCAHO), 136, 284–286, 334
assisted living facilities, 164
home healthcare and hospice agencies, 209
outcomes measurements, 265–266
Journal of General Internal Medicine, 47

K

Kevorkian, Jack, 363, 510
knowledgeable management, 390
Kongstvedt, Peter, 306
Kouzes, James, 401, 407

L

ladder concept, continuum of care, 24
laundry and linen services, in assisted living facilities, 158
law
constitutionality of, 39
history/passage of, 38
vs. regulation, 262
leaders
born or created, 401
charisma of, 401
competent, 403
culture change, role of, 427–428

forward-looking, 403
honesty of, 402–403
inspiring, 403
managers as, 524, 528
as prescient visionaries, 401
providing direction: skills
planning, 408
strategic thinking, 407–408
should be approachable, 402
superior position of, 401
leadership, 399–416, 422. *See also* culture change
assumptions about, 404
definition of leadership, 400
function, 389–390
gaining and improving skills
assess current skills, 415–416
recognize the need for improvement, 414–416
getting voluntary acceptance: skills
conflict resolution, 412
enabling, 410
managing stress, 413–414
mentoring, 413
negotiation, 412
problem solving, 411–412
providing feedback, 411
team building, 413
influencing others: skills, 404–406
communication, 406
managing power/influence, 404–405
motivation, 406
providing direction: skills
decision making, 409
managing change, 408–409
theories of leadership, 400
Leadership Challenge, The, 401, 407
"Leadership in Health Administration," 4
learning organization, creating, 525–526
least restrictive environment, 64
legal and ethical issues
community-based services
decision to accept hospice care, 216–217
inequitable access, 217
patient safety, 216
patients' rights, 216
nursing facilities, 108–110
patient noncompliance, 215–216

legal liability, 395–396
legislation, 262, 268, 273
legitimate power, 405
length of stay, preset limits on, 12
liability costs and tort reform, 315–316
licensed practical nurse (LPN), for community-based services, 214
licensure
administrators of assisted living facilities, 170
for administrators of nursing facilities, 273–274
of community-based professional staff, 209
of community-based service providers, 208–209
confusion over, 274–276
inconsistencies in, 273
of individuals, 271
subacute care facilities, 140
life-and-death issues
ethical dilemmas of, 510
futile care, 511
life care community, 180, 183
life care/extensive contract, 187
life expectancy today, 294
Life Safety Code, 105, 136, 163
living/housing options, long-term care organization, future in, 499–500
living wills, 110, 359
local quality regulations, 267–268
Long-Term and Post-Acute Care (LTPAC), 433
long-term care (LTC). *See also* long-term care system
administrators, 396
consumer demographics of, 486–491
consumer-driven, 490–491
consumers of, 94, 323, 365
age of, 100
care needs, 100
choice of care, demand for, 114, 133
gender mix, 100
insurance, private, 113
demand for, 9
different types of, determining most appropriate, 22
as a dynamic process, 24
in family homes, 7

managed care and, 309, 313

and Medicare, differences between, 298

quality improvement and, 327

regulations, nursing facilities, 266–267

in reimbursement, 326

self-direction of care by recipients, 499

sheltering assets, 77

shift of patients to MCOs and HMOs, 112

spend-down requirements, 76, 300

spending on home and community-based services (HCBC), 207

state efforts to reduce spending, 299–300

Title III, 212

Title XIX, 104

waiver program, 298, 509

Medicaid Act, 9

medical appliances and supplies, hospice care, 201

medical coverage, 107

medical device tax, 48

Medical Facilities Survey and Construction Act (1946), 10

medical social workers, in community-based services, 214

medical *vs.* social model, of long-term care, 93–94

medically indigent persons, 9, 78, 298

Medicare, 292, 298, 382, 436–437, 439

as an entitlement program, 293

certification, home health and hospice care, 208

costs, pressures to reduce, 295

coverage, 199, 208

community-based services, 210–212

home health care, 297

hospice care, 212–213, 297

nursing facilities, 92, 105

skilled nursing services, 297

subacute care, 297

cuts in, 40

development, 293–295

eligibility rules, 313

financial status, 293

future trends in, 507

home health and hospice care, 208

hospital insurance (HI) trust fund, 294

impact on long-term care, 8–9

making it needs-based, 509

managed care and, 309

Medicare Trust Fund, 294

number of people qualifying for, 294

OASIS, 201

PACE, 212

Part A, 293

Part B, 293

Part C, 293

preventive testing, 71

problems, 294

qualifications for administrator, home health agency, 217

quality improvement and, 327

regulations of nursing facilities, 266–267

in reimbursement, 326

hospice care, 199

shift of patients to MCOs and HMOs, 112

for subacute care facilities, 135, 137

technological improvements, impact on, 295

Title XVIII, 104

Medicare Advantage Plans, 47–48, 293, 309

Medicare/Medicaid amendments to SSA, 8–9, 90, 104

Medicare Trust Fund, 294

medication management, in assisted living facilities, 168–171

MedPac report (2003), 124

mental health and mental illness or intellectual disabilities, 97

mentally ill, mentally retarded, use of long-term care, 17

mentoring, 413

merger, 242

Minimum Data Set (MDS), 327–328, 436–437, 443, 444

MIS. *See* management information systems

modified/continuing care contract, 187

"Money Follows the Person" program, 42

moral vision for long-term care, 56

morality, 371

of managers, 371

motivation skill of leaders, 406

multi-level facilities, 26, 30

multidisciplinary approach, long-term care, 94

multiple entry points, 30

N

NAB. *See* National Association of Long-Term Care Administrator Boards

National Adult Day Services Association (NADSA), 199

National Association of Long-Term Care Administrator Boards (NAB), 111, 170, 525

domains of practice, 274–275, 287

Standards of Practice for Long-Term Care Administrators, 275

National Association of Social Workers, 287

National Association of State Units on Aging, 42

National Center for Assisted Living (NCAL), 103, 153, 163, 168

age and gender of residents, 159

National Commission for Quality Long-Term Care, 277, 447–448

National Committee for Quality Assurance (NCQA)

subacute care standards, 136–137

utilization management, 144

National Conference of State Legislatures, 306

National Federation of Independent Business v. Sebelius, 46

National Guideline Clearinghouse, 330

National Health Planning and Resources Development Act (1974), 10